RACE WAR

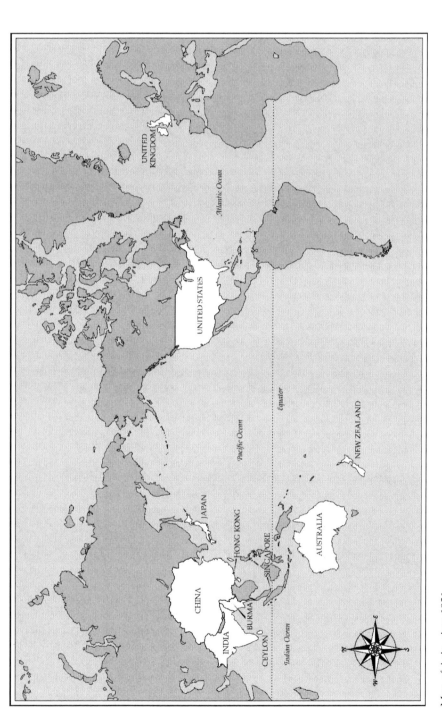

Map of Asia, circa 1931.

GERALD HORNE

RACE WAR

White Supremacy and the
Japanese Attack on the British Empire

New York University Press • *New York and London*

NEW YORK UNIVERSITY PRESS
New York and London
www.nyupress.org

Library of Congress Cataloging-in-Publication Data
Race war : White supremacy and the Japanese attack
on the British Empire / Gerald Horne.
p. cm.
Includes bibliographical references and index.
ISBN 0–8147–3640–8 (cloth : alk. paper)
1. World War, 1939–1945—Pacific Area.   2. World War, 1939–1945—Asia.
3. World War, 1939–1945—Japan.   4. Caucasian race—Social conditions.
5. Racism—Japan.   6. Racism—Asia.   7. Racism—Pacific Area.
8. Asia—Race relations.   9. Pacific Area—Race relations.
10. Japan—Race relations.   I. Title.
D767.H595   2003
940.53'089'009171241—dc22   2003016114

New York University Press books

Contents

All illustrations appear as an insert following p. 124.

Preface

As the Great Depression was unfolding, Robert Abbott, the wealthy African American publisher, sailed eastward to England with his spouse. The experience proved to be a racial nightmare. Upon arriving in London—headquarters of the powerful British Empire—he was refused a room in the prestigious Savoy in the West End, though he arrived with reservation in hand. Why? He was informed curtly that the hotel did not cater to Negroes. He left in disgust and went to several other hotels where he dispatched his fairer-skinned wife to register but in each case when he sought to enter he was blocked at the desk and asked to leave. All told, thirty hotels engaged in this odious practice.[1]

Shortly thereafter, the noted African American jazz musician, Buck Clayton, was on board a ship, sailing in a different direction—actually and metaphorically—westward to Asia. He "suffered," was dismally "seasick," and "really wanted to die"—not because of incommodious treatment but because the choppy waves rocked his vessel. Yet his maritime ailments were quickly forgotten when they landed in Japan: "We were the only ones allowed to disembark. All the white passengers had to remain aboard while the ship was in dock while we Blacks were allowed to go ashore and have a ball. We could come and go as we pleased," he concluded, still wondrous at this reversal of Jim Crow.[2]

Neither Abbott's experience in London nor that of Clayton in Kobe was unusual for the time. In the former, all those not of "pure European descent" were treated like so much chattel within the Empire and in a good deal of North America. Effectively, this was the treatment meted out to the overwhelming majority of the planet's inhabitants—effectively providing an enormous opportunity for the Japanese, who were treated similarly, to "flip the script" and challenge the Empire and its U.S. cousin on the basis of "race." This "reverse discrimination" was

Tokyo's way of appealing to Negroes, not to mention Asians, neutralizing them or even converting them into a fifth column in case of war with Washington and London. This tactic was not altogether unsuccessful.

This is a book about race and racism within the British Empire in Asia. The focus is on Hong Kong, though the narrative ranges from Fiji and New Zealand to India. The narrative is told from both a "top down" perspective, for example, the viewpoints of Europeans in "British Asia" in the pre- and postwar eras and a "bottom-up" perspective, that is, the viewpoints of destitute and interned Europeans, along with those of U.S. Negroes and some Africans and Asians.

The chronology veers from the period leading up to the Pacific War, to the war itself and the immediate postwar era. The thesis is simple: an all-encompassing British racism—amply bolstered by other European powers and particularly by the United States—demobilized the colonized, making them highly susceptible to Japanese racial appeals. This was a major factor contributing to Tokyo's early success in the war. Europeans and Euro-Americans interned by the Japanese authorities during the war received a harsh and sobering taste of racial subordination; and, after the war concluded, a Chinese bourgeoisie was given a boost as a result of the looting, fleecing, and fleeing of many British, not to mention the profitable collaboration of some Asians with Tokyo.

The subtext—but not the principal focus—of this book is the brutality unleashed by Japanese forces, particularly in China. Initially at least, many of those subjected to European colonialism and imperialism welcomed the invaders as liberators from a private hell. However, as the war ground on, it became apparent that this fond wish was far from the truth.

I should make clear early on that if I had been living during the era of the Pacific War, I would have fought against Japan—though I would have been subjected to discriminatory, racially segregated treatment in the U.S. military. Thus, readers should be alert to the fact that my indictment of London—and Washington—is not intended as an exculpation of Tokyo. Instead, I am seeking to show how London's racial policies in particular actually *enabled* Tokyo. Likewise, I recognize—above all—that there were salient factors beyond "race" that shaped the Pacific War, economics, geopolitics, and antifascism in the first place.

In other words, this book is not the latest chapter in the ongoing saga that has become so popular in North America and, to an extent, in the North Atlantic generally—that is, the "good war" fought by the "greatest generation."[3] The physicist Freeman Dyson once concluded that "a good cause can become bad if we fight for it with means that are indiscriminately murderous. A bad cause can become good if enough people fight for it in a spirit of comradeship and self-sacrifice." The historian Michael Sherry has added, "that grasp of moral complexity has weakened amid the recent feel-good politics of nostalgia about America's role in World War II"—and he might well have added, that of Great Britain as well.[4] Thus, as one nuanced study of "Chinese collaboration with Japan" argues, accounts of this complicated era should seek to "break free from the moralistic framework in which wartime history is viewed. . . . which holds the historian's task to be that of assigning 'praise and blame.'"[5]

This approach has been exemplified by scholars in other contexts. The journalist and historian Roger Wilkins has wrestled with the idea that those apostles of freedom and liberty who founded the nation to which he swears fervent allegiance, were slaveholders.[6] He could have added that the victorious North in the U.S. Civil War tolerated a virulent racial segregation, dispossession of Native Americans—and worse—but that does not mean that they deserved to be defeated during this titanic conflict. In short, Japan's claim to be the "champion of the colored races" was fraudulent in no minor way, though inevitably some who fought on her behalf actually believed the claim—just as some who fought for the United States during the Gulf War actually believed this war was fundamentally about human rights and not about oil. But although Tokyo's claim was fraudulent the shock Tokyo administered to the ingrained system of white supremacy—which was an essential underpinning of the Empire and the United States alike—was central to the devolution of the doctrine of white supremacy. Despite this doctrine, however, the Allies did not merit defeat.

To the contrary. The withering experience of the war was critical in compelling a forced retreat from the dictates of white supremacy, as Washington and London most notably increasingly came to see racism as a threat to national security. Britain was compelled to deploy tens of thousands of Africans to fight Japanese troops in India and Burma.[7] Ironically, just as African Americans earlier in the century had pointed to Japan as evidence for the proposition that modernity was not solely the province of those of European descent, London—reeling from their defeat at the hands of Tokyo—pointed anxiously to the success of these

African troops as evidence for the proposition that the Japanese were not superior beings. The United States contained an obstreperous African American population that had been cultivated for decades by Japanese operatives. As the war plodded on, it was evident that London—and Washington—would have to adjust their policies of white supremacy and rules privileging those of "pure European descent."

The enormous atrocities committed by Japan should not obscure the point that the war it helped to trigger led to this result. As Frank Furedi observed in noting the similar impact triggered by another pilloried regime, "other than the Russian Revolution of 1917 the Japanese war effort probably constituted the most significant challenge to the Western-dominated world order"—though, for various reasons, this "is rarely acknowledged."[8]

This underscores the differing kinds of bigotry that Japan and its European and Euro-American antagonists represented. B. V. A. Roling, an eminent Dutch jurist who served on the postwar tribunal in Tokyo that tried Japanese war criminals, has concluded that Japanese chauvinism grew out of discrimination. "In slavery," he has noted, "the feeling of being 'the chosen people' can easily surface." The brusque imposition of unequal treaties on Japan in the nineteenth century and the failure to provide this nation with full membership in the club of imperialists generated a severe counterreaction. Roling adds that "Japan wanted to expel the colonial powers from Asia. But there was no plan to exterminate all Europeans."[9] Thus there was a critical distinction between Tokyo and Berlin.

That there is something to what he says is suggested by the experience of Israel Epstein. In 1942 he was in "Japanese-controlled Hong Kong, where his political activities made freedom so dangerous that he decided to slip into an internment camp. . . . 'I was safer as an enemy national interned with 3000 other foreign nationals,'" he recalled years later, "'than I would have been walking around in Hong Kong.'"[10] It is hard to imagine anyone *choosing* internment in German-occupied Europe. One of the leading scholars of race in Japan has observed that the "Japanese equivalent of white [supremacy] was improbable if not impossible. . . . Whereas racism in the West was markedly characterized by denigration of others, the Japanese were preoccupied far more with elevating themselves."[11]

Though the term World War II is often tossed casually over a complex series of differing struggles, this book seeks to distinguish the Pacific War, which substantially involved attacks on European colonialism and the war in Europe, which primarily involved attacks on sovereign states. This distinction was evident in the war's aftermath: after the liberation of France in 1944, fifteen hundred people were executed peremptorily; after trials which had a trifling acquaintance with due process, about nine thousand more were executed and thirty-eight thousand sentenced to prison.[12] In Hong Kong, as shown later in this book, the number of revenge killings and trials with executions and jail terms was stunningly small by comparison, even given the disparities in population.[13]

In sum, this is a study in "whiteness," not a book about Japan. As the subtitle suggests, this is a book about white supremacy—its high tide, ebbing, and reorientation.[14] The focus is primarily on the British Empire—and its rival-cum-successor in Washington—and its reaction to the racially charged events that were unfolding. Thus, this book should be read as a complement to—and, quite frankly, homage to—the work of John Dower, Yukiko Koshiro, and Christopher Thorne,[15] all of whom have written about the racial interplay between Japan and its non-Asian rivals. The focal point here, however, is much narrower and sharper, that is, Europeans and Euro-Americans, followed by Negroes and Asians. Moreover, unlike the above-mentioned authors, the emphasis here is much less on what was going on in capitals like Washington, London, and Tokyo than on what was taking place on the ground as Japan's racial reversals were being attempted—particularly in Hong Kong. Thus, this story tracks the perilous route from racial privilege to racial subordination to racial accommodation with Europeans and Euro-Americans as our primary guides, registering the shocks and changes.

The book also tussles with the slippery and unscientific concept of "race," a term that has changed in meaning over the years. As it is often said, "race" may be an illusory will-o-the-wisp but "racism" and "white supremacy" are not.[16] Fortunately, the Empire has provided a constructive definition of the latter—as suggested below—with its infelicitous policy of conferring benefits on those of "pure European descent," which tracks contemporary and historical U.S. visions of "whiteness." Those not so blessed, namely, the indigenous inhabitants of Africa, Asia, and the South Pacific, along with African Americans and other "nonwhite minorities" in the United States, were generally excluded from the benefits of "white supremacy." This was a "Pan-European" concept within the Empire that privileged—often subtly, often openly—the English, then the British, and so on. Those whose roots stretched from the Urals to Western Europe were generally accorded preference over those who were not so blessed.[17]

The scholar David Yoo has been among those who have called for a reassertion of the notion of "race," particularly in relation to Asian Americans. "The increasing tendency to view American identity in terms of ethnicity," he says, "has subtly masked the persistence of race in the United States," a process which serves to elide sharp differences between, say, Italian Americans and German Americans on the one hand and Japanese Americans and Chinese Americans on the other. The Nisei, he says, had a "distrust and even hatred of European-Americans" during the war. This phenomenon is best understood within the admittedly elusive—though no less real—context of "race."[18]

Unfortunately, Asian American scholars like Yoo have been much more keen to explore this evasive and fugitive construction than their Asian counterparts, in that "scholarly work on the impact of 'race' in China, Japan and Korea only began to attain a critical mass in the mid-1990s," if then.[19] This omission makes it harder to fully comprehend why Tokyo's racial appeals gained such traction within the Empire and in North America. This is sad in part because, as the prominent Hong Kong sociologist Henry Lethbridge, put it, "The underlying antagonisms that existed between Chinese and British were more racialist in origin (consequently more difficult to exorcise) than economic or political, although"—he adds, quite correctly—"these three factors must be, to some degree, inter-related."[20]

After all, racial discrimination was not solely a "thing in itself" but intimately connected to a larger project that involved political domination and economic exploitation. W. Somerset Maugham, the British novelist who most adroitly addressed Empire in Asia, recognized these connections. As he wrote, "In China it is man that is beast of burden. . . . Coolies are animals." One of his characters, a U.S. expatriate, reflected the insouciant disdain for the Chinese in that—like many of his compatriots—he "lived in China for . . . years but he knows no Chinese and takes no interest. . . . They bore him."[21] In another novel, published in 1925, that led to a lawsuit against Maugham because of his characters' similarities to existing figures, his heroine, Kitty Fane, "had never paid anything but passing and somewhat contemptuous attention to the China which fate had thrown her. It was not done in her set. . . . Kitty had never heard the Chinese spoken of as anything but decadent, dirty and unspeakable."[22]

The tightly interwoven questions of white supremacy and economic exploitation were major reasons why many African Americans saw their fates linked with those of Asians thousands of miles away and why a modicum of sympathy existed for Japan—at least for a while—on both sides of the Pacific. Moreover, British colonial officials often deployed the lessons they had learned in Africa in Asia, and vice versa. These ties were sensed by some U.S. Negroes particularly. Thus, in the 1930s, the influential Negro intellectual W. E. B. Du Bois insisted that it was impossible to understand the black experience in the United States without reference to "that dark and vast sea of human labor in China and India, the South Seas and all of Africa. . . . that great majority of mankind, on whose bent and broken backs rest today the founding stones of modern history." Negroes and Asians, he thought, shared a "common destiny," both were "despised and rejected by race and color; paid a wage below the level of decent living; driven, beaten, [im]prisoned and enslaved in all but name" with the "resultant wealth . . . distributed and displayed and made the basis of world power and universal dominion and armed arrogance in London and Paris, Berlin and Rome, New York and Rio de Janeiro."[23]

Japan's ability to insinuate itself within the interstices of this racialized edifice of exploitation—though it was a colonizing power itself—was facilitated by the stern refusal of those of "pure European descent" to fully accept the new phenomenon of an Asian power. This point has to be qualified, however. As Japan launched its offensive in China in the early 1930s, Henry Stimson, U.S. Secretary of State, was not prone to articulate a fervent denunciation. He said he "did not want to be driven by China, that after all the white races in the Orient had got to stand more or less together." In pursuit of these alleged common interests, Tokyo hired "Ralph Townsend, a former U.S. consul in China, as a propagandist to convince Americans that Japan was 'fighting the white man's battle' against Chinese nationalism." Britain, which had pursued the wrongheaded policy of viewing Japan as its overseer in the region, was similarly reluctant to speak against Tokyo's depredations. Of course, arguably these anti-China and pro-Japan policies were driven by white supremacy in terms of the flagrant disregard for China's basic interests and the utter disbelief that Japan—being a power not of "pure European descent"—could ever mount an effective challenge to the existing racial order. And, as stressed below, both London and Washington were similarly driven by anticommunism, which both united them at certain junctures with Tokyo and made all three powers somewhat leery of a China which had a formidable Communist Party.[24] However, this study will not target anticommunism, unlike previous books I have penned which have addressed this weighty ideology,[25] but "race," which served to divide Tokyo from London and Washington.[26]

Thus, in war it seemed that Imperial Japan was more of a menace than Nazi Germany. The U.S. historian Allan Nevins noted that "probably in all our history, no foe has been so detested as were the Japanese. Emotions forgotten since our most savage Indian wars were awakened by the ferocities of Japanese commanders." Or as the chief of the evacuation of Japanese Americans from the West Coast put it, "'You needn't worry about the Italians at all except in certain cases. Also, the same for the Germans except in individual cases. But we must worry about the Japanese all the time until he is wiped off the map.'"[27]

That the Japanese were often regarded as no more than degraded Negroes was reflected even in children's doggerel. Thus, by the spring of 1942 the rhyme "eenie, meenie, minie, moe . . . catch a nigger by the toe, if he hollers let him go. . . . if he hollers, make him pay, fifty dollars every day" had morphed into "catch the emperor by the toe" with a similar refrain.[28] The Negroes were now needed for the purposes of national unity. However, that the concept of white supremacy was still alive and well was indicated by the substitution of Japanese in their place. From the mouths of babes came a profound—though flawed—"wisdom" betokening a shift in the tectonic plates of race.

Because of severe apprehension about the impact of Tokyo's racial appeals, their opponents began to stress racial equality.[29] Wartime Japanese propaganda, which targeted Negroes, was "successful" in that it "forced the American military to reevaluate its racial hierarchy if it wished to maintain domestic tranquility." The Japanese Foreign Ministry—like many Negroes and Asians—argued that "white racial bias towards the Japanese and discrimination [against] blacks originated from the same source."[30] All of a sudden, "any use of the word 'nigger' in BBC broadcasts was discouraged" and this potent megaphone of the airwaves, just as suddenly, decided that the "word 'natives'" was "derogatory and edited . . . out of Colonial Office radio talks." This was a small part of a concerted policy of racial reform driven by the exigencies of "race war."

Why this left turn was necessary was signaled by Walter White, the moderate leader of the U.S.-based civil rights organization, the National Association for the Advancement of Colored People (NAACP). He acknowledged the impact of the Pacific War on race relations in the United States. He argued that the Pacific War and the fall of the Empire in Singapore specifically, marked "the end of an epoch . . . racially"—a welcome development, since the status quo had been "exceedingly dangerous."[31] The status quo had enabled Tokyo to embark on an "exceedingly dangerous" route toward war and likewise had demoralized Asians and blacks alike, making them more susceptible to Japan's siren song. With no hint of cynicism, the eminent Negro intellectual, Du Bois, declared as the war was in motion, "If Hitler wins, down with the blacks! If the democracies win, the blacks are already down."[32] As it turns out, when the "democracies" won, chastened by their wounding encounter with Japan's jujitsu-like maneuver of turning "white supremacy" into a debilitating weakness, the United States began a painful retreat from racial segregation. Actually, this withdrawal had begun during the war itself, as the exclusionary "white primary" was ruled unconstitutional and voting rights were expanded.

But the greatest changes probably occurred within the Empire, where Asian nations after witnessing the ineptitude and fecklessness of British troops in the face of a challenge from a fellow "colored people"—the Japanese—recognized that "whiteness" and competence were not one. In India in particular, the very heart of the Empire, considerable pro-Tokyo sentiment had been expressed during the war—an indication of the revulsion there to British colonialism and its handmaiden, white supremacy. India's independence from the Empire, which followed shortly after the war's conclusion, and its rapid emergence as the world's largest democracy suggested that there was no necessary contradiction between pro-Tokyo feelings and democracy itself.

Because this study ranges so widely—from the South Pacific to South China to South Central Asia, from North America to Africa—the book is divided into various parts. The following is a brief description of each chapter, so as to allow the reader to dip into particular areas of interest.

The introduction provides a broad overview of the issues to come in succeeding chapters. It discusses the situation in Hong Kong, including the question of race and its intersection with Japan, along with why these issues, which were once so conspicuous, are now so little known.

Chapter 1 presents a portrait of the racial segregation endured predominantly by the Chinese in prewar Hong Kong. It includes a sketch of the creature comforts enjoyed by those of "pure European descent" alongside a picture of the evolution of Japan's encounter with white supremacy.

Chapter 2 examines the positive response of many U.S. Negroes to Japan in the prewar period—a consensus that conspicuously excluded Negro Communists, who faced the brunt of persecution both before and after the war, which contributed to an efflorescence of various forms of nationalism within this community.

Chapter 3 provides a sketch of the Japanese invasion of Hong Kong in December 1941 and shows how the success of this audacious venture was marked by racial accents, particularly the collaboration of many Chinese and Indians with the Japanese.

Chapter 4 examines the internment of Europeans in Hong Kong at the behest of their Japanese captors, the agony they were forced to endure and the racial context that drove this process. Some of the captives came to see that traits among Asians that they had thought were driven by race, actually were propelled by poverty.

Chapter 5 probes deeper into the complex question of the Negroes' response to Japan—particularly Japan's invasion of China—and the growing influence of pro-Tokyo organizations amongst this strategically sited minority.

Chapter 6 scrutinizes the impact of Japan's attack on the evolution of race and gender, most notably by examining what transpired in the internment camps, where Japanese Americans and Japanese educated in the United States—both working on behalf of Tokyo—played a conspicuous role.

Chapter 7 looks at the war in the South Pacific, especially New Zealand and Australia, where white supremacy—which had been deeply entrenched—confronted Japan's racial thrust. A cruelly poignant moment arose in January 1942 when Canberra, seized with fear about the prospect of living under Japanese rule, backed hesitantly away from its "White Australia" policy and reluctantly agreed to accept a complement of Negro troops. Like some U.S. Negroes, many Australian Aborigines and the Maoris of New Zealand also took a strong pro-Tokyo position. In the United States, the Nation of Islam spoke of deep ties to Tokyo as reflected in its idea of the "Asiatic Black Man." Among Maoris, there was the "Ratana" which too was close to Tokyo and a similar movement arose in Fiji.

Chapter 8 looks at the theater of war in the region ranging from the Malay peninsula to south-central Asia, describing the stunning array of pro-Tokyo forces, especially in India, the heart of the Empire, and how white supremacy helped to create this result. The preeminent personalities in contemporary Singapore and Malaysia—Lee Kuan Yew and Mahatir Mohammed—both "collaborated" with Tokyo during the war and acknowledge the boost given by the Japanese occupation to decolonization. The Empire was also dependent on Indians—be they in India itself or in Southeast Asia, Africa, and the Caribbean—but this seemingly ineradicable strength became something of a weakness after the rise of the popular pro-Tokyo Indian National Army, which fought shoulder-to-shoulder with Japanese troops in Burma.

Chapter 9 examines the experiences of African Americans, Africans, and Afro-Caribbeans in the war and shows how white supremacy hampered their ability to contribute to the anti-Tokyo effort despite their indispensable contribution to victory. Like Canberra, London had difficulty in realizing that survival might depend on turning away from fiercely held notions of racial inferiority. This realization came to the fore as skilled Negro personnel were rejected on spurious grounds and tens of thousands of Africans saved the Empire in Burma.

Chapter 10 explores the separate and intertwined relations between, for example, China, Japan, the Empire, the United States, Germany, Mexico, and other nations. Central in this story is the way white supremacy shaped the global context. In particular, Tokyo and Berlin—unlike London and Washington—coordinated their efforts poorly, if at all, because of Nazi racial theories. Fortunately, this weakness helped to doom the Axis. Persecuted Jewish refugees who could not find a home in Europe—or the United States—often wound up in Japanese-occupied Shanghai. Indeed, if the war had ended differently, a conflict between Tokyo and Berlin was probably more likely than that which erupted between Washington and Moscow. And, of course, the Japanese ruling elite's attempt to cobble together a front of "colored peoples" united against white supremacy was designed to obscure its own grab for national supremacy.

The conclusion sums up the story with a focus on the aftermath of the war in Hong Kong, noting, for example, the rise of a Chinese bourgeoisie, the city's growing reputation as a "paradise for collaborators," the trials of accused collaborators, and the racial reforms sparked by a chastened Empire, desperate to maintain its eroding position in "British Asia."

The epilogue updates this story to the present, examining the fates of the Negro-Tokyo relationship, a passel of internees—particularly those who after the war departed Hong Kong for friendlier racial climes in South Africa—the response, years later, by a number of Asians to the Pacific War, the continuing story of racial discrimination in Hong Kong, and the not altogether remote prospect of a future "race war."

Acknowledgments

In researching a book of this type—a venture that involved traveling to five continents—one inevitably incurs debts of various sorts. Thankfully, I was the recipient of a Fulbright fellowship that brought me to Hong Kong University, where I spent a fruitful academic year. The students, staff, and faculty in American Studies, History, and English—in particular—were all helpful and merit my heartfelt thanks; Adams Bodomo notably taught me quite a bit. The History Workshop at HKU is a treasure, not to mention the Public Records Office in this "Pearl of the Orient." My reliance upon their resources can be gleaned from a cursory glance at the footnotes. The library at HKU was essential to my research, containing as it does an incomparable collection of materials on the Japanese occupation and on British colonialism.

The same holds true for the Public Records Office in London, which is a model of efficiency that archives worldwide could well emulate; the BBC Archives are an underutilized jewel. The Australian War Memorial in Canberra and the National Archives of New Zealand in Wellington were both helpful, as were the archives and libraries I visited in New Delhi, Kuala Lumpur, and Singapore. My stay in Bangkok was brief, though enlightening. An earlier Fulbright at the University of Zimbabwe not only led to my writing a book on that African nation but also helped to plant the seeds that led to the present work. Explorations in the well-organized National Archives of Zimbabwe were essential to the initial formulation of this book on Asia. I enjoyed the hospitality in London of Michael Casey, in New Delhi of Carl and Patricia Shipley, in Singapore of Grant Preston, in Tokyo of John Pfeffer.

In the United States, Walter Hill of the National Archives not only has been a reliable guide through this labyrinth but a good friend as well. The library at the University of North Carolina-Chapel Hill, where I was a member of the faculty when this research was conducted, was equally helpful. As the footnotes reveal, archives from the Atlantic to the Pacific provided useful materials.

Introduction

WITH ITS MAGNIFICENT HARBOR, steep peaks, and verdant surrounding islands, Hong Kong is one of the world's most physically imposing cities. The territory's 423 square kilometer area is divided into
four areas: Kowloon, the New Territories, Outlying Islands, and the
center of commerce: Hong Kong Island. This Crown Colony was punctuated by Victoria Peak, thirteen hundred feet above sea level, which
provided an astonishingly panoramic view of the city and outlying islands. But this beauty was rivaled by the splendid beaches of Repulse
Bay Beach. Then there was the quaint fishing village of the Aberdeen
district, where hundreds lived aboard junks and sampans.

The British gained a foothold here after the conclusion of the
Opium War in 1842, then fortified their position by obtaining the New
Territories in 1898. On the eve of the Japanese invasion there were about
1.7 million residents in Hong Kong, including fourteen thousand Europeans and seventy-five hundred Indians—the rest were overwhelmingly Chinese. But it was the Europeans who basked in opulence while
the Chinese were consigned to a desperate, racially blighted plight not
unlike that endured by Negroes in the U.S. South. However, when the
war arrived in December 1941, Japan started pouring molten gold
down the throat of the fabulously rich Croesus that was "British
China," choking it on its ill-gotten wealth.

Though Singapore, hundreds of miles to the south, was viewed as
the most strategically sited outpost of the Empire, others viewed Hong
Kong as possessing more potential—particularly as a gateway into the
fabled China market. This market captivated the city of London with
its dreamy prospect of selling billions of matches and socks.[1] Hong
Kong, the "Pearl of the Orient," was also a center of international intrigue and espionage. Hong Kong was no paragon of democracy either,

because the Chinese had no say in whether they wanted to be ruled from London.

Hong Kong was also a critically important trade entrepot. Even today, Hong Kong with a population of about 7 million has hefty foreign reserves of about $100 billion. By comparison, Brazil, Turkey, Russia, South Africa, and Greece combined did not reach this total—by far—though their combined populations were about fifty times larger than that of Hong Kong.[2] It is, according to the *Far Eastern Economic Review*, "one of the wealthiest places on earth," but now—as in the prewar era—it "suffers from one of the world's biggest economic gaps—a ticket . . . to economic and social instability."[3] And on the eve of the invasion by Japan, this instability was exacerbated by a gaping racial inequality in which tens of thousands of Chinese dwelled in miserable penury while Europeans luxuriated.

Perhaps this is why the Japanese seizure of Hong Kong in December 1941—about a century after the seizure by Britain—and their assault on the Empire in Asia was greeted as a combination of apocalypse and Judgment Day. As one commentator put it, "the psychological damage was even greater than the military defeat." Specifically, the capture of Singapore was "the greatest defeat an Asian army had inflicted on the Europeans since the bearded horsemen of Genghis Khan had swept from the east to the gates of Vienna more than seven centuries before. . . . a door closed on centuries of white supremacy." It was a "battle of East and West, coloured and white. . . . And in losing that battle they lost so much more as well. They lost their psychological superiority, their belief in their right to rule; and when they had lost that, there was little else left to lose."[4]

As the war raged, Ian Morrison conceded that "the supremacy of the white man, and the special status which he claimed, were bound to beget a reaction towards him." But now, he acknowledged reluctantly, "the privileged status of white man in the Far East is a thing of the past. It will not return . . . the white man will have to make his way and create a position for himself on his merits and quality alone. . . . not, as often hitherto, by virtue of the pigmentation of his skins and the warships of his country's navy."[5] He was partially correct: by the end of the century—at least in the United States—the prewar era was referred to as the period of "merits and quality," while efforts to undo the ravages of white supremacy were referred to as the era of an obsession with "pigmentation."

Driving this racial hysteria was many Europeans' fear that the day of reckoning had arrived. Not only would they be severely punished for past racial transgressions but worse, a new racial order would be forcibly imposed—with them at the bottom. This angst was not alleviated by the knowledge that the defeat of the Japanese invaders rested heavily on the often narrow shoulders of Asians and Africans, some of whom were none too keen to rescue those who had persecuted them on racial grounds.

Japanese militarists played adroitly on the feelings of those bruised by the ravages of white supremacy. In their internment camps the "majority" of the guards were Korean and Formosan under Japanese command; in these camps what unfolded was thought to be a new racial order with the latter on top and the European internees at the bottom. Non-Japanese Asians were being instructed to view Europeans as "inferior, subjugated people."[6] In Washington's "eyes, the worst Japanese war crime was the attempt to cripple the white man's prestige by sowing the seeds of racial pride under the banner of Pan-Asianism." The "International Military Tribunal for the Far East. . . . accused Japan of, among other things, 'racial arrogance' in challenging the stability of the status quo that existed under Western rule."[7] Placing the presumed beneficiaries of white supremacy in the bull's-eye was not without a painfully direct effect. The "death rate" of "Hong Kong survivors," that is, veterans of military internment camps, was, according to one account, "23% higher than that of veterans who had served in other theatres."[8]

Ironically, Japan's targeted racial policies had a strangely deracinating impact. Patrick Hardie was a Eurasian, born in Borneo in 1928. He grew up in Singapore where he recalled later a "house-to-house search for the white men" there after the Japanese takeover. His brother "looked very western," meaning "white," but when the Japanese forces arrived he changed his "racial" identity and "called himself a Malay." Later they reported to the newly imposed Tokyo authorities at "Beach Road." The "Japanese got two tables and said, 'What is your father? English? Then you have to go to one side. Those [with] fathers who are Eurasians, they will go to one side.'" And "having white father[s], all these people were brought to Roxy Theatre in East Coast Road, Katong," and were eventually interned. Patrick Hardie, on the other hand, who was not taken for "white" by the invaders, was not interned; instead he became a driver for them. London's policies, which had privileged those of "pure European descent," in one swooping maneuver were reversed by Japan, with consequences that reverberated even after the war's end.[9]

Given the shattering nature of Japan's racial policies in the occupied territories, why is it that these policies are—or were—not better known? John Dower writes that "if one asks Americans today in what ways World War II was racist and atrocious, they will point overwhelmingly to the Nazi genocide of the Jews. When the war was being fought, however, the enemy perceived to be most atrocious by Americans was not the Germans but the Japanese and the racial issues that provoked greatest emotion among Americans were associated with the war in Asia. . . . Japan's aggression stirred the deepest recesses of white [supremacy] and provoked a response bordering on the apocalyptic."[10]

These words suggest that the Pacific War should have left a cavernous imprint on the consciousness of Euro-Americans, not to mention the British. But there was another factor looming that served to vitiate this possibility. James Belich, the leading scholar of the titanic wars that led to a stalemate between the British invaders and the indigenous people of New Zealand, argues that as a result of this humbling episode, the British, like a child awakening from a vivid nightmare, resorted to their "final safety net," which was "to forget."[11] The Japanese racial assault was greeted with a similar syndrome of amnesia.

This blind spot about Asia and race was not simply limited to Japan and the war. The prominent U.S. journalist, Theodore White, acknowledged in 1975 that he had consciously omitted from his "reporting in all the years" he had spent in Asia "the simple dynamics of race hatred. Our presence there was self-defeating because they hated all of us, with historic good reason," he concluded in a thinly veiled reference to the racially marked colonialism endured by so many Asians. Even chief U.S. ally Chiang Kai-Shek, White asserts, "hated white men." White too felt that only the largest U.S. minority group could understand: "Perhaps only black Americans can sense," he averred, "that wild and helpless fury which the Asians felt at the presence of white men."[12] This was the powerful gravitational pull of which Japan took advantage before and during the war.

The scholar Alexander Saxton is no doubt correct that "there were good reasons for supporting the Allied cause in the Second World War; yet it added little to understanding white racism in American culture."[13] This is true, though the caveat might be added that it has added little to our understanding of racism in British culture either. Thus, because these policies are—and were—shrouded, fewer lessons could be drawn leading to deeper understanding of race and racism.

One reason why this wrenching wartime experience has not led to a crystalline comprehension is because as these events were unfolding, the London authorities chose to downplay them. When Japanese racial atrocities targeting Europeans and Euro-Americans were revealed, London noticed that "generally speaking . . . there has been a relative lack of Chinese interest in the British and American disclosures"; worse, it was noted forlornly, "it is also possible that the Chinese appreciate—and secretly sympathize with—the fact that one Japanese aim in perpetrating these atrocities was the humiliation of the white man, as part of the plan for his expulsion from East Asia."[14] In a "secret" memorandum from India, a British official cautioned that "publicity" about the "specific question of ill treatment of white captives should not be undertaken for the present, though a statement in general terms might be issued without reference to race of prisoners." Hence, it was decided that "the point is to emphasise by every means Japanese barbarity towards other Asiatics, but not to bolster up [the] Japanese self-proclaimed role as defender of Asiatics by putting out stories of their barbarous treatment of Europeans."[15]

Thus, in the heat of war the shoots of postwar racial policy and the forced retreat from white supremacy were already evident: a compelled assertion of equality between European and non-European peoples, and further, an assertion of "nonracialism," denying even the relevance of a characteristic that heretofore had been proclaimed from on high.

The United States, in some ways more sensitive than the United Kingdom to such racial questions because of its tortured history of racial slavery and indigenous dispossession, went a step further. In mid-1942 the U.S. Joint Psychological Warfare Committee sent a "secret" proposal to their British allies, warning that "it is essential to avoid giving unwitting aid to the Japanese propaganda attempt to convert the Pacific war into a racialist, Pan-Asia war." It was "advisable to institute a program of propaganda directed toward people in this country to lessen the strong racial prejudice existing in white Americans toward colored races, including the Negro. Such propaganda could not take the form of direct statements regarding this racial prejudice, but could be done indirectly by telling the accomplishments of colored races." It was also "essential to avoid reference to such terms of racial opprobrium as 'little,' 'yellow,' 'slant-eyed,' 'natives,' etc. Within limits of considerable care, it will be possible to meet Japanese anti-white propaganda with the utterances of American Negro leaders."[16]

Again, one detects the compelled contours of postwar racial policy as the war was unfolding: an exquisite awareness of racial sensitivities, which would be derided years later as "political correctness," straining to avoid giving offense to those formerly subjected to such noxious practices systematically; plus, pushing "American Negro leaders" forward, especially on the global stage, so as to deflect concerns about Jim Crow.[17]

The Australians were instructed sternly in "Political War Directives," coded as "Most Secret," to "avoid especially anything that can be construed as an assumption of racial superiority." The only divergence deemed suitable for deployment was "using German racial doctrine as a Nazi-Japanese irritant," that is, "the fact that Germans consider themselves superior to all other nations, considering [Japanese] as fit only to slave for Germany." Turning to Vietnam, it was reported with sobriety that "Annamites have seen the people of the yellow race, the Japanese, show themselves masters of organisation and display at least temporary superiority over Europeans" and thus "it is unsafe to assume . . . a return to complete French control after the war. . . ." Thus Canberra, which had a state-sanctioned policy of racial superiority, was obligated to make at least a rhetorical retreat from these practices.[18]

But this was a retreat through a minefield. British officials, for example, knew that "it is a tricky business to tell [Japanese] that Hitler despises the yellow races; they might answer, 'the only person we [hear] this absurd insult from is *you*.'"[19]

Yet nations that had turned white supremacy into a blunt system were often perplexed by the nuances of racial and ethnic maneuvering. In mid-1942, officials of Britain's Ministry of Information met as the war seemed to be going quite well for Tokyo. "The question was raised whether" they "could make use of the pronouncement by the Japanese that in Malaya and in Thailand they proposed to oust the Chinese from their important trading position for the alleged purpose of giving the Malays a greater share in the country's economic life." Yet, it was noted sadly, "the argument is a double edged weapon." In short, London ran the risk of driving more Malays—in Malaya and the populous Dutch East Indies—straight into the arms of the welcoming Japanese if they publicized Tokyo's demarche.[20] Years of an enforced white supremacy were being entangled in the mesh of seeking to fight a war purportedly for freedom and democracy.

There are other reasons why the racial policies of this horrendous war are not better known. For various reasons, the question of race in the Asia-Pacific region has been obscured intentionally. As the twentieth century dawned and the war in the Philippines gripped the feverish imaginations of many in Washington, the U.S. military in Hawaii "sought to avoid racial conflicts: one general order explicitly stated 'such delicate subjects as . . . the race question, etc., will not be discussed at all except among ourselves and officially.'" There was a decided fear among many officers "who believed, quite as sweepingly, that 'there was a natural bond between the rural Filipinos and the American Negro'" troops and a robust ventilation of the "race question" could only convince these two groups of their mutual hostility toward white supremacy.[21] A corollary to this reticence was the report that during the Pacific War London was "reluctant to initiate an anti-German campaign among West Africans because officials calculated that such propaganda might encourage a revolt against white rule as such. 'Having been encouraged to hate one branch of the white race, they may extend the feeling to others,' warned one memorandum."[22]

Washington, and especially London, faced tremendous constraints in coping with Japan's "race war." At that desperate moment they had to distinguish themselves not only from Japan's racial policies—but also had to distance themselves from their own racial practices. London had to proclaim the exalted aims of democracy of the Atlantic Charter, while seeking to deny democracy to their Asian and African colonies. The British Empire especially was flummoxed by the turn that race took during the war. One approach adopted was an eerie silence about what was going on. Even in the Middle East, it was decided that though "the Palestine question raises great attention . . . one should discuss as little as possible sensitive points like colour" or "racial characteristics."[23]

Consequently, given this orchestrated silence, unearthing the impact of the race war on the British Empire is not easy. Complicating this conundrum is the fact that even before the war erupted, "It is striking how little racist thinking was questioned before the Second World War. Even critical critics of imperialism were reluctant to criticize the racist justification for national expansion."[24] Back then, "few Britons of any class were concerned with the conditions of the people ruled by England. . . . School textbooks barely mentioned the colonies. Those works that did predictably described the colonies in paternalistic and racist terms, as did most popular literature."[25] Even in the early postwar era, "it would be vain to search through the debates of the House of Commons in recent years for any general debate on the problems of the British Empire as a whole or the impact of these problems. . . . In the old days the annual India debate used to be guaranteed to empty the House."[26] Though Japan imposed a brutally racial policy on Europeans interned in Hong Kong, few of the flood of memoirs that emerged from this catastrophic experience even raised this topic, as if it were too tormenting—or dangerous—to recall.[27]

It was a momentous occasion in 1853 when Commodore Matthew C. Perry waded on shore in Japan, ending more than two centuries of self-imposed isolation. At this auspicious moment, he chose to march between two orderlies, "both tall and stalwart Negroes." Though he represented a nation that exalted African slavery, and while docked in Hong Kong had sanctioned a racially insensitive performance of "Ethiopian Minstrels" amid "roars of laughter," for whatever reason "he wished citizens of color to take part" during this epoch-rendering instant. As a precursor of a tendency that was to emerge full-blown in coming decades, the Japanese during this landing "were more interested in the Negroes," the "first they had ever seen."[28]

What motivated Perry? This remains unclear. Perhaps he wished to impress the Japanese with the realization that they too could become enslaved, not unlike "stalwart" Negroes in the Americas. Or perhaps they could simply be subjugated, like those who resided in Hong Kong and India. Whatever the case, what ensued was one of the more extraordinary developments in human history: the Meiji Restoration, the creation of an advanced society by Asians in a blunt refutation of the predicates of white supremacy. As the scholar Peter Duus put it, the Japanese "had transformed themselves into a modern nation mainly out of fear"—fear that they too could be enslaved or colonized. According to Duus, this also helped to induce among many Japanese a sincere desire to overthrow white supremacy. This "would be on a par with, but on a grander scale than either the French Revolution, which emancipated the 'common people' or the Russian Revolution which emancipated the 'working class.' It would be no less than a 'revolution for mankind,'" the liberation of those who were not "white."[29]

Self-defense may have motivated this "sincere desire," for it was evident that Britain was cutting a prodigious swath through Africa and Asia because of the widespread use of African and Asian troops. Undermining white supremacy and alleviating the plight of the dispossessed might help to ease the increasing pressure on Japan itself. The British army that attacked Hong Kong in May 1842 was comprised predominantly of Indians. Throughout the nineteenth century the Indian army was sent on numerous occasions to fight for British interests in campaigns in China, Egypt, and elsewhere. Just as it was the Indian market that accounted for 20 percent of British exports by the 1880s and propelled the island nation to wealth, so it was the Indian army and its huge reserve force that allowed London to confront the huge conscript armies of continental states like Germany, France, and Russia. Lord Curzon was no doubt correct when he said, "As long as we rule India, we are the greatest power in the world. If we lose it we shall drop straightaway [to] a third rate power."[30] Strikingly, Indians—not only on the subcontinent but throughout Asia, notably in Hong Kong—were some of Japan's closest allies during the war.

Japan's fear of possible servitude unless the nation was transformed drastically was heightened by the fact that the British often deployed the ultimate epithet—"Nigger"—not only against Africans but against Asians as well.[31] Indeed, the repetitive pattern in which this quintessential U.S. epithet was used in Asia, along with the equation of Asians themselves with simians—a comparison once thought to be reserved for Africans—points to the toxic unity of a white supremacy that spanned the Pacific.

Hence, the popular African American musician Buck Clayton was moved when on arriving in Shanghai in the 1930s he saw "four rickshaws coming down the street with some white American marines in them. The next thing I heard was the white guys saying, 'There they are. Niggers, niggers, niggers!' And before long one of them threw a brick that they had piled up in rickshaws." These Euro-Americans obviously saw parallels between Chinese and Negroes. So did Clayton. Illustrating the essential unity between and among victims of white supremacy, he joined in the fray alongside the Chinese targets of these epithets and against his erstwhile American compatriots. "Soon fists were flying everywhere," and one of his opponents had the audacity to dislodge "my brand new Stetson hat." Enraged, Clayton "grabbed this cat and put a headlock on him and proceeded to run his head into a brick wall" and "just as a last gesture I kicked him in the butt as he ran." When "it was all over the Chinese onlookers treated us like we had done something that they had always wanted to do and followed us all the way home cheering us like a winning football team. I guess they figured it was something that should have been done a long time before, because I remember one time I saw a marine fall off a bicycle and he promptly got up, went over to a Chinese coolie and kicked him in the ass and then got back on his bicycle and rode on off."[32] This anecdote illuminates simultaneously how some people of European descent treated both blacks and Chinese contemptuously and how this disdain could drive the latter two groups together. Above all, the concept of white supremacy was tailor-made to be exploited by Tokyo.

Yet this was a hard lesson for some to learn. Lewis Bush was interned in Hong Kong where he received a bitter taste of subordination. But his experience did not prevent him from participating in what he termed "nigger minstrels" while interned. He made no connection between these performances and other incidents, for example, when a Japanese soldier came to "our room" to "slap and kick us around, stand us to attention and then harangue us on the iniquities of the American and British. 'You win war,'" the soldier screamed, "'and you make all Japanese like black slaves!'"[33]

Many Europeans and Euro-Americans routinely used the term "monkey"—often deployed against those of African descent—to describe the Japanese.[34] Benjamin Proulx, captive in wartime Hong Kong, referred to the Japanese who imprisoned him as the "cartoon personification of monkey-Japanese. . . . Their bodies were stubby, like apes, but strong."[35] The South African O. D. Gallagher—who had reason to be familiar with racial invective—referred to the Japanese as "apes in uniform" and "slant-eyed flying apes called Japanese."[36] The leading U.S. military figure in wartime China, Joseph Stilwell, not only used the term "nigger" but also "wops" and "gooks"—and "chinks" to refer to the Chinese who accompanied him in the trenches.[37] Years after the war had concluded, this despicable practice was still going strong, as the well-respected historian of Hong Kong, Alan Birch, made an indelicate colloquial reference to "another nigger in the woodpile."[38] In short, many of those of European descent tended to lump together in an all-embracing racism those of non-European descent. This in turn was a generous donation to Tokyo's effort to band together the planet's majority in an all-embracing crusade against white supremacy.

The first statesman to have used the term "yellow peril" publicly was reportedly Germany's Kaiser Wilhelm. He was inspired by the Australian writer, Charles Pearson, whose work had an electrifying impact on the Pan-European world: "It is doubtful that any book with an Australian inspiration has ever had a greater impact among intellectuals in Britain or the United States." The popular Fu Manchu series, the subject of numerous U.S. and British films from the 1920s forward, spoke of the alleged Asian need to "control the world and eliminate the white race."[39] The Kaiser reflected this alarm in 1895 when he "commissioned an artist to draw an allegorical picture depicting the European powers called together by the Archangel Michael, and united in resisting Buddhism, heathenism and barbarism." This fear and loathing among those of European descent was a product of apprehension not only of the potential power of China but the actual and growing power of Japan. They feared an abrupt reversal of fortunes in which the racialized colonization that Europeans had pioneered might be turned against them.

For its part, in the early twentieth century the Japanese elite "knew that, deep in its collective heart, the white race feared domination by the yellow race. . . . It was plain that should Japan and China combine to fight Russia, fear of the 'yellow peril' would become so intense that Germany, France and other countries would most probably intervene." In turn, Theodore Roosevelt felt that "at bottom" Japan tended to "lump Russians, English, Americans, Germans, all of us, simply as white devils inferior to themselves. . . . They include all white men as being people who, as a whole, they dislike and whose past arrogance they resent." As the new century dawned, racial nervousness was surging, with Tokyo near the heart of this troublesome matter.[40]

Bruce Cumings, a scholar of Korea, has written that "in the first decade of [the twentieth] century Japan was flypaper for many Asian progressives,"[41] attracting them in droves as an antipode to European colonialism. The Chinese were also attracted, though China's justifiable post-World War II anger at Tokyo and related reasons has made this a difficult point to raise. One observer has uncovered close ties between the Japanese ultranationalist faction, the Black Dragon Society, and the Chinese hero lauded by Communists and nationalists alike:

Sun Yat-Sen. The BDS "aimed at driving all Europeans and Americans out of Asia" and so did Sun. Simultaneously, after the Bolshevik Revolution in European capitals there was a perception of a growing alliance between Tokyo, Moscow, and the Chinese leadership aimed at their common antagonists, principally London and Washington. When Tokyo and Moscow concluded a treaty in 1925, when others were seeking to isolate the Bolsheviks, the perception of an alliance was strengthened.[42] As Soviet and Japanese influence rose among Sun's forces, the Chinese leader's "speeches became increasingly anti-western. . . . [His] concept of nationality came to imply racial struggle in which China would rid herself of the unequal treaties, extra-territoriality and foreign controls on her economy, while the People's Livelihood implied a socialist state."[43]

Even before the rise of Sun, the Empress Dowager "entered into a pact with the Boxers giving them a free hand against foreign white residents in the country and their Chinese sympathizers such as all Christians were presumed to be."[44] As for Chiang Kai-Shek, he attended the "Shinbo Gykyo (Preparatory Military Academy) in Tokyo; he remained in Japan four years. . . . As a part of his study he served with the 13th Field Artillery (Takada), Regiment of the Imperial Army," where he gained a "working insight into the Japanese language, mentality and strength."[45] As late as the winter of 1940–41, "it was widely rumored that secret meetings were being held there between Japanese agents and representatives of Chiang kai-shek."[46] Chiang was not unique. Amy Li Chong Yuet-ming, the late wife of contemporary Hong Kong's preeminent billionaire, Li Ka-shing, was "fluent" in Japanese.[47] Ironically, the British may have boosted Japan's efforts by vigorously persecuting the most passionate anti-Tokyo forces: the Chinese Communist Party.[48]

Hence, when the Japanese invaded Hong Kong in 1941, some Chinese willingly and eagerly joined the war against the British crown. Quickly there emerged a "sensational revelation," a "plan to massacre the entire European community of the colony." "Zero hour was to have been A.M. on December 13, 1941." Chinese triads, or brotherhoods widely viewed as organized crime formations, were to spearhead this scheme. "Leaders of the underworld were gathered together and a meeting was held between them and police officials at the Cecil Hotel." After hours of vigorous debate—and perhaps the payment of a sizable bribe—the authorities "came to terms with the underworld."[49]

Of course, Sun himself was a "Triad official of long standing"; "overseas Triad branches were fully utilised for the dissemination of Republican propaganda." However, by the war's advent, Chinese triads were split between pro-Chiang, neutral, and pro-Japan formations. The latter worked closely with the invaders and profited handsomely during the occupation.[50]

But the triads were not alone. Tokyo "had little difficulty in successfully recruiting numerous Chinese collaborators or traitors to fill the ranks of the puppet governments" in China. The invaders were "bolstered by the influx of troops from former warlord armies, Nanking's puppet army swelled to nearly 600,000 men." There was "little wonder that the [Communists] charged the KMT [nationalists] and Chiang with being united with the enemy or puppet troops." Thus, the story of Wang Ching-wei, the chief collaborator with Tokyo, "should not be written off lightly as the tale of a traitor to China."[51]

Inevitably, the racialized colonialism forcibly imposed in "British China" played a major role in compelling some Chinese to become "traitors" to an Empire that held no allegiance to them. Similar dynamics no doubt compelled a number of Japanese Americans to cross a similar line. Japanese Americans who fought on behalf of the nation that interned their relatives have received justifiable attention. Less attention has been paid to an untold number—outraged by the illogic of white supremacy—who crossed the Pacific and aligned themselves with Tokyo in the occupied territories. Even before Pearl Harbor there was an "extraordinarily high level of per capita contributions from" Issei in Hawaii to the Japanese war effort. Hanama Harold Tasaki, to cite one example, was born in Maui in 1913, studied at Oberlin College and worked in California. In 1936 he went to Japan and joined the military. Why? Among other reasons, he "had carried a residue of resentment, recalling discrimination against Hawaii's Japanese. One memory remained vivid: at PTA meetings his mother and father had been snubbed by haoles [whites]."[52] He was not alone.[53] Many Asian American expatriates, perhaps because they were seeking revenge for the racism they had endured in the United States, were viewed by European internees in Hong Kong as among the most vicious authorities they had encountered.[54]

But then Tokyo surrendered and Hong Kong was liberated, only to return to British suzerainty where it was to remain until 1997. However, the war had decimated the European colonists, as many were killed or died during internment. After August 1945 some had the wherewithal to repair to the more comfortable racial climes of South Africa, while still others fled the region virtually penniless after their wilting experience. Much of their property had been looted, either by the Japanese invaders or the Chinese. Their roles in the economy had been supplanted during the war by these two groups as well. So when the British fled and the Japanese were ousted, this created opportunities for the Chinese—which horrified many.

One gentleman wrote to the colonial authorities in 1947, "deploring the fact that a number of persons appear to have flourished under enemy occupation." But the "difficulty of obtaining evidence and otherwise establishing the fact of 'collaboration' as the origin of improved fortunes, as distinct from other causes, [was] great." Tseng Yu-Hao and Denis Victor were not deterred by such assertions when they wrote to the crown's representative. Hong Kong was "accused" of being the "Paradise of Collaborators," they sputtered. This was a "black mark" on the colony's reputation. Hong Kong's "leading collaborators are mostly proteges or even members of some high councils of which [Hong Kong's] government has no control." Many of these were "buyers of land in the occupation days" who were now "trying to influence the former sellers to sign the deeds a second time," thus multiplying the indignity.[55] Their appeals went unheeded, not least because at that juncture London required the support or at least sympathy of the collaborators in their confrontation with the growing power of the Communist Party, just across the border on the mainland.

"Race war" is not an alien concept in the Empire or the United States. The rebellion in India in 1857 was viewed in these disquieting terms.[56] In South Africa Jan Smuts noted privately, "I have heard natives saying, 'Why fight against Japan? We are oppressed by the whites and we shall not fare worse under the Japanese.'"

In 1943 as a veritable "race war" was raging in Asia Senator Elbert Thomas of Utah worried about providing aid to China since just as "Genghis Khan got into Europe. . . . we can loose in Asia forces so great that the world will be deluged," that is, in aiding China's resistance to Japan, the United States might wind up bolstering a bigger foe. Congressman Charles Eaton shared this concern. If the "Oriental peoples" were to "have independent and civilized nations," then "eventually the

United States . . . might be pushed off the map." In fact, he advised, "there might be a racial war between the yellow man and the white man in the future [and] we may be liquidated."[57]

Edwin Embree, head of the prestigious Rosenwald Fund, spoke in similarly portentous terms in 1944. Linking the "advancement of the Negroes during the last half-century" with "the general upsurge of colored peoples the world over," he warned that the "balance has shifted radically." The "white man of the Western World," Mr. Embree said, "was being offered the last chance for equal status in world society." He continued, "if the Western white man persists in trying to run the show, in exploiting the whole earth. . . . non-western people may in surging rebellion, smash him into nonentity."[58]

This fear was magnified by the possibility that such a conflict could spill over onto U.S. shores and that African Americans might ally with Tokyo in the "final solution" of the question of the "white man of the Western World." Also declaiming in 1944, W. E. B. Du Bois, who had sought to forestall "race war" on the east bank of the Pacific, felt compelled to invoke this macabre concept again. "The remainder of the Balkans and Russia," he announced, "have been [viewed] as Asiatic barbarism, aping civilization. As quasi-Asiatic, they have come in for the racial contempt poured upon the yellow peoples. This attitude greeted the Russian revolution and [the major powers] staged almost race war to uphold tottering capitalism, built on racial contempt." The "'yellow peril'" he warned, "as envisaged by the German Emperor William II [sic] has by no means passed from the subconscious reactions of Western Europe."[59]

Can we dismiss Du Bois's prophetic words today? Are relations between Japan and China and Asia on the one hand and the Pan-European world on the other still tinged—or saturated—with race, to the point of "race war"? Let us hope not. Still, it is well to reexamine the most recent occasion when "race war" reigned, not least since this phenomenon seemed to work symbiotically with the prospect of "class war" in compelling concessions from otherwise obdurate elites.

I

To Be of "Pure European Descent"

IF A VISITOR FROM THE U.S. SOUTH had arrived in Hong Kong in November 1941, he would have recognized a kind of racial segregation and racially coded deprivation that would have made him feel at home. Lucien Brunet was born in Montreal and was not unfamiliar with discrimination, being French Canadian, but even his otherwise blasé conscience was moved by what he witnessed when he arrived in Hong Kong on the eve of the Japanese invasion. It was "very depressing," he recalled years later. The "poverty" was so widespread, "I could not believe my eyes." The "place was so poor," he lamented. There were a "lot of people without shoes . . . wearing black pants and a hat. Women were doing the same work as [men]"; all Chinese were "treated as non-human," he concluded sadly.[1]

Robert Hammond thought similarly. A missionary born in Hong Kong, the revolting degradation of the region was not new to him. Yet when he returned to China with his family in 1939, he was stunned by what he saw. Above all, it was the sight of the "coolies" that amazed him. "These yellow men" with their ragged clothes were a portrait in penury. "Many had their shirts off and one pant leg rolled up; on their feet they wore grass sandals. Old pieces of cloth were tied around their heads to keep the sweat from running down their faces."[2] The noted physician, Selwyn-Clarke, found "wards full of beri-beri . . . in the late thirties," while "hunger and disease were rife." Cholera, smallpox, and tuberculosis were common.[3]

Like the Negroes of the U.S. South whom they so closely resembled, Chinese and other Asians in Hong Kong had no rights that Europeans were bound to respect. For the longest time, theater tickets were restricted to Europeans.[4] European hotels and clubs routinely restricted entry by Chinese; one museum placed limitations on the hours when Chinese—but not Europeans—could visit. In the nineteenth century a succession of laws required Chinese to carry night passes, a common practice in apartheid South Africa. A Chinese was not appointed to the ruling Executive Council until 1926. Only European children could attend the Kowloon School and the Victorian School.[5] As its name implies, the Central British School was exclusively for British children. Eurasians and Chinese went to Diocesan Boys' or Girls' School and the Chinese had Queen's and King's Colleges.[6]

Luckily, those not of "pure European descent" had some access to education, for Hong Kong lacked a "good public library" and a "town hall," not least because the colonizers were "more interested in its race course, its golf links and its clubs."[7] The highly regarded Hong Kong barrister Percy Chen recalled that Hong Kong "was governed in the same way as a police state is governed."[8] Hong Kong was a "Crown Colony," and in such a system—said the former Governor of the city, Alexander Grantham—"the Governor is next to the Almighty."[9]

There was a stifling residential segregation. Amidst a maze of narrow winding streets and dimly lit passages the Chinese were consigned to housing that had all the commodious features of rabbit warrens. In 1899 a "European reservation" was established in Kowloon. In language that would not have seemed out of place in South Africa at that precise moment, it was noted in passing that the "low lying land between Robinson Road and Carnarvon Road is absolutely unadapted for residences for Europeans and eminently adapted for native dwelling."[10] In 1919 an application was made for a "proposed European Reservation on the Middle Levels east of Glenealy."[11] This apartheid had popular support among many Europeans. In 1930 "homeowners and residents in the reserved area of Cheung Chan" nervously pointed to the "considerable apprehension [that] has been felt lately owing to rumours of tentative attempts by certain people to obtain a footing in the reserved area. . . . Residence in Cheung Chan would become impossible if Chinese with different standards of living and habits were permitted to enter at will." Thus, they felt constrained to bar "admission as residents of non-Europeans and non-Americans."[12]

"British China" might have been a suburb of hell for many Chinese but for the European refugees from the English-speaking world who flocked there it was akin to paradise regained. There was a clearly defined social stratum in which one's place was fixed according to race and nationality, but also on the basis of position, accent, and education. The geography of Hong Kong in the prewar period mirrored this pecking order. There was "The Peak," of course, where only the presence of the wealthy Ho Tungs interrupted an unbroken skein of racial segregation. There one could escape the miasmic heat during the colony's brutal summers, and avoid the peculiar musky scent of Hong Kong, composed of sandalwood, cinnamon, jute, urine, and tar. The affluent Japanese in Hong Kong had encroached only as far as Macdonnell Road, a safe distance from "The Peak." Between Macdonnell and May roads there was a neutral zone in the lower part of which resided the Nipponese, while Portuguese, Jews, Armenians, and Parsees lived in the upper part. Below "The Peak" lived the Chinese masses in dark, dirty, rat-infested low-rise tenements.[13]

When E. H. Parker arrived in Hong Kong in 1903 he was "surprised" to discover that "life in China is much more luxurious than it is at home. Servants and food are so cheap that a dollar goes almost as far there as a pound at home."[14] This idyll rolled on—until December 1941.[15] Perhaps the penultimate symbol of the moneyed and sumptuous life[16] led by most Europeans in the colony before the war[17] was the fact that simple soldiers could employ a barber on a monthly basis for about one pound. For this, they received one haircut a month and a shave every morning—in bed: whether asleep or awake.[18]

It would be a mistake to see this comfortable life in the "East"—not to mention the searing bias that made it possible—as purely the province of the British, or even the English. Far from it. Australians in Melanesia relished similar privileges.[19] And Canada was in the same league when it came to discriminating against the Chinese.[20]

Euro-Americans, no slouches in this ghastly competition, were notorious for their pioneering role in perpetuating the African slave trade. The family of U.S. President Franklin D. Roosevelt was implicated deeply in the lucrative China trade in the nineteenth century, which was in some ways a supplement and substitute of its more ill-famed geographical cousin. His mother's father, Warren Delano, had been a partner in the leading firm, Russell & Company, founded in 1824, which for a while was as influential as the notorious East India Company. It dealt in opium as well as tea. Sara Delano, Roosevelt's mother, lived for several periods during her girlhood at the family home, Rose Hill, in Hong Kong. Her two oldest sisters were born there and married partners of Russell & Company. At Hyde Park, New York, Roosevelt himself was brought up among slightly ostentatious Chinese furnishings.[21]

Yet, like the British, the Yankees too were prone to discriminate against the Chinese. So said Liang Yen who worked with the Office of

Strategic Services—Washington's precursor of the Central Intelligence Agency—in Kunming, China, during the war. There she found that interracial marriages "were not socially accepted and their children—'Eurasian' was a derogatory word—were outcasts among both Chinese and Westerners. . . . There were reports of doors barred, spiteful words, even in the United States." Across the Pacific, Chinese "were thought of as laundrymen, chop-suey vendors. The opportunities for recognition and advancement for which America was famous were not open to them; they were treated as inferiors. I couldn't help feeling a bit of this attitude at first [in Kunming]."[22]

Similar rough conditions persisted in "British China," as homelessness was a common condition for Chinese in Hong Kong. Major Albert Hood, who served in Hong Kong before the war, reminisced that "Many, many of them had nowhere to live, they carried a rush mat with them at night and at night they laid themselves down—and this was in Hong Kong too—and they laid themselves down on the footpath, laid down on their rush mat, rolled over, and they slept there all night just like rows of sausages laid out."[23] This sad reality also left an impression on Andrew Salmon; in the late 1930s "anywhere other than the main central district you used to have to step over these people. The whole streets were covered [with] these street sleepers . . . individuals and families."[24]

Further up the social ladder, Chinese were barred for the longest time from the prestigious Hong Kong Jockey Club. They could not become jockeys or own horses though they were allowed to throw away their money by placing bets. Massive protest in 1915 caused a tactical retreat by the British authorities. It was not until the Japanese took over that these exclusionary practices changed substantially, as a Chinese, Ho Kom-tong, was named chairman. As the leading contemporary Hong Kong commentator, Frank Ching, put it, "The Japanese. . . . involved large numbers of Chinese people at all levels of government in a way never attempted by the British."[25]

By the late 1920s there was segregation in nearly every part of the traveling process. Passengers traveled in separate classes, disembarked in separate ways, and were sold tickets by parallel but separate organizations. Usually there was a special class for foreign [European] travelers with foreign food and furniture, and a Chinese first class, with Chinese food and round tables. There was a barbarous indifference to the hideous conditions in which Chinese passengers ate, slept, bathed, relieved themselves, and promenaded. A launch met all steamers to land saloon—that is, foreign—passengers on a trip to, say, Shanghai, leaving most of the Chinese to take a sampan and endure exorbitant over-charges on the part of "coolies."[26] Hong Kong was little better. For the "first fifty years on the Star Ferry," which plied the choppy waters of the harbor, "no Chinese was allowed to ride first class and no European could ride second class."[27]

A similar pattern obtained on mass transit in Hong Kong. When the British soldier John Sutcliffe Whitehead arrived in Hong Kong in 1938 he was struck by the fact that on "the double-deck tram . . . the top deck was for . . . the well-to-do people we were classified in. And the bottom deck of the tramcar was for the coolies['] class." Though he was from a coal mining family back home, in Hong Kong he was able to ride with the "taipans."[28]

On the other hand, Alice Y. Lan and Betty M. Hu recalled that "prior to the outbreak of the Pacific War, we often had to wait for half an hour or more for the signature of one of the British clerks. Sometimes he was really busy, but often, knowing that we were Chinese, he would pur-posely make us await his pleasure. How long we had resented this."[29]

These mudsills of society—these "non-Europeans" and "non-Americans"—were treated by the Europeans as if they were so much rubbish. Kenneth Andrew was a Hong Kong policeman from 1912 to 1938. He recalled that the "European looked upon the Chinese as being the lowest form of animal life; I have actually seen a European ricksha [sic] passenger throw his fare . . . to the ground rather than risk touch-ing the ricksha-coolie."[30] In Hong Kong and the numerous treaty ports dominated by colonial powers that littered mainland China, Sinopho-bia was rampant.

Like Negro men of the Deep South, Chinese males of all ages were routinely referred to as boys and beaten for the slightest of transgres-sions. Emily Hahn, the U.S. journalist who resided in prewar Hong Kong, once told of an Englishman visiting San Francisco where he had encountered a Chinese "boy" who did not get out of the way as he walked along the street. "Why in a civilized country," he sputtered, "I'd have flayed the bastard!"[31]

Visitors often remarked on this impatient and violent behavior to-ward the Chinese and "the diplomatic records record it" in sickening detail. Violence was "common enough to enter Chinese Shanghai slang: eating waiguo huotui (foreign ham) meant receiving the all too frequent kicks aimed at rickshaw pullers by foreign passengers." When inchoate violence descended into random fatalities, the penalty to be paid was often negligible. London's Consul-General in Shanghai once remarked that a "jury would never bring a verdict of 'guilty' against a 'white' British subject charged with the murder or manslaughter of a Chinese."[32]

Mirroring these horrific sentiments was a British police officer in Shanghai who confided in 1921 that the Chinese "should only be treated as the animals they are." Later he was to describe the Chinese as "yellow pigs" and a "bunch of worthless, treacherous, yellow-skinned reptiles." Bernard Wasserstein, an astute analyst of "Old Shanghai," suggests that "these were not merely the ravings of a disgruntled individual. They echoed a general opinion in the expatriate community— and in official circles."[33]

Rudyard Kipling, the poet laureate of British colonialism, confirms this allegation. "I hated the Chinaman before," he began angrily, "I hated him doubly as I choked for breath in his seething streets." His demented passion reaching a disturbing crescendo, he concluded, "Now I understand why the civilized European of Irish extraction kills the Chinaman in America. It is justifiable to kill him. It would be quite right to wipe the city of Canton off the face of the earth and to exterminate all the people who ran away from the shelling. The Chinaman ought not to count."[34]

These were not simply inflamed rhetorical outbursts. John Sutcliffe Whitehead, who served with the military in Hong Kong, noted pointedly that the "white officer type always was armed." Why? Well, "if there was a bloke in the market place and he was stealing or something like that the usual [cry] in the market place was 'stop thief, stop thief.' With that he'd fire one shot in the air. If that had no avail upon the thief, bang! The next one went into him and they'd pick up the body." With no residual regret, he concluded, "Such was summary justice in Hong Kong at that time," with British soldiers as police, judge, jury—and executioner.[35]

In part, the Chinese may have been stealing in the marketplace because so many jobs were barred to them. Andrew observes that "senior posts" in "Maritime Customs" were "all held by Europeans. . . . The Peak Tramway was operated entirely by Europeans and the cars were actually operated by European crews. . . . There was then no Asiatic and Indian police officers holding gazetted rank . . . and certainly no women police. . . . The judiciary were all Europeans as were most of the legal luminaries. . . . Most of the firemen were Chinese but the drivers were European policemen. . . . The first floor was the living quarters for Chinese firemen. The second floor was for the European."[36] As one writer put it, "In government there was a distinct level beyond which the Chinese, however able and well-qualified, could not rise."[37]

Though Hong Kong University had been initiated by the colonists, its enrollment was limited and its eminently qualified graduates faced all manner of discriminatory barriers. Man Wah Leung Bentley, who was at the university in 1940, remembered later that "the teaching staff"—which was mostly British—that she "encountered at lectures and tutorials showed no interest in their students' progress or intellectual concerns and treated them like strangers." These professors "did not encourage criticism or dissent." HKU "forbade the discussion of political topics and the formation of political clubs . . . for fear of upsetting the status quo."[38] Yet, while HKU regularly turned out graduates of impeccable intellect, illiterate Canadians in the colony could rise higher on the socioeconomic ladder for racial reasons alone.[39]

Sir Shouson Chow, born in 186l, was the first Chinese to join the Executive Council that helped to administer Hong Kong. His admission to this celestial circle was a direct response to the unrest of 1925 in Shanghai where nine were killed by British troops—an event that was echoed in Hong Kong. Perhaps not coincidentally, in 1907 he received the "Order of the Rising Sun (4th Class)" from Japan and soon became the "first person to be knighted in Hong Kong by a representative of the British royal family and only the third Chinese person to be knighted—in a colonial history of nearly 80 years." But in his youth he had to endure the degrading spectacle of setting sail for the United States for education and suffering through "queue-pulling" or the pulling of his pigtail. This was during a time when "British soldiers would beat Chinese people in the streets for no apparent reason." He recalled a time in 1919 when laws were passed in Hong Kong "restricting Chinese from living in certain areas of Cheung Chau." He recalled a time when "the Foreign Office . . . was unashamedly racist, like most of the British policy-makers of the time."[40] Not surprisingly, during the invasion he was viewed widely as one of the chief collaborators with Tokyo.

As late as the eve of the war, a cruel repression enveloped Hong Kong. Police kept a vigilant eye on the Chinese community, harassing, imprisoning, or banishing political activists and censoring mail and literature. Labor unions were virtually impossible to organize. The quelling of activism helped to ossify a racial and economic apartheid that rivaled what was then unfolding in Southern Africa.[41]

Of course, the precious term "European"—this umbrella term that could protect illiterate Canadians—was not defined expansively. While "Europeans" sat atop the racial hierarchy, not all "whites" were created equal. The Sassoon family was one of the wealthiest in Hong Kong; they were friends of Edward VII when he was still the playboy prince of Wales. Yet members of this family were never admitted to the Hong Kong Club because of their Bombay Jewish origins.[42] In fact, in the early part of the twentieth century there was a "Jewish cemetery," just as there was a "Eurasian Cemetery."[43]

But however the term European was defined, few among this group were sufficiently courageous to challenge frontally the racial chauvinism that pervaded Hong Kong. There were honorable exceptions. James Bertram, a New Zealander, recollected that Hilda Selwyn-Clarke—spouse of Hong Kong's leading physician and a prominent member of the tiny political left—"was the only Englishwoman [there] to use her social position all the way on behalf of the struggle of the Chinese people." Conceivably because of her past associations with the "Society for Cultural Relations with the USSR" and "Mm. Kamaladevi" of the Indian National Congress who was "kept under surveillance wherever she moved," Selwyn-Clarke was seen by many as being rather odd and marginal, thus hampering severely her antiracist activism.[44]

Tony Carroll was born in Hong Kong in the late nineteenth century. In 1986 he recalled the suffocating superciliousness of his fellow Britons: "They had this nose-in-the-air attitude, terrible, Chinese had to humble themselves before them and this was deeply resented." Because he was reputedly of Irish and Cuban heritage he could not ascend to the rarified ranks of society. As he recollected, those like him, locally born but of Chinese, Indian, Portuguese, or other ethnicities could not join the Stock Exchange because of racial prejudice. His Irish heritage meant that the Japanese authorities did not intern him during the war, which facilitated his business dealings during this tumultuous period, and through pluck and luck he became a millionaire. Moreover, because they were tossed to the margins of Hong Kong society, he and his influential relatives found it easier in the prewar era to engage in mutually beneficial relations with other outsiders—namely, the Japanese, with whom Carroll had a "long family connection." The Carrolls had begun "what was then the first modern shipyard in Yokohama."[45] William Carroll was indicted for collaboration after the war. The saga of the Carrolls suggests how ingrained British biases could boomerang.

But it was not only those so unlucky to be born Irish or Cuban who could suffer in Hong Kong. Those from Scotland were at times derisively referred to as "Scotch coolies."[46] Professor Walter Brown, a Scotch nationalist who taught at Hong Kong University, objected to such craven practices; he objected to the Anglocentric use of the word "English" when the word "British" would have sufficed. So he devoted hours of his leisure time in the library crossing out such misusages in its books and entering "BRITISH" firmly in the margin.[47]

Needy Scotch doctors were often forced to emigrate to Hong Kong because of lack of opportunities at home or financial inability to buy themselves into a practice; this did not improve their ill-humor toward English elites.[48] "White Russians"—exiles from the Bolshevik Revolution—were "seen by Britons and others to undermine 'white prestige' by the employment they took, their lifestyle, their homes but mostly by the sheer poverty of the majority." Thus, "taboos about specific forms of interaction with the Russians were as strong as those for Asians."[49] Then there were the Portuguese, who—said Emily Hahn—"don't claim to be pure white but they do consider themselves, haughtily, far above the British Eurasians in social standing. The other Eurasians don't share this conviction. Neither do the British."[50]

In "British China," class prejudice—and anxiety—was often deployed to articulate race prejudice. The Chinese were brutalized in order to provide a sense of identity to Europeans as a class, so they could bask in the reality that no matter their status, at least they were not Asian. As one commentator at the time put it, "they take it out on the Chinese so as to make themselves feel big."[51] "They" may not have felt "big" because too often those who decamped from Britain to Hong Kong were—in the words of one London diplomat—"third rate men."[52] The scholar, Charles Boxer, who was interned in Hong Kong during the war, observed that "Hong Kong is the dumping ground for the duds. . . . Any old fool who can't be used elsewhere is dumped out here.'"[53] Queenie Cooper remained realistic enough to conclude that "in England a girl of my class would have been a domestic servant . . . but for five years I've been living in [Hong Kong] like a queen."[54] Fearing that their "third rate" status would stigmatize them, many expatriates

focused their anxiety on the Chinese, clinging desperately to their elevated status. There was a class-cum-racial hierarchy, with the affluent
English at the top of the social pyramid.

To be sure, not all who hailed from the United Kingdom reached
this charmed circle. There was a pointed fear of the growth of a class of
poor Europeans who might undermine the "prestige" of the British.
Often they were deported unceremoniously. European prostitutes, for
example, were "treated with great severity: they were thought to lower
the prestige of [the] white man in the East." The British at times treated
the "lower classes" in Britain as badly as they treated the Chinese in
Hong Kong and, sadly, upon arriving in China these "lower classes"
exacted their ire not on English elites but on the Chinese. "British
China" did become a hotbed of class consciousness but not in the way
Karl Marx might have imagined it. There were intense "snobberies" in
Hong Kong, as "visitors" there "were always struck by the excessive interest Europeans took in questions of status." Gossip and scandal, leav-
ened with "snobberies," were the staff of life among the colonizers in
Hong Kong.[55] The official historian of the powerful trading firm Jardine
Matheson agrees, concluding that "In Hong Kong, far more than Shang-
hai, social life was stuffy, not to say snobbish."[56]

This was no minor matter and the victorious Japanese aggressors
made much of it. In one of the first issues of the *Hong Kong News*, the
journal they published after seizing power, an editorialist proclaimed,
"It is time that equality should be restored to the Asiatics. It was not
uncommon for a Chinese or Indian, who had long service in the government to have to obey the orders of a young upstart, newly arrived
from 'home,' who knew practically next to nothing and who nevertheless received several times more pay. . . . even up to now Chinese,
Indian and other local government employees have not been paid
salaries due while the British officials have still not taken the trouble
to prepare lists of casualties of Hong Kong volunteers."[57] Again and
again the victors hammered this point home.[58] A few days later yet
another editorial noted that the "Eurasian when he seeks employment
is classified as a 'native' and is required to accept 'native' pay. . . . The
Eurasian could [be] of great help to these powers [that is, the United
Kingdom] contributing valuable liaison between the ruling nation
and the native population. Instead, in most British territories, those of
mixed blood are underprivileged, discontented and resentful." Another editorial claimed that "third-raters with a bloated sense of their

own importance . . . incompetent officials" ruled "Asiatic peoples who, irrespective of their capabilities were seldom given the opportunity to rise to positions of high standing. . . . But callow British youths just out of school and half-witted Englishmen were often placed in charge of departments over the heads of Asiatics. . . . To eradicate such abuse of the rights of Asiatics is one of the aims of Japan," which is why Tokyo declared, "Asia for the Asiatics."[59] The razor sharp slash of class privilege dug deeply in Hong Kong, particularly compared to neighboring Shanghai where jurisdiction was shared with other powers.[60]

Even those who were sworn to defend the British Empire often were viewed with contempt because of their social standing—which may be why they exacted their residual anger on the poor Chinese. Major Albert Hood, who served in Hong Kong before the war, felt that the military was "looked down on" by the "European civilians." The latter viewed the military as a "necessary evil."[61] Charles Drage, who arrived in Hong Kong in 1923 to serve with the military, agreed. The "civilians," he thought, "were generally risen in the world a great deal. They were people at home [who] would never dream of having a servant. Out there they probably had three or four servants. And they inclined to be very, very class conscious."[62] Harold Bates was a British soldier assigned to Hong Kong before and during the war. "In those days," he recalled, "a soldier was one step removed from a coolie in the eyes of the Hong Kong expatriates." But there were emoluments to compensate for this degraded status. Bates thoroughly enjoyed the plethora of prostitutes available, not to mention "cricket, football and swimming. It was a thoroughly enjoyable life and I just wanted it to go on."[63]

This reverie was rudely interrupted by the Japanese invasion. But while it lasted, lowly grunts could revel in the perks of colonialism, though racial segregation also inserted itself into prostitution. In accordance with the "1867 Contagious Diseases Act, licensed brothels were segregated for Chinese and Westerners."[64] Prices for sexual recreation, in any case, were remarkably low, reflecting the dire predicament faced by Chinese women. For as little as one dollar one could purchase a sexual encounter, for four more one could spend the night.[65] That many Britons did not hesitate to partake is suggested by the assertion of Harry Sidney George Hale, who arrived in Hong Kong in 1937 to serve with the military. His recollection was that "eighty or ninety percent of the battalion" was riddled with venereal disease.[66]

A closer examination of the brothels of Hong Kong—palaces of sin with a global reputation—suggests why British soldiers found them so alluring. Women there were recruited from the China seaboard and "were trained from their early teens in the arts of love. The client was entertained with stringed instruments, delicately erotic songs and dances of rare beauty. There were two kinds of singing (or 'singsong,' as they were sometimes known) houses. The best known were 'purple mansions.'" As the visitor entered, "a smiling male slave in blue cotton robe would appear, bowing deeply. He ushered the arrival into an immense square room with green white draperies covering the walls. . . . The [women] were customarily dressed in blue or red silk."[67]

Hong Kong was symptomatic of a larger trend. Imperialism has involved not only the export of capital but the export of libido as well. Edward Sellon, a British army officer in colonial India, reflected this libertine attitude; upon his arrival there—as he indelicately put it, he "commenced a regular course of fucking with native women."[68]

Still, the attempt to impose a racial bar in the midst of carnal desire was ironically reflected in the horrendous treatment accorded "Eurasians," or the progeny of unions between Europeans and Asians. Henry Lethbridge, a leading sociologist of prewar Hong Kong, has written that "Eurasians in a European social gathering created a climate of unease and psychological tension. . . . Even highly educated Europeans reacted strongly against mixed marriages." This occurred though Eurasians were "regarded as more reliable and loyal than racially pure [sic] Chinese."[69]

There were "cases in which a Eurasian with British professional qualifications, e.g. medical or architectural [was] engaged in Hongkong [sic] as a member of the local staff, on conditions not to be compared with those accorded his British colleagues with similar qualifications."[70] This discrimination was deeply resented and made a number of Eurasians prime candidates for defection to the Japanese at the time of the invasion.

Kenneth Andrew, a Hong Kong police officer whose beat provided him with more than a passing acquaintance with illicit sexual unions, recalled that before the war "there was a very strict colour bar in Hong Kong. Social relationships between Chinese and Europeans were very much taboo, especially with regard to Chinese females." Upon arriving in the colony in 1912, Andrew found that "I was obliged to sign a document to the effect that during my service I would neither keep nor marry a Chinese female."[71] George Wright-Nooth, who also served in the prewar colony, was told of the "danger of having a Chinese girl-friend, often referred to when learning Chinese as a 'sleeping diction-ary.'"[72]

Why take such extraordinary measures to prevent miscegenation? An answer is best gleaned by posing another query: how could a "white" or "European" community be constructed and "non-Euro-peans" debased, if formally strict lines between the "races" were blithely ignored? Yet, as the experience of the British military sug-gested, it was difficult to bar cross-racial liaisons altogether. What emerged from this spicy stew of contradiction was a crude hypocrisy wherein European men mated with Chinese women alongside sancti-monious condemnation of miscegenation.

A powerful prophylactic designed to bar interracial relationships was the surly hostility directed at Eurasians. Emily Hahn found to her dismay that many of her fellow "foreigners" felt about "Eurasians as our own Southerners do about mulattoes."[73] The attitude of Charles Drage, a British soldier who served in Hong Kong in the 1920s, did lit-tle to dispel Hahn's opinion. He was against marriages between Chi-nese and Europeans. Why? "If you burden your children with mixed blood you are doing a fairly thoughtless thing. They are frightfully at-tractive and sometimes very, very evil."[74]

In the l920s British Empire in Asia, Martin Sharp called on the fa-ther of his potential spouse and bluntly inquired, "Is there any Eurasian blood in you? There was a pause of several seconds and therefore I knew they were Eurasians, for if you put that question to an English-man, he would knock you down. . . . I turned to Pauline and said, 'Am I mistaken? Are you pure white?'" A decade later this prejudice against Eurasians had hardly dissipated. Iris MacFarlane had a "horror and nausea, and a sort of physically drawing away from anybody who was coloured. This was especially true of Anglo-Indians because they could be a threat in that they could infiltrate your world without your know-ing it, unless you were very careful. So you had to learn all the little signs, which you had to learn when you went out. However fair their skins, there were always the little signs—the fingernails, and the ears, and the whites of their eyes."[75]

The scholar Robert Bickers has found similar patterns in British China, adding that "Eurasians were widely disliked, both as partners and as issue; the language used to describe them was often strong, indicating how deeply the taboo was felt." Of course, this "taboo" was wildly skewed, mostly targeting couplings between Asian men and European women and the offspring therefrom. There was a "fear," Bickers writes, "of male Chinese sexual desire for 'white' women." A British naval officer expressed unease at the familiarity between a missionary woman from the United States and her Chinese landlord. "It will always seem queer to me," he asserted wondrously, "to hear a coloured man call a white Christian girl by her Christian name." The "subtext" of this anxiety was "clearly sexual," says Bickers.[76] The prospect of this kind of coupling was so disturbing that in 1925 the "League of Nations set up a special committee to examine the situation. It concluded unhappily that 'the breach of the natural racial barrier . . . affects very deeply the prestige of the Western nations in the Orient.'"[77]

In the late 1930s Esther Holland was planning to marry a Chinese man. She had met him while he was visiting Britain and was told reprovingly, "Esther, you are young and good looking. Why can't you find nice English boy? There are plenty." A concerned European "wrote to [her] brother and asked him what the status of a young British girl who marries a Chinese would be. He wrote me a long reply and said, 'If there is such a girl within your ken, do all in your power to dissuade her. In the first place, she'll lose her British nationality. . . . All the Britishers would look down upon her and she would have no British social standing whatever.'" Unimpressed, she defied convention and married him. Soon she found herself in conversation with another British woman whom she casually informed about her betrothal. She "saw a look of disgust come over her face. Her brows came together and her mouth went down at the corners."[78]

This phobia about Asian men and European women was also a reflection of a patriarchy that saw women as property to be defended as fiercely as any other form of commerce. On the other hand, couplings between Asian women and European men were also frowned on but not condemned as vigorously.[79] The formal taboo against interracial romance extended to the silver screen. In 1930 the British Board of Film Censors forbade English actor John Longden from kissing on-screen the heroine, Chinese actress Anna May Wong.[80]

On the other hand,[81] after the successful invasion, many Britons recalled ruefully that "many of the British cadets, studying Cantonese for the required three years of training, fell in love with these [Chinese] girls as a kind of ritual. . . . Well, of course most of these girls have been drawing pay from the Japanese on the side, probably for years and years. After the surrender, they came out of hiding."[82]

The "stigma" attached to Eurasians was so severe that "before World War II most found it easier to go 'the Chinese way,'" that is, to melt into the Chinese community, though often marriage to a non-Chinese was seen as a halfway house, a step away from racial purgatory.[83]

Generally, Hong Kong was a stunning geographic tableau of racial inequality, with Europeans residing at "The Peak" high above the island, with the Chinese crowded in the sprawling flatlands. The affluent Robert Ho Tung, patriarch of the clan, had to obtain "special permission" to reside in that "exclusive residential district." Their wealth did not deliver the Ho Tungs from the petty and profound biases of their nearby residents. "We had little contact with the neighboring children," Jean Gittins, a member of this prominent family, maintains. "I do not remember ever having been invited to any of their homes. They had no intention, I am sure, of being unkind, although they would on occasion suddenly refuse to play with us because we were Chinese, or they might tell us we shouldn't be living on the Peak." Adding to the indignity of it all was the fact that the nearby "Peak School . . . did not normally admit Chinese children."[84]

The result of this prejudice was predictable: some of the staunchest opponents of white supremacy in Asia—and helpmates to the invading Japanese—were Eurasians. Among them was Lawrence Klindt Kentwell, born in Hong Kong in 1882, the "illegitimate son" of a "ship's captain and a Chinese mother." A "pupil of Sun Yat-sen," he grew up in Hawaii, then studied at Columbia University in New York City before attending Oxford and becoming a barrister. Yet, despite his accomplishments, he felt that the barrier of racial discrimination was handcuffing his very existence. At Oxford his application to join the Officers' Training Corps had been rejected on the grounds "that I was not a person of pure European descent." In 1926 in Shanghai he founded the *China Courier*, an "anti-British journal" in partnership with another Eurasian, G. R. Graves. By 1939 he was on the payroll of Tokyo as he castigated "Britain's own acts of perfidy in this country and . . . the suffering and misery she has caused the Chinese people." He had "no doubt" that he was "regarded as a despised Eurasian, a half-cast [sic] outcast," compelled to suffer "all sort of hidden indignities." His "bitterness" was "full to the brim"; hence his goal was the "[complete] destruction of England."[85] In pursuit of this lofty goal he accepted the post of "Governor" of the British troops interned in Kowloon: there he had plenty of opportunities to realize his malignant dream.[86]

Ultimately the defense of the Empire—and of Britain itself—rested with the more populous United States, particularly after the threat from Japan arose—a threat, ironically, boosted by London's prewar approach of viewing Tokyo as its regional watchdog. The problem with this strategy of relying on the United States was that Washington itself had intractable racial problems that played to Tokyo's strength. This unfortunate reality was clear as early as 1853 when the "black ships" from the United States entered Japanese waters.

After the United States "opened up" Japan many Japanese feared that the fate that had ensnared a good deal of Asia and most of Africa would now come to pass in their country.[87] Carmen Blacker has argued persuasively that the Meiji Restoration—Japan's modernization that followed the riveting episode of 1853—was spurred by the desire "to avoid the humiliating fate which had befallen India and China." The "Opium War was, of course, the event which, more than any other, had served up Japanese fears of Western aggression." This unappetizing encounter with white supremacy allowed Japanese elites to rationalize that it "must use her armed forces to protect [sic] her neighbors in order to ensure her own safety. . . . A man with a stone house," it was said, "was no more secure against fire than a man with a wooden house, if his neighbor's house was made of wood. . . . Japan's intervention in Korea could thus be justified on the plea that it was for the sake of promoting civilisation, and strengthening the whole of Asia against the West."[88]

Colonizing neighbors like Korea was an integral part of this approach, but there was another. As Warren Cohen has put it, "The idea of liberating Asia from Western imperialism was a strong current in Japanese thought from the Meiji times through World War II. For many Japanese the vision was altruistic."[89] Ian Nish agrees, adding that "The racial issue was much more than a bargaining-counter to be surrendered gladly; it was a genuine conviction honestly held. . . . The government was under considerable domestic pressure from the press, the opposition parties and a mushroom growth of new societies" to do something about this festering matter.[90]

Japan's smashing victory over Russia in 1905 was an event that thrilled many Negroes and Asians, just as it horrified many Euro-Americans and Europeans. Simultaneously, in California there was a concerted effort to enforce "white supremacy" in the schools; how this could be done without "upsetting Tokyo," which was becoming ever more powerful, compelled President Roosevelt to confess that he was "more concerned over this Japanese situation than almost any other." This was understandable. Roosevelt was obliged to attempt to reconcile white supremacy with the reality of an ever more powerful—and decidedly "nonwhite"—Japan.[91]

"The world tour" of the appropriately named "American 'great white fleet' in 1907–8" was not unconnected to the rising fear of Japan. In an unusually blunt speech in February 1908 Roosevelt directly linked the issues of race and immigration with the fleet's movement: "'We have got to build up our white civilization,'" he proclaimed, "'and we must retain the power to say who shall and shall not come to our country.'"[92]

As World War I erupted, the perception by many Japanese of impending racial conflict on a global scale seemed to be vindicated. One leading Japanese opinion maker was convinced that his country would inevitably be sucked into a "worldwide race war." After the war in Europe is over, he thought, "The rivalry between the white and colored peoples will intensify; and perhaps it will be a time when the white races will all unite to oppose the colored peoples." This racialist thinking was echoed across the Pacific.[93]

During this same era, a California legislator struck a note toward Japanese migrants in terms reminiscent of how Negroes were being described elsewhere. Demanding segregated schools, he viewed with alarm the "matured Japs [*sic*], with their base minds, their lascivious thoughts . . . sitting in the seats next to the pure maids of California. I shuddered then and I shudder now, the same as any other parent will shudder." Just as the very presence of Negroes helped to bond otherwise squabbling European immigrants into a cohesive "white" community that reveled in the fact that they were not "black," in the Far West of the United States, "Japanese-baiting was a ticket of admission for men who might otherwise have been targets themselves" of anti-Italian or anti-Irish bigotry.[94]

Suguira Shigtetake, a Japanese official in the prewar period reinforced the idea of trans-Pacific racisms by arguing that "world history is the history of rivalry and contention between the yellow and white races. . . . The whites shout about the yellow peril and we are angry about the white peril. . . . The Europeans and Americans . . . are apt to look down on the yellow race with preconceived notions. I think it will be very difficult to abolish racial prejudice."

The Asiatic Exclusion League was gaining momentum, particularly on the West Coast, as they placed a heavy emphasis on Japan. "It is useless," said the AEL, "to expect that people with such different racial characteristics and such different civilization can ever mix with our people and become absorbed into our body politic. They cannot become good American citizens," they snapped, "it is useless to attempt to make them such." These were "minorities" of a new type, however, in that "to the Asiatic, the Caucasian is an inferior." It was noted approvingly, "California has decreed that, whenever it is so desired, the local school authorities may provide separate schools for the Chinese and Japanese children."[95] Some San Franciscans raised the cry, "White men and women, patronize your own race."[96] Japanese immigrants were a "band of spies," it was reported; "they are educated as spies, they have schools in Japan to educate spies." This was a matter of simple survival: "It is a question of which race can dominate and live on this Coast."[97]

The Democratic Party in California mimicked these judgments. Repeatedly its early twentieth century platforms called for "the continuance and strict enforcement of the Chinese exclusion law, and its application to the same classes of all Asiatic races."[98] Hiram Johnson, perhaps the preeminent politician of this era in what was to become the nation's largest state, was a member in good standing of the Native Sons of the Golden West, a leading nativist organization in the forefront of the struggle for the exclusion of the Japanese.[99]

Even before World War II, strains between Washington and Tokyo were rising. As Noriko Kawamura put it, "On the eve of the Pacific War [many] were aware of the grave prospect of interracial rivalry—or even a race war—between the white and yellow races." President Wilson said that he "had been more and more impressed with the idea that 'white civilization' and its domination over the world rested largely on our ability to keep this country intact, as we would have to build up the nations ravaged by the war" and that "he was willing to go to any lengths rather than to have the nation actually involved in the conflict." Wilson "frankly" said that "in order to keep the white race or part of it strong to meet the yellow race—Japan, for instance—[if he felt that] it was wise to do nothing, he would do nothing, and would submit to anything and any imputation of weakness or cowardice" in order to avoid declaring war on Germany.[100]

The Bolshevik Revolution in 1917 also figured into ever more complex calculations about Japan. Early in 1918 a top aide to President Woodrow Wilson told him, "I have never changed my opinion that it would be a great political mistake to send the Japanese troops into Siberia. . . . It would arouse the Slavs throughout Europe because of the race question if for nothing else."[101] This powerful aide, Colonel House, told A. J. Balfour that the unfolding 1918 Japanese intervention in Siberia "may be the greatest misfortune that has befallen the Allies. . . . The race question, in particular, will be sharply emphasized and an attempt made to show that we are using a yellow race to destroy a white race."[102] Thus, some in the higher echelons of the U.S. government were prepared to run the extraordinary risk of allowing Bolshevism to survive in order to foil Japan.

When Japan at Versailles proposed a clause in the peace treaty concerning racial discrimination, pandemonium erupted not only in the United States but in the Empire more generally, especially Australia. "Many societies sprang up" in Japan "to advocate that the conference at Paris should be used for the abolition of racial discrimination. . . . This was widely reported in the press in what became a campaign for racial equality. . . . It had the advantage of being an issue on which Japan could make common cause with China." In sum, moving aggressively against racial discrimination was a genuinely popular matter within Japan and was not solely—at least at first—a matter of mere elite manipulation.[103]

Noriko Kawamura feels that Tokyo's concern in this matter was "genuine." "Tokyo's instructions on this issue were explicit from the very beginning"; after all, the Japanese encountered prejudice while traveling and seeking to immigrate, to a greater degree even than nationals from other countries considerably less developed economically. Nevertheless, the Japanese concern was said to be demagogic in light of their colonization of Korea. Wilson "abstained from voting on the racial question"; it was "obvious that he did not fight for the principle of racial equality. . . . Wilson was well aware of the strong opposition against the racial equality principle in his own country." As ever, the slippery United States sought adroitly to shift the burden of Tokyo's wrath. As a Wilson aide wrote, "It has taken considerable finesse to lift the load from our shoulders and place it upon the British, but happily, it has been done."[104]

The Japanese government and people were irate about what they deemed to be a deliberate affront when this proviso on race was derailed. Emperor Hirohito mentioned this much later. "When we look for the causes of the Greater East Asia War," he said, "they lie in the past, in the peace treaty after World War I. The proposal on racial equality put forward by Japan was not something the Allies would accept."[105] Among those at Versailles were the political advisor to the Emperor, the "American educated Count Sutemi," and "Count Makino" who "spoke excellent English, having spent eight unhappy years as a boy studying in the United States."[106]

Like other Japanese, the Emperor had further reason to be "unhappy" after Versailles. Washington, consequently, twisted itself like a pretzel trying to assuage Tokyo. Wilson's Secretary of State told the president that in discussing immigration exclusion and other matters, he was seeking to "convince them that the question is not a race question but purely an economic question," that is, they were unwanted due to their sizable numbers. However, no one seemed overly concerned about the presence of huge numbers of European immigrants.[107] Versailles later turned out to be a fateful step toward the Pacific War, as many ordinary Japanese could not comprehend why they should be discriminated against. Those educated in the United States and most familiar with it were particularly irate about what they considered to be a betrayal at Versailles.[108]

Informants told the U.S. Embassy in Tokyo in 1919 of the "mass meeting held . . . to discuss race discrimination. . . . Marquis Okuma [declared] the solution of the racial question essential in order to avoid future strife among nations arising out of the present unequal distribution of natural riches."[109] That same year the U.S. State Department was informed that Tokyo "hopes for an abandonment of the existing standards on account of race and color, and the substitution of moral and intellectual standards. . . . Some journals even go so far as to advise withdrawal from the Peace Conference and the League of Nations altogether if the equality of races is not provided for." In that event, Washington was warned, "Japan, at the head of one billion colored people, should rise in protest against the white races."[110]

Washington sought to squirm out of this dilemma. The U.S. embassy in Tokyo issued "an official statement to the press," wherein "regret was expressed that the claims of Japan for race equality were not admitted and it was explained this was due to the fears of the British and American delegates that it had a bearing, not only on the immigration question, but on the treatment of subject races such as Indians and

Negroes in their dominions."[111] The Japanese could either be comforted by the fact that they were allegedly not the primary target of white supremacy, or wonder why the United States was incapable of making meaningful distinctions between the "races." Others, perhaps, may have begun to think they had more in common with the despised U.S. Negroes than they had imagined.

The U.S. allies were not helping matters. One British official in a "confidential" riposte reputedly said that Japanese proposals on racial equality were "an eighteenth century proposition which he did not believe was true. He believed that it was true in a certain sense that all men of a particular nation were created equal but not that a man in Central Africa was created equal to a European." Again, the corollary of this approach was that the Japanese and the African might have things in common that neither had imagined—not least, a common foe in white supremacy. That the "Chinese representative" was "in full sympathy with the spirit of the Japanese amendment" was viewed as irrelevant.[112]

Ordinary Japanese were not willing to accept this passively, as Frances Hewitt, who had spent six years teaching English in Japan, discovered. In an atmosphere suffused with concern about Versailles, "Americans or other white men mistaken for Americans are mobbed and beaten because California happens at the moment to be passing some protective laws. This has happened to me," she said regretfully, "and to friends of mine several times. . . . [Japan]," she concluded, "will test the strength of the League of Nations to the utmost in order to force the world to recognize her people as equals. The moment she accomplishes this the end of the white man is in sight."[113]

Joseph Stilwell, the leading U.S. general in China, agreed. While at Harvard, a Japanese student in 1902 "had told him of Japan's schedule. . . . for a 100 year program of expansion. . . . [with] culmination in a protectorate over all the yellow races." Visiting Japan in the 1920s he found eerie confirmation of his suspicions of Tokyo's intentions. Officials there, he thought, were "seizing every available bureaucratic contact to annoy and domineer foreigners who had for so long walked the East as superiors. 'Made to wait for meal on boat,' Stilwell recorded. 'Japs [sic] already eating.' 'Serving Japs [sic] first and out of turn, e.g. at ticket window, etc. Close scrutiny of papers. Insistence on lengthy questioning. Open sneers met everywhere.'" The erudite Stilwell, who knew how to speak Japanese and Chinese, frequently used racial slurs.[114]

Again, immigration provisos in the United States that discriminated against Japanese were viewed with asperity in Tokyo. The pro-Tokyo *Hong Kong News* focused intently on this matter after Japan seized power in the British colony. Washington, it was stated, "must be thoroughly thrashed in this war and must be taught the serious consequences" of racism. The paper mentioned "the American Asiatic Exclusion acts of 1882, 1917 and 1924; Australia's 'White Australia' policy as well as Canada's anti-Indian, anti-Chinese, anti-South African Negro exclusion laws of 1919, 1923 and 1933 respectively."[115] As late as 1941 Tokyo was demanding that "Japanese immigration to the United States and to the South-western Pacific shall receive amiable consideration on a basis of equality with other nationals freed from discrimination." Tokyo demanded that the "government of the United States . . . guarantee the non-discriminatory treatment of the Japanese nationals in the Philippines Islands," something that Washington was loath to do.[116]

If the British Empire had paid attention sooner—and had been less focused on enticing Tokyo to be their overseer in Asia—they might have noticed Tokyo's demands. When Paul Hibbert Clyde was in Tokyo in the prewar period he was struck by the "anti-British propaganda." Articles in English-language newspapers about "anti-British posters" from the "Asiatic Anti-British League" talked about the need to "Defend Asia: Drive Out Great Britain."[117]

Washington's policies toward Japan reinforced those of Great Britain. Asian nationals—including Japanese—sailing from West Coast ports to Asia in the 1930s were forced to confront a Jim Crow system that Negroes would have recognized easily: there were "First Class and European Steerage Tickets" versus "Asiatic Steerage: Japanese and other Asiatics only will be booked in this class."[118] When landing in Shanghai, these Japanese passengers may have encountered a "Chinese branch" of the Ku Klux Klan, "started with the help of Captain L.D. ('Pegleg') Kearney, an American adventurer, arms smuggler and sometime propagandist for the Chinese revolution."[119]

It was in such a racist environment that the Black Dragon Society arose. This ultrapatriotic, ultrarightist Japanese based grouping were the shock troops of Tokyo's advance and the key ideologues of the assault on white supremacy. They were chiefly responsible for a wave of assassinations in Japan in the 1930s that pushed Japan decisively in their direction. Thus, when a Tokyo publisher, Matsutaro Shoriki, brought the baseball star Babe Ruth to Japan in the 1930s, the BDS murdered Shoriki. They hoped to kill Charles Chaplin "hoping that this would bring on war between Japan and the United States." With a membership of about ten thousand, the BDS were the "Leninists" of the Japanese right wing. During the U.S. war with the Philippines in the early twentieth century, the BDS "shipped arms, fighting men and officers to the Aguinaldo Insurrectos."[120]

As the BDS gained influence in the 1930s and as Japan turned toward militant right-wing nationalism, this had a knock-on effect in the United States. State Senator Tom Collins of Phoenix was told as much by one of his constituents, I. L. Shauer, in 1935: "I have just returned from Japan where I have been living for the past fifteen years." He was concerned about the intensified harassment of Issei and Nissei in Arizona: "Bombings of the Japanese in Salt River Valley last summer and fall resounded across the Pacific." Thus, "it would be very inopportune to pass" an anti-Japanese "alien land law. . . . at present while there is so much tension in the Orient. As you know, Japan is our best customer, and it does seem unwise to do anything that would arouse animosity or ill will with a friendly customer."[121] The United States was tempting fate by pursuing a policy of white supremacy with Japan, where race consciousness was swelling. Furthermore, Japan was also a major economic power whose interests could not be ignored easily.

The British Empire controlled more territory than either Canberra, Ottawa, or Washington and inspired racial prejudice in these three continental giants. Within the Empire and, particularly in London itself, the subjects of the crown were not all equal: they were sliced and diced into racial categories. A typical incident occurred in London in 1937, when a hotel proprietor refused to accept Asian lodgers. Now he "had not . . . the slightest objection to Asiatics." It was "his clientele" that demurred. Failure to adhere to their wishes "would mean the loss of two or three hundred of his regular clients." The British authorities acknowledged that "the existence of [a] certain amount of colour prejudice must be recognized"; still, they worried that if this became widely known in Ceylon—where the rejected lodgers lived—"this information would lead to very serious consequences."[122]

Whereas the United States admitted only those defined as "white" into the hallowed halls of privilege, London accomplished the same thing by using different words. In 1936, for example, the Air Ministry pointed out that "'colour' is an absolute bar to a commission in the Royal Air Force. . . . 'All candidates must be of pure European descent.'"[123]

What did these three words mean? As one British official put it a few years earlier, "The question is really much less of fact than one of expediency. It is not so much whether a man actually has mixed blood which matters, as whether people think so." He was referring to an applicant for a police appointment in Hong Kong who was barred from the job though he claimed that his "great grandfather . . . was a Dutch official." The officials went back and forth on how to define precisely this slippery three-word phrase. One noted that challenging the racial bona fides of applicants could easily transmute into a petty settling of scores. "Cameron is a case in point," he said. "They all said he was 'a nigger' because they didn't like him in Nigeria."[124]

There was a bizarre fixation in London on this rule of "pure European descent." After watching British Tommies bathing in a communal cleansing station, Lord Curzon confessed that he never knew that the working classes had such white skins: those who were not "white" were automatically deemed to be of subordinate class and those of a subordinate class were assumed to be not "white," at least not in the same way as their "betters." Class bias was articulated via racial prejudice and vice versa in an endless loop that Asians and Africans particularly had difficulty escaping.[125]

London enforced these race rules with an energetic relish. A mere thirty-eight months before war erupted in Europe, colonial officials were discussing judicial appointments in the colonies. From Nairobi there was objection to "transfer to this Colony of men from the West Indies who have a 'slight touch of color.'" "I would strongly advise against this proposal," he intoned scornfully. "Kenya is a cruel colony and I am convinced that on the social side the newcomer would be treated as an outsider and that things would be made uncomfortable for him and his wife. I fancy that he would be debarred from memberships of the various European Clubs and that he would not desire to be associated solely with the Indians." From Dar-es-Salaam a colonial official remarked that "the European population here is not very level-headed." It would be easy to "deplore this prejudice and its lack of logical justification—but there it is and I [do] not think I need to say more."[126]

Although he did not, inevitably this issue arose time and time again in an Empire whose benefits were doled out on the basis of color. Perhaps because the very process was irrational, the British authorities often sank into a morass of absurdity in defending the rule of "pure European descent." Why would someone object to officials from the West Indies being transferred to East Africa, for example? Well, in both East and West Africa, according to one administrator, there was a "tendency to suspect colour in anyone who has been been near the [West] Indies and a Kenya settler indignant at being sent to gaol by a 'Negro judge' would raise cain . . . in Nairobi."[127] But why didn't such repulsive policies spark more outrage within the Empire? Well, the official rule was that individuals were not rejected for certain posts because of their color and great pains were taken to hide the reality. As one official put it in 1927, "It is most important that no indication should leak out that men are rejected for the Colonial Services on account of colour."[128] Many subjects of His Majesty were deluded into thinking that they were racially and legally equal.

There were special provisos designed for specific populations. When in 1939 London was soliciting subjects of the Empire to sign up for military duty, one key official said that "we should . . . be most careful to word the announcement as not in any [way] to imply that we regard all 'Colonial British Subjects' as not being of pure European descent, otherwise great offence will be given in some quarters (e.g. in Malta)."[129] Closer to Africa than to London, the Maltese were perpetually concerned that they would be confused with their nearest neighbor and not their patron.

Thus throughout the Empire rules were devised to make sure those with a hint of melanin did not get crucial posts. Yet as the metronome of war pounded ever louder, some officials began to worry that this could compromise the Empire's security. In September 1939 Sir A. F. Richards in a "secret" message responded to frantic queries about "loyalty" in the West Indies. Perhaps it was the press of war that compelled him to acknowledge that "this colour question . . . is one of the biggest questions in the Empire. In my opinion," he continued, "if it is not faced and solved by recession from the 'pure European birth on both sides' rule it will wreck the Empire yet." Plaintively, he lamented, "How can a world Imperial Power with all too few pure white subjects justify this principle—if principle you call it."[130]

Principle it was, observed more often than it was breached. But what would happen if a nation not of "pure European descent" challenged the Empire, challenged it precisely on the basis of "race," promisimg to provide a thrashing comeuppance to the mighty English?

2

The Asiatic Black Man?

IN THE PERIOD PRECEDING THE ATTACK on the British Empire, Japan was—without question—the nation most admired by African Americans. Many reasons account for this now mostly forgotten fact: Tokyo assiduously courted black leaders and, in any case, the latter looked to Japan as a living and breathing refutation of the very basis of white supremacy, that is, that one had to be of "pure European descent" in order to construct an advanced society.[1] Moreover, this admiration for Tokyo was part of a larger identification with Asians generally on the part of Negroes,[2] who saw them as fellow strugglers against white supremacy. Obviously, the Negro-Japan alliance was a nettlesome problem for the United States when it had to rush to the aid of the Empire when challenged by Tokyo. The United Kingdom, then comparatively bereft of such "colored minorities" on its home turf, was not compelled to face frontally the ugliness of racial segregation, as Washington was as a matter of national security and survival. Consequently, the United States moved more aggressively on this front than Britain, which was justifiably terrified that racial reform measures could lead to the progressive unraveling of the Empire. Emboldened Asians (particularly Indians) might ponder why they should be a colony of a distant European nation about the size of Laos. Thus, as the Negro-Japan alliance withered, then disappeared under the intense heat of war and the bombing of Hiroshima-Nagasaki, the United States was in an advantageous position to pick up the scattered pieces of the Empire.

As the United States expanded into the Pacific in the wake of the Spanish-American War of 1898, Washington feared that the black troops they relied on would prove unreliable. Serious consideration was given to "exclude black Americans from service to the Philippines," as it was felt that "there was a natural bond between the rural Filipinos and the American Negro."[3] But this apprehension was minor compared to the worry in Washington about Negroes' fondness for bathing in the stimulating rays of the Rising Sun.

Like many Asians, African Americans were drawn to Japan after its startling defeat of Russia in 1905, which in their mind signaled a crisis for white supremacy. Left, right, and center, radical, conservative, and moderate—black opinion molders of every stripe and persuasion may have quarreled among themselves about domestic matters but all were united in looking longingly toward Tokyo. Joseph Bryant, writing in 1905 in *The Colored American Magazine*, spoke for many when he saw Japan's rise as rebutting "the habit of underestimating the intelligence and ability of other races, a deception common to Caucasian character. . . . Japan has become a world power and with it dies the absolute domination of the world by the Aryan people. . . . It can be safely predicted," he said with confidence, "that within a few centuries, the Asiatics will lead the world in civilization and moral ideas."[4] Tokyo's victory over Moscow "marks the beginning of a new era," said this journal, "in which all races of mankind shall play a part"; this victory "forever destroyed the claims to supremacy of the haughty spirit of the white man."[5]

At times it seemed the "Colored American" was more delighted with the 1905 victory than the "Colored Japanese." This win, it was reported, "has rather set the metes and bounds of the over-strides of the white man, who has always regarded Asia as a part of his scheme of world-mastery." Washington was assailed for backing Moscow at the peace conference: "She sided with wrong and defeat, simply because they hung about the necks of those whose skin is pale. . . . Culture is richer because of the war. Equity and reason thank Japan for their new dignity."[6] Speaking to the Negro Business League in 1905, John Milholland attacked the notion of "race superiority." "What a delusion has vanished at last," he concluded happily, "and before the whole world! What a fallacy was exploded at Port Arthur!"[7]

Prefiguring the Nation of Islam's concept of the "Asiatic Black Man," some Negroes began recasting the Japanese in compatible racial terms after the 1905 victory. "The Japanese race," said Rev. J. M. Boddy, "is neither Mongolian, Semetic, Celt, Teuton, nor Saxon, they must be Hametic, and therefore they must be akin to the Negro race. . . . The Black races of Africa could have easily penetrated Japan." The "Japanese race," it was reported, are of "Turano-African origin, who travelled eastwards through Egypt." There was a "Black Tide," a "sort of gulfstream . . . which begins off the coast of Africa and then goes to Asia." "There is a large infusion of Negro blood in their veins," it was reported. "In view, therefore, of the brilliant master strokes of the Japanese [army], under General Kuroki and Nodzu and Field Marshal Oyama, and the unprecedented achievements of the Japanese naval forces, under the command of the brilliant Admiral Toga [sic], [this] may therefore justly be regarded as the achievements of the Negro race."[8] Indeed, the joint discrimination faced by those of African and Japanese descent in the United States and the fervent praise of Tokyo by some Negroes, had led as early as 1906 to mutterings about a "black American-Japanese alliance."[9]

Japan became the touchstone, the lodestar, for matters local and global. This Asian nation was recommended to Liberia as a "most useful lesson. . . . As Japan aspires to leadership in the east, Liberia should so aspire to figure in the kaleidoscopic changes that ere long must come to the west coast of Africa. . . . Japan has shown that yellow men with guns are all conquerable over white Russians, at least; so let Liberia show what the black men can do with a gun."[10] Keeping the Japanese out of schools in the West showed that "as California would treat Japanese, she would also treat Negroes."[11]

This veneration of Tokyo was of particular concern to W. E. B. Du Bois. This war moved the dapper and diminutive activist to soaring rhetorical heights in 1906, months after the war had ended. "Since 732," he began, "when Charles Martel beat back the Saracens at Tours, white races have had the hegemony of civilization"; but now "the Russo-Japanese war has marked an epoch. The magic of the word 'white' is already broken. . . . The awakening of the yellow races is certain. That the awakening of the brown and black races will follow in time, no unprejudiced student of history can doubt."[12]

Most famously, Du Bois clashed sharply with his fellow black leader Booker T. Washington. But when it came to the question of Japan, the two were as one. In 1912 Washington asserted that "there is no other race living outside of America whose fortunes the Negro peoples of this country have followed with greater interest or admiration" than Japan; "in no other part of the world," he said, "have the Japanese people a larger number of admirers and well-wishers than among the black people of the United States."[13]

Yet, perhaps more than Du Bois or Washington, Marcus Garvey, whose Universal Negro Improvement Association had transcontinental membership (particularly in British colonies in Africa and the Caribbean) and may have included more African Americans than any other organization before or since, was most admiring of Japan and most aggressive in incorporating it into his overall strategy. The U.S. government, which was becoming increasingly wary of the developing Negro-Japan alliance, took somber note of his remarks in December 1918, weeks after the conclusion of World War I: "Garvey also preached that the next war will be between the Negroes and the whites unless their demands for justice are recognized and that with the aid of Japan on the side of the Negroes they will be able to win such a war."[14] Garvey, it was reported, said "that Japan was combining with the Negro race to overthrow the white race because the black man was not getting justice in this country," that is, the United States.[15] Evidently Garvey's views were shared by the membership. As a government agent reported on a UNIA meeting in Springfield, Massachusetts, one speaker exhorted hotly, "I feel like banding my race together, join the Japanese and advance on the Mason and Dixon Line and mop up the devilish 'crackers' down here."[16]

This incendiary rhetoric was backed up by action. Reportedly the *Japanese Commercial Weekly* was helping to circulate Garvey's words in Japan. A representative of this publication acknowledged that "Garvey's statement about the 'day of the war of the races' was good agitation. . . . It is reported that the Japanese are now working to sell a 4,000 ton ship to Garvey."[17] Others from Japan "promised to offer their merchandise at prices much lower than what the U.S. could sell and to convince the Negroes that it would be far more advantageous to throw in their lot with Japan."[18] The Japanese, who often addressed UNIA meetings, hardly sought to dampen the fire-breathing words directed at the "white race." To the contrary, they often threw gasoline on the flames. When Sumio Uesugi attended a Garvey meeting in 1921, this University of Chicago graduate, who "had been speaking at many Negro churches recently," declared that "white people were hypocrites who called themselves Christians" but "always turn [me] down on account of [my] color." Like Negroes in Chicago, he too had a "hard time" in "finding and retaining a suitable lodging owing to his color." Thus, he said, "the white people were afraid of the Japanese Government on account of their growing power and strength."[19]

In California—where a good deal of the nation's population of Asian descent resided—the UNIA was subject to an intense scrutiny. In

1922 the Office of Naval Intelligence noticed that in San Francisco the UNIA leader George Farr was "being financed by local Japanese interests." Recently at the Emmanuel Gospel Mission in the city by the bay, "the music, dancing[,] the crowd were all frivolous. The congregation was composed largely of the mixed foreign population, Mexicans, Hindus, etc. and a number of Negroes." This multiracial assemblage was bent on "anti-Caucasian agitation," as protests abounded—notably from "Hendric, a Hindu" and the "Negroes." "Both the Hindu and the Negro preach among the Negroes, Hawaiians, Mexicans and Hindus, the doctrine of the supposed necessity of the union of all colored races against the whites. And they also preach: 'assert yourself, fellow brothers; hit the white man back twice if he hits you.'" They were buoyed by the growth of the "movement in India, the Bolshevik success in Russia; rise of the Japanese Empire. . . . Their audience is such that it cares little or nothing about the inconsistency of the supposed rise of the colored race against the white." This church, it was thought, "is really one of the worst things that was ever born in the name of Christ's religion."[20] Yet it had a "Hindu" leader, "one of the moving forces in the Gospel Mission," who was "very strong against Christianity" as he alleged that the "whites and the Christians are hardly human, but very much of devils." He spoke French and "knows a number of Japanese."[21]

This was one of many intriguing incidents monitored by the U.S. authorities. In May 1920 they had detected "secret meetings of Negroes," for example, one in New York of "over 1000" with a Japanese speaker who exclaimed, "Let the Negro join the Japanese forces and we will show him to prominence. Every race has had his day except the yellow and the black man. . . . We will give you the ammunition to fight the whites. . . . on the Pacific Coast the two races should join hands." The Negroes, it was reported, "were very much affected by the utterances of this Japanese and they cheered for some time when he concluded his harangue."[22]

Incidents like those involving the shaken Kathleen Skaten were becoming more common. In her handwritten 1921 letter to the U.S. Secretary of War she recounted what she had witnessed in New York City. There was "an argument" with "an angry Negro and an indignant white woman in a train today." The "Negro was glad of the invasion of Japan into America in the rumored war. It would give the Negro an opportunity to 'defend' himself and kill off the oppressor. The idea conveyed was that Japan influence is being used to rouse the Negro [to] the

Jap [*sic*] side." She conceded that she "may be hysterical on the subject of Japan." But this admission could not obscure the larger point that white supremacy was creating a dire challenge to U.S. national security.[23]

In the era before Japan had assaulted the British Empire, the UNIA was not unique within the constellation of Black Nationalism. Garvey was born in the British colony of Jamaica and, strikingly, a disproportionate number of those attracted to his banner also hailed from British colonies. The Pacific Movement of the Eastern World, which "gained a significant black nationalist following during the 1930s" in the United States—perhaps "forty thousand members," with "other estimates" soaring "as high as one million," also attracted adherents from the "British West Indies."[24] If these figures are accurate, it would mean that such groupings attracted a substantially larger Negro membership than organizations within the orbit of the Communist Party, for example—which was one of the few entities with influence among Negroes that managed to resist Japan's racial siren song.

Certainly the Nation of Islam, which began in Black America over seven decades ago and still remains potent, has been the heartiest of the Black Nationalist groups that originally had a pro-Tokyo orientation. From the beginning, stubborn rumors persisted that the notorious Japanese agent, Satohara Takahashi, was "bankrolling the NOI." The Federal Bureau of Investigation charged that these "Muslims and other black nationalists were receiving carbine rifles and sophisticated military weapons from Japanese espionage agents." One Takahashi-sponsored group was "directed toward the extermination of the White Race" while "during meetings and services a large sign [was] always displayed bearing the inscription, 'The Paleface Has to Go.'" Elijah Muhammad, a patron saint of the NOI, was actively engaged in these circles. He emphasized that "the Japanese will slaughter the white man. . . . The Japanese are the brothers of the black man and the time will soon come when from the clouds hundreds of Japanese planes with the most poisonous gas will let their bombs fall on the United States and nothing will be left of it." Like his "colored" counterparts in New Zealand—the Ratana, noted below—Elijah Muhammad also believed that he and his people were somehow related to the Japanese. "The Asiatic race is made up of all dark-skinned people," he stated, "including the Japanese and the Asiatic black man." The implication was clear, he thought: "Members of the Asiatic race must stick together."[25]

This notion that Negroes and Japanese were blood relatives was not peculiar to the NOI. Harry Dean, born in 1864, was the grandson of Paul Cuffee, perhaps the most prominent and affluent Negro of the early nineteenth century. Like his grandfather, he was an "African and proud of it." He too was a sailor and he recounted in some detail his travels to southeastern Africa in the late nineteenth century and the story of "Teo Saga," a "chief" who was "more Japanese than African. . . . The story runs that before the cataclysm South Africa, Madagascar, Sumatra, Java and even Korea and Japan were all connected by land, and formed a great, illustrious, and powerful empire. The people were highly cultured, the rulers rich and wise. When the great flood came over the land it left only the remote provinces. However that may be, one may still find such Japanese names as Teo Saga on the coast of Africa to this very day."[26]

Yet this pro-Tokyo bent was not unique to Black Nationalism. The iconoclastic and militantly anticommunist black journalist, George Schuyler, who proudly called himself "conservative," also bowed in the direction of the Rising Sun. He wrote a roman a clef that posited "race war" as a major theme. He was "fascinated by Japan and by the meaning to blacks worldwide of its great military expansion. At the invitation of the [*Pittsburgh*] *Courier* he wrote a series of articles on the subject that the publisher found too pro-Japan to be printed."[27]

Japan-related themes were a frequent staple of black writers in the wake of the 1905 victory, with revenge against white supremacy as a repetitive theme. In 1913 James Corrothers wrote a story in the *Crisis*, journal of the National Association for the Advancement of Colored People (NAACP), that "situated the problems of black leadership within global affairs by imagining a military alliance of Japan and Mexico against the United States, further supported by black deserters from the U.S. Army and the secession of Hawaii, led by angry Japanese-Americans." The U.S. president had to appeal to "Jed Blackburn," a Jack Johnson type character who "led a force of ten thousand black soldiers on a suicidal counterattack of Japan's invasion of Southern California."[28] J. E. Bruce was another black writer who wrote wishful fiction about Japan defeating the United States militarily. In his plot, the U.S. president had to call for volunteers to prevent this defeat, which led to a reduction in racism against African Americans who were now pivotal to national security—a scenario not far distant from what occurred during the Pacific War and the Cold War.[29]

This work of propaganda was matched, if not exceeded, by the 1921 potboiler by Japanese General Sato Kojiro, *Japanese-American War*. This book imagined the surprise destruction of the U.S. Pacific fleet, the occupation of Hawaii, and an invasion by Japanese forces of the U.S. mainland supported by 10 million Negroes led by Marcus Garvey.[30]

As in nonfiction, Du Bois was also a pioneer in his fictional portrayals of the importance of Japan to Negroes. In his riveting novel, *Dark Princess*—which he once called his "favorite book"[31]—Matthew Towns, the leading black character meets with a Japanese figure who tells him, "I have been much interested in noting the increased political power of your people" and asks, "I have been wondering how far you have unified and set plans. . . . either for yourselves in this land, or even further, with an eye toward international politics and the future of the darker races." He informed Towns of the "Great Council . . . of the Darker Peoples" which was to "meet in London three months hence. We have given the American Negro full representation." Another leading character in this novel, an Indian woman, says of her Nipponese comrade, "He is our leader, Matthew, the guide and counselor, the great Prime Minister of the Darker World." Presumably the Great Leader agreed with her assessment that the "strongest group among us believes only in Force. Nothing but bloody defeat in a world-wide war against whites will, in their opinion, ever beat sense and decency into Europe and America and Australia. They have no faith in mere reason, in alliance with oppressed labor, white and colored; in liberal thought, religion, nothing! Pound their arrogance into submission, they cry; kill them; conquer them; humiliate them."[32]

The black press gave considerable space to pro-Tokyo viewpoints, though admittedly they did not go as far in their bloodlust as the feisty Du Bois of fiction. Banner headlines shouting, "Japan to lead fight for Rights of Colored Races," with references to their being "enterprising and wonderful," were a staple in the Los Angeles-based *California Eagle*.[33] The Japanese were seen as a group to emulate. In 1916 the paper starkly contrasted the "protest" of Japanese in the region to the "obnoxious" film, *The Cheat*, compared to the largely futile protest to the anti-Negro movie, *Birth of a Nation*. The "nation itself, as well as the state," it was stressed admiringly, "have been known to BACK UP [*sic*] when Japan gets busy."[34] Japan was also seen as a model worth emulating in the realm of business. "There are 22,000 Japanese" and "30,000 colored Americans" in the region, yet the former "have this city honeycombed with their business enterprises—they even conduct pretentious places on Spring Street and on Broadway. . . . They employ thousands of Japanese men and women" and "they forever and eternally STICK TOGETHER [*sic*]." Negroes, it was said, "can well emulate the Japanese in business and look to the soil."[35]

Paying obeisance to Japan was not solely the province of California black newspapers. The *New York Amsterdam News*, based in Harlem, often tossed even more hosannas across the Pacific. In a prescient admission, one of their writers in 1934 predicted that "In the next quarter century England will be persuaded to relinquish her grip on India, Hongkong and Canton; and the French and Dutch will be pushed out of Java, Sumatra, Borneo and Annam." The reason was clear in his mind: "Japan's ascendancy means the twilight of the white gods in Asia."[36] But even before that longed-for day of colonialism's retreat, Japan was already aiding the beleaguered. Or so said their well-known columnist, J. A. Rogers. "Will the rise of Japan as a commercial power benefit the darker races?" he asked rhetorically. "Answer: it is already doing so." In Africa the masses wore cotton clothes that were often "filthy," and would "breed lice, typhus and other diseases." But, according to an "overworked doctor in Tanganyika," the "purchase of cheap Japanese rubber soled shoes has done more to check hookworm here than all the efforts of the health department." Rogers had no illusions about the beneficence of Japan, however. "Would Japan be less cruel to the darker peoples than the whites have been?" "I do not think so," he replied. Still, "Japanese cruelty, at its very worst, would find it extremely difficult to equal the record of the white man." After all, he concluded, "What can equal the story of the extermination of the Indians of North and South America; the African slave trade," and all the rest?[37]

Tokyo made good use of the public relations bonanza of having so many Negro adherents. The Japanese authorities translated a novel by the NAACP leader, Walter White, that concerned the lynching of Negroes. "The new edition sold in fantastic numbers, due to a publicity campaign by the Japanese government pointing out that the novel pictured the kind of barbarities which were tolerated and even encouraged in the democracy which had the temerity to criticize Japan for her acts in China."[38]

By the time the great black novelist Richard Wright had been catapulted to prominence, he was a card-carrying Communist and thus not predisposed to paying homage to Tokyo. Yet, when he was growing up amidst the atavistic racism that was Mississippi he was "filled with dread of white people," while his grandmother "sometimes at dusk on the Sabbath . . . would make the family kneel, and she would say a prayer for the Africans, the Japanese and Chinese."[39]

The prayers of Wright's grandmother were not unusual for religionists. The leaders of the African Methodist Episcopal Church—a bellwether among blacks—"believed that the ability of the Japanese to compete with Europeans and Americans on their own terms dispelled the myth of white superiority. Thus, AME leaders wholeheartedly supported the Japanese in the war against Russia." Japan "fascinated church members who demanded information on every aspect of Japanese life and culture."[40]

But it was not just the black poor like the Wright family or black parishioners that were bedazzled by Japan. When a massive earthquake hit Japan in 1923, "wealthy Negroes" were in the forefront of "rushing relief to her stricken cities and towns." As one black paper editorialized, "This is as it should be," since states like California "do not accord the Japanese the same rights and privileges accorded peoples of lighter hue." It was appropriate for affluent blacks—though some were often just a few steps away from poverty themselves—to hurry to the assistance of their fellow "coloreds."[41]

Ironically, the post-1898 expansion of the United States—a clear expression of strength—served to reveal a debilitating internal weakness: the presence within its borders of an alienated Negro minority that could prove fatal to national security, particularly in a confrontation with Japan. This fear was not assuaged in the aftermath of World War I when Negroes were involved in organizing an "International League of Darker Peoples"—akin to Du Bois's fictional creation—which in the "spirit of race internationalism" sent a "Japanese peace delegation" in New York a "floral arrangement" as "a token of friendship and brotherhood." Those involved in these efforts were no ill-kempt hodgepodge but, instead, the crème de la crème of Negro society. The effort was spearheaded by the richest black woman in the country, C. J. Walker— a cosmetics mogul—who "hosted a gathering at the grand Waldorf-Astoria for a small League delegation and S. Kuriowa, a Japanese envoy and publisher of *Yourdo Choho*, a Tokyo newspaper. During the session, Kuriowa . . . was said to have 'assured the delegation of his unqualified and genuine approval of the darker peoples making common cause against the common enemy—race prejudice based upon color.'"[42]

Washington was not idly sitting by as these potentially seditious acts were unfolding. To the contrary, surveillance of Negroes was escalated and the reports agents were filing were not encouraging. In October 1919, for example, came the disturbing story from Los Angeles that "Japan is planning trouble with Mexico against the United States and it is reported that within the next twelve months they are planning [war] in California. . . . The Japs [sic] are enlisting and promising certain things to the colored people on this coast if they will join in with Japan and Mexico when trouble is begun here in California. This information comes through a certain colored man now in this city from Gary, Indiana, he has been displaying a revolver. . . . He said that he had it to shoot up any fresh white fellows with in the event anything was started in this city at any time." This was corroborated by a "Negro bootblack" in Los Angeles who said "that the Japanese had been making overtures to the Negroes to side with them and that in a year or so they would take California and that when they did the Negroes would be treated right."[43]

The U.S. incursion into the Philippines, marking its entry into big power politics, also had the effect of introducing disgruntled Negroes to potential allies. Consider T. Nimrod McKinney, for example. He fought in the Spanish-American war, then resided for almost two decades in Manila, where he was "granted the first government franchise to establish a private detective agency. . . . then entered the brokerage and financial field." At one point he was employed by the "Manila House of Commerce, a firm composed of Japanese and Filipinos." As a result, he could "speak, read and write Spanish and Tagalog." By the early 1920s, like so many other pro-Tokyo Negroes, he was based in Los Angeles where he was "quite an active worker in various enterprises of doubtful character" and was "known to have strong Japanese inclinations for reasons of color." The U.S. authorities had reason to believe he was trying to penetrate their structures on behalf of Japan when he sought a job with U.S. military intelligence. At that juncture he was an organizer for the "American League of Democracy (Negro)" and "lectured and did propaganda work among Negroes against [the] Alien Land Bill." He was accused of being "paid by [the] Japanese Association" after he contributed a "series of pro-Japanese propaganda articles to the "Los Angeles California Eagle.'"[44] Perhaps worse, he was accused of alleging that anti-Japanese laws in California could be extended to "the Negro, the Mexican, the Jew."[45]

There was particular concern in the corridors of power in the United States that Negroes would link their grievances with those of Japanese Americans, creating a synergy that would ultimately incorporate Japan itself. One of the major complaints about McKinney was that he had "sent out literature against the alien land law," seen as discriminatory against Nissei and Issei, "which was furnished and paid for by the Japanese Farmer's Protective Association. The Japanese," the memo added sourly, "are striving to stir up race feeling stating that the Negroes and Japanese must stick together and resist the injuries of the whites." Pro-Tokyo advocates were said to be "disseminating propaganda among the Negroes and endeavoring to make the Negroes believe that the separate schools which have been established for the Japanese will be followed by a law establishing separate schools for the colored children." To that end, "all Japanese consuls in the United States have been directed by their government to make a survey of the Negro situation in the United States."[46]

These consuls had a lot to investigate, particularly on the West Coast where the Japanese-derived population was often larger than that of Negroes, and collaboration between the two groups was not uncommon. Delilah Beasley was a pioneering Negro writer in the Golden State; in the 1920s she came into conflict with irate Euro-Americans who objected to John D. Rockefeller's plan to "erect an International House on Berkeley [campus]"; they "objected to the possible entry of Negro and Oriental students to the areas adjoining the school."[47] In Seattle, workers of Japanese origin "outnumbered blacks in that city through the 1930s" and "held all of the [railroad] station porter positions"—a post traditionally held by Negroes in many parts of the nation—and, thus, worked closely with the mostly black Brotherhood of Sleeping Car Porters.[48] This collaboration was also social. As late as "the summer of 1941" intelligence reports noted that "a closer association between young Japanese and young Negroes in the San Francisco Bay Area was observed. . . . such mixed parties are known to have gone to Oakland, California, to attend meetings of the Nisei Young Democratic Club."

There were also reports about the "training of Negroes" by Tokyo in "New York, New Orleans, San Francisco and Los Angeles"—all convenient ports of entry to the United States. The U.S. authorities intercepted messages from Japanese operatives indicating in the spring of

1941 that "we have already established connections with very influential Negroes to keep us informed with regard to the Negro movement." U.S. intelligence asserted that "Japanese authorities are watching closely the Negroes who are employed in defense production plants, naval stations and other military establishments, particularly in the naval bases at Norfolk, Va., Philadelphia, Pa. [and] Brooklyn, N.Y."[49]

This campaign by Tokyo among Negroes, which was a prominent though often ignored feature of the interwar years, had a basis in material reality. Negroes had reason to believe that Tokyo's effort at Versailles to proclaim racial equality as a principle of international diplomacy would redound to their benefit. A few years later Du Bois explained that the exclusion of Japanese immigrants from the United States—a step that inflamed Tokyo—had resulted from a deal between the South and the West in which the former endorsed the Oriental Exclusion Act of 1924 in exchange for the sacrifice of the Dyer federal antilynching bill.[50]

Hence, the U.S. authorities should not have been surprised by the growth and depth of the developing Tokyo-Negro alliance. In Kansas City in 1933 a "Japanese visited . . . with the object of organizing among the Negroes [an] Anti-White Race Movement." "Nightly meetings" were being greeted "enthusiastically." The "Japanese organizer is said to have promised Japanese assistance in arms, cash and supplies, in a war against the white race." These agents were "covering the entire United States in the interests of the new organization; also that this organization is working in conjunction with the old Garvey (Negro) association. . . . This combined movement is, locally, among Negroes only and will have no dealings with Communists. It has already grown so strong that it has stripped local communistic bodies of practically all their Negro members. . . . Information is extremely difficult to obtain."[51]

As in Kansas City, so in Pittsburgh: From the latter city came reports about Japanese agents holding meetings "attended by a large number of other colored people." They were being told to "dispose of any property they might possess. . . . and go to the Continent of Africa, which the Japanese Government is soon to undertake to colonize; that the Japanese Government will build for them an army; that they will build for them a navy and will see that that they become a formidable nation." This promise to fulfill Garvey's old dream was reported at meetings "intended for [and] attended by Negroes only, and that if even a light-skinned Negro is present at the time [the Japanese agent] makes his address, the invectives against the United States are eliminated from his talk." There was a suspicion that this agent was Filipino since he spoke Spanish, suggestive of the pro-Asian bias involved.[52]

Such meetings were sufficiently well-known to be reported in the black press as the *Pittsburgh Courier* reported that a "Japanese scholar" was offering "free transportation "back to Africa'" along with "75 acres of land, a house, farm equipment, animals and crop seed, all free."[53] This Japanese initiative was also a spur to race changes domestically as the U.S. government, which otherwise excluded blacks from meaningful employment, felt compelled to search for a "good Negro operative" so that "he might find out what is going on."[54]

The Japanese offensive among Negroes had created a dilemma for the United States. The government knew that the only organized and militant anti-Tokyo force among blacks was the Communist Party and their allies. Yet this was precisely the group under harshest attack by the U.S. authorities—which, ironically, bolstered the pro-Tokyo forces. Not least because of Tokyo's anticommunism and Japan's racial appeals, which were seen as contrary to working-class unity, the U.S. Communists kept Japanese agents under surveillance as well. Thus, at the same time that U.S. agents were eyeballing Japanese-sponsored meetings, the Communists and their allies were doing the same. For example, in 1932 an operative of the soon to be defunct "Communist front," the "League of Struggle for Negro Rights," broached a "very important matter. . . . The UNIA is conducting a drive throughout the country, holding mass meetings with Japanese speakers, preparing the masses ideologically in support of the Japanese attack against the Soviet Union and Chinese masses. The line they follow is to point out the unity that should exist between the colored races as against the whites. Such meetings are held here in Chicago and we also know of a few held in Gary. . . . There seems to be a definitely organizationally prepared plan to enlist the Negro masses behind the wagon of Garvey and his movement. As we were informed there are 250 Japanese students touring the country and everywhere speaking under the auspices of the UNIA."[55] But before December 1941 the U.S. authorities were reluctant to ease pressure on Communists, so as to heighten the same on pro-Tokyo Negroes.

For this left-wing grouping was on to something. A black community languishing under the cruel lash of lynching and an ideology that heralded as superior all things "white," was predisposed to lend an eager ear to Japanese agents preaching a radically different message. In

New York, for example, Hikida Yasuichi had "polished his English in a high school in Michigan," then proceeded "to study sociology for one year (1922) at Columbia University." This dapper spokesman of Tokyo, graying and animated, was "often warmly welcomed into the homes of leading [black] citizens."[56] There he was often accompanied by a Negro woman—that a white man of similar or virtually any stature would be reluctant to share such company openly was yet another living rebuke to prevailing racial mores in the United States.[57] Described as "suave and genial," he "often" traveled in Jim Crow accommodations, like those he was seeking to influence. He had a wide-ranging knowledge of black history, having written a biography of the Haitian hero, Toussaint L'Ouverture, and was a frequent speaker at the foremost institutions of black higher education, Tuskegee and Hampton Institutes. He worked in swank Forest Hill as a servant but "maintained a Harlem address at the colored YMCA," an address from which "every year unfailingly he sent his Negro friends Christmas cards—usually a picture of Japan's Rising Sun."[58]

Hikida's profile was similar to that of other Japanese nationals, who came to the United States in the run-up to the blitzkrieg against the Empire, settled in black communities, and worked as menials amongst affluent whites. Besides Forest Hills, Saratoga, New York, Lexington, Kentucky, and the posher sections of Florida were their favorite haunts. They often worked as chauffeurs—a prime position for those seeking unguarded but vital tidbits of information. There they could also more easily propagandize among the legions of Negro servants who toiled alongside them. Like Hikida, they often had Negro women companions—or wives. This revelation had reached a leading aide of President Franklin D. Roosevelt, who learned that there were a "small number of Japanese nationals married to Negresses [sic]," which was viewed as a "fifth column move on the part of the Japanese in creating such marriages to build good will and sympathy."[59]

But the most intimate of relationships was not the only place where the Japanese had insinuated themselves. The famous composer W. C. Handy recalled a cook who traveled about the country for five years as a member of his vaudeville troupe, who later turned out to be an eavesdropping Japanese Army officer. This Japanese crusade was not without effect, or so thought the perceptive black journalist Roi Ottley. "Some Negroes," he thought, "came to look upon the Japanese as belonging to a messianic race, which would lead black men out of bondage. A few Negroes traveled to Japan on grants and subsidies," and returned with stories rivaling those of contemporaneous sojourners to the Soviet Union, who had claimed to have seen the future, while noting that it works.[60]

This vision of Japan as the new Mecca for Negroes was gaining in strength as the war approached. In 1938 the Japanese journalist Masao Dodo spoke in Harlem on what had become a familiar theme. The Harlem community writhing in the parched desert of racial oppression found it difficult to ignore his soothing liquid words that "the Negroes have every assurance that they will be treated better in Japan than the whites." When the great black boxer Joe Louis fought the German, Max Schmeling, in New York City about the same time that Masao was speaking in Harlem, "the overwhelmingly white audience . . . had switched allegiance in an hysterical few seconds from black American to white foreigner as Schmeling's blows staggered Louis."[61] Yet Masao in stark contrast proclaimed that "it thrilled Japanese to know that Jesse Owens had breasted the tape ahead of white men the world over." This fluent English speaker and graduate of the University of California argued that "as a result of Japan selling goods cheaper than white nations to colored people, the white nations clamped high tariffs on all Japanese manufactured goods." His audience, many of whom had fled the poverty of the "British West Indies," often had direct knowledge of what he meant.

Likewise, when Masao proclaimed that "Japan has [no] choice but to match the strength of the white nations or be slaves," a black community which included many who had endured bondage could only nod in agreement. Arthur Schomburg, whose eminence was ratified when his name came to grace the leading national library for research in black culture, expressed the sentiments of many when he declared, "If Japan will help the darker people to gain opportunities, I am ready to shoulder arms for Japan now." Those assembled dismissed concerns about Japan's war against China as if they were so many inoffensive flies: "It was clear," said the reporter present, "that most of those present sided with Japan in its present imbroglio with China. . . . At the same time some of those present criticized other Negroes who want the United States to fight Japan because of its invasion with China."[62] Those who had been paying attention to Tokyo-Negro relations should not have been surprised by this: in 1939 one U.S. operative confessed that "'enlightened Negro leaders' had told him 'that between eighty and ninety percent of the American colored population who have any views on the subject at all, are pro-Japanese as a result of the intensive Japanese propaganda among this racial group.'"[63]

The proliferation of accounts in the black press about Japanese agents addressing black audiences was not solely a product of the latter's hunger for news about Nippon. Tokyo made a concerted effort to bring Negro journalists across the Pacific for visits where they were wined and dined. Months before the strike against the Empire, the United States intercepted a message to the highest levels in Tokyo, meant "to be kept secret." Why the need for surreptitiousness? It seems that an emissary from Tokyo had been "using a Negro literary critic" and "had him open a news service for Negro newspapers. The Negro press is so poor that it has no news service of its own and as I have told you in various messages, had been getting relatively good results and because of the advantage we have in using men like this in our political and subversive activities." That was not all. Much has been made of alleged and actual Soviet spying in the U.S. capital, but Tokyo too felt that "in organizing our schemes among the Negroes. . . . Washington . . . should be our hub." Further, "in the arsenals at Philadelphia and Brooklyn there are also a few unskilled Negro laborers, so I would say in the future there will be considerable profit in our getting Negroes to gather military intelligence for us." "Chicago, Los Angeles and New Orleans" were also targeted.[64]

Thus, as the pulse of an approaching war became ever more rapid, Tokyo thought it possessed an advantage in having a firm base of support among the Negroes, situated strategically within the boundaries of the Empire's chief military ally. This was not an unlikely assumption. However, timely concessions on the racial front by the United States, along with strong antifascist sentiment among Negroes eventually vitiated Tokyo's putative advantage.

3

Race/War

THE BRITISH COULD HARDLY AFFORD to alienate anyone—least
of all Chinese—as they faced the grim prospect of a Japanese invasion.
But such dire realities were far from the mind of the working-class men
fleeing the austere future awaiting them in a Britain fearful of being
overrun by Germany. Harold Robert Yates was "really looking forward
to going to Hong Kong. . . . It was reckoned to be the best station in the
British Army at that time. . . . Generally the standard of living for the
soldiers was much better." His "money went further" to begin with.
There was a "pleasant climate. There was plenty of sport, swimming
and football. And of course there were plenty of women."

Not only was the food of better quality there, but it was "relatively
cheap . . . compared with the U.K." Beer and cigarettes, clothes and
cameras were cheap too. Sure, there were downsides. While he was in
Hong Kong, "occasionally someone would rape a Chinese girl," though
a "lot weren't reported." One ghastly case involved a girl who was "crying and of course she'd been a virgin." But that was a blip on an otherwise happy screen, he thought. "Normally we were finished at twelve
o'clock and we were . . . freed to leave the barracks." The reason they
had such latitude was that they had "barrack room servants" called
"'boys'" who were compelled to "clean anything, except rifles. [They
weren't] allowed to touch rifles," he stressed. This was the system that
obtained in Asia, "but not in [the] U.K. itself."

These luxuries helped to make soldiers softer than they were back
home and, consequently, more susceptible to being swept away by an
invasion. There were "Chinese and Indian constables at that time, the
officers were all British—but the Chinese or Indian constables had no
power to arrest us of course. So we could get away with quite a lot."
And they did, carousing, brawling, and boozing madly. Anyway,
"Hong Kong was absolutely riddled with corruption" and "police took
bribes." The colony had "the best police that money can buy." Yates got

on "fairly well with the Middlesex Regiment but not so well with the Royal Scots. And the Royal Scots and of course the Middlesex didn't get on well," as fierce "fights" were frequent. As he recalled it, "British civilians wanted Chinese and soldiers to walk on one pavement while they used the other," and, as he recalled, there were signs that read, "dogs and soldiers not allowed." If a "girl went with a soldier, you know, she's considered no good," though civilians "admired the Navy a little better than the Army."

But when the war began in 1939 these fusty attitudes changed. Then civilians began "inviting soldiers to their homes." But Yates's attitude was, "if you don't want to know us in peace-time, we don't want to know you in war-time."

Along with these intra-European tensions there was the ever-present problem of tensions with Asians. The Sikhs mutinied in 1940 on Stonecutter's Island, as the "British were trying to get them to wear steel helmets."[1] This violation of their fundamental religious beliefs was an illustration of the British tin ear and tone deafness when it came to dealing with Asians.

U.S. authorities had their ear to the ground and did not like what they were hearing. In July 1940 the State Department was told "of the fear by this Government of Chinese mob violence in Hong Kong which may require a Japanese attack to start it. . . . Many Chinese shops are being equipped with iron grills and show evidence of various forms of protection against mob violence. This Government endeavor[s] for reasons of policy to blame the state of alarm more on external developments than on this internal situation which is undoubtedly potentially serious."[2]

This was true. The United States had cause to suspect the "loyalty of many of both the Indian and Chinese police." The British, it was reported, "had more to fear from dissatisfied elements within the colony than from outside sources." Who were these "outside sources"? Agents of Tokyo? Actually, an agent of Tokyo had informed the gullible U.S. official that "the Indian troops and the police were being incited to subordination by Communist agents."[3]

The confluence of anticommunism and white supremacy greased the path for Japan. Somewhat naively the colonial governor asserted in the spring of 1941, "I am struck with [the] continuing growth of Staff of Japanese Consulate in Hong Kong. Excluding clerks, staff in 1931 when Japanese population was 2205 numbered 5 and remained at that figure until 1937. [The] number has steadily risen and during 1940 averaged 11: today with Japanese population [of] 463 Consular Office number 12, clerical staff has risen from three to eight during this period. With American infiltration [and] Philippino [*sic*] population of 869 American Consulate has only 7 officers with 9 deputy Commissioners, clerks and 5 lady assistants. I have now been asked . . . for visa for two more non-official Consular officers to come to Hong Kong with no indication of what posts they will fill. . . . The functions of such a large staff," he said guilelessly, "can hardly be consular in the accepted use of the term."[4] There was "nothing to be gained," countered the Colonial Office, "by making it difficult for Japanese civilians to enter or remain in Hong Kong."[5]

Still, London was becoming more trusting of Japan, its anticommunist ally, but still maintained an inflexible doubt about the colonized Chinese, who it suspected "were tampering with the safes."[6]

As 8 December 1941 unfolded, Hong Kong was experiencing a typically pleasant day—at least for some. Gwen Priestwood found herself at the posh Peninsular Hotel "waited on by silent, smoothly efficient Chinese waiters." A "perfect orchestra" played "The Best Things in Life Are Free." Other members of the city's elite were "at a dinner given by the Japanese Consulate." Not surprisingly, Madame Sun Yat-Sen was there, along with her sister.[7] Joan Cummack was on her way to play yet another round of golf on that fateful day. She had cheerful feelings about Hong Kong at this juncture. It was "very wonderful," she thought, "it was absolutely paradise. . . . It was a dream, it was beautiful. . . . sailing, parties and the servants." There "were very few foreign women in the colony and a lot of foreign men," which put a premium on women like herself.[8] Meanwhile, just before the invasion Harrison Forman in a radio broadcast from Hong Kong likened the inhabitants of the colony to a "colony of ostriches—and nearly got thrown out for his statement."[9] Few recognized that this effete outpost of Empire was, like a rotten fruit, on the verge of dropping into the hands of Tokyo.

Suddenly this pleasant carousal and avoidance were to be disrupted by another song: as the Japanese invaded "they were accompanied by a powerful gramophone amplifier on a barge which played 'Home Sweet Home' and 'The Last Rose of Summer.'"[10] This was part of a sonic invasion, as the Japanese troops entered Hong Kong emitting "blood curdling yells" that reminded one missionary of "American savages."[11] These dueling sounds were to set the tone for a harrowing seventeen days for Hong Kong, as it fought a losing battle against overwhelming Japanese forces until its ignominious surrender on Christmas Day.

Once again, British racism served to make this surrender virtually inevitable. To put it bluntly, the British failed to utilize the substantial manpower constituted by the Chinese in Hong Kong. When Brigadier R. C. B. Anderson arrived in the colony the composition of the defense corps was "roughly this: they had four companies, one English, one Scottish, one Eurasian and one Portuguese." The "recruiting for the Eurasian and Portuguese companies were no trouble at all but recruiting for the British element was difficult, in fact it became impossible in the end." Why? "The apathy of the British populations not only in Hong Kong but in all places in the Far East and also to the fact that you could never instill into them there was any possible chance of war."[12]

What about the Chinese? As Chohong Choi put it, "The average Chinese male was deemed too small to serve in the army (an inadequate excuse, because his would-be Japanese opponent was not large in stature either) and even if he was big enough, there was not enough arms to equip all who volunteered. Moreover, the reliability of the Chinese was regarded with suspicion by the British, who knew that most Chinese resented Westerners and declared their loyalty to China, not to Hong Kong."[13] There was little enthusiasm in higher circles for forming Chinese military units. Keeping arms out of the hands of Chinese was one of the "oldest and deepest-rooted of all Hong Kong prejudices, dating back to strikes and boycotts of the 'twenties': suspicion of any organisation of the Chinese. It was still the prevailing view of the colonial government, expressed in tardy and grudging recruitment of a small Chinese unit for the Volunteers, that the gravest of all dangers to a British colony in the sort of crisis that had now arrived was from 'the Chinese mob.'"[14] While the Chinese were under strict scrutiny to hinder their carrying weapons officially, historically the colonists had recruited for the police—to cite one example—from Europeans who were "discharged sailors and soldiers, ship-jumpers, beachcombers and prostitutes."[15]

In sum, the colonists felt that the Chinese would not only accept the invaders but would assist them—despite widespread Chinese rancor toward Japan because of the latter's brutal assault on the mainland.

This rancor notwithstanding, many Chinese aided the invaders considerably—or so thought the British. General C. M. Maltby, a top British military official in the region, thought there were numerous "agents and spies" for Tokyo among the indigenous residents of Hong Kong. Although his perspective may have been skewed by the fact that Japanese were "disguised as innocent labourers or coolies," the invaders' "patrols [were] advanced by paths which could have been known only to locals or from detailed reconnaissance." The "possession of these agents and guides with such intimate knowledge counteracted the first great advantage the defence forces normally has over the attack, that is, familiarity with the ground." The "enemy system of intelligence was most complete," replete with detailed maps; they "knew the names of most of the senior and commanding officers" of the British forces. Maltby concluded that there were many "Chinese guides" for the attackers "drawn from the village of Tsun Wan Wai"; a "large number of army transport drivers deserted, some of them taking lorries with them."[16]

Father James Smith of the Maryknoll Mission had a similar experience. He found that "when British lorries tried to move through the streets of Kowloon, Fifth Columnists often obstructed their passage."[17] Simultaneously, G. A. Leiper discovered that "many Chinese . . . drivers had already deserted" and he was "afraid that more would follow."[18] Gwen Priestwood was directly familiar with these Chinese drivers fleeing with lorries. At the height of the invasion, as bullets were whizzing all about, she was asked, "Can you drive a car?. . . . The Chinese drivers have all gone on strike." So she rushed behind the wheel of a truck.[19]

She had little choice. The journalist Emily Hahn concluded that "the failure of transportation" was a "large factor of our defeat." It was "sabotage, mostly. The Chinese chauffeurs had dozens of little ways to do it; they swiped the carburetor . . . or just drained the gas tank, or wrecked the truck."[20] Gwen Dew, a U.S. journalist then in Hong Kong, was irate about what she perceived as Chinese perfidy. "The British police had 50,000 of these enemy Chinese listed on their books previous to the war and were well aware of their activities," she fumed. "I do not know why they were not all arrested and shot at the beginning of the hostilities." She was outraged when she saw that Japanese and their Chinese allies "stormed the cars of Europeans, and men who had worked with the Chinese for twenty years and loved them had to drive through the mobs at tremendous speed to save their own wives and children."

Yet even as the battle for Hong Kong raged, Gwen Dew had reason to understand why there might be inadequate Chinese defense of the Crown Colony. She and others had repaired to the Repulse Bay Hotel as the war intensified. There she found "so-called society women from their villas on the hills." They "had always lived in high luxury, with countless Chinese servants and splendid homes." Now "their mouths had prickly persimmons in them." There was one "dowager duchess" with her "limousine, her flying veils and her scalding tongue," all of which "had been topics of the day in more gossipy times." She was "not a guest of the hotel, but had come from her spacious home on The Peak" at the time of the invasion. From "time to time" the "snipers" would "fire at the hotel and we could hear the answering guns of the British near-by."

Suddenly, Dew's "own private war began." "Mrs. Elegant, let us call her, looked around and in a penetrating voice said: 'what are all these Chinese doing in here? What right have they to be here?'" Since "some of the Chinese were millionaires and well-known Chungking government officials, this was ill-timed, to say the least." Remarkably, the "faces [of the Chinese] turned white." Dew took the high road. "There were also some amahs and servants, but they were all human beings and our allies, as far as I was concerned. 'Why shouldn't they be here?'" she asked. The "dowager duchess" snorted, "'I know more about these Chinese than you do. You people come out from America for a few months and tell us who have been here twenty years how to run the Chinese.'" Dew was "mad!" She exploded: "'You've lived in a pretty house high on the hill, with a score of servants whom you've paid a few dollars a month and that's about all.'"

Another furor erupted when Dew sought to make sure that the Chinese huddled in the hotel were able to get something to eat. "This blew the lid off again. 'The idea of giving all those people food!' Mrs. Elegant sniffed. 'They shouldn't be here at all and they will get plenty of food if we don't.'" Then, lo and behold, a Chinese man showed up with more food. Her "antagonist snatched the plate from his hand and said: 'We don't want any more Chinese in here.'" Dew "exploded" again "as though a shell had made a direct hit. 'Of all the stupid, ill-mannered women I've ever known, you are the worst,'" she cried. She "stated rudely" and fairly, "It has been talk of your sort that has caused international wars in the first place. Here we crouch and our only hope of Hong Kong being saved is if the Chinese army manages to arrive to rescue us. . . . ' She tossed her head like an excited bull and announced to our diverted audience, 'American fool.'"

Begging to differ, Dew thought it was the British fighting forces who were waging war like fools. The Japanese "were able to tap wires and give orders to the British to fire against their own men. . . . Members of the Maryknoll Mission, near Fort Stanley, later told of watching the fighting on the hills opposite them, with British troops on two ridges, who suddenly began firing at one another, killing many. Somehow the Japs [sic] had managed to give such an order, and it was carried out." Presumably one of their fluent English speakers was instrumental here.[21]

Dew's experience was not unique. Her fellow Hong Kong journalist, Emily Hahn, recounted that before the invasion her friend Margaret was "simply laying out anyone with whom she had dealings, especially one Indian gentleman with a dark red fez. When after the surrender, he joined the Japanese, with a glad cry I remembered Margaret's savage rudeness to him and I thought I understood."[22]

This was just one example of an all-encompassing discord that reigned during the invasion. The British Foreign Office was told that when one Briton saw the Japanese land he called police headquarters, "only to be told that it was not their business. He then telephoned to military HQ and the sergeant who replied, when told the Japs [sic] were landing and to inform his [commanding officer] said, 'I can't wake him up at this time, its 11 P.M. and he's gone to bed, he'll be mad if I wake him up.'"[23] He was supine in dreamland—as was British policy.

The invasion of Hong Kong was a nightmare for all concerned, but particularly for the Europeans and Euro-Americans, for unlike the Asians a passing glance revealed them as the probable target of the invaders and their allies. Father James Smith of the Maryknoll Mission discovered "during these terrible and anxious days" that "many came back to the Sacraments after years of laxity; confessions were heard among [them] everywhere, in the streets and in dugouts and pillboxes."[24] Robert K. M. Simpson had taught at Hong Kong University and was a member of the defense corps. One of his "colleagues, widely informed and well-balanced, as he began to see what the end must be, developed the reaction of violently opening and closing his fists and his eyes, whenever he thought of the impending unmentionable catastrophe."[25] There was a "European Sergeant who refused to put on [his] uniform and locked himself in his room and refused to come out."[26] <u>The invasion invoked a massive emotional collapse—a collective nervous breakdown—not least among European men.</u>

Victor Merrett, who served with the military in Hong Kong, felt that "we Britons have been educated that we always win wars and here we were in the middle of something that it was fairly obvious we weren't going to win. And it's [,] as I say [,] deflating. It's a very difficult situation to come to terms with."[27] As the invasion was unfolding, Ellen Field did the unthinkable: her "pride had been so affronted that day," she "thought nothing of going into a Chinese roadside tea shop—a place normally used by coolies—where we were glad to sit down on hard three-legged stools at a long home-made trestle-table, and rest our feet." Her downward spiral continued when she tried to catch a bus but could not: "It was annoying to watch those buses go roaring by, crammed to the doors with Chinese grinning at our plight." These reversals of fortune were so amazing that she started doubting religion: "How can I believe in the Bible, in the Sermon on the Mount," she bewailed, "after what I've seen?" When she arrived at her well-appointed home during the midst of the invasion and discovered that it had been seized by Japanese troops, she acknowledged feeling like a "Jew who had just seen a Nazi scrawl 'Jude' across his shop window."[28]

Gwen Priestwood sensed this cascading anxiety. "All through the siege people squabbled over trifles," she said. "Lifetime friendships exploded with the bombs. Bosom companions quarreled—over nothing." But in exploring this burgeoning apprehension, Priestwood understood—albeit ironically—that the loss of a life of racial privilege was behind all this nervous, querulous concern. In the midst of the war, "the old habit [of] brushing one's hair one hundred strokes a night, something usually performed by one's amah [servant], was forgotten. But the feminist instinct to look one's best never really died. If one had to stop a shell, one might as well stop it with a powdered nose and a trifle of lipstick, and so make it less of a shock for those who gathered up the remains." The strain was too much for Priestwood. She "almost cried. Well, I supposed any woman would have. Here I was, at a great moment of tragedy in the history of the British Empire, a city in flaming ruin around me, surrender to the Japanese a few hours away," and all that she could think of was "silk stockings . . . the most beautiful things in the world."[29] Her compatriot Ellen Field was shocked when she was compelled to deal with a "very officious Chinese clerk" who "made sure that foreigners never got preferential treatment."[30] What abomination awaited them next?

Morris "Two-Gun" Cohen—gangster, Zionist, and former bodyguard to Sun Yat-Sen—had led a dissolute and swashbuckling life, with a lengthy list of convictions including "carnal knowledge of [a] girl under 16 years."[31] Not surprisingly, he was full of bluster and bombast and was not to be intimidated easily. Yet he was trapped in Hong Kong at the time of the invasion and was visibly fearful. His colleague, Solomon Bard, found him "rather frightened. . . . He was just a very ordinary frightened man, as we were all. He was nervous. Very nervous."[32] Robert Simpson, who taught at Hong Kong University, like many Europeans was incredulous about what he was witnessing. "There were some who to the last were simply unable to believe that Britain could lose Hong Kong. . . . It was utterly incredible that Japanese troops could defeat [the] British." A comrade of his signaled the emotional holocaust marked by this defeat when he mused that "to surrender Hong Kong to Japan" was like "relinquishing the right to read Shakespeare."[33]

Benjamin A. Proulx was full of contradictions; he compared the victorious Japanese at length to "apes" before noting with wonder, "They were our conquerors."[34] David Bosanquet reflected sadly that "We had been beaten ignominiously. It had happened so fast. It left us utterly deflated. Our world had collapsed. Many of us, including me, were racked with strange new doubts, apprehensive of what the future held—if there was to be one." It was all so "soul destroying."[35] It was not just being beaten, but being beaten in a context redolent with racial meaning that heightened the distress among those of "pure European descent."

This nervousness was compounded by Japanese propaganda leaflets raining down on Hong Kong. Phyllis Harrop asserted that the "subject matter" of these paper missiles was "anything but pleasant. All definitely aiming at the suppression of the white population and inflaming the Chinese and Indians to turn against us. Many of the leaflets are aiming at killing the white man." They said, "Kill all the Europeans as they are responsible for the war and once they are out of the way the fighting will stop." These words had a military impact, for the British were "afraid to shell Kowloon for fear of frightening the Chinese into riots and saying we are killing their own people, relatives and friends in that area."[36]

One leaflet featured a picture of a "large, fat, white man, supposed to be John Bull. He was completely nude and was sitting on a massive ornate chair. By his side were bags of money spilling out gold and silver coins and on each of his massive knees sat a pretty Chinese girl— also completely naked. Under this effort was printed: 'How the British colony destroys the morals of your womenfolk with their gold.'"[37] A leaflet targeting Indians featured a crude drawing on rough paper showing a Japanese soldier pointing a rifle at an Indian who was sheltering a frightened British officer. The caption read, "We cannot fire while our comrade stands between." Another leaflet showed Indian soldiers carrying a white flag, approaching a party of Japanese. "Come, Indian soldiers," said the caption. "We treat you especially good!"[38] An intelligence summary filed after the war was well under way noted that a "Chinese who recently walked from Kweilin to Ishan . . . noticed several village houses with pictures of Europeans pasted on the walls. Upon enquiry he was informed that these had been dropped by aircraft. . . . The front has the caption, 'Who is dancing with your girl?' overprinted on an ordinary dance hall scene. In the center there are 2 close ups; the first a man and a woman dancing normally and the second, the same couple engaged in a concentrated kiss." The message was that Chinese women were being "stolen" by European men. Another leaflet declared, "Asiatic people should not fight amongst themselves, but shoulder to shoulder drive the Americans and British out of Asia."[39]

The British believed that Japanese propaganda was working and the Chinese were not rallying fervently to the Union Jack. Scribbling furiously a few days after the surrender, E. C. Ford railed against the "Fifth Column activity in the colony." "What made our defeat inevitable," he said accusingly, "was the Chinese, who, being prepared to sell their rotten souls at any time for a dollar, were sniping and hand grenading our troops from housetops and flats . . . near . . . our lines. Caught between the 6" mortars, artillery and explosive bullets of the Japs [sic] in front, the grenades and rifles of the Chinese in near and bombs from above, our lines were repeatedly broken." In fact, when the "Japs [sic] came to take over Jubilee this morning . . . their guide was a deserter from the Chinese Royal Engineers." Then there were the "cowardly Rajputans Rifles (Scum of India) and Royal Scots. The last-named have earned the soubriquet [sic] of 'His Majesty's Fleet of Foot.'"; he viewed the Indians as "useless swine . . . except Punjabis." They lost "a Gunner Robinson. Shot dead by the Indian sentries. . . . Our Indians have had to be relieved by British gunners because they are considered unreliable. At Jubilee and Scutters they have had to be forced out of their shelters at revolver point." Above all, Ford was mortified by the "bitter hostility and fifth column activity of the Chinese in Hong Kong. The majority of these were renegades from the Sino-Japanese war."[40]

Ford's recollections about Indians have been confirmed by others. Sir Arthur Dickinson Blackburn recalled that "Peenyfeather-Evans, the Chief of Police, told me that Sikhs had been practically in a state of mutiny during the last days of the fighting."[41] Like many of the British, he did not seem to comprehend that Asians may have been alienated from London because of its harsh white supremacist policies. The scholar Barbara Sue-White states that "as long as five years before the battle of Hong Kong, a secret cipher telegram reported that two men from the 6th Rajputana Rifles had deserted and probably crossed the border into China to join the Japanese." Though they were derided for their real and imagined pro-Tokyo tendencies, the "Rajputs suffered the greatest casualties of any of the defence forces in the battle for Hong Kong. A mammoth 65 per cent of the men of Rajput C Company became casualties, and every single officer was lost." Such figures may confirm their patriotism to the crown; or it may confirm the opposing charge that these Indian troops were little more than cannon fodder. This latter allegation was confirmed by the debased status of Indians in prewar Hong Kong, for example, the Matilda Hospital was reserved for "British, American and European patients," with "others" conspicuously excluded.[42]

The prewar mutinous sentiments among the Rajputs were shared by the Sikhs. Alan Jackson Wood, who was with the artillery during the war, charged that "all the Sikhs" joined the invaders.[43] The British had found earlier that the Sikhs believed firmly in solidarity, for when "one of their numbers is put into the guard room . . . immediately the rest demand to go in sympathy."[44]

James Allan Ford of the Royal Scots felt that the "real fifth column was the Chinese. . . . a great number of them. I watched them carrying mortar bombs to the grave urns which stood on the hillside." "Some of them probably would feel well disposed to anyone who was against the British because there was strong feeling among the Chinese that the British should get out." When "we left the mainland after the defence of

Gordon Hill we came down by a bus from, I'm not sure where it was. . . . we were fired upon several times by Chinese . . . trying to gun [us] down as we left." Yes, "there were occasions when the Royal Scots fell back"; it was "surprising they didn't run away altogether when there was so little to fight for and so little to fight with." General Maltby was a "Middlesex man. . . . he regarded us as indisciplined and what he really meant [was] that we Scots, we're not English."[45] But it was the Chinese that Ford blamed most; in his novel he spoke of how "Chinese fifth columnists shone signal lights, sniped, spread false rumours and incited desertion, looting and riot."[46]

One British soldier told of "tales of small arms having been buried years before in fake funerals by renegade Chinese working for the Japs [sic]. True? I just don't know, but it was of course feasible." The British acted as if it were true since "about three or four days before the end of the battle we were given instructions to shoot out of hand, any Chinese whether in our uniform or not who we found in the vicinity. . . . So there must have been a reason for this order. Some men I afterwards spoke to in POW camp . . . told me that Chinese were throwing hand grenades at them from buildings behind their front lines."[47]

This hearsay report about the massacre of Chinese by the British during the invasion has been confirmed by Wally Scragg of the military. During the siege, police shot at rampaging looters at random. A "Sergeant who had just returned from a visit to Central described witnessing the summary execution of 70 Wang Ching-wei agents who had been rounded up by Special Branch detectives and Chungking agents: their hands were tied behind their backs and gunny [sacks] were put over their heads. . . . they were shot in batches by Mr. 'X,' using a Thompson gun and then he went along the line of bodies and shot each one in the head with a pistol. It was very professionally done." As the war reached the "doorstep" of Hong Kong, "the Cantonese . . . began to desert. . . . I remember finding tunics in the streets from which the numbers had been removed."[48] Robert Hammond was struck by the fact that "the British soldiers, to keep order in Hong Kong machine gunned thousands of looters and fifth columnists."[49] But these massacres did not decrease the acute anxiety of the Europeans.

As the New Zealander, James Bertram, remembered it, the Chinese were not allowed to do "night patrol" during the invasion since the "Fifth Column scare was at its height." So the Europeans, some of whom were not ready for it, "did the night patrols and the Chinese recruits did a lot of serious trench-digging." But the "one mass group that might have defended Hong Kong with real passion—the Chinese—was never called upon."[50] But how could they be called on when before the war "British soldiers refused to bathe in the same pool" with Chinese?[51] Britain only trained a "few hundred Chinese" in military and quasi-military operations. Years later an observer who signaled the sensitivity of his insight by "wish[ing] to remain anonymous," acknowledged that "had it not been [for] such distrust and bad faith coupled probably with the shortage of weapons . . . hundreds of thousand [sic] Chinese volunteers could have been trained for the defence." There was a "general European . . . fear of the overwhelming Chinese majority" and a withering suspicion that the "local population" would "turn against the Europeans the moment the Japs [sic] attacked." The "battle of Hong Kong," he sighed "was lost before it began."[52]

Myriad sources confirm that the expatriates had "an underlying fear that the Chinese, however law-abiding they might seem, might rise up against them." So it was best to render them militarily impotent. When the Chinese were recruited, albeit sporadically and sparsely, this "raised fears among those in the colony who believed the Chinese might turn on the British." The British were keen to keep the Chinese in their place; the expatriate Solomon Bard was "amazed to discover that there were British volunteers who would refuse even to recognize their Chinese comrades-in-arms if they met out of uniform on the street."[53]

It wasn't simply weaknesses in the military and police that led to the defeat of the British. Sir Arthur Dickinson Blackburn recalled that "in many a gracious home on the Peak or in the Mid-levels, entire Chinese staffs deserted, leaving bewildered matrons, some for the first time in their lives, to grapple with the problems of the pantry." This could only contribute to escalating levels of anxiety among Europeans. On the other hand, he felt that "Eurasians were enthusiastic soldiers. Subtly discriminated against in the cloistered business community of Hongkong, they'd found a source of pride in the Volunteers. They had their own company—No. 3"—which performed admirably, he thought.

Still, apprehension reigned about the reliability of those not of "pure European descent," perhaps for fear that the discrimination they had suffered would sour their attitudes toward British colonialism.[54] Thus, London insisted that a majority of the police force in Hong Kong be recruited overseas because the security of the colony could not be safely entrusted to locally recruited Chinese policemen—the first line of defense in Hong Kong. This was not unique to this Crown Colony: in the African colonies of the Empire often the police in a given district were strangers, recruited in another part of the territory and frequently unable to speak the local language. Police were recruited heavily from India but they were poorly paid, receiving less than half the wages of a European constable. Even some of the "White Russians" were paid less than other Europeans.

George Wright-Nooth of the colony's police force verifies that the "principle of divide and rule predominated in recruiting policy. Below gazetted rank there were Europeans, two categories of Indian, White Russians and Chinese from widely differing regions of China—a cocktail of three races and five languages" with "about a third" being Indians, all of whom spoke "Urdu," that were "divided roughly between Sikhs and Punjabi Muslims." Most of the Sikhs, he said, "were disloyal and took an active part in humiliating and beating the Europeans," while the "Punjabi Muslims generally were very loyal."[55] The "Indian contingent gave little help during the struggle. Their loyalty had been undermined." Closing the barn door after the horse had bolted, after the war the police became majority "Cantonese" for the first time, while an effort was made to "get rid of the Sikh police" and retain "Punjabi Muslims."[56]

Nonetheless, the defeat of the British also had causes other than the debilitating impact of white supremacy on the fighting mettle of Hong Kong. One Hong Konger acknowledged that "with hindsight the defense of Hong Kong was laughable. There were two antique destroyers and a few torpedo boats, five obsolete airplanes. . . . The second Battalion of the Royal Scots had been abroad for seven years and was riddled with VD and malaria and was unfit to fight." Apparently "part of [the military's] equipment went to Honolulu instead of Hong Kong."[57] Then there were the poorly trained soldiers, such as the Canadians who arrived days before the invasion. Lucien Brunet of Montreal later confessed that he had not "seen a hand grenade before in my life" until that tumultuous day in December 1941.[58] Kenneth M. Baxter, who was in the trenches during these battles, recalled that "Lewis gunners [had] mistaken some of us in the bush as the enemy and fired their own people in the back. . . . [He] tried to keep it quiet."[59] E. C. Ford spoke ruefully of the "awful failure of our officers" and the "poor quality of Canadian troops. . . . They would capture a position by day and desert it entirely by night to go and feed. At Stanley they even looted their

British comrades' kit and equipment."[60] Incompetence and inexperience were major factors explaining the overwhelming British loss.

Still, Chinese assistance to Tokyo is startling in light of the anti-Nippon attitude that permeated the Chinese community. In the wake of the Japanese invasion of China in 1931, the "intensity of anti-Japanese feelings was unprecedented in Hong Kong. People spontaneously searched out Japanese goods, destroyed shops, attacked the police for arresting rioters and committed other violent acts of protest. One Japanese couple together with several of their children were savagely murdered. The situation in Wanchai and Yamati, the two areas where the Japanese presence was most concentrated, was so explosive and out of control that the assistance of naval men and the Highlanders had to be enlisted."[61] White supremacy had to have been awfully potent to motivate so many Chinese to aid the Japanese invasion.

But before the disturbances of 1931, a more accurate precursor of the events of late 1941 was the General Strike of 1925. According to Britain's Secretary of Chinese Affairs, this event was "organized and put into effect through triad societies by members." And in December 1941 "the Japanese bought [sic] many of the triad societies, particularly in Kowloon, and when we were forced to evacuate Kowloon the evacuation was greatly hindered by triad societies armed with rifles and in some cases machine guns mounted in lorries, who started indiscriminate looting combined with terrorism and murder the moment our Force began to move out." Tellingly he had detected "no hint of any triad elements in the Left Wing unions"—an anti-Tokyo force that London had successfully suppressed over the years.[62] And it was the triads that had sought to massacre all the Europeans in Hong Kong at the time of the invasion. This was a throwback to 1856, when an attempt was made to poison the entire European community by placing a hefty dose of arsenic into the bread supplied by a Chinese bakery.[63]

In sum, the Chinese "had little influence in the military establishment"; when it was "proposed that the local Chinese be armed and incorporated into the Hongkong [sic] garrison," this was "politely ignored." In no small part because of the tensions generated by the "strikes and boycotts" of the 1920s, as late as 1941 the British "feared an armed Chinese mass almost as much as they did the Japanese"; perhaps not unrealistically, "they worried that their arms might be turned against them."[64]

There were other reasons for sympathy among some Chinese for Tokyo. As the writer Han Suyin recalled it, Pearl Harbor "made the [Chinese] officers almost delirious with pleasure, both because Japan had delivered a big blow to White Power, which would enable the pro-Japan clique to emphasize the failures of the whites, and because the telling criticisms of Chinese chaos, inefficiency and defeat, could now be shrugged off with a triumphant, 'And what about you?'" After all, the Kuomintang—that is, the Chinese nationalists led by Chiang Kai-Shek—"had looked forward to an alliance with the Axis powers, and the entry of America into the war did not modify these long-term views."[65] Edwin Ride, the leading analyst of the Hong Kong resistance and the son of its leader, Lindsay Ride, concurred, terming Chiang and his allies "fascist."[66]

The British defeat led to a racial and political reversal that was to reverberate long after the artillery had stopped firing and the Japanese were driven out of the occupied territories. The New Zealand writer, James Bertram, who was present in Hong Kong, was astonished as he saw these "roles" being "reversed." "It was the dark-skinned warriors," he asserted, "who had the advantage of training and technique; the whites—too often—like the Canadians—had little but their courage." Britain, in the irony of ironies, "was meeting Asiatics who had learnt too well the lessons of the gunboat years." Simultaneously, those who flocked to the Union Jack were not exactly likely candidates—and this too was to resound loudly long after the war. Sammy Kahn, who was Jewish, had been "driven from his native Halle, he was one of the few Volunteers who felt he really owed something to Hong Kong. . . . He had worked so hard to become an 'Englishman.'"[67] It was in order to avoid these cataclysmic reversals, perhaps, that London instructed the Hong Kong authorities—in words deemed to be "Most Secret"—that "the eyes of the world are upon you. We expect you to resist to the end. The honour of the empire is in your hands."[68] But alas for London, there were not enough Sammy Kahns to halt the Japanese juggernaut aided by their Asian allies.

Robert Ward, the U.S. Consul in Hong Kong, realized this. Asked in 1942 why this Crown Colony had collapsed, he recalled that "several of them"—the British rulers—"said frankly that they would rather turn the island over to the Japanese than to turn it over to the Chinese, by which they meant rather than employ the Chinese to defend the colony they would surrender it to the Japanese." Moreover, "when the real fighting came it was the British soldiery that broke and ran. The Eurasians fought well and so did the Indians but the Kowloon line broke when the Royal Scots gave way. The same thing happened on the mainland. This situation was brought very sharply to my mind when I read the statement of a member of the British government that there were more white troops in India now than there had been before in the history of the connection between Britain and India. If the British attempt to defend India with foreign troops brought from a long distance who know nothing of the Indians," he warned ominously, "and regard them as 'niggers,' they are likely to fall just as miserably as they did at Hong Kong."[69]

The British Foreign Office was told that "many of the Chinese police reserves discarded their uniforms and arms. . . . The Indians are being particularly objectionable in searching foreign women, particularly at the ferry points. . . . The Indians are definitely mauling women." Perhaps worse, London was told that "we have lost a dreadful amount of face and prestige over the fall of Hongkong [sic] and we shall never regain what we have lost. Feeling against us has been running for some time now. . . . I am afraid it will not be long before there is trouble in the Colony between the Chinese and Europeans. . . . In Chungking the anti-British feeling is very high. The Chinese up there are very pro-American but one can feel the bitterness between the Chinese for the English."[70]

The prim Sir Arthur D. Blackburn and his prudish spouse had their own particular explanation, resulting from their experience of the invasion. "How is it that Hongkong [sic] was captured so quickly?" he asked. The colonizers were "sabotaged by Wang Ching-wei Chinese. . . . Our troops were completely bewildered by the apparent ubiquity of the enemy as they were being fired on from all sides at once."[71] Australian officials provided another explanation as to why this Crown Colony "was captured so quickly." There was "complacency," they said; "men in key posts [were] said to have been busy at their golf rather than their duty; in the prelude to the invasion, the social life of the colony proceeded just as merrily as in peacetime."[72]

Phyllis Harrop, present during the invasion, agreed that "the Indian police [turned] against us," but that was not the full extent of her concerns. "A Jap [sic] officer asked for the manageress and when she appeared he said, 'Bring me food [and a] couple of English beauties.'"

Stunned, she sought a meeting with "Lt. Col. Iguchi" and together they planned a "brothel system" and she "offered to contact" prostitutes "for him." The swiftness of the British defeat left her dumbfounded. "Words cannot express the feeling that what has been accomplished in a hundred years has completely crumbled in a few days. . . . There are signs of anti-British feelings amongst the Chinese people and I'm afraid the results are going to be anything but bright when the time comes. . . . It is evident that [Chinese] feelings are against us by the amount of looting that has taken place and the way in which homes and houses have been broken into and smashed." The relationship between the British and the colonized had deteriorated to the point that the former felt "we shall be safer in camps than we shall be if we are allowed to remain free."[73]

It was a dreary Christmas Day in 1941 for the Europeans and Euro-Americans of Hong Kong. Almost a century of prosperous existence had come to a crashing end at the hands of the Japanese and their allies. An uncertain fate awaited. The mighty had fallen. Now the invaders were impressing upon the Chinese and other Asians in Hong Kong that a new racial reality was dawning. The U.S. reporter George Baxter acknowledged that "it was plain that humiliation was part of the Jap [*sic*] scheme to convince the natives that the white man had been conquered."[74] The China-born missionary, Robert Hammond, recalled that the victors told the Chinese that "from now on the Chinese would not only be able to have schools and business enterprises, but also would be able to live like the whites had lived with no fear of being cheated out of all their possessions by the foreigners," as had happened so often during the colonial period.[75]

The horror of it all struck Gwen Dew like a thunderclap. In a conscious attempt to lower the prestige of those of "pure European descent" in Hong Kong, the victorious Japanese marched the vanquished through the streets. "They paraded us, the hungry, bedraggled two hundred of us, through the crowded Chinese section." Balefully, she concluded, "We were the perfect picture of the Fall of the White Man in the Far East. A white man lying disemboweled in the dirt, a white woman snatched naked and gang-raped, a parade of whites carrying their own pitiful burdens—these pictures delighted the Jap [*sic*] heart. . . . They are determined upon the rape, the ruin, and the subjugation of the world—particularly the white world."[76] It was "one of the most damnable sights" she would "ever want to watch—the group of prisoners being marched down the road, hands still held high, prodded by bayonets. . . . If you in America," she reminded her terror-struck readers, "could see your own people being marched by those little monkey men with the big bayonets, you would realize what the Japs [*sic*] intend to do to all the white men and all other enemies in the Far East." A young Canadian confided to her, "Some day I'll come back here and get even with these devils" and she "could only echo his wish."[77]

Father James Smith of the Maryknoll Mission noted how the invaders manipulated cigarettes, which quickly became the common currency of a collapsed city. They would take cigarettes and "would toss a pack or two [to] the Chinese sitting on the floor with us but nary a pack to the padres—this perhaps to show in what seat the foreigners were now sitting."[78] Gwen Priestwood felt that she personally—and perhaps all Europeans—were "losing face." As this "March of Humiliation" took place, the "Chinese and Indians stood by, watching me to see how a white woman would take this humiliation by Orientals." Actually, she did not have to join this discreditable procession but the events had given her a burst of race consciousness—"We're all one and the same race," she proclaimed, so she joined her fellow Europeans.[79] Decades later James Allan Ford could not forget the sight of the "Chinese population lining the streets shouting and jeering" as the former rulers shuffled by defeated.[80]

These forced marches were part of an overall Japanese strategy to lower the prestige of those of "pure European descent" in the eyes of Asians. With wide-eyed wonder, the *New York Herald Tribune* reported that "one of [Japan's] puppet Quislings in Burma has demanded the Anglo-Saxons be stripped of their clothing and treated like monkeys or featherless birds."[81] In 1942 the U.S. State Department was informed that "the treatment of Americans and Europeans . . . would seem to be carefully calculated to effect their humiliation and degradation and to be animated in some measure at least by racial animosity."[82] Jack Edwards would have agreed, as he was forced to endure a similar march through the streets of Taiwan.[83]

Clifford Matthews had fought valiantly to defend Hong Kong. But as he witnessed what was being revealed, an epiphany overwhelmed him. He was watching the Chinese as they saw this unique retreat of white supremacy. He "could see it was the end of . . . imperialism in the Far East. They [had] seen the foreigners being humiliated. Some of us picking up cigarette [butts] which were thrown down by the Japanese sentry. Even there . . . I saw [that] obviously this was the end of the whole superior attitude. . . . [Chinese] could see that we were nothing special, we were just human beings. [What] was clear to me [was] that there will be another world after the war."[84] Morris "Two-Gun" Cohen agreed; as he pondered the amazing sight of Europeans being marched through the streets of Hong Kong by armed Japanese troops and witnessed by the Chinese masses, it "struck" him "as being rather like Judgment Day."[85]

4

Internment

AFTER BEING COMPELLED TO RESIDE temporarily in a sleazy brothel, several thousand disheveled and disarrayed Europeans and Euro-Americans were marched off to what became Stanley internment camp. Even this brothel, otherwise a site of degraded pleasure, was fraught with racial tension.

Many Europeans had barely noticed the Indians who resided in Hong Kong before the war, nor were they fully cognizant of how heavily dependent the mighty British Empire was on India itself. Yet, as internee John Streicker put it, the Indian guards at this brothel had "succumbed to the glowing promises of life under the Rising Sun, and foresworn the British Raj, so our pleas of hunger merely delighted them."[1] The Europeans, most of whom were accustomed to commodious surroundings, were not just ignored, they were jammed into small and suffocating rooms, bereft of food and other basic requirements. They could only gape in amazement as the once graceful city they had known was transformed into something alien. Bill Harman, an Australian physician residing in Hong Kong, was appalled by the cutting down of so many trees: belatedly he "began to realize what it must be to be so poor that you have to resort to this to get fuel to cook the daily meal." Looting had stripped the city bare, though he thought that "the worst looting was done by the undisciplined Chinese mobs." There were "armed robberies all over the place," as mercantile sentiments and revenge seeking against the Europeans merged neatly. An escape to the mainland—which Dr. Harman was able to execute miraculously—brought no relief, for in so doing he had to run the gauntlet of the Chinese military, and "the chance of evading them and not being robbed of everything was about nil."[2]

The missionary, Father James Smith, was struck by the "almost total absence of English signs on streets and over buildings and stores." As an emblem of their hegemony, the invaders had sought to obliterate signs of what was now seen as an alien language. In "the lobbies of office building[s], all the tenant names were in Chinese or Japanese, and it was very difficult," he moaned, "to find one's own family doctor"—if one were sufficiently lucky to escape the invaders.[3] This was a telling signal of what was to come. The conquered and increasingly unkempt community of Europeans and Euro-Americans had received a bitter foretaste of the racial humiliation that was to follow when they were subjected to the debasing "March of Humiliation" through the mean streets of Hong Kong. Their fate was to turn on racial and ethnic factors, which were once passively accepted as brands of privilege, but now were to be treated much, much differently. Many were worried that their racial privilege had been destroyed for all time.

David Bosanquet wondered what the Chinese thought of what they were seeing. "Was it contempt that an Asiatic race had so easily humbled so many Europeans who had long dominated the indigenous population" and would the Chinese ever accept passively the status quo ante after what they had seen?[4] The racial reversal was captured by a character in a novel by the U.S. writer Emily Hahn: "They say the English are monkeys in the zoo and this is Pan-Asia."[5]

Conditions were abysmal in this "zoo." The "almost complete absence of toilet paper" was, perhaps, the least of the problems encountered. "Some ladies wore little more than natural sun-tans." The "fight against flies was constant," while "kitchen staffs were at times defiant in their attitude and abusive to those who dared to advise them." The "diet in Stanley camp was, without doubt, monotonous and . . . unsuitable for Europeans." The rice internees were fed had "sand, small stones, cigarette ends, insects and their young, droppings, glass and once, at least, rat carcasses." Some died due to dysentery. A "mild epidemic of chickenpox with 57 cases occurred late in 1944 and early 1945." Some suffered "occasional waves of depression."[6]

After they seized control,[7] there was a "persistent, continuous and very effective racial and cultural propaganda" unleashed by the "Japanese military." The European and Euro-American expatriates who had expected deference as a virtual birthright "were treated less considerately than the higher-class Chinese."[8] A "flood of anti-white propaganda poured over the people of Hong Kong and sprayed out from the colony in all directions." On 24 January 1942, Major General Yazaki, the chief of the newly installed "Civil Administration Department" in Hong Kong, announced curtly, "The object of Japan in fighting this war

. . . [is] to free the Asiatic races from oppression and to drive out the evil influence of the white people." The highest ranking U.S. official in the Crown Colony, Robert Ward, was concerned that this inflammatory rhetoric accompanied by equally fiery acts "may well leave marks that this generation will not erase." He came from a nation where racial segregation was exalted and thus had reason to ponder the larger repercussions of the invasion. This Tokyo "gospel," he continued, "is infinitely more dangerous, more insidious, and affects more deeply the emotions of a much larger section of the world's population than Hitler's." The "central message was a simple one: the dominance of the white man is done."[9]

Ward had grasped the magnitude and breadth of the matter. Tokyo had seized the opportunity to overturn the white supremacy that had been imposed on Hong Kong specifically and Asia more generally. In a lengthy missive aimed at Japanese troops, entitled "Read This Alone and the War Can Be Won," these fighters were instructed sharply: "Once you set foot on the enemy's territories you will see for yourself only too clearly, just what this oppression by the white man means. Imposing, splendid buildings look down from the summits of mountains or hills on to the tiny thatched huts of the natives. . . . These white people may expect, from the moment they issue from their mother's wombs, to be allotted a score or so of natives as their personal slaves. Is this really God's will?"[10]

The Japanese propaganda piece, "The Way of Subjects," asked plaintively, "How were American Indians treated? What about African Negroes? They were hunted as white men's slaves." The Tokyo-based correspondent for the *New York Times*, Otto D. Tolischus, called this a "startling document" in its indictment of "outrageous acts. . . . unpardonable in the eyes of God and man," which allowed Europeans to "spread their dominion over the colored races" and meant that "Asiatics, Negroes and American Indians" were "killed and enslaved." Tolischus was not shocked when Toshio Shiratori, the "official adviser to the Foreign Office and former Ambassador to Italy," declared that "Japan's true aim was to drive the white man out of Asia."[11] By the time they had subdued the ineffective British resistance in Hong Kong, Japanese troops had reached a veritable white-hot mood of resentment against European colonialism.

This topsy-turvy situation also came as a shock to Emily Hahn, the journalist who had fled the quotidian pleasures of the United States for the exotic danger of Hong Kong. She had been the first woman to earn a degree in mining engineering from the University of Wisconsin, then had worked at a hospital in the Congo, resided in Shanghai as the *tsip* (common-law wife) of a Chinese scholar, ducked falling bombs in Chungking, then come to the Crown Colony to write her successful biography of the Soong sisters. With her lovely face and lively mind she rapidly became a fixture in a community otherwise given to blandness. Various adjectives were used to describe Hahn but "bland" was one that was rare. Her open love affair with a married British officer, her pet gibbons which often accompanied her on her jaunts around town, the fur coats that she doffed during the winter, her thigh-length boots and long padded jackets, all lent her an air of eccentricity. She had given up on smoking opium but now puffed on cigars, which further contributed to her idiosyncratic image.[12]

All these affectations—but particularly her well-known relationship with a Chinese man—had served to add to her outré reputation among expatriates. But when she was interviewed by a Japanese official, after their defeat of the British, she found that he "was pleased that an American girl should have married an Oriental. It made him more friendly." This surprising turnabout—what the previous ruling elite saw as a demerit was now seen as meritorious—was to continue. "'According to American law,'" Hahn reminded her Japanese interlocutor, "'this Chinese marriage does not make me Chinese.' 'According to Japanese law,' he said, 'it does. . . . You cannot be interned. We are ejecting all Chinese subjects from the internment camp.'" A European friend scolded her for accepting this racially and ethnically keyed dispensation: "'You ought to stay with your own people, you know.'" The "'British are not my own people,'" she replied with passion, "'I feel more at home . . . with the Chinese.'"

The internment came as a surprise to Hahn—and many others. "We were rather expecting an internment of Jews and Chungking patriots and such," she said at the time, "but internment of all Europeans? Impossible!" Certainly the new conquerors were "fully aware of the social implications of Hong Kong's geography" and "wanted to humiliate the whites as much as they could, and bringing them down from those costly heights"—at The Peak—"to sea level was an obvious and necessary move in the campaign." Whereas the British by means fair and foul had limited drastically the ability of those not of "pure European descent" to reside at The Peak, the victorious Japanese "actually did make a law, later on, which made it punishable for any enemy white left outside of camp to live on the hillside."[13] The world had turned upside down.

It could have been worse. The aristocratic Sir Arthur Dickinson Blackburn, a diplomat from the mainland, who had come to Hong Kong for a visit just before the invasion, was not accustomed to the humble surroundings that Stanley provided, yet he found its beachside location "pleasant"; "there is no real ground for complaint regarding the quarters themselves," he proclaimed early on, though the "lack of privacy," "overcrowding," and the "consequent friction and nervous strain" were a "more serious hardship than the food shortage."[14] John Streicker, who served as Administrative Secretary at the camp, found it a "perfect site, richly endowed with fresh sea air and lovely scenery." There was "very little barbed wire," which gave camps such an ominous air, and what there was—ironically—had been laid by the British.[15] Still, they were so closely packed that the thousands there all seemed to be inhabitants of one household.

Good humor under trying conditions enabled many to survive the ordeal of hardship. William G. Sewell, a humble Quaker, recalled that "if ever we started to grumble we reminded ourselves of the comments of a Jew who had fled from the Nazis to [Hong Kong]. 'If I knew that my family in Europe was nearly as well off as the people in this camp, then I might begin to believe in God—just begin,'" he announced. Sir Franklin Gimson, the top British official detained, looking back at war's end, concluded, "Now that I am able to contrast our treatment at Stanley with that of other camps, I think we were extremely fortunate that we escaped so lightly."[16] He was correct: the "death rate" at Stanley "was much lower than in other camps in Japanese held territories."[17] Stanley was no playground, but it was a far cry from its counterparts in Europe.

However, as Emily Hahn indicated, many thought internment camps were for "Jews" and others deemed to be outcasts, certainly not for the upper echelon of Hong Kong. Sir Franklin initially expected a France- or Belgium-style occupation where Tokyo would rule through officials like himself. Indeed, he seemed willing to serve as a quisling. In a strange letter, days after the surrender, instead of promising sabotage he offered the invaders advice on how to locate "petrol supplies" and tips on how to administer the sprawling metropolis.[18] The Japanese refused his offer to become their lackey. Instead he was "arrested" and "detained" for "thirty hours" before being released "owing to the intervention of Mr. Kimuru, a former Japanese consul in Hong Kong." Still confident, Sir Franklin "got in touch with leaders of the Indian and Portuguese communities and offered to make any representations on their behalf to the Japanese authorities." These "communities" did not need the vanquished to represent them, however, and no doubt some looked forward to gaining an advantage over the once powerful British who had fallen so precipitously.[19]

All told, approximately 1,290 men, 908 women, and about 315 children were detained at Stanley camp.[20] To avoid detention, some rushed to embrace identities that earlier would have been shunned. The lordly Ellen Field was compelled to masquerade as a lowly Irish woman in order to avoid internment, as the invaders did not target Europeans thought to be antagonistic toward London, suggesting that Tokyo was warring against white supremacy, more than "whiteness" itself.[21]

Why was anyone detained, in any case? The conquering Japanese seemed to improvise after their victory. Sir Franklin acknowledged this, adding that the "Japanese at the outset averred the Europeans had been interned for 'their own protection.' Though this contention appeared to be at first sight ridiculous, in reality it proved to have some substance."[22] A number of expatriates concurred.[23]

The time had arrived for the Chinese to wreak revenge on those who had oppressed and exploited them since the Opium Wars and they seized the opportunity aggressively. In Emily Hahn's novelistic rendition of wartime Hong Kong, a character asserts, "After the poor exhibition they have given during the war, the Chinese might tear them [the British] to pieces."[24] As conditions in Hong Kong steadily deteriorated in the following months, these internees—most of whom had become accustomed to a life with a retinue of servants—would have had a hard time fending for themselves.

Despite—or perhaps because of—this "favor" of internment, many faced the future with grave apprehension. Gwen Priestwood had heard "stories of what had happened to the Germans who were interned by the Japs [*sic*] in the First World War: how they came home afterward with no teeth and no hair." This grim prospect so disturbed the fashion-minded writer that she immediately looked in the "mirror, dabbing on my rouge and lipstick and brushing [her] hair." She vowed to "fight to retain my looks as long as possible." As she was about to be herded into Stanley, she "saw a girl take out a vanity and carefully powder her nose. So I powdered mine. Never say die!"

Priestwood and her comrades soon found that their ordinary concerns had undergone a quantum transformation. Still, the misery they endured was nowhere near that suffered by the "10,000 servicemen" interned in Hong Kong in separate camps.[25] The internees were an odd assortment of nationalities: British, Euro-American, Dutch, Chinese, Eurasian, Portuguese, Russian, Turkish, Czechoslovakian, Hungarian, Spanish, Jamaican, and Cuban.[26] This group was in three camps: Indians at Ma Tau Chang, officers in Argyle Street in Kowloon, and other ranks at Shamshuipo.[27] Shamshuipo—similar in many ways to the other sites—consisted of a cluster of small, low, wooden huts squatting on reclaimed land close to a "smelly slum and a fetid, typhoon, junk-anchorage" with "no sewer in the area." The other camps were little better. Earlier the British at Shamshuipo had a "barbed wire fence erected to keep the Chinese out. Ironically, it was the same fence that now kept us in," said one internee contritely. After the invasion, the Chinese "stripped the buildings of everything, leaving intact the barbed wire fence" in an almost psychic foretelling that it would be used against their former rulers.[28] Lucien Brunet, an interned Canadian soldier, recalled this residential horror with "no toilets. . . . full of bedbugs, roaches. . . . no soap."[29]

Because these fighters had been defeated by—and had killed—those who now held them captive, they had to bear a special psychological burden and most likely greater persecution by their captors. Yet both sides, civilian and military, realized that they were experiencing not only a "normal" defeat but a racial debacle as well. Gwen Priestwood realized it when she was playing softball with her captors. One of the Japanese guards "lifted the ball high and a young English girl who was playing managed to catch it. 'Out!' she sang triumphantly. . . . The Jap [*sic*] shook his head. . . . 'Not out, no.' . . . 'Singapore broken, not out.' He swung his bat again. There was nothing to do but honor him. Most of the afternoon was spent pitching to him and catching his drives. Every time, all the white folks would yell 'Out!'—and the Jap [*sic*] would grow angrier and angrier and retort: 'No, not out. Singapore broken!'"[30] David Bosanquet had a similar epiphany—a recognition that the racial rules of the game had changed—when "true to type" the Japanese officer guarding him and his comrades "ordered us to dig" a "communal grave. . . . while the coolies"—the erstwhile beasts of burden during the British colonial era—"sat and watched."[31]

Filled with dread, John Streicker worried that "all the long training the white man has undergone in his adaptation to the East has been undone. Vegetables are insufficiently washed, children eat native products raw, hats are discarded by nearly all, even on the hottest days, flies are everywhere, water is impure. . . . Perhaps," he fretted, "natural native adaptation has replaced the careful but artificial adaptation of the European."[32] He was profoundly concerned that Europeans were making a great leap backward in China and would soon supplant the "coolies" as the pack animals of the region.

He had reason to be concerned. Not long after the internment the already horrible conditions in the devastated city declined sharply. Beyond the barriers of the camps there were credible reports of "cannibalism," or so alleged I. D. Zia, who hailed from Shanghai but who was educated as a physician in Hong Kong. "One neighbor house-wife," he recalled chillingly, "disclosed that the distinction between human flesh and animal meat lay in the fact that human flesh when cooked in a frying pan would bounce up whereas animal meat would not."[33] Inside Stanley, one mother "overheard two middle aged men discussing which of the little ones they would start on if the Japanese stopped sending rations to us."[34] The interned Jean Gittins reports that "by 1944 it was said that human meat was being sold openly in the markets."[35] When a "large mongrel dog strayed" into one camp, "two English soldiers decided to kill the cur, boil him and eat him after dark."[36] Robert Hammond "saw one lady so hungry that she ran out and picked up a large rat that had just been thrown away and started to eat it, skin and all"; with astonishment he saw a man "selling 'lo shi tong' rat soup for ten cents a bowl."[37] A U.S. sailor interned at Stanley recalled that "no meat ever tasted as good as the horse meat I ate there." They also ate weevils since "the doctors in the camp told us they contained vitamins."[38]

A pervasive hunger gripped the camps during the occupation. This contributed to a "severe loss of memory especially for names of former associates and acquaintances, and of names of places." The resultant debility led to "difficulty [in] gripping things . . . Many a piece of crockery or dish of stew falls surprisingly from one's hands."[39] As the captive Ralph Goodwin recalled it, "The Europeans were broken wrecks scarcely able to keep on their feet. So low had their treatment brought them that they could not concentrate, and they were unable to remember the orders shouted at them. This was a source of great amusement to the Japanese, who regarded the Europeans as very inferior beings."[40] That they were given an "elaborate intelligence test" only served to confirm in the minds of many Europeans that they were being treated like so many Negroes.[41] The ravenous craving for food, the unfriendly captors, the racial reversal, all this and more led many to emotional collapse.[42] Numerous "internees did show signs of increased irritability, hypersensitiveness to noise and exaggerated ill-temper. Concentration became difficult for many, and loss of memory and insomnia at night were common complaints."[43]

There were objective reasons for the emotional abyss of the incarcerated. Not only had they been defeated, an enormous setback in itself, but worse in the eyes of many they had been defeated by those not of "pure European descent," thus undermining the very predicates of "white supremacy." The police officer George Wright-Nooth was stunned when some of his fellow Sikh officers "stripped off their uniform, then in their ridiculous red underpants and with their long dank hair let down, except for the topknot with a silver dagger stuck through it, had gone on the rampage. They had rushed around swearing and spitting at European officers and civilians as well as cursing the British government," something they would never have dared to do prior to the invasion. The "bulk of the warders" at the detention camp that he found himself in were "the original Chinese or Indian staff who had merely exchanged their British masters for Japanese." One Indian warder in particular, Rehimat Khan, "commonly known as Redbeard. . . . took immense pleasure in humiliating and beating his European prisoners."[44]

When the Stanley camp was first opened, Sir Arthur Dickinson Blackburn was shocked when the "Japanese put in a number of English-speaking Chinese as block supervisors." The British, for obvious reasons, had thought they knew this language group but now found they did not: the sense of betrayal was boundless and deeply emotional.[45] There were other injuries as well. The journalist George Baxter found it hard to forget the moment when the prisoners were lined up only to find that "many of the Jap [sic] officers and men broke ranks, facing us, calmly unbuttoned their trousers and urinated in our direction. One British woman fainted."[46]

The boisterous "Two-Gun" Cohen was reduced to a pipsqueak after being relentlessly interrogated, then beaten by his captors. All that he could recall at that moment was the distress of Lawrence of Arabia after he had been beaten and raped by Turkish soldiers. On another occasion thirty men in Stanley were sunning themselves on a wall. A Japanese officer drove by and his aide told them it was not polite for white people to sit and look down on the prison. The colonel then ordered the aide to slap all the men. Perhaps as part of the sweeping racial reversal, the Japanese authorities objected violently to any hint—metaphorical or otherwise—that Europeans were looking down on them; that was one reason the Europeans were ordered from The Peak and to the flatlands of Stanley.[47] The Japanese authorities also insisted that their prisoners bow ritualistically when in their presence, which the latter correctly viewed as confirmation of their subordination: they resisted, which led to frequent rounds of slapping and beating. Many of the Europeans and Euro-Americans felt they were braving a racial Armageddon.[48] Priests too had been subjected to indignities,[49] perhaps inspiring further religiosity although they hardly required it.[50]

These trials for the Europeans and Euro-Americans[51] induced emotional turmoil but emotional metamorphosis as well. William Sewell, a Quaker, was interned with his wife and children. He worried about how much food the children would receive during their growing years—or, for that matter, whether they would become food in an emergency. Sure, "patience and humility" were in short supply; moreover the relentlessly "British attitudes did not make things easier. We tended to withhold praise from those who did their duty [and] were very free in criticizing those whom we thought to have failed." On the other hand, selfishness was held in check to an extent as "it was an unwritten law neither to offer nor to receive, lest jealousy should be fostered or obligations made." Reflecting further, "Was moral fibre, after all, we wondered, dependent upon balanced vitamins and health?" Likewise, some came to recognize that those they had formerly derided as "the dirty Chinese" may simply have been too poor to live in a more sanitary environment. The difficult conditions under which Europeans lived at Stanley gave some of them a "new sympathy" for "Chinese labourers" who toiled under similar conditions in the prewar era: this too was a lesson gleaned from their oppression at the hands of the Japanese.[52]

The interned Benjamin Proulx recalled a "system of behavior, almost a code of morals, by which we lived and without which we would have gone mad. . . . We would not, especially in the morning, say one disagreeable word to each other. . . . We would share all foodstuffs, cigarettes and other belongings equally; and we would keep our sense of humor no matter what." If Proulx went to "wash out some clothes, I would automatically grab another man's laundry and wash that too."[53] In what resembled a controlled anthropological experiment, the prisoners reverted to what internee Les Fisher termed "Communism in toto."[54]

Imprisoned Hong Kong police also made an "unconscious decision to stick together." It became "our guiding principle that everything we had except for sentimental possessions was shared. . . . We also shared out any privileges or proceeds from black market sales, chores, cooking or camp duties. We ate as a mess, the same food, the same amount of food and at the same time. We became practical communists and in our case it worked."[55]

This reversion to "communism"[56] was serendipitous—and quite telling—in light of the Allies' heavy dependence on the performance of the Soviet Union. William Sewell perceived a competition to work in groups at Stanley since it provided an "occupied mind and greater chance of physical health." Being "in a [collective]," he thought, "gave a sense of cooperation and friendship." Confirming the "spontaneous communism" that arose at Stanley, he observed that "musicians and preachers as well as teachers"—that is, those not involved in work in the gardens growing food—were seen as "non-workers" and not entitled to as much as those who did.[57]

However, the bonhomie of the camp only extended so far. Kay Franklin, an internee, detected a "lot of informers in the camp," especially among the British soldiers' Chinese wives: "They would do anything for extra food or money. So they'd keep their ears open to hear what was going on and then report to the Japs [sic] to get this extra food. So we had to be very careful."[58]

Even under alien rule, the prosperous continued to enjoy distinct advantages. Just as the British royal family often could bond with Ugandan royalty but not with Ugandan peasants—or British workers, for that matter—the Japanese elites in Hong Kong often felt the same way about their British counterparts. Emily Hahn, who roamed Hong Kong during the occupation because of the benign interpretation of her relationship with a Chinese man, wrote that the Japanese leading official, "Oda," a "confirmed capitalist," "had been severely shocked at the sight of many Hong Kong millionaires he had known, brought low at Stanley. Even enemy rich men are still rich men," she divined, "and Oda felt sympathetic toward them."[59] However, Jean Gittins disagreed. In her view, "Japanese sought to humiliate the elite by assigning them to the poorest type of accommodation in the camp."[60]

In brief, class conflict did not cease simply because conditions were harsh. A number of U.S. sailors were trapped in Hong Kong at the precise moment of the Japanese seizure of power. They railed at the leadership of Stanley being "overweighted with Standard Oil executives and other China Coast tycoons." Despite their leadership roles, they were subject to "demoralization" while the "unionists, who were quickly recognized as natural leaders, provided a striking contrast."[61]

Though the prisoners at Stanley devised a number of organizations to protect their interests, many of them—particularly the "capitalists"—still looked forward to denying a similar level of organization to their workers in Hong Kong upon their release from detention. Sir Franklin Gimson made a note in his diary about a "discussion" with some interned bosses "on trade unions" where he "heard the usual employer's argument that they were not necessary."[62] When it came to unions, these defrocked economic royalists had learned nothing and forgotten nothing. The U.S. Consul in Hong Kong, Robert Ward, writing from the comfort of North America, acknowledged the obvious when he averred, "It is probable too that had there been stronger unions in the Colony, the laboring groups would have felt that they had a larger stake in the continuance of the former Government's rule. . . . The absence of unions provided the Japanese with one situation to exploit in their efforts to discredit the West."[63]

But just as the interned had difficulty overcoming class bias, they had a similar problem transcending the bonds of race. Jean Gittins, a prominent member of the Eurasian community, felt this strongly. Some of the British felt that were it not for the many Eurasians in the camp, there would be sufficient food for them. Racial discrimination had by no means moderated in the face of general adversity, and some people were too bigoted to understand that the food was rationed by the Japanese according to the number of mouths to be fed. Then there were those who, failing to get parcels themselves, became increasingly jealous of those who did. They were envious not of the large business houses whose parcels came regularly and had to be paid for at the end of the war, but of the Eurasian community whose relatives in town sent parcels at great personal sacrifice. "One of our neighbors worked himself into a bad humor each parcel day. He repeatedly advocated the pooling of all parcels, even though less than ten per cent of internees received them, and the contents divided equally between the three thousand others. . . . We were all stunned to find at the end of internment that, instead of eating the contents of their comfort parcels from the Red Cross, they saved intact at least one parcel each, besides tens of corned beef, presumably for a rainy day."[64] This though they were pitiably emaciated. Thus, Stanley could not escape the failings of the society communism had presumably left behind. Europeans and Euro-Americans continued to demand "communism" when the property of non-Europeans was at play and react passively to the accretion of goods by others.[65]

Conflict had to emerge from the Japanese attempt to construct a new racial reality—a reality at odds with the prevailing ethos of white supremacy. As time passed, a black market emerged which reflected the race changes that accelerated with every passing day of the occupation. As John Streicker described it, "A third party became necessary between internees and guards" and "these were generally confined to those with a fluent knowledge of Chinese"—which automatically ruled out most Europeans and Euro-Americans. It was "not surprising" that the "Eurasians"—figuratively born to be the "middle man"—took this role. Although Streicker thought "most of the Europeans felt [this role] either beneath their dignity or disliked the idea of profiteering at the expense of their fellows," the fact was that many of the Europeans had no qualms about "profiteering" before internment.[66]

Certainly, selfishness tinged with racial chauvinism did not disappear with internment. Gwen Dew has written bitterly of the woman she called "Mrs. Elegant," a British dowager who despised the Chinese. While interned, this elderly woman was reluctant to share even a glass of water: "She managed to get to the bucket first, and before even the sick children had a chance, she had five glasses of water! Then she grabbed two dozen lumps of sugar and put them in her pockets and walked off!" Not stopping there, Mrs. Elegant turned on a "very fine man with mixed blood" and called him a "dirty wop" for seeming to question her. Later, at a meeting with Japanese journalists, one gave her a bottle of spirits but a fellow European internee asked if he could carry it, then refused to return it: "'Of course I took it,' he yelled" triumphantly, after denying the episode had occurred.[67]

Of all the tensions in occupied Hong Kong—Japanese versus British, Chinese and Indians versus British, Japanese versus Europeans, and more—some of the sharpest emerged between Euro-Americans and the British. In fact, these various sets of contradictions fed upon and reinforced each other in a sort of feedback loop. Kenneth Andrew, who served with the Hong Kong police from 1912 to 1938, says that often a "pack of American sailors" would "go out and comb the area for "limeys' . . . and when they found any, [they] beat them up severely. Feelings ran so high between the two naval factions that for a time it got to be rather dangerous for a sailor to walk about that area on his own. Once a party of Americans visited every well-known hotel in the city and beat up every British sailor they found."[68]

These strains reflected the declining fortunes of the Empire and the rising challenge of U.S. imperialism. Though Britons like Rudyard Kipling, the former Colonial Secretary Lewis Harcourt, the Duke of Manchester, Lord Randolph Churchill, Lord Curzon, and Joseph Chamberlain had all married U.S. women, George Bernard Shaw better reflected the real state of affairs in his 1929 play "'The Apple Cart' in which the United States in effect makes a takeover bid for the British Empire."[69] Prewar Shanghai was a hotspot for sharp clashes between British subjects and U.S. citizens.[70] According to Harry Hale, Hong Kong was similarly replete with conflict; as he recalls it, U.S. sailors "used to be so roughly handled by the garrison station in Hong Kong that two Americans at one time, if my memory serves me, were killed by artillerymen."[71]

Stereotypes often carry a grain of truth and so it was for the U.S.-U.K. relationship. The British were thought to be more hidebound, wedded to feudalistic class privilege, while the Euro-Americans were said to be more flexible in this regard. But lo and behold, that was precisely the image that emerged from those that braved the camps. George Wright-Nooth, who was British, said that the British were both the most "numerous" and the "most disorganized," while "the Americans seemed the best organized entity with a commendable tendency to work together." The "British community, more divided by class, occupation and prejudice, spent too much effort and energy bickering or complaining. Not untypical of their attitude was the remark of the rotund British matron who, as she watched a group of Americans repairing a stove, remarked, 'Isn't it fortunate that the Americans have so many members of the working class in their camp?'"[72]

Stereotypes aside, there were profound underlying reasons that accounted for the conflicts between the British and the Euro-Americans. The United States was distrustful of British intentions in Asia. In the eyes of the United States, Britain wanted to prolong colonialism and the status quo; disrupting both would facilitate a U.S. advance in the region. This insistent message was difficult for citizens and subjects alike to ignore. Put simply, the Euro-Americans relied on the strength of their economy and the potency of the dollar—both often proclaimed with arrogance—to override British reliance on "imperial preference" and other rigged rules designed to sustain the Empire.

The Jamaican activist, Billy Strachan, observed this reality while he was training for the war in Britain. "The Americans in general," he maintained, "were very unpopular during the war. They were unpopular for two reasons. . . . The white Americans were so well paid and well dressed relatively that whenever they arrived in a pub . . . it was their technique to take out a large wad of notes and put them on the counter and say, 'Now let's drink.' The Englishman, who had far lower wages was very envious." But Strachan also noticed another ironic advantage that the land of Jim Crow enjoyed over Britain. "Now the blacks amongst the Americans," he continued, "were still treated just as American, not as blacks. . . . Strange as it may seem I remember finding myself lining up with the Americans against the English because the blacks were involved. I remember being involved in street fighting at Hitchin in Hertfordshire. A group of Americans and I was on the so-called British side but I went across as a traitor and went on the Americans' side. . . . Ninety-nine per cent of the fights and there [were] fights, broke out over the girl, the English girl was playing up to the American and . . . the fights broke out."[73] As the United States began to move more aggressively against racism than Britain, its sizable complement of blacks and other racial minorities provided it with yet another advantage over its rival.[74]

Thus, it was not long before fissures between Britons and Euro-Americans began to emerge at Stanley.[75] The head of the camp, Sir Franklin Gimson, felt that his erstwhile trans-Atlantic colleagues were much too quick to assume that the end of British rule meant that his words could safely be ignored. Sir Franklin sniffed at one point that "the American representative had also a reputation open to question." Disputes ranged widely between the two; when Sir Franklin objected to a "committee of hospital management," his counterpart from the United States asked him bluntly, "'Have you ever heard of the Boston tea party?'" The thunderstruck Briton could "only exclaim! What?"[76]

The British were "perturbed at the attitude being taken by the Dutch and the Americans who were wanting to run their own affairs without reference to the British. . . . They want direct access to the Japanese. . . . They often prejudice the harmonious relations between ourselves and the Japanese." That was precisely the problem, thought many from the United States. These non-British nationals felt that in order to prolong rule of the Empire—that is, over the interned—Sir Franklin would go to extraordinary lengths to collaborate with the Japanese. For his part, Sir Franklin felt he had no choice in light of the "difficulty" he had with the "Dutch, Americans and Norwegians," which was "one of the most important aspects of the camp."

No doubt Sir Franklin's detractors' worst fears would have been confirmed had they been able to read his diary. He was close to "Zindel," who was "not prepared to indulge actively in any anti-Japanese activity"; Zindel felt that it was possible "to achieve far more by playing up to the Japanese susceptibility to flattery" than by outright opposition. "I entirely agreed with him," said Sir Franklin, "and stated that I found myself in a similar position." Actually, after U.S. citizens were evacuated from Stanley in 1942–1943, he had more room for maneuver—and collaboration—and was able to wangle more commodious quarters for himself in contravention of the wishes of many of the internees. Sir Franklin argued that certain "individuals" who "in their own selfish interests would approach the Japanese direct and obtain special concessions."

Ironically, the subjugated of Stanley were subjected to the same tactic they had mastered to virtual perfection: divide and conquer. This was even more ironic in light of the fact that the prewar British press in Shanghai tended to be more pro-Japan than the U.S.-owned press, in part because London counted on Tokyo to hammer the Chinese Communists.[77] The Northern Irish were beginning to distinguish themselves from the British in order to cut a separate deal and not be stained by the broad brush of London's blunders. An "Australian and New Zealand Society" was formed at Stanley comprised of "about 100 Australians and New Zealanders" interned there. The captors tried to split this group from the British by offering to transfer them to Shanghai in return for doing propaganda broadcasts. "Most" refused but "one or two who showed signs which were not immediately negative" were sent to Shanghai.[78]

As Jean Gittins recalled it, "the small Dutch community, subsequently joined by the Norwegians, numbered well over one hundred. They kept mostly to themselves and in all those years I cannot recall any direct contact I ever had with any of their nationals. The Americans, on the other hand, stood out as the most favoured nation: throughout their short internment"—they were released prematurely by Tokyo, well before the war concluded—"they enjoyed many privileges in food and accommodation which were denied the rest of the camp. . . . I remember the envy we felt towards them."[79] Stanley was not unique in this regard. In camps in the occupied territories generally, "Australians and Americans were likely to make common cause out of being strongly anti-British. And, in general, the British, Australians and Americans—all English speakers . . . were strongly anti-Dutch."

Yet whatever tensions existed between the Allies, they were overshadowed by those between all of them and their Japanese captors. J. P. S. Devereux, a proud Marine major, "would never willingly have lowered himself to talk to a yellow man on equal terms. Now he had to learn to speak lower than low, in the voice of unconditional surrender." He was not alone, as "the yellow man returned the white man's hate and contempt" in spades. In the early days of captivity a Japanese officer was holding a handkerchief to his nose. A POW sergeant asked him if he had a cold. *"Baka! Stupid!* said the Japanese. *You smell bad, you smell very bad."* Later the captor said his prisoner did not smell so terribly. *"Now you smell O.K. You no eat meat since you become pu-ri-so-na.* This story could be read another way: The Japanese liked their white prisoners to be starving." And it can be read yet another way: treacherous tropes of insult traditionally used by Europeans and Euro-Americans—such as suggesting that some groups emit foul odors—against Africans particularly, were now being turned back against the perpetrators by Asians.

That was not the end of it. In the United States it had long been suggested that if one treated a group as if they were slaves, before long the group would begin to believe it themselves and act accordingly. Now Euro-Americans began to be subjected to similar patterns of oppression. In one camp "there was the Dog Man, also an American. . . . He turned himself into a dog. . . . He went around on all fours, lifted his leg to pee and slept curled on the floor. When the guards tried to make him stand on his hind legs he barked at them: when the commandant came around he snarled and bit him on the boot."[80]

Alan Jackson Wood of the British military argued that such aberrant behavior was more typical of his U.S. counterparts. "Americans generally speaking, could not look after themselves as well as the British. . . . Generally speaking if the Japanese knocked a British chap down he'd get up, be knocked down, get up, knocked down. He wouldn't stay down until he was knocked out. The Americans normally would be knocked down once and that was [that], they wouldn't get up." Wood's observation was based on his experience at an internment camp in Yokohama where at one point somebody took down a U.S. flag: "It must have been as a protest to the life which they'd had to live with the fleas and the lice and the general behaviour of the Americans . . . who seemed unable to stand up in adversity as the British did."[81]

Sir Franklin,[82] whose view of the U.S. was becoming increasingly choleric, was even more outraged when he discovered that Tokyo's tactics were having a material impact on those he purported to represent. Under the pressure of internment, national bonds that had been taken for granted were fraying badly. There was a "strong anti-Government feeling" to the point that his "attempt to reconstitute the administration of the camp" with himself "in charge," "would be resisted even to the extent of arousing riots accompanied by war and bloodshed." The legendary and all-important British "prestige . . . suffered by the display of low morale of the British internees at Stanley and by its disregard of the respect due to the higher officials."

The turning point in this intra-British conflict came in April 1942 when a number of U.S. citizens left the camp. Perhaps sensing that ties to a government, even a discredited one based in London, might not be such a bad idea, the formerly rebellious British internees reversed their strategy. A petition asking Sir Franklin to lead the British community was signed by "fifteen hundred." The imperious Sir Franklin then instructed them that the former administrative council were "purely members of an advisory board whose advice I could reject or accept at my discretion." Some of them must have rued their reversal for he came out firmly against "repatriation," since "this was British territory" and a mass departure might "jeopardise the future retention of Hong Kong as a British colony." In other words, British internees should sit tight in the unpleasantness that Stanley was becoming so that the tenuous legal principle of the crown could remain inviolate.[83]

Sir Franklin's attitude was indicative of an incisive fissure within colonialism. As early as 1942, he noted that "the whole legal fraternity in the camp is thoroughly discredited, the lawyers and judges of the Supreme Court included." Sir Franklin continued with evident disdain, "I am disgusted with the whole atmosphere of intrigue which surrounds the Hong Kong community and scarcely can visualise myself as assisting the rehabilitation of a society which is entirely worthless."[84]

This should not surprise us. Wenzell Brown, a Euro-American interned at Stanley, has painted a disquieting portrait of his fellow citizens there. Jake Bayne, the U.S. representative at Stanley, "padded the number of Americans coming into the camp and, by so doing, secured more than a fair allotment of space for our group." By "securing more than our fair share, we deprived the British of a portion of theirs. Bayne boasted openly of his deceit in the matter. No American in the camp raised his voice in protest." Hence, a "tremendous proportion of the suffering endured in Stanley Prison Camp was caused by our own greed, our failure to share and our willingness to submit to petty dishonesties. Within a few weeks the camp was split wide with dissension." Brown objected and "the retaliation taken upon" him "personally was both brutal and contemptible."

This sly maneuvering was a reflection of the diverse makeup of the motley group assembled at Stanley. The China coast "has always abounded in adventurers," says Brown, "young men who go to China to build up a swift fortune through all the devious channels, the strange chicanery, of the Orient. . . . Others are caught by the lure of cheap liquor, becoming more and more dissolute and finally ending up sometimes as waterfront bums, sometimes as wealthy members of the fantastic, corrupt society of the coast. These men, mostly young, and some strangely idealistic Jake Bayne gathered about him. . . . He appealed to all that was greedy and conceited and evil in you and showed you that these faults were really virtues."

Moreover, "to add to the difficulties of the situation, the Japanese released the white prisoners from the jail at the same time and a group of prisoners, the scum of the China coast, mingled freely with people from the Peak. These men had been convicted of every crime from rape to murder, and while there were only a handful of them, they added greatly to the terror and uncertainty of the camp." Brown's friend, Mike Shakhty, was among those who hailed from the "periphery of New York's underworld." He was among the "riff-raff of the Wanchai waterfront" who arrived at Stanley. There were "mixed Asiatic bloods—Chinese, Japanese, Indian, Malayan, Javanese, often with a touch of Negro or European." From these various spheres there arose in camp a "group of Americans" who had "given in, within a prison camp, to a form of fascism at its very worst. We had the spy system, the strong-arm boys, uniforms of a type, ruthless revenge against those who criticized the leader."

Caught among these finaglers, the elite British were akin to the pigeons among the cats. Yet Stanley's Euro-Americans were not solely comprised of soldiers of fortune, for in this camp "half of our men were university graduates. At least a dozen held Doctor of Philosophy degrees. Most of the large universities were represented. Columbia, I think, headed the list. Stanford, University of California, Yale, Harvard, George Washington, Oberlin, Pomona, Lehigh, University of Pennsylvania, Chicago, Duke and other universities and colleges throughout the country had graduates in the camp. The small colleges were represented too, especially among the missionary group." This meant that the "racial" lessons of a "race war" were bound to be transmitted to an influential U.S. audience.

Brown's picture of Stanley diverges sharply from those who have portrayed an abstemious, altruistic communism that arose in the military camps. He felt that a "new aristocracy had sprung up which was divorced from the old class system of Hong Kong. The privileged groups were the physically strong, the politically dexterous and those [who] had got large sums of usable money into the camp. The former heads of big firms, university professors, wealthy widows were on the edge of starvation, while an engineer, a biscuit salesman, a sailor and a high government official drank and dined and held gay parties late into the night. Worst of all, Bayne fraternized with the Japanese."[85]

Stanley was like a laboratory experiment, a stew of various perspectives and persuasions tossed together.

On 5 September 1941 the very proper Sir Mark Young was sworn into office in Hong Kong. The ceremony took place in the King's Theatre on a stage bedecked with mounds of flowers alongside the British flag. Those present included leaders of the Chinese and Eurasian communities, including Sir Shouson Chow and Sir Robert Kotewall,[86] whose knighthood was the most visible symbol of their allegiance to the Crown. Five months and fifteen days later—on 25 February 1942—the same performance was reenacted in the same theater, except there was a a major difference: now allegiance was pledged to another sovereign, Japan.

Strikingly, Sir Robert was even more fervent in February than in September. He was now Law (or alternately Lo) Kuk-wo, reflecting the distance he had put between himself and the Anglo-Saxon heritage he had formerly embraced. At the end of his heartfelt remarks, he led the audience in three rousing "Banzais." Emily Hahn recalled later that "we all joined in execrating Sir Robert Kotewall," since "before Pearl Harbor" he "had been just about the most British-loving Asiatic you could find. A mixed blood himself, Parsee and Chinese and English. . . . he was prominent in all civic politics. . . . The Hong Kong government were proud of Kotewall and did him honour [yet he] was the very first of the great men to welcome the Japanese. It was Sir Robert Kotewall who made speeches at Jap-[sic]inspired mass meetings."[87] Eugenie Zaitzeff of Montreal agreed that "Kotewall and Shou-Son-Chow . . . seem to vie with each other in pro-Japanese fervour and anti-British advocacy."[88]

Sir Robert—or Law Kuk-wo—was not alone. Many did not have the option of switching loyalties so quickly to Tokyo; on the other hand, there was a coterie of Chinese who benefited directly from the occupation, not least because they took the places of now departed or interned Europeans. Robert Ward, formerly U.S. Consul in Hong Kong, noted that in contrast to the "very small participation of Chinese in their [U.K.] government," the Chinese had a "much wider 'popular' base" in the government of the new colonizers.

According to Ward, a "Chinese Manufacturers Union" was formed "at the instance of Japanese." Some union members were also part of the "Chinese Chamber of Commerce," which was "perhaps the first group to contemplate cooperation with the Japanese after their capture of Hong Kong." As in India, the Crown had blocked systematically the development of an indigenous capitalist class that might challenge their British counterparts. By taking a different tack, Tokyo not only gained adherents among critically important opinion molders but also set the stage for Hong Kong's postwar economic boom, as many Chinese businesses "turned their companies into partnerships giving a considerable share of the business to a Japanese."

War is systematic looting, among other things. Tokyo made this process "legal" in Hong Kong. By printing the military yen the Japanese could take whatever they desired in exchange for their paper currency. In any case, Hong Kong made an immediate and continuous contribution to Japan's war effort as a repair dock for naval and merchant vessels, while also serving as one of the principal construction bases for the wooden-ship building program. The cement, rubber goods, and other factories also played their part in the fabrication of materials or articles necessary for the armed forces.[89]

To be sure, Hong Kong suffered hundreds of millions of dollars in damage during the war. However, this damage was skewed: far more "British" as opposed to "Chinese" properties claimed damage. The British made higher claims for "private chattels," "tugs, launches, lighters, waterboats," to cite one example, while Chinese made higher claims for "stocks, growing crops and livestock."[90]

In prewar Hong Kong, the British controlled a disproportionate share of the wealth. A good deal of this wealth was placed on ships and transported to Japan, particularly automobiles, laboratories, the innards of manufacturing plants, and the like. But as the war was unfolding and later, as the British and Japanese left Hong Kong, the Chinese stepped into their places. Shortly after the war, one BBC commentator noted "one rather surprising impression that must come to everyone . . . the tremendous amount of money that appears to circulate amongst the Chinese. The proportion of Chinese patronising the cafes, restaurants and cinemas is vastly higher than before."[91]

Some of the biggest winners during the war were the triads—Chinese organized crime—as they were among Tokyo's chief allies. Some "sabotaged British military equipment and supplied valuable intelligence" to the Japanese.[92] This list included the "Tan Yee Triad Society, originally known as the Luen Lok Tong," led by Wong Wo. During the occupation he was a "detective at the Wachai Gendarmerie" and benefited handsomely as a result. In the postwar era his group mushroomed to "several hundred members" and was "engaged in 'protection' and extortion rackets," along with "prostitution."[93]

"During the Japanese occupation," the "members" of the "Wo Yung Yee Triad Society, also known as the Yung Yee Tong . . . robbed and looted godowns in West Point." The occupiers "allowed the [WYY] society to carry on, as its members acted as detectives and informers for them. The various wharf owners also came to an agreement with the

Triad Societies. This was to let the Triad Societies control the wharves after the war had finished. . . . After the Japanese surrender the leaders of the Triad societies seized the wharves with the intention of running them in their own interests." Historically, the docks had been a focal point for the triads. Before the war, the "coolies" controlled by Tsang Pun "boarded vessels arriving at the different wharves and took the luggage of persons desiring to use his boarding house, from the ship to the boarding house." After the war, these "coolies" were "prevented from boarding the ships" by certain triads. "I get daily complaints from passengers arriving at my boarding house," said one official, "about baggage being stolen and . . . exorbitant charges levied. . . . If a passenger demurs about the charges he is assaulted and during the assault one of his baggage is stolen by the coolie as payment."[94] Despite this banditry, the British authorities reported that "the Chinese public does not support police activity against Triads and the European population has little idea of the crime potential they represent."[95]

Stanley Ho—one of the richest men in postwar Hong Kong—was among the Chinese who benefited from the occupation. Born in 1921, his father fled Hong Kong for Saigon in the 1930s, leaving in disgrace after going bankrupt. During the war Ho escaped from Hong Kong to Macao. Years later, with a glow in his voice Ho recalled that he worked for "the biggest company in Macau during the war, the Macau Cooperative Company Limited . . . one-third owned by the Japanese army. I became its secretary. . . . I had to start by learning Japanese." For most, Macao was a graveyard of hope but for Ho it was "paradise during the war. . . . I had big parties almost every night. Bird's nest, roast pork. . . . I became the teacher of the most important Japanese man in Macao during the war. . . . a man called Colonel Sawa." Each "morning at six" he would send "his car" to fetch Ho to take him to "Zhongshan across the border in China. There," he recounted rapturously, "the two of us would climb together to the top of a small hill. Then he started singing in Japanese and he taught me how to sing with him—and in return I taught him English. I was his English [instructor] for one year, and in that time all the Japanese soldiers in Special Branch would kneel down to him—and to me, as his teacher."

Though the colonel was viewed as no more than a thug by some, to Ho he was a boon companion. His contacts proved useful when Ho "started a small trading company. . . . By the end of the war, I'd earned over a million dollars—having started with just ten. . . . Macao was tiny, and yet a bit like Casablanca—all the secret intelligence, the murders, the gambling—it was a very exciting place. When the war ended, I bought a boat, the first one to start crossing between Hong Kong and Macao. . . . I bought up many of the supplies left by the British army." What of the political morality of what he was doing? Ho "never felt hatred of the pro-Japanese Chinese or the Japanese in Macao. To me they were just people doing their thing and I was doing my thing."[96]

Before the beginning of this successful stint, he "started off with a job as secretary to the Japanese owner of a firm handling imports of rice, beans, flour and other goods shipped from Canton. . . . Six months later [he] became a partner in the company. . . . Stanley's facility with the Japanese language can be traced to these days." By war's end "he was the biggest provider of kerosene in Southeast Asia."[97] "Inadvertently," as one writer put it, "the Japanese war had created vast opportunities for those who cared to seek and cultivate them," people such as Stanley Ho who "made his first million" as a direct result of this conflagration.[98]

Ho's idyll with the Japanese occupiers stands in dramatic contrast to the unhappiness of his encounter with the British after the war. "It was quite a contrast," he said. "I thought I knew the British. When I first started business, I knocked at the door of one of the senior British officials. . . . I walked in and tried to shake hands with him but he was so cold, he wouldn't even shake my hand, just told me to sit down." The British official, on his part, may have been justifiably suspicious of Ho, given Ho's ties to Tokyo. Moreover, years later it was revealed that Ho was on a "10 year old Canadian police watch list on Asian organized crime" as a result of reputed "links . . . to a Macao-based triad gang called Kung Lok . . . involved in drug trafficking, illicit horse racing and casino gambling and counterfeiting." Still, the frostiness with which he was greeted by this British official was not inconsistent with the white supremacist ethos that characterized London's policies.[99]

Still, Ho was not alone. Henrique De Senna Fernandes found the "war years" in Macao to be "terrible, but it's strange, I've never had such happy times either. Every night there were parties."[100] During the occupation a number of Chinese companies—including quite a few from Taiwan and Shanghai—were able to enter a market where previously barriers had existed.[101] This increased penetration of Hong Kong by Chinese capital and the opportunities consequently afforded certain businessmen may shed light on the otherwise confounding words of Robert S. Ward, the U.S. Consul in Hong Kong in the immediate prewar era. "A Chinese informant" of his, he reported, "who left Hong Kong in the fall of 1942 and who has fairly wide contacts both in Hong Kong and Chungking, states . . . that there has been and is very little underground activity, directed at hampering Japanese control; the situation in Hong Kong is, he believes, different from that in Europe. . . . The Chinese, he says, may hate the Japanese military, but he tends to regard the ordinary Japanese as of the same race as himself, an attitude which makes for easier camaraderie between them. There are thus no deep loyalties, no sound historic or political bases, from which the desperate underground activities which characterize Yugoslav or Greek resistance could spring in Hong Kong."[102] In other words, in Europe sovereign states primarily were dislodged by Berlin, while in Hong Kong a corrupt colonial state was overthrown. This state was unable to inspire the kind of fervent loyalty that drove the antifascist resistance in Europe.

5

War/Race

WHEN THE PACIFIC WAR COMMENCED, London and Washington faced a vexing problem: after tirelessly cultivating a disaffected Negro population over the years Japan had won legions of adherents. At a time when the black population on the West Coast was still relatively small,[1] migrants from former British colonies in the Caribbean—many of whom were reluctant subjects of a faraway monarch—had streamed north to New York City. Thus, Harlem, which had the largest and most diverse black population in the nation, had become the epicenter of this potentially seditious pro-Tokyo posture. Consequently, as Hong Kong was reeling under a Japanese assault in January 1942, a meeting of black leaders voted "36 to 5 with 15 abstaining, that African Americans were not 100 percent behind the war" against Tokyo. A 1942 poll conducted among black New Yorkers found that "18 percent" said "they would be better off under the Japanese and an additional 31 percent . . . declared that their treatment would be [the] same and only 28 percent . . . said it would be worse."[2]

The black press, which routinely carried gory stories about lynchings and disenfranchisement, also carried stories of Negroes visiting Germany where they encountered fewer problems than, say, on a journey to North Carolina. As late as 1944, the *Pittsburgh Courier* carried a series of articles by African American pianist John Welch recently freed from wartime internment, reporting on the basis of his experience that "there is 'no color problem' in Germany."[3] This was a continuation of past trends. When Du Bois visited in the 1930s he was "received with an exceptional courtesy everywhere in Germany, a dispensation that contrasted almost bewilderingly with the treatment accorded to Jews." Even Berlin sought to exploit the Achilles heel of the United States by making overtures to the Negroes. Actually, as David Levering Lewis put it, "popular sentiment" among Negroes held that "more Nazis lived in the South than in Germany."[4] This was most likely the opinion of an unnamed sixteen-year-old black girl in Columbus, Ohio, who won an essay contest during the war on the subject "What to do with Adolf Hitler." Her idea was to put the "Fuhrer into a black skin and make him spend the rest of his life in America."[5] Hence it was hard for this oppressed minority to align with their oppressors, even when confronted with a foe as demonic as Hitler.

In the spring of 1932, Hitler himself entertained a Georgia-born Negro, Milton S. J. Wright, at a dinner party at a fashionable Heidelberg watering hole. Even Jesse Owens (the Negro sprinter whose victories at the 1936 Berlin Olympics were said to have been a major setback to the Axis) told the Negro journalist, Roi Ottley, "candidly—as one Negro to another— . . . the Nazis bent [over] backward in making things comfortable for them, even to inviting them to the smartest hotels and restaurants."[6]

The Negro response to Germany should be seen as more of a comment on London than on Berlin. Decades earlier Negroes had been told that if they fought Germany in the "war to end all wars," they would benefit. Instead colonialism continued, falling heavily upon those of African descent. Hence, as London was under heavy assault from Berlin as the Pacific War approached, the Colonial Secretary was told that there was insistent "anti-British talk" brewing in Jamaica, a colony that supplied numerous black migrants to Harlem. Jamaicans had a hard time understanding why it was unacceptable for Berlin to deprive European nations of sovereignty, but acceptable for London to do the same in the Caribbean. This alarmed the Jamaican Left, which moved a supportive pro-London resolution noting that "many of the inhabitants of Jamaica" were "apparently inclined to be [Axis] sympathizers."[7] Neighboring Haiti too had long admired Japan.[8]

Further north in Bermuda there were similar currents. In the fall of 1940 a "Bermudian" recalled that "not so long ago a former Bermuda governor established birth control clinics to limit the Negro population. This plan was defeated by determined New York West Indians. If the Negro race is going to be treated in a British Crown Colony as the Nazis handle their subjugated peoples, then by all means let us have Hitler's new world order."[9]

This was alarming, though comprehensible. NAACP leader Walter White recalled later that "during the dark days immediately following" the commencement of the Pacific War, "bitterness against the Japanese seemed to find expression in Southern communities through acts of violence against Negro soldiers."[10] Not least because of the historic lumping together of all who were not "white," some Euro-Americans found it difficult to distinguish between their actual Nipponese foe and their presumed Negro compatriot. In December 1941, as Hong Kong reeled under a fierce Japanese assault, the black intellectual William Pickens was amazed to find a radio commentator in Los Angeles referring to the Japanese as "Ethiopians" in discussing "slant-eyed people and other Ethiopians like that."[11] Blacks and "Southern communities" were reacting to comments like those of the national hero, Charles Lindbergh, who asserted that the colored must be met frontally by the lily-white, that "a Western wall of race and arms which can hold back either a Genghis Khan or the infiltration of inferior blood," must be hastily constructed.[12]

Feeling—in retrospect incorrectly—that the triumph of London and Washington would further augment white supremacy, "the black press tended to view the war as a race war, seemed anxious to explain war excesses on the part of Japanese as reactive, and tended to be more condemnatory of atrocities on the part of whites, whether Americans or Europeans."[13] The journalist Roi Ottley found that "a survey of the leading Negro newspapers since the war began reveals no letters-to-the-editor condemning Japanese treachery and few editorials castigating the Japanese foe, a fact which might suggest that many Negroes have been neutralized."[14] The black conservative icon George Schuyler wondered about the uproar about Japanese treatment of Europeans and the corresponding reticence about how Negroes were treated in the South.[15] The words of the *New York Amsterdam News* columnist, A. M. Wendell Malliet—who happened to be Jamaican—were typical. "Japanese hospitality can only be equalled by their pride and sensibilities," he acknowledged. So, in this year of 1944 when reports of Japanese atrocities had stirred the conscience, he found these accounts questionable. After all, "the atrocities, insults and humiliations which are being heaped upon white captives by the Japanese are the fruits of the white man's prejudice and race hates. . . . They intend to show the white man . . . he's just like other men. . . . A Japanese officer compelled a Philippines soldier to slap an American captive several times on his face. The meaning here is clear. . . . World War 3 is already in the making and . . . the white race may not then survive."[16]

Hugh Mulzac, a member in good standing of the Black Left in the United States and a native of the British colony of St. Vincent, echoed the sentiments of many blacks when he said "there was a strong feeling among colored Americans in 1941 that the colonial powers be allowed to destroy each other. As a former British subject I felt this keenly."[17] As one black writer put it in 1940, as London faced the grim prospect of being vanquished, the Europeans had "spilled the blood of the colored race in conquering them, and then spilled again the same blood to protect themselves from Germany. This is double execution. Keep the colored people out of white men's wars. This war is God's vengeance on the 'democratic' butchers."[18] J. A. Rogers, the popular black historian and columnist, agreed. "England has cause to be panicky," he announced more than a decade before the Pacific War. "Of some 475,000,000 persons in the British Empire there are about 425,000,000 colored." And "of that number perhaps one in a thousand really loves a white man."[19]

Although many Negroes were apprehensive about the anti-Comintern axis that included Japan, Germany, and Italy, others accepted it because of their antipathy to the United Kingdom and the United States. Tokyo's "tie-up with that abominable gang" was "due to provocation by American statesmen. . . . We passed an immigration exclusion law branding the Japanese as an inferior race." However, Philip Francis of Harlem foresaw that this "new gangster partnership . . . double-crossed itself, because in lining up Japan, a colored race against Britain and the United States, it only served to cement the two so-called Anglo-Saxon nations in the face of common danger, the defeat of white nations by a mongrel combination." In any case, speaking in the fall of 1940, he was reluctant to join the "Anglo-Saxons." "As members of the black race, we ought to be on the watch for the grouping and re-grouping of nations and the effect that such actions will have on the future of African peoples."[20]

The alienation of Negroes was a propaganda coup for Japan which it exploited adroitly. One wartime scholar noted that Tokyo "chose "Briton' and, to a lesser degree, "American'" as their "scapegoat" in this process, seeing the former's colonial rule over erstwhile sovereign states as simpler to exploit. The attack on the United States, on the other hand, stressed the "Americans' contempt for non-whites, their scorn of colored peoples and their mistreatment of Negroes within their midst." The "Negroes," according to a Tokyo broadcast to other Asian states, "hate the United States." Filipinos, who needed no introduction to U.S.-style white supremacy, were subjected to "frankly racial appeals" by Tokyo and "told that the white Americans despised them as racial inferiors," while Japan promised equality.[21] If need be, Tokyo could point to the Negroes as living confirmation of their indictment of white supremacy.

The nagging perception that Tokyo was the sole force standing between Negroes and a continued escalation of white supremacy led many blacks to rationalize, if not justify, Japan's creeping encroachment, then war against China. Hubert Harrison, a native of the former Danish colony of St. Croix, Virgin Islands, who came to be known as the "Father of Harlem Radicalism," hailed the rise of Japan early on and derided the idea of the "United States as the champion of China against Japanese aggression." Harrison, who—unusually—was close to the Black Left and the Black Nationalists, recalled the events of the 1890s when in the wake of Japan's war against China, the "four powers . . . proceeded to take what they had denied Japan. England took Wei Hai Wei, Germany took Shantung, Russia took Port Arthur and France also took her slice. . . . while the white powers were stripping China the United States did not assume any ethical role." So why would the United States now object to Japan taking her "slice" of China if not for racial reasons, he mused? Speaking in the early 1920s, he maintained that "to men of color it seems that [the United States] does so now only because Japan, as a colored nation, has assumed in China a prerogative exclusively appropriated hitherto by the dominant and superior whites."[22] He cited approvingly Motosada Zumoto, editor of *The Herald of Asia*, who stated angrily that "if the West persistently refuses to listen to the voice of Reason and Justice" on China and related matters, "and aggravates the antagonism of culture by injecting race prejudice, it is not inconceivable that the result may possibly be war between the races, incomparably more calamitous than the late great war and wider in extent."[23]

With painfully unrealistic hopes, many Black Nationalists sought a way out of their conundrum of backing Japanese rapacity in China while objecting to the same in Africa by fervently praying that the two Asian giants would combine. Du Bois was among those who succumbed to this notion.[24] Others saw Japan's plunder of the planet's largest nation as a form of "tough love," meant to harden China so it could better confront white supremacy. Some thought the Japan-China conflict had been wildly exaggerated by London and Washington for their own narrow interests.[25]

While Du Bois in his later years became a devoted admirer of Communist-ruled China,[26] in the 1930s his irascibility in discussing the Chinese knew no bounds. They were "extremely separatist," he thought. "They do not know Europe. They have no idea of human cruelty . . . current in Europe. China does not even realize the insult of the American Chinese Exclusion Act," he said in amazement. But Japan was different, he felt. Du Bois, a socialist of sorts and a friend of Soviet Russia, sought to reconcile this nation with Japan[27] as this unlikely prospect steadily slipped away in reality.[28]

Du Bois tended to see the Japanese as robust in their encounter with white supremacy and Chinese as pusillanimous—a notion that was confirmed in his mind when he visited Shanghai in 1936. When he raised the question of racial indignities with the Chinese leaders—who had just denounced Japanese aggression in their country—they "made no reply. . . . They talked long, but they did not really answer my question" concerning Anglo-American outrages.[29] Du Bois, like other Negroes, found China's abrasive approach toward Japan and mildness toward the Empire rather curious; it reminded many blacks of a distasteful phenomenon in the United States where certain Negroes were fire-breathing combatants toward their own kind but timorous when dealing with Euro-Americans.

This suspicion of China and the Chinese as being much too quick to seek accommodation and collaboration with the "white" powers, as opposed to Japan, which was seen by contrast as utterly confrontational, soured many Negroes on the Middle Kingdom. During this 1936 visit to Shanghai, Du Bois recalled "sitting with a group of Chinese leaders at lunch." Rather "tentatively," he told them that he "could well understand the Chinese attitude toward Japan, its bitterness and determined opposition to the substitution of Asiatic for an European imperialism." Yet what he "could not quite understand was the seemingly placid attitude of the Chinese toward Britain."[30] Indeed, he thought "the fundamental source of Sino-Japanese enmity was in China's 'submission to white aggression and Japanese resistance to it.'" The Chinese, he thought, were "Asian Uncle Toms of the 'same spirit that animates the 'white folks' nigger' in the United States."[31] With a wave of the hand, Du Bois dismissed concerns about violation of Chinese sovereignty by Japan. "In 1841," he argued, "the English seized Hong Kong, China with far less right than the Japanese had in seizing [Manchuria]."[32]

When all was said and done, many Negroes simply had a high opinion of Japan and the Japanese and a correspondingly low evaluation of China and the Chinese. James Weldon Johnson was neither a Black Nationalist nor a Black Leftist; in fact, he was an early leader of the NAACP. Yet after attending a 1929 conference on Asia he was candid in asserting that he had "boundless admiration for the energy, the enterprise, the genius for organization and execution, and that uncanny efficiency of the Japanese." Besides, they were assertive in the face of racism, unlike their Asian neighbors.[33]

Unfortunately, it was often difficult for some Negroes to distinguish between Chinese Americans—who on the West Coast were often in clawing competition with blacks for jobs—and China itself. Thus, in 1928 the black press was ablaze with stories about how the "railroads and the Pullman company fearing a strike of their colored Pullman porters are beginning to introduce Oriental workers into their service."[34] In places like Mississippi, some Chinese sought to escape bias by distancing themselves from Negroes. Thus, a Negro newspaper reported with apparent delight in 1928 on the high court barring a "Chinese boy from Mississippi white schools." The court said that the "term 'white race' is limited to the Caucasian race, that the term "colored race' includes all other races."[35]

As late as 1942, when the Japanese rape of China was no secret, many Negroes still had difficulty breaking with Tokyo's line. By this juncture a wartime U.S. government had become less tolerant of such opinions, censoring and jailing those sympathetic to Japan, thus underscoring how deeply felt these opinions were. Weeks after the fall of Singapore, a *Pittsburgh Courier* writer asserted confidently in a front-page story, "Between the Japanese and the Chinese, the Negroes much prefer the Japanese. The Chinese are the worst 'Uncle Toms' and stooges that the white man has ever had."[36] "In this country," he continued bitterly, "as soon as he gets a chop suey place, which is anything like decent, the first thing he does is put up a color bar."[37] Even as the war unfolded, the conservative George Schuyler, on the other hand, noted that in Ogden, Utah, "The only two restaurants open to colored soldiers, were run by Japanese. . . . If Uncle Tom's children want a hotel room in that locality, they must go again to the Japanese." This was, "to say the least . . . ironical."[38]

Such biting editorial opinion at the expense of China and Chinese was not new. Shortly after the plunder of Nanking in 1937, in the runup to the blows inflicted on the Empire, an *Afro-American* editorial made "the case for Japan" and backed the war against China. James Ford, the Black Communist, was astonished. He issued a blistering critique—but his was a view tainted by communism and, in any case, contrary to the pro-Tokyo sentiment so prevalent then.[39] But William Pickens was no radical. He too had a long-term relationship with the NAACP, and he too had boundless admiration for Nippon. As for their war against China, he declared in 1932 that "We do not like war but we do like the Japanese: they are the first colored nation to refuse to take orders or to be bluffed by white Europeans and Americans in generations. In that act," he concluded portentously, "they have ushered in an epoch; they have actually put an end to 'white supremacy' in the world."[40] He did not stop there. ""White supremacy' was slain in Manchuria. . . . with all the evil things they are doing in their attack on China, that is the one good result they have achieved; and it is almost, perhaps altogether, a compensation for the evil. . . . Whether they set out to do that or not, the Japanese are re-creating Asia. Our present Western 'sympathy' for the 'poor Chinese' is thoroughly hypocritical. . . . We have treated them worse in our country," referring to the pogroms that often greeted Chinese immigrants on the West Coast. Pickens was no dummy; in 1932 he possessed sufficient foresight to see that "in the immediate future the resisting Chinese are going to be a far greater threat to white domination in Asia than Japan ever could be."[41] Yet he too was blinded by the Rising Sun.

George Schuyler was a fervently anticommunist black conservative who ultimately hailed McCarthyism. Yet in 1940 he was hailing the "Japanese digestion of China," since it "continued the progressive deflation of white supremacy and arrogance in the Orient. Where white men once strutted and kicked coolies into the street, they now tread softly and talk in whispers," he noted approvingly. "The Japanese have done a fine job in making the white man in Asia lose 'face' and shattering the sedulously nurtured idea of white supremacy. Of course the white people hate them because they fear them." This "war" was "wonderful," he thought, since it was deflating white supremacy and fomenting race equality.[42]

These conflicting currents help explain why one black columnist felt that the Japanese war on China had "sharply divided Negro opinion," though there was decided agreement that the invasion was a "necessary means towards a most desirable . . . end, namely full manhood status and freedom for the Negroes of the world and the colored races in general." The awesome burden of white supremacy had distorted the vision of too many Negroes, he thought. "This passionate desire to see some arrogant white imperialistic nations crushed by some colored group has led many astray," this "[idea] that the success of Japanese imperialism will be the means of our racial salvation" explained the reasons for black support of Japan's action.[43]

Of course, there were noted exceptions to this anti-China, pro-Japan bias among Negroes. A leading "Chinese air ace" helping Peking to repel Tokyo's assault was a U.S. Negro. "E. Vann Wong" was a native of Greenville, South Carolina, where he was born in 1908 as Edward Vann; he "took the name of Wong to make his Chinese brothers feel more at home with him." He had unsuccessfully tried to enlist with the U.S. armed forces, when he "heard that in China, ability counted and not race." So he crossed the Pacific, where he proceeded to shoot "down a long [list] of enemy planes during the Sino-Japanese war."[44] Likewise, when the "Old Harlemite," Chu John passed away in 1942, this Chinese man who owned the "World Tea Garden on Lenox Avenue and 140th Street" was remembered with honor.[45] Still, on balance, Harlem possessed a decided fervor for Nippon and a wary skepticism of the Middle Kingdom.

Japanese agents in communities like Harlem had the advantage of being able to circulate easily for these areas had attracted a sizable Asian American population. This group and the Negroes with whom they shared neighborhoods had been consigned to the most run-down, decrepit, dilapidated section of Harlem. In August 1940 the journalist Marvel Cooke decided to "saunter down around 110th Street and Lenox Avenue" and found the "effect . . . startling." For "lining the avenue for almost two blocks are countless small shops, groceries, laundries, souvenir and notion stores and chop suey restaurants. On every window can be seen Chinese names, often inscribed in Chinese characters." It would be a "herculean task to determine how many Chinese actually live in this little settlement. . . . nor is it any easier to attempt to determine the total Chinese population of Harlem."[46]

Three thousand miles due west was San Francisco facing the Pacific and it too had a similar makeup. "The Japanese colony and the Negro colony in San Francisco are close enough neighbors to provide many contacts," said one writer. Further, "they share some things in common. The color line is not noticeable as it is elsewhere. This had made it possible, my agents learn from loyal Negro sources, for Japanese to spread racial propaganda." Writing in March 1942 as the outcome of the war hung in the balance, this analyst asked nervously, "Who do you suppose is tearing down air-raid shelter signs and defacing other notices designed to prevent confusion and save lives?"[47]

Even Japanese fiction manifested a strong interest in Negroes and their potentially subversive role in the United States. The Japanese novel ""Michibeisen Miraiki' (Forecast of Future American Japanese War) written by Lieutenant Commander Kyosuke Fukunaga and prefaced by Admiral Kanji Kato, both of the Imperial Japanese Navy," published in 1933, concerned a "fictitious battle between the American and Japanese navies in which the Japanese emerge victorious. One incident relates that a Negro mess boy, won over by the Japanese, procured information as to the time United States warships would pass through the Panama Canal after the commencement of hostilities between the United States and Japan. The Negro mess boy leaves the fleet at Havana after planting a time bomb which resulted in the fictitious destruction of the Battleship Oklahoma while it was passing through the Canal lock." Such efforts helped to move some Negroes to contend that they envisioned a "race war" unfolding "in which the Japanese were the champions of oppressed Negroes in the United States and of 'colored' people the world over."[48] Japanese agents could swim like fish in this ocean of color. Not surprisingly, days before the bombardment of Hong Kong, Yoshici Nagatani, who was Japanese and a "prominent businessman and expert [on] America" saw the "color problem" in the United States as one of its major "weaknesses."[49]

Evidently Washington felt the same way, for "immediately following" the launching of the Pacific War, the New York Police Department "invaded Harlem and began rounding up Japanese suspects." But even this setback provided dividends for Negroes. For "with the exception of marked facial distinction there is somewhat of a striking similarity in hue between the Japs and many Harlemites." Thus, "colored policemen" were deployed en masse and "played an invaluable role in the mass arrests," exhibiting their indispensability in a world where color mattered. In addition to Chinese shops, lower Harlem also was distinguished by its "Jap restaurants." In a final flourish, as they were being marched to the gallows, "many of the sons of Nippon . . . declared 'me colored man, too.'"[50]

So began—as the Pacific War was launched—a witchhunt in the Harlems of the United States, though Washington claimed that there were real witches out there, namely, "many colored persons prominent in New York and Washington political circles" who "may have received Japanese money." The bibliophile Arthur Schomburg, who "widely introduced" Japanese figures throughout the United States, was singled out for special scrutiny. The visitors "would travel Jim Crow and visit colored homes as their guest lodger" in places like "Tuskegee and Hampton." This endeared them further to Negroes, who were unaccustomed to such gestures of solidarity from the residents of powerful nations. However, the authorities' intense scrutiny of Schomburg in 1941 was wildly misplaced, as he had passed away in 1938.[51] Such was the nervous hysteria that accompanied the Pacific War.

Old habits die hard, however. Many in the United States desperately wanted to maintain racial segregation though they recognized that the Japanese challenge had made it untenable and this conflict could create an enervating dissonance. Roy Wilkins of the NAACP was stunned in January 1942 when he encountered the authorities in Washington "trying feverishly to arrange Jim Crow air raid shelters."[52] Of course, if Tokyo had invaded Washington, such segregation would have facilitated them in their effort to intern Euro-Americans immediately—as they had done in Hong Kong—while relying on Negroes in their administration.

James Thornhill was part of a sizable and organized pro-Tokyo constituency among U.S. Negroes. As he was being carted away in manacles in 1942, A. H. Johnson, an FBI agent in Chicago, warned that black membership in pro-Japan groups exceeded a hundred thousand—many, many more than the number of Negroes in pro-Moscow (and anti-Tokyo) associations, the usual target of FBI harassment and surveillance.[53]

One of these groups was the Tokyo-backed Pacific Movement of the Eastern World, which had "revived with new intensity" after the successful seizure of Hong Kong and Singapore. This "alarmed. . . . responsible Negro leaders," as "several thousand St. Louisans joined the movement and tens of thousands elsewhere." In March 1942, black columnist A. M. Wendell Malliet counseled that "pro-Japanese sentiment among colored people is said to be growing in the United States," buoyed by Tokyo's victories.[54] For the longest time Mimo D. Guzman, "alias Dr. Takis," had "operated a little hall on Lenox Avenue with a sign board carrying the inscription 'The University of Tokio.'" He "told Harlemites that rifles would be furnished them by the Japs [sic]."[55] Born in 1894, he had enlisted in the U.S. Navy before being "dishonorably discharged" in 1920, then started a "thriving business as a herb doctor among his followers."[56] Pro-Japanese sentiment was not quelled by reports that Australia was resisting the dispatching of black troops there because of concerns about white supremacy. This was "one of the most bitter experiences that any race may be called upon to face," it was said, that is, rescuing those who despised you.[57]

There was said to be a massive Tokyo "spy ring" in Harlem that held "regular meetings" of its "well-organized and well-financed group of agents." Germany too was considered a "friend of the black race" since it was "exterminating [the] European enemies and exploiters" of the Negro, thus saving the latter time and trouble. An "octoroon colored woman" served as "liaison, together with two Japanese and two or three whites." Negroes were told that the "present leader of the Japanese had an African mother and a Japanese father." It was "predicted that when we (Japanese) win, we will have [FDR] picking cotton and Stimson and Knox riding [us] around in rickshaws."[58] These gatherings were among the "many meetings held by federations and congregations at which the silent but gracious little sons of the Mikado have been interested listeners." As one black journal put it, "The colored laborer with wife and children at home, who is turned away from the door of industry, whose advertisement reads 'Colored men not wanted' is a virgin field for [Tokyo] propaganda."[59]

The U.S. government did not dismiss the efforts of black advocates of Tokyo as empty rhetoric. On the contrary, the government detained and placed many Negroes on trial in the fall of 1942 as Japan continued to rampage through Asia. Almost ninety were arrested, including Elijah Muhammad, leader of the group that was to become the Nation of Islam, who—it was reported—was "found hiding under his mother's bed." Keith Brown, Assistant U.S. Attorney General was explicit. These Negroes, he said, were part of a "conspiracy" to "corrupt the patriotic, loyal and law abiding colored population of Greater New York and more particularly the community known as Harlem." In his view they had crossed a dangerous line by saying that "colored United States soldiers should not fight the Japanese." Among the "forty two specific statements" he cited, the one that rankled particularly was that the defendants had resisted conscription on the grounds that they "might shoot the wrong man."

James Thornhill was among those convicted. Born in the Caribbean, in the U.S. Virgin Islands, he contemptuously referred to the United States as the "United Snakes of America." "It will only be a matter of time," he contended confidently, "until the Japs are running the United States." Indeed, "they will eventually rule the world." Thus, he instructed Negroes, "you should learn Japanese." When "they tell you to remember Pearl Harbor, you reply 'Remember Africa.'" After all, "the white man brought you to this country in 1619, not to Christianize you but to enslave you. This thing called Christianity is not worth [a] damn. I am not a Christian," he declared. "We should be Mohammedans or Moslems." Thornhill's gumption got him a conviction and an eight-year prison term, though "three members of the jury, including the forelady were colored."[60]

Leonard Robert Jordan (also known as Robert Leonard Jordan) was also among those targeted. He was a small, nattily dressed man with a passionate flare to his nostrils, which dilated when he spoke.[61] A Harlemite residing at 239 West 116th Street, he was born a British subject in Jamaica, and was "in central South America in 1914 in the Navigation Department of Great Britain and later served for the Japanese Steamship Company. He is alleged to have made the statement that while in Japan he found the Japanese to be very friendly to the Negroes and that he had the privilege of studying the customs of the Japanese and becoming a member of an outstanding society in Japan." Jordan, who claimed to have served with the Japanese Navy and was reported to have been their agent since 1922, declared that "Japan was going to form a government in Africa which the Negroes could rule under Japan." This may have been the least of the inflammatory statements he routinely made from various street corners in Harlem.[62] The eloquence and sharp debating skills of the "Harlem Mikado" was "said to have driven a number of competing street speakers to introduce Jap [sic] propaganda in their talks to hold their audiences."[63] The fiery Jordan allegedly "intended 'cutting off the heads of a lot of colored people'" when he took charge, most notably those not as enthusiastic about Tokyo as himself.[64] The fates of Washington elites would be a mite better, however. The president would be reduced to "picking cotton" while his two top Cabinet members "would be riding me around in rickshaws"—a common fate prescribed for the mighty.[65] Jordan was reported to be "backed by Japanese money with substantial weekly allotments."[66]

In November 1936, "Robert O. Jordan," the "President-General" of the "Ethiopia Pacific Movement" based at 204 Lenox Avenue in Harlem wrote Japanese Foreign Minister Hachiro Airta. The head of the EPM, whose "chief business advisor" was "T. Kikuchi," was explicit in noting that "we the dark race of the Western Hemisphere . . . are putting our entire confidence in the Japanese people with the hopes that in the very near future we will be one hundred percent united and when this [is] accomplished, we will desire [a] very close relationship with the Japanese government." Yet, he warned, if Japan were to back Italy in its invasion of Ethiopia, "this would completely wreck the progress we have made in this direction and naturally this will lessen the faith that the sons and daughters of Africa had placed in the good government of Japan." Jordan was certain that Tokyo would not disappoint, for "according to history, we are sure the Japanese people always show a good feeling toward their colored brothers of the world. We have great faith in what the future holds for the dark races under the excellent leadership of Japan."[67]

The attempt by Black Nationalists to reach out to Tokyo was a reflection of their desperate plight, besieged as Negroes were by lynchings, poverty, as well as mundane indignities. Their desperation is also reflected in their contemporaneous effort to get Britain, a land otherwise known as the epicenter of global white supremacy, to intervene on their behalf. Thus, in 1933, "the members of the Pacific Movement" told "Your Majesty" that "we are suffering [sic] here. In the southern part of the states they lynch and burn them unmercifully with no other reason than that we are black. We do not know why they have to treat us with such hatred. We are writing you because when the first slaves were brought from Africa America belonged to England. . . . We want to go back to our Native Land Africa. . . . We are requesting that you enable us to do so. . . . This is not our country and we do not want to stay here, we want to go back home."[68]

Many in Harlem were indignant about the so-called "Harlem Mikado." One newspaper influenced by the Black Left was dyspeptic in its assessment. Jordan, it said, was part of an unlikely "BB Plan." This plan also implicated "Black Followers of Buddhism [who] preached

Buddhism as the religion of people of color the world over [as] the key to racial success." Under this scenario, "American Negroes who became Buddhists automatically won Japanese citizenship, would get chances to visit Japan, study science and professions, receive military and naval training." This fiendish plot was said to have "over 11,000,000 followers in Burma," and millions of others in the rest of Asia. "Success of the plan would mean establishment of a black empire in Africa," a prospect that probably delighted the paper's readers, alienated as so many of them were by colonialism in their ancestral continent.[69] The paper's "investigations" revealed that "the scope of the world B [sic] Plan of the Japanese is almost unbelievable," supposedly exposing "the cunning of an Oriental group" that had "gone back to the wars of the Crusaders in the interest of Christianity."[70]

The FBI was convinced that the Negro Nationalists were part of a plot to create a force of pro-Tokyo blacks and Asians who would be utilized by the Japanese armed forces when they invaded the United States. The scheme included Policarpio Manansala, a Filipino, linked to Japan's race-conscious Black Dragon Society, a paramilitary—indeed, Leninist—elite of activists and thinkers.[71] Manansala was among a motley array of the discontented and disaffected who spearheaded Tokyo's crusade in the United States. Another was "Eugene Holness" (also known as Lester Holness and Lester Carey) who vowed to "fight for Japan with every drop of my blood." He was a leader of the Ethiopia Pacific Movement, "second in charge" behind Jordan. Like his commander, he had been born outside the United States and was "active as a street speaker."[72] Then there was Joseph Hilton Smyth—a tall, sallow man with a long forehead—and his spouse Annastean Haines, a "brown-skinned beauty." Smyth founded the "Negro News Syndicate" with active assistance from Tokyo.[73] Others included David D. Erwin, a "cook," and General Lee Butler, a "janitor."[74]

It was left to a black columnist to point out that "white metropolitan newspapers are making much of the fact or fiction that the men [arrested] are British West Indians," many of whom found it difficult to understand why they had to pull London's chestnuts from the fire lit by Tokyo.[75] Harlem was just a leading indicator, however. There was a "pronounced inclination" among black children generally "to play the Japanese" in games, "since 'they are fond of imagining that they are in a position to avenge themselves against white oppressors.'"[76] One analyst found that Tokyo had "turned" for spying to "the

American Negroes, a massive force of largely disgruntled citizens, many of whom had a racial axe to grind against white Americans." Japan, it was reported, had "established . . . contact . . . with influential Negroes who had promised to keep the Japanese informed about the operations of Negro organizations."[77]

Congressman John Rankin of Mississippi railed vigorously against these trends. Desegregation, he suggested, was all a Tokyo plot for "if these agitators will let the Negroes alone, we will [not] have trouble with them."[78] But to Congressman Rankin's dismay, Harlem was not alone. FBI field offices from the Atlantic to the Pacific were filing reports as the Japanese advance unfolded, indicating that Washington faced real problems in keeping a restless mass of pro-Tokyo Negroes in line. In Detroit—to cite one example among many—George Clarence Myers, a nineteen-year-old Negro, was indicted in 1943 for sabotage in connection with his activities at the Chrysler plant, where he toiled as a janitor. Myers "kicked off gauges from a machine" which caused a "delay in the production of tank motors." Scrambling to stay ahead of events, Detroit quickly hired more Negro bus drivers to pacify black ire. It was not just the U.S. ruling elite that was compelled to undertake racial reform in the face of a race war. Negroes themselves, inspired by the Japanese example of driving Euro-Americans to the brink, received further confirmation that the idea of white supremacy itself was at root just a confidence game. Undermining such seditious talk would require major racial reform: as a matter of national security the United States found out the hard way that being a major power and retaining racial segregation could be fatally incompatible.[79]

Surely many Euro-Americans had reason to think so. A reporter from the *Afro-American*—a paper that a few years earlier had supported editorially Japan's invasion of China—told Eleanor Roosevelt that he had attended Negro meetings "where Japanese victories were slyly praised and American defeats at Bataan and Corregidor brought amused and knowing snickers."[80] Ms. Roosevelt's good friend Walter White of the NAACP, who could—and did—"pass" as a Euro-American from time to time, also sparked concern. The authorities in Dallas were alarmed when in February 1942, as the startling fall of Singapore was being consolidated, this usually mild-mannered functionary was reported to have said that "America had incited Japan's attack on the United States for 50 years with its color prejudices." Speaking before a crowd of two thousand Negroes and one hundred Euro-Americans, White supposedly asserted that "racial and color prejudice had also resulted in the loss of Singapore and is threatening the Burma Road. He stated that if something is not done immediately for democratic equality of the 13,000,000 Negro minority in the United States he would not answer for the horrible consequences."[81] Ultimately this tension between raw white supremacy and national security was to be resolved in favor of the latter, though White's NAACP was loathe subsequently to acknowledge this connection.

Early in 1942 the writer Isaiah Berlin observed that "both members of the Administration and others are a good deal perturbed by development of [the] Negro problem under influence of colour propaganda by Japanese." In his view, the United States was being compelled to endure racial reform as a result of this external pressure; thus, Washington was "encouraging employers to look more favorably on black workers." Moreover, all this was placing pressure on the Empire as the United States sought to deflect attention from its own racial dilemma to the equally nettlesome matter of "colonialism in Africa," which was primarily a European burden.[82] This gave momentum to anticolonialism in Africa.

Many Negroes wondered why the racial consequences of the war—which they commented on and debated regularly—did not seem to be of similar public concern to their Euro-American compatriots. At a particularly tense moment in early 1942 when Japan seemed to be on the verge of upsetting the applecart of color, columnist A. M. Wendell Malliet mused that "although the racial aspect of Japan's fight is being willfully ignored and written down in the United States, the fact is that the racial phases and activities of the Japanese are considered and understood as dangerous in other capitals of the United Nations, especially London."[83] It was as if the race changes brought by the war were too painful to contemplate.[84] Malliet, an unheralded intellectual, was regarded as the "only Negro commercial publisher"; after arriving in the United States from Jamaica in 1929, he had worked for Oxford University Press.[85] He was no neophyte. Yet, while hands were wringing in London and Washington about the fall of Singapore, he felt that "to others, especially the colored races, it may be good news." Today, he continued almost hopefully, "as never before in the long and ghastly history of western civilization has the future of the white race hung so dangerously in the balance."[86] The "belief" that this war was a "'a white man's war' is rapidly gaining adherents among colored people in the United States," he wrote.[87]

It was clear that unless profound racial reforms were undertaken, the security of the United States could be in serious jeopardy. Carter G. Woodson, the doyen of black historians, also was not particularly depressed by the seizure of Hong Kong and Singapore, a fact that had caused him—like other Negroes—to be "questioned by white Government officials." He was unrepentant, however. "I can't blame the white Americans," he ventured, "for being suspicious of our loyalty now, because they have done enough devilment to have their suspicions justified."[88] Du Bois did not disagree. He felt that the "British Empire has caused more human misery than Hitler will cause if he lives a hundred years. . . . It is idiotic to talk about a people who brought the slave trade to its greatest development, who are the chief exploiters of Africa and who hold four hundred million Indians in subjection, as the great defenders of democracy."[89] Adam Clayton Powell, the black Congressman from Harlem, was of like mind; as he saw it, in the fall of 1942 "the difference between nazism and crackerocracy is very small. . . . crackerocracy is a pattern of race hatred."[90]

From the other shore, the black conservative George Schuyler concurred. In mid-June 1944 most of the United States was elated about the nation's prospects in prevailing in the war. But Schuyler was thinking different thoughts. "The Europeans," he noted caustically, "have been a menace to the rest of the world for the past four hundred years, carrying destruction and death wherever they went. . . . True, this system of world fleecing directly benefited only a handful of Europeans, but indirectly it benefited millions of supernumeraries, labor officials and skilled workers. . . . Europe has been a failure as well as a menace," he concluded wearily. "The European age is passing. One can derive a certain pleasure from observing its funeral."[91]

On the other hand, the fact that Schuyler could emerge as one of the harshest critics of white supremacy—though he was the nation's preeminent black conservative—exposed the fault lines of black conservatism and the nation itself. For it was apparent that under pressure from Japan, Negro conservatives could espouse a philosophy that hardly comported with that of their Euro-American counterparts. Moreover, the prevalence of white supremacy meant that Negroes of virtually all ideological persuasions could flee from the banner of the nation in times of stress and strife, severely calling national security into question.[92]

These angry and passionate words emerging from all corners of the black political spectrum were often matched by comparable actions in the streets of a racially torn nation. On the Pacific coast there were "ominous reports of Negroes 'choosing' white people," that is, assaulting them randomly. George Schuyler felt that a "change comes over many of these Negroes when they migrate [north]." There "they are ready to break the law, slice the throat or shatter the eardrums of some white person they have never seen before on the slightest pretext."[93]

In Los Angeles in 1944, J. F. Anderson was upset with the "pugnacious attitude of the colored people who have come here in droves. . . . People tell me that . . . they have what they call 'Shove Tuesday'; on that day the Negro folks emphasize themselves in every way they can, even to shoving white folks off the sidewalk if they feel inclined to do so. . . . If the colored folks are not set right on these questions," he warned, "there will be trouble in this state."[94]

Governor Earl Warren of California was told a similar story that year. O. L. Turner of San Mateo said that a "dastardly attack was made by a Negro sailor upon the person of a 24 year old wife and Defense Worker." Ruefully, he noted that the "Japs [sic] who were driven out of this community were far more safe for our white girls and women than are the hosts of Negroes that have moved in and taken the place of the Japs [sic] . . . and I am no Jap [sic] lover." With exasperation, he pleaded, "How would YOU like to have this or any other Negro . . . attacker hold the knife to your wife's throat—or your daughter's or even your own?"[95] Apparently the situation had deteriorated to the point where L. G. Brattin felt moved to confide to Governor Warren a "plan which is determined to be used in disposing of the entire Negro race." With understatement, he added forebodingly, "The plan will be a revelation to the entire population of the United States for its very boldness."[96]

Theodore Roosevelt McCoin suspected that this diabolical plan was already in force. In the fall of 1943 he was moved in desperation to write the president himself because of the awful experiences he was compelled to endure "working for E.I. Du Pont at Hanford, Washington." For he and "other Negroes is getting very bad here [sic], one killed by white men, cursed and whipped. . . . the white men on this job hate a Negro man." "We don't want their women," he cried, "we don't want to [be] white, we want to be treated right." Despite his tormenters' fears,

"Every day the white men take the Negro woman in the car and the Negro man can't say nothing." Most ominously for FDR, he mentioned in passing that as a result of such racial persecution, "they"—not "we"—"will never win the war."[97]

Washington did not make things easier by countenancing a vile form of discrimination against Filipinos too, while Japan was telling those who resided in the Philippines that they too would receive a better deal if Tokyo ruled. When news broke in 1943 that California might seek to repeal laws banning intermarriage between Filipinos and those of European descent, Governor Warren was besieged with angry mail. His press secretary hastened to clarify that Warren had "no authority to abrogate the law."[98] But John D. Stockman of Hollywood fumed, "We should have a law against association of Filipino men with white girls, making them guilty of mesalliance [sic] and immediate arrest and deportation of the Filipino and the girl given a mental test." Why? "The more segregation we have," he reasoned, "the fewer race wars we will have." Desegregation was insane, he declared. "While the best of our manhood are fighting one Mongoloid race to keep it from exterminating another, we don't want them to find when they come home that we have allowed a good California law to be abrogated," he concluded with impeccable illogic.[99]

Miguel Garcia was an intended victim of Stockman's anger. In November 1944 he alleged that he "was refused employment" by the American President Lines "as a Purser because he was a Filipino"; that "no Filipinos have been employed as Pursers" bolstered his claim.[100] Filipinos could take solace in the fact that they were not the sole objects of bigotry; in 1941 the shipyards of Richmond, California, were refusing "applications from Negroes, Filipinoes [sic], Japanese and Chinese."[101]

The sons and daughters of India were expected to hold the line against Japan's advance, while meekly accepting their place in the Empire. As if this were not enough, in the United States—which purported to be more enthusiastic about Indian independence—they continued to be "subjected to a legal discrimination that denies them the privilege of naturalization." Ramlal B. Bajpai, then of Washington, D.C., bombarded Governor Warren with clippings about his countrymen fighting with the Allies in Burma. But like most politicians the future Chief Justice was reluctant to risk the anger of his constituents, who held white supremacy dear.[102]

Hong Kong, early twentieth century. Uninterrupted British colonial rule in Hong Kong lasted approximately one hundred years—until the Japanese invasion in December 1941. During that period, the Chinese were segregated racially in a manner not unlike patterns then extant in the U.S. South. Also, like African Americans in the latter region, the Chinese in Hong Kong were a rich source of cheap labor, as this "tote that barge/lift that bale" photograph suggests. *Courtesy of the Library of Congress.*

Hong Kong, early 1920s. The Prince of Wales is feted on his first trip to his colonial possession. London was wary about arming the Chinese for fear that the weapons would be turned against the British. This in turn made it easier for Japan to seize this Crown Colony in late 1941. *Courtesy of the Library of Congress.*

A Japanese soldier beats a prisoner of war during Japan's brutal wartime occupation. The Pacific War generated apocalyptic ideas about "race" that were different from notions in the European theater. Both London and Washington hesitated to speak openly about this, not least since it was perceived that many Asians and Africans would sympathize with Tokyo's claim of wreaking vengeance against "white supremacy." Thus chastened, both the Empire and the United States moved tentatively toward racial reform after the war's conclusion. *Courtesy of the Library of Congress.*

Colombo, Ceylon (now Sri Lanka), February 1942. Australian officers touring the city. A key outpost of the British Empire, Australia also pursued racially coded policies that made it difficult for the Empire to refute Japan's claim to be "champion of the colored races." *Courtesy of the Australian War Memorial.*

London, 1919. The British Empire was heavily reliant on "coloured" soldiers—a reality that was evident as early as World War I—yet it continued to pursue policies favoring those of "pure European descent." This too complicated London's effort to refute Japan's claim to be "champion of the colored races." Moreover, the Empire's reliance on these soldiers allowed them to transgress otherwise impermeable race-gender boundaries by interacting in intimate settings with women of "pure European descent." *Courtesy of the Australian War Memorial.*

Singapore, 15 February 1942. At the Ford Motor factory, British forces surrender unconditionally to their Japanese counterparts. Many Asians and a number of African Americans interpreted this event through a racial lens and viewed it as a turning point in their centuries-long struggle against "white supremacy." London's racially coded policies were not useful in galvanizing opposition to Japan's assault on the British Empire in Asia. *Courtesy of the Australian War Memorial.*

Service at a lonely grave — 'Railway'

Anaquin, Burma (now Myanmar), 26 September 1945. A ceremony unfolds at a grave believed to be of ten men—the crew of an Allied B-24 bomber shot down by an Anti-Aircraft unit of the pro-Tokyo Indian National Army—buried earlier by Japanese forces on 3 January 1945 in a bomb crater from a previous raid. Subhas Chandra Bose on the INA was viewed as a hero in his native India on a par with Gandhi and Nehru, not least because of his strong opposition even during the war to London's racially coded colonial policies in his homeland. Ultimately, Japanese forces were evicted from Burma, a critical battleground during the war. A major reason for the Allies' success was their ability to throw into battle tens of thousands of African and African American troops. Paradoxically, by prevailing against the Japanese military in Burma, black troops helped to restore the sagging racial image of the British Empire, whose defeat at Singapore was widely interpreted as evidence of Japanese superiority. *Courtesy of the Australian War Memorial.*

Unfortunately, in California and the West in general, people of Japanese ancestry were not able to escape the long arm of prejudice. They were persecuted, expropriated, interned. Du Bois was "one of the very few Negro leaders to" affix his signature to an "open letter condemning Roosevelt's internment of Japanese Americans," a sin that he "interpreted" as "conclusive proof of the racial origins of the Pacific War."[103] Du Bois's occasional antagonist, Roy Wilkins of the NAACP, was struck by the internment of Japanese Americans in relation to the comparatively benign treatment of German Americans and German spies. "The good white people," he said, "keep saying over and over again that this is not a race war, but some of the things they do speak louder than the things they say."[104]

George Schuyler was no less critical of this mass jailing, as he saw it as a dangerous example that could be extended easily to Negroes themselves. "More ominous," he said in 1943, "the Native Sons of the Golden West [in California] has suggested that citizenship also be taken from Afro-American citizens. . . . Once the precedent is established with 70,000 Japanese-American citizens, it will be easy to denationalize millions of Afro-American citizens." Thus Negroes, he counseled, "must champion their cause as ours. . . . Their fight is our fight. . . . and the sooner we realize it the better." To those who argued that the Japanese Americans be ignored since allegedly they had ignored Negroes, Schuyler answered sarcastically, "We are now expending our money and our lives and undergoing privation in order to save the Dutch, Belgians, Norwegians . . . British . . . and yet THESE people have never championed our cause."[105]

But Du Bois and Schuyler were far away from the cockpit of intense struggle. In Los Angeles itself, where "Little Tokyo" quickly became "Bronzeville," many Negroes were exhilarated by the opportunity presented by the internment, thus exposing the frailty of "race" politics. Even before Hong Kong was subdued and days after the bombing of Pearl Harbor, the National Negro Business League chortled that "Negroes have the greatest opportunity ever offered in the state of California." Meeting at the headquarters of the black-owned Golden State Mutual Insurance Company, the "consensus" was "that somebody must take the place of these alien farmers and fishermen. . . . There lies the opportunity of the Negro." One speaker contrasted the presumed loyalty of the Negroes with that of the soon-to-be interned: "You don't have to distrust a Negro face in a boat plying in California waters; nor would you need to fear a traitor in our lettuce fields."[106] Soon there were elated reports that a "race woman takes over Jap [sic] café."[107] The major complaint was that Euro-Americans seemed to be getting more of the booty than the Negroes.[108]

There were contrary voices, but these could give no comfort to white supremacists. Alphonse Henninburg, a Negro and a former official at both the historically black Tuskegee Institute and the National Urban League, was blunt: "I feel that the attitude which now is being developed against these Japanese-Americans is a part of the total pattern of color in this country. It seems to me that prejudice against Japanese and Jews is indicative of the increasing tension between Negroes and whites."[109]

The distinguished writer, Pearl Buck, was all too aware that growing discontent on the racial front could weaken the war against Japan. NAACP leader Walter White cited her words prominently: "The persistent refusal of Americans to see the connection between the colored American and the colored peoples abroad, the continued, and it seems even willful ignorance which will not investigate the connection, are agony to those loyal and anxious Americans who know all too well the dangerous possibilities." The message from Tokyo, Walter White suggested, was: "See what the United States does to its own colored people; this is the way you colored people of the world will be treated if the Allied nations win the war!"[110]

How could the Empire or Washington respond credibly to this pointed query given their own bloodstained records? "Psychologically," wrote a senior State Department official, "Japan might well obtain such a secure place as the leader of the Asiatic races, if not the colored races of the world, that Japan's defeat by the United Nations might not be definitive." That is, white supremacy would be eviscerated even if the Allies won—a sobering thought for many.[111] Hiroshima-Nagasaki extinguished this question but its invocation showed that despite its supposed assets, white supremacy brought with it powerful liabilities.

The attraction of some Negroes, particularly those outside the United States, to right-wing European powers suggested that Tokyo also was drawing upon a general disaffection with the Allies that went beyond common racial sympathies and that would make some susceptible to calls for sedition. After the war, for example, there were "three hundred Negroes being held at Drancy" in France "as Fascist intriguers. . . . Several articles to justify anti-Jewish decrees in Paris during Marshal Petain's regime, appeared in *Miroir de la Guadeloupe*, a weekly newspaper published by Negroes in Pointe-a-Pitre." "Under the Nazis few Negroes were victims of day-to-day brutality, as meted out to the Jews."

At the same time, Berlin recognized that they could manipulate the frequently bruised feelings of victims of white supremacy, even of those who had decided to throw in their lot with the Allies. "Hans Habe reports that in the prisoner-of-war camp in which he was interned" by Germans, "Negroes alone among the prisoners were permitted weekly walks in the nearby village. They were given one cake of soap for every four men, a privilege never granted white prisoners. Their food was improved. . . . the Germans made change with elaborate ceremony." A number of the "top German officers" in Paris "had maintained Negro mistresses." The case of a U.S. Negro musician was emblematic. He became a French citizen, then was seized by the Germans, who made him a leader of a prisoner-of-war camp orchestra. "I could never have done that in free America!" he said with no small irony. In a nutshell, this summed up the dilemma faced by Washington, the chief supporter of London during the Pacific War. For some Negroes, the U.S. record on race seemed hardly better than that of Berlin and, to their mind, lagged considerably behind that of Tokyo. With the war's conclusion, more sober U.S. and U.K. elites realized that such a state of affairs was not sustainable.[112]

6

Race Reversed/Gender Transformed

THE BRITISH AUTHORITIES WERE VERY CONCERNED with the presumed enemy within the gates of U.S. territory.[1] Weeks after Hong Kong surrendered and just as Singapore was about to do so, the Foreign Office briefed the United States on "lessons" to be drawn from the attack on Pearl Harbor. "For some days before" the assault on U.S. territory, "Japanese girls had been making 'dates' with sailors for that Saturday night and most of them saw that the sailors were filled up with liquor. This was remarkable because it is apparently unusual for Japanese girls to mix with the sailors. Also a Japanese restaurant keeper near Pearl Harbour gave drinks on the house. On Friday many Japanese quit their jobs and did not turn up on Saturday morning." During the bombing, "attempts were made to obstruct military traffic by such means as drawing lorries across the roads by Japanese truck-drivers. . . . Some of the local Japanese expected an uprising and a seizure of Hawaii by force. One Japanese restaurant keeper, who owned a restaurant close to Pearl Harbour, appeared at the height of the attack dressed in the uniform of a Japanese officer. . . . He was promptly shot." It has been suggested," said London ominously, "that many of the [Japanese aviators] were Hawaiian born Japanese." Some that crashed had "McKinley High School . . . rings and Oregon State rings." Expressing astonishment and bewilderment at the hybrid Asian American community that had arisen in the race-obsessed United States, the lengthy report continued that in Hawaii "the Orientals cooperate and there is none of the Sino-Japanese animosity which exists in Asia. The Japanese, as the most pushing, active and well-organized, run the Chinese."[2] These overheated assertions were not only suggestive of the temper of the times, but also foreshadowed the internment of Japanese Americans in the western United States—though, tellingly, not in Hawaii itself.[3]

This anti-Nippon attitude quickly gained currency in western Canada, principally in British Columbia. The clear message that emerged from a Cabinet-level confab that convened in Ottawa in January 1942 was that citizens of Japanese ancestry should be used as leverage to improve conditions for Britons in Hong Kong. There was earnest concern, on the other hand, that if they mistreated Japanese Canadians, the Japanese would retaliate against internees in the occupied territories.[4]

This was part and parcel of London's difficulty—both before and during the war—in deciding how those of Japanese ancestry under Britain's jurisdiction should be treated. The Japanese community in Hong Kong was relatively small, about twenty-two hundred all told in 1931. However, under British rule they were discriminated against.[5] An attempt before the war to have Japanese doctors "admitted to practice" in Hong Kong "stirred the antagonism of many."[6] Afterwards, this bias was rationalized on the grounds that during the invasion "Japanese agents worked as waiters, barmen, hairdressers and masseurs, or at any trade in which customers were given to sharing confidences. Japanese bars in Wanchai were among the most popular in town. A pint at Nagasaki Joe's was ten cents cheaper than anywhere else and the girls in Japanese bars seemed especially solicitous." The "finest hairdresser" in Hong Kong, who in "seven years cut the hair of two governors, the commissioner of police, the officer in charge of Special Branch, the colonial secretary and the [Hong Kong and Shanghai Bank] chairman," in late December 1941 "presented himself" as a "commander of the Imperial Japanese Navy."[7] Thus, it was thought after the fact, Japanese doctors in Hong Kong could have perpetrated much damage.

One Hong Kong police officer noted sorrowfully that a man he now knew in an internment camp as a "lieutenant in the Japanese Army-Mizuno," had "run a sports shop in Wanchai" prior to that.[8] In prewar Hong Kong "Yamashita" was the "best barber in the Hong Kong Hotel barber shop. . . . Then after the surrender . . . Yamashita had appeared in uniform."[9] The British sailor George Harry Bainborough recalled a "hotel in Hong Kong called the Chitose," a "bar with Japanese women used to be in this place." A "fellow" officer told him that when the "Japs [sic] caught him he was interviewed by an interpreter, the interpreter, no less, was one of the girls from the Chitose."[10]

How did Japan, a nation as large in square miles as California, imagine it could take on not only the United States but the Empire, with its virtually inexhaustible supply of African and Asian troops and resources? Admiral Isoroku Yamamoto, "head of the Combined Fleet and

Japan's chief naval advisor at the [crucial] Naval Disarmament Conference" of the 1920s declared that "for victory to come to Japan in any war between her and the U.S.," Tokyo would have to "cross the Pacific Ocean, seizing springboard islands en route, invade the West Coast and then march 3000 miles over great mountains, across scorching deserts and great plains, fighting every inch of the way against a resolute nation of 130 million souls and at the end of a line of communications growing steadily to a length of 10,000 miles" and "to make victory certain we would have to march into Washington and dictate the terms of peace in the White House."[11] The task was daunting. Converting white supremacy into a defect was an active element in the Japanese imaginary, as they had a justifiable reason for thinking that their antagonists had powerful enemies within the gates, in the form of the masses of "coloreds" in the United States and within the Empire in Asia. As the top U.S. Asianist, Owen Lattimore, put it, many of the colonized and the colored saw it as a conflict "between their old masters and would-be new masters"; the latter "might turn out to be worse . . . but was that a difference worth fighting for?"[12]

Cleverly, the Japanese ruling elite motivated the Japanese masses—particularly the armed forces—by telling them their mission was to liberate billions from the tyranny of a racialized colonialism. Nogi Harumichi, a Japanese national, later recalled that his teacher would say in class, "I've been to Shanghai where signs say, 'Dogs and yellow people—no entry!'" Harumichi observed, "My feelings resonated with him. I burned with a desire to act. Given an opportunity, I want[ed] to go to the front. I want[ed] to go to China. . . . That's what we all said." Hata Shoryu, a war correspondent in Burma, asserted that "the colored people of Asia had been exploited by the 'have' nations of Europe and America, so this was a war to liberate Greater East Asia. We mesmerized ourselves with such arguments. They were quite appealing, actually—and if you didn't agree, you couldn't survive." Korjima Kiyofumi, a soldier, was inflamed when talking to a Japanese American: "He told me about how Japanese-Americans were horribly ill-treated in America, that they were placed in camps, and still oppressed [despite] the outstanding record of the All-Nisei 442nd Regimental Combat Team."[13]

A booklet for soldiers instructed them that their "task is the rescue of Asia from white aggression."[14] Unfortunately for those they were tasked to liberate, the Japanese troops often engaged in a brutal banditry. Nevertheless, there was no denying that the propaganda these troops were fed was powerful, not least because it was not wholly inaccurate. White supremacy had provided Tokyo with powerful kindling with which they could set Asia afire. "Once you set foot on the enemy's territories," Japanese troops were told, "you will see for yourselves, only too clearly, just what this oppression by the white man means. . . . These white people may expect, from the moment they issue from their mother's wombs, to be allotted a score or so of natives as their personal slaves. Is this really God's will?"[15]

Caught up in the frenzy of distaste for white supremacy, one Japanese general inquired, "Why should the United States, Britain and other powers which had every opportunity to advance their own vital interests now cry, 'Thief' if Japan so much as looked at neighboring territory?"[16] Japan's chief propaganda organ in Hong Kong added that "one reason why Japan was deemed a warlike country was because. . . . with 95 percent of Africa, 99 percent of the South Sea Islands, 100 percent of Australia and 57 percent of Asia under the control of European countries and the United States, Japan had to struggle to keep her independence. If Japan did not fight, she might possibly have become subject to some European power or America."[17] Once the Empire had opened the door to colonial exploitation, it was difficult to claim that the status quo should be frozen, that only Japanese seizure of territory was wrong but London's was quite permissible. Accepting such logic would only serve to rigidify white supremacy.

Before the 1941 invasion of Hong Kong—and even after—there had been an outflow of Nisei and Issei from North America, spurred in no small part by bigotry targeting them.[18] This was no more than grist for Tokyo's mill. Dozens of Japanese Americans fought with Tokyo in the 1895 war against China. Racism in the United States drove many more to reside in Manchuria in the 1930s; in fact, in the period leading up to the Pacific War tens of thousands of Japanese Americans went back and forth between the United States and Japan.[19] In 1933 alone there were "18,000 Nisei living in Japan."[20] The abysmal treatment of Japanese Americans during the war impelled some to swear allegiance to Tokyo or make little effort to return to the United States.[21] In 1943, the Japanese authorities in Hong Kong announced that "over 50,000 boys and girls . . . returned" to Japan proper.[22] A few months later, "75 American-born youths of Japanese parentage. . . . volunteered as student pilots in the Army and Navy air corps."[23]

With their detailed and intimate knowledge of Jim Crow in the United States, these Japanese Americans in Asia were powerful propaganda weapons, bolstering Tokyo's claims about rescuing Asians from white supremacy.[24] In November 1942, when optimism still reigned about an ultimate Japanese victory, "a group of 12 Nipponese evacuees" from the United States spoke out in Shanghai against white supremacy and the treatment in North America of their compatriots.[25]

Some Japanese American migrants wound up in Hong Kong with the triumphant Japanese. There they were able to revel in the historic reversal that had converted those who had once persecuted them into their subordinates. Commenting about a colleague, Emily Hahn wrote, "Suddenly, you see, that Japanese blood of his which had kept him feeling sore and inferior all his life. . . . Suddenly it was a damned good thing to have after all."[26] After the surrender in Hong Kong, a "British officer walked over to one of the civilians and said, 'Pardon me, but do you speak English?' The Japanese turned his back. 'I do not speak English,' was all he said, in a clear American accent."[27] The interned Hong Kong police officer, George Wright-Nooth, described Niimori Genichiro, for example, as a "Japanese/American with pointed ears." He had "lived for years in Ohio, where he owned a sideshow in an amusement park. He coupled the worst attributes of an American gangster with the cruelty of the worse Japanese. He addressed everybody as 'youse guys.'" He had an "evil reputation" and was "senior of the official Japanese interpreters in Hong Kong."[28] Ellen Field noted that "Nimori . . . spoke perfect English. . . . with only a very faint American overtone due to the many years he had lived in New York. . . . His tone was cold, arrogant and contemptuous. He was always sharp, rude and impatient with us."[29]

Li Shu-Fan, a Chinese surgeon in Hong Kong, has written of "Sato, a graduate of the University of Missouri," who "never lost a chance to revile the Anglo-Saxons in fluent English with the accent of the midwest." Like many of his fellow Japanese who had endured a sojourn in the United States, he too engaged in "one of the main aims" of the invaders, which was to "stir hatred in the Chinese against white foreigners. This aim at times amounted to an obsession."[30] Gwen Dew, the U.S. journalist interned in Hong Kong, encountered a one-armed aide to the invaders who wore a ring with an insignia from the University of Michigan; "Mr. Kondo," had gone to school there during the World War I era.[31]

When Japan took over the *Shanghai Times* in December 1941, "an American educated Japanese was appointed editor" and "the staff of the paper included a Filipino, Conrado A. Uy." Keeping them company in Shanghai was a "Lieutenant Matsuda, an American-educated officer" and "Ikushima Kichizo," an "Episcopal Christian who had studied at Amherst College . . . and Cambridge," who worked for Japan's Naval Intelligence. Takami Morihiko was "an American as well as a Japanese citizen. A dark-skinned, square jawed, bearded young man," he was "well-built and of medium height" and "was said to look "more Hawaiian or Filipino than Japanese." Born in New York City in 1914, he was the "son of a Japanese-American doctor who was head of the city's Japanese residents association. He was educated at an expensive private school in Lawrenceville, New Jersey and spent one year at Amherst." Despite—or perhaps because of—his extensive experience in the United States, he wound up in Shanghai working for Japanese Naval Intelligence, where his English-language skills came in quite handy.[32] Also to be found in wartime Shanghai was "Kazumaro Buddy Ono," a graduate of Compton High School in Southern California in 1932. He felt he "had been treated like a yellow whore by white men," so he said, "to hell with the United States." The POWs who encountered him spoke of his "special hostility towards whites."[33] Japanese Americans were also to be found in Singapore. When Lee Kuan Yew, the future leader of this city-state then occupied by Japan, went to be "interviewed" for a position with a Japanese news agency, the man sitting on the other side of the desk "turned" out to be "an American-born Japanese, George Takamura, a tall, lean, fair-skinned man who spoke English with an American accent."[34]

What was striking about this participation of Nissei and Issei in Japan's military occupation was that it was virtually coterminous with the Empire in Asia itself—and often stretched beyond. Intelligence officers in India got wind of Tokyo's "intentions to send espionage parties into Nepal." How was this sensitive information uncovered? An "informant" overheard a Japanese "officer" who was "educated in a university in America from which he graduated. He is aged about 25 years, strong built" and "fluent in Gurkhali."[35] In wartime Singapore, Charlie Gan recalled vividly "one Japanese whom my wife was working with. He spoke beautiful English. Oh! First class. And [a] very understanding man, very much westernised in his ideas, very friendly."[36] He was believed to hail from North America.

Soon Kim Seng had a similar experience in the "Lion City." Born in Burma, he arrived in Singapore in 1933. "The most interesting person[s] that we met," he recalled later, "[were] two Japanese brothers, they were repatriated from America. . . . could not speak Japanese, could not read and write Japanese. They only speak American [sic]." He was "very happy to meet someone who could communicate and we did have a very jolly good time. . . . They were frank" with him and he had "a very pleasant experience" with them.[37] Tan Cheng Hwee, also of Singapore, was interrogated by a man from Japan during the war. "The Japanese who questioned me," he recalled later, "knows English. He told me he was not educated in Singapore."[38] Samuel Eric Travis, the Director of Henry Waugh and Co. in prewar Singapore, confessed that he "suffered considerable physical maltreatment" during the war; in a sworn affadavit he detailed his unpleasant memories of a "fat American speaking interpreter."[39] An Indian resident in Singapore encountered a Japanese officer during the occupation "who was [once] in America" and "could speak English well."[40] He made no comment about his treatment.

When the *New York Times* correspondent Otto D. Tolischus was arrested in Tokyo, his torturer—whom he contemptuously referred to as "The Snake"—reminded him angrily, "I have been beaten and spat upon in America." Then he "hit" the dazed Tolischus forcefully and "spat" in his face. "I'm going to get even with somebody," he snarled: later the bruised and battered journalist learned that his assailant was "Yamada," who "was supposed to be a graduate of the University of California, a former Federal court interpreter at Oakland, and a former YMCA secretary."[41]

Tolischus's abrasive experience was illustrative of something else: these Japanese from North America who were assisting Tokyo were often more brutal than Japanese who had not resided in the Western Hemisphere. They seemed to be exacting retribution for the racial indignities they had suffered. In the Woosung internment camp near Shanghai, there was a "camp interpreter named Ishihara"—colloquially known as "The Beast of the East" because of his aggressive tactics. He "spoke excellent English, which he had learned while working in Hawaii." At the camp at Mukden, "Cpl. Eichi Noda" was "particularly disliked by the Americans"; he "had been born and educated to the high school level in the San Francisco Bay Area." He often "took the opportunity to beat Americans. For his cruelty and enmity toward Americans, Noda was called 'The Sadist' or 'The Rat.'" At the prisoner-of-war camp in Fukuoka, "the interpreter for Mitsui mining company, an American-born Japanese who went by the name of 'Riverside'—the California city he was raised in—was at times an informer and grew to be strongly disliked by most of the Americans." It was an "American born Japanese named Uno" who conceived of the idea of "a daily scheduled radio broadcast by POWs to their families back home." He was arranging to bring POWS from the occupied territories to Japan for this purpose when a New Zealander objected: "He was promptly dragged from the room, beaten and taken away."[42]

Reverend Joseph Sandbach of the Stanley internment camp in Hong Kong has spoken of "Colonel Toganarga. . . . years before he'd been in America and had been engaged in fair-ground business." He was a "rough, tough character. And he was no good to us at all from the word go."[43] Martin Boyle had enjoyed thoroughly the pleasures, carnal and otherwise, of prewar Guam, but his preoccupations were interrupted abruptly with the arrival of Japanese invaders. He wound up interned in Osaka where he encountered, "The Sheik, a tough, thoroughly Americanized villain who returned to Japan from the United States . . . in some sort of administrative capacity. . . . He was the spit image of the city slicker whose picture is now on the wrapper of a well-known brand of American contraceptives, and that's why he got his nickname—the only name I ever knew him by." Boyle despised him. "He roared . . . command[s] in perfect English," he added with disgust. Moreover, he was violent toward his charges. "The Sheik [was] the only man I ever saw who was able to knock a man down with one blow of his bare fists. The Sheik was an ornery son-of-a-bitch."[44]

Jack Edwards had a similar experience while imprisoned during the war in Taiwan. He recounted a guard there who "spoke English with an American accent." He was born in the United States. Before being transferred to Taiwan, Edwards was incarcerated in a camp on the Malay peninsula. There he encountered an "engineer with a strong American accent . . . born in the USA." In an incident that illustrates the value of the Japanese Americans to Tokyo, a fellow prisoner said, "I wonder if this little yellow bastard in charge today will stop somewhere for a woman; while he is in there we can nip off and find some grub." He was stopped short when a Japanese American guard said, "Say you guys, this little yellow bastard has pulled up, but not for a woman. Now you get the hell out and find some food!"[45]

It would be a grievous error to assume that all Japanese Americans were models of cruelty. Such an assumption could not account for Kiyoshi Watanabe. He studied at Gettysburg Seminary before winding up at Stanley as an interpreter. He thought he may have been the "only" Christian among the occupiers. Some saw this as an explanation for his tenderness and gentleness toward internees, and for his rejection of advice to "stick to your own kind, to your own people."[46] Mary Erwin Martin was sufficiently moved by her treatment at Stanley, that she swore in an affadavit about the "kindness my husband and I received"—he was London's consul in Chungking—at the hands of Tako Oda; she forwarded this message to the Tokyo War Crimes Trials that were then trying him. Yes, she conceded, this thirty-five-year-old former student at Amherst College and former diplomat in Washington had an "aggressive personality" and was "extremely bad tempered at times." And yes, he was a "member of the Black Dragon Society," notorious for its radically racial outlook. Nevertheless, she could hardly forget the "kindnesses shown by Mr. Oda to my husband" and to herself, which were "innumerable."[47]

The interpreter at the Argyle Street camp was named "Matsuda," but was "affectionately known as 'Cardiff Joe' as he spoke excellent English with a Welsh accent." He was seen to be closer to Watanabe than to Ishihara, Noda, or others renowned for their physical tactics.[48] He had "married an English wife and had lived for some years in London, working as a shipping clerk."[49]

George Stoddard was aboard the "heavy cruiser USS Houston" which "went down in the Battle of Sunda Strait, one of the early naval battles of World War II on March 1, 1942." He wound up in the infamous Changi camp in Singapore, then in 1943 was dispatched to "Yahata Branch Camp #24, near a steel mill on the Sumi Saki Strait." The "Japanese guards," he recalled in 1985, "were supposed to speak only Japanese to us . . . But some of the Japanese people had been educated in the United States" and "would come and talk with us in English."[50]

Many Japanese migrants had fond memories of Japan. The fact that ties between Tokyo and the Allies were worsening because of discriminatory immigration policies—which affected them and their relatives directly—endeared Japan to them further. Just as the Allies expressed concern about the fate of their nationals interned by Tokyo, Japan expressed concern about those interned by the Allies. Frank Fujita, one of the few Japanese American soldiers to be interned by Japan,[51] acknowledged that the Japanese treated internees harshly, just as the Allies' treatment of Japanese prisoners often left much to be desired.[52]

More than once, Japanese propagandists were aghast at the treatment of Nissei and Issei.[53] This was one of their chief complaints.[54] Those interned in Hong Kong read about Professor Ken Nakasawa, a former faculty member at the University of Southern California, who was interviewed in Tokyo about the internment. He had been held by the Los Angeles police, beaten, and "lost three of his front teeth" as a result.[55] "Special radio broadcasts" were "directed to the United States in an effort to have the Washington government correct" such matters.[56]

The pro-Tokyo attitudes of some emigrés may have been somewhat artificial, if the opinions of London's prewar Consul in San Francisco are any guide. The Consul's "Japanese man servant . . . informs . . . that he is required by the local Japanese consulate . . . to make a monthly contribution of $5.00 towards the cost of the war in China." This was not just an isolated case, but allegedly applied to "all propertied or wage earning Japanese in the state of California."[57]

Yet whether Japanese Americans were voluntary or forced adherents to the cause of Imperial Japan, the question asked by Yuji Ichioka remains: "What is the meaning of loyalty in a racist society"?[58] Shouldn't allegiance be mutual? Should one—can one—be loyal to a state that does not uphold its end of the social contract, when it treats a significant portion of its citizenry in an apartheid-like fashion? Miya Sannomiya Kikuchi would have understood this predicament. Growing up in California in the early twentieth century, this Japanese American woman was familiar with bigotry. But "the stronger she felt that white Americans were prejudiced against her, the harder she studied"—something of a metaphor for the evolution of Japan itself since 1853. In all her classes, Jewish Americans and Japanese Americans were "the smartest," which she "ascrib[ed] . . . to the discrimination both groups faced." But when she went in 1913 to the Grand Guignol of bias that was Alabama, she was shocked and "became bitterly critical of Southern racism."[59] How then could she subscribe to the belief that the United States was the locus of all that was good and Japan the epicenter of evil?

This was the grim situation faced by many Japanese Americans. One Nisei who requested repatriation to Japan in 1944 had the distinct "feeling that a person of technical or professional training cannot find full scope for his activities in the United States because of race and caste lines." This "man" was "excellent in his field" and he was only one amidst "so many cases of persons who have . . . requested repatriation or expatriation for similar reasons." This raised the "question of whether the United States [was] not likely to lose many of the best trained and talented people among its people of Japanese ancestry," to Tokyo's benefit.

In the moving words of one Nisei: "I feel that I've made every attempt to identify myself with this country and its people. But every time I've tried I've got another boot in the rear. . . . I realized that any white foreigner who came here had a better chance than I had. . . . I have a Japanese face that I can't change. . . . Look at the difference in the way they treated the Italians and Germans and what they did to us. You can't tell me that having a Japanese face didn't make a difference. . . . I figure that if it happened once it can happen again. . . . I can't see much improvement during my life. The Negroes have been in this country for generations and look how they are treated."

"I don't expect an easy time in Japan," he continued. "I know how tough things are. . . . but when I get turned down for a job it will be because there isn't a job, and not because I look different from someone else." The logic of white supremacy was driving U.S. citizens straight into the arms of Tokyo. "I don't think I'll ever forget evacuation," he vowed, "if a gang rushes me and piles on me, even if there are five or six of them, I'll get every one of them, no matter how long it takes to track them down. . . . I'm not afraid to die, and I'll fight for any country that treats me right, but I've gone through too much to talk about democracy in this country any more."[60]

Such angry despair was one reason why Tokyo radio broadcasts to foreign audiences were able to employ "a large number of Nisei." One such person was Kanai Hiroto, educated in Pasadena, who was an "interpreter" for the hated and feared secret police, the Kempeitai: he "interrogated U.S. fliers" who had been captured, and led them to decidedly perilous fates.[61]

The brutality of the Japanese Americans came as a rude awakening to their victims, who had come to view all those not of "pure European descent" as inferior. Lt.-General William Slim of Britain didn't think of the Japanese as humans but as "soldier ants."[62] The leading publication of U.S. press mogul Henry Luce "compared the Japanese soldier to a cockroach, "superbly adapted to getting along on almost nothing.'"[63] One of his magazines considered the Japanese "automatons in uniform."[64]

In 1941 Air Chief Marshal Sir Robert Brooke-Popham, commander of Allied Forces in Southeast Asia, attempted to boost his troops' morale by belittling the martial qualities of the Japanese. Myopic creatures, he called them, incapable of night fighting, lacking in automatic weapons, inferior in the air.[65] British Major-General A. R. Grassett "believed, like many British servicemen, that the Japanese were an inferior race. . . . In mid-November two courageous but almost untrained Canadian battalions disembarked at Kowloon: 'When do we get to grips with the goddamned little yellow bastards?'" one soldier asked in a sentiment reflecting the attitudes of many.[66] The British soldier, Harold Robert Yates, was told that "because of their slant eyes, Jap [sic] pilots would not be able to bomb accurately." Even after this bizarre perception was dashed in the rubble of Hong Kong, it persisted: "In the early days at least, some were heard to say, after witnessing the precision with which the Jap [sic] planes bombed and machine-gunned, 'They must be Germans in those planes, they're so good.'"[67]

Lance Sergeant Andrew Salmon, who served in Hong Kong, avows "We had a very poor opinion of the Japanese. . . . This business of saying that they can't fly at night-time and everything—we really believed those things. . . . I don't think we took them seriously."[68] Gwen Dew reflected the views of many expatriates when she proclaimed, "When one tries to think of one great contribution Japanese brains have given to the world in music, art, literature, science, or modern inventions, there is not one to be called. They have been expert copyists, but never creators."[69]

The U.S. elites were little better. There was a "popular belief" among them "that the Japanese were members of a lesser race," as "not a few Americans believed that one westerner was equal to five to ten Japanese." Chohong Choi contends that "even to this day Asians are thought to be inferior pilots to Westerners due to the myopia factor. This misconception is a factor in the reluctance of many airlines (even Asian ones) to hire Asian pilots."[70]

This imprudent dismissal of Japanese capabilities was not mirrored by comparable condemnation of other antagonists. One British lieutenant said, "Somehow one could imagine . . . that one would have a drink and a cigarette and a cup of tea with a [German] prisoner but once having met the Japs [sic] one can only imagine kicking their heads in. They look like animals, they behave like animals and they can be killed unemotionally as swatting flies. And they need to be killed, not wounded, for as long as they breathe, they're dangerous."[71] Harold Robert Yates of the British military concurred, adding, "I don't think you'll find a British soldier who will talk about a German soldier in a disparaging manner. . . . There's only two enemies who have ever made the British soldier actually hate them. One were the Indian mutineers and the other, of course, is undoubtedly the Japanese. None of us I don't think would ever [have] a reunion or meet any Japanese soldier. . . . A British soldier will call a German 'Jerry,' which is rather an affectionate term to us. . . . But a Jap [sic] was never given a nickname like that." Decades after the war, he continued to maintain, "I still hate the Japanese."[72] Lt. Col. Graeme Crew agreed, declaring bluntly, "We hated their guts."[73]

This animus was reciprocated, in the sense that it was widely thought in Japan that the Europeans and Euro-Americans wanted to reduce them to the level of Native Americans and Negroes. This perception led many Japanese to confront white supremacy fiercely. They felt that their nation must subdue the Empire and their allies in order to escape this unpleasant fate; ineluctably, in the right-wing atmosphere then prevailing in Tokyo, defensiveness was transformed into chauvinism. The U.S. journalist, Gwen Dew, then interned in Hong Kong, was subjected to a disquisition by "Colonel Toda" of the Japanese military, who "went into a long dissertation about Greek and Roman civilization, how it changed from time to time, with the inference, of course, that now Japan was going to take charge of the history of the world, and our era of white influence has ceased."[74] Ellen Field met a Japanese officer in occupied Hong Kong who would not allow her to deliver medicine to the camp for interned soldiers. Abruptly he reminded her, "If British soldiers' stomachs are not strong enough to expel these germs, it proves how weak they are. Japanese are immune to this disease. This demonstrates the decadence of the white race."[75]

Nevertheless, this chauvinism must be seen in the context of the palpable fear among common, ordinary Japanese—not being of "pure European descent"—that they could suffer the fate of Negroes or the colonized Hong Kong Chinese. Indeed, this real fear is what made the chauvinism so effective. Gwen Terasaki, a Euro-American married to a Japanese diplomat, was in Japan during the war. It was assumed that she did not understand the language. So a "harassed mother told the crying child on her back to hush or she would give him to the foreigner, me. The child immediately choked off his cries and became fearfully silent."[76]

Japan stoked these fires of fear. One of their propagandists derided U.S. pretensions in light of the tens of thousands of American illiterates—a disproportionate percentage of whom were racial minorities.[77] In the Empire and the United States there was much to-do about the "Yellow Peril." Well, argued Japanese propaganda, "We are more justified in saying that our world today is menaced by the 'White Peril' which is infinitely more dangerous than the "Yellow Peril.'"[78] With pride, Japanese elites claimed that the "war that has been thrust upon" Tokyo "is certain to be the greatest leveller of class and race, irrespective of colour or creed, since the French Revolution."[79] General Douglas MacArthur confirmed the explosive nature of Tokyo's racial appeal when he claimed that Japan "might try to overrun Australia in order to demonstrate their superiority over the white races."[80]

The mutual recriminations between these bitter antagonists are reflected in the attitudes of some Chinese immigrants, who like Japanese Americans, found themselves collaborating with Tokyo not least because of their own bitter experience of white supremacy. The most notorious of this group was George Wong, who participated in torture on behalf of the occupiers in wartime Hong Kong. During his postwar trial, one witness testified that Wong was an "American citizen who had torn up his papers. Before [the] war, he had nothing to do with Japs [sic]. But since [the] war he had torn up his papers because it was a war between yellow and white races. He said he hated Americans."[81] A young man in his thirties, Wong had roots in Hoi Ping, Kwangtung. Wong operated an auto repair shop on Nathan Road before making the fateful decision to throw in his lot with Tokyo.[82] He was not alone. The U.S. Consul in Hong Kong, Robert Ward, spoke contemptuously of a "renegade Chinese named Ts'ao, a graduate of West Point and from a good family, who had become a panderer, a dope-smuggler. . . . a collaborator with the Japanese."[83]

This collaboration began early on. On 8 December 1941, one "B. Mishima" was jailed by the British as the invasion was unfolding. He was treated harshly and given little water and food. "I still recall," he said a year later, "an incident which occurred on the day when we first entered Stanley Camp. When they saw the Japanese entering the camp, the Chinese inmates in the prison put up their thumbs, indicating triumph for the Japanese forces. Their act was seen by the British guards who severely reprimanded the prisoners."[84]

When the invaders seized a radio station in Hong Kong, one of the first things they did was to install an "Australian Chinese" announcer who, in the words of internee John Streicker, "appeared to like the Japanese an awful lot and us not at all. . . . Naturally we christened her Lady Haw Haw."[85] T'ien-wei Wu contends that Tokyo "had little difficulty in successfully recruiting numerous Chinese collaborators or traitors to fill the ranks of the puppet governments" in China and Hong Kong.[86] Frank Ching maintains that "the British were distinctly embarrassed by the fact that all the men they had appointed to senior positions had cooperated with the Japanese."[87] In fact, says Wing-Tak Han, "the Japanese administration was much more embracing than that of the British; it included people from all levels in society."[88] There was a "strong anti-British sentiment," in particular "among well-to-do Chinese."[89]

Japanese propaganda stressed the "discriminatory treatment" accorded Chinese in North America, including Canada where the King was still sovereign.[90] I. Y. Chang recalled bitterly that "those of us who lived in the sea ports and big cities of Asia" have noticed "the clubs and homes of the Oriental are open to all races without any barrier of colour or race," while "the opposite is the case with European clubs and homes."[91]

There was a "large body of opinion [in] what was regarded as the 'left' of the [KMT]" who agreed with Eugene Ch'en—a "wartime informant for the Japanese"—and his pro-Tokyo sympathies. Ch'en Kung-po "had been one of the founders of the Chinese Communist Party in 1921" and had graduated from Columbia before becoming one of Tokyo's key collaborators. The leading British diplomat, John Keswick, complained that Chinese nationalist "underground channels to occupied China were 'double circuits' from which 'the Japanese seem to derive more benefit . . . than the Chinese.'" Among this latter group in Shanghai were the "Chinese-American collaborationist Hubert Moy"—who attended Columbia University—and his "mistress," Marquita Kwong.[92] In that vein, Emily Hahn had a Chinese friend in Hong Kong named "Bubbles" who "before the war . . . must have been a Japanese agent. She had specialized in American seamen and British soldiers, young men who were inclined to credit Chinese girls, especially pretty ones, with the most impeccable romantic and patriotic sentiments. Naturally, they thought"—wrongly, as it turned out—"Chinese girls would love Chiang Kai-shek and hate the Japs [sic]."[93] The British in particular had few allies. The interned officer George Wright-Nooth conceded that "Strangely it was usually better to fall into the hands of the Communists rather than the Nationalists. The former's hatred of the Japanese was intense, whereas if the Nationalists thought there was more money in it for them they would often hand escapees over."[94]

Ellen Field's own experience corroborated this observation. During the war, a U.S. pilot was shot down near Hong Kong. He "managed to crawl into the undergrowth where he lay hidden until he saw a Chinese peasant. Supposing that all the Chinese in Hong Kong were still loyal to the British, he had called the man and asked him to bring help, giving him, as a token, his U.S. navy ring. But the Chinese had betrayed him, going straight to the Japanese gendarmerie."[95] The collaborators from the Chinese diaspora had plenty of company.

Why would they side with Tokyo in light of the bloody massacres in Nanking and elsewhere and the debasement of the occupation? The answer is not so much that they liked Tokyo but that they disliked more London and its policies of "pure European descent." Moreover, the leading force contesting Japanese hegemony in China, the Communist Party, had been subjected to destructively negative publicity by European and Euro-American propagandists. The fact that by war's end Chinese were "occupying judicial and executive posts with responsibilities unknown before the war," shows how biased the British had been toward the Chinese.[96] Similarly, as the Europeans were chased into exile from Hong Kong or interned, the Chinese often took their places, including quite a few from the Japanese colony of Taiwan.[97]

The invaders probably made their deepest inroads among the Indians, then in open rebellion against British colonialism and predisposed not to view the vanquished as allies and heroes. Why? To cite one example among many, the mother of the U.S. historian and presidential advisor Arthur Schlesinger, Jr., visited India in the early 1930s; she asked a British official how to say "thank you" in Hindustani. He refused, telling her "No white person ever thanks an Indian for anything."[98] When the Chinese writer Han Suyin visited India in 1942, she did "not remember meeting any Indian who was not a servant, a bearer, a something-wallah. . . . In the hotels no Indians stayed as guests; these edifices were only for the British, or diplomatic guests, such as us." But "in the back streets of Calcutta, just behind the hotel . . . I saw scribbled upon a wall 'Long Live Subhas Chandra Bose,'" a reference to the pro-Tokyo Indian leader.[99]

Han Suyin's observations in India, including the scribbled graffiti, indicated the source of the difficulties faced by the British in forging a united front with Indians in Hong Kong. Indian sympathies were often with their brethren back home and with Tokyo's position in Hong Kong. A British "internal intelligence" report from Hong Kong filed during the war noted that "the Indians are in the words of one refugee 'belonging number one people.' In other words they are receiving excellent treatment from the Japanese. They have many representatives in the Government, several being highly paid. The Indian police are solidly behind the Japanese."[100] Indian "officers and men were subjected to intense propaganda and a large number were persuaded to work for the Japanese administration." The chief of Japanese counterintelligence in Hong Kong "endeared himself in particular to the Indians in Hong Kong and therein lay his most powerful weapon against" the anti-Tokyo resistance.[101] The British writer Phyllis Harrop agreed. "The Indians are being especially favoured," she acknowledged. "They have been allowed, or should I say, encouraged, to stage an 'Independence Day.' This is, I suppose, to help in the Japanese attack on India."[102]

Mohammed Sadig was one of many Indians who collaborated with Tokyo in Hong Kong. One witness against him, swearing on the "Koran," said that Sadig stated, "When the Japanese are ruling India you will not be sent back to India but to England."[103] Sadig's alleged remarks were representative of a virtual tidal wave of anti-British sentiment in the Indian community of Hong Kong in the aftermath of 8 December 1941. Gwen Dew "saw an Indian knock down an aged British doctor who did not understand his order that a road was temporarily closed. A number of times Indian guards kicked women, or hit them with guns."[104] Emily Hahn saw "Indians everywhere" in occupied Hong Kong: "renegades from the British regiment that had been stationed in Hong Kong and former policemen and watchmen who had a grudge against the English and were glad to welcome their new conquerors. In this part of town they were under the command of a white man named Grover and his Eurasian henchman, John. Grover had run a butcher shop in Hong Kong and had passed as English until Pearl

Harbor. Then he suddenly claimed to be 'stateless.' Probably he was White Russian."[105]

The invaders made a special effort to woo the Indians. When "B. Mishima," a Japanese journalist, was arrested on 8 December 1941, he was jailed in Hong Kong. What struck him was the "kindness shown to me by the Indians [on staff]," which "gave me the impression that they realised that Indians and Japanese were all Asiatics and they would be close to each other." A year after this incident he mournfully recalled that "at the time of the British surrender, the British took no notice of the many dead bodies of Indian soldiers which were scattered along the roads." When Mishima saw "such treatment of the Indians," it "made [him] shed tears for our Asiatic people."[106] True or not, such words were appreciated by an Indian population that had been ground down over the years by the colonialists.

Before their arrival, the Japanese authorities emphasized, Indians "were often treated as unwanted children." Worse, "in order to achieve the best results, communal distinctions"—differences between and among Hindus, Muslims, and Sikhs—were played up by the British. These differences, said Hong Kong's new rulers, "have been the chief drawback against India's attainment of her lofty aims" and "should be banished from the affairs of Indians living in Hongkong."[107] Soon thereafter, an editorial in the *Hong Kong News* hailed the formation of a "Muslim-Hindu Friendship" association in Malaya.[108] In August 1942, as India itself was in turmoil as a result of the "Quit India" movement, Japan freed a "few thousand Indian war prisoners"; "all of them," it was said, "have expressed their desire to co-operate and work with the Nipponese."[109] Banner headlines in occupied Hong Kong spoke of "thousands" attending "mass meeting[s]" demanding "freedom" for India.[110] That same year, "Indian independence day was observed for the first time in Hongkong." "[Mr.] Singh, a prominent member of the Sikh community" said that Britain "had been in possession of Hongkong for the last 100 years and during that time they humiliated the Indians to the extreme."[111] Shortly thereafter, "preparations for the publication of the first Indian newspaper in Hongkong" began, to be edited by yet another Sikh, "Mr. Hukam Singh."[112]

Tokyo seized the opportunity to press home a message that would not be forgotten once London returned to rule Hong Kong. In July 1942, the *Hong Kong News* editorialized that "one of the black marks of Hongkong under British rule was the policy of fostering prejudice among the Chinese against the Indians." The British, they charged, "brought Indian troops and policemen to this country" and were "the first to start a gigantic propaganda machine to fan fear and dread in Chinese and other Asiatic minds against the Nipponese. . . . While the Nipponese attitude towards the Indian has always been one of sympathetic understanding, the same could not be said of the Chinese attitude, due to British perfidy."[113]

Indians resident in wartime Osaka, Japan, according to Martin Boyle who was interned there, were none too sympathetic to the Allies either, although they too were prisoners of war.[114] That was the dilemma faced by the Empire: because of their treatment of Indians in the past, some Indians now preferred imprisonment over dodging bullets on the battlefield.

Naturally, the Japanese distinguished between Indian and British prisoners. Their instructions regarding the interrogation of prisoners of war stated bluntly that the "means of obtaining [a] statement" will "vary with nationality." The need to "rouse anti-British feelings" among the Indian troops was stressed. "Contrast treatment of British and Indian troops. Point out slave attitude of Britishers towards Indians. Stress patriotism of Eastern Asiatic Indians and activities of INA." "British and Indian troops must be kept in different camps and receive different treatment. Indian troops must be treated by [Japanese] officers and men as if they were brothers. . . . Awaken in them a sense of superiority over the British." Chinese troops were to be treated similarly. "Point out common racial homogeneity of China and Japan." British troops should be reminded of "American atrocities . . . to women in England." Generally speaking, the rule of thumb was, "Do not kill Indians; kill whites but not officers, or those who understand Japanese."[115]

The Empire had its own special approach to Indians, as well. The "racial arrogance" of the Japanese should be emphasized, it was said, "along with 'Japanese sharp practice in commerce. (It remains to be seen whether we have enough evidence for this)." Their "treatment of women" should also be stressed, but the British—who were not exactly renowned for their advanced theory and practice in this realm—added cautiously, "This needs to be handled with the greatest possible care and quite impersonally." London was hoisted on its own petard in launching this crusade. "In dealing with all items in this section," it was said prudently, "it will be necessary to bear in mind [Indian National]

Congress criticisms of the British and either avoid instances where unfavorable comments on the British might be made or else discuss such comments quite frankly."[116]

Japanese racial ideology was sufficiently flexible to allow for a special appeal to disgruntled Europeans too. The collaboration of "White Russians"—that is, refugees from the Bolshevik Revolution—with Japanese forces in China and throughout Asia was well known. More generally, disaffected minorities reached out to Tokyo. A petition from "citizens of Ukrainian descent" complained about the Polish government.[117] The beleaguered Macedonians beseeched Tokyo to assist them in their struggle against "Greek and Serb domination."[118] The Ukrainian population "in Eastern Galicia" sought Tokyo's support in fighting "persecution."[119] Thus, viewed widely as leader by default of the majority of the "colored" world and having made decided inroads in Europe itself, Japan thought it was well poised for global domination.

Tokyo's crusade also had far-reaching consequences in the realm of gender, as conquest and its handmaiden, submission, inevitably do. Just as the various "Marches of Humiliation"—in which the captives were compelled to walk through masses of Asians while the often smaller Japanese troops held the Europeans and Euro-Americans at bay at gunpoint—were designed to have maximum psychological impact, convincing all sides that the era of white supremacy was over, Tokyo also had other aims with regard to their new captives: in particular, they sought to break down the notion of racial supremacy that rested firmly on the shoulders of the men of the allegedly "superior race."

Like the "breaking" of a mustang or, more precisely, the taming of a newly enslaved African, the Japanese sought to dehumanize their captives. George Wright-Nooth, interned in Hong Kong but born in Kenya where his father was an army officer, needed no introduction to racial serfdom. He noted that his captor had a "normal way of addressing internees, all Europeans were 'hairy apes'"—thereby reversing prewar usage when Japanese were routinely referred to as "those monkeys."[120] This reference to Europeans as simians crept into fiction of the era.[121] Such indignities—both profound and trivial—were shattering to the psyche of those who had come to believe in the alleged verities of white supremacy.[122]

Solomon Bard, interned in Hong Kong, was among the many who had begun to see the experience of the internees in stark gender terms.

"The Japanese," he said, "were exceptionally cunning (or perceptive?) in selecting an effeminate, spineless Royal Army Service Corps officer, one Major Boon, to act as liaison officer between the camp and them."[123] Major Boon, seen by many of the interned as a collaborator, had also, in their eyes, lost a prized possession: his manliness. Lewis Bush described him as an "effeminate looking individual, well-shaved, powdered and perfumed and well-uniformed with a slender waist which seemed to indicate that he used corsets." They gave him a "nickname," ""Queenie." Many of the men felt the loss of their masculinity deeply and "performed" what they felt in various ways. Lewis Bush was the master of ceremonies at an event featuring a "beauty chorus of handsome young men dressed as girls" with Japanese captors as the audience. "Our girls were a tremendous hit," he thought; they "looked quite fascinating."[124] In the penultimate scene, the lead "girl" threw his bouquet to a Japanese officer—we do not know whether either blushed.

Les Fisher was not amused. Sure, "the leading 'lady' was certainly a "wow' and was kissed by some of her fans when she came amongst the audience. Although this was looked upon as good fun," Fisher "could not but help feeling that it was all wrong psychologically."[125] Sonny Castro didn't think so. He was the object of affection, the "leading lady," a "wow." He described himself as a "slim lad who dressed as a lady and did a man's job of it too." Born just as World War I was ending, in 1978 at the age of fifty-nine he had the "looks" even then of someone "about 20 years younger." At Sham Shui Po in Hong Kong where soldiers were held captive, he was known as "Sonya," "Carmen Miranda or simply . . . the 'Sweetheart of Shamshuipo.'" He dressed as a woman with "brick dust for rouge and Chinese ink for mascara. Wigs were made of old rice bags." The site where he performed, extravagantly known as "The 'Hippodrome' staged a new production each month and the 'run lasted three months.'" Years later he continued to relive the "command performances for the Japanese." They "often came backstage to look at us ladies," he recalled blushingly, "and sometimes they'd give us some sweets and cigarettes. Once," Castro said, "a guard picked me up for a working party and told me to bring a strong friend. When we got to the place where we were supposed to dig, he told my friend to do the work, while I was told to sit there and teach him to sing 'My Blue Heaven.'" "No actress alive or dead had better notices," said one writer understandably.[126]

This kind of performance was not peculiar to Hong Kong or "unique to the British," though "they were the ones who raised it to the highest art," their "male prisoners taking female parts. . . . attractive young men who could [act] like attractive young women. They drew wolf-whistles, stage-door Johnnies, even Japanese guards bringing gifts, cigarettes, candy, perfumed soap."[127]

In such an intensely homo-social environment, homosexuality flourished. In one camp "something like twenty-five homosexual couples were getting counseling from one of the American doctors."[128] There were variations on this theme. Captain "Crumb" Chattey was charged before the war in Hong Kong with "homosexual offences with a Chinese 'boy.'" "Disgrace, dismissal and imprisonment followed," but he was released to fight the Japanese and "displayed outstanding courage and leadership in the battle for Stanley."[129]

Otto Schwarz of the United States found himself in a cell with "two Englishmen. . . . One of them was very feminine in behavior and also very timid. . . . 'Red' Krekan took on the role of being a sex-hungry sailor from China. He started making passes at the Englishman just for the hell of it, and we had more fun over that. This poor Englishman . . . I believe he would have died if we didn't get out of there." Sure, "there were a few incidences" of homosexuality that he "knew of. . . . There were incidences of homosexuality among the British that I heard of." Just as during stage shows, "They had one Australian officer" who was "dressed . . . as a female." There was "standing room only" for the latter performance.[130]

In Australia, as in the United States, "one of the key obsessions that sustained the continued existence of segregation" was the hoary chestnut that "white women could only be partners of white men," with Negroes—men and women alike—viewed as "hypersexual" and dangerously and compellingly attractive. At the same time, there was thought to be a "high incidence of homosexuality among Black American troops stationed in Australia," which both ratified and challenged these more traditional notions.[131]

Of course, in these camps—more specifically in Hong Kong—there was hetero-sexual coupling as well. "One would imagine," thought internee Lewis Bush, "that love-making was the last thing to bother about in such circumstances. But there were a number of full-blooded young men and many healthy and lonesome women. Unfortunately there were many tragic love affairs, broken marriages and the infidelity of some whose husbands were across the water in the prisoner of war camps in Kowloon." In these camps, where resurgent spirits fought tenaciously against death, "the cemetery was popular with camp lovers."[132] As Emily Hahn put it, "a freshly dug grave is one of the most private places you can find."[133]

The *Stanley Journal* published by the internees included such "Stanley Proverbs" as "never put off till tomorrow the man you can do today" and a poem about the "Camp Gigolo" (he was "young and quite good looking and reasonably dressed, yet he's often designated as Stanley's major pest.") There was also the admonition, "My son, beware of the damsel who telleth you that thou are one in a hundred for there is no doubt thou might well be that," suggesting once again that sexual intercourse is the poor person's grand opera.[134] Of course, the cemetery was also popular with those bone-tired and haggard with hunger and seeking a bit of rest, with nary a thought in their minds—nor the energy—for a romp through the tombstones.

It was remarkable how the former burghers of Hong Kong, many of whom were dismissive of the mating habits of their alleged racial inferiors, engaged in behaviors they might have denounced officially months earlier. At Stanley "there was a regular red light district. . . . A girl for a tin of bully beef" was the going rate. A "brothel of sorts" was established.[135] John Streicker, Administrative Secretary at Stanley, noted soberly that "very often between persons, one or both of whom had a legal partner elsewhere," affairs ensued. "This caused comment at first but soon became accepted."[136] "One sensational marriage" at Stanley, "of a young man of 25 to an old lady of 60" initially drew criticism, but after a while it too ceased to be of interest.[137]

Many of the men at Stanley were "holding women responsible for lowering morals, promiscuity and the increase in babies" that resulted. It is unclear, however, how the women could have had babies without the men's participation. Some men had difficulty adjusting to the fact that their decreased status and the transformation brought about by internment of necessity had fundamentally altered gender dynamics. Why should women defer, for example, to men who were deferring to the Japanese who were supposedly their racial inferiors? Consequently, the women became more assertive. Many said that internment "had changed them," some had "gained more tolerance" and "another internee spoke for many when she said: "My husband had a lot of trouble adjusting to the 'new me.'"[138]

Her husband was not alone in having difficulty accepting new realities. Father Meyer, a Catholic priest who was interned at Stanley, was opposed to abortion and made no effort to hide his views. Some women might have argued that if he was opposed to abortion, he should avoid having one. But this would not have deterred this determined man of the cloth who "feared a loosening of morals if such operations were allowed to be conducted indiscriminately. He objected to the attitude that children now should not be born in the camp owing to the general conditions prevailing."[139] This "might lead to a general belief" that abortions "could be lightly undertaken with the result that with this period of the camp's history the moral standards of the camp might be lowered and rather more promiscuous sexual intercourse undertaken."[140] In the spring of 1945 Father Mayer—and he was not alone—expressed his "deepest concern over the apparent ease" with which abortions were done, "not less than seven cases." "Any woman who desired it has been accommodated."[141]

A "surgical board" was established to rule on whether pregnancies should be terminated. In March 1945 the case of "Mrs. E. Philippens" came before the board. Some said that "there did not seem to be any reason to terminate the pregnancy," though one doctor objected, considering it "definitely wrong" to "continue any pregnancy" due to "malnutrition, semi-starvation and avitaminosis." After all, "it was proved in the last war that the children born toward the end of the period of hostilities lost their permanent teeth in their early teens and were mentally very poorly developed."[142]

The women and their allies did not blithely accept such remarks. By the summer of 1945 the "Camp Medical Officer," after a "brisk discussion" with fellow medics, presented a "motion accusing Father Meyer [et al.] of gross impertinence in attempting to interfere with rational medicine. [The motion] was defeated by a large majority."[143] There was another concern—one that was once thought to be a preoccupation of class and race subordinates—namely, that "legitimacy of the child should in no circumstances be allowed to influence the decision to terminate or otherwise a pregnancy."[144]

Some interned men—and women too—were concerned with the tendency of some women to become a bit too friendly with their captors in order to garner favors.[145] Emily Hahn "discovered that many women have a Sabine complex; they can't wait to get into bed with the triumphant Romans, even when the Romans happen to be duck-bottomed, odorous Japanese. . . . "After all, they must have felt, "'we are desperate; there is security only with the Japanese. Never mind what they look like; they whipped the proud British in record time. . . . If I can capture a Japanese protector, my family will eat.'"[146] Sir Franklin Gimson of Stanley observed that "the Japanese generally did not cause any difficulty which the presence of many women in the camp might have occasioned, though I regret to record there were some of the latter who were only too ready to receive the attentions of the former."[147] In her roman á clef about the occupation, Hahn writes of "Dorothy [Macklin]" who "had run through a series of affairs, choosing her lovers with an eye to gain and ease."[148]

Nevertheless, interned women in nonsegregated situations still had to rely on men to some extent—and vice versa—to help protect them from the excesses of the occupiers. During the war, "white women were particularly prone to assault, rape and public abuse in Japanese Manchuquo" or Manchuria.[149] However, Sir Arthur Blackburn of Hong Kong was "told by people who were in Kowloon when the Japanese came in that the behaviour of the latter towards European women was good, though numbers of Chinese and half-caste girls were taken off, obviously for use in soldiers' brothels."[150] Li Shu-Fan estimates that there were "10,000" rapes during the invasion alone, a figure reputedly confirmed by a "deluge of maternity cases" in October 1942. Even if this figure is inflated, most of the sexual aggression was aimed at Chinese women. By some accounts, the occupiers had peculiar social habits that did not bode well for women generally. "In pre-war days," said I. D. Zia, "it was the custom of the [Japanese] family to offer their grown-up daughter to their guest of honor as a bed-partner. . . . Bearing in mind this custom the soldiers did not think of 'rape' as a serious crime."[151]

John Streicker, a leader at Stanley, felt that comments from abroad were unhelpful. In March 1945, "the Japanese press . . . gave much publicity to the suggestion of a well-known American Senator that all Japanese internees should be sterilized. As may well be imagined, this was considered a poor idea by the British and Americans who were still interned at the time. Apart from anything else it was extremely unlikely that the Japanese would use anything like such up-to-date methods as the Americans."[152] Gender anxiety was not solely a preoccupation of the interned. Liang Yen recalled that in wartime Kunming, China, "There were times . . . when I found myself alone with one or another of the Americans. And sometimes I had to exercise a certain amount of persuasion, once or twice a certain amount of force."[153]

But things were especially difficult for European and Euro-American women as their elevated status had crumbled, along with their racial privilege, and they now had to compete with more numerous Chinese and Indian women for favors. Bernice Archer points out that "prior to internment all Europeans in Hong Kong had at least one servant, most had two or three. Many of the women had been in Hong Kong a long time and had therefore done little in the way of laundry, cooking, shopping and general housework."[154] This changed dramatically with internment.

Like a seesaw, the fall in the status of women of European descent was accompanied by the elevation of a number of Chinese women, who became intermediaries between Stanley and the larger society. Tobacco was an all-important currency and a palliative for hunger. A "monopoly" in this valuable commodity was "first obtained by the Chinese wife of a British policeman," who had been interned. Then "other Chinese wives went into business." They were part of a larger phenomenon of the rise of a soon-to-be-fabled Chinese capitalist class in Hong Kong borne on the back of the war and European degradation.[155] As Emily Hahn put it in her roman á clef, "Japanese and Chinese guards and the Formosans who were put on the job later," made "friends" with the common-law wives or Chinese wives of internees and the latter were catapulted up the socioeconomic ladder. The "aristocracy altered" fundamentally, which was of enormous import in terms of race and gender. A Chinese woman became "queen of the market."[156]

The fall in status of many Europeans and the rise of once lowly Asians is illustrated by Alan Dudley Coppin, interned at Sham Shui Po, who was once a prosperous businessman. He "found that a lot of Chinese shopkeepers were quite practical in doing business with the Japanese . . . They managed to make peace with the Japanese Army there and made good profits." He also "witnessed a lot of Chinese, Taiwanese and Koreans collaborating" and was shocked to find that "some collaborators there had been spies in Hong Kong too" before the war. The broader point, however, is that Coppin "lost almost everything" due to the war: "his business, his property and his wealth. . . . He left Hong Kong as a sad man and returned to the U.K. in 1945" at war's end.[157] But while he was falling, male—and female—Asians were taking his place.

Some European and Euro-American women adapted to the newer conditions, though old habits died hard. As Gwen Priestwood escaped to the mainland, dodging Japanese troops and Nationalist bandits alike, "she was also careful to take" her "powder compact and Elizabeth Arden lipstick." The "plan" was that "Anthony should be in charge and" she "should take orders—'provided they are reasonable orders,'" she "added mentally, womanlike." Priestwood was wrestling with the change from her previous status as a sheltered socialite to her present role as a desperate escaped prisoner. Her male comrade was little help. "Those old flannel trousers you're wearing," he said. "I don't like to see foreign women dressed like that—and it's bad for the peasants and coolies to see you so poorly dressed." Even on arrival in "bomb-torn Chungking," she "began to realize, it was up to a white girl to do her bit to maintain white prestige—even if she had escaped from a prison camp and marched and ridden across China for weeks. 'I'll buy a dress,' I promised.'" She took a bath, stepped out of the tub and stared in the mirror, then noted "with some satisfaction that the rigorous Japanese diet had, at least, given me a pretty decent figure." Priestwood was trying hard to pretend that the intertwined worlds of race, gender, and class had not been decisively transformed.[158]

The Euro-American, Gwen Dew, was tickled that some questioned her rooming with a man in camp. "This was funny," she mused, "for I had been assigned to rooms with men since December 20 and under war conditions everyone becomes merely a human being, not a man or woman, and there is no false modesty."[159] Dew's avant-garde approach showed just how much gender relations had been transformed—if only temporarily.[160]

Perhaps the final fall from grace for the women of Stanley came when they were forced to wear khaki shorts because their few changes of clothes had turned to rags. "Having been made locally for dispatch to Africa where they were intended to be bought at cut rate by natives," now they were eagerly grabbed up by the former mollycoddled mistresses of Hong Kong.[161] On the other hand, Sir Franklin Gimson is probably correct in suggesting that "women endured privations better than men possibly because domestic duties eliminated to some extent the opportunity for morbid introspection and criticism of administra-

tion." Men had further to fall and often received the brunt of the occupiers' assaults. Their identities were more bound up with the Empire
and thus they were more likely to crack when the Empire itself crumbled.[162]

There was a "tradition" in the Empire of "merging a sense of authority with the white racial identity," Suke Wolton noted, citing George
Orwell, whose "legitimacy as a representative of the rule of law, even
when dealing with a mad elephant, seemed to be intimately bound up
with the prestige of being white." Actually, this tendency was not specific to the Empire. In 1896 the *London Times* "regretted the Italian humiliation" in Ethiopia, 'complaining of the disrepute it had brought to
all white armies: "the chief feeling expressed is one of sincere regret, not
merely because by this defeat the prestige of European armies as a
whole is considerably impaired.'"[163]

Women were also under immense pressure as reflected in the self-
policing of those outside Stanley who were tending as best they could
to their loved ones in the camps of interned soldiers. As Emily Hahn observed, "Any woman who forgot herself and broke the rules of the
men's prison camp was the object of our indignation. We kept watchful
eyes on the girls who had bad reputations for being emotional. It was
always the same ones who smiled, or waved at their husbands behind
the barbed wire, or otherwise loused up the proceedings and we knew
it. We were savage against these women. . . . I was as bad as the rest of
them. I joined in cursing the Portuguese girls who giggled, passing
camp." The Japanese were not charmed. Sometimes there was "mass
punishment" for all the women, which brought down further collective
wrath upon the heads of those directly involved.[164]

Such pressures led directly to the formation of the British Women's
Group in April 1942, which quickly agreed that the "Dutch ladies" and
the "Maryknoll Sisters" could be invited to their meetings. In early 1943
the British Women's Group observed that "a year ago the presence of
women had . . . been largely resented" in the camp; but now "this feeling had died down, especially as the women had contributed very
greatly to the harmonious running of the camp. The women were working in clinics, diet and community kitchens as well as in the hospital
and school." The group also decided that "the use of the word
'Eurasian' . . . was deplored and it was agreed that a letter be sent to the
Council pointing out the need for more careful wording." The men also
had become more sensitive under conditions of duress; "some" had

"requested that they should be taught to darn and patch their clothes before the women were repatriated."

But this compelled sensitivity had its limits. "In the minds of the men," according to the minutes of the BWG, "women did not count in the camp. . . . 'we don't want any women in our meetings!'" they said. Thus, "the women organized work squads and were doing a nice, quiet job when suddenly they were given a man supervisor." The women promptly rebelled. "After that they respected us as they thought at any time we might be a strong political block who would vote as one." Further, the men expected that complaints about "delinquent and noisy children" would be taken up by "the women's group. . . . It was, however, agreed that it was a camp problem"—and not just a problem for or of women.[165]

The experience of interned women beyond Hong Kong was both similar and different.[166] Unlike their counterparts in Hong Kong—and reflecting Tokyo's improvisation and lack of an overall plan for the internees—a group of four hundred women and children were segregated from male internees in Sumatra.[167] Sister Jessie Elizabeth Simons, an interned Australian nurse, recalled that some of her comrades sought to make themselves appear as unattractive as possible.[168] Shirley Fenton Huie, also interned in Indonesia, had a different recollection, emphasizing how interned women traded sexual favors for the necessities of life.

Like some of her male counterparts elsewhere in Asia, the traumatizing experience of internment "taught" Huie "to understand better the attitude of poor and underprivileged people. Coolies often used to carry around with them a piece of material about one metre long and, say, half a metre wide. My mother confessed that she had often wondered why they carried such a piece of material, sometimes slung over one shoulder, sometimes wrapped around the waist. It was not until we ourselves were reduced to the state of coolies that we learned to appreciate the uses of a rag! In the first place," she marveled, "one can use it to wipe one's brow, one's hands, one's neck, one's armpits . . . anywhere! In the second place, it is always handy to wrap something in, and especially if one intends to steal something, say, for instance, a dropped cigarette, a piece of wood from the Commandant's kitchen, a piece of handy firewood. . . . Just nonchalantly drop your rag to cover the object, and leave it there for a while. If nobody seems to have noticed anything, pick up the rag when leaving, at the same time making

sure the object in question is wrapped inside . . . It can be used as a turban, a scarf or can serve as a bandage in case of accident [or] to tie up
some firewood." Increased empathy for the underprivileged, a status in
colonized Asia that had hitherto been thought largely to be divinely in-
herited and/or racially driven, grew under the intense heat of oppression, and led to the subsequent loss of support for colonialism. As Huie
wrote, "For those of us who survived, it probably did us a lot of good.
Most of us lived very spoiled lives in the Indies before the war and I
think the camp taught us new perspectives. We learnt that class barriers
are only artificial and came to place a greater value on the everyday
things of life."[169]

The moral state of the interned was reflected in the treatment of
children. "The presence of women and [particularly] children" in Stanley, "however unfortunate it may have been, gave the camp population
the semblance of a normal community and may well have been responsible for its mental stability, as only one case of serious mental dis-
order occurred."[170] Nevertheless, interned children suffered disproportionately and insidiously in a way not unlike what had happened to enslaved African children over the centuries. A report in 1948 observed
that "European children who were interned vary from one to three
years behind the general standard of education, and in certain subjects—history, science and geography—they are even more re-
tarded."[171] In the "higher age groups" there was "very definite evidence
of retardation, lack of concentration and inability to apply knowledge. . . . It seems probable," the report concluded sadly, "that they will
never reach normal standards."[172]

The trauma induced by the war continued to reverberate years
later.[173] Ralph Malcolm Macdonald King, a former Hong Kong solicitor,
still overwrought long after the war had ended, found that "for a period
of time after the war I was unreliable in the sense I did odd things,
strange things."[174]

"Odd" and "strange" were also terms used to describe the impact
of internment on collapsing marriages. At Stanley, questions arose over
the "divorces" "pronounced" by Sir Atholl MacGregor. Were these
proclamations valid? One man had obtained a divorce in this unortho-
dox manner in June 1942 and his spouse had remarried on the basis of
its validity. She remarried in Singapore, and after the war he wanted to
remarry in Britain. Was she a bigamist? Would he be deemed one?[175]
Margaret Sams faced a related dilemma. Interned at Santo Tomas in the

Philippines, she had more problems with her fellow Americans and their ethos than with the Japanese. The Americans' antipathy toward her soared when she fell deeply in love with a fellow internee, though her spouse was interned in a neighboring camp.[176] Gender bias may have been involved in the animosity between her and her camp mates.[177]

As for the Japanese, they had to endure a gender reversal after the war. "Male writers" tended to "typically rely on metaphors of linguistic and sexual subordination." Their "stories" were "often told from the perspective of an adolescent boy and suggest that the occupied society, like the narrator himself, has yet to attain, or has been stripped, of its masculinity." With "remarkable consistency, male writers from both mainland Japan and Okinawa have articulated their humiliating experience of the defeat and occupation in terms of the sexual violation of women."[178]

7

The White Pacific

BRITISH SETTLERS IN AUSTRALIA in the latter part of the eighteenth century began to create a "successful" white supremacist system in the Pacific. As the Pacific War approached, this system provided Japan with a lush opportunity to appeal to the downtrodden who were not of "pure European descent."

The settlement of New Zealand was also an illustration of this pattern. The indigenous Maoris had fought the Europeans to a virtual standstill before acceding to nineteenth-century treaties that were largely ignored subsequently. New Zealand had attracted a sizable Chinese population as well. As war loomed on the horizon, the Chinese did not fall silently in line behind Wellington despite the Japanese siege of China. In July 1941, the "Association of New Zealand Born Chinese" instructed the Prime Minister that "unless we be granted Imperial citizenship with Imperial privileges, . . . the government has no moral or ethical right to compel Chinese subjects to fight overseas in defence of territories in which in peace time they have not even the rights of free entry and residence. . . . [There is] a definite discrimination against them in spite of their birth as British subjects, because they are of 'Chinese race,' as distinct from those of 'European race.' Is it fair to discriminate against them on the one hand, and to ask them to offer their lives on the other?" This pointed query drove postwar racial reform from New Zealand to North America, as those not of "pure European descent" refused to be cannon fodder in war, even wars deemed just. The New Zealand-born Chinese did not stop there. "As far as we can ascertain," they asserted, "we New Zealand born Chinese enjoy the rights of a British subject only within New Zealand. . . . We do not however enjoy the rights of a British subject as do others of 'European race' in other parts of the British Empire."[1]

Pearl Buck has told the tale of her preaching to a Chinese man, telling him, "If you reject Christ you will burn in hell." Reputedly, he replied, "with a twinkle, 'Besides if heaven is only full of white men, I should be very uncomfortable there. I had rather go to hell, where the Chinese are.'"[2] Many New Zealand Chinese would have agreed most heartily. Racial reform occurred when it intersected with national security: it seemed that only the prospect of being overtaken by racial revenge could erode the calcified system of white supremacy. The British Empire teetered uncertainly on a shaky foundation of racial prejudice: when those within the Empire began to challenge this injustice, racism—not to mention the Empire itself—had no choice but to retreat or, minimally, redefine itself. When in the 1930s Tokyo "complained about" discriminatory policies concerning the entry and immigration of Japanese nationals, Wellington sought to secretly continue its normal rules concerning Euro-Americans, while continuing to discriminate against the Japanese. But it no longer did so openly. Of course, the Japanese embassy only needed to keep a keen eye and ear open, coupled with a bit of investigation, in order to ascertain whether Japanese nationals were being allowed into New Zealand like Euro-Americans or Europeans. It was precisely this kind of bias that helped to mobilize the Japanese public against white supremacy and, despite Tokyo's defeat in the war, these were the kinds of policies that fell apart as a direct result of the Pacific War.[3]

Surely, the Japanese embassy only needed to listen to local politicians to ascertain bias toward the Japanese. Particularly after their resounding shellacking of Russia in 1905, Wellington began to look nervously over its shoulder, worried that they would be next on Tokyo's hit list. This precipitated an early version of the post-World War II campaign by New Zealand to move away from the declining power, the United Kingdom, and toward the ascending one: the United States. For it was early in the century that one Wellington parliamentarian raised his voice against the "yellow peril," adding, "I would rather live in the most abject manner under Uncle Sam's flag than I would tolerate the monkey-brand [Japan] any time." The then prevailing London-Tokyo alliance, whereby the United Kingdom viewed Japan as its junior warden in the region, upset Wellington. Said one editorialist in 1908, "As the champion of the white ascendancy in the Pacific, America, therefore, represents the ideals of Australia and New Zealand far better than Britain has hitherto been able to do in this respect."[4]

But the challenge presented by the comparatively tiny Asian population paled when compared to that presented by the Maoris, whose numbers in New Zealand—not to mention their martial traditions— were considerably more substantial. Moreover, the Maoris were not grateful immigrants escaping the endemic war and famine of China for the bounty of New Zealand. No, some Maoris felt their land had been invaded and wondered whether they would be worse off if they were invaded again—this time by fellow "non-Europeans" from the north.

The triumphant British invaders who created New Zealand tried to establish white supremacy in their new homeland. They placed barriers in the path of those not of "pure European descent" who wished to move there; the 1921 census revealed that there were 671 Indians— mostly from the Punjab—and a mere 3,266 Chinese, mostly from Canton. Poll taxes were used to keep Asians from voting: such measures were abolished in 1944 under the threat of Japanese-inspired pressure and subversion.[5]

This biased policy was dictated not only by the requisites of Empire but also by the interests of local organizers.[6] These interests help explain why the Chinese were "the only racial immigrant minority that suffered the indignities of thumb printing" even when departing the nation.[7] Anti-Semitism was also strong and persistent in New Zealand over the years.[8]

Bias against the indigenous Maoris gave rise to the Ratana Movement, said to have begun in New Zealand in 1918. As of 1934, "of 74,000 Maoris in the Dominion, 40,000 [were] adherents." It engaged in "faith healing" and was grounded in Christianity.[9] As early as 1925 a key leader of this movement visited Japan and quickly became a close ally of Tokyo. He had met a "Japanese lad" who wanted to "learn the Maori language," and this had helped spark his interest in Japan. "I was invested with a Japanese costume," he said proudly after his return, "and also the entire members of my [delegation]."[10] While there, "Ratana," as he was called, was "said to have stated that he was officially received in Japan; that he laid the grievances of the Maori race before the Government of Japan; that the country had agreed to take the Maori race under its protection and would redress these grievances. He claimed to have made a compact on behalf of the Maori race with Japan and dramatically flourished a dagger, which he said was given him by a representative of the Japanese government in token that the pact so made would be carried out even if blood must flow in its enforcement." Some in the Empire deemed these words to be "grave disloyalty," but the question remained: why should the Maoris owe allegiance to a regime that had been so lacking in loyalty to so many of its "sub-jects"?[11]

Gradually the New Zealand authorities began to see Ratana's ties to Tokyo as potentially dangerous, though it was hard to disentangle these suspicions from a preexisting racial bias. In 1926, J. G. Coates, the "Native Minister," referred dismissively to "the so-called 'Ratana Bank,'" which some thought might have been a conduit for Tokyo gold. The Native Minister sniffed offhandedly, "Personally I do not think that any of the followers of the Ratana movement are capable of successfully running any banking institution."[12] Others were not so sure. One New Zealander felt that Ratana's ties to Tokyo were "sowing the seeds of un-rest under cover of spiritual uplift," and "sowing the seeds of belief that unlimited marvels of material benefit will accrue through the Japanese connection," just as the pro-Japan and all-black U.S.-based Nation of Islam would be accused of doing subsequently.[13]

In the same vein Sir James Parr, the Minister of Justice, was in-formed that "Ratana had stated that he had wedded . . . the Maori race to the Japanese." An Auckland solicitor confided that a "native client" said that "Ratana had just brought back with him a young Japanese, and that Ratana had, at his meetings at his settlement, informed the people that as the King of England had refused to assist the Maoris in their claims to their lands under the Treaty of Waitangi, the Japanese were going to help them to secure their rights by force." To do so, it was said, "the Japanese were eventually going to send warships here." "Ratana is endeavouring to transfer the allegiance of the Maori race to the Japanese," was the nervous conclusion delivered to the Minister of Native Affairs.[14]

This conclusion was based in part on a growing militancy in the Ratana Movement, emboldened by its ties to Tokyo. While traveling aboard a Japanese steamer, Peter Moko of the Ratana Movement con-fessed boldly, "I had to slap the face of the American and the New Zealander too" after "they insulted our girls and our whole party."[15] Other "insults" to Maoris, this time by Rhodesians who "had extended toward them the treatment they were used to giving the Kaffirs [in-digenous people] of South Africa" were met with a similar brusqueness, unusual for that time and place.[16] Just as some U.S. Negroes claimed to be "Asiatic" and related to the Japanese, Ratana suggested that Maoris and Japanese "belong to the lost tribes of Israel. . . . Many of the Maori words have a similar pronunciation to those of the Japanese and have the same meaning. . . . Professor Whyteman of Tokio [*sic*] University in-formed. . . . that he had spent 15 years of research in these matters and had come to the conclusion that the Japanese, Maoris, Philippinos [*sic*], Hawaiians, Malays and many other races were related."[17] When the Ratana Movement refused to share the benefits of faith healing with Pakehas [Europeans]—"no benefits for Pakehas" was their forceful as-sertion—it was apparent that New Zealand, a far-flung outpost of the Empire, would have to make severe adjustments.[18]

New Zealand's neighbors in the South Pacific also had troubled racial relations. While the U.S. South was in the midst of severe racial violence, Fiji in the 1870s was undergoing similar troubles at the hands of an organization that bore many similarities to the Ku Klux Klan: this almost led to a "racist war."[19] Fiji's population was a mix of indigenous people, Indians, and Europeans—with the latter, of course, at the top of the heap.[20] The Indian population, the bulwark of the Empire but also the prime source of its weakness, were reluctant to serve during the war—not least due to unequal pay compared to those of "pure Euro-pean descent." According to a leading scholar of Fiji, this reluctance an-gered the Europeans, who "deliberately stirred" among the indigenous people the "fear of Indian domination"—which has continued to cause instability in Fiji to this day.[21]

Thus, as the Pacific War approached, London had good reason to think the Empire would be threatened, with the aid of those who had been subjected to white supremacy. Nevertheless, the Empire pro-ceeded as if the prospect of disloyalty among subjects of the Pacific was unimportant. In the spring of 1941, the War Cabinet stated firmly that Cook Islanders and Samoans could serve with the military "provided" they were "full blooded whites and up to but not including persons of half-European blood." With typical understatement, it noted that "in western Samoa considerable discontent has been caused by the blood limitation. . . . And local born men of British nationality and European status, but who are of half, or more than half, Polynesian blood, strongly resent their exclusion from the privileges of serving the Em-pire." The War Cabinet wondered whether they should be placed in Maori units or "would resent" it, or whether they should be "formed into a separate unit."[22]

The Japanese Navy was well aware of British fears. They "appar-ently based [their] plans" for war "at first quite seriously on gaining the support of the Maoris and agitating them against Great Britain. This was to be achieved [with] submarine or parachute landings in areas where Maoris were concentrated."[23] Fortunately for New Zealand it did not come to this. But after the war, Wellington quickly moved to ease some of the heavier racial burdens upon the aggrieved, in order to do away with this internal threat to national security.

Australia is as large in territory as the United States, but its current population is approximately the size of Southern California's. Large in size and relatively small in population, with a murderous record against the indigenous people, it was a perfect target for Japan. "Racism was written into the Defence Act which governed the composition of Australia's forces—it specifically excluded 'full-blooded' Aborigines from enlistment," while "descriptions of the Japanese as baboons, apes and monkeys . . . recall white descriptions of Aborigines as 'monkeys' in the early days of Australian settlement," said one scholar tellingly.[24]

The Australian mining magnate W. S. Robinson put his finger on the problem when he declared that "Australia and New Zealand have a total population of 9,000,000 whites. Their neighbors are 1,000,000,000 of the coloured races—only a few hours away by air. . . . Australia and New Zealand are in the uncomfortable position of having most to lose and the greatest chance of losing it."[25]

How true. But Canberra—like Wellington and London and Washington—proceeded blithely, as if white supremacy would reign eternally.[26] Canberra was not unaware of the sense of outrage that its policies were creating, particularly in Japan. In the spring of 1919, as world concern was mounting about the victorious Allies' unwillingness to accept racial equality as a principle of the postwar settlement, a British diplomat in Tokyo forwarded a lengthy missive detailing the anger in Nippon. "It is difficult to understand what is at the bottom of the sudden ebullition of feeling on this subject," he said, seeming perplexed, "how far it is real, how far artificial." Still, he continued, "It is practically the one topic of discussion and great dissatisfaction is expressed on all sides at the failure so far of the Japanese Delegates at Versailles to obtain the insertion in the Covenant of a clause abolishing this discrimination." Warily he observed that "in his speech before the Japan Society at New York Viscount Ishii, the Japanese Ambassador is reported to have said that nothing would contribute more to universal peace than the rectification at the Peace Conference of racial discrimination and that a League of Nations with racial discrimination would be a miserable contradiction, a danger rather than a safe-guard." Signaling the importance of what he had noted, he sent a "copy of this dispatch to the Governor-General of Australia and to Washington."

The British emissary included reflections on a February 1919 meeting of the "Japanese Association for the Equality of the Races," that he had attended, a meeting also "attended by several hundred delegation of statesmen, scholars, newspaper men, ronin, and other Japanese . . . A fair representation of intelligent Japanese," in other words. There were "27 Japanese societies and organizations" at this lengthy meeting at the "Seiyoken Hotel." One speaker spoke for many when he proclaimed, "The world does not belong to the European alone. In point of popula-tion, Japan and China have more people than all the other nations and until race discrimination is abolished there can be no League of Na-tions." Lt. General Kojiro Sato noted that "unless one goes abroad . . . one cannot realize how the colored races are treated in America and other foreign countries. He said that he would remind his audience of the history of Hawaii. . . . He told of the intolerance in America toward the colored races. 'Who has seen Negro men eating in a respectable restaurant in America,' he asked. . . . 'The same thing may be said of the lot of the Hindoos.' . . . He said that the Japanese are not treated so badly but as elder brothers to those oppressed colored races, Japan cannot keep silence."

That was not all. "Dr. Soyejima, a scholar," said, "abolition of race discrimination should be made a condition of Japan in joining the League of Nations. Especially this point should be emphatically im-pressed upon the minds of Americans." But the United States was not the only target. "Mr. Shimada of the Kenseikai" noted Germany's "at-tempt at the time of the Sino-Japanese war to oppress Japan," which "failed, for Russia and France which were Germany's partners realized their mistake in joining hands with Germany against Japan. That broke down the race barrier." Similar forcefulness, it was said, would be needed to tear down other racial barriers. This was a militant meeting, with those assembled criticizing the diplomats for not being sufficiently forceful on these pressing matters of concern. This suggests that Tokyo's decision to make opposition to white supremacy a major ele-ment of its policy toward Europe and Euro-America—a policy that eventuated in war—was not solely generated at the Imperial Palace or the Foreign Ministry.

Despite these storm signals in its vicinity, indicating growing cyclonic distress with white supremacy, Australia sailed blindly on its racial course. High-level Australian operatives were well aware of the Black Dragon Society, which began shortly after the Meiji Restoration to "work for Japanese world conquest." J. L. Hehir of the Australian military reported that members had taken an "oath" to "sleep only four hours each night as a sign of [their] vigilance . . . to eat sparingly. . . . to commit harikiri if commanded." Race was their trump card and they were said to have members in Australia itself.[27]

The Empire was aware that Japan was playing the race card in its attempt to undermine London. In late 1937 Reginald Clarry informed "My Dear Eden,"—referring to the once and future Foreign Minister, Anthony Eden—of "poisonous anti-British documents" that Tokyo was circulating. These were not being furtively circulated. On the contrary, there were full-page advertisements "in one English and five leading vernacular newspapers in Japan," the text of which was also submitted to the U.S. Congress. In forceful words Tokyo assailed Britain for "cruelly massacr[ing]" the indigenes of Australia and New Zealand and selling "slaves" from Africa. "Recall History of British Empire before Accusing Japan in Current Crisis" another ad advised.[28]

Yet, like a hopeless alcoholic who cannot turn down a stiff martini, Canberra could not resist pursuing a policy of white supremacy, which to its mind had served it well over the decades. In 1928 a furor erupted in Australia in the wake of the persecution of visiting American Negro musicians. Five Euro-Australian women were on trial for cavorting naked with these men; "1000 male voyeurs" showed up at court to watch and listen, illustrating the "apparently perverse sexual fascination that visiting American Negroes held for Australian women and men." Like night following day, the local press regularly insulted the Negroes during their stay.[29] This was followed by a "run of attacks on dagoes [sic], Greeks, Jews, Chinamen and Asiatics." In other words, some Australians considered that discrimination against the reviled "colored races" was not enough and had to be extended, even to some Europeans. But how could Canberra confront Japan if it were to cut itself off from a good deal of Europe? Such was the logic of racial chauvinism, an illogical policy which found it difficult to know where to draw the line of exclusion. Thus, the leading Australian politician, Billy Hughes, who had been unyielding in his opposition to racial equality at Versailles, snorted, "Are we to be subservient to the dago [Italian]?. . . .

We believe in the White Australia Policy, and a British White Australia policy at that."[30] With this Hughes dropped the veil, and exposed the reality that "white supremacy" was a disguise shrouding the supremacy of the British Empire and, like one Russian doll within another, the supremacy of an English elite.

But this was a reality not often revealed and those who were not part of the enchanted circle of elites preferred to soak up whatever residual racial privilege they could garner. For example, Winston Churchill asserted baldly that "the Australians came of bad stock." After all, it was a "country established originally as a convict colony and subsequently settled by large numbers of working class Irishmen." His feelings were shared widely within Britain's ruling class, if only subconsciously, and they acted to exacerbate the enmity between the two countries.[31]

This perception evidently did not prevent W. E. Prentice from enjoying racial privilege. For when this Australian arrived at Port Moresby in Papua New Guinea in the prewar period, he recalled lovingly that "all troops had Papuan Native house-boys, one per ten other ranks, one per sergeant and one per officer, who did the troops' washing and ironing plus mess-boys and cooks assistants." Furthermore, almost all troops had a "compulsory siesta from 12:30 P.M. to 1:30 P.M. This was an extension of the British Raj, for troops on Tropical Service."[32] How could such military luxury prepare the Empire for combat with the battle-hardened Japanese? White supremacy thus carried the seeds of its destruction and spontaneously generated its gravediggers.

As the wail of war approached, the colonial authorities in Hong Kong took preventive steps. But they were trapped within a paradigm of race that undermined their attempt to soften the punishing blows of war, thereby demoralizing the Chinese on whom they would have to depend if Japan invaded. In the months leading up to the Japanese invasion, the authorities began to evacuate women and children, getting them out of harm's way. The evacuation of a small percentage of British subjects not of European descent, however, was of lower priority than that of their "white" counterparts. As the evacuation began in 1940 it was limited sharply by ethnic and racial considerations. Emily Hahn, the U.S. writer residing in Hong Kong at the time, observed that this proviso "implied that thousands of Eurasians and Portuguese who held British passports were not considered worth saving from danger, though the non-Asiatic women and children were. These Asiatics, always sensitive and considering themselves badly treated (which they were) blew up."[33]

This was not solely the fault of the colonial authorities. Australia was the logical site of decampment for these evacuees in that it was far from the presumed theater of war, yet close enough for them to return if the threat of war diminished. But in November 1940 Australian officials dashed plans for a nonracial evacuation, for they agreed to "accept white British subjects who might be evacuated" but "persons not of pure European descent were not eligible for admission." An exception was made for "coloured or partly coloured wives of white British evacuees."[34]

Residents of Hong Kong were well aware of the "White Australia" policy. They also may have been aware that the tiny Chinese population of Australia, sited particularly in Darwin on the northern coast, had been repatriated to Hong Kong in recent years, thereby relieving Canberra of "expense." Most of the Chinese "were brought to the Territory many years ago for railway construction work on the line running south from Darwin."[35] Thus Canberra was sending the Chinese into zones of conflict just as they were welcoming Europeans into safer climes.

Strikingly, it was the Chinese legation in Canberra that spoke up on behalf of their brethren in Australia, suggesting that white supremacy inexorably generated Chinese nationalism. In December 1941 this mission complained that "Chinese residents" in Darwin were "not receiving equal treatment with the Australians in the matter of evacuation. . . . All expectant mothers, women and children, and all aged and invalid persons are being evacuated from Darwin, but no Chinese were included." The official reply from Canberra was that "no discrimination is to be shown between Chinese and other residents."[36] But official replies meant for Chinese eyes were one thing, the reality was often quite another. This also underscores another aspect of the defense of the lie that was white supremacy—mendacity.

The Australians argued fiercely that there were other issues at play. In a "most secret" report on the "Japanese Intelligence Service," it was noted that "the detection of enemy agents among Chinese in Australia presents an extremely difficult problem." There were "nearly 7000 male Chinese in this country . . . including some who have escaped from Hong Kong," and a "thoroughly reliable source" alleged that "a group of Chinese, after having been trained in Hong Kong were to be sent via

New Guinea to Australia presumably by submarine, as espionage agents."[37] How could Canberra root out these spies if even more Chinese were flooding in as evacuees from Hong Kong, they asked? How could Canberra tell the difference between Chinese and Japanese? Yet, like the United States, Australia did not seem as concerned with the possibility of infiltration by, say, German agents. Canberra could argue in damaging mitigation that there were some—presumably of "pure European descent"—who also may have been subjected to discriminatory practices: The Consul General of Holland in Sydney reassured Canberra that some Dutch citizens wanted to come to Australia from Singapore: "All these people are well-to-do," and included "no Jews or undesirables."[38]

Jean Gittins of Hong Kong was Eurasian and belonged to one of the leading families of the city. Yet on reaching Manila after the 1940 evacuation order, she found that "passengers were divided into two categories: those of pure European descent were sent on to Australia; the Eurasian families were returned to Hong Kong." It "mattered not" to the Anglo-American authorities who collaborated to enforce this scheme that "these people" returned to Hong Kong were "British nationals, nor [did it matter] that they were families of deceased members of the British fighting forces."[39]

Canberra seemed obsessed by the prospect of an influx of Chinese, even those who were servants to Europeans. A newspaper clipping indicating that "about 3000 women and children taken from Hong Kong for safety will come to Australia"[40] ignited a flurry of cables and memos. As a result the minister decided that "women evacuated from Hong Kong should not be allowed to bring coloured amahs to Australia."[41] The Interior Department in Canberra followed up by instructing the "Colonial Secretary" in Singapore to "kindly refrain from granting passport facilities for Australia in favor of coloured amahs whom European employers propose to bring to Australia for the duration of war or indefinitely."[42] The Interior Department had no choice, given the debate in Australia over the propriety of bringing in more "Asiatics as servants." Ruby Board of the National Council of Women in New South Wales argued that this "would introduce a system which Australia, with its White Australia policy, has always . . . opposed." The president of the "Feminist Club . . . Mrs. P. A. Cameron also opposed" the plan since it was at odds with the "White Australia policy."[43]

Even after the war had begun, the Department of Interior ruled that "as it is desirable that these [coloured] servants be returned to their own countries as soon as possible, it is suggested that their exemptions should not be extended for more than one year."[44] Many European employers from Hong Kong and elsewhere had fallen on hard times and had begun to dismiss their servants. Canberra was worried that they would stay on, thus disrupting the "White Australia" policy. Though these servants might be put in harm's way in raging war zones, for Canberra yielding to the sentiments of its Asian allies was not a priority.

In addition to Chinese servants, Canberra was also trying to deport "Chinese wives of Army personnel in Australia." It "has always been a problem," wrote one official, "to find suitable accommodation for them; the fact that the population of Australia is 98% British stock and that there is no admixture of 'color' makes it difficult both for the Chinese wives and the white people with whom they come in contact. Furthermore, they are unwanted by the white wives of military evacuees. It seems a great pity that these Chinese wives should ever have been evacuated from Hong Kong."[45]

But this official was not the only one to be upset. "Mrs. Alice Standard" of Hong Kong had been evacuated to Brisbane, and found to her dismay that she—like others—had plummeted precipitously on the class ladder. This was causing her no small amount of anxiety. "Aussies," she groaned, "have caused us nothing but heartache." "Why," she cried, "did they have to pick this country to send us to, these Aussies don't like the English people, they show it in a lot of ways, even the school kids fling it in our faces, that we are living on charity."[46]

"Mrs. Trinder" seemed to agree with Mrs. Standard, or so thought one Australian official, who complained that she "has occupied a great deal of the time of the staff in this office and I can say, without hesitation, that she has been one of the most difficult evacuees with whom we have had to deal." He "was inclined to think that Mrs. Trinder, when in Hong Kong, enjoyed unrestricted recreation by reason of the fact that she then had servants to care for her children; but conditions here are different."[47] Europeans in Hong Kong had had even more servants at their beck and call than Euro-Australians, and were in a panic without them.

This Australian bias created a gaping opening for Japanese propaganda. A stinging editorial in the Tokyo-administered *Hong Kong News* charged in April 1942 that Britain consciously was seeking to fight on the "homeland of a coloured people" rather than, for example, in New Zealand or Australia. It charged that "white women and children were evacuated and the inevitable war suffering was the lot not of the privileged whites but of the downtrodden coloreds . . . and the white race intends to have it so until the end if they can." Why was London so worried about Australia, but not about, say, Burma or Malaya, it was asked. Because the latter were "not the homelands of precious white folk" and London wanted to "conserve equipment for the defense of white lands."[48]

This set the stage for what was to come. The Australian, Desmond Brennan, recalled that on the eve of the Japanese offensive in December 1941, he was on duty in Malaya and had "lunched with the officers, three of whom were British, and I remember Lt. Collins warning us about our current perception of the Japanese. We all thought they were little short sighted [sic] men with buck teeth, whose rifles were old scrap iron and whose bullets would not fire." Bathing in the warm aura of racial privilege, "that night" Brennan and his comrades were "allocated an Indian soldier as a 'servant.' . . . He wanted to take my shoes and socks off and so I agreed to do that at most, but when he commenced to massage my feet, I thought perhaps this servant idea wasn't too bad after all." As Japanese bombers approached, preparing to blast racial privilege, Brennan's Indian servant "lay across the door of my hut after tucking my mosquito net in securely and assuring that his large knife was able to be drawn readily."[49] Brennan was lucky that his "Indian servant" did not wield his weapon against him, his erstwhile master—as so many former servants did.

The Japanese assault on Asia sent shock waves through Australia and New Zealand. Kevin Ireland grew up in New Zealand during the war. Years later he still could recall vividly "that most terrible time of national fear, impotence . . . the year of the Japanese." New Zealand had explored many "taboo" issues over the years, including "sex" and "incest," but the possibility of a Japanese invasion had been neglected, he thought, because of the mass anxiety it ignited. The "curious thing," said Ireland, "was how our cockiness reasserted itself immediately" after Midway, though "our arrogance was proportionate to the depth of fear from which we had just been released." One factor remained constant, however: like the soldiers of the Allies, "in our school [sic] boy games we preferred to shoot imaginary Germans; the Japanese were too far beneath our contempt." They were "sub-human," "malevolent freaks." Still, Ireland conceded, "there was no doubt that we had all been in shock" during the war as the prospect of a "Japanese invasion nightmare still casts a shadow on our character."[50]

The lurking fear in New Zealand was that the "Japanese invasion nightmare" would combine with an internal uprising of the Maoris seeking revenge against British colonization during the past century. Wellington closely watched the activities of the Japanese in the region for this reason. In February 1939 Wellington worried about whether a Japanese firm should be allowed into the country. They noted carefully that the "part Samoan" employee of the firm would "manage the business," a fact that no doubt seemed strange to a New Zealand accustomed to keeping such a person in a subordinate position. "Up to the present," it was said, "we have successfully avoided accepting Indian immigrants (British subjects) from Fiji. . . . It is felt that once a Japanese business gets a footing it will be difficult to curtail any extension of trade which is certain to follow."[51] By including those not of "pure European descent" in matters of high commerce, the Japanese—perhaps intentionally—upset the preexisting system of racial preference, thereby worsening relations between the indigenous people of the Pacific and the Empire.

Months after the Japanese had declared war, A. E. Mulgan of the National Broadcasting Service asked the Prime Minister to authorize "broadcasting sessions for Maoris." Why? A key informant had reported that he was "very definitely worried about the attitude of the Maoris. They are not wholly loyal and apt to panic very easily. Also, disloyal ideas and views have been deliberately put into their heads." Mulgan was no less concerned: "We have been aware of a certain apathy among the Maoris ourselves and were startled to hear, from the Manager of one of these native settlements in a wild part of the Raglan district, that every one of the Maoris on his settlement said frankly they would welcome the coming of the Japanese. The Home Guard tried to get volunteers among these natives and were blandly told that they wanted the Japanese to come, because they would get back their land from the Pakehas."[52] Earlier there was a report that an "alarming revolt has broken out in New Zealand and the Maoris have protested against military service on religious grounds."[53]

Te Puea, one of the most influential women in New Zealand's history, was among those suspected of disloyalty during the war and thought to be "anti-British and pro-Japanese." Like many of the indigenous people, the bigotry to which she had been subjected had left her unclear in her own mind as to how much allegiance she owed to Wellington. Many Maoris declared that they would defend New Zealand against an invasion but would not fight abroad.[54] In April 1942, as war escalated, Wellington also worried about a "Fijian named Apolosi, of dangerous subversive tendencies, who it is feared might be contacted by the Japanese and used as a focus of discontent." Apolosi, it was reported, "is a full blooded Fijian with a dangerous influence over sections of the Fijian people."[55]

From fears of Maori and Fijian subversion, Wellington's attention turned to the prospect of Asian unrest. The presence of Chinese New Zealanders gave strength to the idea of "possible employment of Chinese nationals by the Japanese for espionage purposes." In the "early stages of the Sino-Japanese war, a Japanese Captain in the Intelligence Service who posed as a Chinese Officer under the name of 'Wong Ah Bew' was responsible for a lot of successful [fifth] column among Chinese. This enemy agent speaks Cantonese and four or five other Chinese dialects and in addition is described as somewhat Chinese in appearance. It is also reported that he was used successfully by the Japanese at Hong Kong and later in Malaya and Singapore. He was last heard of at Hong Kong where it is reported the Japanese have established an espionage organization." Japan, the Consul General was warned, "will make every effort to affect the entry of this agent . . . in the guise of a Chinese for espionage purposes."[56]

If suspicions of the Chinese were rife, those of New Zealanders of Japanese ancestry were apocalyptic.[57] Even Japanese American seamen—even those born in the United States—were "classed as enemy aliens for the purpose of alien control in New Zealand."[58] Thus, Wellington began to worry that any Asian might be a spy. In the early stages of the war, as Tokyo easily vanquished Hong Kong and Singapore, many Chinese New Zealanders were viewed suspiciously. The discovery of Japanese documents stamped "most secret" that suggested that Indians might be deployed as a "Fifth Column," gave rise to fresh trepidation.[59]

Many Maoris did indeed enlist to fight abroad. But their experiences often caused them to resent racial privilege in New Zealand even more than before. In 1944 one "returned Maori soldier, Major Harawira" complained that the "colour bar is more obvious in New

Zealand than in England." Worse, he "had observed more alarming signs of the colour bar in New Zealand today than after the last war. He himself had the door slammed in his face at one boarding house." Much was made by Wellington of turning the martial traditions of the Maoris against Tokyo, but how could this be done effectively while they were being subjected to bigotry at home?[60]

Certainly the dynamics created by the war—especially the prospect that the racial status quo imperiled national security—fomented a severe crisis for white supremacy. In fact, New Zealand and Australia had created the worst of all worlds for the kind of war they were forced to fight. They had alienated the indigenous population both at home and throughout the region and had created a right-wing ethos that fostered the growth of pro-Tokyo sentiments among the émigré population from Europe. Many of them had been maltreated as a result of prevailing chauvinistic British attitudes.

In 1943 Canberra developed a lengthy list of "potential 'quislings' in the event of an invasion," a list replete with White Russians—anticommunists who had fled the Bolshevik Revolution—who had been welcomed to the "lucky country" on account of the "White Australia Policy."[61] Italians in the prewar era would have been more welcome in Australia than the Chinese; yet now as the flames of war were leaping, leading officials in Canberra were warning their counterparts in Wellington that "Italians constitute the largest alien group in Australia and the most difficult to handle" in light of their decided lack of sympathy for the Allies.[62]

But both New Zealand and Australia worried during the war about the reliability of their indigenous populations. And because Australia had a larger land mass to defend and a worse record on race relations, Canberra may have worried more than its neighbor. One official 'pinpointed the deeply ingrained public fear widespread during and after the war that Aborigines, because of the ill-treatment they had received would link up with a potential Asian invader to Australia. "It's time white people in the south realized the danger of their attitude towards natives. They despise them and refer to them as 'niggers.' This sort of thing made the native very bitter. . . . The attitude of the white people . . . has turned the natives into a fifth column."[63]

A few months after Pearl Harbor a "secret" report detailed the hysteria felt by Canberra at that tense moment. Reverend E. C. H. Gutenkunst of Adelaide asserted that "these aboriginals have openly stated the Japs [*sic*] told them that the country belonged to the blacks, had been stolen from them by the whites and that 'bye and bye' they (the Japs [*sic*]) would give it back to them (the blacks)." The Director General of Security in Canberra added that "the aborigines in Cape York Peninsula have for years been fed and given tobacco by Japanese luggers," which suggested there was an alliance between them. Yet another informant reported that the indigenous people "are not to be trusted and are more likely to assist the Japs [*sic*] than the whites. The reason being that the Japs [*sic*] have consistently made presents, etc., to them over a period of years in return for the favors of their women, etc."[64]

Given the fear that the indigenous people would rally en masse to Tokyo's banner, it might be imagined that Canberra would be enlisting Aborigines enthusiastically. But it was not. Like Hong Kong, it feared placing weapons in the hands of the oppressed lest they be turned on it. Professor A. P. Elkin of the University of Sydney questioned the "refusal of the military authorities to accept for military service various aborigines of mixed blood in New South Wales." He acknowledged that "there has been some discussion in the press of late that the aborigines might help the Japanese if they were to attempt a landing." He confessed, "This is quite possible" since "during the past ten years or so they have [seen] the Japanese as a very kind folk." Besides, "they hold many grudges" against Canberra. "Disaster" could have been avoided in "Burma and Java" if a hand had been extended to the "natives." But some thought that arming the indigenous people would lead to an even greater disaster.[65]

A few months after this initial warning a high-level administrator in Brisbane was informed that "the aboriginals living in Cape York Peninsula cannot be trusted to help the Allies in the event of a Japanese landing." Reassuringly, he added the now dated—but telling—comment that he did not "subscribe to the theory of Communistic sympathies [with] which they are reported to be imbued." Previously, "the Japanese . . . during their fishing excursions . . . became very friendly with" the indigenous people. Signaling how the press of war enkindled race changes, he recommended that to "build up a better feeling toward the white man" in order to counter Japan, the indigenous people should be given "flour, sugar, native tobacco."[66]

Apparently Japan had made a long-term effort to cultivate the indigenous people of Australia. In Japan "Wakayama [was] tucked away in the south-east corner of Honshu. The people from this region have by tradition followed Nakimini-Fudo, the God of the Sea." They became pearl divers off the coast of Australia early on. They "maintained their pre-eminent position right up to 1941 when over 500 of them were providing Broome with the wherewithal to develop its wealth and livelihood."[67] Broome was strategically situated in underpopulated western Australia, only nine hundred kilometers from the Portuguese colony of East Timor to the north.

The Japanese effort appears to have been successful, as an "intelligence report" complained of the "doubtful loyalty" of "blacks." The "matter is worthy of the closest attention," it said, particularly since the indigenous people had "an invaluable knowledge of Queensland topography [that] would be of inestimable value to the enemy in an overland drive. That the enemy would have little difficulty in soliciting many of these people's services is born[e] out . . . by the writer's own experience. These half-educated half-castes and aboriginals have been largely influenced by Communist and anti-capitalist propaganda for many years and can almost invariably be swayed by the agitator. They are extremely class conscious and consider that they have had a raw deal from the white man. These sentiments are not displayed to the white man's face but are most evident when the coloured group are together in groups. There is little doubt that the Japs [sic] would find many of them willing helpers."[68]

Yet another official warned that the aboriginals in northern Australia might "retaliate" because of the indignities they had suffered over the years. Further, "the Japanese have treated the Torres Strait Island native as a friend, visiting in their houses and treating them as equals"[69]—a policy seen as downright seditious. The leading Australian jurist, Charles Lowe, declared that "evidence was given before me that the natives of Melville Island were in all probability more favourably disposed towards the Japanese than towards us."[70]

Just as even paranoids sometimes have real enemies, so Canberra may have had real reason to suspect sedition. As one aborigine put it years later, "during the war, some whites regarded Aborigines as security risks. They were too! When you've got a decision to make whether you would back the Australian people or the Japanese who would be kinder to us, I would have backed the Japanese if they had been kinder to me. Why not? We [are] still a security risk. Until Australia can accept the fact that we are not second-class citizens in this country, we will remain a security risk. I'll sell out to someone who will be kinder to me, thank you very much. Why not?"[71] Why not, indeed, was a hard question for Canberra to answer. In response, Australia and its allies, such as the United States, began to recognize that steps toward racial justice, no matter how halting, were the only way to keep this question from being posed, let alone answered.

Like Wellington, Canberra also feared that its Chinese population either might join with the invading Japanese or that the Japanese would masquerade as Chinese, providing an effective cover for internal subversion. In a "secret" report on "tactics of Japanese troops," Canberra belatedly admitted with chagrin that "we underestimated the enemy." An analysis of "Japanese methods" showed that when Tokyo's troops successfully invaded Hong Kong, they "entered many Chinese homes and confiscated all available Chinese civilian clothing." They "used this disguise to infiltrate unobserved through the streets." In Shanghai "clean shaven Sikhs" were "known to have come down to this area with the Japanese," claiming to act under the "authority of Subhas Chandra Bose" (the pro-Tokyo Indian patriot) and rallying the Indian community. This was another worry for Canberra, given the proximity of Indians from Fiji, New Zealand, and Australia itself.[72]

Then and now, some of the best intelligence on the region was produced by Canberra's emissaries; though perhaps knowledge of the hostility to its "White Australia Policy" in the region often led Canberra to exaggerate the dangers of internal and external Asian subversion. The well-connected Australian legation in Chungking reported weeks after Japan's astounding victory in Singapore, that "British prestige" was "never lower than it is today." "Chinese hostility to Britain" was "sometimes quite open," laced with "expressions of contempt." The legation acknowledged belatedly that "the British have not been popular in China for some generations" and there was an "ineradicable preference for the Americans among the Chinese." The ground beneath the feet of the Empire was eroding: things had become "exceedingly difficult," because there was also a "strong pro-German party in Chungking, especially in the army" and China might want to cut a separate deal. Did the putrid policy of "pure European descent" have anything to do with this? Well, no, the legation felt that "the evil lies deep in the Chinese character, which with its lack of civic consciousness and sense of social responsibility tolerates corruption." Still, with rare candor F. W. Eggleston—Canberra's representative in China—conceded that "it is difficult for European military empires to defence successfully possessions which are fully populated by native races whose interest in the contest is small."[73]

Fears about the Chinese were conjoined with apprehensions about their presence in Australia itself. Though Canberra had discriminated against its Chinese population systematically and had sought to bar the Chinese from evacuating from Hong Kong to Australia—both policies had helped to place the nation in dire peril—it could not seem to avoid bias. Thus, Canberra monitored carefully during the war an unlikely site of sedition: Chinese restaurants. The Deputy Director of Security in Brisbane asserted that "by paying fantastically high prices for businesses Chinese groups are taking over a large part of Brisbane's café and catering trade." Shockingly, "every Greek restauranteur in Brisbane has received an offer for his business." Though China was officially an ally of Canberra, while fascist elements dominated in Greece, Australia was little concerned about the latter. It was more concerned about the impact of the Chinese on its hallowed "White Australia Policy." It wanted to know where the Chinese were obtaining the funds for their purchases and thought the purpose was "Japanese espionage," since the eating places "would be a likely place for pro-Japanese to learn much of the movement of ships, etc. and an avenue likely to be exploited."[74] Although Canberra well knew that many Chinese resented Tokyo because of the latter's plunder of Nanking and other outrages, it concluded that its own policies were despised more than those of Japan.

Sadly, there was a basis for this perception. As the Malay peninsula was about to be overrun by Japanese troops early in 1942, the Governor of the Straits Settlement sent a hurried message to Canberra. "I am afraid that I must let you know that the decision to admit only fifty Chinese and fifty Eurasians in the first instance has caused acute bitterness and uneasiness here." The population of the Straits was "600,000" and "85%" were Chinese. "It is absolutely essential," the Governor continued, "that we should have this assistance but we cannot expect much if we are unable to obtain even temporary asylum for wives and children of those who wish to send them away." He wanted to send "5000," which Canberra thought might be five thousand too many.

But the Governor would not relent. A few weeks later the peninsula was under perilous siege and he wrote to "venture most earnestly that the Commonwealth Government will reconsider." China, he felt driven to remind, "is fighting on our side. The Chinese in Malaya have contributed much in money and kind to amenities for Australian troops here." Canberra remained reluctant.

In "secret" deliberations, the "War Cabinet" in Canberra dealt with "complaints of Chinese that special arrangements were made for the evacuation of white British residents and not the Chinese" from Malaya. When hundreds of Chinese from Hong Kong wanted to depart for Australia, "the majority belonging to the educated classes and possessing ample means . . . the admission of these Hong Kong Chinese was not approved. . . . although entry was desired for a limited period only." Why? Well, if Hong Kong were to remain indefinitely in "enemy hands, there would be no alternative but to permit the Chinese to remain in Australia notwithstanding the White Australia Policy." This was unacceptable. For "difficulties in securing accommodation amongst the ordinary Australian community would be very real. The same considerations apply in regard to the question of the admission of Chinese and Eurasians from Malaya." But because it was "highly important" that those barred take "no offence," and Canberra wanted to forestall such an eventuality, it would admit a "small number" of Chinese women: "no male person should be admitted."[75]

Although China and the Chinese were allies of Australia and although China was far away from Canberra, throughout the war the Australians feared a mass influx of refugees. The arrival of "Chinese and other coloured persons" on Australia shores, they feared, would disrupt prevailing racial patterns.[76] In the midst of the war—a war in which Tokyo was able to gain traction by purporting to be opposed to white supremacy—the Australian authorities seemed to agree with a headline from a local newspaper that proclaimed, "Australia must remain white."[77]

The "other coloured persons" that worried Canberra included dark-skinned Melanesians from the north, in the land that came to be known as Papua New Guinea. The evacuation from PNG in 1942 was racially marked as well. The *Sydney Morning Herald* claimed Papuans protected the Japanese by guiding them in jungles." This was a double-edged sword for, in a pattern to be replicated throughout the region, the evacuation of the Euro-Australians led directly to the "successful propulsion of Papuans into all leadership positions," again signaling how the war fomented race changes.[78]

Slowly Canberra was awakening to the consequences of being an island of "whiteness" in a sea of color, as it sought to keep up with events it could not entirely control. Thus, in a "secret" communication an Australian diplomat expressed his anxiety about developments in the neighboring New Hebrides, a French-U.K. condominium. The United States favored the United Kingdom in this marriage and Australia was worried about the "social consequences" of this, as the "natives" would now be exposed to the alleged "openhandedness" of the "Americans."[79]

In the language of the Empire, all those who were not "European" were deemed to be "coloured." Being "coloured" they were deemed to be unfit to settle in Australia, no matter how desperate their situation. Why? Canberra's view of the Chinese was similar to the attitude of some right-wing regimes to those who were Jewish, in that "the Chinese principle of dual nationality, their tendency to form enclaves and their reluctance to assimilate" made them unsuitable as immigrants. The authorities knew that Australia ran the "risk of isolation on the racial question" because of its policies, and devised cunning means to avoid indictment. "The slogan 'White Australia' . . . should be avoided," they said as the war plodded on, as it "would range opinion against us." Instead, the question should be reframed: "Ceylon excludes Indians, Thailand excludes Chinese, Japan restricts the Koreans." They also sought comfort in the thought that "fellow feeling is not sufficiently highly developed among oriental races to make really dangerous the prospect of a combined challenge to Australia." Canberra should continue to make a "vague affirmation of equality," since "Australia is no longer strong enough nor sufficiently protected by the United Kingdom to be able to ignore world opinion." The policy should remain the same but the packaging (as in an adept advertising agency) should change: "The name 'White Australia Policy' should be dropped with advantage and without any change in policy."[80]

The war also accelerated Australia's long-term shift from a historic reliance on London to closer ties with Washington. But this shift brought further complications, for unlike the United Kingdom, the United States had a huge Negro population that was not predisposed favorably toward white supremacy. The United States too had to make changes on this front in order to placate the African American minority and prevent them from tilting toward Japan. This was particularly so since Washington had to rely heavily on black troops.

These considerations presented a major problem for Canberra. In January 1942 Japan was on the march, having seized Hong Kong and given clear indications that Singapore would fall soon. Australia seemed tantalizingly within Japan's reach. But instead of responding eagerly to any offers of aid from Washington, Canberra balked, appearing to value white supremacy more than simple survival. Or perhaps it found it difficult to adjust to the new reality that, far from guaranteeing its survival, white supremacy jeopardized it.

Repeatedly the United States was said to be "pressing for a percentage of black troops which would mean a number so great as to create serious problems here." A "secret" memorandum stated unequivocally that "by decision of [the] War Cabinet no coloured troops from the United States will be stationed in Australia," though graciously they would be allowed to pass through on their way to another assignment. This was no off-the-cuff remark but the product of deliberation. It was preceded by a "confidential" report from the Department of Labour and National Service in Canberra, which stated unequivocally that deploying African Americans—even as "waterfront labourers in Brisbane"—"would have the most disastrous consequences."[81] In early February 1942 a "secret" report was filed concerning a "convoy of American troops which had arrived at Melbourne" and encountered "Customs officials [who] refused permission to a number of coloured troops to land." After much argument back and forth, "it was directed that this restriction should be withdrawn."[82]

In April 1944 Canberra was in the familiar position of declaring that "any fresh American Negro troops to be sent to the South West Pacific will be sent directly to New Guinea." It was also "likely that those already on the Australian mainland will be transferred to New Guinea as soon as they can be absorbed." One reason for this was that the Negroes had rebelled against the bias they had experienced; thus, it was said, "the situation regarding Negro troops in the area is tense, the Negroes claiming that there is discrimination against them in courts-martial."[83] Despite the fear of invasion, Canberra kept a tight lid on the total number of Negro troops. In August 1942, there were only 7,258 all told, most toiling on the docks, airports, doing roadwork, and the like; this number included 1,561 in Port Moresby, 242 in Sydney, and 116 in Brisbane.[84]

Although Canberra was required to accept these Negroes, it had not agreed—nor had its Euro-American counterparts for that matter—to treat them fairly. In fact, those within the Empire believed that they had a restraining influence on the more bigoted impulses of the Euro-Americans. Early in 1943 Britain's High Commissioner in Canberra forwarded a memo he had obtained from his colleagues stating that "British soldiers and auxiliaries should try to understand the American attitude to the relationships of white and coloured people and to appreciate why it is different from the attitude of most people in this country." The British should "be aware of the differences of attitude among Americans themselves, according to whether they come from the Southern States of the Union" or the North. "It is a matter of deep conviction in the South that the white men and women should not intimately associate with the Negroes." So Australians should "be friendly and sympathetic towards coloured American troops—but remember that they are not accustomed in their own country to close and intimate relationships with white people." The memo also made disparaging comments about Negroes that vitiated the point about British liberalism: "Like children Negroes commonly inspire affection and admiration."

Racial liberalism was not the dominant theme of Australia's policies toward Negroes. In a report coded "most secret," sharp words were spoken about a "coloured American Service Men's Club in Albion Street, Sydney" that was causing consternation. Although "American coloured troops are barred by regulations from the greater part of the city," the report stated, there were "odd disputes between coloured women and white women" who were "obvious prostitutes." Reflecting the age-old fear of miscegenation, the authorities were instructed to "prevent street women loitering in the vicinity of the Club."[85]

Interracial relations were charged. There were "frequent" and "violent" clashes between black and white U.S. troops down under. Though Australian Communists and some unions crusaded for racial equality, others were not as welcoming. One Negro soldier said that the first time he was called "black"—this was not deemed a neutral or descriptive term then—was in Australia. However, a positive outcome of this difficult situation was that the "aggressive retaliation" of the Negroes "against perceived discrimination provided an effective education for Aborigines. . . . These first contacts with Negroes laid a basis for learning and provided a model for later Aboriginal activists."[86]

Such realities gave the Australian elites further reason to seek to curtail the admission into Australia of U.S. Negroes. Thus, in 1942, at a time when it was unclear whether Australia would be ruled in the future by a Japanese viceroy, Canberra gave an "instruction" that "action be taken to discourage Australian troops from fraternizing or drinking with American coloured troops." Though such activities were a sine qua non of forging cohesion among those who might be on the verge of making the ultimate sacrifice, Canberra objected. Like London, Canberra cited the precedent set by Washington: "Such fraternization is not permitted or thought of on the part of American white troops and it is undesirable that it should continue on the part of Australian troops." Such "an association was deleterious to discipline among the U.S. forces and the issue of this instruction was in conformity with the wishes of the U.S. Army." The working class was split. The "Trades and Labour Council" of Ipswich protested sternly to the Prime Minister against these "racial superiority theories which are Fascist in character," but its words were met with obstinate resistance.[87] When two thousand Negro laborers arrived in Townsville the trade unions objected in no uncertain terms.[88]

In Queensland, "black Americans were subject to highly formalized residential, occupational and recreational segregation both within the U.S. armed forces as well as those constructed by their host community."[89] But all this harassment and suffering endured by Negro troops and Aborigines was not for naught. For it was evident, even before the war concluded, that the "forces for change" generated by the conflict gathered "considerable momentum" and "induced an often reluctant Government to liberalize immigration policy" and related racial practices.[90] An integral part of this process was the disrupting presence of Negro troops. The "international pressures" they provided were a catalyst for the improvement of the lot of Aborigines; these pressures, not "domestic policies," drove racial reform, according to one scholar. As one indigenous Australian put it, "The black American had a big effect in the coastal areas in Queensland where there were large numbers of them stationed. We met and talked to them. This laid a basis for learning. . . . This change in outlook is terribly important—revolutionary in a way. It has laid the basis for all the other changes that have occurred in the post war years."[91]

Something similar occurred in neighboring Irian Jaya, north of Australia, which shared a land mass with Papua New Guinea and where Canberra exercised its hegemony both before and after the war. During the war itself, one "keen Papuan observer" remarked, "This [U.S.] army had men with dark skin who lived in the same way as the whites. We even saw black officers. Then we were sure that our people too could live differently than they had been living."[92]

Japan spread the news of racial inequity far and wide. In the neighboring French colony of New Caledonia, reported the pro-Tokyo *Hong Kong News*, Governor Christian Laigret "had openly charged Negro American troops stationed in Noumea of misbehaviour and of being [the] "terror of the white women in New Caledonia.'"[93] The South Pacific, a model of white supremacy, was a major target of Japanese propaganda. Reality there, the paper said, presented a "scathing indictment" of the Empire. But with the rise of Tokyo, "the white man in the South Seas is now in grave danger of being hoist by his own petard."[94] Japanese propaganda repeatedly threatened Australians and New Zealanders—even when it may have intended otherwise. Thus, Totehiko Konishi in September 1942 reassured them that after the Japanese invasion and conquest, "a century would be required for Nippon to outnumber the white Australians"; "to Asianize" this vast land would not be "feasible," though part of the Empire provided "ideal places for Nipponese settlement." That the "whites" were promised that they would "not be treated in the same category as Chinese and Indonesians" was not exactly reassuring,[95] particularly since it was acknowledged that "for the development of Australia, the importation of Chinese labour seems to be the only solution."[96]

These observations reflect the impact of the war—including the presence of Negro soldiers and the pervasive, often frightening, Tokyo propaganda—on the Empire in the South Pacific. The "Official War History" drafted in New Zealand notes that "the crucial widening of the Native (now appropriately, Maori Affairs) Department occurred during the war years and the war affected and accelerated the change. [The] chief elements contribut[ing] to this effect" included "increasing racial consciousness of the Maori during the years of recruiting and fighting."[97] It was in 1944 that there was a "conference of representatives of all the Maori tribes . . . the first conference of its kind that [had] ever been held." The Prime Minister spoke, and the indigenous people made land claims that were to roil Wellington for years to come.[98] The war experience itself propelled this consciousness and militancy. For "people who had the greatest respect for the prestige of the white man saw him engaged in menial occupations."[99]

Make no mistake: race relations in the South Pacific were not magically transformed by dint of war. To the contrary. Peter Hall, a Eurasian, matriculated after the war at a school in Sydney. He observed, "I was called 'Tojo' probably because I came from "China.' . . .

In later years as the Australian sun tanned me, I was nicknamed 'Wog.' You just had to grin and bear it, otherwise you would never get any peace."[100]

Hall's experience was not unusual. Canberra had developed special rules for "non-European students" who wished to study there that were not free of discrimination.[101] Without a doubt this was part of a larger immigration scheme that sought by various means to extend the shelf-life of the "White Australia" policy. Weeks after the Japanese surrender the cleric Dr. Wilson Macaulay felt compelled to remind Canberra that "the phrase 'White Australia' has a deadly sound in Oriental ears—it means the same type of racial superiority as Hitler's 'herrenvolk' and is equally objectionable."[102] In its defense, Canberra could point to analogous policies of its chief ally, Washington. In the immediate postwar era an "American army chaplain . . . advised [soldiers] to think twice before marrying a Filipina because of the prejudice they might encounter" in North America.[103]

But the United States, which was reigniting a Cold War against its most recent ally, the Soviet Union, was also revising its racial policies to better engage in this conflict. Australia, on the other hand, seemed more interested in presenting a happy face of racial concord while continuing the same old antebellum policies. Thus, the National Maritime Union of the United States, whose merchant seamen often sailed into Perth and other Australian ports, took issue with the continuing "attempt to discriminate against Negro seamen." They had read an article in the local press about Australian women dating these visitors: "We have tried to reason with the girls who have been frenziedly embracing their black lovers," said the periodical, "begging them not to go. But they have no reasoning power." But why? "By our standards," said the journal, the Negroes were "sex-crazed and liable to go mad after drinking very little alcohol." They left in their wake "many half-caste children running around. . . . [They] came . . . from the north with plenty of spending money" and produced a "degrading spectacle of Australian white girls rushing the wharf to vie for the attentions of the Negro members of the crew." This generated a "revolting sight of local girls hysterically mauling black men and begging them with tearful voices to stay. According to white Americans, in no other Pacific port do white women behave in such a depraved and abandoned fashion. And for this reason Sydney has become the favorite port of call for Negro seamen. . . . Some of our 'Boong Molls,' as we term them in the police force, reserve themselves exclusively for the black men. They watch the shipping news carefully for arrival dates of American ships."[104] Ferdinand Smith, the Negro leader of the seamen, was "horrified and shocked beyond credulity at the monstrous libel" of these words, but it just showed that the war had not changed everything.[105]

8

Asians versus White Supremacy

WHITE SUPREMACY GENERATED AS STURDY and resolute a response in the region from the Malay peninsula to India as it had in the South Pacific. Unlike the latter, for the most part the former did not involve settler states of the type and magnitude of New Zealand and Australia. Here colonialism was more in line with that found in Hong Kong. And here was a reaction that Hong Kongers would have found familiar.

As in Black America, Vietnamese patriots, chafing under French colonialism, were heartened by Japan's defeat of Russia in 1905.[1] This was echoed in India, the heart of the Empire. Subhas Chandra Bose, an Indian hero who fought side by side with Japanese troops against the British, speaking in Tokyo, proclaimed, "Japan's victory over Russia in 1905 was the harbinger of Asia's resurgence. That victory was hailed with great joy not only by the Japanese but also by the Indians."[2] Likewise, Jawaharlal Nehru, a founding father of the world's largest democracy, also spoke warmly of Japan's momentous triumph. He "invested in a large number of books on Japan" and began to study their example for insight into what it might mean for his own country. The victory, he exclaimed, was a "great pick-me-up for Asia." Like others in the region, he watched with rapt attention as the number of Chinese students going to Japan rose from five hundred in 1902 to thirteen thousand in 1906. Yet another Indian leader, R. B. Bose, helped organize a "Conference of Pan-Asianists" in Nagasaki in 1926, attended by Chinese, Vietnamese, and Indians, among others. This conference presaged the future role of India and the Indian diaspora as the headquarters of pro-Tokyo sentiment in Asia.[3] In the prewar era, the Empire had a "barely concealed fear of the Japanese appeal" in the region.[4]

This pro-Tokyo sentiment should not be overestimated: it was not universal, particularly among Communists, who had some support in both India and China. But the Empire appeared more fearful of the

Communists than of Tokyo. In the prewar period they ruthlessly suppressed the former, while entering into an alliance with the latter. This had the predictable consequence of strengthening Japan-inspired nationalism, while weakening their predators, the Communists.[5] The Empire could have strengthened anti-Japan feeling but often took actions that pointed in a different direction, for example, in the 1930s when they deported the Vietnamese Communist, Ho Chi Minh, from Hong Kong—where he had been residing for seven months—to an uncertain fate.[6] Indeed, a former colonial governor of Hong Kong and Singapore was quite blunt in his "objection . . . to any Chinese political organizations whatsoever functioning here, communist or non-communist."[7] The British repressed political expression among Asians, but in so doing weakened organizations such as the Communists that were adamantly opposed to Japanese imperialism.

Similar trends occurred in Malaya. Mustapha Hussain "was an avid reader and a member of the British Left Book Club," a "left-wing socialist," and a "happy-go-lucky fellow," who would have "remained" that way "if he had not been discriminated against in the civil service by white Europeans." This "racial discrimination made him a bitter diehard Malay nationalist. Nationalist anger consumed his soul." Hence he moved closer to Japan and worked with the Japanese when they occupied his homeland.[8]

Hussain's anger was generated by white supremacy. Even as the blaze of war was beginning to crackle in Southeast Asia, the Empire reaffirmed that "in Malaya . . . the colour bar is strictly enforced by the Colonial Office both in the Malayan Civil Service and the professional departments." According to the eminent Sir George Maxwell, former chief secretary in the government of the Federated States of Malaya, the color bar had been introduced earlier in the century because "fear arose that the Civil Service might be inundated by candidates from India, unconnected with Malaya; and the Colonial Office altered the regulations and required that all candidates should be of pure European descent." Sir George noted, "In the Medical Department there is a large number of Asiatics domiciled and educated in Malaya, British subjects . . . they have diplomas. . . . But for no other reason than their colour, they can get no further than the 'subordinate grade.'" And "in the Agricultural Department, Mr. Gunn Lay Teck, a Chinese . . . [graduate] of Cambridge . . . has a better degree in agriculture than the European head of his branch in the department. He too because of his colour has not been able to get beyond the rank and pay of a subordinate."⁹

These policies created fertile soil for pro-Nippon sentiment on the Malay peninsula. Throughout the prewar era the British feared that not only Japan but also "Russia" were "now working independently to reach the same goal—the elimination of white influence in the East."¹⁰ (It is unclear why Moscow would be interested in doing this, unless its ideology automatically barred it from admission into the hallowed halls of "whiteness.")

Only months after the Japanese takeover, even British writers were proclaiming a "very practical revolution in race relationships."¹¹ Given the Empire's practices, it did not take much to bring this on. Lee Kuan Yew, the founding father of Singapore, recalls that "the best local graduates" had "much lower salaries" than the British. This conservative politician years later remained contemptuous of the legerdemain necessary to maintain the illusion of white supremacy. "Any British, European or American who misbehaved or looked like a tramp," he later recalled, "was immediately packed off because he would demean the whole white race, whose superiority," he added with a dash of sarcasm, "must never be thrown in doubt." But whatever mystical faith there was in the alleged "superiority" of the "whites" was crushed by the Japanese invasion, as "stories of their scramble to save their skins led the Asiatics to see them as selfish and cowardly." Lee, who collaborated with the Japanese, said the "three and a half years of [the] occupation were the most important of my life." He was not alone in benefiting from the occupation, gaining power (that he never relinquished afterward) when the British and other Europeans were ousted from leading posts. Said Lee, "The luckiest and most prosperous of all were those like the Shaw brothers who were given [by Tokyo] the license or franchise to run gambling firms in the amusements parks."¹²

Though present-day Malaysia (with a Malay majority) and Singapore (with a Chinese majority) often disagree on many things, it is striking that the preeminent figure in Malaysian history, Mahatir Mohammad, agrees with Lee Kuan Yew on the importance of the Japanese interregnum. "It completely changed our world," he said. "Not only did the Japanese forces physically oust the British, they also changed our view of the world." He studied Japanese and remains friendly with Tokyo. "For those who went to Japanese schools and were willing to learn the language, the Japanese Occupation was not too painful. Of course," he adds, "people of Chinese origin suffered more and many were killed or held in captivity." But as for himself, he was "not violently opposed to the Japanese." He even accepted some key arguments of the Japanese right. "Even today some Japanese will argue that their occupation of Asia was not so much an act of aggression towards the Asian nations, as it was an attempt to free us from European colonial rule. There is at least some truth to that argument. . . . The success of the Japanese invasion convinced us that there is nothing inherently superior in the Europeans. They could be defeated, they could be reduced to groveling before an Asian race, the Japanese."[13]

The Japanese themselves were contemptuous of their British adversaries. Masanobu Tsuji was an architect of the Japanese campaign. Years later he marveled at the fact that the "British Army had blown up the bridges and abandoned several thousand Indian soldiers on the north bank of the river." The British Army, he concluded, slightly bemused, "excels in retreat." Perhaps worse was their utter disregard for their Indian comrades: "In the Japanese Army there would have been no blasting until it was certain that the last of our comrades in arms had crossed the river." Although Masanobu Tsuji did not say that this disregard may have been motivated by white supremacy, his contempt for the British Army was clear: they "looked like men who had finished their work by contract at a suitable salary, and were now taking rest free from the anxiety of the battlefield."[14]

Colonialism on the Malay peninsula had prepared the ground for a Japanese advance. Lim Chok Fui was born in Singapore in 1936 in a neighborhood which had "no such facilities as water closets or tap water. We had to get water from wells. . . . Living conditions at the time could be regarded as similar to those in a rural area or those in a farming village in China." His home was a bungalow of "900 square feet. . . . divided into living spaces for four families" with "each family" having "one room." There were four in his family. A "common toilet was shared by all the families. It was a hole dug in the ground with a roof which was actually a zinc sheet."[15] Meanwhile, the British resided in regal splendor. "The European colony was a mere handful of about 8000" with "Scotsmen predominating," and they lorded it over those not of "pure European descent."[16]

This racial supremacy had an intra-European class bias, of course. Many British troops felt that London "did precisely nothing to make life more tolerable for the airmen up in Khota Baru." There was even a dearth of "good drinking water." Nonetheless, the troops lived in greater comfort than non-Europeans. Among some Navy men, even their "boy" had a "boy" or servant.

As in Hong Kong, the Empire adopted color-coded evacuation policies. When war threatened, London was reluctant to evacuate about seven thousand "Chinese workmen" at the docks in Singapore— though this group was to become the heart of the anti-Japanese movement—since "the reception areas would be either Australia, India, Ceylon or South Africa. The first and last of these countries have hitherto held strong views on the subject of Asiatic labour."[17] As in Hong Kong, in Singapore Japan relied heavily on a unique crew of "shrewd men, the barbers." They "automatically gave all white customers an anti-hangover massage whether they wanted merely a shave or hair-cut," which relaxed them and made them more willing to engage in casual conversations that often yielded a mother-lode of intelligence.[18] Although there were only "3500 souls" in the prewar Japanese community in the region, the white supremacist policies of the British enhanced their effectiveness.[19]

In any event, the British, being outnumbered, could not have held off a credible invasion, particularly as London had alienated the Chinese, Indians, and Malays. Moreover, intra-European conflict weakened them further, as white supremacy was no more than a cover for British, then English supremacy. The case of David Marshall indicates that those who did not fit the proper national origin profile were also subject to exclusion. "I applied to join the Singapore Volunteers Corps," he said, "and it was with some difficulty that they finally accepted me as I was neither European, nor a Chinese, nor Eurasian; but they finally placed me with the odds and sods, East Europeans and some English volunteers."[20]

Harvey Ryves had typical colonialist attitudes. He complained of the "general inefficiency of Asiatics, particularly Malays, when left to their own initiative. They have little idea of method or coordination among themselves." But somehow this "inefficiency" disappeared when the Japanese invaders arrived, as "many of the Malays . . . were established Fifth Columnists," especially "schoolmasters." Perhaps recognizing that by maltreating the Malays the British may have helped to foment sedition, Ryves found that the colonizers had a "fifth column mania." "They suspected nearly every Asiatic who was unlucky enough to find himself near the fighting zone." In "Kedah, an unfeder-ated state with an anti-British tendency . . . Fifth Columnists" were no-tably active. "Malays were caught signalling to Japanese aircraft. . . . It is also true that a good deal of signalling was done on Singapore is-land."

Worse, "of the European troops, very few could distinguish a Malay from a Tamil, a Chinese or Japanese," since the "vast majority of military units knew next to nothing about the country. . . . Perhaps two out of every hundred British soldiers had a rudimentary knowledge of Malay, the lingua franca . . . and possibly the easiest language in the world to learn." Ineluctably, racial bias marred relations between "whites" as well, as the "phobia was so bad that not only Asiatics were distrusted but also responsible Europeans." There was some justifica-tion for this in fact, as "the Australians earned themselves a deservedly bad reputation for looting—on every possible occasion they took what they could lay their hands on."

The decadence of the Empire was so deep that even as the Rising Sun was seizing Hong Kong, life in supposedly impregnable Singapore continued unchanged. In January 1942 Ryves "joined in the general he-donistic way of life. Dancing went on nightly at Raffles; the Sea View Hotel, the Adelphi and Cyrano were full of diners day and night. . . . Drunken Australian soldiers lurched their way around the streets. . . . It was a bacchanalian feast." The "gaiety was garish and spurious with a touch of the last days of Pompeii about it. . . . Everyone was drunk in varying degrees."[21] Like the Australian government which could not see that its white supremacist rejection of Negro troops could jeopard-ize its own existence, the colonists in Singapore were out of touch with reality.[22]

But the revelry did not last long. The Australian, Raymond Bur-ridge, was stationed on the Malay peninsula. "The Australians," he re-called years later, "were not very popular with the British civilians in Singapore and Malaya as the British looked on the Australians as mere 'colonials.' . . . Our opinions of the General Staff commanding Singa-pore was that they were centuries behind the times and no good as lead-ers, except at golf or cricket perhaps. Our opinions of the peoples of Malaya were quite negative, except for the Chinese and Gurkha troops and civilians. The Malays and Indian troops and civilians were pro-Japanese and after the fall of Singapore, [they] marched us into Changi Gaol. . . . No, not the Japs [sic] but Sikh Indian troops who had been our allies the day before." During the inevitable "March of Humiliation" when the Japanese forcibly marched the vanquished and beleaguered Europeans through the streets, many of the colonized were "spitting on us as we marched into Changi Gaol and calling us. . . . dog Britishers."[23]

When Malayans "saw British and Australian POWs, who only several months before ruled Singapore and Malaya, doing menial work that only indigenous people had done, and begging for cigarettes," they could not help but be moved. "The sight impressed" one "cadet, reminding him of the dawn of a new era in Asia and of a new Malaya for which he had trained." This cadet was now being trained by the new occupiers, the Japanese, and he could not avoid comparing them—favorably—to the previous occupiers: the British. The training included a forty-mile march. "What was most impressive during the march was that the Director and the instructors too, walked with the students every inch of the way. The British, they thought, would have driven in a car." Among other things, the authorities chose to ban the film "Gone with the Wind." The film had been scorned by many African Americans and other "colored people" for its positive portrayal of plantation slavery in the United States while it was embraced by many "whites," who helped make it one of the more lucrative films of the twentieth century. With every maneuver, Tokyo signaled its hostility toward the European colonizers, and its apparent willingness to embrace the concerns of the oppressed.[24]

Victor Krusemann was born in Malacca in 1918. He joined the Malacca Volunteer Force in the prewar era but was not pleased with it. "I never met any European before the war who treated you as an equal. They always behave[d] [like] they were . . . superior than you. . . . You see thing[s] that made a lot of local people really angry and they were pleased that the Japanese fellows had come, because [of] the way they were treated. . . . In the beginning, they thought the Japanese had come to liberate them." This sentiment was widely held throughout the region.[25]

Joginder Singh concurred—he was born in 1919 in Malacca and was part of the segregated defense force that was overrun.[26] Certainly few non-Europeans[27] regretted the end of the Empire initially.[28] "I don't care who rules Singapore," said Tan Cheng Wee. Unfortunately for Tokyo, its misrule quickly led to substantial hardship and eroded whatever goodwill it had had coming in.[29]

K. M. Regarajoo was not Eurasian but Indian, but he shared Kruse-mann's feelings. Born in 1915 in India, he migrated to Singapore in 1929. He was a founder of the Indian Youth League, which by 1941 had ten thousand members. Though he helped in 1937 with Chinese relief during the Japanese invasion, he was not a supporter of the Empire. Why? The British "had superior feelings toward Asiatics, that's all. . . . They show discrimination." India was a "slave under the British people. . . . That is the feeling [of] every Indian," he claimed.[30]

Dr. Tan Ban Cheng, born in Singapore in 1929, recalled all the "toy stores" owned by the Japanese: "They sold a lot of cheap goods" and "they were very polite," which distinguished them from their British counterparts.[31] Heng Chiang Ki, born in Singapore in 1923, did not recall the Japanese stores but did remember that there were "a lot of prostitutes" among them, which made them popular with many men. So, "on the day they came in," he said, "every house had a Japanese flag. . . . Even my house, we had one made." The change in rulers did not bother him particularly: "Whoever was the boss makes no difference actually." It was "still a colonialist country." Unlike those who have recounted Japanese brutality toward the Chinese, he felt differently, averring that the Chinese had an advantage over Malays and Indians since they could "write "kanji'" and could, thus, "pick up Japanese faster."[32] Given the exploitative conditions of the Empire, the new occupiers were understandably popular at first.[33] Kip Lin Lee recalls the British denouncing the new occupiers as "cruel," but in his view "this was far from the truth." He was a "Peranakan," an important ethnic group on the peninsula, and was "fifth" or sixth generation in the region. His father, like many others, had been "pro-British." But "when the surrender came, he made one remark . . . 'Well, what's the difference, it's a change of masters.'" The Japanese "walked in here practically. That's when the British prestige came down, I think for good. After that in Singapore, I think no one really respected the British at all." He felt that "Malays had it easy. The Japanese did not bother them that much. The very fact that they did not have to [go] into concentration camps seemed to prove the point." The new occupiers also "assumed . . . that the Indians did not care for the English. And they were in a way quite right." The Chinese, of course, were different, he thought.[34]

Ismail Zain, a Malay born in 1912, also recalled the sheer joy of the British defeat. "Actually among the Malays, they welcomed the Japanese," since unlike the former colonizers, "they were very friendly, they were nice to all the people. . . . They always offer you a cigarette, that and that. They used to talk [sic] all the jokes." By contrast, "the British, they look down upon you if you are a junior staff. They don't give you cigarette, like that. . . . They are not friendly, they won't talk to you in a friendly manner. But the Japanese do that. I appreciate that." The British, he thought, had a "superiority complex. . . . but the Japanese, no. They treat us all alike. . . . They treat us like friends, whether they are high ranking officers or not. . . . But the British, no. They won't do that."

The ground had been prepared for the invasion in the 1930s by the Kesatuan Melaya Muda or "Malay Youth Movement," whose "duty was to help the Japanese intelligence." They formed the basis for the "heihos," the indigenous collaborators, of which there were "quite a lot. In Singapore alone I think nearly 10,000. . . . They were in uniform." Like those who had been impressed with Japanese stores, Ismail Zain felt that goods were cheaper as a result of the occupation. Thus, he was "happy" about the British surrender.[35]

Dr. F. A. C. Oehlers, who was Eurasian, felt likewise. Born in 1921, his brother was the first Speaker of the Parliament in Singapore. Eurasians who were "first generation" were "given red badges" and not interned, unlike those of "pure European descent." But because of his "Occidental heritage," he—like others similarly situated—was "viewed with suspicion." He learned Japanese and, like others, had fond memories of these new colonizers: "There were many decent ones among them. . . . They used to come along to the house" and the "nucleus of a kind of camaraderie, a friendship . . . developed."[36]

Clearly, the Malays were subjected to systematic anti-British propaganda,[37] which may account for their negative attitude toward London and their positive feelings about Tokyo. Moreover, many associated the end of colonialism—which was seen as inseparable from white supremacy—with the demise of the Empire, which too was associated with Tokyo. Thus, Sho Chuan Lam, born in 1927, recalled that the new occupiers "used to tell us how the British had exploited the Asians. . . . At times they made us feel very proud that we [were] Asians, telling us that all this culture and civilization started with the Chinese and other Asians. I remember one Japanese even told me [that] although they did not like the Christians, he said Jesus Christ was also an Asian."[38] Patrick Hardie has a similar recollection. In "every Singapore theatre" during the occupation, "before they start the film, this is the word, [sic] have to be shown on the screen. They said in Malay: 'Alhamdulillah, East Asia sekarang sudah dikembali ke bangsa Asia. Marilah kita bekerja bersama—sama untuk Asia Timor Raya'—so it says that 'Asia have gone back to the Asian people. So therefore we must work together for the sake of Southeast Asia.'"[39]

This propaganda offensive by the new colonizers began from day one.[40] As in Hong Kong, they marched the Europeans, bedraggled and defeated, through town, providing a living symbol of the fall of white supremacy and the rise of a new order.[41] Gay Wuan Guay was struck by the "long marches to Changi Jail, to Sime Road. It was a pitiful sight!" They saw their former "bosses marching haltingly, lamely and some of them begging for water." Singaporeans "were no longer cringing like before" when they "stammered . . . 'yes, sir.' . . . and could hardly reply when they were addressed by a European or Englishman. But now they could look at a European straight in the eye. Somehow or other the psychological breakthrough happened." This was the beginning of a "new spirit of independence among the young people. Even the older people (the leaders) felt that it was time, they realized that the white supremacy was a myth; that it was time that independence should be taken seriously. . . . That was the beginning of this political awakening. . . . We felt the British were not superhuman, supermen, as we used to think."[42]

The Japanese methodically ingratiated themselves with the local population.[43] But then again, anything they did in this sphere would have made them stand out, given the abysmal policies of their British predecessors. Zamroude Za'ba was born in Malaya in 1921 and worked with the new occupiers as a clerk in the police department during the war. As she recalled it, the "good thing" about "those Japanese there" was that "they could speak Malay rather well," unlike the British; in turn, she learned Japanese.[44] Mary Lim, born in Malacca in 1922, had a grandmother who also learned Japanese, simply "by hearing their conversation. . . . They come quite often to my grandmother, at my grandmother's invitation. . . . So that's how she picked up Japanese. . . . They were very nice to my grandmother."[45] This friendliness coupled with opportunities for education and the advancement of locals was in dramatic contrast to the Empire. As Robert Chong noted, "In a way, working with them, they impart their full knowledge to you. That's why I give them full credit for that. They teach you sincerely and they will encourage you wholeheartedly. Definitely."[46] Tan Ban Cheng also compared them favorably over the British.[47]

Lt. M. M. Pillai of India was part of the British military and served on the Malay peninsula but even he observed that compared to their European counterparts, "the Japanese could get to the heart of the Asiatics by sitting down and talking with them on terms of perfect equality. . . . It would have been a miracle if any European had condescended to do that. This was the trump card of the Japanese." Furthermore, "in all Japanese retail shops in Singapore the salesmen were Malays or Indians," while "Eurasian girls were employed by the Japanese as steno typists, telephone operators and as sales girls." The "Sultan of Johore had given concessions to the Japanese in his state to work the iron ore mines and the Japanese owned many rubber estates in the states. Many Japanese had become Mohammedans and this flattered the Malays a good deal." At one point "at a meeting of the nine rulers of the states which was held at the Adelphi Hotel, the Sultan of Johore was reported to have stated that there was Japanese blood in the veins of some of the Malay Sultans."[48]

Conventional wisdom[49] holds that the new colonizers favored the Indians and Malays and persecuted the Chinese,[50] as an extension of the war taking place in China.[51] But Charlie Gan, born in Singapore in 1919, disagrees with this generalization. "From the point of the Japanese being harsh or cruel to us, we didn't really experience that, especially after the initial occupation, say about a year later. I think we enjoyed quite a peaceful life in Singapore." No, he continued, the Malays and Indians were not favored. "Not that I know of. . . . Skin alone doesn't work if the fellow is useless to them. They must be useful to them."[52] F. A. C. Oehlers did not feel that the Japanese ignored "skin." To the contrary, Europeans of every stripe were interned and wives too even if they were married to "local people"—but "their offspring . . . were not, funnily, because they were considered to be Singaporeans."[53]

Whatever the subsequent recollections, the fact is that the major anti-Japanese forces during the war "were almost exclusively Chinese." The Chinese forces "could not rely on either the Malays or the Indians, amongst whom no comparable movements existed."[54] Ironically, these same anti-Nippon forces—often Communist-led—were later forced into a bitter conflict with the returning colonialists from London after the war ended. This conflict prefigured the longer and better known war in Vietnam.

The friendly recollections of Japanese rule may not have been ex post facto fabrications.[55] As late as November 1943, a "secret/confidential" report of the Allies acknowledged that "the Malayans on the whole appeared to be indifferent as to whether the British returned or not."[56] Once more, this says more about the Empire than it does about Tokyo.

Even after the Japanese were forced out of power in Singapore and the surrounding region, their presence was considerable. The methodical propaganda offensive they had conducted against white supremacy, the unforgettable sight of unkempt and subjugated Europeans marching off to an uncertain fate with Japanese soldiers pointing bayonets at their backs, the positions occupied by Malays in particular after the fall of the Empire—all this and more ensured that the status quo ante would no longer prevail. Although Arthur Alexander Thompson, a Eurasian born in Singapore in 1925, was quite critical of the new colonizers, even he admitted that "with the Japanese coming to Singapore, they have taught the people one thing. . . . that the people here should get independence." Moreover, after the war "all the British had gone back to their homes and our own people took over all these top posts. Before that you'll never be able to take up [major] posts. . . . We had few local people who were Inspectors. There were British Inspectors. . . . The principal Commissioner of Police, all [were] Europeans. Even the General Hospital too, the Sisters [nuns] always [British], no local person could be a Sister. That's true, that was the case. And the same thing goes to the City Council. . . . Municipal Commissioners, they were all Europeans, all English people on top and none of our people were able to run the department being right at the top. We always worked down below."[57] But after the invasion, this changed for good.

Ismail Zain also detected some change among the British after the war. "They changed a little bit. They are not so proud, not so arrogant as before. They were very arrogant before, you know." This war, he thought, was a "blessing in disguise. . . . If not for this war, I don't think Asian nations that are already now independent could get independence so soon."[58] After the war, Ng Seng Yong also had a "very poor opinion of the British, very poor . . . because they let us down badly. Through their propaganda we were mostly misled. . . . Later on we found that in fact the British has got no quality. No quality as far as fighting spirits is concerned, they got nil. . . . For me personally I have one thing to say that the Japanese invasion practically changes the destiny of Southeast Asian people. . . . Had it not been for the Japanese war, we would still be calling the British our masters. . . . Had it not been for the [Japanese] . . . I [would] probably still be working as a clerk. . . . I won't be what I am today."[59] Tan Ban Cheng agreed. Previously, "a lot of Asians had a sort of inferiority complex." Then the Japanese "instilled in us . . . the fact that we could do a lot of things, also as good as any other people in the West." After the war, "people did not look so much toward the West for their direction, for their dominance in our affairs."[60]

F. A. C. Oehlers recalled that previously there was an "in-born feeling, this feeling was inculcated in us—that the white man was lord, you know, and you were second-class," though "we had so many competent Singapore people, local people, who were teaching and getting half the salary that young recruits from England were getting. Things like that irked us." They were "not permitted to enter Tanglin Club. . . . not permitted to [set] foot in the Swimming Club." But the occupation "made us see also, like it did everybody else; that the white skin, the white person, the white man, wasn't [as] all-powerful as he declared himself to be in the colonial era. And if anything good did come out of the Japanese Occupation, it was independence. And I'm sure independence would have been a long time coming if not for the war. . . . not only in Singapore, all over in India, Ceylon. We got to know that the British Empire was not invincible."[61]

Tan Wee Eng, born in Singapore in 1919, discovered that after the war, "the British I noticed were little bit more humbler [sic], before that they were real colonialists." But after their defeat they were "more civil. I noticed that in my own department. And they became more friendly—everyone that I knew. . . . I found I could make friends easily with all my British [associates]" who had formerly thought themselves "superior." Before they were "ordering you about" with "no sort of warmness, no friendship, just work and purely work and literally you were like slaves or labourers to them. There was not much friendship involved. . . . They were . . . snobbish, snooty" as if "they belonged to [a] different society or different class or different creed." Before "the Chinese were left out" of the sports competition for "the Naval Dockyard in the Singapore Cup" but afterward that changed. Before he had to go to "the canteen for Asiatics, they called it . . . [through] the back door." But afterward he could go where "they were serving the officers. So I went there and I ate the British set-lunch. Beautiful! I enjoyed [it] and paid like a duke of course. . . . Beautiful steaks, pork-chops, chicken, mash potatoes. . . . I enjoyed it very much. . . . It was like heaven returned after the Japanese occupation." Thus, he found the arrival of the Japanese "very good, personally I think. To me, it was a blessing in disguise . . . It was the sparkle, the dawn of awakening for Asian people. . . . And not only that, I think the dawn of Afro-Asian people also. The Japanese taught us that Asians can fight, can stand up and do things for themselves and not to depend on foster fathers. . . . It led to the fall of the British Empire."[62]

Like the Ratana in New Zealand and some Negroes in the United States, the attempt to trace blood ties between the Japanese and Malays was symptomatic of an increasingly close relationship between Tokyo and those who were hostile toward white supremacy. Again, London was well aware of this gathering storm but found itself incapable of responding effectively, possibly because such action might have meant disrupting prevailing racial practices. Thus, in its annual report on Siam in 1937, London's emissary in a "confidential" report spoke of a "typically stupid piece of Japanese propaganda," that is, a "speech delivered by the military attache at a cocktail party given by him to the Bangkok press. In this oration he made the egregious statement that the present situation in China might lead Japan to wage war with the white races."[63]

This "stupid propaganda" fed on colonial practices. Mrs. U. M. Streatfield recalled that in Bangkok in 1931 there were "about a thousand Europeans living and working there and perhaps five hundred of these were British. The rest were Danes, Americans, Germans, French, Dutch, Swiss and many others but the communities mixed a good deal. At any party there might be six or seven nationalities present." It was an "astonishing place for parties of every sort"—"we went to a great many parties" and "played a great deal of bridge," she observed fondly. This ostentation hardly embraced the Siamese. Though Bangkok may not have been as bad as Bombay, where "at night multitudes slept in the streets" and the dainty had to "step over sleeping bodies," it was not Valhalla either.[64]

Hence, it should have come as no surprise to the Empire to learn from one of its agents in the summer of 1944 that "the Siamese appeared to work in harmony with the Japanese and it is considered that an attempt to drive the Japanese from Thailand would not be welcomed."[65] The British seemed paralyzed by such threats. They had hoped that Tokyo would pulverize the Communists throughout the region, and in the prewar era were reluctant to do anything to interfere with this possibility. Tokyo often was given the run of the Empire because of its sterling anticommunist credentials. Thus, another "confidential" report in 1938 from the British legation in Tokyo spoke of a "Burmese engineer" who noted that the "Japanese are sending commercial travellers and other business and professional men to Burma with instructions to spread anti-British and Pan-Asia propaganda." Their informant chose to "pass as a Japanese," spoke "Japanese fluently," had had a "Japanese wife," and was in a unique position to uncover acts of subversion by Tokyo.[66]

Tokyo's "Pan-Asia propaganda" in Burma[67] seemed to be vindicated when the British evacuated Rangoon and other areas. When the war began, "motor convoys" were used "mainly for Europeans, Anglo-Burmans or Anglo-Indians employed by the Burmah Oil Company. . . . There was preferential treatment for Europeans and Anglo-Indians."[68] Ho-yungchi spoke sarcastically of "Dorman-Smith," the "British Governor of Burma" and his "stroke of sheer genius." This "bumbling colonial governor had segregated black and white refugees. The whites were either evacuated to India early, aboard ship, or were flown out on Indian Airways or China National Aviation Corporation planes. The natives were sent out on what became known as the 'black trail.' . . . An estimated 400,000 black refugees tried to escape by these trails. . . . The forlorn fugitives died by the tens of thousands from starvation and disease." Not only were the "Indians" of Burma "barred from white trails" but "so were the Chinese."[69]

"Colonel the Rt. Hon. Sir Reginald Dorman-Smith" in numerous "secret" dispatches from Burma agreed. As early as January 1942 he was reporting that a "Thakin fifth column was extremely active" there. "They led Japs [sic] around our forces and created all necessary disturbances."[70] After the biased evacuation process, "Morale has definitely deteriorated especially among Indian community. Servants are now wanting to leave. . . . It is now being said that Europeans will look after themselves and leave others to their fate." But the feisty Sir Reginald had not given up all hope. "Two of [the] main human instincts," he thought, "are Love and Fear. It may well be that this part of the world do not love us. What we have to do is to make them fear the Japs [sic]."[71]

But soon pessimism set in. By March 1942 Dorman-Smith was admitting that the "Japanese occupation has generally been accepted with

a grace which must be gratifying to the Japanese. The Thakins have actively co-operated in every way with them and where necessary have
applied persuasion to bring their fellow Burmans into line. . . . It is definitely disappointing that after all our years of occupation of both
Lower and to a lesser degree Upper Burma we have not been able to create that loyalty which is generally associated with our subject nations.
But I fear that we must accept the fact that we have not repeat not in-
ducted that sort of loyalty which will withstand adversity."[72]

Just as many U.S. Negroes had difficulty during the war accepting
that London was the hero and Tokyo the villain, many in Burma did
too. Some nationalists felt that Tokyo "represented a resurgent Asia
against European domination." As in the United States, those who were
close to the Communists vehemently disagreed.[73] But, as elsewhere, the
Communists had been so effectively destabilized that the path was
smoothed nicely for the rise of Japanese-oriented nationalists.

London's reluctance to arm Africans on African soil or the Chinese
on Chinese soil was matched by its hesitation to arm the Burmese in
Burma. In 1939 the Burma Defense Forces "contained only 472 Burmans
as against 3197 Karens, Chins and Kachins." It was deemed "imprudent
to enlist Burmans in a force which might have to be used against their
fellow countrymen."[74] On the other side, Japan was enlisting forces of
all kinds. Even animals were included. For example, "trained" monkeys were taught to "carry a length of string to the top of a tree, loop the
string over a strong branch near the top and then drop the string to the
ground. A strong rope was fastened to the string and the rope was easily pulled over the branch and back to the ground. A Japanese soldier
would then climb up the rope whilst his companions anchored the
other length. Reaching the top the Japanese used it as . . . a visual signaling station."[75]

Bolting the prison gate after the inmates had fled, London now recognized that the new regime in Rangoon was popular in part[76] because
it was "opening . . . some of the higher posts in Government services to
those who had not learned English in school, the friendly attitude towards the common people by their co-religionists the Japanese, whom
they believe would raise their standard of living more so than the
British had done or would do." Almost incredulously the British noted
that "there was no discrimination made by the Japanese between Indians and Burmans, Hindu-Moslem animosity was now not heard of in
Burma."[77]

Izumiya Tatsuro, who was Japanese, was intimately involved with the struggle in Burma, including training the renowned "30 comrades" (Aung San among them) in military warfare. As he reviewed the military situation before the war, he could only smile in anticipation. "There were only 25,000 British troops. Moreover, of these, only 4000 were truly British; there were 7000 Indians and the rest was made up of Karens, Kachins, Gurkhas, etc." During "the period of British rule, the Burmans who comprised 70% of the population, were kept at arm's length while the hill races like Karens and Kachins were used as mercenary soldiers." The Empire's reliance on minorities handed the disaffected majority to Tokyo on a platter. "When the war broke out," Tatsuro said with glee, "the Burmese people welcomed the Japanese everywhere. The instances indeed [were] many." As they entered villages, "there was the undisputed call of the blood that came from our being fellow Asians, and there was a feeling of intimacy." Subsequently, the Burma Independence Army—like the Indian National Army—fought shoulder to shoulder with Tokyo against the Empire.[78]

Tokyo also had devoted considerable attention to Islam, the dominant faith in the nation that was to become Pakistan as also in Indonesia, the world's largest predominantly Muslim nation.[79] The 1943 celebration in Tokyo of the seventy-seventh birthday of Viscount Naganari Ogasawara was typical.[80] A number of Muslims were present. Over the years, Ogasawara had forged solid relations with Yemenis in particular—whose territory was held dear by London, particularly the strategically located port of Aden.[81] The BBC acknowledged in 1942 that Tokyo's bulletins directed at Muslim audiences were "'good and well-liked.' . . . Tokyo broadcasts in other languages draw fantastic pictures of rioting and revolution throughout the Arab countries" and the Islamic world generally.[82]

The colonialists' definition of subversion was peculiar. The Dutch complained that in Indonesia "Japanese shopkeepers, under instructions from their officials, treated their native customers with a friendliness and civility."[83] Because this contrasted sharply with Dutch practices, it was viewed suspiciously. Indonesia, the world's largest predominantly Islamic nation and rich in oil and other resources, emulated the Malay peninsula in welcoming the invaders. Patrick Hardie, in wartime service for the Japanese in Singapore, recalled driving the Indonesian national hero, Sukarno, to "Government House together with General Itagaki." He overheard him say he was on his way to "Rangoon," no doubt to confer with pro-Tokyo forces there.[84]

The Allies were aware of the close relationship between the Indonesians and Japanese. In Indonesia it was widely predicted that a "government of yellow men would replace the whites in Java and would thereafter relinquish the government to the natives themselves."[85] The Australians had good reason to monitor this relationship. A "most secret" report in 1942 noted that there had been "ten years of Japanese penetration in the Dutch East Indies." The notorious Black Dragon Society of Japan, it said, had financed the "education of some fourteen students who were sent to Arabia and Egypt in 1935." This was all part of a crusade to have Tokyo "proclaimed Protecter of Islam." The Australians could not believe that anyone would deign to treat the Indonesians courteously, scoffing at the fact that Japanese "shop-keepers" in Indonesia sought to "treat their native clients with particular friendliness" and tried to "treat the native races as equal." The behavior of the Japanese was cynical, unfair, and dirty pool, the report suggested.[86]

As the occupation of Indonesia continued, the Empire became increasingly pessimistic about the return of their Dutch ally to power. Days before D-Day in Europe, a "secret" communication lamented that "Japanese propaganda would appear to be effective on the Indonesians [who] now adopted a hostile attitude toward the Dutch. When asked why this should be, source replied that the Indonesians considered the Dutch inefficient as they were unable to keep the Japanese out of Dutch East Indies."[87] This was a major legacy of the Japanese occupation: white supremacy or the notion of European superiority was the glue that had held colonial empires together; however, when Japan showed that this "superiority" was a chimera, the colonized felt cheated. They felt tricked; they were angry about what they had endured and were determined that it would not happen again—even at the hands of fellow "coloreds."

Nevertheless, the unpopularity of the Dutch allowed the Japanese to integrate into the fabric of Indonesian society. Other than the "Dutch-Indonesian half-breeds," who were considered "extremely anti-Japanese," much of the population, according to one study, including the "overseas Chinese" were relatively pro-Tokyo. The expulsion of the Eurasians and Europeans resulted in a "tremendous upward rise in socio-economic status" of the indigenous people.[88]

The Dutch had repressed the nationalist movement in Indonesia while the Japanese worked with it and, to cite one example, "considerably built up the archipelago's radio network." While the Dutch had sought to squash the Indonesian Reds, the Japanese established schools with instructors known to be close to the Communist party that, inter alia, taught classes in Marxism. Admiral Mayeda of Japan "and the naval intelligence officers who helped him run the schools soon came to give principal emphasis to the study of communism. They stressed the need for nationalization of production but the chief emphasis of their teaching was negative, anti-imperialism and anti-capitalism being the dominant themes." Why? This may have been a way to split the PKI, the party of Indonesian Communists, then allied (like Communists globally) with the leading "imperialists," including the Dutch, in an anti-Comintern alliance.[89]

Decades after the war this alliance persisted. The leading Indonesianist, Benedict Anderson, found it unfathomable that in the 1960s, the Indonesian Communist Party, one of the largest in the world at the time, had "rallies" that "feature[d] anti-Western songs composed under the brutally repressive—and anticommunist—Japanese occupation regime of 1942–1945."[90]

Europeans faced similar problems in neighboring East Timor. In 1942, as the Japanese landed, a unit of "about 600 troops, mostly natives, retreated to the mountains from the town without defending it and gradually disintegrated." Even the haughty Sir Henry Robert Moore Brooke-Popham had to concede in a "most secret" telegram that the Portuguese "young officials" who were forced to flee were "Fascists."[91] Would the new colonizers from Japan be worse than them?[92]

India was the heart of the Empire. Indeed, there could be no Empire without this massive, subcontinental nation, not only because of the wealth it generated but also because of its "human capital" that provided laborers, soldiers, and the like throughout the Empire. Not surprisingly, India was also targeted early on by Japan, though given the unpopularity of London in Delhi, Indians were courting as much as they were being courted. As early as 1912, London in a "top secret" document suspected that "Japanese Spies" were active in India. An Indian patriot, R. B. Bose, was suspected of conspiring to murder a leading British official; Bose fled to Japan.[93]

Acknowledging that India was chafing under British rule,[94] censorship was tight. Thousands of miles away the Negro writer Lester Walton noted that London "suppress[ed] in India all cinematic portrayals of whites thought to compromise white supremacy and colonial rule." In "99 percent of the films shown in India," he wrote, quoting an Empire analyst in 1921, "the characters are all white people. There is a white hero, a white heroine, a white evil woman and a white villain. . . . Such scenes [of the latter two] shown to illiterate Indian audiences can have no other effect than to lower the prestige of the white woman and the white races in general." This "moral whitewashing," wrote Walton, "this attempt to hide the truth and cause East Indians to believe all Caucasians are 'angels [robed] in spotless white,' is merely wasted energy."[95] This cinematic distortion was not ignored by the Indians themselves. Just as war was about to explode in Europe, M. K. Gandhi dispatched a mission to Hollywood to "urge American film companies to cease depicting the great Indian people as little better than savages."[96]

London disagreed. But a major problem for the Empire was that Indians were to be found not only in South Asia but all the way from the South Pacific to Southern Africa—not to mention Guyana, Trinidad, and the United States itself. A wide net against subversion would have to be built as a result. Another problem was that India and Indians were the epicenter of pro-Tokyo sentiment in the Empire. This was as true for the Malay peninsula, where the Indian population was prominent in the working class, as it was for South Asia.[97]

London was not dumb to this reality. In a "secret" transmission (that ultimately reached Delhi) the British Consul-General in San Francisco reported a typical incident to Foreign Minister Anthony Eden before the onset of the war. Ram Mohan Bagai, an Indian, had arrived in San Francisco "on board the Japanese [ship] in which he had embarked at Kobe," bringing a message from Nehru about "independence."[98] Bagai was an Indian in the diaspora who was close to the independence movement.[99] The reputation of these "diasporans" was so prominent that even Germany considered "possibilities to make use of Indians residing in the United States for the Axis powers."[100] Bagai, who graduated "with honors" from Stanford and the University of Southern California and had lived in the United States since the age of two, called British rule in India "fascism." He also declared that "we are Caucasians, correctly, not Asiatics."[101] Bagai had to concede that Indians were colonized. Yet if people of such high status condemned British rule, what might others think?

London responded by trying to stir up trouble between India and its presumed patron, Japan. When the Indian National Congress failed to make a statement condemning Japan after a "Kobe Mosque dispute in Tokyo," the British made an issue of it, apparently oblivious to its implications for Buddhist-Muslim or Hindu-Muslim relations.[102] In neighboring Afghanistan the Empire went further, cooking up "propaganda material stressing the detestation of [the INC] for all things Japanese. . . . This is because of rumors in this country that Congress are supporters of Japan and would welcome the Japanese in India."[103] Again, the impact on interethnic relations was ignored. But even the most virulent anti-Japanese propaganda that was devised by Indians expressed its antipathy to white supremacy.[104]

London had good reason to worry about Japan-India relations.[105] According to one conservative estimate, of the "60,000 Indian prisoners-of-war" captured by Tokyo after the invasion of the Malay peninsula, "about 25,000 joined the Japanese-sponsored . . . Indian National Army." Many of these were Gurkhas, who had a reputation for fierce fighting. The Indian National Congress of Gandhi and Nehru "exploited the INA for all it was worth" in its effort to gain independence in the midst of war.[106]

Racial discrimination facilitated the mass defection of thousands of Indians formerly serving with the British military. "Indian officers were not admitted as members of a large number of clubs in Malaya," wrote Shah Nawaz Khan, an officer of the 14th Punjab regiment who later led an INA brigade against the British in Burma. "There was an order by the Railway Authorities of the Federated Malay States that an Asiatic could not travel in the same compartment as a European, and the fact that both held the same rank and belonged to the same unit did not seem to matter in this respect." Lieutenant-Colonel Mahmood Khan Durrani, later decorated by the Viceroy of India with the George Cross for resisting Japanese torture, made the same point. Such resentment was nurtured by Tokyo.[107]

Tokyo made great strides in quickly winning over sizable portions of the Indian and Malay populations.[108] The anti-Tokyo chiefs were disproportionately made up of Communist leaders of Chinese origin who had been pounded by the British before the war, and who were deserted by their former British allies soon after the war ended.

Indians from other parts of the world also organized anti-British activities.[109] In April 1943 there was a major conference of Indians in the disapora in Tokyo, with representatives from Thailand, Japan, Manchuria, "Borneo and Celebes, Sumatra, Philippines. . . . China. . . . Indo-China and Andamans," along with Malaya. The conference denounced the Empire's policies of "jailing of leaders" and repression. A leading Japanese military man in contrast stressed that "through cultural relations and Buddhism, we, Nipponese have had traditional respect and affection for India for more than 2000 years and it has indeed been unbearable to us to see the present slavery that India is undergoing under the rule of Great Britain."[110] For their part, representatives of the India Independence League enumerated the sins committed by the Empire, not least the fact that it had "exterminated the entire aboriginal races of America and Australia to make room for themselves."[111] Later they scoffed at the Atlantic Charter, since "it leaves out of its scope countries like India." It was no more than a "fresh lease for Asiatic slavery," they gibed. They contrasted it with the Tokyo-backed "Greater East Asia Assembly with its insistence on the elimination of racial discrimination."[112]

The human touch, alien to white supremacy, helped to win over many Indians. Fujiwara Iwaichi of the Japanese forces was struck when he ate "Indian dishes" with an Indian officer after his surrender, and was told, "I cannot think of an occasion when Indian officers have ever had dinner together with British officers with whom we have fought side by side. Despite our firm request that Indian dishes be put on the menu at the officers' club, it was turned down by the British Army." This Japanese major, serving in intelligence, played a pivotal role in the founding of the INA and remained a hero in India years later.[113]

But the greatest hero for defecting Indians was Subhas Chandra Bose. The Indian writer P. A. Narasimha Murthy is not alone in observing "the only other leader who equaled, even surpassed him in impressing the younger minds was Jawaharlal Nehru"—even today—despite his fighting shoulder to shoulder with Japanese forces in Burma against the British Empire and their allies.[114] Bose was not alone. After the seizure of Hong Kong, the INC was grappling with the question of whether it should ally with India's colonial oppressor, London. In a "confidential draft" the INC wrestled with the fact that the Empire was "determined to maintain and intensify their imperialist hold and exploitation of the Indian people." How could Indians back London when "the whole background in India is one of deep-rooted hostility and distrust of the British government?"[115]

Bose was "extremely friendly" with local Communists despite their hostility toward Tokyo and support for the Allies during the war. It would be "utterly wrong," says Gautam Chattopadhyay, to see him—and by implication other victims of white supremacy—as a "kind of quisling of the Axis powers." There was his "refusal" to fight the Soviet Union or the Burmans who turned against Japan in 1945. Chattopadhyay argues that "Aung San in Burma, Soekarno . . . in Indonesia, in fact all anti-imperialist leaders of Southeast Asia with the solitary exception of Ho Chi Minh . . . followed [Bose's] strategy."[116]

"Bose's strategy" included a powerful appeal to Indians scattered throughout Southeast Asia. The Empire knew that the pro-Tokyo "so-called 'Indian National Army'" had an "estimated strength of force in Malaya" of "16,000/20,000." "Tamil civilians recruited in Malaya predominate." The Tamils, who played a key role in both South India and Ceylon, were often bitterly hostile to the Empire.[117]

Tamils and other Indians predominated in the army that was sworn to uphold the Empire in Asia, which presented a problem that resonated even after the end of the war. Weeks after the bombing of Hiroshima a "secret" report from the "Intelligence Bureau" in India noted the proliferation of Indians taking "exception to [the Indian National] Congress' repeated assertion that Subhas Bose and his followers were 'misguided' in seeking Japanese aid. . . . [Bose] was merely using the Japanese as his tools," said one Indian, "just as the British employ coloured troops to fight their battles for them." In India, "the almost universally expressed view has been that Bose and his INA although misguided in hoping to obtain freedom through Japanese help acted with the highest motives of freedom. . . . From this follows on an equally widespread demand, supported by almost all shades of Indian opinion . . . for extreme leniency" toward the INA, a sentiment that could hardly be ignored.[118]

Damodaran K. Kesavan of Malaya, born in Kerala, India, in 1918 was among the many who joined the Indian National Army (INA) early on. While interviewed in 1981, he still recalled the Japanese phrase—"Aji, Ajino, Ajia!"—Asia for Asians—"that was their slogan." Kesavan, suitably impressed, collaborated closely with the Japanese during the occupation and even learned the language. "The language construction," he said, "was just like our Indian language—construction of sentences and everything just like our Indian language." The Japanese-speaking Kesavan joined the "big crowd" that assembled "in our streets" when Tojo arrived. He was also part of the throngs that greeted Subhas Chandra Bose when he arrived in Singapore. It was raining and Bose was offered an umbrella. Brushing it aside, he inquired, "Can you provide [an] umbrella for all these people?" The crowd was visibly moved by his altruism, as Bose switched effortlessly between English and Hindi.

When asked if the Japanese had encouraged him to join the INA, he was forthright: "No . . . no . . . no. Never. Never." He was not alone, as INA ranks were flooded with "engineers . . . and all professional groups." There was a "full cross-section" of the "Indian" population in the INA, the "whole of India" was represented. "Nobody was concerned about the religious feelings of the others." There were more "Sikhs" than others but then "they formed the bulk of the [pre-occupation] army." "All" of his "relatives" joined, since, unlike the British, "We felt a sense of dignity and freedom from the Japanese."[119]

K. M. Rengarajoo, born in 1915, also recalled vividly that rainy rally with Bose in Singapore. Sheets of precipitation were falling "but not a single soul moved." He too agreed that there were Indians from "all walks of life," including "a lot of wealthy Indians." The "Indian Muslim" was "giving full support" too, though "they couldn't get the approval of the Japanese higher authority" to form a separate organization. The residence of Bose when he visited Singapore, at "Meyer Road No. 61" became a veritable shrine, despite—or perhaps because of—his fervent stand against the Empire.[120]

Narayana Karuppiah was born in India in 1925; he too joined the INA and studied Japanese and was a devotee of Subhas Chandra Bose, comparing him "equally" to "Prime Minister Lee Kuan Yew . . . Had he been alive, and had he reached India, Nehru would not [have] become the Prime Minister. Definitely. [Nehru] would have been the Foreign Minister." When he met with Bose one day in Singapore, Bose advised him to go to Tokyo for advanced training. He did so. But on the day he arrived—a day on which Bose happened to be in town—the United States bombed. "We surrounded him," so that "even if there were any bomb, the shrapnel wouldn't [hit] him." It did not and Bose went on to address a rally of "thousands" in "Hibiya Park" in Tokyo.

Karuppiah was quick to point out that the INA training in Japan was paid for by Indians themselves—"everything," he insisted. Contrary to London's claims, Japan "did not do anything, not even a single cent for us." At the military academy in Tokyo, there were also "students from Thailand, Burma, Manchuria, Machuko, Philippines, Singapore and Indians."[121]

Despite the transparent reasons why Indians and others deserted the Empire at its moment of need in Singapore, some Britishers had difficulty coming to grips with this reality. Sir Henry Robert Moore Brooke-Popham, writing from the safety of Australia in 1942, pointed to the "low morale [of] Indian troops" as a "prime cause" of the "failure" in Malaya. This, he snorted, was "due" to the "eastern races" being "less able to withstand" the "strain" of "modern war." On the other hand, he thought that "special mention is due to [the] white population for devotion to duty."[122]

The Indian diaspora presented complications for the Empire beyond the Malay peninsula. In 1943, a "confidential" message to the future Prime Minister, Clement Atlee, reported that although there were only "2547 souls" among the "Indians in S. Rhodesia," they still created an "Indian problem." The "set-aside [of] a residential area for the Asiatic[s]" in one capital neighborhood was rejected by Europeans in "Belvedere," since the reserved area was too close for comfort.[123] As in southern Africa, a similar dilemma confronted the Empire in the South Pacific. According to a New Zealand analyst, during the "Pacific War when Europeans and [indigenous] Fijians supplied all possible manpower against the Japanese, the Fijian Indian community did absolutely nothing—only a handful of Indians engaged in non-combatant units."[124]

London had to be concerned about this growing estrangement and disaffection within the broader Indian diaspora, particularly in Africa, which provided tens of thousands of troops for the Empire. By early 1945 the Colonial Office was taking worried note of the "known attitude on racial relations of the white communities of the Union of South Africa, Southern Rhodesia and Kenya colony." One clear reason was the fierce opposition to this "attitude" by Indians who often faced discrimination in all three nations. "The Indians," the Colonial Office said, "have now come to regard the European communities from the Cape to Ethiopia as a bloc endangering the Indians' political welfare and other interests."[125]

Then there was nagging fear about the Indians of British China. U.S. intelligence in a "restricted" report in 1944 anxiously noted that the

Indians there "largely belong[ed] to the Sikh community. A revolutionary movement, dating from the years of the last war, fed by resentment
against the British and influenced by Chinese nationalist activities,
flourished in Shanghai." In fact, Japan was the "center of Indian nationalist activities in eastern Asia. . . . It is probable that few Indians
would have been found to prefer British to Japanese domination." The
report described Subhas Chandra Bose as a "former Congress president
with a large following in India, an able leader, widely considered to be
a sincere patriot." Even before the war there were "Ghadr (revolution)
societies, affiliated with similar organizations on the West Coast of the
United States and elsewhere . . . which conspired for the overthrow of
the British government in India." Like other "coloreds," Indians "generally looked to Japan as the leader of Asia," the report said. The sympathy of this U.S. report for Indians languishing under British colonialism in Asia could only be of somber concern to London.[126]

Of course, the Empire had its own worries about Indians in China—
and the Chinese in India. In 1944 it was noted that "no Indians were interned at Shanghai and they were not required to wear arm bands. The
Free India Movement frequently held parades at the race course which
invariably degenerated into anti-British demonstrations. British political prisoners in Warm Road Gaol were roughly treated by the Indian
guards. The Indian population on the whole were anti-British and they
assisted the Japanese to the best of their ability."[127] A high-level Japanese official confirmed that representatives from the Indian community
in Hong Kong participated in many strategy sessions in Tokyo during
the war.[128]

Though Nationalist China was supposedly an ally of the Empire,
London was also concerned about the migration of Chinese to what it
deemed its turf. In 1944 Britain's Chungking legation observed that
"our information, such as it is, does not in general support the theory of
'Chinese colonisation.'" That was something of a relief, given China's
huge population, but they could not ignore that "Chinese schools in
India cater only for a small number of Chinese children." There was a
troubling "increase in restaurants under Chinese management,"
though it was evident that this was "due to their popularity with the
British and armed forces." But that was small beer compared to "Chinese banking activities which may perhaps have more significance."[129]

Overall there was a "marked increase in Chinese activity in India"
since the war had commenced. There were "seamen" and "deserters"

and "evacuees"; "consular activity and intelligence," "remittances" and "trade." This "secret" report did believe that "Chinese colonization in India has begun" and was being encouraged by the Nationalists, which was of even more concern given that their government had more than one pro-Tokyo sympathizer.[130] Yet how could the Empire complain about supposed Chinese colonialism in India—no matter how real or imaginary—unless colonialism was only to be practiced by those of "pure European descent"?

U.S. intelligence had different concerns. It was studying the notion that the "growth of nationalism in the Far East" was driven in different ways by London and Tokyo. As early as the 1920s, Washington observed the formation of the "Asiatic Society" in Japan, "an organization constituted by the Japanese in their efforts to excite race hatred . . . by using the [immigration] Exclusion Law as an argument for the union of Asiatic races." Indians were essential to the formation of this grouping, according to a "confidential" report. Its purpose was "the reawakening of all Asiatics against the white peoples of the world and the unity of Asiatic nations." The feared ultrapatriotic Black Dragon Society of Japan was integral to this organization, which was determined to move "against white despotism" and their "arrogance toward Oriental nations."[131] When in 1943 a large assemblage of Asian nationals—including a sizable number of Indians—met in Tokyo to work for the "abolition of racial discrimination," U.S. intelligence's fears were confirmed.[132]

Yet for all the upset caused by the Indians of Malaya, Singapore, Africa, and China, it was the Indians in India itself who posed the biggest headache for the Empire. L. H. Landon of the Empire's military discovered this to his dismay. As the war commenced, he was on holiday in eastern India. "When we broached the subject of resistance to the Japs [sic] . . . their answer was always the same." Random Indians would remark generally, "A hundred years ago we were a warlike nation . . . causing you to send in an army to pacify us. But in the last hundred years we have learned the art of peace; you have allowed us no new weapons or warlike activity—we are no longer a fighting race. Yet you ask us, with our spears and muzzle loaders, to resist the Jap [sic] Army, while you, with your tanks and aeroplanes and guns and modern equipment and training, are now fleeing before these same Japs [sic] out of Burma!" Landon found this to be a "reasonable—and unanswerable—argument."[133] It was hard to convince Indians after decades of warping colonialism that they should align with the devil they knew, rather than the one they didn't.

Japanese propaganda stressed the obvious underdevelopment brought about by London, telling the Gurkhas—whom the Empire relied on heavily—that they were "merely a soldier slave" to the British.[134] Apparently such appeals were effective. A "secret" report revealed that "Gurkhas" were working with Japanese forces in northern India.[135] A BBC-directed "private and confidential" "Review of Japanese Broadcast Propaganda" noted that in the prewar era Japanese radio broadcasts "in Hindi [were] one of the chief mouthpieces for the Indian Independence movement." The reviewers were struck by the fact that "most evils of the Far East are attributed to capitalism and capitalism is suggested regularly to listeners as a purely British and American system." Just as some Europeans conflated opposition to the status quo with communism, Tokyo—a capitalist nation for sure—often slyly conflated the status quo with capitalism. In this way, Tokyo added its voice to Moscow's, at a time when the Great Depression was in full swing.

The old-time religion of anti–white supremacy rhetoric was not absent either. As late as September 1940, Japanese broadcasts in Hindi were reassuring Indian listeners that "Japan has no intention to subjugate China but to free China from white domination." Looking to the future, Tokyo also sought to "devote considerable attention to reaching child audiences overseas."[136] The effectiveness of this anti-London propaganda became clear when the "Quit India" movement—consisting of huge strikes and the like—was launched against the British in the midst of the war. In a "secret telegram," London feared that it was "originally timed to coincide with the end of the rains and the moment most favourable for a Japanese attack on India."[137]

The rhetoric emanating from the "All India Congress Committee" routinely referred to the colonizers as the "usurper government." What about the real prospect of Japanese invaders, the Indians were repeatedly asked? Should not the "Quit India" movement be postponed until this threat had passed? This was in October 1942 when a Japanese invasion appeared imminent. But the AICC would not retreat. "Some mealy-mouthed and chicken-hearted people," it replied, "will, of course, suggest that the fight for freedom in such a situation be given up. . . . This is a council [sic] of despair and slavery." To the contrary, "there is greater reason for us to further intensify our fight for freedom in the event of a new invasion."[138]

The "fall of Rangoon," specifically the way in which it was evacuated, may have given Indian patriots added encouragement during the "Quit India" movement. "The British . . . evacuated all their men using all available modes of transportation and had literally abandoned the Indians there." Many Indians escaped to India and complained bitterly about their sense of betrayal, thereby inflaming public opinion.[139]

As the Empire braced for an invasion of India, Washington—bound in an alliance with a tottering London—grew ever more concerned. A small but well-placed Indian American community was also sending troubling signals to the White House. Reverend Swami Prabhavananda of Los Angeles wrote that his nephew, a "British-Indian subject," had come to the United States for higher education. Now he was being drafted. The swami wanted to know the "cause for which he has been asked to go to war. He cannot say to fight for the cause of freedom, for the people of India have not even the right to wish for freedom."[140] The White House had difficulty in responding.

M. K. Gandhi told President Franklin D. Roosevelt in early July 1942, "the Allied declaration that the Allies are fighting to make the world safe for freedom of the individual and for democracy sounds hollow so long as India and, for that matter, Africa are exploited by Great Britain and America has the Negro problem in her own home."[141] These words, which echoed the line coming from Tokyo, said more about London's anomalous position of fighting a war ostensibly for democracy and freedom while denying hundreds of millions of Indians the same.

India was of great strategic importance during the war. Vice President Henry A. Wallace stated correctly as the "Quit India" movement was unfolding that India was the key to the Allies' strategy of defeating Japan. For only via "India alone" could the Allies supply or spark the "recovery of Burma." It was the Allies' "only industrial plant between Great Britain and Australia."[142]

Among the many reasons for the developing rift between London and Washington, the question of India was certainly one. The rising power also naturally wished to replace the waning one. Washington questioned London's stranglehold over huge markets in the Empire through the device of "preference." And many in the United States wondered whether their ultimate sacrifice was simply designed to preserve the Empire. These strains and tensions came to a head in India where FDR's "Personal Representative," William Phillips, criticized Winston Churchill, who he said, "gives the impression that personally he would prefer not to transfer any power to an Indian government either before or after the war and that the status quo should be maintained." But this was incompatible with the Atlantic Charter, which "has given the [Indian] movement great impetus"; a "new idea" was afoot and "sweeping the world," namely, "freedom for oppressed peoples."[143] How could the Allies confront Japan effectively while allowing tiny (white) Britain to rule over huge (colored) India?

Phillips, the U.S. emissary, grew increasingly critical of the Empire with every passing day. He found "increasing anti-British sentiment" in India and with good reason. Mysore had rubber but was "not permitted to produce automobile tires," as it was "turned over to the Dunlop Tire Company, British owned." Indians thought justifiably that the British did not "welcome full development" of their nation due to "competition." "Everywhere" he went in India, he found "a feeling of frustration, discouragement and helplessness."[144] India appeared about to fall into the hands of Tokyo.

In April 1943, as the whole world seemed riveted on a battle to the death between the Axis and the Allies, Phillips found "very little thought given to the war among Indians." They felt "they have nothing to fight for. Churchill's exclusion of India from the principles of the Atlantic Charter is always referred to in this connection. . . . Twenty thousand [Indian National] Congress leaders remain in jail without trial and the influence, therefore, of the Congress party is diminishing while that of the Muslim League is growing." This set the stage for the internecine conflict that gripped the subcontinent and ultimately led to the birth of the predominantly Muslim state of Pakistan. Worse, as other diplomats had found in Malaya and Thailand, Phillips concluded that "it is hard to discover, either in Delhi or in other parts of India, any pronounced war spirit against Japan, even on the part of the British." Indians were ignoring the high-flown rhetoric of the Allies and "coming more and more to disbelieve in the American gospel of freedom of oppressed peoples." They had found a friend across the border in China, as "Chinese apathy and lack of leadership and, moreover, Chinese dislike of the British, meet a wholly responsive chord in India." Phillips reported that "color consciousness is growing more and more," along with "a vast bloc of Oriental peoples who have many things in common, including a growing dislike and distrust of the Occidental."[145]

Privately, the U.S. president was being told that there was ample reason for Indian alienation. They had been drawn into the war "without the formality of consulting Indian leaders or even the Indian legis-lature." Quite naturally, he thought, they felt the Allies were fighting "only for the benefit of the white races," as Tokyo had long said. The In-dians fighting for the Empire were doing so for "purely mercenary" rea-sons. They suffered from "poor morale," that was only exceeded by the "attitude of the general public." By May 1943 "lassitude and indiffer-ence and bitterness" had increased. Yet when Washington raised these issues with London, it replied, "this is none of your business." But the United States was carrying the major burden of the war and saw little reason not to question the Empire's policies. Though the Empire may have been oblivious, Roosevelt's man detected growing "anti-white sentiments of hundreds of millions." The mighty "peoples of Asia"—and he was "supported in this opinion by other diplomatic and military observers"—had begun to "cynically regard this war as one between fascist and imperialist powers."[146]

Phillips's words were reflected in increasing disillusionment in the United States with the idea of Empire, stemming from the prospect of losing India to a Japanese antagonist whose racial appeals were res-onating loudly throughout Asia. One of the major tragedies—no, crimes—of the war took place in this pivotal year, 1943: the famine in Bengal, which claimed the lives of tens of thousands. Anti-Empire sen-timent was strong in Bengal. It was "always a site of unrest" and the famine had led to "much increased evidence of pro-Japanese sympathy among the peasants who are said to be hopeful of a Japanese invasion in the belief that the Japanese would bring them rice from Burma."[147] The famine did not quell pro-Tokyo sentiment in Bengal.

Phillips's blistering condemnation of the Empire did not go down well in London. It is unclear if this U.K. anger might have had anything to do with the fact that "one of" his "confidential letters" to FDR was leaked and disseminated in the press, along with the "equally mysteri-ous publication" of a "cable" from Delhi alleging that he was a "persona non grata."[148] However that may be, Phillips's views reflected a grow-ing consensus in the United States that the Empire, as constituted, was unsustainable, and certainly should not be supported at the cost of U.S. lives and resources.

The respected writer, Pearl Buck, was typical of this trend. India, she told Eleanor Roosevelt, was "so filled with bitterness against the English that we must look for revengeful massacres against all white people on a scale much greater than have taken place in Malaya and

Burma. This I know." U.S. troops in India, she predicted, "must be prepared for a revenge which may fall upon them, too, only because they are helping white men whom the Indians hate." She considered her letter so explosive that she went to extraordinary lengths to insure that only the Roosevelts read it. "I am typing it myself so that I have no copy. Please destroy it when you are finished with it." The president told his spouse, "You can tell Pearl Buck that I have read her letter . . . with real interest. I am keeping her letter in my files."[149]

Washington promptly embarked on a massive counteroffensive both to distinguish itself from London and to present its best face to Asians, particularly Indians. The president was told in the spring of 1942 that Japanese American troops should be sent to "strategic ports of India" for "counter-propaganda" against Tokyo and its Indian allies. This would be more effective than an "Anglo-Saxon appeal."[150]

Of course, U.S. criticism of the Empire was not new, considering that it was born in revolt against London. A quarter of a century before the Pacific War, Secretary of State William Jennings Bryan had written, "British rule in India is far worse, far more burdensome to the people, and far more unjust . . . than I had supposed."[151] But the hothouse of war had exacerbated tensions.

It was not only the Empire's inflexibility on the "color bar" abroad that disappointed Washington. There was even greater concern about the "effect of the sterling bloc on Anglo-American-Indian relations," as a "serious source of Anglo-American-Indian friction."[152] This was good for Britain, bad for the United States. Nor was this closed system of trade and currency good for the colonies either—here the interests of these colonies and Washington and, ironically, Tokyo converged, for destroying "preference" was an aim shared by the United States, Japan, and India. As it stood, the Empire was in dire need of radical reform, particularly in the financial realm.

Thus, through means subtle and blunt, the United States accelerated the delicate process of disentangling itself from its erstwhile ally, Britain. Early in 1944 an aide to FDR was preparing a statement for him on Japan. "The words 'Japanese-occupied' should be substituted for the word 'colonial' since the expression 'colonial territory' would be offensive to the Burmese and play into the hands of the Japanese Propaganda Ministry." Suggesting that Japan be expelled from colonial territory, in other words, might imply the return of the much despised British, intimation of which would be a propaganda coup for Tokyo.[153]

Yet with all the concern about Japanese influence in traditionally British spheres of influence, those at 10 Downing Street appeared oblivious to the undercurrents of the situation. In August 1942, as the Quit India movement gathered speed in India, Churchill told Roosevelt that "you could remind Chiang that Gandhi was prepared to negotiate with Japan on the basis of free passage for Japanese troops through India."[154] The prime minister appeared to overlook the fact that Chiang himself was not estranged from Tokyo. So why would linking Gandhi to Japan cause alarm in Chungking? This was the dilemma for the Empire: by inflicting the "colour bar" on Asia it had alienated Asians. This did not bode well for the future of the Empire. However, moving away from the system of "racial preference" would have been met with hostility by the legions of "third-raters" from Britain who sustained the Empire in Asia.

In addition, the Communist Party of India—like its counterpart in the United States[155]—was keen to back the Allies, particularly after the German attack on the USSR in June 1941. But most Indians were not keen to provide succor to the British. Thus, the party "condemned" the August 1942 rising in India as "folly" and had extreme difficulty explaining its opposition to Bose. The party, said one contemporary observer, "was in an uncomfortable position of appearing to back the government against the patriots." When Congress leaders were arrested in 1942, the fissiparous tendencies were worsened, leading to the splitting of India and the creation of Pakistan. In sum, the events set in motion by Japan's race crusade were of incalculable consequence.[156]

Yet, as many Singaporeans acknowledged, the invasion of the Empire by Japan with all its brutality and death spelled doom for British colonialism in Asia. Certainly it guaranteed that the postwar world would face substantially different racial realities than those that obtained before 1941.

9

Race at War

OF THE NEARLY FIVE HUNDRED THOUSAND MEN in the U.S. army in 1940, only forty-seven hundred were Negroes, all serving in segregated units. Black officers could be counted on one hand—three chaplains, a colonel, and a captain. The navy allowed Negroes to enlist only as messmen. The marines and the air corps excluded Negroes completely. In the most notorious example of this system of racism, blood stored for the wounded was also segregated.[1] Negroes were largely excluded from the naval training academy at Annapolis, Maryland. The "Bureau of Naval Personnel believed that 'the Negroes' relative unfamiliarity with the sea' gave them a 'consequent fear of water.'"[2] Conveniently this also fed into stereotypes about Negroes' alleged unfamiliarity with bathing and the resultant odors they were said to emit.

This was not the optimal armed force with which the United States would be forced to engage Japan in a "race war." If nothing else, it allowed Tokyo to make special appeals to those Negroes who would have to be conscripted and dragooned in order to meet this unique challenge. U.S. national security could be severely threatened. Closing the racial gap between black and white was, as a consequence, not a matter of benevolent and idealistic altruism but that of tough-minded and hard-headed calculation.

Thus, "the largest number of black POWs were located in the Philippines. There were twenty among the more than two thousand POWS from the Los Banos camp. . . . Freed black prisoners told how they were offered better treatment by the Japanese in exchange for cooperation in an anti-white campaign."[3] Even before their capture, Negro troops seemed to be favored. When a "troop transport being fired upon by Japanese was found to contain Negroes . . . Thereupon the Japanese ceased their firing and took the Negroes aboard the ship." The FBI, known to pamper white supremacists, conceded angrily that the

"Japanese attempted to gain favor among the Negroes through frater-nization and increased friendliness."[4]

Yet what may have angered the FBI was the fact that the urgencies of war compelled a halting retreat from white supremacy. In the Philippines there was a fight between "white" and "colored" internees in one camp. During the normalcy of peacetime, this might have led to the lynching of the latter, though it was sparked by an anti-Negro racial slur. But now there was worry that the Japanese captors might hear of it and use it as yet another example of U.S. "race prejudice." Thus, a "trial was duly held and both men were given 60 days' probation."[5]

Racial segregation repeatedly provided added ammunition—figuratively, perhaps literally—for Tokyo, but like a heroin addict who could not resist an injection, London and Washington found it difficult to dump age-old policies although their survival was at stake. Walter White of the NAACP was dumbfounded to discover that "white American troops" in the United Kingdom "had told the townspeople that Negroes had tails, that they were illiterate, that their color was due to disease." Correspondingly, when Negro troops spoke of "the enemy," they referred not to the Nazis across the Channel but to their "white fellow Americans." Tokyo responded with glee: "See what the United States does to its own colored people; this is the way you colored people of the world will be treated if the Allied nations win the war!"[6] White confirmed Tokyo's belief when in June 1942 he pointed to "disturbing rumors" from the "Orient of Southern soldiers treating Indians and Chinese as they are accustomed to treat with impunity Negroes in darkest Mississippi."[7] Long-standing behavior patterns that mandated that those not of "pure European descent" should be accorded inferior treatment could not be reversed quickly just because a worldwide war was raging.

Even efforts to reverse these patterns often seemed to confirm Tokyo's propaganda. In February 1945 many senior white staff officers in the 93rd Infantry Division received a pamphlet entitled "You and the Native," prepared by the command of General Douglas MacArthur. Drawing upon a seductive pseudo-scientific racism, the document suggested that Asians displayed the characteristics of children: "The native has always looked up to the white man. He admires him because of the marvelous things that white men at large can do—make electric torches, fly airplanes, etc. He is also rather afraid of the white men, with all the power of their civilization behind them. Therefore he is afraid of you. The soldier is advised to meet with the native, but as an adult with a child. Don't forget to maintain your position or pose of superiority even if you sometimes have doubts about it."[8] Even the antifascist Asian could be excused for concluding that this pamphlet was no more than a recruiting broadside for Tokyo.

Walter White could only confess to the "bewilderment . . . created throughout the Pacific . . . by the prejudice of some American white soldiers" and their "attempt" to "spread race hatred."[9] He recalled encountering a white soldier from Mississippi "playing with a group of dark-skinned children" in Guam. White asked him if he would do the same at home and was told, "These kids are not niggers."[10]

Such episodes were not conducive to the military's morale or Negroes' fighting spirit. In "Dutch New Guinea" there were complaints that Negro soldiers did not want to fight the Japanese, cutting and running when they appeared. White investigated and was hesitant to help those who were skeptical of Negroes' ability to hold their own on the battlefield. Still, he conceded reluctantly that some Negroes were "breaking under fire, retreating to safety."[11] The alleged unreliability of Negro troops—a highly sensitive matter—was of great concern to Secretary of War Henry L. Stimson.[12]

Reports trickling in from the South Pacific confirmed White's perception that Negro troops were not altogether enthusiastic about the war they were fighting. The "commanding general" of the "93rd infantry division" was told that there was a "marked resentment of various kinds" among the men. "Some resent being in the war at all. They say it is a white man's war and when things are over the Negroes at home will be worse off than before."[13] A Negro soldier in the dreary forests and mountains of "Dutch New Guinea" may have been the author of those encapsulating words of the black experience during the Pacific War: "Just carve on my tombstone, 'here lies a black man killed fighting a yellow man for the protection of the white man.'"

To be fair, Negroes were not the only ones with grave doubts about the Pacific War. A Native American said of his people, "They feel that this country was taken away from them by white men and for that reason they should not now be required to help in case of invasion or attack." A Native American soldier recounted that "In Okinawa . . . I was almost shot by soldiers on my own side who mistook me for the enemy when I came out of a cave. One of my white buddies came out just in time to save me." One of his so-called comrades shouted at him, "Get out of there, you damn Jap [*sic*]!"[14]

Goaded and prompted, the United States took extraordinary measures to combat a white supremacy that previously had been accepted as virtually god-given. Special antiracist films were made, and pamphlets intended to indoctrinate soldiers in the new and developing antiracist consensus were made obligatory by the press of war.[15]

The Japanese were not standing still as the United States moved to reform its centuries-long policies on "race." A Japanese prisoner of war captured in the Philippines began to read material that would later be characterized as "Afrocentric." He was taken by the points made about the "racial superiority of blacks" though he could not "readily agree with this fanatical author, but belonging as I do to a race that the world regards as second class, I applaud his frontal attack on racial prejudice. No doubt it was because of the damage my own racial self-esteem had suffered that I was so drawn to pictures of blacks in the magazines I read." He became even more sympathetic toward Negroes when he saw how Negro prisoners were treated by the Euro-Americans they encountered. He asked a Euro-American guard what he thought of his compatriots, Negroes. "Niggers are cowards in combat," the guard snarled, "and I'm betting we'll have all kinds of trouble with 'em once this war is over because we buttered them up so much in the services." He was struck by the stark contrasts between the two groups of U.S. citizens, for at the camp Negroes "whatever their status, the manner in which they went mutely about their work with their eyes to the ground contrasted sharply with the free and easy manner of the white men I had seen. In essence," he concluded sadly, in a chilling reminder of the fate he thought he had eluded by waging war, "they still acted like slaves."[16]

But it would take more than antiracism on paper and celluloid to reverse centuries of white supremacy. In the spring of 1944 as the war dragged on, Brigadier General Leonard Russell Boyd who had oversight of Negro troops in the South Pacific, conceded that the very structure of racial segregation hampered unit cohesion and battlefield readiness. "Our officer problems are multiplied by having mixed white and Negro officers in the same companies; however, we never place whites under colored officers in accordance with directed policy." But just as the irreligious often discovered the deity as bullets whizzed past their heads, General Boyd found that "racial problems are no problem during actual combat. Here we have died-in-the-wool southerners sleeping in the same 2-man foxhole with colored officers and there is no friction."[17]

General Boyd may have been overoptimistic, for throughout the war there were sharp interracial tensions in the military. At times those "2-man foxholes" were a picture of mortal combat—though Japan was not the target. Not atypical was a riot that rocked a naval ammunitions depot in June 1943. The following month more than seven hundred Negroes of the 80th Construction Battalion staged a protest over segregation aboard the transport that was carrying them to their duty station in the Caribbean, where they would have encountered further antipathy toward the Empire. Guam, a frequent site of battles with Japan, was also a site of frequent conflict between "white marines and black sailors . . . over relations with local women. . . . Sailors began to arm themselves illicitly with rifles and knives,"[18] as the Japanese adversary sat back contentedly.

But Japan knew that the racial segregation practiced so assiduously by its adversaries was like adding a fully armed battalion to Tokyo's already well-armed forces. It kept close tabs on the subject, methodically filing documentation on "influential Negro Leaders today" (Du Bois was listed as an "intellectual leader"), "important Negro publications,"[19] "discrimination against colored seamen," and information on the "Double V" campaign against fascism abroad and at home spearheaded by the black press. Details on black troops were collected as well, including the names and ranks of officers, along with the racial breakdown of various U.S. states—information that might prove helpful in case the mainland had to be invaded. Tokyo also kept records about the sizable and growing black population of Liverpool. Tokyo had data on Negro illiteracy, death rates, occupational status, education, and population. Tokyo took note of an editorial underscoring that "examples of race discrimination in the U.S. are being used by Axis radio propaganda to weaken the will of Negro troops . . . in the Southwest Pacific and Africa." No doubt Japanese leaders were happy to see their radio broadcasts being cited in the U.S. press, for example, when they told their listeners "[FDR] stated recently that he was against race discrimination. One might ask the President why he was segregating Negroes."[20]

Part of the problem was, again, that Negro soldiers—like Negro civilians back home—had doubts not only about their white fellow citizens but also about their Chinese allies. The well-respected black publisher and writer, Charlotta Bass of Los Angeles, questioned "Madame Chiang Kai-Shek" when the latter visited Los Angeles in the spring of 1943. When Bass asked her about her "country's attitude toward race prejudice as practiced in the United States," she was disconcerted by Madame Chiang Kai-Shek's response; Bass had "no idea that such a question would rebound so unfavorably. But it brought the creamy little lady to her feet instantly and she beat a hasty retreat. On the way out she mumbled, 'That is a national question.'"[21]

Bass was particularly shocked as reports of the Chinese visitor being harassed during her tour of the South were well-known. Moreover, unlike Japan in the aftermath of World War I, China lost considerable black support when it seemed less enthusiastic than Japan in pushing for a racial equality proviso in the postwar dispensation. This was consistent with other reports about Chinese attempts to keep Negro troops out of China.[22] There were frequent complaints about "Jim Crow by [the] Chinese army" and "anti-racial attitudes" against Negro soldiers. As a result these qualms were conflated with pre-existing questions about Chinese Americans creating a bog of suspicion. As one Negro put it, "I've noticed some of the Chinese restaurant and laundry owners in Harlem. They play dumb when you mention community problems, pretend that they are white when the word race is mentioned, and yet they'll ask us to support such deserving drives as the Chinese Relief, etc."[23] Black San Franciscans had to contend with "numerous derogatory references" to themselves in local Chinese newspapers.[24]

Many Chinese were reluctant to identify with Negroes, who waged a two-front campaign against racism abroad and at home. In so doing, they chose to ignore the clear parallels between their plight and that of their darker brethren, which was revealed—appropriately enough—by one Harry S. Truman: "I think one man is as good as another so long as he's honest and decent and not a nigger or a Chinaman. Uncle Will . . . says that the Lord made a white man out of dust, a nigger from mud, then threw up what was left and it came down a Chinaman. He does hate Chinese and Japs [sic]. So do I. It is race prejudice I guess. But I am strongly of the opinion that Negroes ought to be in Africa, yellow men in Asia, and white men in Europe and America."[25]

At bottom, Negroes believed that the racial animus directed at Japanese soldiers and civilians alike was similar to their own experience—and to what might await them once the war ended. This too was extremely demoralizing. To the black press, the tendency of U.S. troops to keep as trophies the teeth and bones of dead Japanese soldiers was a macabre replay of what had happened to the victims of lynching in the South.[26] When the scalps of Japanese soldiers were taken and displayed as triumphant prizes, others recalled the recent decimation of Native Americans.[27]

In 1944 Adolph Newton of the U.S. Navy found himself on board a ship in the Philippines. This Negro saw "the body of a Japanese pilot . . . lying on the deck behind the cockpit," and was stupefied when he noticed that "white fellows started to curse him, then someone pulled out a dirk and plunged the blade into the lifeless body; then more people began to stab the body." He "was bothered by the way they treated the body." Not only did they stab it repeatedly, but someone pulled the teeth from the body, and "they called him awful names. I stood there and wondered if they would do that to me. From somewhere came the answer: Yes! It all reminded me of the pictures I had seen of the lynching of Negroes in the southern part of the United States." Newton had just sailed from San Diego where he "saw signs in almost every window with the words 'No Colored Allowed.'" On board he had endured conflicts with his fellow sailors who continually played "boring hillbilly records," while he liked jazz. The pummeling of a Japanese corpse was just one more reminder to him that fighting a race war alongside whites ineluctably led to tensions.[28]

Japan was aware of the cruelty with which its troops were treated, and like Negro soldiers, it too connected this to white supremacy. "Symbolizing the zenith of 20th Century American barbarism," it reported, "is the grim picture of President Roosevelt at his huge desk in the White House fondling a letter opener made from the forearm of a Japanese soldier." This was akin to the "American brutality and atrocity as shown in their lynchings and other discriminations committed against innocent Negroes." This meant that "the peoples living in East Asiatic countries will not be exempted from falling prey to American mob psychology and sacrificed upon the altar of American barbarism if the enemy should win the war."[29] This "barbaric conduct of the American fighting forces . . . is not so very surprising when one realizes that the personnel is selected from people who are characteristically capable of such shocking cruelty as lynching a fellow citizen for no other reason than being of a different colour."[30]

Japanese propaganda made much of racial prejudice in the United States. When in 1942 thousands of Negroes protested in Manhattan against job discrimination, the pro-Tokyo *Hong Kong News* asserted sarcastically, "It would be a good thing if President Roosevelt, before proclaiming his beliefs concerning nations outside the United States, would first put his principles into practice at home."[31] This was part of a barrage of propaganda in Japanese news media during the war, roaring about the ugly reality of U.S. racism. Naturally they focused on the sorry situation of the Negro soldier. An editorial found something tragic about the plight of the Negro soldiers in the American Army who "are being forced to fight on the side of injustice, gross discrimination and tyranny against the very forces which are working to wipe these things out of the world.'" To "be born black or brown or any other colour but white," it said, "has always been considered an unpardonable sin by the American people."[32] When "U.S. Negro soldiers" were "involved" in "race riots" that "spread to Britain," it made front-page headlines.[33] With thinly concealed ridicule,[34] the *Hong Kong News* observed that "It has been customary for the American politicians to mistreat and exploit the Negroes during peace-time and draft them as soldiers in case of war by offering them empty promises in order to fill up the dearth [of] labor power and fighting force."[35]

The lamentable lot of Negro civilians came in for censure. "Negroes & Whites clash in Detroit" was one gripping headline in 1943.[36] This clash was said "to be a prelude to wholesale Negro-white wars" in the United States.[37] When the eminent Negro jurist, William Hastie, was barred from the National Press Club in Washington for racial reasons, the *Hong Kong News* seemed even more outraged than he was.[38] When the notorious Senator Theodore Bilbo of Mississippi advocated "removal of Negroes from the U.S.," he was said by Japan to have "declared war on his coloured fellow Americans."[39] When "U.S. Negroes" were "barred from participating in presidential elections," this too captured the headlines.[40] Japanese propagandists even quoted "Waubuno, Chief of the Delaware tribe of Red Indians" at length on "the white man as an Exterminator of Other Races."[41] Japan's war was said to bolster the chief's efforts.[42] This was "more than a war of emancipation," it was "also a war of ideology."[43]

Such news stories were accompanied by coverage of Negro activities within the newly minted Japanese Empire. In 1943 it was reported that "Roy Brooks, clever Negro boxer, was yesterday crowned Welterweight Champion of the New Philippines by virtue of a clearcut win over Jimmy Villanueva before 9000 fans at Rizal Stadium. . . . In the semi-finals Jeffries Ware, two-fisted Negro slugger" also triumphed.[44] The Japanese press prominently reported the tax problems of the heavyweight champion, Joe Louis—the "Brown Bomber"—at the hands of the U.S. government he had supported so assiduously.[45]

The United Kingdom faced a racial dilemma no less daunting than that of the United States. It may even have been more so, for it had to defend territory—such as India and Burma—with tens of thousands of African and Afro-Caribbean troops, not to mention indigenous people often hostile to John Bull. Moreover, it faced the unique challenge presented by Marcus Garvey's Pan-Africanism, which sought to organize the colonized against London. Even before Garvey's rise, London had been monitoring trans-African threats. Hence, in 1913 London kept a close eye on "Alfred C. Sams" who then was in Oklahoma but claimed to hail from the "Gold Coast;" a British colony. He was "inducing Negroes" there to "emigrate" to Africa, which London found disquieting.[46]

But the bête noire in London's eyes was Garvey himself. He was under tight surveillance. In 1926 an experienced colonial hand reported in a "confidential" dispatch that "from my experience in the Political Intelligence Department . . . and in Malaya, I do not feel easy in my mind as to the results of the arrival of this fanatical Negro agitator in Jamaica."[47] Both the British Consul General in New York and the Embassy in Washington were informed earlier of the "large meeting of Negroes" in Manhattan where the "fanatical Negro agitator" "spoke at length on the Indian situation." That these cables were forwarded to the Prime Minister—and the King himself—shows how concerned London was.[48] The Empire, which had truly global responsibilities, had representatives who had served in Asia and Africa and drew upon their experiences in the one to shape their response in the other. In turn, their "subjects" often sought to join hands across the oceans.

In 1928 after Garvey had been unceremoniously deported from the United States to Jamaica, British officials there continued to keep a watchful eye upon him. They considered their communications sensitive: "This ought to be a secret despatch," began one message, since "I do not want it to be on permanent record there." Making the connection between those of African and Asian origin, R. E. Stubbs observed that the portly Jamaican "reminds me curiously of Sun Yat-Sen. There is the same devotion to an idea—possibly spurious but, if so, wonderfully well counterfeited; in Sun's case the unification and independence of China; in Garvey's the improvement of the status of the black races. . . . The same childish vanity, incessant talk of 'my organization,' 'my party,' 'my ideals.'" Stubbs talked at length about "anti-white disturbances," suggesting at one point that Garvey's "vanity has led the man into absurdities."[49]

But the term "absurdities" might be more appropriately applied to the racial policies of the Empire, heavily dependent on those not of "pure European descent" to defend its white supremacist policies. As early as 1921 the Foreign Office stated that the United Kingdom and its putative ally the United States were "all equally interested in avoiding a discussion" of the subject of racial discrimination—which only happened to be a matter in the forefront of the minds of the troops it ultimately had to rely on. But while acknowledging that there was "no subject more fundamental" for the "ultimate settlement" of tensions in the Pacific, the Foreign Office affirmed that the question of racial discrimination had no solution since the "white and colored races cannot and will not amalgamate." "One or the other must be the ruling caste," it said. As late as March 1941, the Foreign Office continued to unambiguously oppose the principle of racial equality, as one brave Briton had proposed issuing a statement that made it "clear that the white races and the dark races are not unequal." Making such a statement, he said, would undercut Tokyo's increasingly open appeals. Many greeted this idea as if they had been asked to relocate to Jupiter. More diplomatically, Sir Horace Seymour dismissed the proposal on the grounds that the Australians would never accept it. Yet by 1944—under the gun of war—the principle was accepted, suggesting once again that there is nothing like the prospect of being overrun to advance racial reform. A close student of these events maintains that "the old fear of racial revenge" on the part of those once dismissed as mere "coloreds"—that is, the bulk of the Empire—was salient in prompting a change of heart.[50]

Jamaicans and U.S. Negroes, in league with Tokyo, had been protesting British rule in Africa at least since 1905. The Empire feared that Japanese businesses would undercut their British counterparts on the African continent, thereby strengthening Tokyo's hand in Asia.

Thus, in 1936, Thomas Stanway, writing from Durban, complained to the Under Secretary for the Colonies about the "wholesale dumping of cheap Japanese cotton and silk goods into our colonies." He had just visited "Mombasa, Zanzibar and Dar es Salaam" and found "ports" there "flooded with Jap [sic] goods at the expense of our own. Lancashire and Yorkshire used to have the whole of this trade," he added with acidity, "and now they have been robbed of it by a ruthless competitor with whom it is quite hopeless to compete."[51]

In 1939, as the Empire was about to plunge into war, a Glasgow executive charged that "in East Africa the [U.K.] position was, if anything, worse than it had been. The Japanese were cutting prices drastically to levels that could not be economic even for them and were ruining the whole market," particularly in the bedrock industry of "sewing cotton." Thankfully, he said, in West Africa "the position . . . was not quite so bad."[52] But a few years earlier, even British executives in West Africa were singing the blues about the Japanese onslaught. Over a brief two-year period, from 1934 to 1936, the "very valuable business for such enamelled articles as wash basins, cash bowls . . . etc. has passed almost entirely to Japan at prices considerably below the cost of production in this country," that is, the United Kingdom.[53]

Although Berlin was professedly an ally of Japan, for reasons of geography and history German firms often allied with British ones in Africa—which brought the two European giants into conflict with Tokyo. Thus, in the pivotal year of 1936 a German diplomat told London that his nation "had a regular and considerable trade in cheap earthenware and enamelled ware, exported mainly through British firms, to British West Africa, especially Nigeria. This trade is now . . . in danger of being wiped out by the competition of cheap Japanese products." He enquired whether "we might contemplate checking these Japanese imports by means of quota restrictions, as has been done in the case of textiles."[54] London was "rather inclined to welcome this approach. While the suggestion that discriminatory duties should be imposed against one foreign country expressly to safeguard export trade to another certainly opens up a rather terrifying prospect should it be adopted widely in trade negotiations," it reasoned, "it has always seemed to us that as regards the Empire's trade with Germany the best reply to the latter's claims for territorial adjustment is the institution of some system of trade regulations by which 'good customers' are favoured at the expense of bad ones."[55] In other words, London was quite willing to accommodate Berlin at Tokyo's expense, although Germany—by dint of geography if nothing else—was a clearer and greater danger to the British Isles.

But just as the ardor of many U.S. Negroes for all things Japanese collided with their hunger for the property to be seized from Japanese Americans as the war began, Tokyo itself faced a similar dilemma between supposed principle and "larger" goals when Italy invaded Ethiopia—the Jerusalem and Mecca combined for blacks globally. Highly cognizant of Addis Ababa's significance, Tokyo had courted Ethiopia devotedly over the years—a fact carefully monitored by U.S. military intelligence, which was well aware of its importance.[56]

Yet if the economic challenge provided by Tokyo was menacing, the social challenge was deemed greater. A U.S. official reported with amazement on plans for a merger through marriage of branches of the royal families in Tokyo and Addis Ababa respectively. "In 1932 Prince Lij Alaya Ababa, nephew (or cousin) of the Emperor of Ethiopia, visited Japan," and like "many another sojourner in Japan, found the Japanese women pleasing and memorable." One thing followed another, and in "June 1932 stories appeared in the press to the effect that Prince Lij had requested a Tokyo lawyer to find for him a suitable Japanese bride." In London such a request would have brought chuckles, while in the U.S. South it might have led to the prince's bloody demise, but in Tokyo there were "applications from approximately 60 Japanese girls." The skeptical U.S. analyst explained this amazing maneuver in the context of Tokyo "endeavoring to organize a Pan-Asiatic movement and get into working order a League of Colored Peoples with Japan at its head." While his analysis was probably accurate, the United States—like the United Kingdom—could only stare in bewilderment as the crafty plot unfolded, while U.S. Negroes were electrified by this gesture.[57]

But many Negroes were dismayed by Tokyo's response to the Italian invasion of Ethiopia. Initially the influential and extremely race-conscious Black Dragon Society of Japan held a meeting in Tokyo to protest against Mussolini's invasion as yet another "fresh example of white imperialism." The BDS was joined by like-minded ultra-right, patriotic, and allied factions within the military and government.[58] The Japanese Embassy in Rome was placed under police guard and all the leading Italian newspapers ran front-page stories on Japanese policy toward Ethiopia. Tokyo was understandably concerned that important sections of the "white race" were upset about the implications of

Japan's rise to power for the illogic of white supremacy, and suspected that these powers were itching for an opportunity to defeat it. Equally, if not more important, Tokyo hesitated to offend its anticommunist soul mate in Rome and therefore backed down from its brief defense of Ethiopian sovereignty, to the dismay of Pan-Africanists worldwide.[59]

Tokyo's retreat did not dampen the enthusiasm of many blacks globally for Japan, a power that appeared to defy white supremacy. U.S. intelligence remained ever alert to this reality. Islam had established an important foothold in North America with the advent of the organization that became known as the Nation of Islam. Islam itself had been in existence for more than a millennium and in its orthodox form was dominant in large swathes of Africa and adjacent regions. Japan, said U.S. officials, "is in an unequaled position to capture [the] goodwill" of Muslims globally and had "met with signal success in the pursuance of this program." Islam, it was said, is "outspokenly democratic, untroubled by racial and social bias. A Negro from Nigeria, for example, has served as the Chief of the General Staff of Ibn Saud, the most powerful personality of modern Arabia." The "acute nationalism" of the Islamic world was "directed necessarily against western imperialists," which has "made all westerners suspect if not invariably unpopular." Tokyo was "persistent in broadcasting their anti-western policy to the Muslims in proclaiming their pride as members of the Asiatic or 'colored' front." Its "anticommunist policy" was also "gratifying" to Muslims, it was reported. Japan proclaimed that there were parallels between Shinto and Islam and promoted an "ominous alliance between fanatical Japanese patriotism and Muslim ethno-religious fanaticism," that is, a "dazzling promise of 'Japanislam' [sic]."

In pursuit of its ambitions, Japan was distributing scholarships to students. Some prominent Japanese had even gone so far as to convert to Islam. In strategically situated Afghanistan—a dagger pointed at the Empire's heart in India—"Japan" had deftly "been able to capitalize on four fears: of Russia, communism, England and the Hindu Congress Party." The guileful Nipponese were said to preach an anti-Hindu message in Kabul and a pro-Hindu message in Delhi. Now, worried U.S. intelligence analysts, the same model that had worked so well for Japan in the Islamic world was being exported to Latin America, a heavily Catholic region with a modicum of blacks. In one propaganda broadcast Tokyo was said to have asserted that the "Bible has now become the Book of the Japanese," a "new translation of the Old Testament by

Japanese scholars" was "well under way." "Is the Islamic venture to branch off into a Catholic policy?" the U.S. authorities asked anxiously. What was to be done? Creative officials noted with satisfaction that "in the Near East and the Balkans much can be made of Japanese hostility toward whites." In other places, such as Kabul and Delhi, Japan had tried to be all things to all people. Nothing was said about undermining white supremacy as a necessary condition to eroding Japan's appeal.[60]

By the time Hong Kong was seized, Whitehall may have wished it had been less stubborn on the racial front. Frankie Zung would have been defined as a Negro in the United States. According to the writer Emily Hahn, "his face was memorable because you don't see many Negroid faces in the Far East. Mr. Zung was only half Negro (or rather half West Indian; he insisted on the distinction) but it showed up in his features and coloring far more than did his Chinese half." Yet, there he was, in Japanese occupied Hong Kong, collaborating energetically against his ostensible sovereign, London. Why? "The Japanese," he told Hahn, "liked any colored person in the world, anyone at all, as long as he wasn't white. They made big promises to all the colored races. . . . Africa and everywhere else." Zung was married to a Euro-American but because the occupiers were "so delighted over a white woman marrying a Negro"—a potential capital offense in North America—"they freed her without any argument. . . . She was a blonde . . . very blond."

As Hahn and Zung strolled through the battered streets of what had once been described as the "Pearl of the Orient," "people didn't look surprised at seeing us together, as they would have before the war." Hahn herself confessed that before the war "if I had noticed Zung walking with his blond wife, I would have been amazed." With grudging reluctance, Hahn—who had escaped internment herself because of the occupiers' pleasure at her own previous intimacies with a Chinese man—argued that in Hong Kong "the Japanese have certainly succeeded in wiping out the color bar." The "Peak," the neighborhood previously reserved for those of "pure European descent," was now home to the likes of Frankie Zung. Turnabout was fair play, thought Hahn. "The British were cruel with their color distinctions and now they are being treated in the same way, dosed with their own medicine. It is just. It is only fair that I, an American white woman, should be wearing wooden clogs while Mrs. Zung has new patent leather shoes. . . . 'That's our weakness,' I mused. 'That's the big drawback to our winning this war. We'll win but we'll still be up against the color bar and all the resentment it stirs up. The Japs [*sic*] had a chance,'" she reflected perceptively, with their "Asia for the Asiatics" line. "It sounds well. They missed the boat, but they've got a head start with people like Zung."[61]

It was to eliminate this "head start" that Britain belatedly gave up the more egregious aspects of white supremacy. But it was not easy; it was wrenching and required old thought patterns to be changed. Fortunately for him Anthony Hewitt did not bump into Frankie Zung when he had his nerve-racking escape from the clutches of the occupiers. Instead, as he surreptitiously crossed China he encountered Percy Davis, yet another "Jamaican-Chinese half Negro born in the West Indies. . . . exceptionally tall . . . with strong wide shoulders and features more Negroid than Asian." He had a head of full "black and curly hair." Davis "used to own the World Radio Company in Kowloon," in Hong Kong but was now leading the resistance against the Japanese just across the border. His brother, Lee, was a "Communist guerilla." According to Ah Ting, another Red fighter, Percy Davis was a top Red "leader" himself, "the chairman here, the big man . . . the big boss."[62]

Percy Davis's fight against Japan was typical of many in the Empire who overcame their doubts and threw in their lot with London in hope of a better day. Billy Strachan was in the same category. Born in 1921 in Kingston, Jamaica, when war clouds loomed he sought to be a pilot for the Royal Air Force. But he remembered his home, where "there was an elite group of white men from Britain who headed all government organizations." This "small group . . . ran the country with a dictatorial rod. They lived in ultra-luxury" in "vast great houses with a number of servants" dressed as if they had stepped out from the set of the television program "Upstairs, Downstairs." There was "no free education" and at his school "the whites were so rich and so arrogant they didn't care about the blacks." All in all, there was "terrific racism."

But even so, he wasn't prepared for his experience in the United Kingdom itself where he went to train as a pilot in order to save the Empire that had been so unkind to him. There had been a "mass recruitment of West Indians . . . in 1943" and the more that arrived, the more intense was the racism. He had "never been called darkie . . . before" this. He was terribly "annoyed" by the "animosity and jealousy" he faced, which was ironic thanks given the sacrifice he offered.[63]

This "mass recruitment" was unenthusiastically received in certain quarters of Strachan's homeland. George Powe recalled that in Kingston on "every corner you went people would discuss and talk about the War and many people said that they would not fight for Britain because Britain had enslaved us for a number of years and so on." Still irate years after the war had ended, Powe added angrily, "Show me a black serviceman who claimed not to have encountered any prejudice in the U.K. during the war and I'll show you a liar!"[64]

Powe's anger was understandable. In June 1944, as the invasion of Normandy signaled a new phase in the conflict, Sir Frederick Leggett was instructed that "the better dance halls in Liverpool are still closed to the West Indians and feelings of bitterness increase because nothing appears to be happening."[65] Thus, at "Reece's dance hall in Liverpool, the manager has frankly explained that he imposed a ban of coloured persons because white American officers who used the hall objected to the presence of coloured people on the dance floor."[66] One angry Yank had bolted from one club muttering, "I would not have a bloody drink under the same bloody roof as any bloody nigger."[67] Sir George Gater was instructed that "the colour bar difficulties on Merseyside and at Manchester, which have been stirred up by the Americans are seriously affecting the well-being and social life of the West Indian technicians and trainees."[68]

To be sure, blacks and whites from the United States had exported their penchant for marathon brawling to the United Kingdom. Even as the war was winding down in 1945, there was yet another "report on [a] disturbance between American personnel and coloured members" of a club. Just before midnight one summer's day, Lawrence Silver, a Negro, said that one of his colleagues, who was white, said, "Look, there's a f—-king nigger there." The response to this call was predictable: "let's go beat him up," several people said, referring to the now startled Silver. However, Silver collected himself, ignored and evaded the gathering mob, and "continued on his way to the Coloured Colonial Social Club." Here he gathered his own retinue of "thirty or forty" comrades and returned to thrash his interlocutors soundly.[69]

On the other hand, people like Billy Strachan who wanted to fight Japan were perversely "lucky" in that London was not opposed to refusing the aid of Jamaicans like him. This was the dilemma faced by Leo March. In September 1939, as war was erupting, he offered his services to the Empire: "I am a fully qualified dental surgeon, trained at the Royal Dental Hospital of London," he began. He wished to join the RAF (Royal Air Force). "Although I was a British subject and fully qualified for the position I could not be selected as I was not of pure European descent," he moaned. Thus, he found himself stranded in London and "unemployed."[70]

Even as the Empire seemed on the verge of being overrun by predatory Japanese troops, London was unwilling to accept offers of aid by people not of "pure European descent"—particularly for posts beyond simple soldiering. This also applied to "Dartmouth Cadetships and direct entry cadetships," where the "practice of the Interview Committee" was to "reject boys who evidently have a colour strain."[71] They hoped to "secure the exclusion of any candidate whose appearance is so Negroid that it will make it difficult for him to take charge."[72] Because the appearance of fair play and democracy had to be maintained, elaborate subterfuges were deployed to obscure the sordid reality. A "confidential" communication stated that "it should still be the duty of the Committee to look out for boys who may have a colour strain," though "it is undesirable, in view of the delicacy of the question, that written official instructions in regard to it should be incorporated in the memorandum."[73]

The Empire also "rejected on the grounds of race an American black pilot who had applied to serve as a ferry pilot guiding planes between Montreal and Great Britain." "Qualified" African-Americans had also been denied employment with the British Purchasing Commission in Washington; a black doctor from New York, who had volunteered to come to Britain to help because of the widely publicized shortage of physicians in London during the Blitz was rejected by the Ministry of Health. Even when London moved to suspend such practices due to the demands of war, "they made it clear that this was 'for the duration only' and resisted making any statements about what would happen after the war."[74]

One reason African Americans were offering their skills to London was because their own country was often as hidebound as the Empire in matters racial. The United States—influenced by outright racists—was often unable or unwilling to discard its white supremacist policies, despite the presence of a burgeoning Negro population which often compelled it to retreat from such principles. London—which ruled uneasily over sullen "coloured" peoples—was obsessed about keeping them out of high-level posts so as to maintain the illusion of European superiority, and keeping them far away from their borders (and, as was often said, "their" women). Thus, the Empire often had to go to greater lengths than the United States in order to enforce white supremacy.

It also resorted to bizarre tests of "racial purity," the likes of which generated global moral outrage when practiced by Berlin. In a typically "confidential" memorandum, the Civil Service Commission searched energetically for a "touch of the tar brush" in a potential employee. The "evidence before the [Board] was purely visual; the candidate had crinkly black hair, a café au lait complexion and protruding lower lip. . . . For this reason the Board felt some hesitation about reporting the case."[75]

The "colour bar" was being imposed even as the Empire was in a desperate fight for survival with a minimal margin of error, particularly on the part of the Royal Air Force—both a sturdy shield and a sharpened sword. Yet London continued to reject the applications of those not of "pure European descent" for vital posts such as "aircraft apprentices." The son of Viola Smith of Cornwall was "very slightly coloured" and she had noticed that "your qualifications of entry" mandated that "the candidate must be of pure European descent." Her son was "intelligent" and "good looking." She could hardly believe that despite his excellent qualifications he "would be barred from the RAF for a very slight touch of colour."[76] Officials "regretted" it was "not possible to make a departure" from this racial "requirement."[77] After all, there were cases of "gentlemen who admit to be 'slightly coloured'" who "very often prove on inspection to be as black as one's boots." Of course, they said gallantly, the purpose of the "colour bar" was nothing as crude as "racial discrimination" or "narrowmindedness." It was to "spare the feelings of men of colour whose British comrades might not appreciate their presence." The unforgiving compulsion of war ultimately compelled the British to relax their rigid color consciousness, though they freely admitted that "whether we should continue to allow admission of non-Europeans after the war seems . . . to be another matter."[78] Before the relaxation of the "colour bar," Tom Taylor, a "very distinguished University boxer" from Balliol College, was "given the highest recommendation" for a post with the RAF. But this native of the Gold Coast also bumped into the bar and came out second best.[79]

As war erupted in Europe in 1939, the Colonial Office realized that "adverse feeling is being aroused" because of the "exclusion" of men in these regions "from commissions in the Royal Force." It was warned that "grievances felt on this score may constitute a serious handicap to

British war-time propaganda."[80] A far-sighted official went so far as to say, "I sometimes think that colour-prejudice (from which I do not claim to be free) may one day prove to be a crack on which the Colonial Empire may split."[81]

Yet, to hear London tell it, the Empire was often dragged reluctantly into backing a "colour bar" because of the protestations of its chief ally and subtle rival, the United States. This argument was disingenuous at best. The Empire unilaterally rejected U.S. Negro pilots and doctors who offered assistance and tried to bar them from their bases in the Caribbean. A novel solution devised by London was to require black Britons to wear a badge to distinguish them from black Americans. Future Prime Minister Harold Macmillan thought it a splendid idea. Despite protests from various quarters racial segregation remained virtually intact in Britain throughout the war, which handed Tokyo a propaganda bonanza. Little wonder that conservative commentator George Schuyler declared that the Empire was the foundation of racial prejudice and discrimination in the modern world.[82]

In September 1942 the "War Cabinet" affirmed that "we were justified in pressing the United States authorities to reduce as far as possible the number of coloured troops sent to this country." London felt that it was simply trying to meld varying—but united—perspectives on white supremacy for the sake of the overall longevity of the racial project. "The average white American soldier does not understand the normal British attitude to the colour problem and his respect for this country may suffer if he sees British troops, British Women's Services and the population generally drawing no distinction between white and coloured." Guidelines were proffered on how the British should respond to Negroes, with the strict proviso that "it is most undesirable that there should be any unnecessary association between American coloured troops and British women."[83]

London seemed to feel that U.S. blacks stirred up anti-racist sentiments among blacks from the Empire, and therefore should be kept separate. This was not a new thought. As early as 1920 a "confidential" missive from colonial offices from the African nation that was to become Malawi reported that "two American Negroes . . . came" there. One of them, a preacher, had married the niece of the notorious John Chilembwe, whose uprising shook the foundations of the Empire in Africa. His familial connection to an "American Negro" was considered duly important.[84]

The exigencies of war had heightened apprehensions about the strategically placed U.S. minority. In a "most secret" communication in the fall of 1943, an official granted that "in an ideal world we should certainly wish to avoid having British African personnel serving alongside American coloured troops." Why? Because "if British African troops were to be placed in the position of receiving direct orders from American white personnel, there would be unending trouble." Parenthetically, the British authorities noted that the "main points of difference" between African and African American troops were the latter's "higher standards of education," the presence of "Negro officers," and "American political ideals." The Empire was also concerned that blacks from the United States might impart seditious notions to their African brethren.[85] All this made the United States—a headquarters of white supremacy—more appealing to many Africans and Asians, thus contributing to its growing ability to challenge the United Kingdom, not least within the Empire itself.

London was very worried about the deployment of U.S. Negro troops in British colonies in West Africa, where their presence was thought to be disruptive. London firmly "recommended to Washington that no coloured troops" be sent to "the Gambia" or "Freetown," Sierra Leone.[86] Such an idea, it said, "clearly contains the seeds of trouble."[87] The proposal was "strongly objected to by the American commander in Accra, as by [London] and local governments."[88] Soothingly—and evasively—the "War Department" in Washington in words deemed "most secret" assured London that "there is no intention of using United States coloured troops in West Africa."[89] It did not say how this decision would affect the worldwide deployment of troops in a global struggle for survival against wily and well-armed foes.

The "Negro troops supply a great part of the labour of the United States army," Prime Minister Winston Churchill was told, "and as we have been pressing the Americans to increase the proportion of construction troops in their build-up, it would be difficult for us to ask them to reduce the percentage now," just because London did not want Negroes in Britain itself.[90] So London would have to steel itself and accept a horde of "coloured" men.

But accepting them did not mean accommodating them, and soon the "most secret" fact was revealed that "35% of the total population of U.S. soldiers imprisoned" in the United Kingdom were "coloured." The alleged "existence of the drug marijuana" was said to be a major reason;

this substance had to be monitored carefully since "if given to women, it may excite their sexual desires either as a cigarette or ground up in food."[91] For whatever reason, London maintained detailed lists of the crimes said to be committed by Negroes but none of crimes perpetrated by others.[92] In any case, according to the Duke of Melbourne, crime was not the only problem presented by these Negroes. "There are up to the present moment 34,875 coloured troops in this country," he announced in October 1943, and "there is a serious subversive element about them which I do feel can do much to bring about a great deal of unpleasantness in the relationship between our two countries."[93] They had been influenced by the stated democratic aims of the war, the leveling rhetoric from the chief ally of the United States—the Soviet Union—and the cry for racial justice enunciated by Japan, and they were not inclined to accept cheerfully the commands of white supremacy.

What else were these desk-bound bureaucrats so afraid of? Again, in "most secret" language, the Foreign Office recalled bitterly that the "presence of [U.S. Negroes] in Trinidad has been the constant source of embarrassment and has given rise to actual disturbances in Port of Spain," Trinidad.[94] Just imagine what would happen in Africa, where the basis for complaint was even more substantial and the populations substantially larger? This concern about U.S. Negroes infecting their counterparts in the Empire was something of a turnabout for London, in that in the 1920s the Foreign Office had felt that "the West Indian native considers himself to be in every way so superior to the Negro of the southern states that there is no likelihood for the present of an undesirable reaction resulting from Negro movements in the U.S. on [sic] the Negro subjects of the British West Indies."[95]

Evidently times had changed, for something that had not been a particular problem for the Empire earlier was now seen as a threat to the health of the colonial project generally. "Employment" of a "few coloured drivers in Leopoldville led to representations by the Belgian authorities and Americans had to withdraw them." This group of "coloured" soldiers were also "employed in East Africa and . . . difficulties were experienced as a result."[96]

It was not as if London had an easy time controlling African troops: far from it. The Basuto of Southern Africa caused all kinds of headaches for colonial bureaucrats. A British report observed that Basuto troops in West Asia "share the life of British soldiers and [do] the same work for less money, which naturally makes [them] dissatisfied." They "cannot stand the strains of a long war." In early 1945 the report worried that "there is no remedy except victory within the next few months." It did not consider extending equal pay for equal work.[97]

Africans had also been sent to Palestine, where Jews and Arabs were jockeying intensely for position in an exceedingly tense environment in anticipation of a British withdrawal. The British decided that the "Basuto troops . . . cannot be relied upon in the present emergency," for "any moment now" they "may go on strike." "These troops are now a liability not an asset." Somehow the Basuto had got the idea that they were "being exploited because they are Africans. . . . This idea is becoming more and more deeply rooted and no arguments will change these ideas." They had become "useless as a defence against any but casual individual thieves."[98] Thus, the crisis in the Middle East that was to bedevil the prospects for peace for generations to come was exacerbated in part by the increasingly discredited policy of white supremacy.

The rebelliousness of the Basuto was not the only African problem that faced London. In a "confidential" report in early 1945 the military grappled with the "difficulty" presented by the "growing claim to equality irrespective of race on the part of Africans. . . . The situation is that when in contact with the enemy, British and Africans . . . work together admirably and on equal terms. When such a unit is withdrawn for rest, the Africans expect to remain on equal terms with their British comrades, while the latter naturally prefer to exclude them from their billets, canteens and entertainments. There results a feeling of unfair discrimination and colour bar prejudice."[99]

London was asking Africans to sacrifice their lives perhaps for the Empire. Africans, in turn, demanded a modicum of respect. The British "were warned that the Bechuana" of Southern Africa "would take offence if they were sworn at, or if they were called 'blacks' or 'niggers,'" but these old habits died hard. Thus, Africans were "suspicious and distrustful" of the British. Moreover, they had seen the British up close and now saw their frailties, which shattered the Empire's image of total and awe-inspiring superiority. In "two years," the Africans "had seen a great deal of the White Man at close range and they had lost much of their respect for him." Not only that, they saw that not all Europeans resided in majestic grandeur—"in Sicily and Italy they found white people living in poverty and filth"—which also reduced the prestige of an Empire based not only on English, but British and *white* supremacy as well. "Here also the Africans for the first time resorted to white prostitutes and this must have destroyed much of the white man's prestige in their eyes. . . . Obviously they felt there is not much difference between us and the white man after all."[100]

How true. But what did this mean for the long-term prospects for the Empire, not to mention the immediate task of fighting a protracted war? Not surprisingly, by mid-1944 a "top secret" report observed that "generally" among many of the African troops "there has been a definite decline in morale. . . . they are tired." This was the result of the tension between upholding white supremacy on the one hand and fighting a war ostensibly premised on democracy on the other. But London explained it as a result of the fact that the African "has not the education nor the outlook on the war and its issues which help the European to overcome this war weariness."[101]

Both Africans and British had to grapple with the spectacle of Italian prisoners of war making artificial limbs in West Africa for wounded African soldiers. It was hard for Africans to continue to see "whites" as a cut above them while interned and subordinated Italians in Africa were being compelled to labor on behalf of Africans.[102]

London was sensitive to the issue. In Nairobi, Kenya, there were separate facilities for "coloured prisoners" and "the German POW," who—as a further reminder of their subordinate status—were "accommodated in the female section." Colonial officials were quick to point out that the Germans were "entirely shut off from the other Prisoners' quarters," thus preventing Africans from seeing subordinated "whites" in Africa. Moreover, London avoided placing Africans among Europeans—even if the latter were a foe. Thus, the point was made forcefully that "at no time were these men ever mixed up with coloured criminals."[103]

Similarly, in Jamaica colonial officials were sensitive to the "serious objections to use of coloured troops for guarding German civilian internment camps." Reluctantly they conceded that it was "not possible to provide other troops for the purpose." Though the Foreign Office "strongly opposed the use of coloured troops as guards," racial sensitivities had to be ignored. Why? As noted, it was a problem to secure "other troops" for this task, but there was also a sort of "mutually assured destruction" between prevailing racial biases and this was a line that London hesitated to cross. That is, the British feared that the Germans might have the presumed inferiors guard British POWs, which would be a humiliation piled on the insult of internment.[104] And it was not just blacks that London was concerned about either. In Trinidad, "internees" were "housed in a number of hutments . . . which are divided into two sections, one for Jews, and for non-Jews," though the prisoners were mostly German.[105]

If unlucky enough to be captured after risking their lives for the Empire, men of African descent often had to endure the comments of insensitive fellow inmates. Richard Thorpe, a Jamaican, had the misfortune of being interned in Hong Kong with Wenzell Brown. One day while fantasizing—most likely induced by hunger—"we," recalled Brown, "talked to a great, soft Negro mammy dressed in a red print dress who proudly showed us her pickaninny, naked save for the red kerchief she had tied about his head."[106] Brown did not reflect on why in this moment of peril his thoughts had wandered into the grossest of racial stereotypes.

The Pacific War precipitated a massive crisis for white supremacy. The mighty Empire was reduced to asserting that "it has become abundantly clear that the [Africans] are exploding the myth established by the Japs [*sic*] during the original conquest of Burma that they are unsurpassed as jungle fighters."[107] The powerful proponents of white supremacy had sunk to the point where they were extolling the might of allegedly inferior Africans to undermine the idea of superiority of Japanese fighters over Europeans. The message to the Africans was clear: if they were so mighty, why were they languishing under colonial rule, supervised by Europeans apparently unable to fight their own battles? If British troops were taking flight in the jungles of Burma pursued by smaller Japanese, why should they react any differently if confronted by Africans?

This thought had crossed the mind of white supremacists. "One Rhodesian analyst worried that the war—which forced Salisbury to train Africans as welders, drivers and the like, who perforce saw the world along with the Rhodesian troops they accompanied—was the biggest challenge to colonialism since the end of the slave trade." Still another Rhodesian worried that "the prestige of white man depends (whatever the politicians may think) largely on the ability to do things better than the black man," and this "prestige" was shaken profoundly by the war.[108]

It was easy to see why the racist regime of Rhodesia would be apprehensive about the war. The Empire came perilously close to being vanquished in Asia and probably would have been but for the fact that up to "100,000 West Africans" served in the "SE Asia and India Commands" (this did not include the many thousands from East and Southern Africa who served similarly). West Africa had "the largest colonial force in the world fighting overseas and by far the greatest portion of it" was in the critical battlegrounds of "Burma or Assam." In some instances their numbers and contributions outweighed those of the British.[109] All told, "167,000 soldiers"[110] from Sierra Leone, Gold Coast, Nigeria, and the Gambia alone fought for London. Despite their massive effort on behalf of the Empire and the Allies, as Lt. J. A. L. Hamilton pointed out, they received "little publicity" in official and memoir accounts.[111] After the war ended, London seemed to want to downplay their contribution for fear that it might provide a rationale for anticolonial activities.

At the moment of the most intense combat, however, the Empire did not stint in its praise for the Africans. One analyst, for example, complimented the West Africans for their mettle at the crucial battle of Imphal.[112] In a "most secret" report in 1942 "Downing Street" wrote that "West African toops should be sent to the Far East for employment in jungle warfare."[113] British officials in India agreed, adding that the "advantage of West African troops" in Burma "is that they are used to jungle," while "East African troops are at present highly mechanized and not so used to jungle." Both "East and West African troops" had "fought well in . . . Africa operations and should be able to compete with Japanese."[114]

Despite their contribution to the survival of the Empire, these brave soldiers often had to contend with harassment and insult. The official publication of the East African Command included insulting, stereotypical drawings of Africans—combined with racially insensitive attacks on the Japanese—and the usual incongruous rhetoric about fighting for freedom and democracy.[115] Traveling from West Africa to India, a number of African soldiers "escorted by a European officer" stopped in Durban. As Captain P. B. Poore recalled it, the Africans "could not read" and therefore "sat on 'white only' seats and totally ignored the segregation laws." However, the British chose to ignore this flagrant violation of racial norms, aware as they were of the ongoing war and the Africans' contribution. Captain Poore was also sensitive to the issue. "I had a sergeant known as 'sergeant bend down' because he used to beat the Africans to punish them. This I had to stop . . . We were about to fight the Japanese and it would be useful to have 150 Africans to help us." That the war saved Africans from frequent canings was just one more example of how this conflict forced the Empire to shed some of its harsh practices. Colonel F. K. Theobald dryly observed that "in West Africa regulations permitted us to award up to 12 strokes of the cane for certain offences. When we arrived in India this was frowned upon and we were told that this regulation would not operate there."[116]

It was well that the Empire opted for tactical kindness, for the Africans proved indispensable upon arrival in Burma. "I always let them do the talking to the Burmese as they were so much better and obtained information I could never have got," observed Captain Poore. But although the Africans were essential to the mission, they received third-rate treatment. Captain Poore and his fellow British had "been issued with Indian made patrol boots" that "were light and felt great" or "gym shoes" while the "African went bare foot." One reason the Empire was able to prevail against Japan is that it had an almost inexhaustible supply of Africans and Indians that could be thrown heedlessly into combat, without regard for common standards of humanity: Tokyo did not have a comparable advantage, even if their own deployment of Koreans and Formosans is taken into account.

But the services provided by the Africans may have been a disadvantage for the Empire, in that they softened the British in their confrontations with the battle-toughened Japanese. Colonel F. K. Theobald admitted "that life under active service conditions in the jungle life was in some ways more comfortable for officers than it would be with British troops. My boy [sic] would try and wash my aertex battle dress blouse and denim trousers every day. He carried a charcoal iron and there would be an immaculate crease in my denim trousers." That was not all. His "boy" also "carried 40 [pounds] of equipment" since his "orderly" and "bodyguard. . . . did not carry a load."[117] The class-bound British military seemed to be preparing for a picnic or a photo shoot for a safari rather than fighting a war against a cunning opponent.

The Empire at times clumsily undermined its advantages. The "Sierra Leone Battalion," for example, "had many Polish officers." As they were "unable to speak English they could not be put in charge of English troops," so they were shipped out to West Africa. It is unclear how African troops commanded by Polish-speaking officers performed in battle. Captain Poore could not understand why morale "seemed to be dropping like a stone, and a great many people were becoming jittery, both European and African." He recalled an "African Sergeant" who was "very different from the others, he was well educated to University standard and an excellent map reader. He had a chip on his shoulder," perhaps "because all British Sergeants were senior to him, although they were not well educated and he could out-perform them." Typically, Captain Poore compared Africans to "children," but he made no connection with his condescending language, speaking instead of their "rather disappointing performance in the Kaladan," which led to a "rumor going around" that they "would not be used again."[118]

Some Africans may have been overjoyed not to be "used again," for in an "attempt to reduce the casualty rate among Europeans the commanding officer ordered that patrols were to be led by African sergeants. No matter how militarily well-intentioned," said one writer sympathetic to London, "his order could have been interpreted in the battalion as a readiness to conserve Europeans officers' and NCOs' lives at the expense of African ones."[119] Hence it was not unusual for African troops to flee from the Japanese "without a single man—private, corporal or sergeant—doing his duty." On one occasion "so quickly had the platoon fled that they had not fired a single shot" and "had suffered no casualties."[120]

Not using African troops would prove to be a difficult promise to keep, because British soldiers in South Asia often were targeted by the Japanese—and angry Africans too. In what might rank as the reigning metaphor of the racial transformation that accompanied the war, "British personnel were ordered to paint their faces black and 'copy the gait, bearing and mannerisms of their own troops.'" Why? "By their account, British officers did not paint themselves black to avoid Japanese snipers but to protect themselves from being killed by African soldiers."[121] John Nunneley disagreed. In his opinion, "a white man amongst black soldiers was always the prime target of Japanese fire. . . . All Europeans now coated their faces and hands with black cream and removed rank badges." Characteristically, during the British retreat from Burma to India in 1942, the "BIA" or Burma Independence Army "hunted down and killed" a number of British soldiers, Ba Maw, a "leader with Aung San trumpeting: 'The boys were jubilant at the thought of having drawn white blood so cheaply!'"[122] White supremacy backfired in the jungles of Burma. The vaunted pale skin, once a symbol of preeminence had now become something of a liability. This was a harsh lesson; the retreat from Burma mirrored a retreat from the more egregious aspects of white supremacy.

Maltreated, ill-paid, poorly clad, the tens of thousands of African troops were on the verge of mutinous rebellion. The highly charged atmosphere of war provided the catalyst for an experiment that often careened out of control. This caught the attention of Japanese propagandists. In 1944 "Anglo-U.S. atrocities against [their] own coloured troops" were "exposed." These "shocking" deeds were directed at "West African troops." "Corpses of West African troops, their heads and stomachs split open as if they were shot at close range. . . . by the [U.K.] supervising troops to compel the West Africans to advance to the rescue of the trapped British forces." They were "mercilessly driven at points of bayonets to advance blindly against the Japanese forces." One "prisoner revealed that he was captured by British slave traders in Tanganyika from where he was sent to Ceylon and thence to India." Some of them were "burned alive."[123]

The Empire might have countered that this account was inflated, but it accords with other recollections of the outrageous treatment accorded African troops. Such was the case in Ceylon—now Sri Lanka—the tear-drop shaped island off the southern coast of India, in 1943. There two "Sinhalese women and one man were fired on and wounded by persons alleged to have been East African soldiers." This led to a fierce debate in the highest councils of Colombo. Said one Ceylonese, a "Mr. A. Ratnayake," "Why on earth are there African forces in Ceylon? Why should there be an African force in Ceylon? . . . Ceylonese are fighting in Africa, whilst Africans are brought to defend Ceylon. Can you imagine Chinese being sent to defend England?" Apparently he had not realized that the Empire was reluctant to place weapons in the hands of colonial subjects in their own nations.

But Mr. Ratnayake was not the only Ceylonese incensed about Africans in his country. "Mr. Abeywickrama" said: "One day I saw a procession of women going into the interior. I asked them where they were going and they told me that [they] were leaving their homes because they were informed that the Africans eat children, that their best food was the flesh of infants." He sought to rebut this colonial myth: "I told them that these soldiers were not cannibals." But so useful had this myth been in subjugating Africans that it was hard to dispel, though now it had become utterly counterproductive. In any case, Mr.

Abeywickrama was not particularly enlightened, speaking sardon-
ically of the "broad-lipped Africans. They are a most ugly sight. It is
awful to look at these fellows. . . . I tried to convince them that these
Africans were not cannibals but they refused to believe me. They say,
'These people are brought here to eat up the Japanese when they land
in Ceylon.'" He was taking no chances: "Wherever the African soldiers
are billeted, steps must be taken to see that the authorities have a
barbed-wire fence of 5 or 6 strands all round. . . . People seem to believe
that they are cannibals because they are so nasty. Nobody understands
their language; they simply mutter something."

Contradiction was piling on contradiction as the Empire was forced
to send Africans abroad to meet a Japanese challenge that frontally assaulted the soft underbelly of London's major weakness: race. How
could subjugated "Ceylonese" reject the imprecations—no matter how
hateful—of those apparently intelligent and powerful persons who had
colonized them? But how could an effective defense be mounted
against Tokyo in South Asia when the colonized were at each others'
throats?[124]

In neighboring India there were repeated references to "murders
and murderous assaults committed by Americans and American Negroes on Indians," including a "forcible kidnapping of Indian girls in
American jeeps." In "1943 and 1944" there were "four cases of
manslaughter. . . . by members of American forces" against "civilians."[125] These were only some of the problems raised by the presence
of troops from a nation where white supremacy was virtually sacro-
sanct. Delhi maintained a "large number of files concerning incidents in
which Americans are involved," particularly "misbehaviour" by
"American troops in Calcutta."[126] Interestingly, only African Americans—among the broad swathe of U.S. citizens—were specifically identified by "race."[127]

The Empire was slipping slowly into a devolutionary spiral from
which there would be no return.[128] Adding fuel to the flames, the Empire consciously set out to demonize the Africans, apparently oblivious
to the ramifications of such a maneuver. Colonel F. K. Theobald conceded that "our propaganda people were supposed to have made a
record of the sound of bones being crunched up which was supposed to
be a record of our 'cannibals' eating Jap prisoners."[129] Meeting Tokyo's
racial challenge with a wicked dose of racism did not comport with the

Atlantic Charter and the other lofty documents that supposedly were driving the Allies' war effort.

Often shoeless, despised at every turn, no more than cannon fodder for their alleged "betters," African troops had reason to be in ill-humor, if not mutinous. After "13,000 African troops" were "repatriated from France" and were about to be demobilized" in West Africa, "trouble" began. It was late 1944 and "these men had been prisoners of war in France up to the time of liberation." "Several French women" were reportedly "molested by" them. "Arms were smuggled ashore and they were in possession of large sums of money"—or at least "large" compared to the meager sums they usually had. "They were in an uproar, they "mutinied," and this was a "serious" matter.[130]

Speaking of the French, despite their dismal colonial record, Colonel F. K. Theobald of the British military felt that even Paris did a better job than his own country. A number of the Togolese, he recalled, "had been taught the language," that is, French, whereas those of the neighboring Gold Coast spoke a pidgin English that was hardly intelligible to most English speakers.[131] More than a half-century after the war had ended, Bakary Dibba of the Gambia still recalled vividly the dearth of enthusiasm in his village. At one rally to drum up interest "there was no volunteer" so they "started to use force. . . . When they saw you, they would just grip you and take you." He was put aboard a ship bound for India, but all was not lost for it was there that "young men from different ethnic groups worked together for the first time for a common cause." This was a useful rehearsal for the anticolonial struggle that was to follow after the war. But Mr. Dibba concluded by reflecting gravely on why he had fought. "They're the same," he said, "the British, the Japanese; they were fighting all for the same thing—sovereignty. . . . I don't regret fighting for the colonial masters. But at the end of the day, they are all the same." There was no difference—at least for Africans—between fighting for the British Empire or the Japanese Empire, or so he said.[132]

Meanwhile, Robert B. Hammond, a missionary born in Hong Kong, had endured a traumatizing captivity at the hands of the Japanese during the war, but managed an early departure in 1942. When he landed in freedom in East Africa, Mozambique, after a lengthy cruise from China, he was visibly moved. "Such love, such wondrous love that God should love us and give His Son to die for us that whosoever believeth on Him should not perish but have everlasting life! This includes the Africans too!" he added generously.[133] Perhaps the "black pilot" from the United States whose plane crashed as he was attacking Hong Kong in an attempt to free the likes of Hammond, then "was dragged behind a lorry through Kowloon until he died," would have understood this comment all too well.[134]

10

Race World

RACE MADE MORE CONVOLUTED and intricate the ability of allies on all sides of the war to come together. Even when seemingly absent, as in relations between Washington and London, the infamous "colour bar" provided fertile soil for the growth of ethnic and other differences. Such differences also made it more difficult to confront Japan's particular challenge to white supremacy. The ever present race factor made some Chinese hostile to the Empire even as Tokyo rampaged through Asia; it allowed some Mexicans to look skeptically toward their colossal northern neighbor. It complicated relations—thankfully—between Tokyo and Berlin. It helped to propel the war, then prolonged it.

A "vigorous anti-British" attitude characterized the great Chinese patriot, Sun Yat-Sen, as late as the 1920s, not to mention many of his compatriots. To those of "pure European descent," and "to the denizens of the Treaty Ports he came to seem a virtual Bolshevik." In particular "[his] new relations with Russia drew Western fire." At his "last major address" in Kobe in late 1924, he spoke of a subject dear to the hearts of his Japanese hosts, "Pan-Asianism." Like Nehru and Du Bois before him, he too pointed to Japan's defeat over Russia as a turning point in the devolution of white supremacy. "We regarded that Russian defeat by Japan as the defeat of the West by the East," he proclaimed. This was a continuation of Sun's nationalism, as "the first cause in which Sun Yat-Sen and his Japanese friends collaborated was that of Philippine independence," a collaboration which had begun as early as 1898. Sun's position on the controversial race question was as blunt as that of his Japanese friends. As Marius B. Jansen put it, "the idea of an Asiatic union under Japanese leadership to combat Western imperialism was not merely the contrivance of Japanese imagination. . . . For Sun and his friends, China and Japan had so much in common that there was no reason why they should not work together." As Sun once put it during one of his many visits to Japan, "If there were Europeans here tonight . . . they would not be able to tell the Chinese from the Japanese."[1]

In fact, "in the first decade of the twentieth century, tens of thousands of Chinese youth sought a modern education in Japan," at a time when they were few and far between in the United States and the United Kingdom.[2] In 1905, "buoyed by Japanese success against Russia and angered by American mistreatment of Chinese immigrants, Chinese students, some [just] returned from study in Japan, organized an anti-American boycott, arguably the first sustained nationalist movement in Chinese history."[3] At that conjuncture, in the aftermath of Japan's victory over Russia, Tokyo "occupied in the regard of the Asiatic revolutionaries the place later held by Moscow."[4] As a young traveler, Sun often masqueraded as Japanese to avoid harassment, for, as he put it, "when the Japanese began to be treated with more respect, I had no trouble in passing. . . . I owe a great deal to this circumstance, as otherwise I would not have escaped many dangerous situations."[5]

When the Japanese authorities were tried as war criminals after 1945, they sought refuge in their relationships with the colored, particularly Sun. According to Yasaburo Shimonaka, Japan founded the "Greater East Association" which was "based upon the following articles: blood is thicker than water; China and Japan are brother countries." All this was motivated, he argued, by Sun Yat-sen. "Sun Yat-Sen was the origin of this principle and Matsui was the echo."[6] Kumaichi Yamamoto, former Japanese Ambassador to Thailand, argued that the concept of the Greater East Asia Co-Prosperity Sphere, Pan-Asianism, and all the rest all came from Sun.[7] But these ideas were rejected.

One Soviet writer also pointed to "close ties between the Black Dragon and . . . Sun Yat-sen. For many years he collaborated with the Black Dragon Society. . . . Sun Yat-sen as well as the Black Dragon [Society] aimed at driving all Europeans and Americans out of Asia. In all biographies of Sun Yat-sen written for Europeans and Americans, this aim was usually disguised. To him, however, it was a guiding principle." Indeed, argues this analyst, by the time of his death Sun was not only allying with Tokyo but also with Moscow in common opposition to the British Empire and the United States.[8]

Sun was not alone among the Chinese in being influenced by Tokyo, however. Rebecca E. Karl points out that early-twentieth-century rhetoric in China on race could have been lifted wholly from then reigning discourses in Japan. "In the numerous essays on events in the

Philippines published in China between 1899 and 1903, the Filipinos were repeatedly referred to as *tongzhong* 'pioneers of the yellow race' in the global struggle against the 'white race.'"[9] It was the Empire's antipathy toward Chinese independence that drove Sun himself to Japan.[10] Signaling the reality that there was a long-standing tie between race consciousness and the right wing in Tokyo is the fact that the leader of the chauvinistic Black Dragon Society, Toyoma Mitsuru, "persuaded the Foreign Office to change its mind and allow Sun Yat-sen to land in Japan and sheltered him during his stay. He also sheltered Chiang Kai-shek."[11]

Chinese nationalism—like nationalism in the "colored" world generally—was long attracted to Japan, as Sun's example exemplified. Another transnational trend was the fact that Communists—in this case, the Communist Party of China—were profoundly immune to this attraction. But it was precisely the Communists who were the major target of persecution by London and Washington, and by removing the nationalists' natural predators, they coincidentally provided a healthy boost to Tokyo. When Tokyo's dreams were dashed in the ashes of Hiroshima-Nagasaki, the Communists naturally emerged as the logical inheritors of China. They continue to cite their role in the anti-Japan movement as a source of their legitimacy.

But even some admirers of post-1949 Beijing have conceded the role of Japan. According to the leading Marxist intellectual, Hu Sheng, Chinese students in Japan "gave [Sun] a most enthusiastic welcome."[12] Owen Lattimore, a leading U.S. specialist on Asia, observed in 1945 that "Americans usually overlook the important [fact] that Chinese who have studied in Japan are much more numerous than those who have studied in America, are equally influential in politics, administration and business and much more influential in the army. . . . Chinese graduates of West Point and Virginia Military Institute have therefore rarely got anywhere in China," while "Chinese officers who have studied in Japan form powerful cliques. . . . in the politics of China."[13] To be sure, this pro-Japan orientation declined after World War I when Tokyo moved aggressively to take over Chinese territory previously under German jurisdiction. Nevertheless, their shared anticommunism and antipathy to the Empire served to bind certain Japanese and Chinese elites together.

For just as many Chinese for a while looked to Tokyo, they looked askance at London: neither approach was helpful to the cause of the

Allies when the Pacific War began. Lee Yiu Wa argues that London—not Tokyo—became the "main target" of Chinese nationalism after World War I.[14] White supremacy served as midwife to this incipient birth of Japanese-Chinese friendship, for at Versailles "on only one issue debated . . . were the Chinese and Japanese delegates of one mind, and that was the proposal to amend the League of Nations covenant so as to recognize racial equality."[15] Just as the construction of "whiteness" elided differences between and among the English, Irish, Scotch, and Welsh, Japan's racial appeal allowed tensions between and among them and other Asians, particularly the Chinese, to be minimized: dialectically, "whiteness" and white supremacy fed into Japan's own effort at racial construction.

The animus toward London was fueled in part by the way the Chinese were treated in the United Kingdom. They were barred from the seamen's union, for example. Britons went so far as to treat "black immigrants and sailors much better than they treated Asians" generally.[16] Like other "coloureds," these seamen "did not regard the war as in any way "theirs.'" In fact, one scholarly study has concluded that "the body of evidence upon which this study is based offers little support for the theory of World War II as a people's war, indeed it points to the contrary conclusion."[17] Thus, it should have come as no surprise to the Empire when those who saw themselves as heirs to Sun—Chiang Kai-Shek and the Kuomintang (KMT)—in the prewar period leaned toward Tokyo, even as it was nudging, then shoving, the Empire. On the other hand, one must not underestimate the profound disappointment of those Chinese who looked admiringly toward Tokyo, when it became clear that Japanese imperialism was no savior.[18]

On the whole, pro-Tokyo sentiment was driven not only by Chinese anticommunism—which, after all, was shared by London—but also by antipathy toward white supremacy. Chiang, who spoke Japanese and had undergone military training there as well, had also expressed an early interest in Germany, where he also considered doing some training, "published articles on German military practice," and "studied the German language." Thus, "from 1928 to 1938 Chang kai-Shek's [sic] government had closer relations with Germany than with any other foreign power." There were obvious contradictions in this alliance; Chiang objected to Germany's ban on "mixed marriage" which he deemed a "betrayal."[19]

Chiang "knew . . . well" the "father" of the head of the ultrapatriotic Black Dragon Society of Japan. They had become acquainted when he was a cadet in Japan. Moreover, "he knew many officers who were members of the Black Dragon."[20] Inescapably, the KMT also had a fondness for Japan. As late as the 1930s, London was "shocked" when the KMT "hinted that China might 'join Japan in a policy of exclusion of Great Britain from [the] Far East.'" This was "significant," thought Sir John Simon, the Chancellor the Exchequer, since it would mean "the Yellow Peril would become not a mere abstract conception but a harsh and pressing reality."[21] When Britain finally assisted China in 1938, a key factor was reluctance to see China fall under the aegis of Japan—just as its previous reluctance had been grounded in sympathy for the KMT's and Japan's hostility to the Communist Party of China. When in late 1940 Washington supplied the KMT with $100 million, this was "not unprompted: the Japanese overtures to Chiang . . . throughout the autumn and the fear of his capitulation to these had goaded the United States into this expensive gesture."[22]

Even some Chinese scholars rationalize the willingness of the Nationalists to sympathize with Tokyo and to reject a complete alignment with the Allies. Lee Yiu Wa has written that "in fact, the 'Open Door' and the 'New Order' were more or less the same as China, as a sovereign state, had no place at all in both cases. . . . Japanese colonialism and European domination were thus the same thing."[23]

Moscow seemed to be the only outside power that could come to China's insistence. Its assistance to the Chinese Communists is well known. O. Edmond Clubb has noted that while "Britain and the United States were continuing their profitable trade with the Japanese, the Soviet aid to China was substantial and critical. Over 200 Soviet pilots were killed in action flying planes with Chinese insignia."[24]

This created a dilemma for the Empire. It had to choose between acquiescing to Japan to better combat communism, or accommodating the Communists so as to better combat Japan. Ultimately, London acceded—albeit minimally—to the latter without enthusiasm. A British thinker commented that beginning in the 1930s "Russia and Japan were . . . working independently to reach the same goal—the elimination of white influence in the East." This illustrated how some in the Empire had conflated "whiteness" with militant defense of the status quo. The KMT too faced no easy answers: consorting with Japan—and London's antagonist, Berlin—was a kind of fool's gold, promising more than it delivered. But their alliance with the Communists only pointed up the KMT's weaknesses, among which was corruption, and simply paved the way for its demise. As for the Chinese people themselves, their overall posture is described in the book of the same name: passivity, resistance, and collaboration.[25] And collaboration was not limited to the leaders of the KMT alone.[26]

The leading Chinese nationalist, Wang Ching-wei, headed a "puppet" regime in China established by Tokyo. He too had studied in Japan and, interestingly, was a leader of KMT "leftists," just as Chiang led the "the right-wing." He was also a "hero of the republican movement and a close associate of Dr. Sun."[27] But he was a "staunch" opponent of the Communists and was motivated in part by his hatred of white supremacy, which led to his pro-Tokyo posture. The British writer, Cedric Dover, deemed him a "significant character," but "he hated white men" and the "colour bar." Japan, he thought, "at least respects China as a nation."[28] T'ien-wei Wu, though highly critical of Wang, avers that his "case should not be written off lightly as the tale of a traitor to China."[29]

Thus, for various reasons the anticommunist forces led by Wang and Chiang—whose past or present was linked with Tokyo—were not in an ideal position to lead the war effort. And they may not have been alone. When the Vietnamese Communist leader, Le Duan, "first visited China to gain better health in 1952," he was stunned. He "was struck by the fact that the region he visited (probably Guangxi or Guangdong) had not waged any guerilla struggle against Japan during the Japanese occupation despite its huge population. Le Duan claims that Ho Chi Minh confirmed this impression."[30] When the Hong Kong hero of the anti-Japan struggle, Sir Lindsay Ride, was on the mainland, he "met a Japanese who had been an intelligence worker in Yenan during the war. He told" the former professor that "most of his intelligence" during the war "had been based on rumors, but he had had one really good source—a commander of the KMT!"[31]

Throughout the war there were strong suspicions that Chiang and Wang may not have been the bitter antagonists that they were presumed to be. Chohong Choi writes that "a big reason why Japan was able to firmly establish herself in China was because Chiang cared more about eliminating the [Communists] than dealing with the Japanese."[32]

During a good deal of the Pacific War,[33] "the fighting between the Chinese and the Japanese in parts of the interior was by now quite half-hearted." Leading KMT forces were using "American resources to fight the Reds instead of the Japanese"—a move that Tokyo heartily supported—while since early 1942 top KMT leaders "had been in regular secret radio contact with Zhou Fohai," a key Wang supporter in Shanghai. After the war, Zhou was not tried as a traitor but instead became a key figure in the Chiang regime. There was a "widely rumored story that what Wang . . . did was done with the tacit approval of Chiang . . . all along."[34] Many senior British officials felt that there was a "'virtually undeclared peace' between the Chinese government and the Japanese invaders."[35] The Nationalists' attempt to "drive a wedge between Britain and the U.S." also seemed to be designed to give Japan a boost.[36]

"Many Chinese generals (42 in 1943 alone) went over to [Japan] taking hundreds of thousands of their troops with them." London had allied with Tokyo in the prewar era, which facilitated Japan's appeal to Chinese elites. Thus, in the prewar era the British press in Shanghai tended to be more pro-Tokyo than the U.S. news media. In the prewar era, Tokyo and London collaborated in "repressing resistance activities by citizens of China."[37]

On this score, certain U.S. elites were in accord with the Empire. "In public, President Hoover denounced the Japanese takeover [of China], but he supported it in private."[38] As late as 1935, the publishing empire of Henry Luce implied that the KMT "in alliance with Japan, might create a progressive new order in the Far East. TIME [magazine] saw the Japanese Army as a bulwark against Russia and Communism."[39]

As they examined their intelligence files during the war, the Empire found confirmation for its suspicions that the KMT and other nationalists had decided not to sever relations with Japan. This was not altogether unexpected since nationalist Negroes, Maoris, Aborigines, Indians, and others had either an open or veiled affection for Tokyo—so why not the nationalist Chinese? "Farstan T. Sung" had served as the Nationalist Chinese Consul-General in Melbourne, Sydney, Johannesburg, and Vienna, not to mention being "Adviser to the Chinese Ministry of Finance and General Director of the Opium Control Authority." After the war it was found that he had "carried letters and photographs from" Mozambique to "Lisbon" for the Axis, "successfully evading the British control at Freetown."[40]

"Intelligence Reports" filed from Hong Kong in 1944 were deemed sufficiently sensitive to be considered "secret." The "Chief of the Central Ward of Hongkong, Sun To-hok and his predecessor Hsien Ping-shi" appear to have been key collaborators of the Japanese occupation forces. "The former was [KMT] representative of Kwangtung Province during the first All-China Representatives' meeting in 1924 and the latter during the third meeting. Both were active [KMT] members and are still remembered by many people in the [KMT]."[41]

Sir Frederick Eggleston had reservations about the KMT, which he revealed in 1943 as the war dragged on. He wrote from Chungking that during the course of "personal and confidential" talks with the Dutch Ambassador, he inquired about the "rumour that Chiang kai-Shek has asked, by way of Nanking, for an assurance from Japan that if he went for the Communists the Japanese would not take advantage of such a move. He said he had no doubt this was true and then proceeded to say that there was a considerable amount of liaison between Chungking [Chiang] and Nanking [Wang] and with the Japanese authorities. . . . Chungking did not intend to fight seriously as long as Japan did not make [their] position difficult while Japan did not want the burden of holding the whole of China and would not take hostile action unless she was harassed by China. Meanwhile the relations between the people and especially the merchant banking class were becoming freer. People passed between the occupied territory and Free China very freely; banks had no difficulty in doing business in Shanghai and other towns held by the Japanese and there was a large amount of trade."[42]

This was not the first time that probing questions had been raised about the relationship between Chinese nationalists and Tokyo. Another "most secret" communication in 1943 discussed the KMT cutting a separate deal with Tokyo. Tokyo had flown an emissary to "Kuang-Chowwan" where a "special 'plane' was sent by Chiang . . . to bring him from Kuantung. . . . The United Nations was extremely disturbed at this development."[43] Again, it is not easy to distinguish anti-Empire sentiment from pro-Tokyo collaboration.[44] When Singapore and Hong Kong were seized by Tokyo, for example, anti-Empire feelings were a major reason.[45]

Yet the Empire had no reason to be confused, since it knew that white supremacist ideas—along with years of patient tilling by Japan—were responsible. Its own intelligence in 1944 revealed the signs. In Kweiling lyrics in "a parody of a popular song" went: "Once the East

Asiatics extricate themselves from civil war, the death knell for the British and American devils will be sounded."[46]

The most consistent and organized opponent of such thinking was the Communist Party of China. But the Allies were strongly opposed to them, even when they had no choice but to join hands with them. Lindsay Ride fled from Hong Kong to the mainland, where he was pivotal in organizing resistance to Tokyo. He acknowledged that the "most active, reliable, efficient and anti-Japanese of all the Chinese organizations" was the Communist Party and "their control extended right through the Japanese occupied areas, even through the New Territories and into Kowloon." He emphasized, *There was no overland route into or out of Hong Kong other than through Red territory, and no one, be he Chinese or Westerner, could pass in or out without Red help or permission. . . .* [emphasis—LR]" But "as far as the Central Government was concerned, the Reds were public enemy No. 1; the Japanese came a poor second; any hostilities taken by the Chinese in this area were invariably against the Reds and not against the Japanese." Why were there not more escapes from Hong Kong? Quite simply, "It was commonly believed that the Chinese had all turned pro-Japanese" and escapees would be "handed over" to them.[47] The Communists were not the only ones who felt that the Nationalist "resistance" often was targeted conveniently at Tokyo's chief foe: themselves.

In a "most secret" missive, the British-led resistance in China admitted that the Communists "can be regarded as an indigenous growth, not an offshoot of Russia," which contradicted the reigning theory that Communists from Moscow to Madras to Manhattan were one and the same. The report also noted that "accommodation between Chungking [Nationalists] and Japan" was a "very lively [possibility]." The Empire was caught between Communists they despised and Nationalists they suspected of collaborating with their immediate foe. The bill for white supremacy was coming due: "There is a latent anti-Western feeling which might in ordinary circumstances coalesce with the anti-Western drive by Japan," it warned.[48]

The Communists presented a grave obstacle for London.[49] Though cooperation with them seemed unavoidable—as was cooperation with their supposed patrons in Moscow—London realized that in the long run, the interests of Reds and the Empire clashed irreparably.[50] But even the Reds, supposed avatars of the class struggle, were making an argument similar to that of their arch-enemy, Tokyo—and pointing up once more the untenable position of London. The Chinese Communist, "Li Ta-Chao, for one, explicitly argued that in global terms the class struggle had taken on the form of a racial conflict."[51]

Whether it stressed class or race, the Empire wanted to have nothing to do with the Communists. Lindsay Ride early on had "suggested to his superiors in Chungking and New Delhi that in the short term at least it would be more profitable for the Allies to support the Communists rather than the Nationalists."[52] However, such advice risked inviting persecution after the war when the question was asked, "Who lost China?"

After witnessing the British debacle at Singapore and the loss of Hong Kong, many Chinese, on the other hand, believed that the Allies' cause was lost—even setting aside any predisposition to sympathize with Japan. This was all the more reason to collaborate passionately with Tokyo. Antipathy toward the Empire's policy of white supremacy, together with the instinct to kick the mighty "whitey" now that it had fallen, created further animosity toward London. British "prestige," such as it was, was at "an all time low," thought Ride. There was "disgust and contempt for the decadent British; anti-British feeling was rife on all sides." Further, "If the defeated British were considered to be a world power, why not the defeated Chinese," thought the Nationalists.[53]

This metastasizing disrespect was manifested in the sobriquets for the Royal Air Force, such as "Run-Away-Fast" or "Run-Away-First." This was "an obvious legacy of the Burma campaign," thought Ride, who was disturbed by it all. He considered launching a pro-London propaganda campaign but doubted if the Nationalists would buy it by itself. So he proposed "conjoining" it with a strong "anti-Japanese" and "blatantly pro-Chinese" campaign. This had the advantage of directing energy toward their presumed common opponent—Tokyo—and diverting attention from the Empire's dismal performance in the war. But from London's point of view, it raised disturbing questions about why the Chinese should not be administering Hong Kong, particularly in light of the Empire's demonstrated incompetence.[54]

In September 1942, Ride, a former official at Hong Kong University, stated what had become painfully apparent to many: the non-Communist Chinese were now openly organizing an "anti-British" unit called the "Overseas Chinese Volunteer Unit." Their slogan: "1st enemy the Japanese, 2nd enemy the British." Many were from Hong Kong and exiled on the mainland and had representatives in "Kukong, in Kweilin, in Liuchow and Kwong Chow Wan." Disappointingly, "most of the members are Malaysian Chinese, British subjects." "Most of the leaders have only recently come out from Hong Kong and many of them were living in the University [community] where the atmosphere was, if not pro-Japanese, pro Wang Ching-wei."[55]

But surely Ride should not have been surprised by this development. He must have known that even anti-Japanese Chinese often refused to escape from occupied Hong Kong with their European counterparts on account of their lingering antipathy toward white supremacy. Their refusal had serious consequences for the Europeans since the Chinese often knew the terrain better, could more easily fit in and escape detection, and were more likely to receive assistance from mainlanders. Thus, when George Chow, a Chinese Canadian, escaped from Hong Kong he did so alone, leaving his compatriots behind; while he escaped rather easily, they endured a tormenting experience.[56]

It was evident that white supremacy of the old type had become thoroughly counterproductive. Concessions, when made, had a ring of insincerity, as if giving up white supremacy was more difficult than relinquishing life itself. In 1943 Japanese occupation forces moved to eliminate extraterritoriality in Shanghai. "Two days later"[57] London and Washington signed new treaties with Nationalist China abrogating the hated extraterritoriality, and extending Chinese laws and jurisdiction to the city. But like the Emancipation Proclamation in the United States that freed enslaved Africans in regions that the federal government did not altogether control, the Anglo-American concession was half-hearted. General Li Chai Sum was appreciative though pointed, noting that practices like extraterritoriality had provided fertile soil for the growth of "such theories as Pan Asiaticism [sic] or White Man's Aggression."[58]

China's lack of sympathy for London complicated the war effort. In 1944 the British legation in Chungking informed Anthony Eden that "generally speaking . . . there has been a relative lack of Chinese interest in the British and American disclosures about [Japanese] atrocities. . . . It is also possible that the Chinese appreciate—and secretly sympathize with—the fact that one Japanese aim in perpetrating these atrocities was the humiliation of the white man, as part of the plan for his expulsion from East Asia."[59]

Similarly, London knew that "Indians [were] better treated than Europeans" during their internment in Hong Kong but was reluctant to broadcast the awkward fact.[60] The Empire's Commander in Chief in India was perplexed by this stance.[61] Unfortunately, because Japanese atrocities against Europeans were downplayed for fear it would delight Asians, great swathes of Asia such as India, the Malay peninsula, and elsewhere today have difficulty accepting the enormity of Tokyo's crimes during the war.

But what of atrocities against the Chinese? Here it was thought that London had gone overboard, as when it reported that the Japanese had placed "some thousands" of Chinese on "six junks," towed them to sea, "and abandoned them." One British official asked in awe, "How could 'some thousands' of Chinese be put on six junks—and if the junks had sails, etc., why should they just be towed out to sea and then left? Atrocity stories of this sort don't seem to hold water."[62] Others thought that "atrocity stories," even when accurate, were designed to delay opening a second front in Europe.[63] Even a top news editor from the well-respected British Broadcasting Corporation was a "little concerned about the reporting of news of the fighting in China in our Japanese news bulletins.... The news contained in these communiques is unreliable. I have been told that Chinese official communiques are written more as propaganda than as news, and on various occasions heavy fighting has been reported in areas where there are known to be no Chinese troops."[64]

The Empire was perplexed about how to report on Japanese outrages. There was "propaganda value," it thought, in the "Hong Kong atrocities" but the "value in Europe is today low." Why? Because reportage would "create the impression that we have manufactured a lame story to cover up a poor show."[65] How could the mighty Empire credibly report that their alleged racial inferiors had soundly defeated them, and committed barbarities to boot?

London's perplexity indicated the conundrum created when white supremacy went to war. In 1942 the embattled colonial government in India wrote: "The point is to emphasize by every means Japanese barbarity towards other Asiatics, but not to bolster up Japanese self-proclaimed role as defender of Asiatics by putting out stories of their barbarous treatment of Europeans."[66] Thus the policy of white supremacy had led to the downplaying of admitted atrocities against Europeans, which in turn encouraged Tokyo to commit even more crimes in the name of fighting white supremacy.

The question of how to report on Japanese atrocities confounded the Empire. The Viceroy, writing to an official in India, reported with exasperation that "Japanese propaganda is working hard to present the war in the Far East as a matter of Asiatics (yellow and brown) against Europeans. In order to ram home this theme, they regularly put out stories of (1) insulting behavior of European and Dominion troops towards Indian troops; (2) neglect of safety and comfort of Indian troops by their white officers; (3) preferential treatment of Europeans in arrangements for evacuation (4) irreproachable behaviour of Japanese toward Asiatic prisoners of war and inhabitants of occupied territory. In fact they are doing all they can to inflame the lowest passions, which racial and colour prejudice can stir up"—as the Empire knew only too well.[67]

The suggested policy—admitted atrocities against Europeans had to be downplayed while those against "Asiatics" had to be emphasized—was, in a sense, surprising. Whereas it was once thought that the lives of the latter were worth less than those of the former, the compulsions of war meant the old notion had to be turned on its head, at least on paper. In any case, after the war ended it became impossible to return to white supremacy in the old way.

As if the Empire did not have its hands full fighting Tokyo —not to mention dealing with Moscow—it also had to come to grips with persistent probing from Washington. The problem for London was that it was heavily dependent on Indian troops, who were increasingly attracted to various anti-British groups. In the prewar era "India always paid the maintenance costs of about 20 percent of the British army and 10–20 per cent of [the] RAF, indirectly subsidizing their net estimates to the same degree."[68] London might be able to survive by keeping all its various foes off balance, turning one against another, while allying with yet another. But its rivals were not blind to the fact—as the historian Christopher Thorne put it—that "as a world power, Britain herself had been in decline since the last third of the nineteenth century, to the point where . . . her position had come to rest essentially on a series of bluffs."[69] As the crucial month of December 1941 approached, it was apparent that these brazen bluffs were being called by virtually all the parties, including a progressively stronger Washington.

It was likewise clear that there was a palpable difference between the war in Europe and that in the Asia-Pacific region. For the most part, the former involved restoring the sovereignty of nations or resisting threats to sovereignty, while for the most part the latter involved—or so thought certain European powers—restoring colonial empires. These closed empires did not have the "open door" so necessary for the penetration of U.S. business. The United States had its own interests in Asia that did not necessarily include playing second fiddle to the Empire indefinitely.[70] Thus, it was no source of surprise that London and Washington would clash more severely in the Asia-Pacific theater than in Europe. Anglo-American naval cooperation flourished in the Atlantic but not in the Pacific, where Douglas MacArthur and Chester Nimitz maintained separate intelligence organizations from London, even though the Royal Navy had been largely absent from the region since its debacle in Singapore in 1942.[71] And despite the unrivalled importance of the Middle Kingdom during this conflict, when it came to China London "would not" share "their counter-intelligence files freely with the Americans."[72] Overall, in the Asia-Pacific the United States practiced a kind of "jackal" imperialism, feeding hungrily and amply on London's "possessions," while all the while presenting itself as a more reasonable alternative.[73]

This had not escaped the attention of London, which knew that despite its state-sanctioned white supremacy, Washington—and other powers—presented themselves as more progressive on the racial front in Asia. Thus, the British-controlled "Shanghai Club" on the mainland excluded the Chinese, in contrast "with the Cercle Sportif Francaise, to which access was much less restricted, the American Club (Chinese members from 1929) and the German Club Concordia (Chinese members from 1917)."[74]

Differences between the British and the United States were also prevalent in Hong Kong.[75] There the British resistance leader Lindsay Ride was candid about his dislike for the Yankees. "I was violently anti the major American . . . policy in China which appeared to us to be China for the Americans and Wedemeyer and to hell with everyone else." Washington, the British thought, was not above currying favor with the Chinese at London's expense, presenting itself as the liberal alternative. Thus, "there was a hostile belief among the Chinese leadership that the [organized British resistance] was being kept in South China by the British mainly for the purpose of keeping a foot in the Hong Kong door." This view "received a good deal of support and encouragement from the" sly and artful "Americans."[76] Disingenuously, the British would argue, many Americans were often moved to make a "striking observation" about "the intensity of anti-British sentiment within the Chinese government . . .

rooted in the suspicion that the British wanted to keep China weak and divided in order to maintain their own imperial strength in Asia."[77]

The status of Hong Kong was a sore point between the Empire and those in the United States who wished to inherit Britain's leading role. The State Department deemed it "politically undesirable" for U.S. troops to retake Hong Kong, then hand it back to London. Winston Churchill was determined, however, that "never would we yield an inch of the territory that was under the British flag." This had occurred to President Roosevelt, who was threatening to "go over Churchill's head in an appeal to the King and the parliament." This only fueled suspicion in London. A poll revealed that more than half the U.S. population objected to the return of Hong Kong.[78]

The popular image grew of the effete though sophisticated Empire continually bilking the naïve though increasingly powerful U.S.[79] The Empire found this image quite distasteful. London realized that there was an "American aversion to being actively associated with restoring 'colonial rule' especially in areas where they believe that it has made us unpopular." Washington had a "sincere if unfounded belief," it thought, "that they are more popular than we in these areas, and that. . . . it is a positive military advantage . . . if they are . . . not closely associated with us."[80] Years later a British Foreign and Commonwealth Office official recalled that "the problem was . . . to get back into Hong Kong before the Americans and certainly before the Chinese nationalists."[81]

In a "most secret" missive in early 1944 one bureaucrat was stupefied by "the tenacity with which those who oppose us in America seek to eliminate us from the Far Eastern scene." The "secret" reply, penned by the key political advisor to Lord Mountbatten, charged hotly that London "may have to conduct our war against Japan on much the same lines vis-á-vis the Americans as the Japanese and Germans now adopt in fighting us—namely, a certain friendly interest and exchange of information and assistance but no common plan, collaboration, or sacrifice of interests."[82]

Just as white supremacy had benefited from the dexterous manipulation of ethnic differences between the Chinese and Malays and Indians in Singapore, for example, Japan was now trying to deepen the wedge between the British and Euro-Americans. Jan Henrik Marsman, who escaped from wartime Hong Kong, recalled that during his detention "throughout the Japs [sic] showed they hated the English worse than any other nationality, and always they showed no love for the Americans but they always saved the dregs of their hatred for Englishmen. Englishmen were given the most brutal treatment of all."[83] According to the well-connected U.S. journalist Emily Hahn, who was not interned in wartime Hong Kong, the occupation forces had a "feeling toward the British" of "ruthless, revengeful hate." They had a milder approach toward the United States, hoping to take advantage of Washington's well-known desire to supplant the Empire by cutting a deal with the United States.[84] As usual, the Chinese Nationalists pursued a parallel strategy, though for ostensibly different reasons. Chiang's policy was to "drive a wedge between the British and Americans while obtaining benefits from each."[85] None of this had evaded the attention of London.[86]

The United States had its own divide-and-conquer strategy, or so thought London. "Britain realized that the Dominions"—principally New Zealand and Australia—"mistrusted Japan and feared that the United States wanted to persuade them to follow the U.S. lead." As late as 1919, the "War Office" in London still saw the United States as a "potential threat." "Even then [U.K.] statesmen recognized that British and U.S. interests clashed. . . . [while] few politicians regarded Japan as a threat [and] wanted close ties with it." In the 1920s Churchill thought there was not the "slightest chance" that "Japan would attack Britain 'in our lifetimes,' an argument which, however wrong, was shared by virtually every decision maker."[87] Just as the Empire was trapped between the Chinese Communists and Tokyo, it was also trapped between Japan and the United States, both of whom thought they knew the correct answer to a question that London would have preferred to ignore: who should be the logical inheritor of the Empire?

The British resistance in China was highly suspicious of China's so-called U.S. allies, which was unhelpful in overcoming the common adversary. They believed that U.S. intelligence—the Office of Strategic Services (OSS)—"issued instructions to their secret agents to penetrate [the resistance]." They knew this because a U.K. "agent," an "American subject by birth but a resident" in Hong Kong, had decided to become a double agent. According to this "top secret" communique, this man "had gathered that certain members of the [resistance] official staff were already in the pay of the OSS."[88]

The scholar Lee Yiu Wa has observed that "after 1933, the devotees of rapprochement with Japan dominated the British government and this direction was supported by the Foreign Office and the Treasury."[89] As late as 1937, U.S. radicals were charging that London's desire to scotch the ambitions of Washington meant that the Empire was willing to ally itself with Tokyo. According to the *Daily Worker*, "the proposed Anglo-Japanese agreement 'to guarantee the integrity of China' is actually designed to divide China up into British and Japanese colonies and strike a blow against American interests and the American open-door policy."[90]

Those who thought that the intensity of war would put an end to the animosity between Britain and the United States may have been surprised by the goings-on in Stanley camp in Hong Kong. In the internment camps this divide-and-conquer strategy was deployed nimbly against those who had developed it into a fine art in Asia and Africa. Sir Franklin C. Gimson, who acted as a kind of pro-consul of Stanley camp in Hong Kong in that he had expressed an early interest in operating on behalf of Tokyo, was quite sensitive to the Yankees' tendency to disregard his authority.[91]

John Streicker, the Administrative Secretary of Stanley, noticed that "neither the American nor Dutch representatives attended the British Communal Council meetings." In any case, "it is doubtful whether they would have accepted even if they had been invited," which they decidedly were not.[92] Gwen Priestwood agreed. Bill Hunt, a leading "American capitalist" at Stanley had no affection for the Empire; "one way to make Bill fix anything, the gossip went, was to tell him the British had tried and failed."[93]

Actually, the experience of internment brought both ethnic and class distinctions into sharp relief. As one writer put it, "the Americans seemed the best organized entity with a commendable tendency to work together." The British, on the other hand, were "divided by class, occupation and prejudice."[94]

Thus, the conflict between London and Washington provided Tokyo momentum and complicated the war effort. During the war David Bosanquet escaped from Hong Kong to the mainland, whereupon he encountered an American.[95] Though the American was "very derogatory about the Japanese," he took a British attitude toward the military, which he deemed "beneath his dignity. Fighting was the task of the coolies"—a view greeted with contempt and incredulity by the author. Bosanquet's travails did not cease there. On board ship from India to home in Britain, the American "ignor[ed]" Bosanquet "entirely" and "turned to the steward" and stammered with derision, "God dammit, you've got a Limey with you."[96]

This peevish attitude was rather mild compared to what other Britons encountered. In India on occasion during the war, "an irate American officer might suggest, 'Why don't we fight the British instead of the Japanese? That would be a popular war.'" This prompted a "theme song: . . . . "the Limeys make policy, Yanks fight the Japs [sic]/And one gets its Empire, and one takes the rap.'"[97]

Japan's assertion that it was aggressively moving to destroy white supremacy proved to be a powerful mobilizing tool in a world comprised overwhelmingly of Asians, Africans, and Latin Americans. But it was also a risky and hazardous maneuver. For all the major powers—save one, Japan, and, possibly the Soviet Union headed by a Georgian—could be loosely defined as "white," and their socioeconomic systems were geared to exploiting the very "coloreds" Japan was supposedly determined to liberate. Moreover, the primary "white" power Japan was allied with—Germany—represented the epitome of racial supremacy that supposedly Tokyo had decided to obliterate. This contradiction was profoundly consequential. It served to undermine Tokyo's appeal among U.S. Negroes who were within the orbit of the Communist Party and whose regular work side by side with Euro-Americans tended to disprove the idea that all "whites" were beyond the pale.

Moreover, how could Tokyo be sure that its so-called comrade in arms, Germany, would not be driven by the logic of its racial dream to turn on Japan since, at the end of the day, if Tokyo's hopes were realized, Berlin was also a potential loser? In fact, had Japan won the war a "hot war" between Japan and Germany was more likely to follow than was a "cold war" between the United States and the USSR in the aftermath of an Allied victory. John Morris, who was employed by the Japanese Foreign Office before the war as a language adviser and who maintained good contacts there throughout, "remarked that at the time he left Japan, people were saying openly that if the Allies lost the European war, Germany would be Japan's next objective."[98]

The notion of a German double-cross had crossed the minds of Japanese elites as late as 1941. At one high-level meeting in Tokyo—weeks before the assault on Hong Kong—the question was posed starkly: "What we should always keep in mind here is what would happen to relations between Germany and Great Britain and the United

States, all of them whose population belongs to the white race, if Japan should enter the war." Why should this be a concern? Because "Hitler has said that the Japanese are a second-class race, and Germany has not declared war against the United States. Japan will take positive action against the United States. In that event, will the American people adopt the same attitude toward us psychologically that they do toward the Germans? Their indignation against the Japanese will be stronger than their hatred of Hitler." This comment was prescient. Hara Yoshimichi, "president of the Privy Council, a group of distinguished leaders who advised the Emperor . . . often asked questions in the Imperial Conferences on behalf of the Emperor." He was blunt: "I fear, therefore, that if Japan begins a war against the United States, Germany and Great Britain and Germany and the United States will come to terms, leaving Japan to herself. That is, we must be prepared for the possibility that hatred of the yellow race might shift the hatred now being directed against Germay to Japan, thus resulting in the German-British war's being turned against Japan. . . . We must give serious consideration to race relations, exercise constant care to avoid being surrounded by the entire Aryan race—which should leave Japan isolated—and take steps now to strengthen relations with Germany and Italy."

But Japan too was enmeshed in contradictions all its own that allowed for no easy exit. The Japanese leader pleaded, "Don't let hatred of Japan become stronger than hatred of Hitler, so that everybody will in fact gang up on Japan." Tojo, who was to pay the ultimate price as a chief engineer of Japan's racial policies, added, "The points are well taken. . . . I intend to take measures to prevent a racial war once war is started. I should like to prevent Germany and Italy from making peace with Great Britain or with the United States."[99]

While the Allies dealt with internal rifts not only between London and Washington but also between Moscow and its partners, the tensions between Tokyo and its allies were considerably more acute. A Soviet writer captured this reality in 1944. "Unquestionably Hitler's Germany is not overpleased with her Far Eastern ally. . . . Japan is pursuing her own aims and apparently has no intention of coordinating her East Asian affairs with Hitler's strategic plans. It is impossible to conceal Japanese-German difference in estimating the general military situation."[100]

The BBC also knew about the deep divisions that often marked Tokyo-Berlin relations. It reported that "the Japan-German pact did not appeal to the people of Japan. . . . Both Italy and Germany supplied China with arms and supplies of every kind from 1937 onwards. . . . The German military mission under Falkenhausen directed the operations around Shanghai in 1937, thus costing the Japanese thousands of lives. . . . Although officially at war with Chungking, the German government has always taken a very conciliatory attitude towards it in their pronouncements: while the German press delights in reporting on conditions in Nanking, China in such a way as to discredit the puppet Government and indirectly the Japanese."[101]

Part of the BBC's propaganda arsenal was an intercepted letter from a high-ranking German excoriating the Japanese, terming them "yellow subhumans," "little yellow animals in uniform," "cleverer than world Jewry," and more scathing intended insults.[102] The BBC knew—though it kept it "confidential"—that the "Japan translation" of *Mein Kampf* "omits as one would expect the whole of the famous passage in Chapter XI where Hitler denies that Japan has any culture of her own."[103] It noted that in a well-known Japanese journal in late 1942, a prestigious professor "condemn[ed] the pitiless exploitation of Europe by the Germans."[104]

Likewise, the scholar Louise Young has also suggested that Tokyo's fear of a "white united front" to squelch its plans for racial revolution were not far-fetched. She writes that "long experience with racial discrimination by Europeans, Americans and British colonists in Canada, Australia and New Zealand led Japanese to interpret Western diplomatic opposition in racial terms." Thus, one Japanese writer complained—not altogether inaccurately—of "the current control of the League [of Nations] by the white race." Hence, "the specter of a solid phalanx of white powers united against Japan led to gloomy scenarios of economic blackmail and worse."[105]

Japan's rulers were also justifiably anxious about Berlin's ability to deflect wartime hatred toward the Pacific. Stephen Ambrose comments that "there was not much room for racism in a war that pitted German soldiers who had American cousins against American soldiers who had German parents. Fully one-third of the U.S. Army was of German descent (not to mention the Supreme Commander in the European theatre, whose name was Eisenhower; the Commander of the air bombardment of Germany was named Spaatz.)" The European front could hardly compare with that in Asia, which involved "that most racist war of all."[106]

When the writer John Toland interviewed Ohshima Hiroshi, Japan's Ambassador to Germany, he sensed Hiroshi's anxiety about Japan's relationship with Germany. According to Toland, Hiroshi recalled that "Hitler didn't know about Japan at first. In 1922 he wrote *Mein Kampf* in which he didn't speak particularly well of Japan." (This was a gross understatement.) Thus, during the war there was "not much done in cooperation" between the two powers; they "exchanged information," but not much more. Later Hiroshi asserted that "Goering complained to me saying that 'your general is helping Jews in north Manchuria.' I had it investigated and found it was true. The Jews never did any harm to Japan, therefore, there was no reason for us to reject them. Not only that Rothschild and Schiff but also in Germany such Jews as Greenburg had furnished military funds for Japan. . . . I further told Goering that Japan was using Jews who had escaped (from the Nazis) in such activities as collecting information on Russia (therefore they were useful)."[107]

Hiroshi was not being misleading: Tokyo did diverge sharply from its alleged ally on the bedrock question of anti-Semitism.[108] Dr. Karl Kindermann was Jewish and lived in Japan throughout the war. While there he "had been specially protected by Japanese friends who were high in the ranks of the . . . [ultra-patriotic] Black Dragon Society." This was part of a larger Japanese plan not to participate in the incineration of Jews but to rescue them and deploy their resources and skills on behalf of Tokyo.[109] A striking number of besieged German Jews—even antifascists—looked not to Europe or North America for refuge but to Japanese-occupied Asia.[110] Japanese diplomats like the legendary Sugihara Chiune saved thousands of Jews on the eve of the Shoah by issuing visas from European posts such as Lithuania.[111] Solomon Bard, interned in Hong Kong, detected no anti-Semitism among his captors. They "made absolutely no effort to distinguish those in the camp who were Jews," he recalled later, "Nazi doctrine in this respect did not reach as far as us."[112]

Catherine Davis was in Japan during the war. "There was quite a large Jewish Orthodox colony from Syria, Egypt, Mespotamia, who were in the cotton business; some were immensely wealthy and constantly threw huge parties among themselves, with every kind of luxury, while the rest of the population was practically starving." She was located in Kobe and added that "the Chinese were also chiefs of the Black Market and we managed to get what we wanted from them."[113]

The Empire recognized in the fall of 1942 that "relations between the Nazis and the Japanese appear to have been particularly strained at Shanghai. But technicians with European training are badly needed, as Nazis are unwilling to cooperate except on terms of [inequality] or even superiority galling to the Japanese conqueror, [thus] the Jews have been called in."[114] In fact, according to the *Canadian Jewish News*, "after Adolf Hitler's accession to power, Shanghai was the only place where a Jew persecuted by Nazism could emigrate without a visa or family sponsorship."[115] James Ross, who studied the matter intensively, argues that "the documents show that the Japanese distrusted the Gestapo. . . . The Japanese occupiers in Shanghai could be cruel and certainly were familiar with anti-Semitism but they never succumbed to—or even comprehended—the anti-Jewish hatred that consumed their German allies. . . . The Japanese did restrict the European Jewish refugees to a ghetto after May 1943 but not to placate the Gestapo. They were more concerned with security issues, such as reports of black market activity among the refugees."[116] Jacov Wilczek, now a doctor in Haifa agreed, adding, "The Japanese occupying forces of Shanghai were neither racists nor Jew-haters." On "many occasions," he said of his experience under Japanese rule, "the Japanese emphasized that they were not racist."[117] Perhaps this is why there was a long-term collaboration between "white Russian Emigrants"—including those who were Jewish—"and the Japanese army in the Far East," notably in the area surrounding Harbin. "The Japanese occupation of Harbin in February 1932," said one commentator, was "joyously welcomed by the numerous Russian emigres."[118]

At the same time, British propagandists acknowledged other differences between Tokyo and Berlin.[119] The BBC decided that on their broadcasts to Tokyo "only non-Japanese scholars of the language ought to speak in broadcasts in Japanese. Japan is a far more deeply nationalist country than Germany or Italy and the hatred aroused among Japanese listeners for a 'traitor' speaker would be likely to outweigh the effect of the broadcast."[120] This also suggests that there was more unity in Japan behind the war than in Germany.

In short, Tokyo-Berlin relations were far from ideal. John Morris, a contract worker with the Japanese Foreign Office before the war, was allowed to write "anti-Nazi articles" with impunity, an act that led to his being "reported . . . by the German embassy. . . . I was writing articles in denunciation of Japan's closest ally," he remarked. He agreed that "the

Japanese dislike of the Germans arose from the Nazis' extreme arrogance and the fact that they made no attempt to disguise their contempt for the Japanese."[121] As he was leaving Tokyo, he noted that Japanese people were saying quite openly that if the Allies lost the European war "Germany would be Japan's next objective. In fact, I once heard it said quite seriously that the Japanese army put the nations of the world into three classes; enemies, neutral enemies, and friendly enemies. Japan's Axis partners making up the last class."[122]

His perceptions were confirmed in Shanghai. A 1942 police report noted that "thought is gradually gaining ground among Germans and Italians . . . that all trade possibilities will disappear. The ever-increasing military and economic might of Japan is evidently beginning to worry her Axis partners who consider there may be no limit to Japan's expansion." According to a British intelligence report, the Japanese "were treating all whites, whether enemies or friends, exactly alike." A "repatriated American missionary recalled an incident when a German lady on horseback was stopped at the barrier where Great Western Road crosses the [railroad] to have her pass examined by the Jap [sic] sentry. He made her dismount and kept her waiting for some time during which time her horse dropped a lot of dung. Returning, the sentry ordered her to clean up the place, refused to lend her a brush and dustpan, and made her remove the filth with her hands."[123] Such antipathy was not just a product of Shanghai's peculiar environment. In the fall of 1944 Canberra reported that "German nationals in Hong Kong are being carefully watched and it is rumored that they are liable to be interned at any time pending new developments."[124]

The wellspring of racial ideology was different in Tokyo, as opposed to Berlin—or London and Washington, for that matter. In Japan these doctrines grew out of the anxiety and hysteria caused by the U.S. intervention there in the 1850s and by Britain's seizure of Chinese territory. One scholar has concluded that "It is difficult in fact to find anything in seventeenth or eighteenth century Japan which resembles a coherent ideology of race." It was mostly post-Meiji, that is, part of the anxious rush to modernity in the 1860s. Moreover, "German Nazi ideology failed to attract much of a following in Japan."[125]

The prickly and barbed differences between Tokyo and Berlin were manifested in ways large and small. The "Japanese in general disliked the National Socialist members' arrogance and contempt for the Japanese and [the authorities] kept a permanent tail on the German

Ambassador to Japan, General Eugene Ott and the German military attache."[126] Gwen Terasaki, a Euro-American married to a Japanese diplomat, noticed this taut unease. After being interned with German officials in the United States after the assault on Pearl Harbor, she quickly noticed that "the Axis powers were incomparable at several points." Again, after decamping in Mozambique she attended an "Axis party" that "was not a success. This was the beginning of my conviction that the Tripartite Pact appealed to none of the people represented by the signatories. . . . How unnatural and even hostile the Germans and the Japanese were to each other in all their relationships," she marveled. While residing in Japan she realized "the hostility I was to experience toward myself throughout the war occurred almost without exception because I was mistaken for a German."[127]

Jan Henrik Marsman had a similar experience, as Japanese forces were conducting mopping up operations in December 1941 in Hong Kong. At the Peninsula Hotel "one morning a very bulky and officious looking German with a big swastika on his arm band strode toward the entrance, stopped, clicked his heels, gave the Nazi salute, and trumpeted: 'Heil Hitler!'" He "apparently expected some sort of response. But the sons of Hirohito continued their pacing without any heiling or even momentary hesitation. The German moved forward to enter the hotel. Japanese bayonets blocked the way. Some guttural conversation followed, apparently the sentries wanted to see the Nazi's pass. . . . The German grew very angry and shouted: 'Out of my way! Let me pass!' Japanese steel didn't give an inch. More hard words followed, and two other Japanese soldiers came up. One grabbed the German by his neck and the other yanked him around by his midriff. Together they threw him into the street."[128]

Akira Iriye is correct in saying that "although they shared their hostility toward the Anglo-American [nations], too much separated Germany and Japan—racially, culturally, and historically—to turn the alliance into anything more than a marriage of convenience. Even after Pearl Harbor, Germany and Japan never organized a combined force or established combined chiefs of staff, unlike their enemies."[129]

Germany knew and did not appreciate the fact that Japan never declared war on the nation they saw as the root of all evil, the Soviet Union. The latter reciprocated by not declaring war on Japan until August 1945. Iriye has pointed to the conspicuous fact that "many people in Japan, including some in the army, were envisioning a grand alliance" with Moscow.[130] This is one of the many reasons why the thesis of a "firmly conceived conspiracy between" Berlin and Tokyo "was not proven" at the Tokyo War Crimes trial. Instead, it was "conclu[ded] that Japan's association with the Tripartite Pact was for defensive purposes to protect their move south in the Pacific and to keep the U.S. out of the China war. . . . Japan continued to act with independence, not in a global conspiracy with the Nazis."[131]

Personal anecdotes confirmed this conclusion. Hans J. Massaquoi was born in Germany of parents who were African and German and grew up there during the war years. One of his coworkers in the midst of this titanic conflict told him, "Don't think that they [that is, Japan] will be satisfied with being the rulers in Asia. . . . As soon as this war is over, the Japanese will send a special hit squad to Berlin and assassinate Hitler. After that, they will take over the entire world."[132]

One scholar has gone further, suggesting that the blanket term "fascism" does not describe the differences he has perceived between Tokyo and its wartime allies. "A wide gap in fact existed between the doctrines and regimes of Imperial Japan and those of Italian fascism and German nazism. . . . The Italian-German influence on the Japanese regime was confined to economic and legal and economic 'management fascism.' . . . Japan's alliance with Italy and Germany was no more the effect of ideological proximity than was the alliance of the Western democracies with the Soviet Union." "Political parties were suppressed in 1940" in Japan "but their members continued to sit in the Lower House, an unimaginable state of affairs in Italy or Germany at that time."[133]

Japan may not have acted in concert with Germany but it surely sought to enlist other nations—particularly those today described as "Third World" nations—in their crusade. This was particularly the case for Mexico, which bore a long-term grievance against its northern neighbor not least because the latter had seized a good deal of its territory in the nineteenth century. The white supremacy involved in the relations between Mexico City and Washington added to Tokyo's desire to intervene in their strained bilateral relationship. If Japan could open up a front on the southern border of the United States, its dream of establishing a new racial order would be that much closer. This thought also had occurred to the press baron, William Randolph Hearst, who in 1917 produced a film "which showed Japanese and Mexican troops looting, murdering and raping as they invaded the United States."[134] Although

Japan's plan perished well before the onslaught in Hiroshima, it was not for lack of trying—particularly in the prewar years—by Tokyo.

A few years after its enormous victory over Russia in 1905, complaints arose in southern Arizona—on the Mexican border and in territory that only recently had belonged to Mexico—that Japan was extending its reach across the Pacific. "Vile Japanese," it was said, were "halted at [the] border. . . . with more than $20,000 in good hard cash in their possession and the allegation that they had $11,000 more in [the] bank in San Francisco. . . . Inspector Jones has recently turned a number of various characters back," including a "spy" who was now "under arrest."[135]

Washington had concluded early on that Tokyo had imperialistic designs in the Western Hemisphere. A "great outcry" greeted Japan's putative plan in 1912 to purchase an "enormous tract of land in Lower California," Mexico.[136] At the same time the U.S. Ambassador was arguing that "recent anti-American disturbances" were accompanied by "very strong appeals made through a number of Mexican papers to the people of this country to cultivate the friendship of the Japanese, making very clear insinuations as the advisability of an alliance with them in case of trouble with the United States." This appeal was "the subject of much comment among the members of the diplomatic corps here," as was "the possibility of a secret understanding between the two countries."[137] Theodore Roosevelt asserted that it "seems incredible that Japanese should go to Mexico with any intention of organizing an armed force to attack us from the Mexican border in the event of war with Japan" but others were not so sure—perhaps not even TR himself.[138] For in a "personal and private" letter to President Taft, he worried—justifiably—that "Japan or some other big power [might] back Mexico" in case of war with the United States.[139]

These matters were developing as Mexico was in the throes of the first and one of the most significant revolutions of the century. Soon Washington came to believe that Tokyo was fishing energetically in the troubled waters of its southern neighbor. In the midst of this conflict a well-informed U.S. commentator waxed insightfully on "the Japanese problem. . . . I will wager that within twenty-five years the United States of America and Japan will clinch in one of the bitterest wars in history." This was no small matter. "The safety of our country and of the white race," he declared, "depends on our protecting China against the scheming of policies of Japan." With foreboding, he added, "The issue will not be a question of European backyards that will be involved, but it will be a question of which race shall inhabit the globe."[140]

Congressman William H. Murray of Oklahoma agreed. He linked Mexico to Japan and added that the "right policy now might determine the future political map of the world; it may determine whether republican government shall endure upon this continent. It may determine whether Mexico is to become a white man's country or to be under the control and domination of Asiatic races. It may ultimately determine not only the perpetuity of our own Republic, but the civilization of the Aryan race. The pages of history are replete with the rise and fall not only of nations but of races. . . . Is history to repeat itself and at the end of another hundred years to witness the dawn of the twenty-first century with the world's domination by Japanese and Chinese, both in point of number and empire? The Mexican problem," he added with a flourish, "may answer this question." He also saw a distinction between German interventions in the hemisphere and that of Japan. "To colonize America by European monarchies would be to destroy our Republic, but would preserve white civilization. To colonize the American continent with the Asiatic races would destroy our civilization as well as the Republic. . . . There are worse things than war. To be dominated by an inferior race or to witness the destruction of the Christian civilization is a hundredfold worse than war."[141]

These presentiments of doom arose in the midst of revelations about a shocking plan—the "Plan of San Diego"—to liquidate all Euro-American males in the southwest, retaking land seized from Mexico decades earlier, and establishing independent Negro and Native American republics on the emptied land. This plan apparently involved not only Mexicans and Mexican-Americans but also the Japanese.[142]

Mexico's notable antipathy toward "gringos" was not matched by resentment toward the Japanese. They were decidedly not "the targets of the anti-foreign hatred directed at most other nationalities" as xenophobia took flight. "By the fall of 1915 South Texas was on the verge of race war" and fingers of accusations were being pointed in the direction of Tokyo.[143] When word emerged from congressional hearings that Tokyo might be aiding Pancho Villa, whose forces had sacked Columbus, New Mexico, thunderous hysteria erupted in the United States.[144]

This extreme agitation reached new heights when a Mexican mission was dispatched to Tokyo in 1918. U.S. intelligence remarked on the "unusual attention" that was "shown the Mexicans by the Japanese."

There were "several conferences and banquets" and the visitors were "permitted" to "visit the government arsenals, military and naval academies and private factories capable of turning out military supplies and apparently every opportunity was given them to study the manufacture of munitions." The purpose of the visit could only be "supply of war munitions, particularly machine guns and small arms" since "all the Mexicans connected with this mission have been openly hostile to the United States and have been insisting in their talk with the Japanese that the United States is a 'big tyrant' and is consistently [taking] liberties [with] Mexico."[145]

As the revolution wound down by the 1920s—and as left-wing forces relatively immune to Tokyo's racial appeals grew in strength— U.S. concern about the Japan-Mexico relationship eased. But in 1932 U.S. intelligence fixated on an article by General Juan Merigo, who said that in case of war between the United States and Japan, Mexico would not necessarily align with the former, "due to the hatred." In case of war, he said, "Mexico would . . . become the ally of Japan. That not only Mexico but Peru, Chile, Argentina, Honduras, Guatemala, Salvador, Costa Rica, Nicaragua, Colombia and Venezuela—countries which have reason to dislike the United States—would also ally themselves with Japan. . . . If a national plebiscite were taken the Mexican people would vote to go to war, but as allies of Japan." This officer was "greatly loved by his men" and was "extremely well-posted on military affairs," so his words had to be taken seriously. Merigo did not mention the thousands of Brazilians of Japanese descent, particularly in the key urban center of Sao Paulo. But Washington could not afford to ignore his words.[146] For the "Plan of San Diego" alone showed that white supremacy was dragging down those who heretofore had accepted this doctrine as if it were gospel.

Conclusion

In the Wake of White Supremacy

THE ATOMIC BOMBING of Hiroshima and Nagasaki effectively ended the Pacific War and with it Tokyo's dream of a complete racial reversal. On the other hand, the changes that had been wrought in the theater of war had been so deep-seated and profound that it was no longer possible to return to the status quo ante.[1] Hong Kong witnessed the decline of racial segregation and the arrogance that accompanied it, along with the rise of a cadre of indigenous capitalists. Many had become wealthy by collaborating with the Japanese, which set them apart from the prewar Chinese compradors allied to British business interests. Their rise also served to further discredit the notion of white supremacy. As a leading Hong Kong academic, Henry Lethbridge, put it—controversially though not inaccurately—the "occupation worked ultimately to the benefit of the leaders of the Chinese community. . . . The British Mandarinate collapsed in 1941; it has never been replaced."[2]

When Eugene D. Williams of the United States arrived in Japan just after the war, he was staggered. "No one who has seen it," he wrote, "can visualize the damage done to the industrial portions of Japan by our Air Force. Officers who have just arrived here from Europe say that it looks a lot worse than it does there." He was impressed with the people, who "seem to work all the time like ants." They "appear to accept their subjugation and defeat with equanimity and to be very friendly to us." But he added, ominously, "I do not believe that they actually are. . . . My personal opinion is that they have a vast capacity for hypocrisy and underneath it all they hate our guts."[3] But intense bombing of Japan culminating in Hiroshima was, in part, an expression of such intense animosity.

Williams may have been mistaking simple adjustment to a new reality for something more sinister—which, of course, was typical of dealings by Euro-Americans and Europeans with the Japanese over the decades. The Hong Kong solicitor, Ralph Malcolm Macdonald King, must have had a particularly nasty experience, for he concluded years after the war, "I wouldn't trust a Japanese now as long as I saw him. . . . Sooner or later they're going to come back. They're going to be [the] scourge that they were before. I would never trust them . . . they are an untrustworthy race."[4]

Some dissented. Norman Cliff, a son of missionaries in northern China who was interned in Japan, upon being freed remarked about his former captors, "Just as they had been enthusiastic conquerors, so they were now enthusiastic losers. . . . What an amazing race the Japanese were!"[5] John Streicker of Stanley partially agreed. He recalled that as the war wound down, his captors "became ingratiating. One would expect it of them and one must expect it in the future," for "outwardly he is your most hospitable host, inwardly he is your dangerous competitor."[6]

Sterling Seagrave thought he had uncovered a central reason for Japan's alleged dissimulation. "If a robber steals $100 billion," he asked, "and successfully hides the money before he is captured and jailed, and then is released after seven years for good behaviour, did he fail or succeed?"[7] In other words, Japan was driven by the desire to mask its unjust enrichment. Seagrave's assessment was echoed by another analyst, who estimated that in Hong Kong alone, "goods worth $10,000 million were taken off during [Japan's] 44 month stay."[8] Much of this property had belonged to the British, which suggested the dimensions of London's loss—and the point that Japan's desire for racial reversal was not thwarted even in defeat. The undoing of the British Empire, whose heart was in Asia, was largely attributable to Japan.

Russell Clark, an Australian reporter, arrived in Hong Kong in August 1945 just after the Japanese surrender and was able to witness the surreal effects of Tokyo's invasion. Many of the cars and much of the city's physical plant had been shipped in previous years directly to Japan, giving the city a strangely empty feeling. The narrow serpentine streets of Hong Kong were littered with the detritus of war. The once proud Hong Kong University, which sat majestically on a hill, was a shrunken hull of its old self, with the library and laboratories alike thoroughly looted. Japanese propaganda had charged that HKU provided a damaging "Occidental influence [which] in many cases had the effect of imparting to Asiatic students an inferiority complex"—but now it would have to be rebuilt anew.⁹ A good deal of the prewar population had fled and those who remained appeared to be spiritless wraiths. As he surveyed the destitution and haggard appearance of the newly freed internees, he was moved to his racial core: "I have never in my life before been so ashamed," he said, "of being white and British. . . . I wanted to . . . hide myself because I was the same colour and belonged to the same race."

What he saw were virtual human skeletons with rags for clothes, ravenously hungry, and scrounging for cigarette butts. The "poor, unvarying diet had affected the eyesight of many of them—in some cases to complete blindness." Their craving for food had "affected their powers of concentration. Their minds wandered and refused to grasp and hold on to a fact or a line of thought or conversation. Often as you talked to them, you would see them shake their heads like a punch-drunk fighter." The "dead were lucky. It was the living who suffered," he concluded. "We are gentlemen (I use the racial 'we.')," but not the recently deposed rulers. His sympathy for the internees was matched by his abhorrence for their captors: "We hate the Japanese and . . . we shall not forget. . . . Now, beaten, they were suddenly ridiculous little savages again who had tried to ape the white man"—the implication being that only the "white man" was allowed to rampage and engage in racial subjugation. He was clear in his mind about what was at stake: if the Japanese had won, "we should have been slaves—*his* slaves—and in the very real sense of the word. . . . It was very different from Europe's war. This was racial—a war against savages."

His attitude—and that of others—toward certain Chinese was similar. A "new code of ethics and honour" had developed, particularly toward "any Chinese driving a car." He was "fair game. He had either stolen it from the Japs [*sic*] or was working for them. In either case your right to it was greater than his." He and others like him had yet to jettison the prewar notion that certain things, no matter how commonplace, such as driving a car, were reserved for those of "pure European descent," and those who violated this dictum merited little more than a sound thrashing. It would take a while for him to discard this now antiquated idea, just as it would take him a while to understand that a cadre of affluent Chinese had arisen in the postwar dispensation.

Clark and many others of "pure European descent" were possessed of unbridled racial fury in the immediate aftermath of the war—a fury that at times made no distinction between the Japanese foe and the supposed Chinese ally. "The white man is too good," he said. "He doesn't teach the kind of lessons the yellow man is likely to remember. Instead, he treats the yellow as though he were white." "And the yellow man leers and smiles to himself. . . . My view is that they are savages, but savages on their way up. . . . In another five hundred years—or perhaps a lot less—they can become a frightening menace." But what was to be done?

For the time being, Clark was wandering around the rubble-strewn streets of Hong Kong in search of like-minded people. He spoke to a European doctor who mentioned that he had lived in Japan for twenty-five years, including the war. "I thought they loved," he said sadly. "I *know* they loved me. . . . Yet when the war started and they were told to hate all white men, they turned on me like wolves. Then they were told they weren't to hate the white man any more. So they came back, and they were the old friends I used to know." He spoke to some Chinese who also had noticed reversals that seemed opportunistic. One in particular recalled that some British had become friendly for the first time. With rancor he noted when one "used to say that although the Chinese can own a house on The Peak, he cannot live in it—that The Peak is reserved only for whites. . . . [or] if you marry a Chinese or Eurasian girl your Public Service career is finished and your social status wrecked." The British, he asserted distastefully, "would not give the local Chinese a chance for advancement. Before the war no Chinese could ever get a really worthwhile job." With firm conviction he declared, "It will be different when China take back Hong Kong." Said Clark warily, "Wherever you looked or listened on every hand, this was being said, in a hundred ways, . . . 'when China takes back Hong Kong.'"[10]

Unfortunately for the Chinese, London had no intention of returning Hong Kong though it recognized fully that it could not resume its old ways of ruling—though this was not immediately apparent.[11] When Sir Cecil Harcourt met with his Japanese counterpart on 31 August 1945 on board the HMS Indomitable, he heard loud complaints that "British sailors attacked the Japanese soldiers" in Hong Kong, even after the surrender, though "the Chinese populace as a whole has not committed acts against the Japanese."[12] But the Europeans, who had suffered terribly during the war and had been subjected to ample race-baiting themselves, were in no mood for rational discussion. That innocent

Chinese might have been swept up in this revenge was not their primary concern.[13]

Vice Admiral Sir Cecil Harcourt arrived in Hong Kong in 1945 just after the Japanese had been defeated, at the same time as Russell Clark was walking the rubbish-strewn streets. Now chastened after the brutality of war, he was dismissive of his fellow Europeans "returning to Hong Kong . . . who did not realize that they had to have a 1946 outlook; that outlook is imbued with a spirit of national pride in China and the national sovereignty of China. The 1941 outlook is absolutely taboo. There seemed to be some who were either unwilling or unable to understand this, but if they continue in ignorance of the change they will be heading for trouble." Sir Cecil wanted to overturn decades of racial segregation and "put Chinese in positions of responsibility in the Government" and attack the "colour bar problem." The prohibition against Chinese living in The Peak must be replaced with a system whereby "everywhere a man is judged by his merits and character and not by the colour of his skin." Thus, prior to the war, "the majority of policing in Hong Kong was done by Indians. . . . In this new Chinese national spirit they will not be policed by foreign races."[14]

Alexander Grantham concurred. He returned as Governor in 1947, having first arrived in Hong Kong in the 1920s. A "marked decline in social snobbishness was one of the first things I noticed after my return," he said. "The "taipan" and the senior government official were no longer regarded, nor did they so regard themselves, as demi-gods. . . . I observed, too, a greater mixing of the races." Grantham was contrite in the wake of the Japanese occupation. "It is the mental arrogance on the part of some Europeans towards Asians that has created as much, if not more resentment than the physical aggressions like the establishment of colonies and territoriality," he exclaimed. "The basis of the arrogance is the assumption that the European is inherently superior to the Asian, taking such forms as the exclusion of Asians from clubs, downright rudeness or a patronizing manner." That era was over: "The age of the 'blimps' is over, though a few of them still remain, even in Hong Kong. The insularity and provincial mindedness [of] some of the leading businessmen. . . . also struck me. . . . Such a narrow outlook seemed strange in one of the great commercial centres of the world."[15]

Perhaps. But this "great commercial centre" had just undergone an occupation that had left those like Grantham and Sir Cecil eager for change, while other "blimps" were not so sure. Fortunately for the former, many of the latter had departed for greener pastures. Hong Kong's prewar population of two million was down to about 600,000. According to the historian G. B. Endacott, a conspicuous factor in the ability of the new colonial officials to implement their more capacious vision was that "so few of the old colonials returned and so many new Europeans came to take their places." With their departure an "old" form of racism also exited. Moreover, "political uncertainty and British impoverishment through the sacrifices of the war discouraged the inflow of British capital into the Colony and the Chinese increasingly expanded small businesses." The war "inevitably temporarily undermined Britain's economic strength and impaired her influence in the world while Asians developed greater national self-consciousness." This, along with an "increasing number of Chinese [who] entered the professions" created a refurbished economic system that simultaneously allowed for less space for the old type of racism.[16]

However, in the immediate postwar era, as the internees—many of them no more than bags of bones—emerged stumbling from the camps, some of them hungered for a revival of antebellum white supremacy. The recently released internee, William Sewell, thought that "many" from Stanley "were endeavoring to re-establish the status quo, not realizing that a new order was struggling to birth in Asia." They did not recognize that "life could never be the same in the Far East. . . . Asia for the Asiatics had struck responsive chords in the hearts of youth" and "any shreds of false superiority had gone from the British and Americans." Perhaps naively, he thought that now that the war had ended, "Won't we all find it easier to identify with those who suffer?"[17]

This hope reflected the chastened mood of the colonial authorities and the British generally in Hong Kong. A few days after the respected *South China Morning Post* resumed publication in 1945 after the end of the occupation, a front-page item complained about the "vertical" race relations that had prevailed. Now a "horizontal," more nonracial approach was desired, not least because verticality had "provoked much resentment of which the Japanese later took full advantage." But people like Russell Clark who rousted Chinese from automobiles suggested that change would be resisted; so did the "seeming neglect of the Chinese population for the first fortnight of our freedom." This sparked "bitterness," though the "blimps" were happy to report that "we are getting back to the old Hong Kong all right." It was true: "Old conservatism dies hard."[18]

But die it must. For not only had the British been humiliated at the hands of those not of "pure European descent," they had suffered tremendous losses during the war. White supremacy had been borne on a wave of wealth and had difficulty sustaining itself in the face of the gargantuan financial setback sustained during the war. The formerly eminent Sir C. Grenville Alabaster claimed that as a result of the war he had lost "furniture, household goods, silver, cutlery, glass, carpets, pictures, clothes, bedding . . . jewelry, motor car, wireless set, masonic regalia, etc."—all "looted by the Japanese."[19] The Managing Director of the Hong Kong & Shanghai Hotel said that he was "requested" by the "Commissioner of Police" to "destroy all spiritous liquor" as the invasion unfolded; this was worth about "$275,000—including about $75,000 worth transferred from the Peninsula Hotel."[20] The Jesuits suffered "heavy . . . material losses." The "entire contents of Loyola and Wah Yan College, Kowloon, were gone. Ricci Hall was badly damaged."[21] Claims like this proliferated. Some were compensated and some were not. And, of course, some claims may have been inflated.

Then there was the flight of local residents. The British often had a strong desire to depart Hong Kong after Japan's defeat. This was particularly true of senior civil servants. Junior officers, who might stay, did not have the clout of their elders in the new environment.[22] Furthermore, many police records were destroyed during the Japanese occupation, which made it difficult to substantiate claims about lost property or to know who needed to be monitored in a city that had quickly become a sunny site for shady figures.[23] Many of the old European police officers had either been interned or fled,[24] which created more jobs for the Chinese and put more money in their hands.

This abrupt and radical change—from Chinese penury and British snobbery to the British fleeing in rags while some Chinese gained financially—led to considerable social unrest. Virtually on the day of the Japanese surrender, Sir Franklin Gimson told the Colonial Office of his "concern . . . in the first place, [that] the local leaders of the Chinese are accused, perhaps on very inadequate grounds, of cooperating with the Japanese. . . . and have lost the confidence of the local Chinese community." That was just one of his concerns: "My own views are that in the previous constitution the Chinese were not adequately represented on the Councils and I am strongly in favour of the introduction, not necessarily in the Central Government but in the local Government, of a more democratic constitution based on a wide franchise."[25]

In late August 1946 the "Kowloon Riots" erupted, realizing Sir Franklin's worst fears. "Europeans and non-Chinese were once again the centre for the crowd's attention and stones were hurled . . . at all vehicles driven by or carrying Europeans as passengers. . . . Some of the mob stopped buses and inspected passengers for Europeans or non-Chinese. . . . An Indian pedestrian was said to have been mobbed and his turban torn off his head." The Royal Air Force "headquarters at Kadoorie Avenue" was stoned. What was the immediate cause for this conflagration? As in similar cases in the United States, it was sparked by police brutality involving a Portuguese officer and a Chinese hawker, who was kicked to death.[26]

Europeans, even those who were not "blimps," were becoming increasingly uncomfortable in Hong Kong. One European advocated a "Let's Get the Hell out of China" movement; his letter had to be "reprinted. . . . because of the heavy demand. . . . Hundreds of clippings of the letter are believed to have been sent home." This anti-China screed denounced a "civilization [that] matured 2000 years ago and has not progressed one iota since." The writer maintained that during the war, the Chinese were "surrendering every major city and [were] avoiding all combat." Sure, he remarked with disdain, the Chinese were "higher on the evolutionary [sic] ladder than the animals they maltreat so viciously at every opportunity." He was infuriated about the loss of extraterritoriality and suggested that retaliation include "pass laws" in "our countries forcing all Chinese to get residence certificates," while compelling them to "relinquish control of any business they might have in favor of our nationals."[27]

This writer's anti-Chinese polemic reflected the fact that the Chinese in Hong Kong were making steady economic progress in the postwar era. The seeds of this phenomenon had been sown before the war. Cyril Luckin, who arrived in Hong Kong in 1934, recalled that there were a "number of quite good building contractors, mainly Chinese, although I think there was a great deal of Japanese money behind them as well." The "one and only cement works in the area was owned by a Japanese company," for example. He noted that "the Japanese were quite prominent in the business community" and sometimes had Chinese partners.[28]

But the major expansion in Chinese capitalism in Hong Kong was a direct outgrowth of the wartime environment when, for example, "Chinese insurance companies were operating," while "all British and allied firms were taken over or liquidated. . . . Their offices were either commandeered" or "lay abandoned." By "May 1942 Japanese firms were encouraged to start up; and so were Chinese firms—provided they handled essential products such as food or textiles."[29] Alan Dudley Coppin, interned at Sham Shui Po, "found that a lot of Chinese shopkeepers were quite practical in doing business with the Japanese, especially along the road around the Shamshuipo Camp. They managed to make peace with the Japanese Army there and made good profits."[30]

According to W. K. Tang of Hong Kong, the postwar progress by the Chinese would have been even more significant but for white supremacy. "If Britain desires her Chinese employees to cooperate heartily with her," he said, "she must do away with racial discrimination. You must realize the fact that in all Government Departments and British-owned firms, Europeans rank the first, local-born Europeans the second, non-Chinese and Indians the third and Chinese the last and the least paid."[31] Yam Shing agreed. In European-owned firms a "foreigner holding [a] junior position [was] collecting salary and allowance double or more than that of a Chinese holding a senior job. . . . Many foreign girl typist[s]" earned "much more than that of the Chinese chief clerk. Thus, candidates for jobs are not chosen [on] grounds of abilities and qualifications." With exasperation he concluded, "There is no justice at all."[32]

A number of Europeans disagreed. One argued that the Chinese should not be treated equally—or even well—for this only made them hate Europeans. Allegedly a Chinese had told him, "The kinder you are to us, the more we hate you!" This perverse philosophy conveniently justified the most egregious forms of white supremacy. Chinese "do not appreciate kindness," it was said. Why do they lack senior posts? "When a Chinese is given a position of responsibility the first thing he thinks of is how to get 'tea money' in the easiest and safest manner."[33] As the Chinese pushed vigorously for equity and against white supremacy, they were told that it was the British who had liberated Hong Kong and deserved the spoils, and if the Chinese did not like it, they should go west to the mainland.

But tensions were rising on the mainland too. In late 1946 almost fifteen thousand marched in protest in Peking after U.S. soldiers were charged with raping a Chinese woman. One banner read provocatively, "We doubt that the Americans are any better for China than the Japanese invaders."[34]

Many Europeans and Euro-Americans were outraged by what they considered the effrontery and short-sightedness of Asians. Where were the mass atrocities of Chinese perpetrated by Europeans and Euro-Americans? they asked. However, they failed to see that their reluctance to retreat from the more egregious aspects of white supremacy had allowed for the rise of Tokyo in the first place, and that the continuation of racial inequality only jeopardized the hard-earned peace. Thus, as late as the summer of 1947 those of "pure European descent" were still debating whether they should segregate the Chinese racially on the many ferries that plied the waters of Hong Kong. Supporters of the measure claimed that the alleged Chinese tendency to expectorate unduly would "stir up racial prejudice" if the ferries were not segregated.[35]

Many Chinese were outraged by such claims, particularly the suggestion that the European should "take the law into his own hand by thumping the next [Chinese] offender as hard as possible regardless of consequences." One Chinese responded, "One might as well suggest that we have segregation between the Chinese and non-Chinese because the non-Chinese suffer more from B.O. [body odor] as many who have discovered who sit behind foreigners on hot days in summer."[36]

Just as buses became the flashpoint for confrontations over racial segregation in the United States, in Hong Kong the ferries did so. European women were charged with being the key transmitters of bigoted ideas. "Britain's worst ambassadors are the women," said one man bluntly. On the Star Ferry, he saw "two British women" sitting next to a Chinese man in "European dress." They "exclaimed in high dudgeon, 'Is this a British ferry or not?'" Then they walked off. Didn't they realize, he asked, in a reference to Tokyo, that "the racial discrimination of former years paid sorry dividends in the long run?" The British need to "take stock of new conditions in this old world of ours. . . . A white skin," he concluded in words that many found hard to accept, "does not mean superiority."[37]

Leslie Wade, a Eurasian formerly with the RAF, had just returned to Hong Kong after an absence of nine years. He was "amazed to find no change whatsoever in the general attitude" in the colony. "The snobbery, the smugness, the lack of tolerance. . . ." He wondered "whether being mixed blood hasn't something to do" with the often chilly reception he received from the colonizers. "Barriers as far as joining clubs" remained. "I am beginning to realize," he said, "why so many Eurasians prefer to be known as Chinese."[38] Wade had hit on something, said one interlocutor. The "memories of Stanley, Shamshuipo and other camps are gradually fading away and the old superiority complex is asserting itself." Sadly, he observed that "it is a strange but true thing that wives of Europeans arriving in Hongkong for the first time are naturally friendly and willing to make friends with anyone no matter what their race or colour but when they have been here for some months, one can see the gradual and subtle change taking place. . . . [They distance themselves from] anything that is not pure Nordic or Celtic is Asiatic or Eurasian."[39] Eurasians in Singapore were organized, but not those in Shanghai or Hong Kong. Why? "Here there seems to be a fear or a heavy complex—wherefore the mixed of blood seek absorption in one side or the other." Things were so bad for those with even a hint of "Asiatic blood," that he suggested that "the United Nations might be asked to establish somewhere in the world a common nation where all the products of mixed marriages would be welcomed."[40]

It was not simply a problem of tetchy, unreconstructed white supremacists versus benign Chinese. As noted, a number of Chinese elites had been collaborators, particularly those tied to the KMT. After the war, for example, some of the leading members of the notorious Japanese military police, the Kempeitai, went to work for the KMT.[41] The "armed strength of the [pro-Tokyo] Wang Jingwei regime from its regular army down to its peace preservation and police units was absorbed into the [Chinese] Nationalist forces."[42] But however odious their political connections, their "maliciously anti-British" approach was grounded in justifiable opposition to continued British rule in Hong Kong.[43] Britain's dilemma was that the alternative to the KMT—the Communists—was firmly opposed to colonialism in Hong Kong and, in any event, the postwar climate made a U.K.-Communist alliance impossible. Thus, London could not deploy the age-old tactic of leaning toward the left (that is, the Communists) in order to keep the right (that is, the KMT) off balance. In 1948 the leadership of Hong Kong University warned in a "confidential" message against "over-exhorting" the "British way of life" among students. Why? "We may provoke the wrong reactions" among Chinese, who are "fairly evenly divided" between the "fascist Chiang Kai-shek" and the Communists. Then there was the ubiquitous "America," ready to pounce whenever the Empire seemed to be floundering.[44]

In fact, the British sought "to impose a check on loose publications of a political nature hostile to the recognized government of China," meaning the KMT.[45] In return, the KMT in a "confidential" message requested an outright "ban on the circulation of . . . [CP] booklets in Hong Kong." This would receive a favorable hearing.[46] Yet London was faced with an insoluble problem in that leading elements in the KMT wanted a speedy end to British colonialism in Hong Kong. Only weeks after the Japanese surrender the British conducted a raid on KMT headquarters in Hong Kong,[47] an indication of the increasingly touchy relations between the KMT and London.[48] The raid was followed by a decision to bar the Nationalists from engaging in military recruiting, though their struggle against the Communists was becoming increasingly desperate. This action by the British was seen as strange in leading capitals where the anticommunist struggle enjoyed strong support.[49] But London persisted in its policy.

London had a further problem. Numerous Japanese soldiers had stayed on in China after the war and their role in that nation's affairs was "of considerable importance." After the surrender, "Japanese officers in and around Nanking were treated like honored guests instead of defeated enemies. . . . For at least a year before Japan's surrender, throughout China rumors circulated to the effect that Chiang's regime had entered into a secret agreement with the Japanese. According to these reports, in return for Japanese help in fighting the Communists, both before and after the end of the war, the Nationalists would undertake, following Japan's surrender, to protect the Japanese in China and their property as well." As late as January 1947 there were "eighty thousand Japanese troops" in Manchuria "under the command of Chiang." The "Americans became increasingly willing to wink at Chiang's use of the Japanese against the Communists. . . . Many Japanese in China agreed to serve the Nationalists," a process facilitated by the preexisting relationships forged by many high-level KMT men trained in Japan. The Japanese continued pushing—even as the war ended—their alleged "mutual racial interests with China" and "an Asiatic combination against the West." Of course, the Communists deployed Japanese troops of their own who leaned left, but they were vastly outnumbered by their counterparts.[50] This alliance between the KMT and Japanese military may shed light on why the British were suspicious of various Nationalist activities in Hong Kong.[51] The British also believed that the KMT was involved in drug dealing.[52]

In 1946 the British were able to capture a letter from Ogata Shunsaku, a leading Japanese figure in Macao. "We should thank especially the Chinese authorities in Canton," he said, "for their treatment [of] the Japanese forces and civilians." He was "appointed as advisor to the Canton Headquarters of the Chairman of the Military Commission. . . . in order to take part in the great reconstruction of China in [the] future." He added, "It is a great error to think that Japan has been defeated,"[53] not least since leading KMT figures like General Wu Te-Chen had "studied in Japan."[54]

In addition to the relationship between the KMT and Japan, the British also kept track of other currents. The British Embassy in Chungking informed the Foreign Office in early 1946 about an "anonymous article in the 'Yunnan Daily News' [which] demands with extreme asperity that Siam treat Chinese residents properly now that China is a Great Power." The Embassy considered this outrageous; next, it was thought, the British would be asked to treat Chinese "properly." Likewise, much was made of a translated article from the Shanghai newspaper, *Ta Kung Pao*, about the supposedly unsettled legal status of Kowloon—an essential component of colonial Hong Kong.[55]

Some British advised a more conciliatory approach in this increasingly complicated situation. An editorial in the *Post* regretted use of "the terms 'European' and 'Chinese.'" No, it said, "the emphasis should be on 'British.' . . . Obviously if we expect the locally-born to be militantly pro-British, it is necessary to convince them that they are British."[56] The "traditional reluctance to confer full British rights upon the Hongkong-born" must be rejected, it said. But the British were trapped once again. Those who wished to return to old-style white supremacy were haunted by the specter of communism gaining ground, particularly among the working class, while many of the Chinese who had collaborated with Japan were profiting handsomely from their wartime activities. Which segment of the population should the colonizers seek to collaborate with?

This was one of many aspects of Hong Kong's growing and well-deserved reputation as "the Paradise of Collaborators." This reputation derived in part from the British attempt to besmirch those not of "pure

European descent" who had escaped poverty during the war. Tonya Lee, for example, dates the rise of Chinese affluence in Hong Kong to 1939—not December 1941—when many British departed: "This opened up the way at long last for many Eurasians and others of half-caste blood to fill the gaps left and thereby be recognized for their skills. More and more Chinese also were taking their rightful place in positions previously reserved exclusively for Europeans brought out on contract."[57]

Nevertheless, after the war, many Hong Kong residents were "dismayed and disgusted at the number of Chinese collaborators and outright traitors who are now resident in, and enjoying the amenities of this Colony," particularly alleged traitors from Shanghai. "Prominent among the traitors now enjoying sanctuary," one resident claimed, "are . . . the principal shareholder in a Gambling House, Shanghai, the funds from the licensing of which were used by the Japanese Gendarmerie. . . . This man was a close associate of the notorious Woo S. Pao, leader of the Gestapo . . . a man who was formerly a coolie employed by a tobacco factory and who, through the influence of Japanese Gendarmerie, amassed such a fortune that he was able in the spring of 1943 to purchase an aeroplane which was presented to the Japanese Forces." The writer, who described himself as an "ex-internee," had "personally encountered" these men but "the list is very long." Why were they "allowed to live in safety and luxury, occupying the best houses and, in many cases, well established in business financed with the proceeds of their collaboration?"[58] Another resident, who described himself as a "Chinese refugee," wrote that the "leading collaborators, friends of Isogai, Tojo, Noma, and Tanaka are still important and great men of the Kuomintang."[59]

There were curious connections between some of the Chinese and Japanese. A Japanese man known as "Hiraoka" had been in Hong Kong for "some years previous to the Pacific War" and was "the owner" of "properties" in Causeway Bay and Kowloon, among others. These "were found upon inspection" in 1946 "to be partly occupied by employees of the Wing Fat Printing Co.," which was also partly owned by Hiraoka. Now he was interned in Kowloon and this company was being run by some Chinese, who were apparently his business partners.[60] This was not an isolated example. A "secret" report detailed that the "Ying King Restaurant" in Wanchai-Hong Kong was "being run on [the] basis of fifty-fifty partnership with Japanese capital," and local

Chinese; the former included "some other Japanese Naval people who were in Hong Kong during the war." The manager was "Mr. Chang."[61] Intriguingly, later the police reported on an August 1948 meeting of five hours' duration at this restaurant with one hundred twenty people present, representing "74 guilds" of the "General Labor Union."[62]

Tseng Yu-Hao and Denis Victor vainly sought to bring the subject of collaboration to the attention of Governor Mark Young. "Those who made good as the Mikado's supporters," they asserted, accumulated "ill-gotten fortunes." The collaborators were now safe, while "internees, ex-political prisoners and other loyal subjects" were suffering. They demanded that the collaborators "should be stripped of their wealth." There were "many purchases of houses . . . in anticipation of an Axis victory. . . . Many buyers of land in the occupation days are trying to influence the former sellers to sign the deeds a second time, alleging that Hongkong's authorities shall defend enemy rights if the sellers or vendors refuse to adhere to the Mikado's adherents' demand." They demanded a confiscatory "ninety per cent tax" on "occupation land deals" which would also "solve the problem of the budget deficit." They also wanted "thorough investigations . . . into the sources of income of those who bought land under the enemy occupation."[63] Separately, Victor complained of "collaborators who purchased homes, concubines, and automobiles with ill-gotten gains of the occupation days."[64] Although the Attorney General was understanding, he averred that it was "impracticable here as elsewhere to attain the ideal of redistribution and removal of inequity"—wouldn't that be akin to the new enemy, communism? That remedy would "merely create a problem within [a] problem."[65]

However, some people were not satisfied. T. K. Cheng objected strenuously to the fact that "five thousand buyers of land" under the occupation had their purchases "legalized" after the war. Although those who professed "loyalty" to the crown could not engage in commerce, the actions of collaborators were ratified to their benefit. Was this just? he asked.[66] A self-professed "law man" raised pointed questions about "those Chinese who have had accumulated a worldly treasure in free China during Japanese occupation by way of smuggling, speculation and hoarding." Shouldn't they be pursued by prosecutors?[67]

H. C. Wu had been an "educationist" in Hong Kong. "During the Japanese occupation," he told the authorities, "a great number of citizens co-operated with the enemy." Worse, "During the occupation, many collaborationists who voluntarily worked for the enemy, seized the opportunity of Japanese influence and through their reckless enterprises have amassed great wealth."[68] He demanded that this property be seized and auctioned.

Mr. Wu was to be disappointed. For not only would redistributing wealth raise ticklish questions about how British wealth in Asia had been accumulated in the first place, but the Empire needed those who had collaborated to join them in the new battle against the Chinese Communist Party—the leading voice raised against collaborators and for redistribution. How could London back the same cause as its leading opponent? Perhaps this is why the suspicious activities of C. L. Hsu were met with a halting collective action. The Japanese occupiers would routinely loot from the British, then use this booty to enter into barter contracts with Chinese businessmen. Thus, the authorities in Hong Kong had "received private information in November [1945] that [Mr. Hsu] collaborated with the Japanese Army authorities, that he could get for his Iron Works whatever raw materials he wanted. On our investigations Mr. C. L. Hsu brought in a contract made with the Japanese Army Authorities for Y4,880,000.00 worth of Army mess cans. Mr. Hsu maintains that there was a balance of MY [Military Yen]976,000 due him at the time of the Japanese surrender, and that instead of accepting the Yen he requested and obtained a certain amount of merchandise (the cost of merchandise is very much in excess of the amount due, that is, considering the black market value of the Yen). It is our contention that the seizure of goods from the godowns by the Japanese was illegal, and that, as they had no title, they could not give these away in settlement of a debt. The merchandise in question has been taken into custody."[69] Mr. Hsu of the Diaward Steel Works in Hong Kong begged to differ, of course.[70]

London was finding that it had to contend with a newly enriched Chinese elite in claiming property that had belonged recently to the Japanese occupiers. In September 1945, days after the formal Japanese surrender on the battleship Missouri, Brigadier D. M. MacDougall, newly ensconced in the Peninsula Hotel in Kowloon, had to deal with the entreaties of General Nang Bun Yue of the Chinese Nationalists. The latter had spent "two days" at the Kowloon Docks where he went to "inspect all Japanese articles and materials . . . and which they inform me are to be handed over to the Chinese National Government." With customary British reticence, the Brigadier noted that this was a "very complicated" matter. "We had ourselves a very large stock of materials at the time of the Japanese occupation, much of this stock has been used by the Japanese for manufactures. . . . Thus the Mission and ourselves will have claim and counter-claim in respect of such materials. . . . materials which are in dispute."[71] The newly assertive Chinese wanted not only to control Hong Kong itself but they also wanted the spoils of war. This could only serve to make London's postwar role in Asia "very complicated."

In October 1945 the Japanese Navy turned over "large quantities of weapons, military supplies and food stored on Sancho Island, Wanshan Island and La Tsi Wei" to the Nationalists "with a view to selling them in order to obtain cash."[72] That same month the Nationalists seized "ten ships of the Japanese in Hainan Island, and those ships [were] used for transporting coal from Formosa."[73]

For reasons of their own,[74] the defeated Japanese were keen to make sure that the Nationalists' needs were attended to.[75] Britain was not opposed to having Tokyo serve as its primary interlocutor in postwar Hong Kong, "since neither Chiang Kai-Shek nor Chinese residents in Hong Kong were about to applaud the [British] liberators."[76] Likewise, London had no alternative but to accept the rise of the once derided Chinese on the economic ladder.

With the fleeing and looting of the British, some Chinese were well-placed to take advantage of the situation. When one Chinese businessmen in Wanchai-Hong Kong heard that "some old machinery . . . from Japan" would be coming from Tokyo as part of the reparations, he made it clear that "if there is any confectionery or biscuit machinery . . . we should like to get [it]."[77] On the other hand, Chan Tsan Kan, Manager of Po Sing Shoe Company, had a different complaint. He claimed that he had refused to collaborate with the occupiers and their machinery wound up in Canton "after the liberation," where "it was taken over by the Chinese Military Administration." Fundamentally, after the surrender many businesses sent a "wish list" of what they wanted from property that had once belonged to the Japanese. This allowed considerable room for corruption and shady practices, but it also provided a substantial bounty to certain Chinese businessmen.[78] Around the same time a "large number of Refinery electric motors were shipped to Canton" as part of Japanese materials taken from the colony, then returned. Further, "a large number of tanks were sent to an alcohol factory near Tsingtao."[79]

Truth be told, some British were competing with the Chinese for the booty left behind by the Japanese. Thus, in mid-1946 the Colonial Secretary in Hong Kong was informed that one of his colleagues was "seeking information about enemy assets which may be being held by Chinese."[80] One "Lt. Donald . . . spoke in a mysterious manner about buried Japanese gold and other assets hidden away in the Colony." He was "trying to squeeze money out of Japanese in Macao by under-hand methods on behalf of the British Government and openly boasts of this. He is probably adopting the same methods in Hong Kong," it was said.[81]

The point was that with Europeans fleeing Hong Kong en masse, Chinese businessmen were uniquely situated to take advantage of the situation. The British had not faced such a disadvantage since their original invasion in the nineteenth century. Even simple hawkers—the quintessential small businessperson—proliferated in the postwar environment, often peddling goods that formerly had belonged to Europeans. Yoshimitsu Abe, chief of staff of the Japanese 38th Division during the Hong Kong invasion, commented that "after the occupation, Chinese refugees opened markets in Kowloon and Hong Kong but the majority of their transactions consisted of stolen goods."[82] The courts in Hong Kong felt compelled to validate this pilferage in a September 1946 ruling. Dr. Harry Talbot demanded the return of five pieces of furniture from "Mrs. Lam," but his claim failed since she had purchased these items—looted by the Japanese during the war, then obtained by her in September 1945—"in good faith."[83]

A British woman faced a similar though bigger obstacle. She had been the "registered owner" of a property that had been "taken over [by] the Japanese authorities during [the] war" and "the structure was demolished." She "never received any compensation" and by 1948 it was "being utilised by the government as part of the existing aerodrom at Kai Tak." Her chances of being compensated were quite slim. This was how some Chinese had escaped from dire poverty while some Europeans were expropriated.[84]

Likewise, the Japanese were able by such means to make a quick comeback in Hong Kong, as the British turned their attention decisively on the Communists. Less than two years after their surrender, the *Post* editorialized about "Japan's revival," and the recrudescence of her "old tricks of subsidies, patent-stealing, deliberate imitation and ruthless undercutting." There were justifiable "British objections to Japan's industrial revival," because she was such an "unprincipled and dangerous competitor."[85] Thus, "Japan has remained since the early postwar years the principal source of Hong Kong's imports," as capital has continued to flow to Tokyo in a steady stream.[86] Though Japan lost the war, white supremacy and the constructed "preference" for British products that accompanied it suffered an irreversible setback.

Though World War II is the blanket term used to refer to the conflagration that ended in 1945, it consisted of various conflicts throughout the planet. Germany primarily was dislodging—or seeking to dislodge—sovereign states. Japan was ousting for the most part—or seeking to oust—a semi-colonized regime in China and corrupt colonial empires. This difference, though it could not be grasped as the war raged, ironically became clear when the war ended. The leading historian of Hong Kong, G. B. Endacott, has written that this "partly explains why no individual or group was prepared openly to confront the Japanese during the occupation as some French patriots did against the Germans."

In Hong Kong, "thirty-one persons appeared before the Military Courts up to 30 April 1946. . . . One was sentenced to death and hanged. . . . After the restoration of civil rule on 1 May 1946 a total of twenty-nine suspected collaborators, including one woman, appeared before the magistrates." After 1 May, twenty-eight were found guilty, including six Indians, seven Europeans or Eurasians, and fifteen Chinese, he said.[87] Meanwhile, the scholar Henry Lethbridge has observed that "in France . . . some thirty to forty thousand collaborators were executed, often summarily at the hands of the mob. In Hong Kong a few Japanese . . . and some Chinese underlings, informers and torturers were lynched or manhandled; but after a few weeks things simmered down."[88]

Actually, the "war crimes court" in Hong Kong "ceased to function" on 31 March 1948.[89] According to the *South China Morning Post*, a record of twenty were sentenced to death and ninety were sentenced to prison terms.[90] In late February 1948 Hong Kong's Commissioner of Prisoners asserted that "there are today 99 Japanese in custody at Stanley Prison. Five have been convicted and sentenced to death. . . . Sixty-six have been convicted and sentenced to imprisonment."[91] Even these numbers, paltry as they are, are useful. They can be compared with the declaration of a journalist weeks after the war, who said: "I think at least 75 per cent [of the] population of Hong Kong and the occupied zones of China should be considered as war criminals."[92] A convicted collaborator went a step further, charging that "more than 95 percent of the people in Hongkong during the occupation had to work for the Japanese for a living and I can see no reason why only 10-odd of us are to face such trials."[93] Another observer took a more qualified approach. There were many forms of collaboration, he said: those who "betrayed loyalists to torture and death," those who did it for "profit," and those who "forced many a starving person to work for the Japanese." It was "officially decided" that only those in the first category "should be tried . . . Thereby many who are still at heart pro-Japanese have escaped, to flaunt their wealth in our faces."[94] Moreover, the British had to rely on the Japanese more than they initially desired "since neither Chiang Kai-shek nor Chinese residents in Hong Kong were about to applaud the liberators." As a result the British were unenthusiastic about witch-hunts targeting Japanese or their Chinese collaborators.[95] Consequently, "some collaborators," claimed another commentator with regret, "are becoming wealthy."[96]

This pattern was not unique to British colonialism, nor to Hong Kong. A major collaborator in the Philippines, Claro M. Recto, was a noted nationalist and opponent of Washington after the war.[97] In fact, a mere "0.6 percent of the wartime leadership" in the Philippines "was convicted" for collaboration, while "74 percent was never in court. There was no bloodbath in which the mob ruled at the end of the war, and there was no purge either internal or external." As in Hong Kong, a "quarantine of silence has been placed around the collaboration question" in the Philippines. There were immense horrors there, though according to the historian David Steinberg, "many of the atrocities of the Death March and the humiliations of the prison camps were perpetrated to demean Americans before Filipinos."[98] Even the detentions and trials of suspected collaborators were suspicious, as they were often used as a means to settle scores and exact private revenge, as was the case at times in Macao.[99] Something similar was occurring in Hong Kong.[100] This was not unusual.[101] Moreover, those fleeing to Hong Kong from the mainland seemed to be victims of score settling by their envious opponents.[102]

The Hong Kong Chinese had the added burden of being represented by a government that remained highly suspicious of them. Furthermore, the procedure they had to endure to obtain redress from the government was quite discouraging. Ronald Hall, the Consul General of the United Kingdom in Canton, explicitly observed that "It has been the policy of HM Government for a number of years not to afford protection in China to persons of Chinese race even when they possess British nationality, unless they have obtained (or at least applied for and failed to obtain through no fault of their own) certificates divesting them of their Chinese nationality."[103] Thus, Hong Kong Chinese who fled to the mainland and who often had more substantial assets than many of their new compatriots, were subjected to extortion and revenge seeking with little hope of aid from "their" government.

London's dilemma in dealing with collaborators was revealed further in the spring of 1945. The Acting Attorney General of Hong Kong, George Strickland, was compelled to state in the spring of 1946 that "We should not accede to requests for seizure of property belonging to collaborators wanted by the Chinese authorities. A fortiori, it is unlikely that it is intended that property of Hongkong collaborators within our jurisdiction should be confiscated."[104] However nobly motivated, this measure also had the added impact of protecting collaborators from the full reach of the law.

Of course, not all actual or suspected collaborators were able to escape justice—or vengeance. In February 1946 the "colony's first treason trial" took place and the "court. . . . was filled with a large crowd of spectators," some of whom were related to the defendant. Espionage and torture were among the numerous charges against George Wong, a Chinese man who spoke fluent English.[105] His lawyer, Hin-shing Lo, declared that Wong was not a British subject, though he was of Chinese nationality, and cited "Captain Elliot's proclamation" of 1841 that in Hong Kong all "British subjects" will "enjoy" British law while "natives of the island of Hongkong shall be governed according to the laws, customs and usages of China." Japanese rule, in any event, terminated the sovereignty of the King and allegiance to him.[106] Further, argued the counsel, "The duty of allegiance is reciprocal to the duty of protection. . . . When therefore a state is unable to protect a portion of its territory from the superior force of an enemy, it loses for the time, its claim to the allegiance of those whom it failed to protect."[107]

Wong, forty at the time of trial, was a native of Hoi Ping, Kwang-tung, and lived for a while in North America, where he honed his English. He came to Hong Kong in 1939 and soon was operating an auto repair shop on Nathan Road. As early as 12 December 1941—a few days after the invasion—he was reputedly spotted working with the Japanese. He was alleged to have said, "I knew Japanese military officers six months before the attack on Hongkong."[108]

The trial was a ping-pong match of charge and countercharge. The defendant was asked pointedly, "Did you not say to Tony Yvanovich that 'this is a war between the yellow and white races.'" Wong replied, "I can't remember. If I did, it was part of a story from the newspapers." "Why did you tell a lie about your American papers and say you hated the Americans?" Wong proclaimed, "I told them I had returned from America, which I did not like, and to which I did not want to return."[109] The much despised Inouye Kanao—otherwise known as "Slap Happy" because of his penchant for punching internees—also came to testify. "You said, "[I] hate you whites because in Canada I was called a yellow bellied, slit-eyed bastard.'" "I never said that," Wong declared hotly.[110]

Wong's lawyer moved to quash the indictment against him. "Not being a British subject, the Treason Act of 1351 [sic] did not apply to him. . . . [and] he was acting as some sort of Chinese agent." Wong acknowledged that "my Counsel submitted that during occupation Chinese inhabitants owed no allegiance to the British," but "that is not my view. During occupation, my view was that Chinese should be loyal to [the] Chinese government. . . . I owe loyalty to China as a Chinese. . . . I had been in China Military Service. . . . What I did . . . I did for China and her Allies." But other witnesses disagreed that Wong was a simple Chinese patriot. No, said one witness, "he always boasted about Japs' [sic] invincibility." Another testified that Wong "said Japs [sic] wanted a group of Australian-born Chinese or people who know Australia well to go there with Jap [sic] invaders." Grace Lau testified that Wong came to her house for interrogation accompanied by a "Eurasian." Wong, she said, "explained that his scheme was to get a group to guide the Japanese to invade Australia, adding that the best qualification was to be Australian-born." Wong was disbelieved. He was convicted, received a "sentence of death," and was executed. Soon his tearful spouse, Yoke Shim, was reduced to inquire whether "you could allow me to bury my husband's dead body myself."[111] This was "the first time in the history of a colony that a traitor has been hung here," reported the Post. That he was Chinese and something of a second-class subject was not lost on many.[112]

Tsui Kwok Ching met a similar fate. Prior to the war he was a clerk at Taikoo Sugar Refinery and a Sergeant in the Police Reserve. He was "not a British subject but had been . . . resident in the Colony—22 years." He was said to have been involved in torture: M. A. Da Silva "accused" him of having "burned him with a hot poker."[113] So Leung, a former member of the police force in Hong Kong, was accused of torture as well. He too was not a British subject but had lived in the colony since he was sixteen years old. This traffic constable was said to have used a "bamboo whip" against Da Silva and to have applied the gruesome "'flying aeroplane' torture." A number of Chinese petitioned the government stating that "He had no real intention to assist the Japanese. . . . He rendered invaluable assistance by protecting both our property and ourselves from the Japanese." So Leung said that he was told by the British authorities to continue working under Japanese rule and he simply followed their instructions; he claimed to have aided the Allies by aiding the Chinese guerillas. No matter. He was tried and convicted of high treason and was executed.[114] He was hung at Stanley.[115]

Some of the most despised and reviled collaborators were those of Asian descent—like George Wong—who had spent time in North America. Inouye Kanao,[116] the infamous "Slap Happy" or "Kamloops Kid," born in 1916 in western Canada, exemplified this pattern. Of Japanese origin, he was sent back to his ancestral homeland in 1926. Then he returned to Canada, then came back to Japan in a round-robin trans-Pacific journey. He was "conscripted" for service in Manchuria in 1936, never having "denounced" Japanese citizenship and having retained his Japanese passport.[117]

Kamloops, British Columbia, was not exactly a comfortable sanctuary for those of Japanese origin, which may explain his frequent jaunts across the Pacific. There was an active "Anti-Mongolian Association" there that tried to bar Asian and Japanese immigrants. "Normally government refused to employ Asians." When exceptions arose, "local observers quickly protested and the [Asians] lost their jobs."[118] Japanese immigrants "lost the franchise in 1895" in British Columbia and after Tokyo's epochal victory over Moscow in 1905, there were brutal anti-Japanese riots and widespread panic.[119]

Inouye argued vehemently that because "he was, at all material times, a Japanese subject and had not renounced such nationality," he could not credibly be tried for high treason toward a government to which he had not pledged allegiance. Furthermore, the policies of "pure European descent" meant that the government had not pledged its allegiance to him. "The fact remained," the government said in reply, "that he, at all material times, was also a British subject." The "Chief Justice" of Hong Kong declared that the fact that he might be a Japanese citizen was "immaterial. . . . He came to Hong Kong as civilian and voluntarily joined the Tokyo branch of the Japanese Gendarmerie and committed atrocities." He was charged with twenty-eight overt acts of treason, mostly involving interrogations. A number of internees suggested that he punctuated his English translations with frequent beatings.[120]

No, said Inouye, whose grammar and handwriting were superior to that of many of those who were prosecuting him, "I was a civilian interpreter." He confirmed that he was in the "anti-espionage" branch of the Japanese military, but denied that this had a nefarious significance. Moreover, he added, "I was not treated as though I was in all respects a Canadian. I was not allowed to vote in B.C. or become a doctor or hold a government job. There was also racial prejudice. I was very embittered against the Canadian people." He contrasted this maltreatment with what he encountered in Japan: "If Nisei have Canadian or American citizenship they are regarded with suspicion when they return to Japan but not after they register in Japan." Thus, he said, "When I returned to Japan I was treated as if I had lived in Japan all my life." Still, in the murky madness that often characterized Japan, Inouye recalled, "I was put under water torture in Japan by the Gendarmarie because I had Nisei friends who went back to America and enlisted."[121]

Inouye, who "earlier on admitted that he spoke English better than Japanese," had a grandfather who was a "big shot" in Japan. "Inouye Chotakara" was a "railway magnate, President of the Keio Electric Tramways of Tokyo, inventor of the Fuji spun silk, a member of Parliament and a member of the House of Peers. He had an uncle, Inouye Matsumto, who also had a large business in Tokyo and another uncle, Kimura Tokataro, was one of the leading lawyers in Japan." His English language fluency helped to provide him with the nickname "Yankee" and allowed him in the prewar era to get a job as an interpreter in Hong Kong, followed by Singapore and Osaka, where he was "discharged owing to bad health." He got a job in an "import and export firm in Kobe," but later returned to Hong Kong to join his Chinese wife. He claimed that this was where he was conscripted in 1942 (this statement was viewed as contradicting his earlier assertion that he was conscripted in Manchuria in 1936).[122]

"Slap Happy" found it difficult to refute the harsh recollections of him by internees. He was a "bastard," said Kenneth Baxter, a Scottish internee.[123] Lucien Brunet of Quebec recalled sadly the time when "Captain Norris of the Winnipeg Grenadiers argued with the Kamloops Kid and he hit Norris in the face and punch[ed] him [in] the chin. . . . Later on, Atkinson tried to intervene and tried to stop it. Kamloops Kid turn[ed] to him and hit Atkinson on the legs. . . . [Inouye]," he concluded, "was an awful chap."[124]

Such contradictions were a part of the uphill climb he had in exonerating himself. Inouye had received bad advice from counsel, which initially claimed on his behalf that he was a Canadian citizen. His effort to deny this predicate placed him in jeopardy for violating antitreason laws, and was rejected. He pressed on, questioning the validity of a war crimes court trying a British subject.[125] But his occasional shout of "Long live the Emperor" could not have helped his cause in Hong Kong.[126]

There were several problems with his prosecution. In "summing up," the judge in the "Supreme Court of Hong Kong" noted that "several members of the jury are Chinese and although you may still speak English, still it is not always easy to follow a legal argument in a language other than your own."[127] Though dismissively tossed aside, the authorities took seriously his claim that he could not be tried for treason because he was not a British citizen. As early as October 1945 a "secret priority" message to London inquired, "Can administration prosecute residents who are not British subjects but who by virtue of residence in Hongkong prior to December 1941 enjoyed His Majesty's protection and committed serious offenses?"[128] This profound due process consideration was cast aside and he was convicted and sentenced "into execution" on 26 August 1947 "by causing" him to "to be hanged by the neck until he is dead.[129] Such "war criminals," said one judge, "belonged to a black or evil race."[130]

Inouye was not the only one to be cast into this racial purgatory, nor was he the only man of Asian descent with roots in North America to be accused of collaboration. In the autumn of 1946 William L. Bryce, an army veteran from Los Angeles—a survivor of the "death marches" of Bataan and Corregidor—was stunned into disbelief while strolling down the aisle of a local Sears outlet.[131] He saw a man, Tonoya Kawakita, who thanks to Bryce's alertness, was tried for treason in 1947 in the Southern District Court of California. Kawakita was born in Calexico, California, in 1921 to Japanese parents. In 1939 he obtained a U.S. passport for a trip to Japan where he was to be educated at Meiji University. By 1943 he was employed by a Japanese firm as an interpreter and after the war he returned to the United States.

He was indicted and found guilty, and in 1952 the U.S. Supreme Court affirmed his death sentence and a $10,000 fine. However, as Tokyo-Washington relations improved in the face of their joint struggle against Moscow, President Dwight D. Eisenhower commuted his sentence to life and, finally, in 1963 President John F. Kennedy allowed him to be deported back to Japan.

Few in dusty, hot Calexico could foresee that Kawakita's life would take such twists and turns. He recalled, "I engaged in football [and] basketball and I was assistant manager of the athletic activities [during] my senior year." He insisted that he was a Japanese citizen during the time in question, when he was supposedly engaging in treasonous acts, and therefore could no more be accused of being guilty of treason to the United States than he could be accused of committing treason against the Soviet Union. Yes, while in Japan he had lived with Takeo Miki, a "very important person" and member of Parliament. But he was also a "Boy Scout," hardly training ground for a traitor, he thought. He was so sure that he had done nothing wrong during the war that he returned to the United States. If he had done all he had been accused of doing, why would he return to Los Angeles and enroll at the University of Southern California, as he did? Would a guilty man have done this? Sure, he may have slapped a few "British and Canadians," but was this treason? His lawyer, Morris Lavine, who was a tiger in the courtroom, was more direct: "Your honor," he said, "all I intend to ask is whether there were Japanese-Americans on the grand jury itself." If not, a case could be made for illegal bias and a tainted indictment that must be tossed out. The judge ruled that "that would be immaterial" and tossed out Lavine's allegation instead. Lavine would not yield, disclaiming immateriality: "I don't think so, not from my view of it." He insisted, "Were [there] any Japanese-Americans on any grand jury during a period of seven years?" The judge responded that "during the past seven years no person of Japanese ancestry has actually been drawn or has sat on any grand jury in this court," but he refused to rule the indictment

invalid. Once again, white supremacy—in this case, exclusionary policies targeting Japanese Americans—was providing succor to those presumed to be pro-Tokyo.

During his trial, Kawakita was also accused of being "slap happy"
during the war. The grand jury indictment said that he "impose[d] punishment on one Thomas J. O'Connor. . . . assaulting, striking and beating [him]. . . . repeatedly knocking him into the drain or cesspool." He
was involved in "striking and beating . . . Alexander Holick with a
wooden sword or club to compel" him "to work faster." He struck Marcus A. Rael "because. . . . [he] had become ill with a fever and was then
and there unable to continue the work to which he had been assigned."
His "cruel, inhuman and degrading punishment of Woodrow T. Shaffer" included "forcing him to kneel for several hours on a platform with
a stick of bamboo placed on the inner side of the joints of his knees and
to hold at arms length above his head a bucket of water."

Masueto Nasato, a U.S. sergeant, born in Italy in 1904, came to the
United States in 1926. He was on the Bataan "death march," then was
transferred to Camp Oeyama. "Kawakita was not a gentle soul," he
thought. "He picked on me more than anyone I was able to see. . . . He
would bait me and tell me how Japan is going to win the war" and was
"very, very rough in his language." But he denied that Kawakita had
mistreated him or others unduly.

Marcus A. Rael disagreed sharply. He "didn't know" that Kawakita
"could speak Spanish." He discovered this the hard way after he said in
Spanish in his presence, "Aqui viene este quatro ojos son of a bitche
[sic]" or "here comes the four-eyed son of a bitch." "I called him. . . .
well, he slapped me in my face." Later, said Rael, he "hit me over the
head with a stick."

Maury Rich, another POW, also had unkind things to say about
Kawakita's performance. Once he told the internees that "San Francisco
was being bombed," and then told them "We will kill all you prisoners
right here anyway, whether you win the war or lose it." At his initiative
prisoners were "forced to punch each other as hard as they could for
punishment and if some of them didn't punch so hard, why, the defendant and some of the others would go up and down the line and knock
him down to the ground in the snow and beat them up. That went on
for about an hour."

James T. Phillips, another internee, recalled Kawakita saying that
"Japan would win the war if it took a hundred years." The defendant

also contended that "the Japanese were far superior to the American people and if the American army had Japanese officers, why, they could whip the world." Once Kawakita was said to have seen David Huddle chewing gum; the internee testified that he "grabbed me by the shirt collar and told me to open my mouth. Well, I didn't have a chance to swallow the gum and I tried to conceal it under my tongue. And when I opened my mouth he saw the gum. He says, 'You lie,' and he drew back—he held me with his left hand by the shirt collar, and he drew back with his right and he hit me three times in the nose and just broke my nose."

Johnnie E. Carter alleged that on "one particular night he was sitting there, and he asked me, he says, 'Why do the Americans hate to die and the Japanese like to die?'" Carter offered a tepid reply and "he answered me by hitting me over the head and across the back." Woodrow T. Shaffer was mortified when Kawakita "knocked" a prisoner "into the cesspool," then told the unfortunate soul to "submerge until his head just showed," at which point the Japanese American "struck" the man "with sticks when he refused to submerge" further.

The bespectacled Kawakita, who was about 5'4" and 145 pounds, sat impassively in suit and tie at the defendant's table as these damning charges were made against him. His high cheek bones and broad shoulders and slightly hunched back sat still as his fate was being decided. Interestingly, when talking to his Japanese colleagues during the war, "All he ever talked about was his high school days, the pretty scenery and things like that." Meiji Fujisawa had known Kawakita in California and, like him, had moved to Japan where his helpful comrade got him a job as an interpreter. But Fujisawa was no help at the trial and one can imagine Kawakita sinking deeper into his chair as his fellow "interpreter" said, "I heard from other Japanese employees that Kawakita was mistreating prisoners of war." Kawakita may have slumped even further when Fujisawa said that he saw his erstwhile colleague carrying a "wooden sword . . . about two and a half feet"—a visible symbol of Imperial Japan—around the camp. Yes, agreed Merle Chandler, "It was built like a Japanese officer's sword."

Kawakita was doomed. The judge was harsh, noting the "zeal with which the defendant practiced his treachery in many ways, but perhaps most eloquently by his nicknames—'efficiency expert' and 'empire builder'—given him by the American prisoners of war. . . . He fervently wished Japan would win the war, hoped and believed she would win, but feared she would not. If Japan won, he planned to re-turn to the United States and—as he boasted to American prisoners of war—be a 'big shot' because of his knowledge of the language and the people." His "brutal slave-driving tactics" were also denounced.[132] Kawakita was duly convicted and some of the denizens of Los Angeles drew the inappropriate lesson that they were justified in interning Japanese Americans, while others drew the appropriate conclusion that perhaps the kind of white supremacy that had driven an outwardly normal North American into the arms of a U.S. foe should be recon-sidered.

The problem was that Kawakita was not the sole Japanese Ameri-can to cross the line—or, at least, to be accused of crossing the line. Iva Toguri was born on the fourth of July in 1916 in Watts, Los Angeles, and graduated from UCLA. She voted for the Republican Wendell Wilkie in 1940, then found herself trapped in wartime Tokyo shortly thereafter. Matters were complicated by the fact that she was not fluent in Japan-ese. Yet on skimpy evidence she was accused of being the notorious "Tokyo Rose," whose seductively appealing radio broadcasts from Japan were intended to demoralize the U.S. populace, including sol-diers. Although there were no fewer than twenty-seven Japanese-American "radio girls," she was unlucky enough to have her fate sealed by an all-white jury.[133]

Then there was Isamu Ishara, a thirty-six-year-old interpreter for Japan, toiling at a POW camp of twelve hundred in China. Educated in Hawaii, he was "charged with administering the water and electric treatment [torture]. . . . beatings. . . . under-feeding prisoners and steal-ing their food and cigarettes."[134] He did not escape condemnation. Nor did yet another interpreter, identified simply as "Takemoto." A resident of Hong Kong before the war, he had served as the "propietor of the curio shop, Nikko and Co., in the Hongkong Hotel."[135]

Nimori Genichiro, fifty-three, was also a "civilian interpreter." He was on the ill-fated Lisbon Maru—the "only Japanese on board who could speak English"—and was said to have ordered sentries to fire into the holds of the ship, killing Allied soldiers. He had become a Christian at Cornell College in Mount Vernon, Iowa, and had "spent various pe-riods in New York, Connecticut and Iowa." He spent "eighteen years" in Dayton, Ohio, "where he first worked in an amusement park, learned the trade and later became manager." He denied using the term "bas-tard" as was charged to describe internees; no, he used the less elegant "son of a bitch," a distinction which failed to impress those who were trying him.[136]

Given the magnetic appeal of Subhas Chandra Bose and the Indian National Army, Indians in Hong Kong came under heavy scrutiny after the war and were thought to be prime candidates for treason trials. Although not as many were placed in the dock as first suspected. One defendant ensnared was Wadmull Chattulani. He arrived in Hong Kong on 27 November 1941 on a business trip from Kobe, Japan. He said, "I am [an] Importer and Exporter and provision dealer in Kobe since 1925," who had got caught in the war and was unable to return to Japan. "Being Indian," he said, "I stayed in [the] Sikh Temple" and "started a business in Hong Kong—and was forced to work on behalf of the occupiers" as an interpreter and translator, allegedly under dire duress. He continued to carry a British passport and was charged with aiding the enemy.[137]

The sixty-one-year-old Chattulani, a native of Hyderabad and Sind in the Indian subcontinent, spoke fluent Japanese. One witness testified that Chattulani said he "was neither British nor Indian but held Japanese paper. . . . He told me he had a Japanese wife and showed me a picture of his daughter dressed in a kimono."[138] His fate was sealed, as was that of his countryman, Fakir Mohammed Arculli, who too was charged with aiding the enemy. He too was multilingual, speaking "Japanese, English and Chinese," not to mention several Indian languages.[139] This forty-one-year-old journalist received a three-year sentence.[140] Others were punished as well. Mohammed Yusuf Shah, for example, had been with the Hong Kong police since 1935 but was arrested in September 1945 for high treason, for which he received seven years of hard labor.[141]

The Hong Kong police force had incorporated numerous Indians on the well-worn colonial principle that indigenous people should not be employed in such sensitive positions. But this principle proved faulty when the enchanting allure of the Indian National Army captivated so many Indians, which led to a belated postwar purge and the hiring of more Chinese.[142] But Indian cops from Hong Kong were not the only ones drawn to the INA. A number of "Indian merchants were arrested in Hong Kong by Allied Occupation forces." At least five were "arrested" for collaboration, one of them a "special political detective for [the] Japanese Gendarmerie."[143] But the numbers detained and those actually imprisoned were comparatively small, not least because India itself was undergoing a difficult independence struggle and London was reluctant to alienate this large nation further. Those seen as traitors in Manchester—for example, the INA—were viewed as heroes in Calcutta.

Thus, though many of them were purged from the police, the authorities proceeded cautiously in reining in a community widely thought to have engaged in mass sedition. As the first anniversary of the surrender approached, the "Indian community was asked to register," but "as far as" the colony's Solicitor could "ascertain this rule applied to no other section" of the colony—an indicator of the suspicion with which they were viewed. Though acknowledging that "race, religion and caste, here as in India draw out hard and violent feelings," what was causing the Solicitor "great anxiety" was something else. "Indians who had collaborated with the Japanese were given contracts or employment with the Government or free passages out of the colony while a very large body of Indians (and Malays who have always been regarded for practical purposes as members of the Indian community through inter-marriage, social intercourse, etc.) who had remained loyal and more than loyal during the period have been usually overlooked on the question of obtaining fitting employment."[144]

An exception to the simple story of white supremacy was the obvious pro-Tokyo tilt of the "White"—or anticommunist—Russians. Throughout Japanese-occupied Asia they earned a well-merited reputation for their slavish adherence to Japanese dictates. Hong Kong was no exception. On the other hand, their treatment in postwar Hong Kong underscored the continued viability of the doctrine of white supremacy in that although they drove cars and exhibited other signs of affluence, they did not attract British scrutiny—unlike Chinese collaborators, for example. Some complained about how these Russians "made various degrees of fortunes in gold bars, duress notes, etc." during the war and were now "living in ease" in Hong Kong. But such complaints were infrequent.[145]

There were also some Irish collaborators, many of whom had legitimate grievances about British rule in their homeland and others who felt they were not receiving their full due from white supremacy. Among this group was Frank Henry Johnston. He was a radio broadcaster for Tokyo occupation forces in China. His life had been one mishap after another prior to that time. He was convicted of stealing while living in Florida and later stole jewelry from the actress, Delores Del Rio. He was deported to Ireland but somehow slipped back into the country. Convicted again of robbery, this time he shipped out as a sea-man to Asia.[146] He was sentenced to ten years' imprisonment in 1947 for aiding the enemy. Born in Shanghai in 1905, his odyssey also suggested that, even after the war, white supremacy had not been extirpated alto-gether. When he asked to be repatriated to the United Kingdom from Shanghai, the "Chinese authorities stated that . . . the Chinese prison was unsuitable for the housing of Europeans and that the diet was strictly Chinese" and likewise unsuitable for him.[147] Of course, Chinese prisoners were not so blessed.

There was also W. J. Carroll, a "British subject of Irish parentage," who was placed on trial in part—according to a "secret" message—"in view [of] public reaction if prosecution for treason [continues] only of Chinese and Indians" and "none of non-Asiatic British subjects," though it was unclear whether he was of "pure European descent."[148] Carroll was hard to ignore. He had acted as a "broker" for the Japanese, buying "chemicals" and "metals," and "later was in charge of the Kowloon branch" of a Japanese firm which "acted as buying agents for the Japanese Navy." He was "educated at St. Joseph's College between 1927 and 1930" in Hong Kong.[149] The much despised Carroll was ac-cused of being part Japanese, which he denied hotly. It was an allega-tion "which I very much resent. I have documentary proof of my parentage. . . . My mother was born in Santiago, Cuba."[150] Despite his prominent role during the occupation, he also received a relatively minor sentence upon conviction—a six-month prison term. But his lawyer argued that this former "President of a Sharebrokers' Associa-tion" was "finished so far as Hongkong, so far as the Far East is con-cerned. His case is different from that of the average lower class Chinese or Indian who may have been convicted because of collaboration be-cause, in either of these cases, the man may lose his identity and suc-cessfully conceal his record in the teeming millions of China or India." According to the lawyer, collaboration was not the mortal sin for Chi-nese or Indians that it was for one of European heritage.[151]

The much censured Major Cecil Boon was also a collaborator. This former POW in Hong Kong quickly made a separate peace with his cap-tors and soon "adopted the Japanese custom of wearing his hair cut short and he also wore his shirt outside his trousers in the Japanese style." He also "forced his group commander to speak to him in Japan-ese."[152] Speculation about racial discrimination in the prosecutions of collaborators grew when he was found not guilty on all charges.[153]

C. M. Foure, editor of the pro-Tokyo *Hong Kong News* during the war, was said to be cut from the same cloth as Boon. A "former Royal Navy Commander," he had commanded a gunboat in Canton in 1930. When Chinese mobs attacked a "European settlement," he "opened up on the crowds," an act "for which he was dismissed." He became "violently anti-Establishment" as a result, though not necessarily "anti-British." He was "something of an outcast from conventional society and had few friends." Back in Hong Kong he "went native," residing in a "low class Chinese slum." He was also thought to have moved to the left politically, which makes his alliance with the racial appeals of Japan all the more striking. A former internee noted that "Most could not forgive his rabid communism or that militancy with which he had advised the Chinese trade guilds before the war. He was regarded as a traitor to his class, if not to this country" and his "race." Perhaps he thought that given white supremacy, it was inevitable that Tokyo would prevail.[154] John David Provoo of the United States was "an American" who was also said to be "Japanese-hearted." He "spoke Japanese fluently" and taught the language in "Japan before the war." He too came under legal fire.[155]

Then there were the much despised Eurasians, who contributed their share to Tokyo's war effort and were punished afterward. "D. W. Luke, a Eurasian clerk" was said to be "the first Government servant to offer his services to the Japanese." One of these people of "mixed-race" was said to be William Chang, alias Khan Mohammed, "a half-bred Chinese Negro who claims himself [to be] an Indian." And "Frank Lee, alias Lesson," who was "employed by the Texaco Oil Co. before the war" was "said to be a Negro."[156] Another in the list was a traditionally defined Eurasian, Joseph James Richards, who was tried for high treason. Before the war he worked for the Japanese Consulate as an "informer," then for the *Hong Kong News*—the pro-Tokyo sheet—during the occupation. Apparently his mother was Japanese, for his father was a "British Consul." "In spite of that fact he received very little consideration, whereas on the other hand the Japs [*sic*] appreciated his services."[157]

Days after the surrender, the authorities put forward a "secret" and "unanimous recommendation" that Sir Robert Kotewall "be detained and brought to trial [this] being the only way in which to convict or clear him satisfactorily in the eyes of the world."[158] However, his activities and connections past and present were far too significant for such a powerful personage to be derailed easily. During the famous 1925 strike in Hong Kong he was "employing bands of men . . . recruited from the underworld" to beat strikers. "After a time [this] new force got out of hand" and "went over to the Triad society." Apparently Sir Robert also had connections to a 1937 Japanese venture which involved sending "an agent Lam Kin Yan, a Formosan, to organize from the Triad Society a fifth column cell" which "distinguished itself after the Japanese declared war by its overt help to the enemy."[159] But Sir Robert was a fish too big and dangerous to land and the immediate postwar surge against the Communists ruled out the possibility that he would be successfully prosecuted.

The major war crimes trials were not held in Hong Kong but in Tokyo and they were very different from their counterparts in Europe. For as Yukiko Koshiro has put it, "The Tokyo War Crimes Trial was marked by Eurocentrism in its legal ideas, its personnel, its historical thinking and, as some observers have commented, by its racism."[160] This statement, particularly the reference to racism, is not as provocative as it may initially seem. B. V. A. Roling of the Netherlands was one of the eleven judges at this important trial. He has declared that while "racial discrimination may have been one of the roots of the Pacific War," this could hardly be said about German and Italian aggression in Europe. The Holocaust notwithstanding, "Tokyo had more judges than Nuremberg—eleven instead of four, and we had twenty-eight defendants, five more than at Nuremberg." This was not the only major distinction he drew between the two postwar trials. "Nobody wanted to defend Hitler. That was impossible. You can't defend the man who was behind the genocide of the Jews and Gypsies. It was quite different in Japan. The Japanese defended the action of Japan in this Asian land and in the world, to liberate Asia and to change the world. And they had a case, in this respect. . . . [The] Tokyo Trial was far more difficult and complicated than the Nuremberg one. Nuremberg was a clear case of aggression to dominate the European continent."

Judge Roling viewed a number of Japanese leaders, including the Foreign Minister, in a surprisingly sympathetic light, arguing that "less than a quarter of a century later, the U.N. was doing precisely that which had earned Hirota the death sentence," that is, aggressively confronting colonialism. Washington, he thought, took Tokyo more seriously than Nuremberg. Secretary of War Henry Stimson was "afraid that" the verdicts of the former "would be applicable to the mistreatment of blacks in the United States."

I do not entirely agree with Judge Roling's biting opinions. But it is striking that his ideas were shared, to a degree, by those of the sole Indian judge who, said Judge Roling, "really resented colonial relations. He had a strong feeling about what Europe did in Asia, conquering it a couple of hundred years ago. . . . This war of Japan to liberate Asia from the Europeans, the slogan, 'Asia for the Asians,' really struck a chord with him. He had even been involved with the Indian army that fought with the Japanese against the British." Whenever this Indian judge, Radhabinod Pal, "appeared in court, he unfailingly bowed to the defendants, whom he regarded as men who had initiated the liberation of Asia," although reportedly upward of 20 million Asians perished in this brutal conflict.[161]

What is so dastardly about white supremacy is that it has caused some to overlook Tokyo's depredations and prompted certain Japanese to justify their war making. Reportedly, after the war Emperor Hirohito "called attention to racial tensions in the background to the Pacific War. He began by noting that the Great Powers had rejected 'Japan's call for racial equality, advocated by our representatives at the peace conference following World War I. Everywhere in the world discrimination between yellow and white remained, as in the rejection of immigration to California and the whites-only policy in Australia. These were sufficient grounds for the indignation of the Japanese people.'"[162]

Even before the war ended, the colonial authorities were moving to eliminate the more egregious aspects of white supremacy in Hong Kong. Indeed, "During the war a secret draft, prepared in the Colonial Office . . . stated that there should be no discrimination, statutory or otherwise, on racial grounds in post-war Hong Kong; every public servant should be required to qualify in Cantonese." By November 1945 Chinese were "occupying judicial and executive posts with responsibilities unknown before the war."[163] After the chastening experience of Japanese occupation, a "new sense of egalitarianism was in the air. In London, the Secretary of State for the Colonies announced that the age of racial discrimination was over. In Hong Kong, the governor, proclaiming an end to inequality, repealed laws such as the one forbidding Chinese to live on The Peak."[164]

It would be naïve, however, to think that this racial reversal came easily or without contradiction. In Singapore, which was not atypical within the Empire, "discrimination in employment in the colonial and civil service continued as standard after the war, the only difference being that colour was no longer specified in the rules, it was just noted at the interview." After the war, colonialism was no longer justified on the basis of race. Instead, paternalism became the rationale, that is, the supposed "economic and practical dependence" of the colonies.[165] Despite such subtle shifts, important economic consequences followed from the changes that occurred in Hong Kong.[166]

These seismic changes were part of a larger development in the Pacific Basin—in fact, globally. In Canada, the home of the much scorned "Kamloops Kid," "things began to change at the end of the Second World War. . . . Anti-Chinese discrimination receded perceptibly."[167] The same happened in the United States. There, "World War II brought about the first cracks in the wall of Asian exclusion. . . . Japan had been successfully exploiting Asian exclusion in its wartime propaganda, and Congress felt compelled to respond to the charges that it was discriminating against the citizens of an ally." Congress responded. "For the first time it allowed Chinese to naturalize and become American citizens; it also struck from the books most of the Chinese exclusion laws." In the summer of 1946 "Congress also extended naturalization rights to Filipinos and Indians."[168] Chinese who had been derided as "Japs" [sic] earlier in the century, were now being courted, almost desperately. A "retired Navy officer told a congressional committee. . . . that the Chinese exclusion law was worth 'twenty divisions' to the Japanese army" during the war. A Congressman declared that the "Chinese Exclusion Law had to be repealed" for the "salvation of the white race." If this did not occur, he said, "then all of Asia is apt to go with [Japan]. Then you will have a race struggle in which we are hopelessly outnumbered that will last, not for 1 year or 5 years, but throughout generations to come."[169]

That was not the only retreat[170] by the major powers.[171] On 10 November 1943 the Empire began to retreat from its noxious policy of the opium trade.[172] Of course, the British did not execute a complete one-hundred-eighty-degree reversal. When the ship *Windrush* arrived in the United Kingdom in June 1948 bearing 492 Jamaicans—the first in a major postwar influx—they were not welcomed as representatives of a colony that had stood by the Empire during its most trying moments.

Even the Labour Party "correspondent . . . saw in this influx the hidden hand of 'Uncle Joe' Stalin. 'Do you think,' he confided . . . 'this sudden influx of 400 West Indians is a subtle move of Russia to create for us in another twenty years time a Colour Question here?'"[173] This was consistent with prewar policy when a "Tory M.P. for Tottenham" suggested that "German Jews were better off in concentration camps than they were in Britain." In the 1930s "immigration officers were sending Jews back to Germany."[174]

Australia was little better. Jean Gittins, a Eurasian from Hong Kong, who migrated to Australia after the war, quickly observed a "phobia" toward the Chinese. This was reflected in the notorious witticism that "two Wongs do not make a white." She was asked by an immigration officer if she were Chinese. "Fifty percent," was her reply. He responded, "Can you make it a little less?" She refused and complications ensued. "It seemed that a person's looks were all that mattered," she sighed.[175]

These were simple signs of what was to come in the tottering, though still viable Empire. In July 1945, even before the war had concluded, Lindsay Ride of the Hong Kong resistance told the Colonial Office in a "personal and confidential" message that he had "copies of [an] application" for a soon to be opened postwar position, but "I note," he admonished, "there is a clause about European parentage." The increasingly sensitive Ride inquired gently, "Is this meant to debar Chinese? . . . We have one or two excellent Chinese officers whom I think you should take . . . especially . . . Francis Lee. . . . He was my secretary in HKU."[176]

Other reforms were easier to accept in that they did not necessarily challenge the preeminence of those of "pure European descent." Thus, in 1946 a colonial bureaucrat advocated more radio broadcasts to the Chinese in Hong and more libraries too, since "It cannot be said that the Chinese are not fond of reading." It is "necessary," he said, "to establish at least one good library in Hong Kong and one in Kowloon with a travelling library book service to all districts of the New Territories." Drawing on his previous colonial experience elsewhere, he added that "such a system has been carried out with great success in Northern Nigeria, Trinidad, Jamaica and elsewhere."[177]

Setting up more libraries in Hong Kong was actually part of a self-described process of "dissemination of propaganda." That it was "very largely a continuation of the Psychological Warfare Unit" shows how the war continued to resonate even after the cannons were stilled. There were to be "British Council releases in the newspapers and Chinese magazines." The intention was not to "indulge in a Story Book Secret Service" but "having somebody . . . who is able to walk around talking to the Chinese, listen[ing] to them and generally speaking, to ascertain their point of view on current matters." This was viewed as critical when the concept of colonialism itself was under siege. "Staff salaries should be drastically revised and increased," especially for the all-important "translators," without which the colonists would be deaf and dumb. Perhaps not surprisingly, the "European papers welcomed" the new initiative while "the Chinese press" was "slightly suspicious."[178]

Chinese skepticism about British intentions was foremost in the minds of those seeking to reconstitute the defense forces of Hong Kong after the war. The question of who should be allowed into this force was a leading agenda item in a late December 1946 meeting. "It was agreed that five main communities had to be taken into consideration . . . British (excluding Scottish) . . . Scottish . . . Portuguese . . . Eurasians . . . Chinese." There "were two diametrically opposed view points on this subject, some members of the Committee holding that the Corps should be entirely mixed without regard to race and others being of the opinion that it would be preferable to maintain the racial units as in the old Corps." Such meetings were held throughout the Empire. The choice was simple: should the policies of "pure European descent" and segregation that had led to the occupation prevail, or should another course be pursued?

It was decided to do some of both. "The Committee finally agreed that the most satisfactory solution would be to have all the technical personnel, Headquarter staff and Armoured Car Squadrons completely mixed without regard to race." The "two rifle companies would, however, be divided into British, Scottish, Portuguese, Eurasian and Chinese platoons." This "arrangement would eliminate any criticism on the score of racial discrimination and at the same time satisfy the undoubted demand for some continuation of the tradition of the racial units of the old Corps, though on a considerably diminished role." Naturally, there were no Chinese—who formed a mere 95 percent or more of the population—at this meeting.[179]

These tentative steps toward equality, halting in nature, were not welcomed warmly by many Europeans. By early 1948 the "Council of European Civil Servants" expressed a "vague resentment that lower paid, especially Chinese, workers have received proportionately higher gains" in salary.[180] "European Officers" were also concerned about more mundane matters, such as the desegregation of toilets. "Formerly the lavatory accommodation for European officers . . . consisted of accommodation at the north end of the ground floor . . . Since the reoccupation the former place has been used by Chinese staff. . . . Although the entrance door is clearly marked 'for Officers only,' complaints have been received from European officers that they cannot always gain access to this accommodation as Chinese staff . . . including amahs [maids], always seem to be using the place." The "Director of Public Works" instructed his subordinates to instruct "non-European staff that they are required to refrain from using this lavatory."[181] In other words, segregation that before the war would have been justified on racial grounds was now rationalized on class grounds, that is, by job category.

"Race" had been near the center of the construction of the Empire, for reasons major and minor, and its surgical removal was not easy. Creech Jones, writing from Downing Street in London in early 1947, noted that the United Nations was taking up the race question. But this external pressure could only accomplish so much and no more. "I am far from suggesting," he said, "that all discriminatory legislation can be immediately swept away in Colonial territories. Some may be required in the interests of the local or non-European races. . . . Some may be incapable on broad political grounds of any immediate change."[182]

Nine years later, the matter was still being debated. In Hong Kong there was still "some racial differentiation in the prison." Apparently the Matilda Hospital, "or a part of it, [was] reserved for Europeans."[183] Dr. Clifford Matthews, a Eurasian who fought to defend Hong Kong in the face of the Japanese invasion and was interned for his troubles, continued to be turned away from Matilda Hospital. "As we are Eurasian. . . . [they] told us, at the time, that was only for the British. I found it humiliated [me]. . . . You could not go into the Hong Kong Cricket Club" for a while too after the war, though that did change.[184] In 1956, Dan Waters found that "even today mixed marriages can raise eyebrows" in Hong Kong. His Chinese "wife, as a young girl on leaving college in 1956 was unable to join the Hongkong Bank as a secretary, because it only employed Chinese as janitors."[185]

However, Hong Kong was more progressive than other parts of the Empire. In Africa, of course, racial discrimination was a given and was a cause for war in Kenya. In "non-African colonial territories," the situation was little better. The "Native Administration Ordinance of North Borneo" gave "power to impose collective punishment on the inhabitants of native villages which harbour criminals. . . . In the Gilbert and Ellice Islands regulations make it an [offense] in an Ocean Island for a non-European employee to be absent from his quarters at night or to be found in a European settlement or a native village at night without a permit." Laws dealing with trade unions were "completely free from any kind of racial differentiation with the possible exception of Singapore and the Federation of Malaysia."[186] The Pacific War had weakened white supremacy within the Empire, now evolving into a "Commonwealth," but it had not eliminated it.

Epilogue

HONG KONG, with a phenomenally high level of concentrated wealth, remained a colony until 1997. This was partly the result of circumstances: the Nationalists, mired in corruption and infighting, could not mount an effective challenge to London, while the Communists, intermittently viewed as a prime foe by Washington, could not do so either.[1]

But more than a half century after the conclusion of the Pacific War, Hong Kong continues to wrestle—not always successfully—with the Empire's legacy: white supremacy. This was not the only form of bias that had to be confronted. In mid-1946 the "Chinese Civil Servants' Club" filed a petition for "back pay," which the British viewed with disfavor. The civil servants argued that "those who escaped to free China fared even worse" than those who had stayed in Hong Kong, not least because "people in the interior of China had a prejudice against [Hong Kong] refugees, especially Hong Kong civil servants." Optimistically they concluded—prematurely, as it turns out—that "racial discrimination having happily been part of and parcel of the past," they were certain that London would comply with their modest request. This petition foreshadowed an ongoing rift between Hong Kong and mainland China that continued after the city's reversion to Beijing. The mainland Chinese may have been suspicious about civil servants precisely because they had worked on behalf of the colonial regime.[2]

Ironically, the courts—the presumed bellwether of justice—were among the worst transgressors of the norms of equality. The Chinese have been systematically and pervasively discriminated against during the postwar era. While their British peers were hired on expatriate terms and given generous allowances for housing and plane fares for home leave, Chinese jurists were treated to far less desirable terms and conditions.[3] This may explain why Edward Lau has found that more "non-Chinese" offenders were escaping punishment by the criminal justice system. Asked one commentator cautiously, "Would it not be because some of the non-Chinese offenders (in particular the whites) were more powerful and influential than most Chinese offenders?" Lau's study "grew out of the persisting suspicion about . . . the 'strange' make-up of Hong Kong's judiciary—a one-sided domination of non-Chinese judges over a Chinese society."[4]

"Strange" indeed. "Barristers qualified from England, Northern Ireland and Scotland gain admission as a barrister in Hong Kong more easily than barristers from other Commonwealth jurisdictions." But the government consistently "has taken the view that racial discrimination is not a significant issue in Hong Kong."[5]

This mantra was repeated over the years, as if repetition would make it true. Thus, in mid-1998, Peter Lo Yat-fai, Acting Secretary for Home Affairs, asserted that "Hong Kong does not have the 'historical background' for laws against racial discrimination." This was after an investigation by the *South China Morning Post* revealed that "many nightclubs operate a colour code, charging Indians and Chinese customers for admissions while allowing white people to enter free of charge."[6]

Early in 2000, Deputy Secretary for Home Affairs Leo Kwan Wing-wah concurred with the viewpoint that such corrosive prejudices did not merit government action: "Legislation is not the cure for everything," he claimed. "Punishment may polarize the society." Yet, according to Anna Wu Hung-yuk of the Equal Opportunities Commission (EOC), "compared with legislation on discrimination on grounds of gender, family status and disability, there is no well-defined mechanism according to which a victim of racial discrimination can complain."[7] That is, in Hong Kong "it is illegal to discriminate on the basis of gender or disability but the territory has no laws against discrimination on the basis of race."[8] Meanwhile, "English language teachers who are not white are routinely discriminated against when they apply for jobs." The government "has consistently refused to legislate against racial discrimination in the workplace and commercial establishments, which puts it in breach of a United Nations convention."[9] As of early 2000 the EOC had received "64 complaints alleging racial discrimination over the past three years," but it was "powerless to act" because of the absence of a law. Anna Wu Hung-yuk thought this was just the "tip of the iceberg."[10]

Even after 1997, the Hong Kong government saw no particular problem with this. The leading global weekly of the city, the *Far Eastern Economic Review*, complimented the city's leader, Tung Chee-hwa, for his "rare display of prudence" when he "admitted that he was reluctant to seek a law to specifically ban racial discrimination." Laws, thought the U.S.-owned publication, "aren't meant to shape how people think, an idea with Orwellian overtones and uncomfortable reminders of 1930s Germany." Indeed, such laws "may lead to the erosion of liberty."[11] Popular columnist Bernard Fung agreed, but on different grounds. He wondered why the cry for such laws had only arisen after "the main perpetrator, the colonial administration, has bolted. Filipino maids and white professionals may seek the commission's redress for grievances, real or imagined, against the Chinese, who never had such recourse when they were victims." "Not once," he fumed, "have the paid consciences of humanity championed the cause of the truly persecuted, and even wrongly persecuted—the mainlanders. . . . But since the intellectuals, with whom the equal opportunists are allied, wish at heart to hang the lot of them and smite their government up north, the commission keeps mum on their profound prejudice. To them, the only good Chinese is a dissident."[12] The Citizens' Party disagreed, insisting that an "anti-race bias law" was "needed now."[13]

However, the points raised by Fung were difficult to refute and suggested that white supremacy had mutated and taken on a new form. Those of "pure European descent"—or "Westerners" as they were almost universally called, though many of them hailed from Australia and New Zealand which are east of Hong Kong—disagreed sharply. Many of them were furious when the Accredited Advertising Agents of Hong Kong, a heavily Chinese organization, in the midst of an awards ceremony urged the Chinese to "exorcise" foreigners from the city. They mailed a kit containing a "picture of a white man with a bruised face wearing [a] T-shirt. The obvious implication is [that] the 'gweilo' has been beaten up by the Chinese."[14]

This symbolic annihilation was followed by a version closer to reality. In August 2001 a "bouncer . . . told a court [that] the Wan Chai bar he worked for charged Pakistani, Filipino and Nepali men up to $300 for entry while letting white men in for free. The testimony came after the bouncer was accused of assaulting a European man who had been allowed into the club for free while his Filipino-American friend was asked to pay." This was "company policy." The defendant—the "bouncer"—said the "policy" of racial difference in admissions was based on the premise that "white people are easier to control in these situations—they listen to us" and thus did not have to pay a fee, unlike Asians who presumably did not "listen" and caused trouble.[15]

Finally, in November 2001 it seemed that a consensus was growing that laws against racial prejudice in Hong Kong might not be such a bad idea after all. "All of the foreign chambers of commerce surveyed strongly backed a law against racial discrimination, citing it as essential for Hong Kong to achieve the Government's plan of becoming 'Asia's World City.'" Adding their collective voice to this call were the "Chamber of Property Consultants, the Association of Restricted License Banks and Deposit-Taking Companies, the Hong Kong Hotels Association and the Society of Hong Kong Real Estate Agents." However, "the Chinese Chamber of Commerce"—perhaps wondering why such laws were not imposed when the British had ruled—said the "law was 'unnecessary' and the Hong Kong Employers of Overseas Domestic Helpers" (who were sensitive to their perceived discrimination against Filipinas) said "race discrimination was not a problem in Hong Kong."[16] This was no minor matter. Peter Woo, chairman of the Hong Kong Trade Development Council, announced portentously that by 2005 this former British colony "will be one of the world's two most important centres for business alongside the United States."[17] Yet the United States had moved aggressively after the war to pass laws formally repealing white supremacist statutes and had sought tentatively to build a reality that matched its rhetoric of being a "melting pot" and "gorgeous mosaic" of various races and ethnicities. Some suspected that competing with the United States might drag Hong Kong magnetically in the same direction. This, perhaps, was the final irony: the nation that had pioneered the construction of white supremacy might now influence one of its victims to move against racial discrimination.

Though Japan had been expelled from Hong Kong and the occupied territories and was said to be held in utter contempt by Asians because of its wartime role, as a new century dawned, it was found that "things Japanese have become immensely popular across East Asia, especially among young people, many of whom adore Japanese music, movies, television, animation, fashion and food. . . . In South Korea," where anti-Tokyo sentiment was very real, "Japanese-culture cafes and teahouses are quickly replacing American fast-food restaurants and European-style coffeehouses as the preferred meeting places for college students, Japanese rock and jazz bands are more popular than their Korean counterparts and many soap operas, game shows and television dramas are direct copies of Japanese programs. In Hong Kong, newsstands cannot stock enough copies of Japanese comic books and fashion magazines. Japanese TV dramas have huge followings. . . . The number of Asians studying Japanese has increased 29 percent in the past five years."[18] A lineal descendant of the KMT, former Taiwanese President Lee Teng-hui "who attended college in Japan and spoke fluent Japanese . . . once shocked people by saying he felt more Japanese than Chinese while growing up."[19]

As tensions between Beijing and Washington rose in 2000–2001, like Japanese Americans a half-century earlier Chinese Americans found themselves in the bulls-eye. Hong Kong columnist Frank Ching took note of the case of Wen Ho Lee, the Taiwanese American scientist falsely accused of passing atomic secrets to China, as evidence of a growing hysteria that was only surpassed when New York City was subjected to a terrorist bombing in September 2001. This downturn in U.S.-China relations was "bad news for Chinese-Americans," as "most Americans don't distinguish between Chinese and Americans of Chinese descent."[20] Caricatures formerly reserved for wartime Japanese Americans were dusted off and smoothly and seamlessly transferred to Chinese Americans, who were portrayed as having "thick glasses, buck teeth and heavy Asian accents."[21]

Questionable stereotypes were not the sole province of the United States, however. In the spring of 2001 Yoshinori Kobayashi hailed the "Japanese Army which the artist says, 'sent a shock to the eyes of white people from racist Western powers who only regarded colored people as monkeys.'" His drawing showed Japanese soldiers thrusting their bayonets forward, next to huge guns of battleships and fighter jets, as pale men with British and U.S. flags look on wild-eyed and frightened, with perspiration flowing down their cheeks.[22] This cartoon was a simple reflection of the resurgence of prewar-style nationalism in today's Japan.

This echo of a war that had long since passed into the pages of history was not unique. Less bellicose aspects of the impact of the Pacific War were evident in the person of Adrienne Poy Clarkson, Governor-General of Canada. In 1942, when she was three years old, she was in

Hong Kong "waiting to board a ship for evacuation to Canada, a country then legally closed to Chinese immigration. A colonial inspector skeptically eyed the family, including" the future political leader, "then announced loudly that they did not look like Canadians to him."[23]

African Americans' infatuation with all things Japanese faded rapidly after the war. Even the Nation of Islam in its later incarnations hardly bothered to claim its Japanese connections, though it stood by its original notion of the "Asiatic Black Man." Leonard Robert Jordan, the so-called "Harlem Mikado" who had stirred up such controversy with his pro-Tokyo rhetoric in the prewar era, was released from prison in 1949, and disappeared into obscurity.[24] When the shooting stopped, few paid attention to the story of Earl Whaley, a "popular orchestra leader who left" Los Angeles in 1935 for Shanghai, then found himself in a Japanese prison camp. This Negro musician's "knowledge of Japanese and familiarity with seven Chinese dialects won him a position of interpreter."[25]

Yet his fascination with things Japanese survived in the person of one of the most prominent and influential black musicians of subsequent generations: John Coltrane. In fact, he was a living reminder of the Japan-India nexus that had been so central to the Pacific War. His wife recalls that he listened constantly to "Japanese music . . . the shakuhachi and koto and some of their beautiful instruments."[26] Much of his music was based on the principles of the Indian raga, just as he was "fascinated by [the] Indian water drum." At his home in New York, there were "few records in his library, but what he [had was] almost all folk music from India."[27] After his premature death, the banner of Asia was waved by the rappers, the Wu-Tang Clan, whose imagery harked back to a strain of the old Nation of Islam, combined with Chinese martial arts.[28]

Of course, the impact of Asia on African Americans was not limited to those in the music business. Perhaps the most powerful African American in the corporate sector, Richard Parsons—President of AOL-TimeWarner—studied at the University of Hawaii, the region of the United States with the highest percentage of Asian Americans. There he learned a lesson that illuminates the entire epoch spanning the pro-Tokyo period among Negroes to the disappearance of this sentiment in succeeding years. "You were sort of adopted by all the other people of color as being aligned with them in a kind of global warfare with

whites," he recalled later, "and you were adopted by all the whites because you were aligned with them for being from the mainland."[29]

Others had a different perspective. A Eurasian, Clifford Matthews,
who fought in Hong Kong, later confessed that he did "not feel bitterness at all" toward Japan. "I feel more angry against Germany for all
their acts toward the Russians and Jews," he confided. "I never felt bitterly towards the Japanese at all because I knew there was a real . . .
racism too among British towards them and towards Chinese."[30] John
Streicker, a leader at Stanley camp—and no doubt many others—vehemently disagreed. Japan, he thought, "had learned to run before it could
walk." Undoubtedly unaware of the condescension of his words, he
found a "nasty and vicious period of infancy" in this advanced nation,
in "which the spoilt child was never smacked by its western godpar-
ents," though "it may yet be not too late to re-educate this erring race."
In the same vein he asked, "Will the beaten nation grow to a vicious, in-
corrigible delinquent, hating always the great powers sent to chastise
her, or will she, like a beaten dog, nuzzle the hand which administered
the beating?"[31]

Such provocative comments should be read in light of the curious
fact that many of those interned in Hong Kong embarked for a kind of
freedom in racially divided societies in Africa or Malaya, which
launched a bitter struggle against the main anti-Tokyo force: the Communists. John Fleming, a Scot and former partner in a major Hong Kong
firm, had been interned at Stanley but after the war he left for South
Africa where he "set up a cattle ranch near East London."[32] Ben Wylie,
once interned in Stanely, left for Durban.[33] William Aneurin Jones and
his spouse, Evelyn—known to friends as "Johnnie"—were interned at
Stanley and both died in apartheid South Africa in 1972.[34] Pen-
nyfeather-Evans also apparently found the charged racial dynamics of
South Africa congenial, as he left internment in Hong Kong—and his
previous post as Chief of Police—for this politically divided land. Major
George Gray of Hong Kong "retired to Kenya where, as a District Commander of the Police Reserve, he saw action against the Mau Maus."
Then it was off to South Africa for him too.[35] Lance Searle, upon being
freed from internment, immediately "transferred to the Malayan Police
where he became well-known for his Special Branch work against the
Communist terrorists during the Emergency there."[36]

Those of African descent had reason to think that the rise of Japan
and the Pacific War was of some consequence to them. The popular

Harlem journalist Roi Ottley observed in 1952 that the European colonial powers "inspire little hope in the hearts of black Africans, for losses in the Far East cause Europe to hold all the more tenaciously to Africa and to deal all the more arbitrarily and repressively with aspirations of blacks."[37] Hyoe Murakami, a Japanese historian who fought in the Pacific War, concurred. "Japan was defeated in World War II," he said, "yet as a result of that war countries of Asia achieved independence, to be followed in turn by those of Africa. . . . To say that Japan liberated those countries would be going too far; yet without that great conflict that extended from Southeast Asia throughout the Pacific and that brought Japan down in ruin, those countries would almost certainly not have achieved independence so swiftly. The same goddess history that punished Japan and the Japanese for their presumption also commanded that the West should stop seeing itself as the sole standard-bearer and arbiter of civilization."[38] Fujiwara Iwaichi, a major in Japanese intelligence during the war, added that after the war, "the white man's control over Asia lasting several hundred years has collapsed and has come to an end. An unprecedented historical achievement has been realized and its impact has been spreading to the Middle East, Africa and Latin America like prairie fire."[39]

The eminent British military historian, Basil Liddell-Hart, did not disagree. The Pacific War—notably the fall of Singapore—meant that "the white man had lost his ascendancy with disproof of his magic. The realization of his vulnerability fostered and encouraged the post-war spread of Asiatic revolt against European domination or intrusion."[40] Chu Shuen Choo, the son of a "planter" born in Malaya in 1921, blamed London for the bias he observed. He was struck by the "unfairness given to the Communists during the victory parade" after the surrender. "They were not given enough recognition for their services during the war," he thought. "It's always the rich people who stand to win all these wars. The winners are always the rich people. It's the middle class and the lower class who suffered the most."[41]

Needless to say, many in Asia—not to mention elsewhere—did not recall Japan's occupation so positively, no matter what the alleged long-term beneficial consequences. After the war, the racial underpinnings of the war were downplayed and newer myths more congenial to white supremacy arose. Thus, in the prize-winning Hollywood cinematic extravaganza, *Bridge on the River Kwai*, Japanese officers exploded in rage because they supposedly did not have the technical knowledge to build a bridge. They were saved from their predicament by British officers who designed and built one for them, using it as training for their men to keep up their morale. But the actual railway was designed by the Japanese and built with forced indigenous and POW labor. Obviously, the Japanese were perfectly capable of building the bridges they needed. That is, contrary to the cinematic myth designed to reinforce white supremacy, they were not technologically inferior to the British at all. This was a myth in which some Europeans and Euro-Americans no doubt found comfort after their forced retreat from white supremacy.[42]

Like a beard that continues to grow on the face of a corpse, the defense of white supremacy continued even after it had been discredited officially. The highly popular writer Gore Vidal would probably have disagreed with declarations of white supremacy's retreat. Some years ago, he caused a "stir by urging the white race to put up a sterner resistance to 'more than one billion grimly efficient Asiatics,'" that is, a "'defensive alliance of the white race—a northern confederacy . . . of Europe, Russia, Canada, the United States.'"[43] Personally, instead of appeals to color I would prefer to see class-based alliances against common oppression. But the collapse of the Soviet Union seems to have almost fatally damaged this idea. Coincidentally, this has had the unintended consequence of bringing the construction of white supremacy back to the forefront, away from the shadows, as Vidal's comment suggests. Much has been made of Shoichi Yokoi, the former Japanese army sergeant, who—after the United States reclaimed Guam in 1944—refused to surrender and hid out in the jungle, living alone in a hole in the ground, until 1972.[44] But paradoxically, it is white supremacy that continues to refuse to surrender unconditionally, although it did so formally during and after the war, and remains salient even today. As the twentieth century dawned, W. E. B. Du Bois stated famously that the problem of the epoch was the "color line." This remains true even though a new century has arrived—a century in which the utterly dangerous and poisonous prospect of "race war" will continue to haunt humanity as long as Du Bois's ominous words ring true.

Notes

NOTES TO THE PREFACE

1. Sheila Tully Boyle and Andrew Bunie, *Paul Robeson: The Years of Promise and Achievement*, Amherst: University of Massachusetts Press, 2001, p. 213; Roi Ottley, *The Lonely Warrior*, Chicago: Regency, 1955, p. 287.

2. Buck Clayton, *Buck Clayton's Jazz World*, New York: Oxford University Press, 1986, pp. 66–67. In recent years, certain Japanese officials have become notorious for their racially tinged assaults, particularly on African Americans. This is a reflection of the fact that since the war Tokyo has not sought to cultivate those believed to be most disaffected in the United States; moreover, the atomic bombing of Japan transformed it dramatically, not only in terms of promoting Japanese pacifism but also by increasing the influence of the United States—a nation that exalted "Negrophobia" for a good deal of its history—throughout the country.

3. The ""Greatest Generation' wrote into the covenants of the housing they built with GI-Bill money: whites only." See *Los Angeles Times*, 26 August 2001.

4. *New York Times Book Review*, 23 May 1999.

5. David P. Bassett and Larry N. Shyu, eds., *Chinese Collaboration with Japan, 1932–1945*, Stanford: Stanford University Press, 2001, p. 17.

6. Roger Wilkins, *Jefferson's Pillow: The Founding Fathers and the Dilemma of Black Patriotism*, Boston: Beacon, 2001.

7. See, e.g., Ashley Jackson, *Botswana, 1939–1945: An African Country at War*, New York: Oxford University Press, 1999.

8. Frank Furedi, *The Silent War: Imperialism and the Changing Perception of Race*, London: Pluto Press, 1998, p. 179.

9. B. V. A. Roling and Antonio Cassese, *The Tokyo Trial and Beyond*, Cambridge, U.K.: Polity, 1994, pp. 25, 65.

10. *Far Eastern Economic Review*, 5 April 2001.

11. John Dower, *War without Mercy: Race and Power in the Pacific War*, New York: Pantheon, 1986, p. 204.

12. See, e.g., Henry Rousso, *The Vichy Syndrome: History and Memory in France since 1944*, Cambridge: Harvard University Press, 1991; Peter Novick, *The Resistance versus Vichy*, New York: Columbia University Press, 1968; Pierre Pean, *Une Jeunesse Française: François Mitterrand, 1934–1947*, Paris: Fayard, 1944.

13. This book focuses primarily on areas of Asia occupied by European colonizers, principally Hong Kong, the Malay peninsula, India, and so-called "white settler" states, that is, New Zealand and Australia. Areas and nations that had been subjected to Japanese colonialism—for example, Korea and great swathes of China—have as sour a view of their colonial experience as did those who suffered under British colonialism and occupation.

14. David Roediger, *The Wages of Whiteness: Race and the Making of the American Working Class*, New York: Verso, 1999; George Lipsitz, *The Possessive Investment in Whiteness: How White People Profit from Identity Politics*, Philadelphia: Temple University Press, 1998.

15. Dower, *War without Mercy*; Yukiko Koshiro, *Trans-Pacific Racisms and the U.S. Occupation of Japan*, New York: Columbia University Press, 1999; Christopher Thorne, *The Far Eastern War: States and Societies, 1941–1945*, London: Unwin, 1986.

16. See, e.g., Matthew Guterl, "The New Race Consciousness: Race, Nation and Empire in American Culture, 1910–1925," *Journal of World History*, 10 (Number 2, 1999): 307–352. At one juncture in the North Atlantic community, there was a weltanschauung in which there were

twenty, thirty, or even fifty races all progressing toward some unique destiny and possessing peculiar racial traits. Then a "new race consciousness" emerged which divided the world into about five racial groups according to "color," not nationality.

17. For a useful exploration of the construction and intricacy of white supremacy, see, e.g., George M. Fredrickson, *White Supremacy: A Comparative Study in American and South African History*, New York: Oxford University Press, 1981. Recently Dan Waters, a veteran observer of Hong Kong, has written, "Because white Americans, Australians and other whites originated from European stock, the term 'European,' to cover all "Westerners' or 'Caucasians' is common in Hong Kong." See Dan Waters, *Faces of Hong Kong: An Old Hand's Reflections*, Singapore: Prentice Hall, 1995, p. ix. However, when I resided in Hong Kong in 1999–2000 I noticed that the term "European" was rarely used; instead the imprecise term "Westerner" seemed to be the phrase of choice. I found this curious in that it was intended to describe Europeans and Euro-Americans who came from west of Hong Kong, and Euro-Australians and Euro-New Zealanders who came from east of Hong Kong. Moreover, the preference for the term "Westerner" over "white" seemed to me to relate to its "geographic" and ostensibly nonracial character, no small thing in a region that had endured singeing racial tribulations. I discuss the use of such terms in my study of colonial Rhodesia and apartheid South Africa where "it was discovered that boards which used the word 'European' instead of 'white' caused confusion among white tourists from the United States of America, Canada and Australia, among others, who joined the 'non-Europeans' in their inferior situations. Thousands of boards with the words 'Europeans' and 'non-Europeans' were scrapped and replaced with ones reading 'white' and 'non-white.'" See Gerald Horne, *From the Barrel of a Gun: The United States and the War against Zimbabwe, 1965–1980*, Chapel Hill: University of North Carolina Press, p. 306.

18. David K. Yoo, *Growing Up Nisei: Race, Generation and Culture among Japanese-Americans of California, 1924–1929*, Urbana: University of Illinois Press, 2000, pp. 2, 10, 163. I strive throughout to distinguish between "racial" discrimination and other forms of discrimination, for example, that which stems from national origin bias.

19. Barry Sautman, ed., *Racial Identities in East Asia*, Hong Kong: Hong Kong University of Science and Technology, no date, circa 1996, p. i.

20. Henry Lethbridge, "Hong Kong under Japanese Occupation: Changes in Social Structure," in Ian Jarvie, ed., *Hong Kong: A Society in Transition*, London: Routledge & Kegan Paul, 1969, 77–127, p. 95.

21. W. Somerset Maugham, *On a Chinese Screen*, Oxford: Oxford University Press, 1985, p. 78.

22. W. Somerset Maugham, *The Painted Veil*, London: Heinemann, 1978, p. 166.

23. W. E. Burghardt Du Bois, *Black Reconstruction in America: An Essay toward a History of the Part Which Black Folk Played in the Attempt to Reconstruct Democracy in America, 1860–1880*, New York: Russell & Russell, 1956, pp. 15–16. See also Eric Foner, "American Freedom in a Global Age," *American Historical Review*, 106 (Number 1, February 2000): 1–16, p. 3.

24. Walter LaFeber, *The Clash: U.S.-Japanese Relations Throughout History*, New York: Norton, 1997, pp. 169, 186.

25. See, e.g., Gerald Horne, *Communist Front? The Civil Rights Congress, 1946–1956*, London: Associated University Presses, 1988; Gerald Horne, *Black Liberation/Red Scare: Ben Davis and the Communist Party*, Newark: University of Delaware Press, 1994.

26. Matthew Connelly, "Taking off the Cold War Lens: Visions of North-South Conflict during the Algerian War for Independence," *American Historical Review*, 105 (Number 3, June 2000): 739–769, pp. 753, 768.

27. Ronald Takaki, *Double Victory: A Multicultural History of America in World War II*, Boston: Little Brown, 2001, pp. 148, 171.

28. See, e.g., *New York Herald Tribune*, 5 April 1942, and Gunnar Myrdal, *An American Dilemma: Volume II, The Negro Problem and Modern Democracy*, New Brunswick: Transaction, 2000, p. 1438.

29. See, e.g., Akira Iriye, *Power and Culture: The Japanese-American War, 1941–1945*, Cambridge: Harvard University Press, 1981.

30. Sato Masaharu and Barak Kushner, ""Negro Propaganda Operations': Japan's Short-Wave Radio Broadcast for World War II Black Americans," *Historical Journal of Film, Radio and Television*, 19 (Number 1, March 1999): 5–26, p. 5.

31. Suke Wolton, *Lord Hailey, the Colonial Office and the Politics of Race and Empire in the Second World War: The Loss of White Prestige*, New York: St. Martin's, 2000, pp. 48, 50.

32. David Levering Lewis, *W. E. B. Du Bois: The Fight for Equality and the American Century, 1919–1963*, New York: Henry Holt, p. 467.

NOTES TO THE INTRODUCTION

1. See, e.g., Christopher M. Bell, "Our Most Exposed Outpost: Hong Kong and British Far Eastern Strategy, 1921–1941," *Journal of Military History*, 60 (Number 1, January 1996): 61–88.

2. *Economist*, 21 October 2000.

3. *Far Eastern Economic Review*, 26 October 2000.

4. James Leasor, *Singapore: The Battle That Changed the World*, London: Hodder & Stoughton, 1968, pp. 5, 20, 21, 151–152.

5. Ian Morrison, *Our Japanese Foe*, New York: G. P. Putnam's Sons, 1943, p. 49.

6. Yuki Tanaka, *Hidden Horrors: Japanese War Crimes in World War II*, Boulder: Westview, 1997, p. 37.

7. Yukiko Koshiro, *Trans-Pacific Racisms and the Occupation of Japan*, New York: Columbia University Press, 1999, pp. 17–18, 231.

8. Carl Vincent, *No Reason Why: The Canadian Hong Kong Tragedy*, Stittsville, Ontario: Canada's Wings, 1981, p. 244. See also Hong Kong Veterans Association of Canada, *The Royal Rifles of Canada in Hong Kong, 1941–1945*, Sherbrooke, Quebec: Progressive Publications, 1980. On the other hand, the treatment of civilian internees was not as harsh.

9. Interview, Patrick Hardie, 4 April 1985, *National Archives of Singapore*.

10. John Dower, *Japan in War and Peace: Essays on History, Culture and Race*, London: Fontana, 1996, pp. 258–259.

11. James Belich, *The New Zealand Wars and the Victorian Interpretation of Racial Conflict*, Auckland: Auckland University Press, 1986, pp. 235, 321.

12. Edward T. Thompson, ed., *Theodore H. White at Large: The Best of His Magazine Writing, 1939–1986*, New York: Pantheon, 1992.

13. Alexander Saxton, "'The Indispensable Enemy' and Ideological Construction: Reminiscences of an Octagenarian Radical," *Amerasia Journal*, 26 (Number 1, 2000): 86–104, p. 91.

14. From British Embassy in Chungking to Anthony Eden, l5 February 1944, Reel 1, Volume 41789, F1247, *British Foreign Office: Japan Correspondence, 1941–1945*, Wilmington: Scholarly Resources, 1980.

15. From Viceroy to Secretary of State for India, "secret" "XXX," dateline: New Delhi, 1 March 1942; from Government of India, 17 February 1942, Reel 3, Volume 31818, *British Foreign Office: Japan Correspondence*.

16. "Propaganda," "secret," "Digest of the Japan Plan (Final Draft)," 3 June 1942, CAB 119/50, *Public Records Office—London*.

17. Renee Romano, "No Diplomatic Immunity: African Diplomats, the State Department and Civil Rights, 1961–1964," *Journal of American History*, 87 (Number 2, September 2000): 546–579. See also Michael Krenn, *The African American Voice in U.S. Foreign Policy since World II*, New York: Garland, 1998.

18. "Political War Directives, 1943," AWMsp 189/209; 779/5-804/3; 795/3/8, *Australian War Memorial—Canberra*.

19. Emphasis in original. "Propaganda," from William Empson, l2 February 1941, R34/627, *British Broadcasting Corporation Written Archives, Reading*.

20. "Propaganda," "Minutes of the tenth meeting," 16 June 1942, 10:30 A.M., R34/650, *BBC Written Archives—Reading, U.K.*

21. Brian McAllister Linn, *Guardians of Empire: The Army and the Pacific, 1902–1940*, Chapel Hill: University of North Carolina Press, pp. 60, 122.

22. Frank Furedi, *The Silent War: Imperialism and the Changing Perception of Race*, London: Pluto Press, 1998, pp. 164, 184.

23. "Political War Directives," *Australian War Memorial—Canberra*.

24. Furedi, *The Silent War*, p. 6.

25. Victor Silverman, *Imagining Imperialism in British and American Labor, 1939–1949*, Urbana: University of Illinois Press, 2000, p. 78.

26. R. Palme Dutt, *The Crisis of Britain and the British Empire*, New York: International, 1953, p. 19.

27. See, e.g., G. A. Leiper, *A Yen for My Thoughts: A Memoir of Occupied Hong Kong*, Hong Kong: South China Morning Post, 1982, p. 33. Though race is not invoked, much attention is devoted to the impact of the war on his dogs.

28. Samuel Eliot Morison, *"Old Bruin': Commodore Matthew C. Perry, 1794–1858*, Boston: Little Brown, 1967, p. 332.

29. Peter Duus, "Nagai Ryutaro and the 'White Peril,' 1905–1944," *Journal of Asian Studies*, 31 (Number 1, November 1971): 41–48, pp. 42, 47. The author calls for a "more complex assessment of Japanese nationalism."

30. Denis Judd, *Empire: The British Imperial Experience from 1765 to the Present*, London: HarperCollins, 1996, pp. 77, 78.

31. Judd, *Empire*, p. 74–75, 82.

32. Buck Clayton, *Buck Clayton's Jazz World*, New York: Oxford University Press, 1986, p. 71.

33. Lewis Bush, *Clutch of Circumstance*, Tokyo: Okyuma, 1956, p. 197.

34. Ellen Field, *Twilight in Hong Kong*, London: Frederick Muller, 1960, p. 59. When she passed a Japanese soldier in occupied Hong Kong, Ellen Field muttered, "Good morning, you little yellow monkey."

35. Benjamin Proulx, *Underground from Hong Kong*, New York: Dutton, 1943, p. 135.

36. O. D. Gallagher, *Retreat in the East*, London: George G. Harrap, 1942, pp. 110, 149.

37. Barbara Tuchman, *Sand against the Wind: Stilwell and the American Experience in China, 1911–1945*, London: Macmillan, 1970, p. 127.

38. See G. B. Endacott, *Hong Kong Eclipse*, Hong Kong: Oxford University Press, 1978, p. 325.

39. See David Walker, *Anxious Nation: Australia and the Rise of Asia, 1850–1939*, Queensland: University of Queensland Press, 1999, pp. 3, 178.

40. Robert S. Vaillant, "The Selling of Japan: Japanese Manipulation of Western Opinion, 1900–1905," *Monumenta Japponica*, 29 (Number 4, Winter 1974): 425–438, p. 416.

41. Bruce Cumings, *Korea's Place in the Sun: A Modern History*, New York: Norton, 1997, p. 147.

42. B. Nicolaevsky, "Russia, Japan and the Pan-Asiatic Movement to 1925," *Far Eastern Quarterly*, 8 (Number 3, May 1949): 259–295, pp. 260, 270, 272, 273, 277.

43. C. M. Turnbull, "Sir Cecil Clementi and Malaya: The Hong Kong Connection," *Journal of Oriental Studies*, 22 (Number 1, 1984): 33–60, p. 36.

44. W. P. Morgan, *Triad Societies in Hong Kong*, Hong Kong: Government Press, 1960, p. 24.

45. Paul M. A. Linebarger, *The China of Chiang K'ai-Shek: A Political Study*, Boston: World Peace Foundation, 1943, p. 259.

46. Janice R. MacKinnon and Stephen R. MacKinnon, *Agnes Smedley: The Life and Times of an American Radical*, Berkeley: University of California Press, 1988, p. 226.

47. *South China Morning Post*, 5 January 1990.

48. Chan Lau Kit-Ching, *From Nothing to Nothing: The Chinese Communist Movement and Hong Kong, 1921–1936*, Hong Kong: Hong Kong University Press, 1999, p. 177l.

49. *China Mail*, 6 October 1945.

50. Morgan, *Triad Societies in Hong Kong*, pp. 25, 71.

51. T'in-wei Wu, "Contending Forces during the War of Resistance," in James C. Hsiung and Steven I. Levine, eds., *China's Bitter Victory: The War with Japan, 1937–1945*, Armonk, New York: M. E. Sharpe, 1992, 51–78, pp. 64, 72. See also "Statements by Japanese Officers concerning Secret Negotiations between Chinese and Japanese Representatives, early 1944, Prior to the Fall of Kweilin," Box 10, 5072; "[Japanese] Political Strategy Prior to Outbreak of War [by Japanese], Box 9, 5043; "Enemy Publication No. 278, Japanese Account [of] Malaya Campaign, 1941–42," *JAPAL, Imperial War Museum—London*.

52. John J. Stephan, *Hawaii under the Rising Sun: Japan's Plan for Conquest after Pearl Harbor*, Honolulu: University of Hawaii Press, pp. 34, 35. See also Hanama Tasaki, *Long the Imperial Way*, Boston: Houghton Mifflin, 1950.

53. Agnes Keith, *Three Came Home: A Woman's Ordeal in a Japanese Prison Camp*, London: Eland, 1985, p. 7. The author encountered a Japanese American from Seattle toiling for Tokyo in Borneo.

54. George Wright-Nooth, with Mark Adkin, *Prisoners of the Turnip Heads: Horror, Hunger and Heroics—Hong Kong 1941–1945*, London: Leo Cooper, 1994, p. 224.

55. Attorney General to Hon. C.S., 7 February 1947; Tseng Yu-hao and Denis Victor, 25 January 1947, HKRS, 156–1–1045 *Public Records Office—Hong Kong*.

56. Christopher Hibbert, *The Great Mutiny: India, 1857*, New York: Viking, 1978.

57. Christopher Thorne, *The Far Eastern War: States and Societies, 1941–1945*, London: Unwin, 1986, p. 181.

58. *New York Times*, 27 May 1944.

59. W. E. B. Du Bois, "Prospect of a World without Race Conflict," *American Journal of Sociology*, 49 (Number 5, March 1944): 450–456, pp. 451, 453.

NOTES TO CHAPTER I

1. Interview with Lucien Brunet, 26 November 1995, *Oral History Project, Hong Kong Museum of History*.

2. Robert B. Hammond, *Bondservants of the Japanese*, San Pedro, Calif.: Sheffield Press, 1943, p. 7.

3. *South China Morning Post*, 18 November 1971.

4. H. J. Lethbridge, "Caste, Class and Race in Hong Kong before the Japanese Occupation," in H. J. Lethbridge, ed., *Hong Kong: Stability and Change*, Hong Kong: Oxford University Press, 1978, 163–237, p. 178.

5. Peter Wesley Smith, "Discriminatory Legislation in Hong Kong," Paper presented at Hong Kong Baptist University, June 1987, 0842. PWS.Uf, Special Collections, *Hong Kong Collections, Hong Kong University*.

6. Paul Gillingham, *At the Peak: Hong Kong between the Wars*, Hong Kong: Macmillan, 1985, p. 128.

7. Lewis Bush, *The Road to Inamura*, London: Robert Hale, 1961, p. 159.

8. Percy Chen, *China Called Me: My Life Inside the Chinese Revolution*, Boston: Little, Brown, 1979, p. 385.

9. Alexander Grantham, *Via Ports: From Hong Kong to Hong Kong*, Hong Kong: Hong Kong University Press, 1965, p. 107.

10. Letter from T. H. Reid, Esq., 13 August 1899, HKRS 58-1-14, *Public Records Office—Hong Kong*.

11. Proposal, 28 April 1919, HKRS, 58-1-192 (7), *Public Records Office—Hong Kong*.

12. Letter from W. Schofield with attachment, 15 September 1930, HKRS 58-1-87 (8), *Public Records Office—Hong Kong*.

13. Gillingham, *At the Peak*, p. 8.

14. Chris Elder, ed., *China's Treaty Ports: Half Love and Half Hate*, Hong Kong: Oxford University Press, 1999, p. 118.

15. Robert Blake, *Jardine Matheson: Traders of the Far East*, London: Weidenfeld & Nicolson, 1999, p. 242.

16. Emily Hahn, *China to Me: A Partial Autobiography*, Philadelphia: Blakiston, 1944, p. 110.

17. Vertical File—"Biographical," Marjorie Angus, *History Workshop, Hong Kong University*.

18. George Wright-Nooth, with Mark Adkin, *Prisoners of the Turnip Heads: Horror, Hunger and Heroics—Hong Kong 1941–1945*, London: Leo Cooper, 1994, p. 21.

19. Hermann Joseph Hiery, *The Neglected War: The German South Pacific and the Influence of World War I*, Honolulu: University of Hawaii, 1995, p. 76.

20. Wing Chung Ng, "Becoming 'Chinese Canadian': The Genesis of a Cultural Category," in Elizabeth Sinn, *The Last Half Century of Chinese Overseas*, Hong Kong: Hong Kong University Press, 1998, pp. 203–215.

21. Barbara W. Tuchman, *Sand against the Wind: Stilwell and the American Experience in China, 1911–1945*, London: Macmillan, 1970, p. 174.

22. Liang Yen, *The House of the Golden Dragons*, London: Souvenir Press, 1961, p. 234.

23. Interview, Major Albert Hood, 006243/03, *Sound Archives, Imperial War Museum—London*.

24. Interview, Andrew Salmon, 005202/04, *Sound Archives, Imperial War Museum—London*. U. M. Streatfield moved to Bombay in the 1930s; there she was shocked by the presence of the "multitudes" who "slept in the streets, you had to step over sleeping bodies." See Narrative of U. M. Streatfield, 87/1/1, *Imperial War Museum—London*.

25. Frank Ching, *The Li Dynasty: Hong Kong Aristocrats*, Hong Kong: Oxford University Press, 1999, p. 98.

26. Robert Bickers, *Britain in China: Community, Culture and Colonialism, 1900–1949*, Manchester: Manchester University Press, 1999, p. 174.

27. Dan Waters, *Faces of Hong Kong: An Old Hand's Reflections*, Singapore: Prentice Hall, 1995, p. 142.

28. Interview, John Sutcliffe Whitehead, 006020/10, *Sound Archives, Imperial War Museum—London*.

29. Alice Y. Lan and Betty M. Hu, *We Flee from Hong Kong*, Grand Rapids: Zondervan, 1944, p. 56.

30. Kenneth Andrew, *Chop Suey*, Devon: Arthur Stockwell, 1975, p. 122.

31. Ken Cuthbertson, *Nobody Said Not to Go: The Life, Loves and Adventures of Emily Hahn*, New York: Farrar, Straus & Giroux, 1998, p. 132.

32. Robert Bickers, *Britain in China: Community, Culture and Colonialism, 1900–1949*, Manchester: Manchester University Press, 1999, p. 81. See Elder, *China's Treaty Ports*, p. 10.

33. Bernard Wasserstein, *Secret War in Shanghai: Treachery, Subversion and Collaboration in the Second World War*, London: Profile, 1999, p. 12.

34. Chris Elder, *China's Treaty Ports*, p. 214.

35. Interview, John Sutcliffe Whitehead, 006020/10, *Sound Archives, Imperial War Museum—London*.

36. Kenneth Andrew, *Diary of an Ex-Hong Kong Cop*, Cornwall: United Writers, 1979, p. 52.

37. Gillingham, *At the Peak*, p. 11.

38. Man Wah Leung Bentley, "Remembrances of Times Past: The University and Chungking," in Clifford Matthews and Oswald Cheung, eds., *Dispersal and Renewal: Hong Kong University during the War Years*, Hong Kong: Hong Kong University Press, 1998, 105–107, p. 106. Hong Kong University maintained separate statistical categories for "Eurasians" and "Jews," among others. See "Statistics of Pre-War Enrolment [sic] 1937–1941," "Section: Statistics (44)" "file" No. 44/1, "Dead File;" Registrar to Vice-Chancellor, 15 April 1939, *Registry, Hong Kong University*.

39. Norman MacKenzie, "An Academic Odyssey: A Professor in Five Continents (Part 2)," in Matthews and Cheung, *Dispersal and Renewal*, 179–191, p. 184.

40. *South China Morning Post*, 24 October 1999.

41. C. M. Turnbull, "Sir Cecil Clementi and Malaya: The Hong Kong Connection," *Journal of Oriental Studies*, 22 (Number 2, 1984): 33–60.

42. Shinoa Airlie, *Thistle and Bamboo: The Life and Times of Sir James Stewart Lockhart*, Hong Kong: Oxford University Press, 1989, p. 57. See also Cuthbertson, *Nobody Said Not to Go*, p. 136.

43. Varda Priver, "The Jewish Community of Hong Kong," HKRS 365-1-520, *Public Records Office—Hong Kong*; see also HKRS 58-1-23 (51). On the Eurasian Cemetery, see HKRS 58-1-69 (17).

44. James Bertram, *The Shadow of War: A New Zealander in the Far East, 1939–1946*, London: Victor Gollancz, 1947, pp. 80–81.

45. *South China Morning Post*, 11 September 1983.

46. Wright-Nooth, with Adkin, *Prisoner of the Turnip Heads*, p. 30.

47. Norman MacKenzie, "An Academic Odyssey: A Professor in Five Continents," in Matthews and Cheung, *Dispersal and Renewal*, 25–38, p. 25.

48. Lethbridge, "Caste, Class and Race in Hong Kong before the Japanese Occupation," in Lethbridge, *Hong Kong*, pp. 163–237.

49. Bickers, *Britain in China*, p. 72.

50. Emily Hahn, *Hong Kong Holiday*, Garden City: Doubleday, 1946, p. 199.

51. Bickers, *Britain in China*, p. 97.

52. Bickers, *Britain in China*, p. 61.

53. Hahn, *China to Me*, p. 209.

54. William G. Sewell, *Strange Harmony*, London: Edinburgh House, 1947, p. 113.

55. Lethbridge, "Caste, Class and Race in Hong Kong Before the Japanese Occupation," in Lethbridge, *Hong Kong*, 163–237, pp. 170, 179.

56. Blake, *Jardine Matheson*, p. 141.

57. *Hong Kong News*, 9 January 1942.

58. *Hong Kong News*, 31 January 1942.

59. *Hong Kong News*, 20 February 1942.

60. Oral History, Graeme Crew, 006118/04, *Sound Archives, Imperial War Museum—London*.

61. Interview, Major Albert Hood, 006243/03, *Sound Archives, Imperial War Museum—London*.

62. Interview, Charles Drage, 006131/05, *Sound Archives, Imperial War Museum—London*.

63. Vertical File—Biographical, "B-Miscellaneous," Harold Bates, *History Workshop, Hong Kong University*.

64. Kate Whitehead and Nury Vittachi, *After Sex: Sex in South China*, Hong Kong: Chameleon, 1997, p. 32.

65. Kenneth Andrew, *Hong Kong Detective*, London: John Long, 1962, p. 44.

66. Interview, Harry Sidney George Hale, 006125/12, *Sound Archives, Imperial War Museum—London*.

67. Charles Higham, *Wallis: Secret Lives of the Duchess of Windsor*, London: Sidgwick & Jackson, 1988, p. 35.

68. Anton Gill, *Ruling Passions: Sex, Race and Empire*, London: BBC Books, 1995, p. 37. See also p. 67: One British officer went a step further than the energetic Sellon. "I naturally prefer to satisfy myself with a woman, a friend and a lady of my own class," he began soberly before succumbing to an untramelled licentiousness, "but in the absence of the best I gladly take the next best available, down the scale from a lady for whom I do not care, to prostitutes of all classes and colours, men, boys and animals, melons and masturbation."

69. Lethbridge, "Caste, Class and Race in Hong Kong Before the Japanese Occupation," in Lethbridge, *Hong Kong*, p. 177.

70. H. D. Bryan, U. K. Consulate, Kweilin, to Lindsay Ride, 15 January 1943, Folder 88, MSS840, *Lindsay Ride Papers, Australian War Memorial—Canberra.*

71. Andrew, *Chop Suey*, p. 121.

72. Wright-Nooth, with Adkin, *Prisoners of the Turnip Heads*, p. 19.

73. Elder, *China's Treaty Ports*, p. 195.

74. Interview, Charles Drage, 006131/05, *Sound Archives, Imperial War Museum—London.*

75. Gill, *Ruling Passions*, pp. 48, 53.

76. Bickers, *British in China*, p. 101.

77. Elder, *China's Treaty Ports*, p. 184. See also p. 200: Christopher Isherwood, who visited China in 1938, encountered another brand of affection. He visited a "bathhouse where you were erotically soaped and massaged by young men. You could pick your attendants and many of them were beautiful. . . . It was like a sex fantasy." The idea that men of one "race" were being sexually subordinated by men of an allegedly superior "race" was at the heart of the opposition to white supremacy.

78. Esther Holland Jian, *British Girl—Chinese Wife*, Beijing: New World Press, 1985, pp. 20, 33.

79. See Vertical File—Biographical, "Sir Sidney Gordon," *History Workshop, Hong Kong University*. See also *South China Morning Post*, 3 September 1988.

80. Gillingham, *At the Peak*, p. 11.

81. Dan Waters, *Faces of Hong Kong: An Old Hand's Reflections*, Singapore: Prentice Hall, 1995, p. 124.

82. Hahn, *China to Me*, p. 348.

83. Vertical File—Biographical, "Ho Tung Family," *History Workshop, Hong Kong University. South China Morning Post*, 22 July 1989.

84. Jean Gittins, *Stanley: Behind Barbed Wire*, Hong Kong: Hong Kong University Press, 1982, pp. 8, 11, 12, 14.

85. Wasserstein, *Secret War in Shanghai*, pp. 183, 186, 187, 188, 189, 191, 192.

86. "South Pacific Command, Intelligence Summaries No. 9 to 31-1942," 12 February 1942, AWM 422/7/8, #423/11/172, *Australian War Memorial.*

87. Masanobu Tsuji, *Singapore, 1941–1942: The Japanese Version of the Malayan Campaign of World War II*, Singapore: Oxford University Press, 1988, p. 295.

88. Carmen Blacker, *The Japanese Enlightenment: A Study of the Writings of Fukuzawa Yukichi*, London: Cambridge University Press, 1964, pp. xi, 135, 138, 164.

89. Warren Cohen, *East Asia at the Center: Four Thousand Years of Engagement*, New York: Columbia University Press, 2000, p. 351.

90. Ian Nish, *Alliance in Decline: A Study in Anglo-Japanese Relations, 1908–1923*, London: Athlone Press, 1972, p. 271.

91. Theodore Roosevelt to Elihu Root, in Elting Morrison, ed., *The Letters of Theodore Roosevelt, Volume 5*, Cambridge: Harvard University Press, 1952, p. 717.

92. David P. Rapkin, "The Emergence and Intensification of U.S.-Japan Rivalry in the Early Twentieth Century," in William Thompson, ed., *Great Power Rivalries*, Columbia: University of South Carolina Press, 1999, 337–370, p. 350.

93. Walter LaFeber, *The Clash: U.S.-Japanese Relations throughout History*, New York: Norton, 1997, pp. 5, 24, 36, 38, 101, 113. See also Miwa Kimitada, "Japanese Opinions on Woodrow Wilson in War and Peace," *Monumenta Nipponica*, 22 (Numbers 3–4, 1967): 368–389.

94. Fred H. Matthews, "White Community and 'Yellow Peril,'" *Mississippi Valley Historical Review*, 50 (Number 4, March 1964): 612–633, p. 612.

95. Proceedings of the Asiatic Exclusion League, 5 January 1908, Box 1, *Asiatic Exclusion League Papers, Labor Archives and Research Center, San Francisco State University.*

96. Raymond Leslie Buell, "The Development of Anti-Japanese Agitation in the United States," *Political Science Quarterly*, 37 (Number 4, December 1922): 605–638, p. 621.

97. First International Convention of the Asiatic Exclusion League, 3 February 1908, Box 1, *Asiatic Exclusion League Papers, Labor Archives and Research Center, San Francisco State University.*

98. Democratic Party Platform, 1900, Part 6, Carton 1, *Hiram Johnson Papers, University of California—Berkeley.*

99. Native Sons of the Golden West, circa 1915, Part 3, Box 62, *Hiram Johnson Papers, University of California—Berkeley.*

100. Noriko Kawamura, *Turbulence in the Pacific: Japanese-U.S. Relations during World War I,* Westport: Praeger, 2000, p. 62.

101. Colonel House to Woodrow Wilson, 2 February 1918, in Charles Seymour, ed., *The Intimate Papers of Colonel House, Volume 3,* London: Ernest Benn, 1928, p. 403.

102. Colonel House to A. J. Balfour, 4 March 1918, in Charles Seymour, ed., *The Intimate Papers of Colonel House, Volume 3,* pp. 406–408.

103. Nish, *Alliance in Decline,* pp. 269, 270.

104. Kawamura, *Turbulence in the Pacific,* pp. 143, 144.

105. Peter Wetzler, *Hirohito and War: Imperial Tradition and Military Decision Making in Pre-War Japan,* Honolulu: University of Hawaii Press, 1998, p. 10.

106. Sterling Seagrave, *The Yamato Dynasty: The Secret History of Japan's Imperial Family,* New York: Bantam, 1999, p. 103.

107. William Jennings Bryan to Woodrow Wilson, 8 March 1915, *Papers Relating to the Foreign Relations of the United States: The Lansing Papers, 1914–1920, Volume 2,* Washington, D.C.: Government Printing Office, 1940, pp. 400–402.

108. Count Sei-Ichiro Terashima, "Exclusionists Not True to the Principles of American Founders," in Naoichi Masaoka, ed., *Japan to America,* New York: G. P. Putnam, 1915, 64–69, p. 64.

109. Memorandum from U.S. Embassy, Tokyo, 25 March 1919, Box 249, *Stanley Hornbeck Papers, Stanford University.*

110. Memorandum to "the Honorable Secretary of State," 4 April 1919, Box 251, *Stanley Hornbeck Papers.*

111. Memorandum to U.S. Secretary of State, 28 April 1919, Box 251, *Stanley Hornbeck Papers.*

112. Memorandum, 21 September 1944, Box 358, *Stanley Hornbeck Papers.*

113. Letter from Frances Hewitt, 8 November 1919, *Claremont Colleges Library, California.*

114. Tuchman, *Sand against the Wind,* pp. 24, 87, 127, 174.

115. *Hong Kong News,* 2 July 1943.

116. Memorandum—proposal, circa 1941, A 1,3,1,1-3, *Diplomatic Archives—Tokyo.* See also *Documents on Japanese Foreign Policy, Volume I: Japan-U.S. Talks in 1941,* Tokyo: Foreign Ministry of Japan, 1990.

117. "Anti-British Propaganda," *Japan Advertiser,* 9 May 1933, Box 1, *Paul Hibbert Clyde Papers—Duke University.*

118. "Osaka-Shosen-Kabushiki-Kaisha-Kobe-Darien Services," 1928–1939, Folder 1, General Northern Steamship Company, *Kemble Maritime Ephemera, Huntington Library—San Marino, California.*

119. Nicholas R. Clifford, *Spoilt Children of Empire: Westerners in Shanghai and the Chinese Revolution of the 1920s,* Hanover: University Press of New England, 1991, p. 73.

120. Report, 19 January 1942, Box 299, *Stanley Hornbeck Papers—Stanford University.*

121. I. L. Shauer to Tom Collins, 28 February 1935, MS 164, File 13, *Thomas Collins Papers, Arizona Historical Society—Tucson.*

122. Memoranda, 3 March 1937, 2 April 1937, 24 March 1937, CO 54/948/6, *Public Records Office—London.*

123. From the Air Ministry, "Royal Air Force Cadetships: Question of Colour Bar," 7 July 1936, CO 850/80/2, *Public Records Office—London.*

124. Memoranda, "Colonial Service Appointments: Interpretation of Term "Pure European Descent,'" 6 November 1930, CO 323/1110/28, *Public Records Office—London.*

125. Lethbridge, "Caste, Class and Race in Hong Kong before the Japanese Occupation," in Lethbridge, *Hong Kong,* 163–237, p. 167.

126. Memoranda, "Judicial Offices: Appointment of Officers Not of Pure European Descent," 9 June 1936, 4 June 1936, CO 850/84/8, *Public Records Office—London.*

127. "Judicial Appointment to—of Officers Not of Pure European Descent," 2 May 1936.

128. Memoranda, "Canadian Universities Bands—Not of Pure European Descent," 19 April 1927, CO 877/4/15, *Public Records Office—London.*

129. Memoranda, "Defence Utilization of Manpower," 16 October 1939, CO 323/1673/5, *Public Records Office—London*.

130. Memoranda, "Defence Utilization of Manpower. Commissions to Persons Not of Pure European Descent," 6 September 1939, CO 323/1673/5, *Public Records Office—London*.

NOTES TO CHAPTER 2

1. Reginald Kearney, *African American Views of the Japanese: Solidarity or Sedition?* Albany: State University of New York Press, 1998, p. xxvi.

2. As this was the term used predominantly during the times to which I am referring, I will, from time to time, use the archaic term "Negro" to describe those now termed "African American."

3. Brian McAllister Linn, *Guardians of Empire: The U.S. Army and the Pacific, 1902–1940*, Chapel Hill: University of North Carolina Press, 1997, p. 60.

4. Joseph Bryant, "The War in the Far East," *The Colored American Magazine*, 9 (Number 3, March 1905): 133–136, p. 134.

5. "The Effect of Togo's Victory upon the Warfare between Races," *The Colored American Magazine*, 9 (Number 1, July 1905): 347–348, p. 347.

6. "The Peace of Portsmouth," *The Colored American Magazine*, 9 (Number 4, October 1905): 531–532, p. 531.

7. John E. Milholland, "The Negro and the Nation," *The Colored American Magazine*, 9 (Number 5, November 1905): 609–615, p. 611.

8. Rev. James Marmaduke Boddy, "The Ethnology of the Japanese Race," *The Colored American Magazine*, 9 (Number 4, October 1905): 577–585, p. 581.

9. Marc Gallicchio, *The African American Encounter with Japan and China: Black Internationalism in Asia, 1895–1945*, Chapel Hill: University of North Carolina Press, 2000, p. 93.

10. "Liberia's Opportunity," *The Colored American Magazine*, 12 (Number 3, March 1907): 167–168, p. 167.

11. "The California Muddle," *The Colored American Magazine*, 12 (Number 3, March 1907): 168–169, p. 169.

12. W. E. B. Du Bois, "The Color Line Belts the World," in Herbert Aptheker, ed., *Writings by W. E. B. Du Bois in Periodicals Edited by Others*, Millwood, N.Y.: Kraus-Thomson, 1982, p. 330.

13. Booker T. Washington to Naoichi Masaoka, 5 December 1912, in Louis Harlan and Raymond W. Smock, eds., *The Booker T. Washington Papers, Volume 12: 1912–1914*, Urbana: University of Illinois Press, 1982, p. 84.

14. Robert A. Hill, ed., *The Marcus Garvey and Universal Negro Improvement Papers, Volume I, 1826–August 1919*, Berkeley: University of California Press, 1983, p. 306.

15. Hill, *Marcus Garvey Papers, Volume I*, p. 312.

16. Robert A. Hill, ed., *Marcus Garvey Papers, Volume III, September 1920–August 1921*, Berkeley: University of California Press, 1984, pp. 136–138.

17. Robert A. Hill, ed., *Marcus Garvey Papers, Volume II, 27 August 1919–31 August 1920*, Berkeley: University of California Press, 1983, pp. 83–85.

18. Hill, *Marcus Garvey Papers, Volume III*, p. 62.

19. Hill, *Marcus Garvey Papers, Volume III*, pp. 138, 632.

20. Theodore Kornweibel, ed., *Federal Surveillance of Afro-Americans (1917–1925): The First World War, the Red Scare and the Garvey Movement*, Frederick, Md.: University Publications of America, 1985, Memorandum from Office of Naval Intelligence, 18 March 1922, Reel 23, #686.

21. Memorandum, 18 March 1922, Reel 22, #689, *Federal Surveillance of Afro-Americans*.

22. Report, Week ending 12 May 1920, Reel 17, #531, *Federal Surveillance of Afro-Americans*.

23. Kathleen Skaten, 30 April 1921, Reel 22, #1075, *Federal Surveillance of Afro-Americans*.

24. Robert A. Hill, *The Marcus Garvey and Universal Negro Improvement Association Papers*, Volume VII (Berkeley: University of California Press, 1983), p. 506. See also *Negro World*, 14 June 1924.

25. Karl Evanzz, *The Messenger: The Rise and Fall of Elijah Muhammad*, New York: Pantheon, 1999, pp. 104, 110, 135, 138, 144, 145, 404. It is intriguing that the inspiration of the group that was to become the NOI—W. D. Fard—was reported to have been born in New Zealand. His "sidekick" and "best friend" was a "Chinese American."

26. Harry Dean, *Umbala: The Adventures of a Negro Sea-Captain in Africa and on the Seven Seas in His Attempt to Found an Ethiopian Empire*, London: George H. Harrap, 1929, pp. 20, 93.

27. George Schuyler, *Empire*, Boston: Northeastern University Press, 1991, pp. 51, 71. See afterword by Robert A. Hill and Kent Rasmussen, p. 281.

28. Kevin K. Gaines, *Uplifting the Race: Black Leadership, Politics and Culture in the Twentieth Century*, Chapel Hill: University of North Carolina Press, 1996, p. 206.

29. J. E. Bruce, *The Call of a Nation*, no date, Group D, Manuscript F 10-5, *Schomburg Center for Research in Black Culture—New York City*.

30. David Levering Lewis, *W. E. B. Du Bois: The Fight for Equality and the American Century, 1919–1963*, New York: Holt, 2000, p. 392. There was more about Garvey and black unrest in the 1924 book *The Negro Problem*, by one Mitsukawa Kametaro, the founder of an ultranationalist society.

31. Lewis, *W. E. B. Du Bois*, p. 219.

32. W. E. B. Du Bois, *Dark Princess*, Jackson: University Press of Mississippi, 1995, pp. 150, 151, 262, 297.

33. *California Eagle*, 5 September 1914.

34. *California Eagle*, 29 January 1916.

35. *California Eagle*, 2 March 1918.

36. *New York Amsterdam News*, 12 May 1934.

37. *New York Amsterdam News*, 9 June 1934. See also Patrick J. Washburn, *A Question of Sedition: The Federal Government's Investigation of the Black Press during World War II*, New York: Oxford University Press, 1986, p. 261.

38. Walter White, *A Man Called White: The Autobiography of Walter White*, Athens: University of Georgia Press, 1995, p. 69.

39. Hazel Rowley, *Richard Wright: The Life and Times*, New York: Holt, 2001, p. 15.

40. Lawrence S. Little, "A Quest for Self-Determination: The African Methodist Episcopal Church during the Age of Imperialism, 1884–1916," Ph.D. dissertation, Ohio State University, 1993, p. 227.

41. *New York Amsterdam News*, 12 September 1923.

42. A'Leila Bundles, *On Her Own Ground: The Life and Times of Madam C. J. Walker*, New York: Scribner, 2001, p. 258.

43. Kornweibel, *Federal Surveillance of Afro-Americans*, Report by George Holman, 24 October 1919, Reel 13, #0072.

44. Kornweibel, *Federal Surveillance of Afro-Americans*, Memorandum to Assistant Chief of Staff, War Department, 24 July 1924, Reel 23, #372.

45. Kornweibel, *Federal Surveillance of Afro-Americans*, Memorandum from A. A. Hopkins, 26 July 1921, Reel 23, #379.

46. Kornweibel, *Federal Surveillance of Afro-Americans*, Memorandum for Colonel Enochs, 9 May 1921, Reel 22, #0198.

47. Ephemera re: Delilah Leontium Beasley, 1871–1934, *MS 133, California Historical Society—San Francisco*.

48. Eric Arnesen, *Brotherhoods of Color: Black Railroad Workers and the Struggle for Equality*, Cambridge: Harvard University Press, 2001, p. 154.

49. David Lowman, *Magic: The Untold Story of U.S. Intelligence and the Evacuation of Japanese Residents from the West Coast during World War II*, no place: Athena, 2001, pp. 131, 147, 252.

50. Lewis, *W. E. B. Du Bois*, p. 416.

51. Kornweibel, *Federal Surveillance of Afro-Americans*, E. P. Eldredge to Director of Naval Intelligence, 12 September 1933, Reel 20, #547.

52. Kornweibel, *Federal Surveillance of Afro-Americans*, Memorandum, 1 June 1934, Reel 20, #580.

53. *Pittsburgh Courier*, 29 October 1938. See also *New York Amsterdam News*, 30 March 1935; *New York Amsterdam News*, 27 July 1935; *New York Amsterdam News*, 29 August 1936.

54. Kornweibel, *Federal Surveillance of Afro-Americans*, Village President of Madison County, Illinois to Chief, Bureau of Intelligence, 15 December 1933, Reel 20, #559.

55. J. Lawson to B. D. Amis, 5 April 1932, Reel 234, delo 3038, *Records of CPUSA, Library of Congress*.

56. Lewis, *W. E. B. Du Bois*, p. 390.

57. Roi Ottley, *Inside Black America*, London: Eyre & Spottiswoode, 1948, pp. 256, 257.

58. Roi Ottley, *New World A-Coming*, New York: Arno Press, 1968, pp. 329, 330.

59. J. Edgar Hoover to Jonathan Daniels, 11 August 1943, Official File, Box 6, 4245g, *Franklin D. Roosevelt Presidential Library*.

60. Ottley, *Inside Black America*, p. 256.

61. Lewis, *W. E. B. Du Bois*, p. 396.

62. *New York Amsterdam News*, 5 February 1938. See also *New York Amsterdam News*, 7 July 1939.

63. Gallicchio, *The African American Encounter with Japan and China*, p. 107.

64. Intercepted Message from Nomura in Washington, D.C., to Tokyo, 4 July 1941, Box 2, *Frank Schuler Papers, Franklin D. Roosevelt Presidential Library.*

NOTES TO CHAPTER 3

1. Interview, Harold Robert Yates, 005216/10, *Sound Archives, Imperial War Museum—London.*

2. Memorandum to Secretary of State, 10 July 1940, Box 206, *Stanley Hornbeck Papers—Stanford University.*

3. Memorandum to Secretary of State, 9 July 1940, Box 206, *Stanley Hornbeck Papers.*

4. Governor Sir G. Northcote to Secretary of State for the Colonies, 5 May 1941, Reel 12, Volume 27943, FO 371, *British Foreign Office: Japan Correspondence, 1941–1945*, Wilmington: Scholarly Resources, 1980.

5. Memorandum from Colonial Office, 16 June 1941, Reel 12, Volume 27943, *British Foreign Office: Japan Correspondence, 1941–1945.*

6. Memorandum, 30 May 1941, Reel 12, Volume 27943, No. 13179/1/42, *British Foreign Office: Japan Correspondence, 1941–1945.*

7. Gwen Priestwood, *Through Japanese Barbed Wire*, New York: Appleton-Century, 1943, pp. 1, 2.

8. Interview, Joan Cummack, 5 July 1995, *Oral History Project, Hong Kong Museum of History.*

9. George Baxter, *Personal Experiences during the Siege of Hong Kong, December 8th–25th*, Hong Kong Collection: Hong Kong University, 940.5425 B35, circa 1942.

10. John Streicker, *Captive Colony: The Story of Stanley Camp, Hong Kong*, Hong Kong Collection: Hong Kong University, circa 1941–1945, 940.547252 S8, p. 4.

11. "Indexes, Bibliographies, Catalogues," File "Maryknoll Mission," Father James Smith, M. M., "The Maryknoll Mission, Hong Kong, 1941–1946," *History Workshop, Hong Kong University.*

12. Interview, Brigadier R. C. B. Anderson, 005251/04, *Sound Archives, Imperial War Museum—London.*

13. Chohong Choi, "Hong Kong in the Context of the Pacific War: An American Perspective," M. Phil. thesis, Hong Kong University, 1998, p. 47.

14. James Bertram, *The Shadow of War: A New Zealander in the Far East, 1939–1946*, London: Victor Gollancz, 1947, p. 101.

15. Colin Crisswell and Mike Watson, *The Royal Hong Kong Police*, Hong Kong: Macmillan, no date, p. 8.

16. "Supplement of the London Gazette, 29 January 1948," HKMS, 100-1-5, *Public Records Office—Hong Kong.*

17. "Indexes, Bibliographies, Catalogues," File "Maryknoll Mission," *History Workshop, Hong Kong University.*

18. G. A. Leiper, *A Yen for My Thoughts: A Memoir of Occupied Hong Kong*, Hong Kong: South China Morning Post, 1982, p. 38.

19. Priestwood, *Through Japanese Barbed Wire*, p. 14.

20. Emily Hahn, *China to Me: A Partial Autobiography*, Philadelphia: Blakiston, 1944, p. 265.

21. Gwen Dew, *Prisoners of the Japs*, New York: Knopf, 1943, pp. 58, 73, 82, 89, 96.

22. Hahn, *China to Me*, p. 274.

23. Memorandum, 29 January 1942, Reel 2, Volume 35940, F5476/6/23, *British Foreign Office: Japan Correspondence, 1941–1945.*

24. "Indexes, Bibliographies, Catalogues," File "Maryknoll Mission," *History Workshop, Hong Kong University.*

25. Robert K. M. Simpson, *These Defenceless Doors: A Memoir of Personal Experience in the Battle of Hong Kong and After*, Hong Kong Collections: Hong Kong University, MF 2521408, no date, p. 133.

26. Vertical File, "Events—1941 Siege," *Off-Beat*, 3–16 January 1996, published by Police Public Relations Branch, *History Workshop, Hong Kong University.*

27. Interview, Victor Robert Joseph Merrett, MBE, AFS, MSAAT, 006124/10, *Sound Archives, Imperial War Museum—London.*

28. Ellen Field, *Twilight in Hong Kong*, London: Frederick Muller, 1960, pp. 58, 67, 84.

29. Priestwood, *Through Japanese Barbed Wire*, p. 25.

30. Field, *Twilight in Hong Kong*, p. 78.

31. "Vertical File—Biographical, M. A. Cohen," Chief Constable, Edmonton, Canada to C. Becker, Acting Deputy, Attorney General of Alberta, 14 July 1925, *History Workshop, Hong Kong University.*

32. Daniel S. Levy, *Two-Gun Cohen: A Biography*, New York: St. Martin's, 1997, pp. 209, 212.

33. Simpson, *These Defenceless Doors*, p. 133.

34. Benjamin A. Proulx, *Underground from Hong Kong*, New York: Dutton, 1943, p. 124.

35. David Bosanquet, *Escape through China*, London: Robert Hale, 1983, pp. 11, 49.

36. Phyllis Harrop to Colonial Secretary, 7 April 1942, Volume 31820, Reel 3, *British Foreign Office: Japan Correspondence, 1941–1945*, Wilmington: Scholarly Resources, 1980.

37. Freddie Guest, *Escape from the Bloodied Sun*, London: Jarrolds, 1957, p. 32.

38. Robert L. Gandt, *Seasons of Storms: The Siege of Hongkong 1941*, Hong Kong: South China Morning Post, 1982, p. 84.

39. "Kweilin Intelligence Summary No. 73," "Confidential Sheet 25," 3 November 1944, HRRS 211-2-32, *Public Records Office—Hong Kong.*

40. Statement by E. C. Ford, 31 December 1941, "Memos of the Battle for Hong Kong and Impressions of a Prison Camp by R. S. M. (I.G.) Ford. E. C.," Special Collections: Hong Kong University. This memorandum can also be found at HKMS 100-1-6, *Public Records Office—Hong Kong.* See also "English Translations of Japanese Documents in Japanese Occupation in Hong Kong," HKLB 940.547252 E58, Special Collections: Hong Kong University.

41. Sir Arthur Dickinson Blackburn, "An Account of Personal Experiences of My Wife and Myself at Hongkong during the Japanese Attack and Afterwards," Hong Kong Collections: Hong Kong University, MSS 940.547252, 1942.

42. Barbara Sue-White, *Turbans and Traders: Hong Kong's Indian Communities*, Hong Kong: Oxford University Press, 1994, pp. 30, 39, 182.

43. Interview, Alan Jackson Wood, 004792/06, *Sound Archives, Imperial War Museum—London.* See also Gary Wayne Catron, "China and Hong Kong, 1945–1967," Ph.D. dissertation, Harvard University, 1971, p. 27.

44. Oral History, Harold Robert Yates, 005216/10, *Sound Archives, Imperial War Museum—London.*

45. Interview, James Allan Ford, 13128/5, *Sound Archives, Imperial War Museum—London.*

46. James Allan Ford, *The Brave White Flag*, London: Hodder and Stoughton, 1961, p. 215.

47. Vertical File, "Events–1941–1945 War, B. Yates, Esq." *History Workshop, Hong Kong University.*

48. Vertical File, "Events–1941 Siege," *Off-Beat*, published by Police Public Relations Branch, Hong Kong, 3–16 January 1996, *History Workshop, Hong Kong University.*

49. Robert B. Hammond, *Bondservants of the Japanese*, San Pedro, Calif.: Sheffield Press, 1943, p. 24.

50. James Bertram, *The Shadow of War: A New Zealander in the Far East, 1939–1946*, London: Victor Gollancz, 1947, pp. 115, 121.

51. Agnes Smedley, *Battle Hymn of China*, London: Victor Gollancz, 1944, p. 359.

52. Vertical File, "Events, 1941–1945 War," Letter to "Dear Mr. Birch," circa December 1977, *History Workshop, Hong Kong University.*

53. Paul Gillingham, *At the Peak: Hong Kong between the Wars*, Hong Kong: Macmillan, 1985, pp. 130, 174.

54. Blackburn, "An Account of Personal Experiences of My Wife and Myself."

55. George Wright-Nooth, with Mark Adkin, *Prisoners of the Turnip Heads: Horror, Hunger and Heroics—Hong Kong 1941 to 1945*, London: Leo Cooper, 1994, p. 35.

56. Norman Miners, "The Localization of the Hong Kong Police Force, 1842–1947," *Journal of Imperial and Commonwealth History*, 18 (Number 3, October 1990): 296–315, pp. 297, 299, 300, 310, 311.

57. Narrative of Mrs. D. Ingram, 93/18/1, *Imperial War Museum—London.*

58. Interview, Lucien Brunet, 26 November 1995, *Oral History Project, Hong Kong Museum of History.*

59. Interview, Kenneth M. Baxter, 31 March 1995, *Oral History Project, Hong Kong Museum of History.*

60. Ford, "Memos of the Battle for Hong Kong."

61. Chan Lau Kit-ching, *From Nothing to Nothing: The Chinese Communist Movement and Hong Kong, 1921–1936*, Hong Kong: Hong Kong University Press, p. 167.

62. Memorandum from B. C. K. Hawkins, 19 May 1955, HKRS 163-1-670, *Public Records Office—Hong Kong.*

63. Miners, "The Localization of the Hong Kong Police Force," 296–315, p. 300.

64. Gandt, *Seasons of Storms*, p. 22.

65. Han Suyin, *Birdless Summer: China, Autobiography, History*, London: Jonathan Cape, 1968, pp. 235–236. See also Memorandum from Lindsay Ride, 25 April 1945, HKMS 100-1-5, *Public Records Office—Hong Kong.*

66. Edwin Ride, *BAAG: Hong Kong Resistance, 1942–1945*, Hong Kong: Oxford University Press, 1981, p. 5.

67. Bertram, *The Shadow of War*, pp. 122–123.

68. From "Admiralty" to Governor of Hong Kong, "Most Secret," 21 December 1941, HKMS 100-1-5, *Public Records Office—Hong Kong.*

69. Memorandum, 16 September 1942, Box 206, *Stanley Hornbeck Papers.*

70. Memorandum, 29 January 1942, Reel 2, Volume 35940, *British Foreign Office: Japan Correspondence, 1941–1945.*

71. Memorandum from Sir Arthur D. Blackburn, May 1942, Reel 2, Volume 35940, *British Foreign Office: Japan Correspondence, 1941–1945.*

72. Despatch No. 13, Chungking Legation, 5 February 1942, A5954 (A5954/69), #527/15, *National Archives of Australia.*

73. Phyllis Harrop to Colonial Secretary, 7 April 1942, Reel 3, Volume 31820, *British Foreign Office: Japan Correspondence, 1941–1945.*

74. Baxter, *Personal Experiences during the Siege of Hong Kong*, p. 22.

75. Hammond, *Bondservants of the Japanese*, p. 27.

76. Gwen Dew, "Horrors in Hong Kong," November 1942, *Geoffrey Emerson Papers, History Workshop, Hong Kong University.*

77. Dew, *Prisoner of the Japs*, p. 115.

78. "Indexes, Bibliographies, Catalogues," File "Maryknoll Mission," *History Workshop, Hong Kong University.*

79. Priestwood, *Through Japanese Barbed Wire*, p. 31.

80. Interview, James Allan Ford, 13128/5, *Sound Archives, Imperial War Museum—London.*

81. *New York Herald Tribune*, 2 February 1944.

82. Memorandum to U.S. Secretary of State, 14 March 1942, Box 206, *Stanley Hornbeck Papers.*

83. Jack Edwards, *Banzai, You Bastards*, Hong Kong: Corporate Communications, 1989, p. 45.

84. Interview, Clifford Matthews, 25 November 1996, *Oral History Project, Hong Kong Museum of History, Hong Kong.*

85. Levy, *Two-Gun Cohen*, p. 212. Even after the Communists came to power, Cohen maintained positive relations with Peking. In 1955 a "confidential" report to Hong Kong's Secretary of State reported that he had "arrived in Hong Kong and is reported to be leaving for Peking. . . . He is going at the invitation of the Chinese government and with the knowledge of the Nationalist authorities." See "Vertical File—biographical, M. A. Cohen," to Secretary of State, Hong Kong, from Governor's Deputy, 15 December 1955, *History Workshop, Hong Kong University.*

NOTES TO CHAPTER 4

1. John Streicker, *Captive Colony: The Story of Stanley Camp, Hong Kong*, HK 940.547252 S8, *Hong Kong Collections, Hong Kong University*, p. 3–2.

2. Bill Harman to "My Dear," 9 March 1942, MS 7724, *Bill Harman Papers, National Library of Australia—Canberra.*

3. "Indexes, Bibliographies, Catalogues," File "Maryknoll Mission," Father James Smith, M. M., "The Maryknoll Mission, Hong Kong, 1941–1946," *History Workshop, Hong Kong University.*

4. David Bosanquet, *Escape through China*, London: Robert Hale, 1983, p. 40.

5. Emily Hahn, *Miss Jill*, Garden City: Doubleday, 1947, p. 227.

6. Report, "Civilian Internment Camp. Stanley. Hong Kong. Health Report." 6 March 1946, HKRS, 163-1-81, *Public Records Office—Hong Kong.*

7. Undated, unidentified, mimeographed report, circa 1945, HKRS 163-1-81, *Public Records Office—Hong Kong.*

8. Robert S. Ward, *Asia for the Asiatics? The Techniques of Japanese Occupation*, Chicago: University of Chicago Press, 1945, pp. 57, 79.

9. Robert S. Ward, *Hong Kong under Japanese Occupation: A Case Study in the Enemy's Techniques of Control*, "Restricted," "Detailed to the Far Eastern Unit Bureau of Foreign and Domestic Commerce Department": Washington, D.C., 1943, pp. ii, 24, 90, 94, 104 (read at Hong Kong University).

10. Ian Morrison, *Our Japanese Foe*, New York: G. P. Putnam's, 1943, p. 152.

11. Otto D. Tolischus, *Tokyo Record*, New York: Reynal & Hitchcock, 1943, pp. 3, 71, 186–187, 407.

12. Robert L. Gandt, *Season of Storms: The Siege of Hongkong, 1941*, Hong Kong: South China Morning Post, 1982, p. 21.

13. Emily Hahn, *China to Me: A Partial Autobiography*, Philadelphia: Blakiston, 1944, pp. 311, 312, 321.

14. Sir Arthur Dickinson Blackburn, "An Account of Personal Experiences of My Wife and Myself at Hongkong during the Japanese Attack and Afterwards," *Hong Kong Collections: Hong Kong University*, MSS 940.547252, 1942.

15. John Streicker, *Captive Colony*, 4–12, pp. 5–8.

16. Undated Report from Sir Franklin Gimson, circa 1945, HKRS 163-1-81, *Public Records Office—Hong Kong*.

17. Alan Birch and Martin Cole, *Captive Colony: The Occupation of Hong Kong, 1941–1945*, Hong Kong: Heinemman, 1982, p. 50.

18. The text of Sir Franklin's letter can be found in Ward, *Hong Kong under Japanese Occupation*, p. 21.

19. Undated Report from Sir Franklin Gimson, circa 1945, HKRS, 163-1-81, *Public Records Office—Hong Kong*.

20. John Streicker, *Captive Colony*, pp. 7–15. See also "Provisional Lists of Foreign (other than Japanese) casualties, Prisoners of War and Internees in Hong Kong compiled in the month following the surrender of British Forces to the Japanese," circa early 1942, HKRS 112D/S1/1, *Public Records Office—Hong Kong*.

21. Ellen Field, *Twilight in Hong Kong*, London: Frederick Muller, 1960, pp. 101–102.

22. Sir Franklin Gimson, "Account of Internment in Stanley and the Restoration of British Rule to Hong Kong," *Hong Kong Collections: Hong Kong University*, MSS 940.547252 G 49 I, circa 1972.

23. Phyllis Harrop to Colonial Secretary, 7 April 1942, Volume 31820, Reel 3, *British Foreign Office: Japan Correspondence, 1941–1945*, Wilmington: Scholarly Resources, 1980.

24. Hahn, *Miss Jill*, p. 226.

25. Edwin Ride, *BAAG: Hong Kong Resistance, 1942–1945*, Hong Kong: Oxford University Press, 1981, p. 5.

26. Lewis Bush, *The Road to Inamura*, London: Robert Hale, 1961, p. 170.

27. G. B. Endacott, *Hong Kong Eclipse*, Hong Kong: Oxford University Press, 1978.

28. Anthony Hewitt, *Bridge with Three Men: Across China to the Western Heaven in 1942*, London: Jonathan Cape, 1986, p. 4.

29. Interview, Lucien Brunet, 26 November 1995, *Oral History Project, Hong Kong Museum of History*.

30. Gwen Priestwood, *Through Japanese Barbed Wire*, New York: Appleton-Century, 1943, pp. 66–67.

31. Bosanquet, *Escape through China*, p. 45.

32. John Streicker, *Captive Colony*, pp. 13–15.

33. I. D. Zia, *The Unforgettable Epoch (1937–1945)*, *Hong Kong Collections: Hong Kong University*, HK 940.548151 Z6, circa 1969, p. 37.

34. File—Author, "Archer, B." Bernice Archer, "Stanley Interment Camp, Hong Kong, 1942–1945," Bristol Polytechnic, B.A., 1992, p. 78, *History Workshop, Hong Kong University*.

35. Jean Gittins, *Stanley: Behind Barbed Wire*, Hong Kong: Hong Kong University Press, 1982, p. 77.

36. Benjamin A. Proulx, *Underground from Hong Kong*, New York: Dutton, 1943, p. 150.

37. Robert B. Hammond, *Bondservants of the Japanese*, San Pedro, Calif.: Sheffield Press, 1943, p. 28.

38. *National Maritime Union Pilot*, 11 September 1942.

39. Streicker, *Captive Colony*, pp. 13–14.

40. Ralph Goodwin, *Passport to Eternity*, London: Arthur Baker, 1957, p. 61.

41. Robert K. M. Simpson, *These Defenceless Doors: A Memoir of Personal Experience in the Battle of Hong Kong and After*, Hong Kong Collections: Hong Kong University, MF 2521408, no date, p. 168.

42. R. B. Goodwin, *Hongkong Escape*, London: Arthur Baker, 1953, p. 28.

43. Geoffrey Charles Emerson, "Stanley Internment Camp, Hong Kong, 1942–1945: A Study of Civilian Internment during the Second World War," M.Phil. thesis, University of Hong Kong, 1973, p. 138.

44. George Wright-Nooth, with Mark Adkin, *Prisoners of the Turnip Heads: Horror, Hunger and Heroics—Hong Kong 1941–1945*, London: Leo Cooper, 1994, p. 74.

45. Blackburn, "An Account of Personal Experiences of My Wife and Myself." See also Agnes Smedley, *Battle Hymn of China*, London: Victor Gallancz, 1944, p. 362.

46. George Baxter, *Personal Experiences during the Siege of Hong Kong, December 8th–25th, 1941*, Hong Kong Collections: Hong Kong University, 940.5425 B35, circa 1942, pp. 31.

47. Daniel S. Levy, *Two-Gun Cohen: A Biography*, New York: St. Martin's, 1997, pp. 217, 226–227.

48. Thomas F. Ryan, S.J., *Jesuits under Fire in the Siege of Hong Kong, 1941*, London: Burns, Oates and Washbourne, 1944, p. 102.

49. Ward, *Asia for the Asiatics?* pp. 175–176.

50. "Indexes, Bibliographies, Catalogues," File "Maryknoll Mission," *History Workshop, Hong Kong University.*

51. *Church Review*, July 1942, HKMS 110-1-1, *Public Records Office—Hong Kong.*

52. William G. Sewell, *Strange Harmony*, London: Edinburgh House, 1947, pp. 103, 113, 119.

53. Proulx, *Underground from Hong Kong*, p. 135.

54. Les Fisher, *I Will Remember: Recollections and Reflections on Hong Kong, 1941 to 1945—Internment and Freedom*, Totton, Hampshire, U.K.: Fisher, 1996, p. 73.

55. Wright-Nooth, with Adkin, *Prisoners of the Turnip Heads*, p. 77. As with other aspects of internment, it is useful to speculate on whether similar traits developed among enslaved Africans in North America—and whether a residue of such traits continues to persist.

56. Gittins, *Stanley*, p. 149.

57. William G. Sewell, *Strange Harmony*, London: Edinburgh House, 1947, p. 115.

58. Levy, *Two-Gun Cohen*, pp. 226–227.

59. Hahn, *China to Me*, p. 360.

60. Gittins, *Stanley*, p. 50.

61. *National Maritime Union Pilot*, 31 July 1942.

62. Sir Franklin Gimson, "Diary of Events," April 1943, HKMS 100-1-6, *Public Records Office—Hong Kong.*

63. Ward, *Hong Kong under Japanese Occupation*, p. 99.

64. Gittins, *Stanley*, p. 66.

65. Streicker, *Captive Colony*, pp. 5–16.

66. Streicker, *Captive Colony*, pp. 8–11.

67. Gwen Dew, *Prisoner of the Japs*, New York: Knopf, 1943, pp. 117, 142.

68. Kenneth Andrew, *Hong Kong Detective*, London: John Long, 1962, p. 92.

69. Denis Judd, *Empire: The British Imperial Experience from 1765 to the Present*, London: HarperCollins, 1996, pp. 145, 223.

70. Oral History, Major Reginald Graham, 006181, *Sound Archives, Imperial War Museum—London.*

71. Oral History, Harry Sidney George Hale, 006125/12, *Sound Archives, Imperial War Museum—London.*

72. Wright-Nooth, with Adkin, *Prisoners of the Turnip Heads*, p. 89.

73. Oral History, Billy Strachan, *Sound Archives, Imperial War Museum—London.*

74. Oral History, Billy Strachan, 10042/5/1, *Sound Archives, Imperial War Museum—London.*

75. Oral History, Harold Robert Yates, 005216/10, *Sound Archives, Imperial War Museum—London.*

76. Sir Franklin Gimson, "Account of Internment in Stanley and the Restoration of British Rule to Hong Kong Kong," circa 1972, MSS 940.547252 G 49 I, *Hong Kong Collections: Hong Kong University.*

77. Bernard Wasserstein, *Secret War in Shanghai: Treachery, Subversion and Collaboration in the Second World War*, London: Profile, 1999, p. 63.

78. "Diary of Events," March–April 1943, HKRS 163-1-80, *Public Records Office—Hong Kong.*

79. Gittins, *Stanley*, p. 117.

80. Gavan Daws, *Prisoners of the Japanese: POWs of World War II in the Pacific*, New York: Morrow, 1994, pp. 22, 44, 315, 346.

81. Oral History, Alan Jackson Wood, 004792/06, *Sound Archives, Imperial War Museum—London.*

82. Undated report, unidentified author, circa 1945, HKRS 163-1-81, *Public Records Office—Hong Kong.*

83. Undated report from Sir Franklin Gimson, circa 1945, HKRS, 163-1-81, *Public Records Office—Hong Kong.*

84. "Diary of Events," December 1942, HKRS 163-1-80, *Public Records Office—Hong Kong.*

85. Wenzell Brown, *Hong Kong Aftermath*, New York: Smith & Durrell, 1943, pp. 114, 115, 127, 129, 158, 192, 197, 198, 224.

86. Chart of Hong Kong Leaders, 27 June 1944, HKRS 211-2-35, *Public Records Office—Hong Kong.*

87. Hahn, *China to Me*, p. 328. See also Vertical File—Biographical, "Kotewall, Robert," *History Workshop, Hong Kong University*. This file contains correspondence from Andrew Whitfield of Birmingham University concerning CO 968/120/1, at the Public Records Office in London concerning "Colonial Renegades in the Far East."

88. Report by Eugenie Zaitzeff, 6 December 1943, HKRS 211-2-40, *Public Records Office—Hong Kong.*

89. Ward, *Hong Kong under Japanese Occupation*, pp. 24, 42, 58, 60.

90. "The Preliminary Report of the Hong Kong War Damage Claims Commission," circa 1947, HKRS 258-5-7, *Public Records Office—Hong Kong.*

91. "Proposed Record Talk by E. J. Wayne" for the BBC, 10 July 1946, HKRS 41-1-978, *Public Records Office—Hong Kong.*

92. Martin Booth, *The Dragon Syndicates: The Global Phenomenon of the Triads*, Garden City, New York: Doubleday, 1999, p. 174. See also "Chinese Collaborators (Surrender) Ordinance, 1947," HKRS 46-1-14, *Public Records Office—Hong Kong.*

93. Memorandum from G. Moore, CID, HQ, 26 January 1948, HKRS 163-1-670, *Public Records Office—Hong Kong.*

94. Memorandum from G. Moore, 9 July 1948, HKRS 163-1-800, *Public Records Office—Hong Kong.*

95. Memorandum, 11 July 1947, 41-1-2240, *Public Records Office—Hong Kong.*

96. Jill McGivering, *Macao Remembers*, Hong Kong: Oxford University Press, 1999, pp. 107–111.

97. Stanley Ho, Vertical File—Biographical, *Discovery*, April 1996, *History Workshop, Hong Kong University.*

98. Stanley Ho, Vertical File—Biographical, *Kaleidoscope, undated, volume 3, number 1*, History Workshop, Hong Kong University.

99. South China Morning Post, *11 March 2000.*

100. *McGivering*, Macao Remembers, *p. 98.*

101. "Foreign Companies Registered under Japanese Law in Hongkong," 12 September 1944, HKRS 123-5-240-B, *Public Records Office—Hong Kong.* The Chinese companies included Mei Ah Knitting Company, Dah Chung Manufacturing Co. Ltd., Shanghai Commercial Bank, Industrial Bank of China—all of Shanghai. See also "Companies Incorporated in Japan Registered in Hongkong during Occupation," from 1 July 1944 to 13 July 1945, 123-5-240-A, *Public Records Office—Hong Kong.* There were quite a few on this list from Taiwan, including Kabusiki Kaisa Taiwan Ginko (the Formosa Bank Ltd.).

102. *Ward*, Hong Kong under Japanese Occupation, *p. 41.*

NOTES TO CHAPTER 5

1. See, e.g., Gerald Horne, *Fire This Time: The Watts Uprising and the 1960s*, Charlottesville: University Press of Virginia, 1995, passim.

2. Marc Gallicchio, *The African American Encounter with Japan and China: Black Internationalism in Asia, 1895–1945*, Chapel Hill: University of North Carolina Press, 2000, p. 121.

3. Harold Brackman, ""A Calamity Almost beyond Comprehension': Nazi Anti-Semitism and the Holocaust in the Thought of W. E. B. Du Bois," *American Jewish History*, 88 (Number 1,

March 2000): 53–94, p. 70. Hans J. Massaquoi, a black American born in Germany in 1926, lived there throughout the war; though harassed, his dark skin did not cause him to suffer anything like the persecution suffered by the Jews. See Hans J. Massaquoi, *Destined to Witness: Growing Up Black in Nazi Germany*, New York: Morrow, 1999, passim.

4. David Levering Lewis, *W. E. B. Du Bois: The Fight for Equality and the American Century, 1919–1963*, New York: Holt, 2000, pp. 398, 468.

5. H. Van Straelen, *The Far East Must Be Understood*, London: Luzac & Co., 1945, p. 86.

6. Roi Ottley, *Inside Black America*, London: Eyre & Spottiswoode, 1948, pp. 251, 252.

7. To "Hon. Colonial Secretary," 4 September 1941, 1B/5/77/49, CSO 750, 1941, *Jamaica National Archives*. Hubert Julian, the daredevil pilot and soldier of fortune whose roots were in Trinidad was among the black New Yorkers whose anticommunism helped to attract him to the Axis, in this case Mussolini's Italy. See Hubert Julian, *Black Eagle*, London: Jarrolds, 1964, pp. 41, 44, 114.

8. Brenda Gayle Plummer, *Haiti and the Great Powers, 1902–1915*, Baton Rouge: Louisiana State University Press, 1988, p. 29; Hans Schmidt, *The United States and the Occupation of Haiti, 1915–1934*, New Brunswick: Rutgers University Press, 1995, p. 92.

9. *New York Amsterdam News*, 16 November 1940.

10. Walter White, *A Man Called White: The Autobiography of Walter White*, Athens: University of Georgia Press, 1995, p. 220.

11. *New York Amsterdam News*, 20 December 1941.

12. Marc Gallicchio, *The African American Encounter with Japan and China: Black Internationalism in Asia, 1895-1945*, Chapel Hill: University of North Carolina Press, 2000, p. 89.

13. Reginald Kearney, *African American Views of the Japanese: Solidarity or Sedition?* Albany: State University of New York Press, 1998, p. 117.

14. Ottley, *Inside Black America*, p. 266.

15. George Schuyler column, 12 February 1944, Reel 7, *George Schuyler Papers, Syracuse University*.

16. *New York Amsterdam News*, 12 February 1944.

17. Hugh Mulzac, *A Star to Steer By*, New York: International, p. 23.

18. *New York Amsterdam News*, 22 June 1940.

19. *New York Amsterdam News*, 30 January 1929.

20. *New York Amsterdam News*, 5 October 1940. He continued, "Five hundred years of history and experience have taught the white race nothing. Its leaders are just as vicious, rapacious and hypocritical as mankind has ever been, but somebody is now on the gallows to pay, and they should and must."

21. Saul K. Padover, "Japanese Race Propaganda," *Public Opinion Quarterly*, 7 (Number 2, Summer 1943): 191–204, pp. 197–199, 204.

22. *Negro World*, 31 December 1921.

23. *Negro World*, 28 May 1921. See also Jeffrey B. Perry, ed., *A Hubert Harrison Reader*, Middletown: Wesleyan University Press, 2001, p. 230.

24. See, e.g., W. E. B. Du Bois, "Listen, Japan and China," *Crisis*, 40 (January 1933): 20, in Herbert Aptheker, ed., *Writings in Periodicals Edited by W. E. B. Du Bois: Selections from The Crisis*, Millwood: Kraus-Thomsom, 1983, p. 682: "Remember Japan that white America despises and fears you. Remember China that England covets your land and labor. Unite! Beckon the three hundred million Indians; drive Europe out of Asia. . . . Get together China and Japan, cease quarreling and fighting! Arise and lead! The world needs Asia." See also *Negro World*, 31 December 1921.

25. W. E. B. Du Bois, "Japan and China," *The Crisis*, 39 (March 1932): 93.

26. See, e.g., Gerald Horne, *Black and Red: W. E. B. Du Bois and the Afro-American Response to the Cold War, 1944–1963*, Albany: State University of New York Press, 1986.

27. *New York Amsterdam News*, 18 November 1931. J. A. Rogers also thought that the existence of a strong Japan had motivated the United States to recognize the Soviet Union. See, e.g., *New York Amsterdam News*, 28 April 1934.

28. *New York Amsterdam News*, 16 August 1941.

29. W. E. B. Du Bois, *Color and Democracy: Colonies and Peace*, New York: Harcourt, Brace, 1945, pp. 58–59.

30. Du Bois, *Color and Democracy*, pp. 58–59.

31. Lewis, *W. E. B. Du Bois*, p. 414.

32. *New York Amsterdam News*, 15 March 1941.

33. James Weldon Johnson, *Along This Way*, Harmondworth: Penguin, 1941, pp. 198, 200.

34. *Oklahoma Black Dispatch*, 27 September 1928.

35. *Kansas City Call*, 19 October 1928.

36. Patrick J. Washburn, *A Question of Sedition: The Federal Government's Investigation of the Black Press during World War II*, New York: Oxford University Press, 1986, p. 75.

37. *Pittsburgh Courier*, 28 March 1942.

38. George Schuyler column, 12 March 1943, Reel 7, *George Schuyler Papers*.

39. *Afro-American*, 15 January 1938. See, e.g., James Ford, *The Negro and the Democratic Front*, New York: International, 1938.

40. *New York Amsterdam News*, 17 February 1932.

41. *New York Amsterdam News*, 9 March 1932.

42. George Schuyler column, 14 September 1940, Reel 7, *George Schuyler Papers*.

43. *New York Amsterdam News*, 12 March 1938.

44. *New York Amsterdam News*, 30 September 1939.

45. *New York Amsterdam News*, 17 January 1942.

46. *New York Amsterdam News*, 3 August 1940.

47. *San Francisco News*, 2 March 1942.

48. Robert Hill, ed., *The FBI's RACON: Racial Conditions in the United States during World War II*, Boston: Northeastern University Press, 1995, p. 512.

49. *New York Amsterdam News*, 29 November 1941.

50. *New York Amsterdam News*, 13 December 1941.

51. *New York Amsterdam News*, 3 January 1942; Elinor Des Verney Sinnette, *Arthur Alfonso Schomburg: Black Bibliophile and Collector*, Detroit: Wayne State University Press, 1989, p. 167.

52. *New York Amsterdam News*, 10 January 1942.

53. *Chicago Herald American*, 23 September 1942; Eric Walter Clemons, "Japanese Race Propaganda during World War II: A Comparative Analysis of Propaganda Tactics in Southeast Asia and the West," 213–236, p. 227, in Barry Sautman, ed., *Racial Identities in East Asia*, Hong Kong: Hong Kong University of Science and Technology, no date.

54. *New York Amsterdam News*, 21 March 1942.

55. *New York Amsterdam News*, 8 August 1942.

56. *People's Voice*, 8 August 1942.

57. *New York Amsterdam News*, 21 March 1942.

58. *New York Amsterdam News*, 14 February 1942.

59. *New York Amsterdam News*, 21 February 1942.

60. Deposition of Keith Brown, Assistant Attorney General, Southern District Court of New York, Box 1049, R33.18.2.5, C-113-264, *United States v. James Thornhill, National Archives—New York City*.

61. Roi Ottley, *New World A-Coming*, New York: Arno Press, 1968, p. 336.

62. Hill, *The FBI's RACON*, pp. 7, 191, 532.

63. *People's Voice*, 28 February 1942.

64. *People's Voice*, 26 December 1942.

65. Karl Evanzz, *The Messenger: The Rise and Fall of Elijah Muhammad*, New York: Pantheon, 1999, p. 126.

66. *New York Amsterdam News*, 28 February 1942.

67. Robert O. Jordan to Hachiro Arita, 18 November 1936, A461, ET/11, *Diplomatic Archives—Tokyo*.

68. Letter from "Pacific Movement of Chicago, USA," 14 December 1933, CO 554/95/8, *Public Records Office—London*.

69. *People's Voice*, 28 February 1942; *People's Voice*, 7 March 1942.

70. *People's Voice*, 21 March 1942.

71. Ottley, *Inside Black America*, p. 261.

72. Affadavit by Ketih Brown, circa 1942, CR-113-40, R33.18.2.4, Box 1044, *National Archives—New York City*.

73. Ottley, *Inside Black America*, p. 263; Ottley, *New World A-Coming*, p. 337. Other pro-Tokyo elements who were arrested included "Stokley Delmar Hart, president of the Brotherhood of Liberty; Charles Newby, alias Father Divine Nassam, president of the Colored American National Organization. Mrs. A. Moore, secretary of the Brotherhood and 'prophet' Elijah Muhammad." See *New York Amsterdam News*, 26 September 1942. See also *New York Amsterdam News*, 3 October 1942: Among those arrested in Chicago was Frederic H. Hammurabi Robb, "African

born" and influential in the Windy City. He studied at the University of London and obtained a law degree from Northwestern University.

74. *New York Amsterdam News*, 6 February 1943.

75. *New York Amsterdam News*, 26 December 1942.

76. Philip A. Klinkner, with Rogers M. Smith, *The Unsteady March: The Rise and Decline of Racial Equality in America*, Chicago: University of Chicago Press, 1999, p. 172.

77. Tony Matthews, *Shadows Dancing: Japanese Espionage against the West, 1939–1945*, London: Robert Hale, 1993, pp. 25, 27.

78. *Speeches of John E. Rankin of Mississippi in the House, 18 February 1942 and 23 February 1942*, Washington, D.C.: Government Printing Office, 1942, MS 11158, *California Historical Society—San Francisco*.

79. Hill, *The FBI's RACON*, pp. 81, 104, 129, 305, 350, 397. See J. Edgar Hoover to SAC, 28 April 1942, Roll 1, Section 3, #0133, *FBI File on the NAACP*. Most alarming for the United States was the fact that when the Japanese sank two British warships early in the war, two black workers in the War Department itself "called out to each other, "We just got the 'Repulse' and 'Prince of Wales.' Good hunting, eh?" See Klinkner, with Smith, *The Unsteady March*, p. 163. See also Beth Tompkins Bates, *Pullman Porters and the Rise of Protest Politics in Black America, 1925–1945*, Chapel Hill: University of North Carolina Press, 2001, p. 165.

80. Ottley, *Inside Black America*, p. 266.

81. FBI Report, 12 June 1942, Roll 1, Section 3, #0145, *FBI File on the NAACP*.

82. Suke Wolton, *Lord Hailey, the Colonial Office and the Politics of Race and Empire in the Second World War: The Loss of White Prestige*, New York: St. Martin's, 2000, p. 49.

83. *New York Amsterdam News*, 31 January 1942.

84. *New York Amsterdam News*, 7 February 1942.

85. *People's Voice*, 21 February 1942.

86. *New York Amsterdam News*, 21 February 1942.

87. *New York Amsterdam News*, 28 February 1942.

88. *New York Amsterdam News*, 21 February 1942.

89. *People's Voice*, 2 May 1942.

90. *People's Voice*, 12 September 1942.

91. George Schuyler column, 17 June 1944, Reel 7, *George Schuyler Papers*.

92. In 1944 Schuyler wrote of what he termed "the Caucasian Problem." See Jeffrey B. Leak, ed., *Rac[e]ing to the Right: Selected Essays of George S. Schuyler*, Knoxville: University of Tennessee Press, 2001, p. 38.

93. Column by George Schuyler, 20 November 1943, Reel 7, *George Schuyler Papers*.

94. J. F. Anderson to "Dear Sir," 9 December 1944, 3676, *Earl Warren Papers, California State Archives—Sacramento*.

95. O. L. Turner to Governor Earl Warren, 24 February 1944, 3676, *Earl Warren Papers, California State Archives—Sacramento*.

96. L. G. Brattin to Earl Warren, 24 August 1943, 3676, *Earl Warren Papers, California State Archives—Sacramento*.

97. Theodore Roosevelt McCoin to "Dear President," 25 October 1943, RG 211, War Manpower Commission, Regional Central Files, Box 32, Files 4–5, *National Archives and Records Administration—San Bruno, California*.

98. Verne Scoggins to Mr. A. E. Shaw, 15 September 1943, F3640-3655, *Earl Warren Papers, California State Archives—Sacramento*.

99. John D. Stockman to Earl Warren, 5 October 1943, F3640-3655, *Earl Warren Papers, California State Archives—Sacramento*.

100. Memorandum, 15 March 1945, RG 228, Region XII, Box 25, entry n. 70, 12-BR-501, *National Archives and Records Administration—San Bruno, California*.

101. Shirley Ann Wilson Moore, *To Place Our Deeds: The African American Community in Richmond, California, 1910–1963*, Berkeley: University of California Press, 2000, p. 41.

102. Ramlal B. Bajpai to Earl Warren, 21 July 1944, 3656, *Earl Warren Papers, California State Archives—Sacramento*. See, e.g., *New York Times*, 9 February 1944; *Baltimore Sun*, 22 February 1944.

103. Lewis, *W. E. B. Du Bois*, p. 470.

104. *New York Amsterdam News*, 17 July 1943.

105. George Schuyler column, 29 May 1943, Reel 7, *George Schuyler Papers*. The novelist Richard Wright agreed with Schuyler: "If government can force the migration of a whole

section of the population, and then wash its hands of further responsibility . . . that same tactic can be used against other sections of the population, at any time, and in any situation the government chooses to term an emergency." *New York Amsterdam News*, 26 May 1945.

106. *California Eagle*, 18 December 1941.

107. *California Eagle*, 9 April 1942.

108. *California Eagle*, 23 April 1942: "Race in Vancouver fails to profit from Jap [sic] evacuation." See *California Eagle*, 28 August 1942: "Trinity Baptist Makes Use of Jap [sic] Property." An editorial claimed that because of the internment, "the opportunities open to colored people are fairly obvious." See *California Eagle*, 30 April 1942.

109. *People's Voice*, 21 February 1942.

110. Walter White, *A Rising Wind*, Garden City: Doubleday, 1945, p. 153.

111. Christopher Thorne, *Border Crossings: Studies in International History*, Oxford: Basil Blackwell, 1988, p. 270.

112. Roi Ottley, *No Green Pastures*, London: John Murray, 1952, pp. 93, 153, 164.

NOTES TO CHAPTER 6

1. Memorandum, 27 October 1941, NAB 354, FO 371/27986, *National Archives of Singapore*.

2. Far Eastern Department of British Foreign Office, London, to U.S., 17 February 1942, Reel 3, Volume 31821, F1584, *British Foreign Office: Japan Correspondence, 1941–1945*, Wilmington: Scholarly Resources, 1980.

3. Memorandum from Far Eastern Department, British Foreign Office, 20 December 1941, Volume 28062, Reel 20, F14109, *British Foreign Office: Japan Correspondence, 1941–1945*, Wilmington: Scholarly Resources, 1980. For expressions of pro-Tokyo sentiment among Japanese Canadians, see, e.g., Keibo Oiwa, ed., *Stone Voices: Wartime Writings of Japanese-Canadian Issei*, Montreal: Vehicule Press, 1991.

4. *British Foreign Office*, Reel 3, Volume 31823, F2219/132/23, Report on 8–9 January 1942 Conference in Ottawa.

5. Ian Nish, "Overseas Japanese, Overseas Chinese and British Justice, 1931," in Brook Barrington, ed., *Empires, Imperialism and Southeast Asia*, Monash Asia Institute, Centre of Southeast Asia Studies, Monash University, 1997, 113–125, p. 114, *History Workshop, Hong Kong University*.

6. Li Shu-Fan, *Hong Kong Surgeon*, London: Victor Gollancz, 1964, p. 143.

7. Paul Gillingham, *At the Peak: Hong Kong between the Wars*, Hong Kong: Macmillan, 1985, pp. 130, 169.

8. George Wright-Nooth, with Mark Adkin, *Prisoners of the Turnip Heads: Horror, Hunger and Heroics—Hong Kong 1941–1945*, London: Leo Cooper, 1994, p. 52.

9. Emily Hahn, *Hong Kong Holiday*, Garden City: Doubleday, 1946, p. 95.

10. George Harry Bainborough, 005210/04, *Sound Archives, Imperial War Museum—London*.

11. Chohong Choi, "Hong Kong in the Context of the Pacific War: An American Perspective," M.Phil. thesis, Hong Kong University, 1998, pp. 16–17.

12. Owen Lattimore, *Solution in Asia*, Boston: Little Brown, 1945, p. 127.

13. Haruko Taya Cook and Theodore Cook, *Japan at War: An Oral History*, New York: New Press, 1992, pp. 51, 119, 164, 212, 379.

14. Russell Braddon, *The Other 100 Years War: Japan's Bid for Supremacy, 1941–2041*, London: Collins, 1983, p. 17.

15. Masanobu Tsuji, *Singapore, 1941–1942: The Japanese Version of the Malayan Campaign of World War II*, Singapore: Oxford University Press, 1988, p. 295.

16. Robert J. C. Butow, *Tojo and the Coming of War*, Stanford: Stanford University Press, 1961, p. 25.

17. *Hong Kong News*, 3 June 1943.

18. C. Calvin Smith, *War and Wartime Changes: The Transformation of Arkansas, 1940–1945*, Fayetteville: University of Arkansas Press, 1986, p. 14.

19. John Stephan, "Hijacked by Utopia: American Nikkei in Manchuria," *Amerasia Journal*, 23 (Number 3, 1997): 1–42, pp. 12, 30.

20. Yuki Ichioka, "Beyond National Boundaries: The Complexity of Japanese-American History," *Amerasia Journal*, 23 (Number 3, 1997): viii–xi, p. viii.

21. Letter to Fred Farr, 3 February 1943, MS 5685, *Fred Farr Papers, California Historical Society—San Francisco*. See also http://www.nikkeiheritage.org, the website of the National Japan-

ese-American Historical Society and http://scuish.scu.edu/SCU/Programs/Diversity/jarc .html, the website of the Japanese-American Resource Center.

22. *Hong Kong News*, 24 February 1943.

23. *Hong Kong News*, 26 July 1943.

24. *Daily Mail*, 19 February 1943.

25. *Hong Kong News*, 16 November 1942.

26. Emily Hahn, *China to Me: A Partial Autobiography*, Philadelphia: Blakiston, 1944, p. 343.

27. Benjamin A. Proulx, *Underground from Hong Kong*, New York: Dutton, 1943, p. 123.

28. Wright-Nooth, with Adkin, *Prisoners of the Turnip Heads*, p. 224.

29. Ellen Field, *Twilight in Hong Kong*, London: Frederick Muller, 1960, pp. 101–102.

30. Shu-Fan, *Hong Kong Surgeon*, p. 146.

31. Gwen Dew, *Prisoner of the Japs*, New York: Knopf, 1943, p. 183.

32. Bernard Wasserstein, *Secret War in Shanghai: Treachery, Subversion and Collaboration in the Second World War*, London: Profile, 1999, pp. 170, 171, 181, 249, 250.

33. Yuji Ichioka, "The Meaning of Loyalty: The Case of Kazumaro Buddy Ono," *Amerasia Journal*, 23 (Number 3, 1997): 45–71, pp. 58, 59.

34. Lee Kuan Yew, *The Singapore Story*, Singapore: Times Publishers, 1998, p. 63.

35. Memorandum, 15 February 1944, External Affairs, File 29-C-A, 1944, *National Archives of India*.

36. Oral History, Charlie Gan, 11 December 1984, *National Archives of Singapore*.

37. Oral History, Soon Kim Seng, 3 August 1985, *National Archives of Singapore*.

38. Oral History, Tan Cheng Hwee, 22 March 1984, *National Archives of Singapore*.

39. "Various Affadavits concerning Japanese War Crimes," 8 January 1946, WO 311/562, *Public Records Office—London*.

40. Oral History, Shanmugasivanathan, 7 April 1983, *National Archives of Singapore*.

41. Otto D. Tolischus, *Tokyo Record*, New York: Reynal & Hitchcock, 1943, p. 349.

42. E. Bartlett Kerr, *Surrender and Survival: The Experience of American POWs in the Pacific, 1941–1945*, New York: Morrow, 1985, pp. 67, 168, 183, 189.

43. Oral History, Reverend Joseph Ernest Sandbach, OBE, 004784/08, *Sound Archives, Imperial War Museum—London*.

44. Martin Boyle, *Yanks Don't Cry*, New York: Bernard Geis, 1963, pp. 63–65.

45. Jack Edwards, *Banzai, You Bastards*, Hong Kong: Corporate Communications, 1989, pp. 28, 32, 73, 160.

46. Liam Nolan, *Small Man of Nanataki*, London: Peter Davies, 1966, pp. 15, 26, 82.

47. Affadavit of Mary Erwin Martin, 29 April 1947, *History Workshop, Hong Kong University, Geoffrey Emerson Papers*.

48. Notes from Lewis Bush, *Clutch of Circumstance*, Tokyo: Okuyama, 1956, *History Workshop, Hong Kong University, G. A. Endacott Papers*.

49. Field, *Twilight in Hong Kong*, p. 77.

50. Interview, George Stoddard, 21 February 1985, Box 17, Folder 10, *Cruiser Houston Collection—University of Houston*.

51. Frank Fujita, *FOO: A Japanese-American Prisoner of the Rising Sun*, Denton: University of North Texas Press, 1993, p. 159. See also P. Scott Corbett, *Quiet Passages: The Exchange of Civilians between the United States and Japan during the Second World War*, Kent, Ohio: Kent State University Press, 1987.

52. See, e.g., Charlotte Carr-Gregg, *Japanese Prisoners of War in Revolt: The Outbreaks of Featherston and Cowra during World War II*, St. Lucia: University of Queensland Press, 1978.

53. *Hong Kong News*, 22 March 1942.

54. *Hong Kong News*, 6 July 1942.

55. *Hong Kong News*, 9 September 1942.

56. *Hong Kong News*, 23 September 1942.

57. From U.K. Consul General to Sir Ronald Lindsay, 26 July 1938, NAB 349, FO 371/22177, *National Archives of Singapore*.

58. Ichioka, "The Meaning of Loyalty," pp. 69–70.

59. Eriko Yamamoto, "Miya Sannomiya Kikuchi: A Pioneer Nisei Woman's Life and Identity," *Amerasia Journal*, 23 (Number 3, 1997): 73–101, p. 76.

60. War Relocation Authority, "A Nisei Requests Expatriation," 10 November 1944, Box 2, Folder 1, #5, *Carey McWilliams Papers, Claremont Colleges Library, California.*

61. Raymond Lamont-Brown, *Kempeitai: Japan's Dreaded Military Police*, Gloucestershire, U.K.: Sutton, 1998, pp. 46, 103. See also Eriko Yamamoto, "Cheers for Japanese Athletes: The 1932 Los Angeles Olympics and the Japanese-American Community," *Pacific Historical Review*, 69 (Number 3, August 2000): 399–430.

62. Louis Allen, *Burma: The Longest War, 1941–1945*, London: Orion, 1998, p. 610.

63. Robert E. Hertzstein, *Henry R. Luce: A Political Portrait of the Man Who Created the American Century*, New York: Scribner's, 1994, p. 104.

64. Hertzstein, *Henry R. Luce*, pp. 101, 104. See also Joseph Grew, *Turbulent Era: A Diplomatic Record of Forty Years, 1904–1945*, Boston: Little Brown, 1950; John K. Emmerson, *The Japanese Thread: Thirty Years of Foreign Service*, New York: Holt, Rinehart and Winston, 1978; Charles W. Cross, *Born a Foreigner: A Memoir of the American Presence in Twentieth Century Asia*, Boulder: Rowman and Littlefield, 1999; Armin H. Meyer, *Tokyo: An Ambassador's Journal*, Indianapolis: Bobbs-Merrill, 1974.

65. Anthony Hewitt, *Bridge with Three Men: Across China to the Western Heaven in 1942*, London: Jonathan Cape, 1986, p. 2.

66. Robert Blake, *Jardine Matheson: Traders of the Far East*, London: Weidenfeld & Nicolson, 1999, p. 241. See also Robert L. Gandt, *Seasons of Storms: The Siege of Hongkong 1941*, Hong Kong: South China Morning Post, 1982, p. 30.

67. Vertical Files, "Events—1941–1945, War," "B. Yates, Esq.," *History Workshop, Hong Kong University*.

68. Interview, Lance Sergeant Andrew Salmon, 005202/04, *Sound Archives, Imperial War Museum—London*.

69. Dew, *Prisoner of the Japs*, p. 264.

70. Chohong Choi, "Hong Kong in the Context of the Pacific War," pp. 42, 60.

71. Allen, *Burma: The Longest War, 1941–1945*, p. 612.

72. Oral History, Harold Robert Yates, 005216/10, *Sound Archives, Imperial War Museum—London*.

73. Interview, Lt. Col. Graeme Crew, 006118/04, *Sound Archives, Imperial War Museum—London*.

74. Dew, *Prisoner of the Japs*, p. 155.

75. Field, *Twilight in Hong Kong*, p. 146.

76. Gwen Terasaki, *Bridge to the Sun*, Tokyo: Charles Tuttle, 1984, p. 106.

77. *Hong Kong News*, 4 November 1943.

78. *Hong Kong News*, 28 April 1945.

79. *Hong Kong News*, 8 July 1942.

80. David Day, *The Great Betrayal: Britain, Australia and the Onset of the Pacific War, 1939–1942*, New York: Norton, 1989, p. 290.

81. Report on "Rex vs. George Wong," circa 1946, HKRS 41-1-1338, *Public Records Office—Hong Kong*.

82. *South China Morning Post*, 1 April 1946.

83. Robert S. Ward, *Asia for the Asiatics? The Techniques of Japanese Occupation*, Chicago: University of Chicago Press, 1943, p. 90.

84. *Hong Kong News*, 25 December 1942.

85. John Streicker, *Captive Colony: The Story of Stanley Camp, Hong Kong*, HK 940.547252 S8, *Hong Kong Collections, Hong Kong University*, pp. 1–2.

86. T'ien-wei Wu, "Contending Forces during the War of Resistance," in James C. Hsiung and Steven I. Levine, eds., *China's Bitter Victory: The War with Japan, 1937–1945*, Armonk, New York: M. E. Sharpe, 1992, 51–78, p. 64.

87. Frank Ching, *The Li Dynasty: Hong Kong Aristocrats*, Hong Kong: Oxford University Press, 1999, p. 123.

88. Wing-Tak Han, "Bureaucracy and the Japanese Occupation of Hong Kong," in William H. Newell, *Japan in Asia, 1942–1945*, Singapore: Singapore University Press, 1981, 7–24, p. 8.

89. Ken Cuthbertson, *Nobody Said Not to Go: The Lives, Loves and Adventures of Emily Hahn*, New York: Farrar, Straus & Giroux, 1998, p. 215.

90. *Hong Kong News*, 26 December 1942.

91. *Hong Kong News*, 1 January 1943.

92. Wasserstein, *Secret War in Shanghai*, pp. 192, 194, 210, 250, 173.

93. Hahn, *Hong Kong Holiday*, p. 112.

94. Wright-Nooth, with Adkin, *Prisoners of the Turnip Heads*, p. 112.

95. Field, *Twilight in Hong Kong*, p. 198.

96. Peter Wesley Smith, "Discriminatory Legislation in Hong Kong," *Hong Kong Collections: Hong Kong University*, 0842. PWS, Paper presented at Hong Kong Baptist University, June 1987.

97. See "Companies Incorporated in Japan Registered in Hongkong during Occupation, from 1 July 1944 to 13 June 1945," HKRS 123-5-240-A. There were "44 companies" on this list. Quite a few were from Taiwan, including Kabusiki Kaisa Taiwan Ginko (The Formosa Bank Ltd.). See also "Foreign Companies under Japanese Law in Hongkong," 12 September 1944, "6 companies," including 2 Swiss; Chinese companies, including Mei Ah Knitting Company based in Shanghai; Dah Chung Manufacturing Co. Ltd. of Shanghai; Shanghai Commercial Bank; Industrial Bank of China. HKRS 123-5-240-B, *Public Records Office—Hong Kong*.

98. Economist, 28 October 2000. See also Arthur Schlesinger, Jr., *A Life in the 20th Century: Innocent Beginnings, 1917–1950*, Boston: Hougton Mifflin, 2000.

99. Han Suyin, *Birdless Summer: China, Autobiography, History*, London: Jonathan Cape, 1968, p. 243.

100. Internal Intelligence, "Hong Kong," "Sheet 5," Folder 5, *Lindsay Ride Papers*, MSS 840, *Australian War Memorial*.

101. Edwin Ride, *BAAG: Hong Kong Resistance, 1942–1945*, Hong Kong: Oxford University Press, 1981, pp. 146, 174.

102. Phyllis Harrop, *Hong Kong Incident*, London: Eyre & Spottiswoode, 1944, p. 142.

103. Case of Mohammed Sadig, circa 1946, HKRS 76-3-190, *Public Records Office—Hong Kong*. See also Case of Mohammed Yusuf Shah, HKRS 76-3-208, *Public Records Office—Hong Kong*.

104. Dew, *Prisoner of the Japs*, p. 265.

105. Hahn, *Hong Kong Holiday*, p. 153.

106. *Hong Kong News*, 25 December 1942.

107. *Hong Kong News*, 30 March 1942.

108. *Hong Kong News*, 27 August 1942.

109. *Hong Kong News*, 9 August 1942.

110. *Hong Kong News*, 10 August 1942.

111. *Hong Kong News*, 27 January 1942.

112. *Hong Kong News*, 13 June 1942.

113. *Hong Kong News*, 22 July 1942.

114. Boyle, *Yanks Don't Cry*, p. 127.

115. From Southeast Asia Command to Far Eastern Department in London, "Translations of a Cyclostyle Booklet entitled "Notes on Interrogation of Prisoners of War,'" 10 August 1944, Reel 1, Volume 41791, F3867, *British Foreign Office: Japan Correspondence, 1941–1945*, Wilmington: Scholarly Resources, 1980.

116. From Department of Information and Broadcasting, India, to India Office, London, 2 January 1943, Reel 2, Volume 35941, *British Foreign Office: Japan Correspondence, 1941–1945*.

117. Petition from "Citizens of Ukrainian Descent," 23 October 1932, 14601, *Diplomatic Archives—Tokyo*.

118. P. G. Shaneff, President of the Central Committee of the Macedonian Political Organization of the USA and Canada, to Minister of Foreign Affairs, 22 February 1935, 14601, *Diplomatic Archives—Tokyo*.

119. Wasyl Kalyna to Japan, 10 April 1933, 14601, *Diplomatic Archives—Tokyo*.

120. Wright-Nooth, with Adkin, *Prisoners of the Turnip Heads*, pp. 4, 132.

121. Emily Hahn, *Miss Jill*, Garden City: Doubleday, 1947, p. 227.

122. Gavan Daws, *Prisoners of the Japanese: POWs of World War II in the Pacific*, New York: Morrow, 1994, p. 125.

123. Solomon Bard, "Mount Davis and Sham Shui Po: A Medical Officer with the Volunteers," in Clifford Matthews and Oswald Cheung, eds., *Dispersal and Renewal: Hong Kong University during the War Years*, Hong Kong: Hong Kong University Press, 1998, 193–202, p. 200.

124. Lewis Bush, *The Road to Inamura*, London: Robert Hale, 1961, p. 163.

125. Les Fisher, *I Will Remember: Recollections and Reflections on Hong Kong, 1941 to 1945—Internment and Freedom*, Totton, Hampshire, U.K.: Fisher, 1996, p. 170.

126. *Hong Kong Standard*, 28 August 1978.

127. Gavan Davis, *Prisoners of the Japanese: POWs of World War II in the Pacific*, New York: Morrow, 1994, p. 125.

128. Daws, *Prisoners of the Japanese*, p. 315.

129. Wright-Nooth, with Adkin, *Prisoners of the Turnip Heads*, p. 132.

130. Oral History, Otto C. Schwarz, 7 August 1979, Number 497, North Texas State University, *Cruiser Houston Collection, University of Houston*.

131. Kay Saunders and Helen Taylor, "The Reception of Black American Servicemen in Australia during World War II: The Resilience of '"White Australia,'" *Journal of Black Studies*, 25 (Number 3, January 1995): 331–348, p. 337.

132. Bush, *The Road to Inamura*, p. 159.

133. Hahn, *Miss Jill*, pp. 247–248.

134. "The Stanley Journal," 1943, *British Women's Group Minutes*, HRMS 72, *Public Records Office—Hong Kong*.

135. Geoffrey Charles Emerson, "Stanley Internment Camp, Hong Kong, 1942–1945: A Study of Civilian Internment during the Second World War," M.Phil. thesis, University of Hong Kong, 1973, p. 171.

136. Streicker, *Captive Colony*.

137. Notes from Bush, *Clutch of Circumstance*.

138. Bernice Archer, "Stanley Internment Camp, Hong Kong, 1942–1945," B.A., Bristol Polytechnic, 1992, p. 81.

139. Memorandum, 12 April 1945, HKRS 163-1-80, *Public Records Office—Hong Kong*.

140. Memorandum, 13 April 1945, HKRS 163-1-80, *Public Records Office—Hong Kong*.

141. Memorandum, 16 April 1945, HKRS 163-1-80, *Public Records Office—Hong Kong*.

142. Minutes of Surgical Board, 27 March 1945, HKRS, 163-1-80, *Public Records Office—Hong Kong*.

143. Memorandum, circa July 1945, HKRS 163-1-80, *Public Records Office—Hong Kong*.

144. From "Representative of Internees" to "Camp Medical Officer," 18 April 1945, HKRS 163-1-80, *Public Records Office—Hong Kong*.

145. "Diary of Events," September 1942, HKRS 163-1-80, *Public Records Office—Hong Kong*.

146. Emily Hahn, *China to Me: A Partial Autobiography*, Philadelphia: Blakiston, 1944, p. 328.

147. Undated Report from Sir Franklin Gimson, circa 1945, HKRS 163-1-81, *Public Records Office—Hong Kong*.

148. Hahn, *Miss Jill*, p. 250.

149. Lamont-Brown, *Kempeitai*, p. 70.

150. Sir Arthur Dickinson Blackburn, "An Account of Personal Experiences of My Wife and Myself at Hongkong during the Japanese Attack and Afterwards," MSS 940.547252, *Hong Kong Collections, Hong Kong University*.

151. I. D. Zia, *The Unforgettable Epoch (1937–1945)* , circa 1969, HK 940.548151 Z6, *Hong Kong Collections, University of Hong Kong*.

152. Streicker, *Captive Colony, Hong Kong Collections, Hong Kong University*.

153. Liang Yen, *The House of the Golden Dragons*, London: Souvenir Press, 1961, pp. 232–233.

154. Archer, "Stanley Internment Camp, Hong Kong, 1942–1945," p. 71.

155. Emerson, "Stanley Internment Camp, Hong Kong, 1942–1945," p. 219.

156. Hahn, *Miss Jill*, p. 248.

157. Winnie Davis, "Life in Hong Kong Before 1945," for class of Elisabeth Sinn, circa Spring 1994, *History Workshop, Hong Kong University*.

158. Gwen Priestwood, *Through Japanese Barbed Wire*, New York: Appleton-Century, 1943, pp. 76, 77, 182.

159. Dew, *Prisoner of the Japs*, p. 267.

160. Dew, *Prisoner of the Japs*, p. 279.

161. Streicker, *Captive Colony, Hong Kong Collections, Hong Kong University*. See also "The Diary of Inspector Fred Kelly of the Royal Hong Kong Police Force Compiled during His Internment in Stanley Detention Camp, 21 January–31 August 1945," 940.547252 K29, *Hong Kong Collections, Hong Kong University*.

162. Archer, "Stanley Internment Camp, Hong Kong, 1942–1945," p. 80.

163. Suke Wolton, *Lord Hailey: The Colonial Office and the Politics of Race and Empire in the Second World War: The Loss of White Prestige*, New York: St. Martin's, 2000, pp. 8, 41. See also *London Times*, 4 March 1896.

164. Hahn, *Hong Kong Holiday*, pp. 212–213. See also Linda Bryden, "Sex, Race and Colonialism: An Historiographical Review," *International History Review*, 29 (Number 4, December 1998): 806–822; Sonya O. Rose, 'The "Sex Question' in Anglo-American Relations in the Second World War," *International History Review*, 29 (Number 4, December 1998): 884–903.

165. "British Women's Group Minutes," 1942–1943, HKMS 72, *Public Records Office—Hong Kong*.

166. Harrop, *Hong Kong Incident*, pp. 24–25.

167. Betty Jeffrey, *White Coolies*, London: Angus and Robertson, 1954, pp. 31, 45, 67, 97.

168. Sister Jessie Elizabeth Simons, *In Japanese Hands: Australian Nurses as POWs*, Melbourne: Heinemann, 1985, p. 37.

169. Shirley Fenton Huie, *The Forgotten Ones: Women and Children under Nippon*, London: HarperCollins, 1992, pp. 25, 49, 55, 70, 74–76, 82, 90, 97, 104–105, 108–109, 130, 135, 140, 148–150, 167, 172, 179, 185–186.

170. Report on Stanley, 6 March 1946, HKRS 163-1-81, *Public Records Office—Hong Kong*.

171. Archer, "Stanley Internment Camp, Hong Kong, 1942–1945," p. 92.

172. "The Effects of the War Years on School-Children in Hong Kong," *Overseas Education* 19 (1948), *Geoffrey Emerson Papers, History Workshop, Hong Kong University*.

173. Huie, *The Forgotten Ones*, pp. 149, 150, 186.

174. Oral History, Ralph Malcolm Macdonald King, 004655/04, *Sound Archives, Imperial War Museum—London*.

175. "Divorces," circa 1947, HKRS 163-1-503, *Public Records Office—Hong Kong*.

176. Margaret Sams, *Forbidden Family: A Wartime Memoir of the Philippines, 1941–1945*, Madison: University of Wisconsin Press, 1989, p. 65.

177. Report on Santo Tomas, 11 September 1944, A700, 9-11-24, *Diplomatic Archives—Tokyo*.

178. Michael S. Molasky, *The American Occupation of Japan and Okinawa: Literature and Memory*, London: Routledge, 1999, pp. 2, 11.

NOTES TO CHAPTER 7

1. To "Acting Prime Minister" from R. Wang, et al. of "Association of New Zealand Born Chinese," 1 July 1941, EA 1, #83/3/3, *National Archives of New Zealand*.

2. H. Van Straelen, *The Far East Must Be Understood*, London: Luzac & Co., 1945, p. 7.

3. Sean Brawley, ""No 'White Policy' in New Zealand,': Fact and Fiction in New Zealand's Asian Immigration Record, 1946–1978," *Journal of New Zealand History*, 27 (Number 1, April 1993): 16–36, pp. 16, 19. See also Victor Rine, *Machiavelli of Nippon: Japan's Plan of World Conquest: Willed by Emperor Meiji, Developed by Premier Tanaka*, New York: The Wandering Eye, 1932.

4. M. P. Lissington, *New Zealand and Japan, 1900–1941*, Wellington: A. R. Shearer, Government Printer, 1972, pp. 8, 9. See also Alexander Howard and Ernest Newman, *The Menacing Rise of Japan*, London: George G. Harrap, 1943.

5. P. S. O'Connor, "Keeping New Zealand White, 1908–1920," *New Zealand Journal of History*, 2 (Number 1, April 1968): 41–65, p. 52. Ninety percent of the Indians of New Zealand were Punjabi or Gujarati, and most were Hindus. There were also some Sikhs and Indians from Fiji. See W. T. Roy, "Indians in New Zealand," *Journal of New Zealand Federation of Historical Societies*, 1 (Number 8, August 1978): 16–20.

6. Jacqueline Leckie, "In Defence of Race and Empire: The White New Zealand League of Pukekohe," *Journal of New Zealand History*, 19 (Number 2, October 1985): 103–129.

7. Manying Ip, *Dragons on the Long White Cloud: The Making of Chinese New Zealanders*, North Shore City, New Zealand: Tandem Press, 1996, p. 106.

8. Paul Spoonley, *The Politics of Nostalgia: Racism and the Extreme Right in New Zealand*, Palmerston, New Zealand: Dunmore, 1987.

9. Clipping, 22 August 1934, MA 29, Box 9, *National Archives of New Zealand*.

10. Clipping, 25 February 1925, MA 29, Box 9, *National Archives of New Zealand*.

11. *Rotorua Chronicle*, 15 January 1925, MA 29, Box 9, *National Archives of New Zealand*.

12. J. G. Coates to G. Grindley, 17 July 1926, MA 29, Box 9, *National Archives of New Zealand*.

13. Letter, 21 January 1925, MA 29, Box 9, *National Archives of New Zealand*.

14. Memorandum to Sir James Parr, 28 February 1925; E. Blomfield to Sir James Parr, 4 February 1925; K. Pitiroi Mohi to Minister of Native Affairs, 29 January 1925, all in MA 29, Box 29, *National Archives of New Zealand*.

15. Undated Clipping, *Evening Post*, MA 29, Box 9, *National Archives of New Zealand*.

16. *New Zealand Times*, 25 June 1924, MA 29, Box 9, *National Archives of New Zealand*.

17. *New Zealand Herald*, 19 January 1925, MA 29, Box 9, *National Archives of New Zealand*.

18. Clipping, 8 December 1921, MA 29, Box 9, *National Archives of New Zealand*.

19. Caroline Ralston, "The Pattern of Race Relations in 19th Century Pacific Port Towns," *Journal of Pacific History*, 6 (1971): 39–60, p. 45.

20. Charles Weeks, "The Last Exile of Apolosi Nawai: A Case Study of Indirect Rule during the Twilight of the British Empire," *Pacific Studies* 18 (Number 3, September 1995): 27–45, pp. 27, 29, 30, 32, 33, 39. See also Deryck Scarr, ed., *More Pacific Island Portraits*, Canberra: Australian National University, 1978.

21. Timothy J. McNaught, *The Fijian Colonial Experience: A Study of the Neo-Traditional Order under British Colonial Rule Prior to World War II*, Canberra: Australian National University, Pacific Research Monograph, No. 7, 1982, pp. 76, 78, 149.

22. Acting Assistant Secretary to External Affairs and Cook Islands Department, 22 April 1941, EA 1, #83/3/5, *National Archives of New Zealand*.

23. Penelope Griffith, "Dr. Imasu Kawase and the First Book on New Zealand in Japanese," *Turnbull Library Record*, 9 (Number 1, May 1976): 12–17, p. 16.

24. Mark Johnston, *Fighting the Enemy: Australian Soldiers and Their Adversaries in World War II*, New York: Cambridge University Press, 2000, pp. 85, 87.

25. David Day, *The Great Betrayal: Britain, Australia and the Onset of the Pacific War, 1939–1942*, New York: Norton, 1989, p. 325.

26. Hank Nelson, "The Troops, the Town and the Battle: Rabaul, 1942," *Journal of Pacific History*, 27 (Number 2, December 1992): 198–216, pp. 207, 208, 214, 216.

27. Report on Black Dragon Society, undated, PR 88/178, *J. L. Hehir Papers, Australian War Memorial*.

28. Reginald Clarry to Anthony Eden, 28 December 1937, FO 371/22177, NAB 349, *National Archives of Singapore*.

29. Rosemary Campbell, "The Americans of Brisbane, 1942–1945," M.A. thesis, University of Sydney, 1986, pp. 126–127, MS 1192, *Australian War Memorial*.

30. Richard Hall, *Black Armband Days: Truth from the Dark Side of Australia's Past*, Milsons Point: Vintage, 1998, pp. 171, 180, 184.

31. Day, *The Great Betrayal*, p. 240.

32. W. E. Prentice to Stanley Weintraub, 26 June 1986, Misc 157, *Letters concerning Pearl Harbour, Imperial War Museum—London*.

33. Emily Hahn, *China to Me: A Partial Autobiography*, Philadelphia: Blakiston, 1944, p. 204.

34. "Admission of Coloured Persons from Japan for Duration of the War," 12 November 1940, A433 (A433/1), #1940/2/2969, *National Archives of Australia—Canberra*.

35. Memoranda, 20 May 1941, 7 September 1936, A659 (A659/1), #1941, 1/3100, *National Archives of Australia—Canberra*.

36. "Aide-memoire" from "Chinese Legation," circa December 1941; Secretary of Interior to External Affairs, 20 December 1941, A981 (A981/4) #REF 16, *National Archives of Australia—Canberra*.

37. "Espionage (Japanese)," "Most Secret," 10 March 1944, A8911 (A8911/1), #11, *National Archives of Australia—Canberra*.

38. Dutch Consul General in Sydney to Interior Department, 1 January 1942, A981 (A981/4), #REF 16, *National Archives of Australia—Canberra*.

39. Jean Gittins, *Eastern Windows, Western Skies*, Hong Kong: South China Morning Post, 1969, p. 117.

40. Clipping, *Daily News*, 25 July 1940, A433 (A433/1), #1949/2/44, *National Archives of Australia—Canberra*.

41. Memorandum from A. R. Peters, 10 April 1941, A433 (A433/1), #1949/2/44, *National Archives of Australia—Canberra*.

42. From the Interior Department to the Colonial Secretary, 21 April 1941, A433 (A433/1), #1949/2/44, *National Archives of Australia—Canberra*.

43. Clipping, *Sun and Guardian*, 11 May 1941, A433 (A433/1) #1949/2/44, *National Archives of Australia—Canberra*.

44. Memorandum from Department of Interior, 4 September 1942, no. 42/2/2845, A433 (A433/1), #1949/2/44, *National Archives of Australia—Canberra*.

45. A. Hubbard to H. J. Kilpatrick, China Command, "Hong Kong and Shanghai Evacuees—Applications to Leave Hong Kong or Other Overseas Destinations," 21 January 1941, A433 (A433/1), #1940/2/3117, *National Archives of Australia—Canberra*.

46. Letter from "Mrs. Alice Standard," circa 15 March 1941, "Hong Kong and Shanghai Evacuees," A433 (A433/1), #1940/2/2677, *National Archives of Australia—Canberra*.

47. A. D. Cole, Queensland Government Tourist Bureau, to A. Hubbard, 18 February 1941, A433 (A433/1), #1940/2/2677, *National Archives of Australia—Canberra*.

48. *Hong Kong News*, 24 April 1942.

49. Letter from Desmond Brennan, 4 July 1988, Misc 157, *Letters concerning Pearl Harbour, Imperial War Museum—London*.

50. Kevin Ireland, "Nostalgia: The Year of the Japanese," *Metro* (Auckland), 8 (Number 84, June 1998): 172–173, p. 172.

51. Administration of West Samoa to Secretary of External Affairs, 2 February 1939, IT1, EX87/68, *National Archives of New Zealand*.

52. A. E. Mulgan to Mr. McIntosh, 15 June 1942, EA1, #81/1/11, *National Archives of New Zealand*.

53. High Commissioner, London, to Prime Minister, Wellington, 16 September 1940, EA1#84/2/10, *National Archives of New Zealand*.

54. Michael King, *Te Puea: A Biography*, Auckland: Hodder & Stoughton, 1977, pp. 206, 207.

55. Memorandum from Organization for National Security, Prime Minister's Department, Wellington, to Prime Minister, 1 April 1942, "Subversion-Fiji Native"; Memorandum for Under-Secretary of Justice from Secretary, Organization for National Security, 11 March 1942, EA1#82/2/5, *National Archives of New Zealand*.

56. Foss Shanahan to Consul General, Wellington, 15 June 1943, EA1#84/3/19, *National Archives of New Zealand*.

57. "Japanese Language," 14 May 1943, EA1, #84/1/9, *National Archives of New Zealand*.

58. "U.S. Seamen of Japanese Extraction," 27 January 1944, EA1, #89/2/19, *National Archives of New Zealand*.

59. "Japanese Use of Indians POWs as Fifth Column," translated document, 10 February 1944, EA1 88/1/20, *National Archives of New Zealand*.

60. James Mackay, *Betrayal in High Places*, Auckland: Tasman Archives, 1996, p. 75.

61. "Potential Quislings," #ROLL 22/59, A9108 (A9108/3), 6 October 1943, *National Archives of Australia—Canberra*.

62. "Precautions from Minister of External Affairs, Canberra," to his counterpart in Wellington, 13 June 1945, EA1#88/1/15, *National Archives of New Zealand*.

63. Quentin Beresford and Paul Omaji, *Our State of Mind: Racial Planning and the Stolen Generations*, South Fremantle: Fremantle Arts Centre Press, 1998, p. 89.

64. "SIC Plans (detection of Japanese Espionage, Northern Australia and Contact with Aboriginals)," 16 July 1942, A8911 (A8911/1), #266, *National Archives of Australia—Canberra*.

65. Report from Prof. A. M. Elkin, "Co-operation between Aboriginals and Whites in Event of Enemy Invasion," 2 April 1942, A659 (A659/1) #1942/1/3043, *National Archives of Australia—Canberra*.

66. Lt. Henry Nobbs to Deputy Director, Security Service, Brisbane, 25 May 1943, "Japanese Activities among Aborigines," A373 (A373/1) #5903, *National Archives of Australia—Canberra*.

67. Richard Connaughton, *Shrouded Secrets: Japan's War on Mainland Australia, 1942–1944*, London: Brassey, 1994, p. 79.

68. "Extract from HQ . . . Intelligence Report," 16 April 1943, A373 (A373/1) #5903, *National Archives of Australia—Canberra*.

69. Assistant Deputy Director of Security to Deputy Director, Brisbane, 23 March 1943, A373 (A373/1) #5903, *National Archives of Australia—Canberra*.

70. Douglas Lockwood, *Australia's Pearl Harbor: Darwin, 1942*, Melbourne: Cassell, 1966, p. 177.

71. Robert Hall, *Fighters from the Fringe: Aborigines and Torres Strait Islanders Recall the Second World War*, Canberra: Aboriginal Studies Press, 1995, p. 131.

72. "Secret" Report, No. 183, 26 June 1942, A5954 (A5954/69), #527/15, *National Archives of Australia—Canberra*.

73. F. W. Eggleston Report from Chungking, 6 April 1942, "Despatch No. 22," A5954 (A5954/69), #527/15, *National Archives of Australia—Canberra*.

74. Report by Deputy Director of Security, Canberra, 7 September 1943; G. Malley, Deputy Director of Security in Brisbane, 11 January 1945, A8911 (A8911/1) #5; *Brisbane Sunday Mail*, 3 December 1944, *National Archives of Australia—Canberra*. See also J. Morgan to Director General of Security Patents Office, Canberra, "Japanese Espionage Organization," 10 November 1942, A8911 (A8911/1), #3, *National Archives of Australia—Canberra*.

75. "Secret" Memorandum for "War Cabinet," 9 January 1942, "Agenda No. 11/1942," A981 (A981/4) #REF 16, *National Archives of Australia—Canberra.*

76. Memorandum from Interior Department, 2 April 1942, "Chinese and Other Coloured Persons Evacuated to Australia," A433 (A433/1) #1949/2/5470, *National Archives of Australia—Canberra.*

77. File on "Chinese and Other Coloured Immigration," A433 (A433/1) #1944/2/53, *Argus,* 26 January 1944, *National Archives of Australia—Canberra.*

78. Ross Mackay, "The War Years: Methodists in Papua, 1942–1945," *Journal of Pacific History,* 27 (Number 1, June 1992): 29–43, pp. 31, 32, 35, 39, 41. See also *Sydney Morning Herald,* 2 September 1942.

79. Memorandum, "Defence of New Caledonia since Outbreak of War with Japan, December 1941," 17 November 1943, A5954 (A5954/69) #535/2, *National Archives of Australia—Canberra.*

80. Memorandum from External Affairs Department, 23 October 1944, A989 (A989/1), #1944/43/554/2/11, "Migration—Australia Sub-Committee No. (3b), Coloured Immigration," *National Archives of Australia—Canberra.*

81. Report from Australia Government, 11 August 1942; Report from War Cabinet, 19 January 1942; Memorandum from Department of Labour and National Service, 13 January 1942, A981 (A981/4), #WAR 35, *National Archives of Australia—Canberra.*

82. "Secret" memorandum re: "Presence of United States Coloured Troops in Australia," 2 February 1942, A2676 (A2676/1) #1848, *National Archives of Australia—Canberra.*

83. Memorandum, 14 April 1944, "Presence of United States Coloured Troops in Australia," "Defence Co-Ordination," A2684 (A2684/3), #1330, *National Archives of Australia—Canberra.*

84. "Secret" Memorandum, 13 August 1942, A826 (A816/1), #19/312/116, *National Archives of Australia—Canberra.*

85. Memorandum from Office of the High Commissioner for the United Kingdom; Memorandum from Office of Australia Military Liaison," War Section-American Coloured Troops," A1608/1, #B45/1/10, *National Archives of Australia—Canberra.*

86. Campbell, "The Americans of Brisbane, 1942–1945," pp. 130, 136, 145.

87. "American Coloured Soldiers," 1 August 1942, AWM 60 (AWM 60) #75/1/74, *Australian War Memorial—Canberra.*

88. Day, *The Great Betrayal,* p. 324.

89. Kay Saunders and Helen Taylor, "The Reception of Black American Servicemen in Australia during World War II: The Resilience of 'White Australia,'" *Journal of Black Studies,* 25 (Number 3, January 1995): 331–348, p. 337.

90. H. I. London, *Non-White Immigration and the "White Australia' Policy,* New York: New York University Press, 1970, p. 15.

91. Adam Shoemaker, *Black Words/White Page: Aboriginal Literature, 1929–1988,* St. Lucia: University of Queensland Press, 1989, pp. 18, 20.

92. Paul W. van der Veur, "Political Awakening in West New Guinea," *Pacific Affairs,* 36 (Number 1, Spring 1963): 54–73, p. 57.

93. *Hong Kong News,* 28 December 1943.

94. *Hong Kong News,* 19 June 1942.

95. *Hong Kong News,* 14 September 1942.

96. *Hong Kong News,* 15 September 1942.

97. "Official War History," circa 1945, MA 1, #19/1/565, *National Archives of New Zealand.*

98. "Maori Conference," clipping, *Wellington Standard,* 26 October 1944, MA 1, #19/1/535, *National Archives of New Zealand.*

99. "Effect of War on Native Peoples of the South Pacific," *Taranaki Daily News,* 11 January 1951, ITI, #IT 67/12/84, *National Archives of New Zealand.*

100. Peter Hall, *In the Web,* Heswall, U.K.: Peter Hall, 1992, p. 72.

101. Memorandum, 23 February 1951, HKRS 41-1-6669, *Public Records Office—Hong Kong.*

102. *South China Morning Post,* 23 November 1945.

103. *South China Morning Post,* 26 February 1946.

104. *Smith's Weekly* (Australia), 2 November 1946.

105. Ferdinand Smith to Honorable N. J. O. Makin, Australian Ambassador to the United States, 20 November 1946, Reel 34, Part II, #071, *National Negro Congress Papers, Schomburg Center—New York Public Library.* The copy of the article from the Australian weekly can also be found with this correspondence.

NOTES TO CHAPTER 8

1. Tran My-Van, "Japan through Vietnamese Eyes (1905–1945)," *Journal of Southeast Asian Studies*, 30 (Number 1, March 1999): 126–146, pp. 126, 145.

2. Tatsuo Hayashida, *Netaji Subhas Chandra Bose: His Great Struggle and Martyrdom*, Bombay: Allied, 1970, p. 32.

3. P. A. Narasimha Murthy, *India and Japan: Dimensions of Their Relations, Historical and Political*, New Delhi: ABC, 1986, pp. 18, 21, 97.

4. Sudata Debchaudhury, "Japanese Imperialism and the Indian Nationalist Movement: A Study of the Political and Psychological Implications of Possible Invasion and Actual Occupation, 1939–1945," Ph.D. dissertation, University of Illinois-Urbana, 1992, p. 42.

5. Robert H. Taylor, translator, *Marxism and Resistance in Burma, 1942–1945*: Thein Pe Myint's *Wartime Traveler*, Athens: Ohio University Press, 1984, p. 8. See also Frank Trager, ed., *Burma: Japanese Military Administration, Selected Documents, 1941–1945*, Philadelphia: University of Pennsylvania Press, 1971.

6. Document, 21 July 1932, 2/8, *D. N. Pritt Papers, London School of Economics.*

7. "Secret" report from Governor Clementi, 25 February 1930, NAB 658, *National Archives of Singapore.*

8. *New Straits Times* (Kuala Lumpur), 31 May 2000.

9. Sir George Maxwell to Brendan Bracken, 22 September 1942, NAB 460, *British Association of Malaysia Papers, National Archives of Singapore.*

10. Undated note, NAB 478, *British Association of Malaysia Papers, National Archives of Singapore.*

11. Clipping of article by Margery Perham, 14 March 1942, NAB 460, *British Association of Malaysia Papers, National Archives of Singapore.*

12. Lee Kuan Yew, *The Singapore Story*, Singapore: Times Publishing, 1998, pp. 52, 74, 76.

13. Mahatir Mohammad, *A New Deal for Asia*, Selangor Darul Ehsan, Malaysia: Pelanduk, 1999, pp. 15, 16.

14. Masanobu Tsuji, *Singapore, 1941–1942: The Japanese Version of the Malayan Campaign of World War II*, Singapore: Oxford University Press, 1988, pp. 142, 273.

15. Oral History, Lim Chok Fui, 21 August 1981, *National Archives of Singapore.*

16. *Coventry Standard*, 2 January 1943.

17. From "Director of Dockyards," December 1941, UK-ADM, 1/16397, NAB 427, *National Archives of Singapore.*

18. O. D. Gallagher, *Retreat in the East*, London: George G. Harrap, 1942, pp. 16–17, 35, 68.

19. Undated article, circa 1969, NAB 478, *British Association of Malaysia Papers, National Archives of Singapore.*

20. David Marshall to Stanley Weintraub, 24 August 1988, "Letters concerning Pearl Harbour," Misc 157, *Imperial War Museum—London.*

21. Narrative of Harvey Ryves, 84/30/1, *Imperial War Museum—London.*

22. Narrative of Edith Stevenson, circa December 1941, 86/29/1, *Imperial War Museum—London.*

23. Narrative of Raymond Burridge, 31 July 1986, "Letters Concerning Pearl Harbour," Misc 157, *Imperial War Museum—London.*

24. Yoji Akashi, "Japanese Cultural Policy in Malaya and Singapore, 1942–1945," in Grant K. Goodman, ed., *Japanese Cultural Policies in Southeast Asia during World War II*, London: Macmillan, 1991, 117–172, p. 133.

25. Oral History, Victor Krusemann, 2 December 1983, *National Archives of Singapore.*

26. Oral History, Joginder Singh, 16 November 1983, *National Archives of Singapore.*

27. Oral History, Kip Lin Lee, 29 May 1984, *National Archives of Singapore.*

28. Oral History, Gay Wan Guay, 17 April 1984, *National Archives of Singapore.*

29. Oral History, Tan Cheng Hwee, 22 March 1984, *National Archives of Singapore.*

30. Oral History, K. M. Regarajoo, 30 January 1985, *National Archives of Singapore.*

31. Oral History, Tan Ban Cheng, 25 January 1984, *National Archives of Singapore.*

32. Oral History, Heng Chiang Ki, 2 February 1982, *National Archives of Singapore.*

33. Oral History, Charlie Chea Fook Ying, 30 December 1983, *National Archives of Singapore.*

34. Oral History, Kip Lin Lee, 29 May 1984, *National Archives of Singapore.*

35. Oral History, Ismail Zain, 5 September 1985, *National Archives of Singapore.*

36. Oral History, F. A. C. Oehlers, 13 April 1984, *National Archives of Singapore.*
37. Oral History, Patrick Hardie, 4 April 1985, *National Archives of Singapore.*
38. Oral History, Sho Chuan Lam, 5 September 1983, *National Archives of Singapore.*
39. Oral History, Patrick Hardie, 4 April 1985, *National Archives of Singapore.*
40. Sister Jessie Elizabeth Simons, *In Japanese Hands: Australian Nurses as POWs*, Melbourne: Heinemann, 1985, p. 32.
41. See also R. H. W. Reece, *The Name of Brooke: The End of White Rajah Rule in Sarawak*, Kuala Lumpur: Oxford University Press, 1982, pp. 144, 146, 151, 158.
42. Oral History, Gay Wan Guay, 17 April 1984, *National Archives of Singapore.*
43. Oral History, Arthur Alexander Thompson, 29 March 1982, *National Archives of Singapore.*
44. Oral History, Zamroude Za'ba, 22 February 1983, *National Archives of Singapore.*
45. Oral History, Mary Lim, 30 September 1982, *National Archives of Singapore.*
46. Oral History, Robert Chong, 4 June 1983, *National Archives of Singapore.*
47. Oral History, Tan Ban Cheng, 25 January 1984, *National Archives of Singapore.*
48. Report by Lt. M. M. Pillai, no date, NAB 630, *British Association of Malaysia Papers, National Archives of Singapore.*
49. Oral History, Robert Chong, 4 June 1983, *National Archives of Singapore.*
50. Oral History, Robert Chong, 4 June 1983, *National Archives of Singapore.*
51. Reece, *The Name of Brooke*, pp. 144, 151.
52. Oral History, Charlie Gan, 11 December 1984, *National Archives of Singapore.*
53. Oral History, F. A. C. Oehlers, 13 April 1984, *National Archives of Singapore.*
54. Ian Morrison, "Aspects of the Racial Problem in Malaya," *Pacific Affairs*, 22 (Number 3, September 1949): 239–253, p. 241.
55. Steven Runciman, *The White Rajahs: A History of Sarawak from 1841 to 1946*, London: Cambridge University Press, 1960, p. 225.
56. UK-US Report, 3 November 1943, Microfilm Acc. No. 3861, Reel 1, from *National Archives of Malaysia, National Archives of India.*
57. Oral History, Arthur Alexander Thompson, 29 March 1982, *National Archives of Singapore.*
58. Oral History, Ismail Zain, 5 September 1985, *National Archives of Singapore.*
59. Oral History, Ng Seng Yong, 24 June 1983, *National Archives of Singapore.*
60. Oral History, Tan Ban Cheng, 25 January 1984, *National Archives of Singapore.*
61. Oral History, F. A. C. Oehlers, 13 April 1984, *National Archives of Singapore.*
62. Oral History, Tan Wee Eng, 5 June 1985, *National Archives of Singapore.*
63. "Annual Report," 1937, p. 47, FO371/22215, *Public Records Office—London.*
64. Narrative of Mrs. U. M. Streatfield, 87/1/1, *Imperial War Museum—London.*
65. "Information Report No. 64," CSDIC, India, Red Fort, Delhi, August 1944, *National Archives of India.*
66. Report on "Japan and Burma" from U.K. Legation in Tokyo, 26 December 1938, FO 262/1973, *Public Records Office—London.*
67. James Lunt, *A Hell of a Licking: The Retreat from Burma, 1941–1942*, London: Collins, 1986, p. 277.
68. Louis Allen, *Burma: The Longest War, 1941–1945*, London: Orion, 1998.
69. Ho-yungchi, *The Big Circle: China's Role in the Burma Campaigns*, New York: Exposition Press, 1948, pp. 26–27.
70. Dispatch from Burma, 29 January 1942, 86/8/1, *Sir Reginald Dorman-Smith Papers, Imperial War Museum—London.*
71. Dispatch from Burma, 4 February 1942, 86/8/1, *Sir Reginald Dorman-Smith Papers, Imperial War Museum—London.*
72. Dispatch, 8 March 1942, *Sir Reginald Dorman-Smith Papers.*
73. Robert H. Taylor, translator, *Marxism and Resistance in Burma, 1942–1945: Thein Pe Myint's Wartime Traveler*, Athens: Ohio University Press, 1984, p. 8. See also Frank Trager, ed., *Burma: Japanese Military Administration, Selected Documents, 1941–1945*, Philadelphia: University of Pennsylvania Press, 1971.
74. Allen, *Burma: The Longest War, 1941–1945*, p. 13. See also Kazuo Tamayama, ed., *Japanese Soldiers of the Burma Campaign, Book One, January–March 1942: The War as Seen through the Eyes of Japanese Soldiers*, Tokyo: Tamayama, no date, circa 1997.
75. Report, 14 February 1945, Reel 2, Acc. No. 3862, *National Archives of India.* See also "Information Report No. 75," 9 September 1944, CSDIC, India, Red Fort, Delhi, *National Archives of*

India: evidently the Japanese also were "training" monkeys. "About 500 . . . were lined up and were dressed in Japanese uniform . . . to ride ponies."

76. "Information Report," Number 123, CSDIC, India, Red Fort, Delhi, 23 March 1945, *National Archives of India*.

77. "Information Report," Number 75, CSDIC, India, Red Fort, Delhi, 9 September 1944, *National Archives of India*.

78. Izumiya Tatsuro, *The Minami Organ*, Rangoon: Translation & Publications Department/Higher Education Department, 1981, pp. 105, 137, 140–141. In August 1943 a "Treaty of Alliance between Japan and Burma" was drawn up. See Treaty, 1 August 1943, Box 1, Folder 2, *Burmese Archive Collection, Yale University—New Haven*.

79. Harry J. Benda, "Indonesian Islam under the Japanese Occupation, 1942–1945," *Pacific Affairs*, 28 (Number 4, December 1955): 350–362, pp. 353, 355, 357.

80. See also Shirley Fenton Huie, *The Forgotten Ones: Women and Children under Nippon*, London: HarperCollins, 1992, pp. 9, 108.

81. Translation from Japanese, "Commemoration Committee Celebrating the 77th Birthday of Viscount Naganari Ogasawara," Tokyo: Committee, 1943, *Library of the National Institute for Defence Studies, Japan Defence Agency, Tokyo*.

82. From Near East Services to Head of Middle East Section, 9 October 1942, Misc. A-Z Files, E1/1024, *BBC Written Archives—Reading, U.K.*

83. *Ten Years of Japanese Burrowing in the Netherlands East Indies: Official Report of the Netherlands East Indies Government on Japanese Subversive Activities in the Archipelago during the Last Decade*, New York: Netherlands Information Bureau, no date, p. 33.

84. Oral History, Patrick Hardie, 4 April 1985, *National Archives of Singapore*

85. Bernhard Dahm, *Sukarno and the Struggle for Indonesian Independence*, Ithaca: Cornell University Press, 1969, p. 112.

86. Memorandum, "Japan. Relations with Netherlands East Indies," circa 1942, A981 (A981/4), #JAP 158, Part 5, *National Archives of Australia—Canberra*.

87. "Information Report No. 47," CSDIC, India, Red Fort, Delhi, 23 May 1944, *National Archives of India*.

88. Barbara Gifford Shimes and Guy Hobbs, *The Kempeitai in Java and Sumatra: Selections from the Authentic History of the Kempeitai*, Ithaca: Cornell Modern Indonesia Project, 1986, p. 28.

89. George McTurnana Kahin, *Nationalism and Revolution in Indonesia*, Ithaca: Cornell University Press, 1970, pp. 102, 116. See also Anthony Reid and Oki Akira, eds., *The Japanese Experience in Indonesia: Selected Memoirs of 1942–1945*, Athens: Ohio University Center for International Studies, Center for Southeast Asian Studies, 1986; Ooi Keat Gin, ed., *Japanese Empire in the Tropics: Selected Documents and Reports on the Japanese Period in Sarawak, Northwest Borneo, 1941–1945*, Athens: Ohio University CIS: CSAS, 1998.

90. Scott Sherman, "A Return to Java," *Lingua Franca*, 11 (Number 7, October 2001): 38–49, p. 42.

91. Telegram from Sir Henry Robert Moore Brooke-Popham, *Sir Henry Robert Moore Brooke-Popham Papers*, 7 August 1942, 6/9, *Liddell-Hart Centre for Military Archives, King's College—London*.

92. See Motoe Terami-Wada, "The Japanese Propaganda Corps in the Philippines: Laying the Foundation," in Grant K. Goodman, ed., *Japanese Cultural Policies in Southeast Asia during World War II*, London: Macmillan, 1991, 173–211, pp. 202, 205. See also Elmer N. Lear, "Collaboration in Leyte: The Philippines under Japanese Occupation," *Far Eastern Quarterly*, 11 (Number 2, February 1952): 183–206, p. 183. "A significant proportion of the [Filipino] population did collaborate with Japanese rule."

93. "Activities of Japanese Spies in India," 8 June 1943, in P. N. Chopra, ed., *Quit India Movement: Volume 2, Role of Big Business; British Secret Documents*, New Delhi: Interprint, 1991, pp. 117–120.

94. Murthy, *India and Japan*, pp. 21, 97. See also Veena Choudhury, *Indian Nationalism and External Forces, 1920–1947*, Delhi: Capital, 1985.

95. Anna Everett, *Returning the Gaze: A Genealogy of Black Film Criticism, 1909–1949*, Durham: Duke University Press, 2001, p. 167.

96. Louis Ogull to Franklin D. Roosevelt, 31 August 1939, *Franklin D. Roosevelt Papers, Nehru Library—New Delhi*.

97. Debchaudhury, "Japanese Imperialism and the Indian Nationalist Movement," pp. 42, 157.

98. P. D. Butler to Anthony Eden, 18 January 1941, External Affairs [EA], File 374-X, *National Archives of India*.

99. See OS-6, 28, 30, P-1, P-2, 1939, *All Indian Congress Committee Papers, Nehru Library—New Delhi.*

100. Diethelm Weidemann, "Sources on S. C. Bose and the Freedom Struggle of India in the Central State Archives of the GDR," Acc. No. 998, *Nehru Library—New Delhi.*

101. *Los Angeles Examiner,* 2 March 1941.

102. Memorandum, 12 November 1940, EA, File 272, 7-41, 1941, *National Archives of India.*

103. From "Legation Kabul," 12 October 1940, EA File 272, *National Archives of India.*

104. See also H. I. Saith, *India Looks at Japan,* Lahore: Indian Printing Works, no date, circa 1944, p. 81.

105. From U.K. legation, Kabul, 28 December 1940, EA File 272, *National Archives of India.*

106. Charles Chenevix Trench, *The Indian Army and the King's Enemies, 1900–1947,* London: Thames and Hudson, 1988, pp. 194–195.

107. Allen, *Burma: The Longest War, 1941–1945,* pp. 606, 607.

108. Ian Morrison, "Aspects of the Racial Problem in Malaya," *Pacific Affairs,* 22 (Number 3, September 1949): 239–253, p. 241.

109. J. Victor Morais, *Witness to History: Memoirs of an Editor,* Petaling Jaya, Selangor, Malaysia: Life, no date, p. 52.

110. Minutes of Conference of the Representatives of Indians in East Asia, 27–30 April 1943 (2603), Serial No. 6, Doc. No. 31, *India Independence League Papers, National Archives of India.*

111. "Conference of the Committee of Representatives, India Independence League," 27–30 April 1943 (2603), Serial No. 5, Doc. No. 29, *India Independence League Papers, National Archives of India.*

112. *Young India,* 1 (Number 41, 12 December 2603 [1943]), Group 1, Serial Nos. 21–34, *S. C. Bose Papers, National Archives of India.*

113. Fujiwara Iwaichi, *F. Kikan: Japanese Army Intelligence Operations in Southeast Asia during World War II,* Hong Kong: Heinemann Asia, 1983, p. 86.

114. Murthy, *India and Japan,* p. 148.

115. "Confidential Draft," 28 December 1941, 1/1941–42, (Parts 1 and 2), *All Indian Congress Committee Papers, Nehru Library—New Delhi.*

116. Gautam Chattopadhyay, "Subhas Chandra Bose and the Indian Communist Movement: A Study in Cooperation and Conflict," in Sisir K. Bose, ed., *Netaji and India's Freedom: Proceedings of the International Netaji Seminar,* Calcutta: Netaji Research Burreau, 1975, 422–440, p. 425.

117. "Information Report," undated, CSDIC, India, Red Fort, Delhi, *National Archives of India.*

118. Memorandum, "Far East: India—General," 30 October 1945, HS 1/200, *Public Records Office—London.*

119. Oral History, Damodaran K. Kesavan, 19 November 1981, *National Archives of Singapore.* See also Oral History, A. K. Motiwalla, 19 August 1982, *National Archives of Singapore.* Motiwalla, who was born in 1928, recalled that "when the Japanese occupied Singapore, they more . . . Koreans and Formosans in front. . . . they were the people more here [*sic*]."

120. Oral History, K. M. Rengarajoo, 30 January 1985, *National Archives of Singapore.* See also Oral History, K. R. Menon, 26 February 1982, *National Archives of Singapore.* Menon was born in 1907 in Cochin, India, and came to Singapore in 1931, where he served as Secretary General of the Indian Youth League.

121. Oral History, Narayana Karuppiah, 25 June 1984, *National Archives of Singapore.*

122. Report, 2 April 1942, 6/9, *Sir Henry Robert Moore Brooke-Popham Papers, Liddell-Hart Centre for Military Archives, King's College—London.*

123. See, e.g., *Rhodesia Herald,* 21 July 1943; Memorandum, "Indians in S. Rhodesia," 3 August 1943, DO 35/1169, *Public Records Office—London.*

124. "Effect of War on Native Peoples of South Pacific," *Taranaki Daily News,* 11 January 1951, IT1, #IT 67/12/84, *National Archives of New Zealand.*

125. H. S. L. Polak to Duke of Devonshire, 12 February 1945, CO 847/25/4, *Public Records Office—London.*

126. Report by Research and Analysis Branch, "Indian Minorities in South and East Asia: The Background of the Indian Independence Movement Outside India," 8 September 1944, Reel 9, #1, *OSS/State Department Intelligence and Research Reports, Part I, Japan and Its Occupied Territories during World War II.*

127. Memorandum, 16 August 1944, Reel 1, N. 62, Acc. No. 3861, *National Archives of Malaysia, National Archives of India.*

128. Iwaichi, *F. Kikan,* p. 209.

129. Memorandum from British Embassy in Chungking, 26 April 1944, EA, File 182-X/44, *National Archives of India*.

130. From Intelligence Bureau, Delhi, 4 April 1944, EA, File 182-X/44, *National Archives of India*.

131. Report, 17 February 1926, Reel 2, #875, *U.S. Military Intelligence Reports, Japan, 1918–1941*, Frederick, Md.: University Publications of America, 1985.

132. "Joint Declaration of the Assembly of Greater East Asiatic Nations," 1943, in David J. Lu, ed., *Japan: A Documentary History*, Armonk: M. E. Sharpe, 1997, pp. 423–424.

133. Narrative of L. H. Landon, no date, 80/2/1, *Imperial War Museum—London*.

134. Captured Japanese document, 18 April 1944, EA, File 29-C-A, *National Archives of India*.

135. Report, May 1944, EA, File 29-C-A, *National Archives of India*.

136. "Review of Japanese Broadcast Propaganda," circa December 1941, E1/1032, File 1, *BBC Written Archives—Reading, U.K.*

137. "Secret Telegram No. 6664," from Governor General, Delhi to Secretary of State for India, London, 22 August 1942, Acc. No. 647, *Underground Documents of 1942 Movement, Nehru Library—New Delhi*.

138. "Current Topic Pamphlet II," 22 October 1942, "All India Congress Committee," *Underground Documents of 1942 Movement*.

139. Debchaudhury, "Japanese Imperialism and the Indian Nationalist Movement," p. 156.

140. Reverend Swami Prabhavananda to William D. Hassett, 7 September 1944, *Franklin D. Roosevelt Papers, Nehru Library—New Delhi*.

141. M. K. Gandhi to Franklin D. Roosevelt, 1 July 1942, *Franklin D. Roosevelt Papers, Nehru Library—New Delhi*.

142. Henry A. Wallace to Brigadier General, 7 August 1942, *Franklin D. Roosevelt Papers, Nehru Library—New Delhi*.

143. William Phillips to President Roosevelt, 3 March 1943, *Franklin D. Roosevelt Papers, Nehru Library—New Delhi*.

144. William Phillips to President Roosevelt, 7 April 1943, *Franklin D. Roosevelt Papers, Nehru Library—New Delhi*.

145. William Phillips to Franklin D. Roosevelt, 19 April 1943, *Franklin D. Roosevelt Papers, Nehru Library—New Delhi*. For more on these themes, see the book by William Phillips, Ventures in Diplomacy, Boston: Beacon, 1952.

146. William Phillips to Franklin D. Roosevelt, 14 May 1943, *Franklin D. Roosevelt Papers, Nehru Library—New Delhi*.

147. William Phillips to Franklin D. Roosevelt, circa September 1943, *Franklin D. Roosevelt Papers, Nehru Library—New Delhi*.

148. William Phillips to "Dear Ed," Secretary of State Edward Stettinius, 5 January 1945, *Franklin D. Roosevelt Papers, Nehru Library—New Delhi*. See also *New York Times*, 3 September 1944.

149. Pearl Buck to Eleanor Roosevelt, 7 March 1942, *Franklin D. Roosevelt Papers, Nehru Library—New Delhi*.

150. Letter from Marion S. Mayo, 11 April 1942, *Franklin D. Roosevelt Papers, Nehru Library—New Delhi*.

151. William Jennings Bryan, "British Rule in India," no date, circa 1916, X.708 2102, *British Library—London*.

152. William D. Pawley to Franklin D. Roosevelt, no date, *Franklin D. Roosevelt Papers, Nehru Library—New Delhi*.

153. Memorandum to Franklin D. Roosevelt, 19 January 1944, *Franklin D. Roosevelt Papers, Nehru Library—New Delhi*.

154. Winston Churchill to Franklin D. Roosevelt, 14 August 1942, in Warren Kimball, ed., *Churchill and Roosevelt: The Complete Correspondence*, Princeton: Princeton University Press, 1984, p. 563.

155. See, e.g., Gerald Horne, *Black Liberation/Red Scare: Ben Davis and the Communist Party*, Newark: University of Delaware Press, 1994.

156. Victor Kiernan, "The Communist Party of India and the Second World War: Some Remininiscences," 20 November 1987, Acc. No. 1132, *Nehru Library—New Delhi*. Kiernan was a leading party member in Lahore during the war.

NOTES TO CHAPTER 9

1. Philip A. Klinkner, with Rogers M. Smith, *The Unsteady March: The Rise and Decline of Racial Equality in America*, Chicago: University of Chicago Press, 1999, p. 149.

2. Ronald H. Spector, *At War at Sea: Sailors and Naval Combat in the Twentieth Century*, New York: Viking, 2001, pp. 136, 265.

3. Reginald Kearney, *African American Views of the Japanese: Solidarity or Sedition?* Albany: State University of New York Press, 1998, p. 120.

4. Robert Hill, ed., *The FBI's RACON: Racial Conditions in the United States during World War II*, Boston: Northeastern University Press, 1995, p. 389.

5. A. V. H. Hartendorp, *The Japanese Occupation of the Philippines*, Manila: Bookmark, 1967, pp. 270, 271.

6. Walter White, *A Rising Wind*, Garden City, New York: Doubleday, 1945, pp. 16, 153. See also Sherrie Mershon and Steven Schlossman, *Foxholes and Color Lines: Desegregating the U.S. Armed Forces*, Baltimore: Johns Hopkins University Press, 1998.

7. Speech by Walter White, 16 June 1942, Roll 1, Section 3, #0154, *FBI File on the NAACP*.

8. Robert Jefferson, "'Poor Colored People Were Catching Hell All Over': Staging Politics of African-American Identity in the Southwest Pacific Theater and the Politics of Demobilization, 1944–1946," 18, unpublished paper in possession of author. See also Robert Jefferson, "Making the Men of the 93rd: African American Servicemen in the Years of the Great Depression and the Second World War, 1935–1947," Ph.D. dissertation, University of Michigan, 1995.

9. Report by Walter White, 9 April 1945, Part 14, Reel 13, #215, *Papers of the NAACP*.

10. Undated article by Walter White, circa 1944, Part 14, Reel 13, #0087, *Papers of the NAACP*.

11. Report from Walter White, 12 February 1945, Part 14, Reel 13, #155, *Papers of the NAACP*.

12. Entry, 21 February 1945, Reel 9, L: 129, *Henry L. Stimson Diaries—Yale University*.

13. To Commanding General, no date, Box 1, *Leonard Russell Boyd Papers—Hoover Institute, Stanford University*.

14. Ronald Takaki, *Double Victory: A Multicultural History of America in World War II*, Boston: Little Brown, 2001, pp. 24, 59, 69.

15. "Command of Negro Troops," Washington, D.C.: Government Printing Office, 1944, Box 1, *Leonard Russell Boyd Papers*.

16. Ooka Shohei, *Taken Captive: A Japanese POW's Story*, New York: John Wiley, 1996, p. 209.

17. Leonard Russell Boyd to Major General J. E. Hull, 17 May 1944, Box 2, *Leonard Russell Boyd Papers*.

18. Spector, *At War at Sea*, pp. 267, 270.

19. Lists of "Influential Negro Leaders Today"; "Important Negro publications"; A700, 9–10, *Diplomatic Archives—Tokyo*.

20. Franklin Delano Roosevelt to Joseph Curran, 14 January 1942. Material on "Double V" campaign; details on Negro troops; details on racial breakdown of states; material on black population of Liverpool; material on Negro illiteracy, death rates, occupational status, Negro population, Negro education; undated editorial from *PM*; *Commonweal* editorial, 23 January 1942, I460-1-3, *Diplomatic Archives—Tokyo*.

21. Charlotta A. Bass, *Forty Years: Memoirs from the Pages of a Newspaper*, Los Angeles: C. A. Bass, 1960, p. 125.

22. Marc Gallicchio, *The African American Encounter with Japan and China: Black Internationalism in Asia, 1895–1945*, Chapel Hill: University of North Carolina Press, 2000, pp. 172, 195.

23. *New York Amsterdam News*, 17 February 1945.

24. Yong Chen, *Chinese San Francisco, 1850–1943: A Trans-Pacific Community*, Stanford: Stanford University Press, 2000, p. 199.

25. Takaki, *Double Victory*, p. 172.

26. Gallicchio, *The African American Encounter*, p. 183.

27. Takaki, *Double Victory*, p. 170.

28. Adolph Newton, with Winston Eldridge, *Better than Good: A Black Sailor's War, 1943–1945*, Annapolis: Naval Institute Press, 1999, pp. 29, 64.

29. *Hong Kong News*, 14 August 1944.

30. *Hong Kong News*, 16 April 1945.

31. *Hong Kong News*, 23 June 1942.

32. *Hong Kong News*, 23 February 1943.

33. *Hong Kong News*, 29 June 1943.

34. *Hong Kong News*, 4 February 1943.

35. *Hong Kong News*, 18 August 1944

36. *Hong Kong News*, 2 June 1943.

37. *Hong Kong News*, 6 August 1943. Reporting on U.S. Negroes was a main staple of this newspaper. See, e.g., *Hong Kong News*, 28 April 1945 editorial on "The White Peril."

38. *Hong Kong News*, 25 July 1943. See also *Hong Kong News*, 12 July 1945.

39. *Hong Kong News*, 5 April 1944.

40. *Hong Kong News*, 19 May 1944.

41. *Hong Kong News*, 21 July 1942.

42. *Hong Kong News*, 20 May 1944.

43. *Hong Kong News*, 1 November 1944.

44. *Hong Kong News*, 2 June 1943.

45. *Hong Kong News*, 16 October 1942; Joe Louis was often featured in this newspaper. See, e.g., *Hong Kong News*, 5 July 1942.

46. James Guess, M.D., Clarksville, Oklahoma, to Sir Edward Grey, 20 December 1913, , FO 115/1803, *Public Records Office—London*. See also *New York Times*, 11 February 1914; *Galveston Daily News*, 6 April 1914.

47. To Secretary of State for the Colonies, 31 March 1926, FO 115/3120, *Public Records Office—London*.

48. U.K Consul General to U.K. Embassy, Washington, 17 March 1922, FO 115/2766, *Public Records Office—London*.

49. R. E. Stubbs to "My Dear Wilson," 24 February 1928, CO 318/391/12, *Public Records Office—London*. See also CO 323/1518/12; CO 318/432/2; CO 318/391/12; CO 554/78/8.

50. Frank Furedi, *The Silent War: Imperialism and the Changing Perception of Race*, London: Pluto Press, 1998, pp. 4, 14, 19.

51. Thomas Stanway to Under Secretary for the Colonies, 20 January 1936, CO 852/62/6, *Public Records Office—London*.

52. Memorandum, 6 February 1939, CO 852/234/5, *Public Records Office—London*.

53. D. Ryan, Edward Curran & Co. Ltd., Cardiff, to Assistant Secretary of Board of Trade, 26 March 1936, CO 852/62/9, *Public Records Office—London*.

54. Memorandum to G. L. M. Clauson, OBE, 6 July 1936, CO 852/62/9, *Public Records Office—London*.

55. Memorandum from G. L. M. Clauson, OBE, 28 July 1936, CO 852/62/9, *Public Records Office—London*.

56. "Japan's Activities in Abyssinia," 5 December 1933, Reel 15, #123, *U.S. Military Intelligence Reports, Japan, 1918–1941*, Frederick, Md.: University Publications of America, 1985.

57. "Japanese Concession and Monopoly in Ethiopia," 17 January 1934, Reel 15, #126, *U.S. Military Intelligence Reports, Japan, 1918–1941*.

58. Hugh Byas, *Government by Assassination*, New York: Knopf, 1942, p. 198.

59. Richard Albert Bradshaw, "Japan and European Colonialism in Africa, 1800–1937," Ph.D. dissertation, Ohio University, 1992, pp. 337, 343.

60. "Japanese Infiltration among the Muslims Throughout the World," 15 May 1943, Reel 1, *O.S.S./State Department Intelligence and Research Reports, Part I, Japan and Its Occupied Territories during World War II*.

61. Emily Hahn, *Hong Kong Holiday*, Garden City: Doubleday, 1946, pp. 245, 246, 250, 251, 259.

62. Anthony Hewitt, *Bridge with Three Men: Across China to the Western Heaven in 1942*, London: Jonathan Cape, 1986, pp. 86, 88, 100.

63. Oral History, Billy Strachan, 10042/5/1, *Sound Archives, Imperial War Museum—London*.

64. Robert N. Murray, *Lest We Forget: The Experiences of World War II West Indian Ex-Service Personnel*, Nottingham: Nottingham West Indian Combined Ex-Services Association, 1996.

65. Memorandum to Sir Frederick Leggett, 14 June 1944, LAB 26/55, *Public Records Office—London*.

66. From the Colonial Office to Sir Frederick Leggett, 23 June 1944, LAB 26/55, *Public Records Office—London*.

67. Undated letter from L. N. Constantine, LAB 26/55, *Public Records Office—London*.

68. Letter to Sir George Gater, 17 March 1944, LAB 26/55, *Public Records Office—London*.

69. Police Report, 1 September 1945, MEPO 3/2321, *Public Records Office—London; Daily Express*, 19 August 1945; *News of the World*, 20 August 1945.

70. Letter from Leo March, 26 September 1939, CO 323/1673/6, *Public Records Office—London*.

71. Report, 12 November 1942, ADM 178/299, *Public Records Office—London*.

72. Report, 30 July 1943, ADM 178/299, *Public Records Office—London*.

73. Report, 1 December 1942, ADM 178/299, *Public Records Office—London*.

74. Sonya O. Rose, "Sex, Citizenship and the Nation in World War II Britain," *American Historical Review*, 103 (Number 4, October 1998): 1147–1176, p. 1152.

75. Memorandum from Civil Service Commission, 22 December 1942, ADM 178/299, *Public Records Office—London*.

76. Letter from Viola Smith, 23 March 1941, AIR 2/6243, *Public Records Office—London*.

77. W. A. Dickins to Viola Smith, 2 April 1941, AIR 2/6243, *Public Records Office—London*.

78. Memorandum, 1 June 1941, AIR 2/6243, *Public Records Office—London*.

79. Letter "From the Master Balliol College," 4 October 1939, CO 323/1673/6, *Public Records Office—London*.

80. To A. H. Poynton, 29 September 1939, CO 323/1673/5, *Public Records Office—London*.

81. Communication, 11 July 1936, CO 850/84/8, *Public Records Office—London*.

82. Graham Smith, *When Jim Crow Met John Bull: Black American Soldiers in World War II Britain*, London: I. B. Tauris, 1987, pp. 29, 31, 83, 85, 109, 217.

83. Report from the War Cabinet, September 1942, PREM 4/26/9, *Public Records Office—London*.

84. Letter from Government House, Nyasaland, 16 February 1920, FO 115/2619, *Public Records Office—London*.

85. Memoranda, 18 September 1943, 20 September 1943, CO 968/92/2, *Public Records Office—London*.

86. Memorandum, 21 September 1943, CO 968/92/2, *Public Records Office—London*.

87. Undated memorandum, CO 968/92/2, *Public Records Office—London*.

88. Memorandum, 1 February 1944, CO 968/92/2, *Public Records Office—London*.

89. Memorandum, 6 February 1944, CO 968/92/2, *Public Records Office—London*.

90. Secretary of State for War to the Prime Minister, 2 December 1943, PREM 4/26/9, *Public Records Office—London*.

91. Report, 18 November 1943, PREM 4/26/9, *Public Records Office—London*.

92. List of Crimes Committed by Negroes, 21 October 1943, PREM 4/26/9, *Public Records Office—London*.

93. Report from the Duke of Melbourne, 21 October 1943, PREM 4/26/9, *Public Records Office—London*.

94. From the Foreign Office to Washington, 1 January 1944, CO 968/92/2, *Public Records Office—London*.

95. Sir A. Geddes to Lord Curzon, 13 February 1922, FO 115/27/66, *Public Records Office—London*.

96. Memorandum, 27 November 1943, CO 968/92/2, *Public Records Office—London*.

97. Report, 14 February 1945, DO 35/1183, *Public Records Office—London*.

98. Report, 20 November 1945, DO 35/1183, *Public Records Office—London*.

99. Report, "Jan 5/27 1945," DO35/1183, *Public Records Office—London*.

100. "A Short Account of Relations between Bechuana and British in a HAA troop," circa 25 February 1946, DO 35/1183, *Public Records Office—London*.

101. "Visit by Lt. Col. Arden-Clarke," 28 July 1944, WO 204/6670, *Public Records Office—London*.

102. Report, circa 1944, "Prisoners of War in British Territory. West Africa." CO 980/18, *Public Records Office—London*.

103. Report from East African Command, 2 March 1942, CO 980/17, *Public Records Office—London*. See also "Prisoners of War in British Territory. Kenya," 21 April 1942, CO 980/17, *Public Records Office—London*.

104. "Civil Internees in British Territory," CO 980/35, 23 July 1943, *Public Records Office—London*.

105. "Civil Internees in British Territory," 31 August 1942, CO 980/26, *Public Records Office—London*.

106. Wenzell Brown, *Hong Kong Aftermath*, New York: Smith & Durrell, 1943, p. 101.

107. "West Africans in Burma," 02 (660), clipping, SEAC, 24 February 1945, 2 December 1944, *Imperial War Museum—London*.

108. Gerald Horne, *From the Barrel of a Gun: The United States and the War against Zimbabwe, 1965–1980*, Chapel Hill: University of North Carolina Press, 2001, p. 57. See also "Rhodesian African Rifles—Scrapbook," Reel 1, *National Archives of Zimbabwe*.

109. *West African Forces Observer*, 18 June 1945, *Imperial War Museum—London*.

110. *New York Times*, 15 April 2000.

111. Account of Lt. J. A. L. Hamilton, 97/36/1, *Imperial War Museum—London*.

112. "Rhino Review," circa 1944, 9/5–8, *William Dimoline Papers, Liddell-Hart Centre for Military Archives, King's College-London*.

113. Report on "Employment of East and West African Troops," 17 December 1942, WO 193.91, *Public Records Office—London*.

114. From "C-in-C India," to War Office, 9 December 1942, WO 193/91, *Public Records Office—London*.

115. *Jambo*, circa 1944, Misc 4, *Liddell-Hart Centre for Military Archives, King's College—London*.

116. Account of Colonel F. K. Theobald, 97/36/, *Imperial War Museum—London*.

117. Account of Colonel F. K. Theobald, 97/36/1, *Imperial War Museum—London*.

118. Account of Captain P. B. Poore, 92/15/1, *Imperial War Museum—London*.

119. John Nunneley, *Tales from the King's African Rifles*, Surrey: Askari Books, 1998, p. 167.

120. Nunneley, *Tales from the King's African Rifles*, p. 172.

121. Timothy H. Parsons, *The African Rank-and-File: Social Implications of Colonial Military Service in the King's African Rifles, 1902–1964*, Portsmouth, N.H.: Heinemann, 1999, pp. 33, 201.

122. Nunneley, *Tales from the King's African Rifles*, p. 141.

123. *Hong Kong News*, 5 April 1944.

124. "Incident between East African Soldiers and Sinhalese," November 1943, CO 54/985/20, *Public Records Office—London*.

125. Memorandum, 19 October 1944, EA, File 741(9)-F.E./44, *National Archives of India*.

126. Memoranda, 25 November 1944, 13 December 1944, EA, File 890-F.E./44, *National Archives of India*.

127. Memorandum, 16 March 1944, EA, File 890-F.E./44, *National Archives of India*.

128. Memorandum, EA, File 114-FE/44, *National Archives of India*.

129. Account of Colonel F. K. Theobald, 97/36/1, *Imperial War Museum—London*.

130. Memorandum, 2 December 1944, FO 371/42267, *Public Records Office—London*.

131. Account of Colonel F. K. Theobald, 97/36/1, *Imperial War Museum—London*.

132. *New York Times*, 15 April 2000.

133. Robert B. Hammond, *Bondservants of the Japanese*, San Pedro, Calif.: Sheffield Press, 1943, p. 78.

134. George Wright-Nooth, with Mark Adkin, *Prisoners of the Turnip Heads: Horror, Hunger and Heroics—Hong Kong, 1941–1945*, London: Leo Cooper, 1994, p. 238.

NOTES TO CHAPTER 10

1. Marius B. Jansen, *The Japanese and Sun Yat-Sen*, Cambridge: Harvard University Press, 1967, pp. 37–38, 160–161, 209, 210–211.

2. William C. Kirby, *Germany and Republican China*, Stanford: Stanford University Press, 1984, p. 44.

3. Warren Cohen, *East Asia at the Center: Four Thousand Years of Engagement with the World*, New York: Columbia University Press, 2000, p. 311.

4. Richard Storry, *The Double Patriots: A Study of Japanese Nationalism*, London: Chatto and Windus, 1957, p. 18.

5. Yansheng Ma Lum and Raymond Mun Kong Lum, *Sun Yat-Sen in Hawaii: Activities and Supporters*, Honolulu: University of Hawaii Press, 1999, p. 39.

6. R. John Pritchard, ed., *The Tokyo Major War Crimes Trial: The Records of the International Military Tribunal for the Far East with an Authoritative Commentary and Comprehensive Guide, Volume 68*, Lewiston, New York: Edwin Mellen, 1998, pp. 32, 691.

7. R. John Pritchard, ed., *The Tokyo Major War Crimes Trial: The Records of the International Military Tribunal for the Far East with an Authoritative Commentary and Comprehensive Guide, Volume 38*, Lewiston, New York: Edwin Mellen Press, 1998, pp. 17, 924.

8. B. Nicolaevsky, "Russia, Japan and the Pan-Asiatic Movement to 1925," *Far Eastern Quarterly* 8 (Number 3, May 1949): 259–295, pp. 273, 277. See also George McTurnan Kahin, *Nationalism and Revolution in Indonesia*, Ithaca: Cornell University Press, 1970, pp. 119–120: "Many Japanese officers during late 1944 and through 1945 at least up until the Potsdam Agreement appeared confident that Russia would eventually join with Japan against the United States."

9. Rebecca E. Karl, "Creating Asia: China in the World at the Beginning of the Twentieth Century," *American Historical Review*, 103 (Number 4, October 1998): 1096–1118, pp. 1115, 1117.

10. Harold Z. Schiffrin, *Sun Yat-Sen: Reluctant Revolutionary*, Boston: Little Brown, 1980, pp. 61, 63.

11. Lewis Bush, *Land of the Dragonfly*, London: Robert Hale, 1959, p. 135. Even after the Chinese invasion by Japan, a significant percentage of the Japanese bureaucracy and populace opposed this maneuver. See, e.g., Barbara J. Brooks, *Japan's Imperial Diplomacy: Consuls, Treaty Ports, and War in China, 1895–1938*, Honolulu: University of Hawaii Press, 2000. See also Michael J. Green and Patrick M. Cronin, eds., *The U.S.-Japan Alliance: Past, Present and Future*, New York: Council on Foreign Relations Press, 1999.

12. Hu Sheng, *From the Opium War to the May Fourth Movement*, Beijing: Foreign Languages Press, 1981, pp. 327, 345.

13. Owen Lattimore, *Solution in Asia*, Boston: Little, Brown, 1945, pp. 81, 82.

14. Lee Yiu Wa, "The Foreign Policy of an Incompetent Empire: A Study of British Policy Towards the Sino-Japanese War in 1937–1941," M.Phil. thesis, Hong Kong University, 1998, pp. 33–34.

15. Hallett Abend, *Treaty Ports*, Garden City: Doubleday, 1944, p. 242. See also Edward R. Slack, *Opium, State and Society: China's Narco-Economy and the Guomindang, 1924–1937*, Honolulu: University of Hawaii Press, 2001.

16. Victor Silverman, *Imagining Internationalism in British and American Labor, 1939–1949*, Urbana: University of Illinois, 2000, pp. 42, 77.

17. Tony Lane, *The Merchant Seamen's War*, Manchester: Manchester University Press, 1990, pp. 8–9, 156, 172.

18. Yong Chen, *Chinese San Francisco, 1850–1943: A Trans-Pacific Community*, Stanford: Stanford University Press, 2000, p. 200.

19. William C. Kirby, *Germany and Republican China*, Stanford: Stanford University Press, 1984, p. 168. For another viewpoint, see, e.g., Maria Hsia Chang, *The Chinese Blue Shirt Society: Fascism and Developmental Nationalism*, Berkeley: Institute of East Asian Studies, University of California, 1984.

20. John Deane Potter, *No Time for Breakfast: A Record of Seven Years Travel*, London: Andrew Melrose, 1953, p. 158.

21. Lee Yiu Wa, "The Foreign Policy of an Incompetent Empire," pp. 93, 262, 269.

22. Lynn Pan, *Old Shanghai: Gangsters in Paradise*, Singapore: Cultured Lotus, 1999, p. 141.

23. Lee Yiu Wa, "The Foreign Policy of an Incompetent Empire," p. 269.

24. Cohen, *East Asia at the Center*, p. 345.

25. Poshek Fu, *Passivity, Resistance and Collaboration: Intellectual Choices in Occupied Shanghai, 1937–1945*, Stanford: Stanford University Press, 1993.

26. Translation of 28 November 1952 article from *Peking Daily*, HKRS 63-11315, *Public Records Office—Hong Kong*.

27. Lee Ngok, "The Later Career of Wang Ching-Wei, with Special Reference to His National Government's Cooperation with Japan, 1938–1945," M.A. thesis, Hong Kong University, 1966, pp. 1, 2.

28. Cedric Dover, *Hell in the Sunshine*, London: Secker and Warburg, 1943, p. 65. See also the intriguing letter to the *New York Times* of 15 November 1941 on China.

29. T'ien-wei Wu, "Contending Forces during the War of Resistance," in James C. Hsiung and Steven I. Levine, eds., *China's Bitter Victory: The War with Japan, 1937–1945*, Armonk: M. E. Sharpe, 1992, 51–78, p. 64.

30. Stein Tannesson, "Le Duan and China, 1979 and 1952–1979," Paper presented at the International Workshop on "New Evidence on China, Southeast Asia and the Vietnam War," Hong Kong University, 11–12 January 2000.

31. Sir Lindsay Ride, Vertical File—Biographical, *History Workshop, Hong Kong University* .

32. Chohong Choi, "Hong Kong in the Context of the Pacific War: An American Perspective," M.Phil. thesis, Hong Kong University, 1998, p. 111.

33. T'ien-wei Wu, "Contending Forces," 51–78, p. 64.

34. Pan, *Old Shanghai* , pp. 152–153, 158, 199, 203.

35. R. Harris Smith, *OSS: The Secret History of America's First Central Intelligence Agency*, Berkeley: University of California Press, 1972, pp. 248, 268.

36. Memorandum from Upshur Evans, 9 May 1944, Folder 94, *Lindsay Ride Papers, Australian War Memorial—Canberra*.

37. Bernard Wasserstein, *Secret War in Shanghai: Treachery, Subversion and Collaboration in the Second World War*, London: Profile, 1999, pp. 63, 165.

38. Sterling Seagrave, *The Yamato Dynasty: The Secret History of Japan's Imperial Family*, New York: Bantam, 1999, p. 143.

39. Robert E. Hertzstein, *Henry R. Luce: A Political Portrait of the Man Who Created the American Century*, New York: Scribner's, 1994, p. 101. One journalist has written that Jan Smuts, leader of racist South Africa, "was particularly friendly. . . . toward Japan" as well. See Frank Gervasi, *War Has Seven Faces*, Garden City: Doubleday, 1942, p. 55.

40. Memorandum from Francis Patron, U.K. Consul-General in Lisbon to U.K. Consul-General in Mozambique, "China—Collaborators," 9 January 1946, A4144 (A4244/1), #356/1946, *National Archives of Australia—Canberra*.

41. "Hong Kong—Intelligence Reports," External Affairs, A10322 (A10322), #30, f1944, 1–15 October 1944, *National Archives of Australia—Canberra*.

42. Sir Frederick Eggleston to H. V. Evatt, Minister for Foreign Affairs—Australia, 22 July 1943, A4144, #609,/1943, #23761, *National Archives of Australia—Canberra*.

43. From Chungking Legation to External Affairs, 15 May 1943, A989 (A989/1), #1843/150/4/4, *National Archives of Australia—Canberra*.

44. Masanobu Tsuji, *Singapore, 1941–1942: The Japanese Version of the Malayan Campaign of World War II*, Singapore: Oxford University Press, 1988, p. 273.

45. "B. Yates, Esq.," Vertical File, "Events—1941–45 War," *History Workshop, Hong Kong University*.

46. "Kweiling Intelligence Summary," "Confidential Sheet No. 27," 29 September 1944, Appendix B, HRRS211-2-32, *Public Records Office—Hong Kong*.

47. "Report on the Activities of a M19/19 Organization Operating in South China," 30 September 1946, MSS840, *Lindsay Ride Papers, Australian War Memorial—Canberra*.

48. "China—Fact and Fiction," no date, Folder 11, *Lindsay Ride Papers, Australian War Memorial*: This report also noted that Wang's Naking force "consists almost entirely of Chinese. . . . with solid financial interests" and "includes more poets than any other government in the world."

49. Bill Harman to "My Dear," 9 March 1942, *Bill Harman Papers—National Library of Australia*.

50. From British Embassy, Chungking, to Colonel E. D. G. Hooper, 11 April 1944, Folder 111, PR 82/68, *Lindsay Ride Papers, Australian War Memorial—Canberra*.

51. Christopher Thorne, *The Issue of War: States, Societies, and the Far Eastern Conflict of 1941–1945*, Hamish Hamilton, 1985, p. 31.

52. Edwin Ride, *BAAG: Hong Kong Resistance, 1942–1945*, Hong Kong: Oxford University Press, 1981, p. 121.

53. "Report on the Activities of a M19/19 Organization Operating in South China," 30 September 1946, MSS840, *Lindsay Ride Papers, Australian War Memorial—Canberra*.

54. "A Memorandum on . . . British Propaganda," circa 1944, Folder 3-4, PR 82/68, *Lindsay Ride Papers, Australian War Memorial—Canberra*.

55. Lindsay Ride to U.K. Embassy, Chungking, 5 September 1942, Folder 102, *Lindsay Ride Papers, Australian War Memorial—Canberra*.

56. David Bosanquet, *Escape through China*, London: Robert Hale, 1983, p. 52.

57. Wasserstein, *Secret War in Shanghai*, p. 240.

58. Speech by Li Chai Sum, 21 January 1943, Folder 88, *Lindsay Ride Papers, Australian War Memorial—Canberra*.

59. From U.K. Legation in Chungking to Anthony Eden, 15 February 1944, Reel 1, V41789, F1247, *British Foreign Office: Japan Correspondence, 1941–1945*, Wilmington: Scholarly Resources, 1980.

60. Memorandum from Lisbon to Foreign Office, 18 January 1943, Reel 4, V35953, F442, *British Foreign Office: Japan Correspondence, 1941–1945*.

61. From "C.-in-C., India," 15 October [year not noted, circa 1942], Reel 2, Volume 35940, F5476/6/23, *British Foreign Office: Japan Correspondence, 1941–1945*.

62. Report, 17 January 1943, Reel 4, Volume 35953, F442/442/23, *British Foreign Office: Japan Correspondence, 1941–1945*.

63. *PM*, 8 October 1943. See also *PM*, 28 January 1944; *PM*, 30 January 1944.

64. From Japanese Editor to FESD, 22 May 1945, E1/1029/2, File 2a, Acc. No. 10640/1, *Written Archives—British Broadcasting Corporation—Reading, U.K.*

65. Memorandum from "RHAL," 4 March 1942, Reel 1, V35937, *British Foreign Office: Japan Correspondence, 1941–1945.*

66. From the Government of India, 17 February 1942, Reel 1, V35937, *British Foreign Office: Japan Correspondence, 1941–1945.*

67. From Viceroy to Secretary of State for India, 1 March 1942, Reel 1, V35937, *British Foreign Office: Japan Correspondence, 1941–1945.*

68. John Robert Ferris, *Men, Money and Diplomacy: The Evolution of British Strategic Foreign Policy, 1919–1926,* Ithaca: Cornell University Press, 1989, p. 12.

69. Christopher Thorne, *The Issue of War: States and Societies, and the Far Eastern Conflict of 1941–1945,* London: Hamish Hamilton, 1985, p. 38.

70. For an early-twentieth-century view of U.S. interests in the region see, e.g., A. T. Mahan, *The Problem of Asia and Its Effect upon International Policies,* Port Washington, New York: Kennikat, 1970 (originally published in 1900).

71. See, e.g., William S. Stephenson, ed., *British Security Coordination: The Secret History of British Intelligence in the Americas, 1940–1945,* New York: Fromm International Publishing, 1998. See also http://www.h-net.msu.edu/reviews/showrev.cgi?path=30826932407858, and Alan Harris Bath, *Tracking the Axis Enemy: The Triumph of Anglo-American Naval Intelligence,* Lawrence: University Press of Kansas, 1998.

72. Wasserstein, *Secret War in Shanghai,* pp. 199, 203.

73. Nigel Cameron, *Barbarians and Mandarins: Thirteen Centuries of Western Travellers in China,* Hong Kong: Oxford University Press, 1997, p. 337. On "jackal" imperialism, see, e.g., Cohen, *East Asia at the Center,* p. 261. See also John E. Moser, *Twisting the Lion's Tail: American Anglophobia between the World Wars,* New York: New York University Press, 1999.

74. Robert Bickers, *Britain in China: Community, Culture and Colonialism, 1900–1949,* Manchester: Manchester University Press, 1999, pp. 78, 83, 144.

75. Donald Greene to "Professor Weintraub," 30 July 1986, Misc 257 (Item 2433), "Letters concerning Pearl Harbour," *Imperial War Museum—London.*

76. Ride, *BAAG,* p. 123.

77. R. Harris Smith, *OSS: The Secret History of America's First Central Intelligence Agency,* Berkeley: University of California Press, 1972, p. 247.

78. Lanxin Xiang, *Recasting the Imperial Far East: Britain and America in China, 1945–1950,* Armonk: M. E. Sharpe, 1995, pp. 17, 21, 22, 25, 69.

79. Chin-tung Liang, *General Stillwell in China, 1942–1944: The Full Story,* New York: St. John's University, 1972, p. 165. See also Andrew Whitfield, "The Handing Back of Hong Kong: 1945 and 1997," *Historian* (Number 54, Summer 1997): 4–9.

80. Memorandum from Ashley Clarke, 5 April 1944, FO 371/ 41797, *National Archives of Singapore.*

81. E. G. Boxshall to G. B. Endacott, 21 May 1969, HKMS 100-1-6, *Public Records Office—Hong Kong.*

82. Memoranda, circa February 1944, NAB 357, FO 371, 41795, *National Archives of Singapore.*

83. Jan Henrik Marsman, *I Escaped from Hong Kong,* Sydney: Angus and Robertson, 1943, p. 79.

84. Ken Cuthbertson, *Nobody Said Not to Go: The Life, Loves and Adventures of Emily Hahn,* New York: Farrar, Straus & Giroux, 1998, p. 246.

85. Wasserstein, *Secret War in Shanghai,* p. 213.

86. Unsigned memorandum, circa early 1942, Reel 2, V31813, *British Foreign Office: Japan Correspondence, 1941–1945,* Wilmington: Scholarly Resources, 1980.

87. John Robert Ferris, *Men, Money and Diplomacy: The Evolution of British Strategic Foreign Policy, 1919–1926,* Ithaca: Cornell University Press, 1989, pp. 8, 41, 96, 144, 162.

88. Major D. Hall Caine to Commandant BAAG, 28 February 1945, Folder 61, *Lindsay Ride Papers, Australian War Memorial—Canberra.*

89. Lee Yiu Wa, "The Foreign Policy of an Incompetent Empire," p. 64.

90. *Daily Worker,* 10 May 1937.

91. Sir Franklin C. Gimson, "Account of Internment and the Restoration of British Rule to Hong Kong," circa 1972, MSS 940.547252 G491, *Hong Kong Collections, Hong Kong University.*

92. John Streicker, *The Captive Colony: The Story of Stanley Camp, Hong Kong,* HK 940.547252 S8, *Hong Kong Collections, Hong Kong University.*

93. Gwen Priestwood, *Through Japanese Barbed Wire,* New York: Appleton-Century, 1943, pp. 68, 191.

94. Vaudine England, *The Quest of Noel Croucher: Quiet Philosopher*, Hong Kong: Hong Kong University Press, 1998, p. 142.

95. The term "American" is used as a matter of convenience to describe U.S. citizens and is not intended to deny others in the Western Hemisphere the right to claim this term.

96. Bosanquet, *Escape through China*, p. 178.

97. Smith, *OSS*, p. 287.

98. L. D. Meo, *Japan's Radio War on Australia, 1941–1945*, Melbourne: Melbourne University Press, 1968, pp. 50–51.

99. Nobutaka Ike, ed., *Japan's Decision for War: Records of the 1941 Policy Conference*, Stanford: Stanford University Press, 1967, pp. xxvii, 237. See also Miwa Kimitada, "Japanese Opinions on Woodrow Wilson in War and Peace," *Monumenta Nipponica*, 22 (Numbers 3–4, 1967): 368–389, p. 384: "Field Marshal Yamagata. . . . most powerful of the oligarchs was the head of the Choshu batsu (clique) in control of the imperial army. . . . He dreaded . . . a 'white alliance' including Germany and Russia to force Japan to give up her recent gains in China and elsewhere."

100. A. Zhukov, "Japanese-German Relations during the Second World War," *The Communist*, 23 (Number 3, March 1944): 284–287, p. 285.

101. Undated memorandum, E1/1029/2, File 2a, Acc. No. 10640/1, *BBC Written Archives—Reading, U.K.*

102. Extract from intercepted letter, 18 September 1942, E1/1029/2, File 1, *BBC Written Archives—Reading, U.K.*

103. Memorandum, 17–25 April 1942, R34/651, *BBC Written Archives—Reading, U.K.*

104. Memorandum, 5–12 November 1942, R34/651, *BBC Written Archives—Reading, U.K.*

105. Louise Young, *Japan's Total Empire: Manchuria and the Culture of Wartime Imperialism*, Berkeley: University of California Press, 1998, pp. 101, 102.

106. Stephen Ambrose and Brian Loring Villa, "Racism, the Atomic Bomb and the Transformation of Japanese-American Relations," in Gunter Bischof and Robert L. Dupont, eds., *The Pacific War Revisited*, Baton Rouge: Louisiana State University Press, 1997, 179–198, pp. 179–180, 198.

107. Interview with Ohshima Hiroshi, 9 October 1962 and 24 March 1971, Box 43, *John Toland Papers, Franklin D. Roosevelt Library—New York.*

108. Anti-Semitism in Europe was not limited to Germany. See, e.g., Louise London, *Whitehall and the Jews, 1933–1948: British Immigration Policy and the Holocaust*, New York: Cambridge University Press, 2001.

109. Marvin Tokayer and Mary Swartz, *The Fugu Plan: The Untold Story of the Japanese and the Jews during World War II*, New York: Paddington, 1979, p. 257.

110. Victor Klemperer, *I Will Bear Witness: A Diary of the Nazi Years, 1933–1941*, New York: Random House, 1998, pp. 198, 203–204.

111. Pamela Rotner Sakamoto, *Japanese Diplomats and Jewish Refugees: A World War II Dilemma*, Westport: Praeger, 1998.

112. Solomon Bard, "Mount Davis and Sham Shui Po: A Medical Officer with the Volunteers," in Clifford Matthews and Oswald Cheung, eds., *Dispersal and Renewal: Hong Kong University during the War Years*, Hong Kong: Hong Kong University Press, 1998, 193–202, p. 200.

113. Narrative of Catherine Davis, no date, 97/3/1, *Imperial War Museum—London.*

114. Memorandum, 1–8 October 1942, R34/651, *BBC Written Archives—Reading, U.K.*

115. *Canadian Jewish News*, 4 December 1997.

116. Letter from James Ross, circa 1 July 1994, Box 1, *Matook R. Nissim Papers, Stanford University.*

117. Undated clipping, Box 1, *Matook R. Nissim Papers, Stanford University.*

118. Narrative of Jack Smith, circa 1949–1950, Y0077-10.V, *Hoover Institute, California.*

119. "Propaganda," 3 June 1942, CAB 119/50, FO 371/22215, *Public Records Office—London.*

120. W. Empson to ESD, 27 June 1943, E1/1029/2, File 2a, *BBC Written Archives, Reading, U.K.*

121. L. D. Meo, *Japan's Radio War on Australia, 1941–1945*, Melbourne: Melbourne University Press, 1968, pp. 50–51.

122. John Morris, *Traveller from Tokyo*, London: Cresset Press, 1943, p. 141.

123. Wasserstein, *Secret War in Shanghai*, p. 217.

124. "Conditions in Hong Kong and Southern China," 6 October 1944, A3269 (A3269/12), #W1, *National Archives of Australia—Canberra.*

125. Tessa Morris-Suzuki, *Re-Inventing Japan: Time, Space, Nation*, Armonk: M. E. Sharpe, 1998, pp. 82, 95.

126. Raymond Lamont-Brown, *Kempeitai: Japan's Dreaded Military Police*, Gloucestershire, U.K.: Sutton, 1998, p. 30.

127. Gwen Terasaki, *Bridge to the Sun*, Tokyo: Charles Tuttle, 1984, pp. 83, 97, 106.

128. Marsman, *I Escaped from Hong Kong*, p. 94.

129. Akira Iriye, *Pearl Harbor and the Coming of the Pacific War: A Brief History with Documents and Essays*, Boston: Bedford/St. Martin's, p. 123.

130. Iriye, *Pearl Harbor*, p. 6.

131. Galen Irvin Johnson, "Defending the Japanese Warlords: American Attorneys at the Tokyo War Crimes Trial, 1946–1948," Ph.D. dissertation, University of Kansas, 1998, pp. 191–192.

132. Hans J. Massaquoi, *Destined to Witness: Growing Up Black in Nazi Germany*, New York: Morrow, 1999, p. 165.

133. Pierre Lavelle, "The Political Thought of Nishida Kitaro," *Monumenta Japonica*, 49 (Number 2, Summer 1994): 139–165, pp. 139, 142.

134. Walter LaFeber, *The Clash: U.S.-Japanese Relations throughout History*, New York: Norton, 1997, p. 120.

135. *Bisbee Daily Review* (Arizona), 14 August 1907.

136. Philander C. Knox, Department of State to F. H. Allen, 23 May 1912, "Lands on Magdalena Bay," U.S. Congress. Senate. 62nd Congress, 2nd Session, Document 694, 23 May 1912.

137. Memorandum from Henry Lane Wilson, 16 November 1910, in Gene Z. Hanrahan, ed., *Documents on the Mexican Revolution: Volume II, The Madero Revolution as Reported in the Confidential Dispatches of U.S. Ambassador Henry Lane Wilson and Embassy in Mexico City, June 1910 to June 1911, Part 1*, Salisbury, North Carolina: Documentary Publications, 1976, p. 88.

138. Theodore Roosevelt to "Dear Speck," 16 July 1907, in Elting Morrison, ed., *The Letters of Theodore Roosevelt, Volume 5*, Cambridge: Harvard University Press, 1952.

139. Theodore Roosevelt to William Howard Taft, in Elting Morrison, ed., *The Letters of Theodore Roosevelt, Volume 7*, Cambridge: Harvard University, 1954.

140. Irving Goff McCann, *With the National Guard on the Border: Our National Military Problem*, St. Louis, C. V. Mosby, 1917, pp. 53, 60.

141. Remarks of the Hon. William H. Murray, 7 November 1913, Series 501, Box 6, *Thomas Catron Papers—Center for Southwest Research, University of New Mexico*.

142. Mark Ellis, *Race, War and Surveillance: African-Americans and the United States Government during World War I*, Bloomington: Indiana University Press, 2001, p. 22; see also, Gerald Horne, *Black and Brown: African Americans and the Mexican Revolution, 1910–1920* (New York: New York University Press, in press).

143. Charles H. Harris and Louis R. Sadler, *The Border and the Revolution: Clandestine Activities of the Mexican Revolution, 1910–1920*, Silver City, N.M.: High-Lonesome Books, 1990, pp. 8, 80, 98.

144. "Investigation of Mexican Affairs: Preliminary Report and Hearings of the Committee on Foreign Relations, Pursuant to S. Res. 106," U.S. Congress. Senate. 66th Congress, 2nd Session. Document Number 285, Washington, D.C.: Government Printing Office, 1920, p. 1777.

145. Memorandum, 25 June 1918, Reel 1, #33, *U.S. Military Intelligence Reports, Japan 1918–1941*, Frederick, Md.: University Publications of America, 1985.

146. Memorandum from U.S. Embassy, 8 July 1932, Reel 3, #867, *U.S. Military Intelligence Reports: Mexico, 1919–1941*.

NOTES TO THE CONCLUSION

1. See, e.g., "Post Liberation Welfare—Evacuation of West Indians from Hong Kong," 28 December 1945, CO 980/196, *Public Records Office—London*.

2. Henry Lethbridge, "Hong Kong under Japanese Occupation: Changes in Social Structure," in Ian Jarvie, ed., *Hong Kong: A Society in Transition*, London: Routledge & Kagan Paul, 1969, 77–127, p. 78.

3. Eugene D. Williams to H. Moresby White, 21 August 1946, Box 1, *Japanese War Crimes Collections, University of Southern California*.

4. Oral History, Ralph Malcolm Macdonald King, 004655/04, *Sound Archives, Imperial War Museum—London*.

5. Norman Cliff, *Courtyard of the Happy Way*, Eversham, U.K.: Arthur James, Ltd., 1977, p. 126.

6. John Streicker, *Captive Colony: The Story of Stanley Camp, Hong Kong*, HK 940.547252 S8, *Hong Kong Collections, Hong Kong University*.

7. Sterling Seagrave, *The Yamato Dynasty: The Secret History of Japan's Imperial Family*, New York: Bantam, 1999, p. 289.

8. Alan Birch, "'No' Business as Usual," May 1979, *Geoffrey Emerson Papers, History Workshop, Hong Kong University.*

9. *Hong Kong News*, 22 February 1942.

10. Russell S. Clark, *An End to Tears*, Sydney: Star Weekly, 1946, pp. 10, 17, 23, 25, 40, 42, 45–46, 69, 78, 82, 85, 86, 148, 163, 164, 165, 173, 175, 179.

11. Selwyn Selwyn-Clarke, *Footprints: The Memoirs of Sir Selwyn Selwyn-Clarke*, Hong Kong: Sino-American Press, 1975, p. 107.

12. "Report of Preliminary Negotiations with Japanese Representatives Held by Rear Admiral C. J. H. Harcourt, C.B., C.B.E., on Board HMS Indomitable at Hong Kong on Friday, 31st August 1945," HKRS 163-1-81, *Public Records Office—Hong Kong.*

13. Christopher Somerville, *Our War: How the British Commonwealth Fought the Second World War*, London: Weidenfeld and Nicolson, 1998, p. 293.

14. Vice Admiral Sir Cecil Harcourt, "The Military Administration of Hong Kong," *Royal Central Asian Journal*, 34 (1947): 7–18, pp. 14, 15, *History Workshop, Hong Kong University.*

15. Alexander Grantham, *Via Ports: From Hong Kong to Hong Kong*, Hong Kong: Hong Kong University Press, 1965, pp. 104, 107.

16. G. B. Endacott, *Hong Kong Eclipse*, Hong Kong: Oxford University Press, 1978, pp. 317, 319, 320.

17. William G. Sewell, *Strange Harmony*, London: Edinburgh House, 1947, p. 186.

18. *South China Morning Post*, 19 September 1945.

19. Sir C. Grenville Alabaster, OBE, KC, to Colonial Secretary, 8 May 1947, HKRS, 41-1-4329, *Public Records Office—Hong Kong.*

20. Managing Director to Colonial Secretary, 2 January 1947, HKRS 41-1-1898, *Public Records Office—Hong Kong.*

21. Thomas F. Ryan, S.J., *Jesuits under Fire in the Siege of Hong Kong, 1941*, London: Burns, Oates and Washbourne, 1944, p. 173.

22. See, e.g., *South China Morning Post*, 18 November 1984.

23. "Confidential" memorandum from Chief Commissioner of Police in Hong Kong, 11 January 1946, File 190/INA, *Indian National Army Papers, National Archives of India.*

24. "Catalogues, Indexes, Bibliographies," File—"Police Museum," Ng Chi-wa, ed., *Police Museum*, Hong Kong: Police Museum, 1994.

25. Sir Franklin Gimson to G. E. J. Gent, 2 September 1945, HRKS 163-1-81, *Public Records Office—Hong Kong.*

26. *South China Morning Post*, 29 October 1946. See, e.g., Gerald Horne, *Fire This Time: The Watts Uprising and the 1960s*, Charlottesville: University Press of Virginia, 1995, passim.

27. *South China Morning Post*, 6 November 1946.

28. Oral History, Cyril A. Luckin, 005190/05, *Sound Archives, Imperial War Museum—London.*

29. Alan Birch, "'No' Business as Usual," May 1979, *Geoffrey Emerson Papers, History Workshop, Hong Kong University.*

30. Winnie Davies, "Life in Hong Kong before 1945," Student Paper for class of Elisabeth Sinn, circa Spring 1994, *History Workshop, Hong Kong University.*

31. *South China Morning Post*, 12 December 1946.

32. *South China Morning Post*, 14 December 1946.

33. *South China Morning Post*, 17 December 1946.

34. *South China Morning Post*, 1 January 1947.

35. *South China Morning Post*, 1 August 1947.

36. *South China Morning Post*, 2 August 1947.

37. *South China Morning Post*, 14 February 1948.

38. *South China Morning Post*, 2 August 1947.

39. *South China Morning Post*, 8 August 1947.

40. *South China Morning Post*, 17 August 1947.

41. Raymond Lamont-Brown, *Kempeitai: Japan's Dreaded Military Police*, Gloucestershire, U.K.: Sutton, 1998, p. 155.

42. David P. Bassett and Larry N. Shyu, eds., *Chinese Collaboration with Japan, 1932–1945*, Stanford: Stanford University Press, 2001, p. 13. See also Sybilla Jane Flower, "British Prisoners of War of the Japanese, 1941–1943," in Ian Nish and Yoichi Kibata, *The History of*

Anglo-Japanese Relations, 1600–2000, Volume II: The Diplomatic Dimensions, 1931–2000, New York: St. Martin's, 2000, pp. 149–173.

43. *South China Morning Post*, 24 February 1948.

44. Memorandum to Walter Adams, 29 November 1948, *Vice-Chancellor's Office. IUC Correspondence, 16 July 1948–27 July 1950 Registry, Hong Kong University.*

45. Memorandum to Colonial Secretary, 13 December 1947, HKRS 163-1-610, *Public Records Office—Hong Kong.*

46. C. Y. Liang, Secretary in Ministry of Foreign Affairs, to Colonial Secretary, 17 March 1948, HKRS 163-1-610, *Public Records Office—Hong Kong.*

47. Memorandum, 13 October 1945, HKRS 169-2-119, *Public Records Office—Hong Kong.*

48. From "Staff Officer (Intelligence), Hong Kong," to "Chief of Staff," 11 October 1945, HKRS 169-2-119, *Public Records Office—Hong Kong.*

49. Memorandum, 7 March 1947, HKRS 163-1-401, *Public Records Office—Hong Kong.*

50. Donald G. Gillin and Charles Etter, "Staying On: Japanese Soldiers and Civilians in China, 1945–1949," *Journal of Asian Studies*, 42 (Number 3, May 1983): 497–518, pp. 497, 499, 500, 505, 508.

51. Sir Cecil Harcourt to T. W. Kwok, Special Commissioner for Kwantung and Kwangsi, Ministry of Foreign Affairs, 17 January 1946, HKRS 169-2-150, *Public Records Office—Hong Kong.*

52. Memorandum to the Colonial Secretary, 7 December 1948, HKRS 411-1-4018, *Public Records Office—Hong Kong.*

53. Translation of letter from Ogata Shunsaku to "Dear Brother Seisaku," 2 June 1946, HKRS 163-1-120, *Public Records Office—Hong Kong.*

54. *South China Morning Post*, 14 October 1947.

55. From U.K. Embassy, Chungking, to Foreign Office, London, 14 February 1946, HKRS 169-2-235, *Public Records Office—Hong Kong.*

56. *South China Morning Post*, 6 February 1947.

57. Tanya Lee, *Tanya: Child of the East Wind: An Autobiography*, Port Macquarie, Australia: Persimmon Publications, 1992, p. 117.

58. *South China Morning Post*, 1 October 1947.

59. *South China Morning Post*, 14 January 1947.

60. T. P. Gregory to W. F. C. Jenner, circa 1946, HKRS 251-3-24, *Public Records Office—Hong Kong.*

61. Memorandum, 16 July 1946, HKRS 163-1-120, *Public Records Office—Hong Kong.*

62. Report, 10 August 1948, HKRS 41-1-4251, *Public Records Office—Hong Kong.*

63. Tseng Yu-Hao and Denis Victor to Governor Mark Young, 25 January 1947, HKRS 156-1-1045, *Public Record Office—Hong Kong.*

64. *South China Morning Post*, 25 December 1946.

65. Attorney General to "Hon. C.S.," 7 February 1947, HKRS 156-1-1045, *Public Records Office—Hong Kong.*

66. *South China Morning Post*, 30 April 1947.

67. *South China Morning Post*, 1 May 1947.

68. H. C. Wu to "Dear Excellency," 21 November 1945, HKRS 170-1-460, *Public Records Office—Hong Kong.*

69. Custodian of Property to Secretariat, 6 April 1946, HKRS 170-1-755, *Public Records Office—Hong Kong.*

70. C. L. Hsu to Col. W. M. Thomson, 13 March 1946, HKRS 170-1-755, *Public Records Office—Hong Kong.*

71. Controller of Dockyards, Hong Kong, to Brigadier D. M. MacDougall, 28 September 1945, HKRS 170-1-755, *Public Records Office—Hong Kong.*

72. General Chang Fa Kwei to Vice Admiral Sir Cecil Harcourt, 20 October 1945, HKRS 169-2-131, *Public Records Office—Hong Kong.*

73. "Chinese Military Delegation, Hong Kong," to Vice Admiral Sir Cecil Harcourt, 29 October 1945, HKRS 169-2-132, *Public Records Office—Hong Kong.*

74. Ibid.

75. "Liaison Office, Kowloon," to "Hon. C.S." 4 September 1945, HKRS 163-1-26A. See also "Confidential Memorandum of Agreement Relative to Japanese Surrender at Hong Kong," circa September 1945, and "Investigation into the Seizure of Property by the Japanese in the Colony of Hong Kong. Statutory Declaratory of Keiji Makimura," 18 December 1945, HKRS 165-4-1, *Public Records Office—Hong Kong.*

76. Roger W. Buckley, "From Reoccupation to EXPO—Hong Kong-Japanese Relations, 1945–1970," *Journal of Social Science*, 28 (Number 1, 1989): 45–57, p. 46.

77. San Diego Confectionery to Colonial Secretariat, 16 May 1947, HKRS 41-1-2145, *Public Records Office—Hong Kong*. See also List of Recipients of Japanese Reparations in Hong Kong, circa 1946, HKRS 41-1-2388-4, *Public Records Office—Hong Kong*.

78. T. F. Wu to Colonial Secretary, 7 June 1947, HKRS 41-1-1294-1, *Public Records Office—Hong Kong*.

79. "Register of Property Appropriated by the Japanese and Later Removed from the Colony," 18 February 1947, HKRS 41-1-915-2, *Public Records Office—Hong Kong*. See also "Local Companies Re-Registered in Japan during Occupation," circa 1946, HKRS 123-5-236, *Public Records Office—Hong Kong*.

80. "For Colonial Secretary," 25 July 1946, HKRS 163-1-120, *Public Records Office—Hong Kong*.

81. DSB to Hon. C.P., 30 July 1946, HKRS 163-1-120, *Public Records Office—Hong Kong*.

82. Affadavit, 7 December 1946, Yoshimitsu Abe, in R. John Pritchard, ed., *The Tokyo Major Crimes Trial: The Records of the International Military Tribunal for the Far East with an Authoritative Commentary and Comprehensive Guide, Volume 58*, Lewiston, N.Y.: Edwin Mellen Press, pp. 27, 526.

83. *South China Morning Post*, 22 September 1946.

84. F. Zimmern & Co., Solicitors, to Colonial Secretary, 8 April 1948, HKRS 156-1-398, *Public Records Office—Hong Kong*.

85. *South China Morning Post*, 16 June 1947.

86. Buckley, "From Reoccupation to EXPO," p. 51.

87. Endacott, *Hong Kong Eclipse*, pp. 238–239, 245–247.

88. Lethbridge, "Hong Kong under Japanese Occupation," p. 116.

89. *South China Morning Post*, 1 April 1948.

90. *South China Morning Post*, 2 April 1948.

91. W. Shillingford to "Dear Sir," 26 February 1948, HKRS 125-3-407, *Public Records Office—Hong Kong*.

92. *South China Morning Post*, 17 October 1945.

93. *South China Morning Post*, 7 December 1946.

94. *South China Morning Post*, 6 February 1947.

95. Roger W. Buckley, "From Reoccupation to EXPO-Hong Kong-Japanese Relations, 1945–1970," *Journal of Social Science*, 28 (Number 1, 1989): 45–57, p. 51.

96. *South China Morning Post*, 12 April 1948.

97. Claro M. Recto, *Three Years of Enemy Occupation*, Manila: People's Publisher, 1946.

98. David Joel Steinberg, *Philippine Collaboration in World War II*, Ann Arbor: University of Michigan Press, 1967, pp. 48, 163, 164. See also Larry Bland, et al., eds., *George C. Marshall's Mission to China, December 1945–January 1947*, Lexington, Virginia: George C. Marshall Foundations, 1998.

99. Unknown to General Cheung Wai-cheung, Magistrate of Chungsan, 19 November 1945, Box 17, #59, *J. M. Braga Papers, National Library of Australia—Canberra*.

100. Testimony of Lo Kong, circa 1946, HKRS 163-1-387, *Public Records Office—Hong Kong*.

101. Note from Acting Attorney General, 8 November 1946, HKRS 163-1-169, *Public Records Office—Hong Kong*.

102. Memorandum, circa 1946, HKRS 163-1-170, *Public Records Office—Hong Kong*.

103. Ronald Hall to "Sir," 24 October 1947, HKRS 163-1-172, *Public Records Office—Hong Kong*.

104. George Strickland to "Hon. F.S.," 23 May 1946, 163-1-70, *Public Records Office—Hong Kong*.

105. *South China Morning Post*, 27 February 1946.

106. *South China Morning Post*, 1 April 1946.

107. *South China Morning Post*, 10 April 1946.

108. *South China Morning Post*, 2 April 1946.

109. *South China Morning Post*, 13 April 1946.

110. *South China Morning Post*, 17 April 1946.

111. "Report" on "Rex vs. George Wong," 1946, HKRS 41-1-1338, *Public Records Office—Hong Kong*. See also *South China Morning Post*, 27 February 1946, 1 March 1946.

112. *South China Morning Post*, 11 July 1946.

113. Report on Tsui Kwok Ching, circa 1946, HKRS 41-1-1349, *Public Records Office—Hong Kong*.

114. Memorandum from Judge E. H. Williams, 31 July 1946; Petition to government of Hong Kong, 12 August 1946, HKRS 41-1-1376, *Public Records Office—Hong Kong.*
115. *South China Morning Post,* 21 August 1946.
116. Kanao or Kanawa Inouye and related spellings are also used.
117. "Confidential" documents, 5 September 1947, HKRS 163-1-216, *Public Records Office—Hong Kong.*
118. Patricia E. Roy, *A White Man's Province: British Columbia Politicians and Chinese and Japanese Immigrants, 1858–1914,* Vancouver, B.C.: University of British Columbia Press, 1989, pp. 86, 121, 122.
119. W. Peter Ward, *White Canada Forever: Popular Attitudes and Public Policy Toward Orientals in British Columbia,* Montreal: McGill-Queen's University Press, 1990, pp. 68, 103, 180.
120. Peition from Inouye Kanao," 15 August 1947; Memorandum from the "Chief Justice," 22 July 1947, Memorandum from Inouye Kanao, 15 August 1947, HKRS 163-1-216, *Public Records Office—Hong Kong.*
121. Memorandum, circa 1947, HKRS 163-1-216, *Public Records Office—Hong Kong.*
122. *South China Morning Post,* 26 May 1946, 28 May 1946.
123. Oral History, Kenneth M. Baxter, 31 March 1995, *Oral History Project, Hong Kong Museum of History.*
124. Oral History, Lucien Brunet, 26 November 1995, *Oral History Project, Hong Kong Museum of History.*
125. *South China Morning Post,* 27 February 1947.
126. *South China Morning Post,* 18 April 1947.
127. Memorandum, 22 April 1947, HKRS 163-1-216, *Public Records Office—Hong Kong.*
128. To War Office from CINC Hong Kong, 22 October 1945, 169-2-167, *Public Records Office—Hong Kong.*
129. Colonial Secretary to Commissioner of Prisons, 19 April 1947, HKRS 163-1-216, *Public Records Office—Hong Kong.*
130. *South China Morning Post,* 6 April 1946.
131. *Los Angeles Times,* 20 September 2002.
132. *U.S.A. vs. Tonoya Kawakita, Records of the District Court of the U.S. for the Southern District of California, Central Division,* No. 19413, Boxes 1126, ll47, 1148, Record Group 21, *National Archives and Records Administration, Laguna Niguel, California.*
133. Russell Warren Howe, *The Hunt for "Tokyo Rose,"* Lanham, Md.: Madison Books, 1990.
134. *South China Morning Post,* 2 January 1946. Contrast the case of Cleveland Tom, a "Jamaican of Chinese Race" who joined the Hong Kong Volunteers in November 1940, fought during the invasion, and was "detained" by the Japanese thereafter. Boldly, he escaped and "joined the Chinese guerillas." Tom said, "From June 1943 until the end of the war I served with the Chinese American troops as interpreter being sent with them at one time to India." He returned to Hong Kong in November 1945, but now needed help in returning to Jamaica—a plea that was unlikely to be met favorably. See Case of Cleveland Tom, circa 1946, HKRS 41-1-1568, *Public Records Office—Hong Kong.*
135. *South China Morning Post,* 3 August 1946.
136. *South China Morning Post,* 14 September 1946.
137. Statement from Wadmull Chattulani, 16 October 1945, HKRS 76-3-137, *Public Records Office—Hong Kong.*
138. *South China Morning Post,* 15 October 1946.
139. Case of F. M. Arculli, circa 1946, HKRS 76-3-107, *Public Records Office—Hong Kong.*
140. *South China Morning Post,* 30 October 1946.
141. Case of Mohammed Yusuf Shah, circa 1947, HKRS 163-1-427, *Public Records Office—Hong Kong.*
142. Files on Indian police, some of whom fought with the INA, circa 1946, HKRS 230-2-2, *Public Records Office—Hong Kong.*
143. Memorandum to CINC, Hong Kong, 7 March 1946, HKRS 169-2-167, *Public Records Office—Hong Kong.*
144. Memorandum from A. El Arculli, 20 June 1946, HKRS 163-1-203, *Public Records Office—Hong Kong.*
145. *South China Morning Post,* 24 May 1947.
146. Memorandum, circa 1947, HKRS 76-3-255, *Public Records Office—Hong Kong.*

147. Memorandum, 15 February 1951, HKRS 41-1-6765, *Public Records Office—Hong Kong*. See also *South China Morning Post*, 16 May 1947.

148. From "C in C Hong Kong" to "War Office," 17 April 1946, WO 203/5296b, *Public Records Office—London*.

149. *South China Morning Post*, 3 September 1946.

150. *South China Morning Post*, 13 November 1946.

151. *South China Morning Post*, 14 November 1946.

152. *South China Morning Post*, 29 August 1946.

153. *South China Morning Post*, 21 September 1946.

154. George Wright-Nooth, with Mark Adkin, *Prisoners of the Turnip Heads: Horror, Hunger and Heroics—Hong Kong, 1941–1945*, London: Leo Cooper, 1994, p. 98.

155. Robert S. La Forte, ed., *With Only the Will to Live: Accounts of Americans in Japanese Prison Camps, 1941–1945*, Wilmington: Scholarly Resources, 1994, p. 68.

156. "Most Secret" memorandum, no date, File 191/INA, *Indian National Army Papers, National Archives of India*.

157. Memorandum, 7 May 1946, HKRS 76-3-48, *Public Records Office—Hong Kong*.

158. Minutes of War Activities Committee, 23 October 1945, HKRS 169-2-5, *Public Records Office—Hong Kong*.

159. "Most secret" memorandum, no date, File 191/INA, *Indian National Army Records, National Archives of India*.

160. Yukiko Koshiro, *Trans-Pacific Racisms and the Occupation of Japan*, New York: Columbia University Press, 1999, p. 18.

161. B. V. A. Roling and Antonio Cassese, *The Tokyo Trial and Beyond*, Cambridge, U.K.: Polity, 1994, pp. 20, 47, 55, 67, 87. The historian Richard Minear agrees with Judge Roling: "But Japan was not Germany; Tojo was not Hitler; the Pacific War was not identical with the European war. . . . The categories and assumptions of Nuremberg broke down completely in their application at Tokyo." See Richard Minnear, *Victor's Justice: The Tokyo War Crimes Trial*, Princeton: Princeton University Press, 1971, p. 134.

162. Herbert Bix, *Hirohito and the Making of Modern Japan*, New York: HarperCollins, 2000, p. 596.

163. Peter Wesley Smith, "Discriminatory Legislation in Hong Kong," 0842. PWS. Uf, Paper presented at Hong Kong Baptist University, June 1987, *Hong Kong Collections, Hong Kong University*.

164. Frank Ching, *The Li Dynasty: Hong Kong Aristocrats*, Hong Kong: Oxford University Press, 1999, p. 126.

165. Suke Wolton, *Lord Hailey, the Colonial Office and the Politics of Race and Empire in the Second World War: The Loss of White Prestige*, New York: St. Martin's, 2000, pp. 145, 146.

166. Jon Halliday, "Hong Kong: Britain's Chinese Colony," *New Left Review*, no date, circa 1975, File—Authors, *History Workshop, Hong Kong University*.

167. Wing Chung Ng, "Becoming 'Chinese Canadian': The Genesis of a Cultural Category," in Elizabeth Sinn, *The Last Half Century of Chinese Overseas*, Hong Kong: Hong Kong University, 1998, 203–215, p. 204.

168. Bill Ong Hing, *Making and Remaking Asian America Through Immigration Policy, 1850–1990*, Stanford: Stanford University Press, 1993, p. 36.

169. Ronald Takaki, *Double Victory: A Multicultural History of America in World War II*, Boston: Little Brown, 2001, pp. 118–120.

170. Shian Li, "The Extraterritoriality Negotiations of 1943," *Modern Asian Studies*, 30 (Number 3, 1996): 617–650, p. 629.

171. Andrew Coe, *Eagles and Dragons: A History of Americans in China and the Origins of the American Club*, Hong Kong: American Club, 1997, p. 142.

172. N. J. Miners, "The Hong Kong Government Opium Monopoly, 1914–1941," *Journal of Imperial and Commonwealth History*, 11 (Number 3, May 1983): 275–299, 275.

173. Clive Harris, "Post-War Migration and the Industrial Reserve Army," in Winston James and Clive Harris, ed., *Inside Babylon: The Caribbean Diaspora in Britain*, London: Verso, 1993, 9–54, p. 10. See also Partha Sarathi Gupta, *Imperialism and the British Labour Movement*, London: Macmillan, 1975.

174. Paul Foot, *Immigration and Race in British Politics*, Harmondsworth, U.K.: Penguin, 1965, p. 110. See also Ronald Segal, *The Race War*, London: Jonathan Cape, 1966.

175. Jean Gittins, *A Stranger No More*, South Yarra, Vic., Australia: Gittins, 1987, pp. 113, 116.

176. Lindsay Ride to D. M. MacDougall, Colonial Office, 16 July 1945, HKRS 211-2-38, *Public Records Office—Hong Kong*.
177. Memorandum from T. J. Rowell, 5 November 1946, HKRS 41-1-1603, *Public Records Office—Hong Kong*.
178. Memorandum from S. A. Gray, 27 April 1946, HKRS 41-1-1603, *Public Records Office—Hong Kong*.
179. Minutes of the 6th Meeting of the Volunteers, 27 December 1946, HKRS 163-1-412, *Public Records Office—Hong Kong*.
180. "Letter from Council of European Civil Servants," 23 February 1948, HKRS 163-1-580, *Public Records Office—Hong Kong*.
181. Memorandum from Director of Public Works, 30 January 1948, HKRS 156-1-1168, *Public Records Office—Hong Kong*.
182. Memorandum from Creech Jones, 8 January 1947, HKRS 46-1-164, *Public Records Office—Hong Kong*.
183. Memorandum, 8 February 1956, HKRS 41-1-2941, *Public Records Office—Hong Kong*.
184. Oral History, Dr. Clifford Matthews, 25 November 1996, *Oral History Project, Hong Kong Museum of History*.
185. Dan Waters, *Faces of Hong Kong: An Old Hand's Reflections*, Singapore: Prentice Hall, 1995, p. 145.
186. "Appendix A, circa 1956, HKRS 41-1-2941, *Public Records Office—Hong Kong*.

NOTES TO THE EPILOGUE

1. Gary Wayne Catron, "China and Hong Kong, 1945–1967," Ph.D. dissertation, Harvard University, 1971, p. 27. Of course, beginning in the early 1970s with the visit of U.S. President Richard M. Nixon to Beijing, China's status as a foe of Washington altered dramatically.
2. Petition from "Chinese Civil Servants' Club," 30 July 1946, General Correspondence, 1945–1946, *Registry, Hong Kong University*.
3. Patrick Yu Shuk-siu, *A Seventh Child and the Law*, Hong Kong: Hong Kong University Press, 2000; Marjorie Chui, *Justice without Fear: Recollections of a Chinese Magistrate in Colonial Hong Kong*, Hong Kong: Ming Pao Publishing, 2000.
4. Edward K. N. Lau, "The Influence of Race on Sentencing in Hong Kong," M.Soc. Sc. dissertation, Hong Kong University, 1990, pp. 46, 77.
5. "Equal Opportunities: A Study on Discrimination on the Ground of Race," A Consultation Paper, Home Affairs Branch, Government Secretariat, February 1997, HKP 303.387 E64, *Hong Kong Collections, Hong Kong University*.
6. *South China Morning Post*, 28 July 1998.
7. *Hong Kong Standard*, 11 January 2000.
8. *Financial Times*, 7 March 2001.
9. *Financial Times*, 21 November 2000.
10. *South China Morning Post*, 30 January 2000.
11. *Far Eastern Economic Review*, 28 June 2001.
12. *Hong Kong Standard*, 8 February 2000.
13. *South China Morning Post*, 9 December 1999.
14. *South China Morning Post*, 13 July 2001.
15. *South China Morning Post*, 30 August 2001.
16. *South China Morning Post*, 5 November 2001.
17. *Financial Times*, 7 November 2001.
18. *International Herald Tribune*, 7 December 1999.
19. *New York Times*, 10 February 2000.
20. *Far Eastern Economic Review*, 20 January 2000.
21. *San Francisco Chronicle*, 14 April 2001.
22. *New York Times*, 25 March 2001.
23. *International Herald Tribune*, 26 October 1999.
24. Albert L. Allred, Chief Deputy Clerk, U.S. District Court, Eastern District of Michigan, 14 June 1949, R33.18.2.4, Box 1044, *National Archives and Regional Administration—New York City*.
25. *Los Angeles Sentinel*, 3 January 1946.
26. Lewis Porter, *John Coltrane: His Life and Music*, Ann Arbor: University of Michigan Press, 1998, p. 274.

27. Carl Woideck, *The John Coltrane Companion: Five Decades of Commentary*, New York: Schirmer, 1998, pp. 34, 39.

28. Nikitah Okembe-Ra Imani to H-Afro-Am@H-NET.MSU.EDU, 5 October 1999.

29. Caroline Clarke, "Take a Lesson," *Black Enterprise*, 31 (Number 9, April 2001): 127–132, p. 130. See also Caroline Clarke, *Take a Lesson*, New York: John Wiley, 2001.

30. Interview, Clifford Matthews, 25 November 1996, *Oral History Project, Hong Kong Museum of History*.

31. John Streicker, *Captive Colony: The Story of Stanley Camp*, HK 940.547252 S8, *Hong Kong Collections, Hong Kong University*.

32. *South China Morning Post*, 27 January 1973.

33. *South China Morning Post*, 22 April 1948.

34. *South China Morning Post*, 27 July 1972.

35. Sir Arthur Dickinson Blackburn, "An Account of Personal Experiences of My Wife and Myself at Hongkong during the Japanese Attack and Afterwards," MSS 940.547252, *Hong Kong Collections, Hong Kong University*.

36. George Wright-Nooth, with Mark Adkin, *Prisoners of the Turnip Heads: Horror, Hunger and Heroics—Hong Kong, 1941–1945*, London: Leo Cooper, 1994, pp. 250, 257.

37. Roi Ottley, *No Green Pastures*, London: John Murray, 1952, p. 9.

38. Hyoe Murakami, *Japan: The Years of Trial, 1919–1952*, Tokyo: Kodansha, 1982, pp. 17–18.

39. Fujiwara Iwaichi, *F. Kikan: Japanese Army Intelligence Operations in Southeast Asia During World War II*, Hong Kong: Heinemann Asia, 1983, p. 306.

40. Lecture by Basil Liddell-Hart, circa 1965, *Basil Liddell-Hart Papers, Liddell-Hart Centre for Military Archives, King's College—London*.

41. Oral History, Chu Shuen Choo, 15 August 1985, *National Archives of Singapore*.

42. Louis Allen, *Burma: The Longest War, 1941–1945*, London: Orion, 1998, p. 628.

43. *New York Times Book Review*, 1 June 2001. See also Gore Vidal, *The Last Empire: Essays, 1992–2001*, Garden City: Doubleday, 2001.

44. Asahi Shimbun Correspondents, compilers, *28 Years in the Guam Jungle: Sergeant Yokoi Home from World War II*, Tokyo: Japan Publications, 1972.

Index

Abbott, Robert: racial discrimination in London, vii

Abeywickrama, Mr. (a Ceylonese): on Africans eating children, 247–48

Accredited Advertising Agents of Hong Kong: racial reversal by, 321

Afghanistan: Japanese propaganda in, 232

Africa: Japan's contribution to independence, 326; postwar racial discrimination, 317–18. *See also* Africans

African-American press: *Afro-American,* 112, 120; *Amsterdam News* (New York), 51; *California Eagle* (Los Angeles), 50–51; *Colored American Magazine,* 44; *Crisis,* 49; news service in Japan, 59; *Pittsburgh Courier,* 49, 111; pro-Japan sentiments, 50–51; on WWII as a race war, 107

African Americans, 43–59; aid to victims of Japanese earthquake (1923), 52; air ace in Sino-Japanese War, 113; alienation among, 52; alliance with Japan, 15, 43, 48–49, 53–54, 55–56; animus toward Japanese soldiers to, 226; anti-white violence, 123; applicability of Tokyo War Crimes Trials, 312–13; in armed forces, 149, 183–84, 220–28, 238–41; Asian Americans among, 113–15; Asians' fate and theirs, xiii, 43; in Australia, 181–82; benefits from internment of Japanese Americans, 125–26; Britain and, vii, 94, 106, 236, 347*n*79; British treatment of, vii, 94; China compared to Japan to, 110–13; Chinese Americans and, 111; in Communist Party, 268; conservatives among, 122–23; doubts about their reliability as soldiers, 43, 222; fictional collaborator with Japanese, 114; Filipino bond presumed, 7, 43–44; first ones seen by Japanese, 8; Hitler as an, 106; Japanese agents among, 57, 113–14, 117; Japanese Americans, relations with, 54, 111; Japanese as role models, 50–51; Japanese husbands, 57; in Japanese internment camps, 220; Japanese military intelligence, 59, 114, 119–20; Japanese propaganda aimed at, xiv, 55, 59, 108, 220–21; Japanese racially tinged attacks on, 329*n*2; Japanese-sponsored back-to-Africa movement, 55–56; Japanese-supplied guns, 116; Japan's advantage among, 59; Japan's alliance ex-

plained by, 108; Japan's appeal, vii–viii, xiii, 57–58, 324; job discrimination, 124, 227; London hotels' treatment of, vii; meetings with Japanese and non-whites, 46, 47, 55–56; in Mexican-Japanese alliance, 53; Nazi Germany to, 105–6, 127; in Plan of San Diego, 277; playing Japanese in kids' games, 119; pro-Japan sentiments, 43–48, 115–20, 127; revocation of their citizenship, 125; right-wing Europe's attraction, 126–27; Russo-Japanese War's effect, 32, 44–45, 49; Singapore's fall to, 121–22; Sino-Japanese War to, 58, 109–13; soldier's epitaph, 222; in the South, 1; surveillance of, 47, 53–55; travelers to Japan, 54; travelers to Nazi Germany, 105; using them to deflect criticisms of Jim Crow, 6; vote on backing the war, 105–6; West Coast population, 54; WWII as a race war, 105–8. *See also* Black nationalists

African Methodist Episcopal Church: support for Japan in Russo-Japanese War, 52

Africans: in British armed forces, ix–x, 9, 244–49; in defeating Japanese, 3; distrust of Britons, 241; reluctance to fight Japanese, 14; reports of cannibalism, 247–49; U.S.'s attraction to, 239; white supremacy to, 241–43

Afro-American: report of snickering at American defeats, 120; support for Japan in Sino-Japanese War, 112

Afro-Caribbeans: migration to Harlem, 105

Ah Ting: Communist guerilla, 234

Akira Iriye: on Japanese alliances, 274

Alabama: Grand Guignol of bias, 137

Alabaster, C. Grenville: wartime losses, 285

All India Congress Committee: colonizers to, 214

Ambrose, Stephen: on racism as motivation for war, 270

American Club (Shanghai): Chinese membership, 264

Americans: badges to distinguish black Americans from black Britons, 238; in China, 153; a Chinese American's hatred for, 141; collaboration with Japan, 311; in internment camps, 93–95, 96, 98; unpopularity in Britain, 94. *See also* African Americans; Chinese Americans; Euro-Americans; Japanese Americans

Communist Party, China (CCP): Allied opposition to, 259; "an indigenous growth," 259; British cooperation, 259–60; British persecution, 12, 143; as captors, 143; Chiang's use of Japanese against, 290–91; common opponent of Britain, Japan, U.S., xiv; founders, 142; ingratitude toward, 326; Koumintang ban on its publications, 290; nationalists and, 259; opposition to collaboration with Japan, 13, 143; opposition to Japan, 12, 253; in postwar Hong Kong, 319; redistribution of collaborator's wealth, support for, 294

Communist Party, India: backing the Allies, 219

Communist Party, Indonesia (PKI): schoolteachers, 205

Communist Party, United States: African Americans in, 268; anticommunism toward, xiv, 56; backing the Allies, 219; Negroes and, 48, 55; surveillance of Japanese activities in U.S., 56

Conference of Pan-Asianists (1926), 187

Cook Islanders: in British armed forces, 163

Cooke, Marvel: on Chinese Americans in Harlem, 113

Cooper, Queenie: on being a third-rate queen, 25

Coppin, Alan Dudley: on Chinese businesses in internment camps, 153–54, 287

Corrothers, James: race war fiction, 49

Cotton industry: Japanese-British competition in Africa, 230

Council of European Civil Servants (Hong Kong): opposition to racial reform, 316–17

Crackerocracy: Powell on, Adam Clayton, 122

Crew, Graeme: on hatred for Japanese, 140

Crisis: Corrothers' story in, 49

Crown Colonies: governors in, 18

Cuffee, Paul: prominence, 49

Cumings, Bruce: on Japan's attraction to Asian progressives, 11

Curzon, George Nathaniel, Marquis of Kedleston: on India in Britain's power, 9; on whiteness of working class skin, 40; wife, 93

Da Dilva, M. A.: accusation against Tsui Kwok Ching, 301

Daily Worker (newspaper): on proposed Anglo-Japanese agreement about China, 267

Dark Princess (Du Bois): race war fiction, 50

Davis, Catherine: on Chinese and Jews in Japan, 271

Davis, Lee: Communist guerilla, 234

Davis, Percy: anti-Japan sentiment, 234

Dean, Harry: on blood relations between Negroes and Japanese, 49

Decolonization: independence for Asian states, 14–15; independence in Africa, 326; U.N. confrontation with colonialism, 264–65; U.S. opposition to restoring colonial rule, 264–65

Delano, Sara: family home in Hong Kong, 19

Delano, Warren: in China trade, 19

Democracy: Britain as its defender, 122; in British policy making, 7; pro-Japan feelings and, xv; as a rationale for war, 215

Desegregation: as Japanese plot, 120

Devereux, J. P. S.: on talking to Japanese captors, 96

Dew, Gwen: on Chinese perfidy during Hong Kong invasion, 64–65; disquisition of Japan's place in the world, 140; on dowager in Stanley internment camp, 92–93; on Indians in occupied Hong Kong, 144; on Japanese Americans in Japanese occupation forces, 132; on Japanese as copyists, 139; on Japanese humiliation of whites, 77–78; on racism's persistence during Hong Kong invasion, 65–66; on rooming with men, 154

Dibba, Bakary: on fighting for Empires, 249

Diosesan Boys' School (Hong Kong), 18

Diosesan Girls' School (Hong Kong), 18

"Dr. Takis." *See* Guzman, Mimo D.

Dog Man (prisoner in internment camp), 97

Dorman-Smith, Reginald: on failure to induce loyalty in Burma, 201–2; on fifth columists in Burma, 201

Dover, Cedric: on Wang Ching-wei, 256

Dower, John: on American reaction to Japan's racial policies, 4; writings of, xi

Drage, Charles: on children of mixed marriages, 29; on European disdain for British military in Hong Kong, 27

Du Bois, W. E. B.: attitude toward China, 110; attitude toward Japan, 110; on blacks' and Asians' destiny, xiii; on Britain as defender of democracy, 122; combining Japan and China, 109; *Dark Princess*, 50; on Germany winning WWII, xv; on internment of Japanese Americans, 125; to Japan's government, 224; Nazi Germany's treatment of, 105; problem of the epoch, 327; race war fiction by, 50; Russo-Japanese War's effect, 251; on Russo-Japanese War's impact, 45; in Shanghai, 110; on Sino-Japanese enmity, 110–11; on "Yellow Peril," 15

Durrani, Mahmood Khan: on racial discrimination in India, 207

Ho Chi Minh: deportation from Hong Kong, 188; lack of resistance to Japanese in China, 256; Subhas Chandra Bose and, 209

Ho Kom-tong: in Hong Kong Jockey Club, 20

Ho Tung, Robert: living at The Peak, 31

Holick, Alexander: Tonoya Kawakita victim, 305

Holland, Esther: marriage to Chinese man, 30

Holness, Eugene (also known as Lester Holness, Lester Carey): arrested, 119; in Ethiopia Pacific Movement, 119

Homosexuality: among African-American troops in Australia, 149; among Britons, 149; homosexual defender of Hong Kong, 149; in Japanese internment camps, 149

Hong Kong: Aberdeen district, 1; areas of, 1; Kowloon (see Kowloon); New Territories, 1, 259; Outlying Islands, 1; police (see Hong Kong police); Repulse Bay Beach, 1; size, 1; Victoria Peak (see Peak, The)

Hong Kong, before World War II: American consulate, 61; Asians in, 17; British armed forces in, 22, 27, 30–31, 40; British foothold (1842), 1, 9; Britons in, 25–26, 62; Canadians in, 23; cemeteries in, 24; Central British School, 18; Cheung Chan, 18, 23; Chinese in, 1–2, 12–14, 17–18, 20, 22, 24; collaboration with Japan, 14, 31; compared to colony of ostriches, 62; Contagious Diseases Act (1867), 27; cost of living, 19, 60; as Crown Colony, 18; Delano in, Sara, 19; democracy in, 1; Diosesan Boys' School, 18; Diosesan Girls' School, 18; diseases, 17, 27; distribution of wealth, 101; education, 18, 31; employment patterns, 22–23, 26; Eurasians in, 24, 26, 28–32, 167–68; European Reservation, 18; Europeans in, 1, 14, 17, 18–19, 22–26, 26–27, 71, 74; evacuation of women and children, 167–71, 179; Executive Council, 18, 23; firemen, 23; General Strike (1925), 74; government, 18, 20; Indians in, 1, 24; intrigue, 1; Irish in, 24; Japanese Consulate, 61–62; Japanese in, 19, 61–62, 74, 129, 286; justice system, 22–23; Kings's College, 18; Kowloon School, 18; labor unions, 24, 74, 91; libraries, 18; mass transit, 21; Matilda Hospital, 70; miscegenation in, 28–29; murder cases in, 22; Peak School, 31; Perry in, Matthew, 8; place in British Empire, 1; plan to massacre Europeans there, 12–13; political activism, 23–24; population (1941), 1; Portuguese in, 24, 25, 167–68; poverty, 2, 17, 20; prostitution, 26–27; Queen's College, 18; racial discrimination, 21–22, 28; racial inequality, 2, 17–18; residential segregation, 18–19, 31;

rickshaw drivers, 21–22; Rose Hill, 19; scent of, 19; Scotch in, 25; "singsong" houses, 28; Sinophobia, 21–22; snobbery/gossip, 26; social classes, 18; Star Ferry, 21; theft, 22; town hall, 18; trade, nineteenth century, 19; U.S. view of situation, 61; venereal diseases, 27; Victorian School, 18; Wanchai, 74; White Russians in, 25, 73; Yamati, 74

Hong Kong, Japanese invasion (Dec. 8-25, 1941), 60–79; anti-Empire sentiment, 258; British complacency during, 76; British defeat, 2, 63, 67, 68, 75–77, 78–79, 85; British massacre of Chinese, 71; British surrender, 63; Chinese collaboration with Japan, 12, 64–65, 69–73, 300; collaboration with Japan, 12, 28, 64–65, 69–73, 75, 300; desertion by Chinese drivers, 64; desertion by Chinese servants, 72; discord during, 66; emotional collapse during, 66; fear induced by, 68; fifth columnists during, 64; German-Japanese relations, 274; humiliation of whites after British surrender, 77–78, 147; Japanese agents, 64; Japanese called "Ethiopians," 107; Japanese in Chinese civilian clothing, 177; Japanese propaganda, 68–69, 77; looting during, 77; Rajputana Rifles' casualties, 70; rapes during, 152; religious revival during, 66; reporting the Japanese landing, 66; Singapore during, 192; squabbling during, 67

Hong Kong, Japanese occupation (1941-1945): anti-white propaganda, 81–82; British resistance, motive for, 264–65; camaraderie among Chinese and Japanese, 104; cannibalism, 87; capitalism encouraged, 100–101, 153–54; Chinese Chamber of Commerce, 100; Chinese fleeing to mainland, 299; Chinese in, 279; Chinese Manufacturers Union, 100; Civil Administration Department, 81; collaboration with Japan, 25, 84–85, 95, 100; collaborators in, 233, 279, 289, 298, 299–303, 308–11; damages in, 101; destruction of police records, 285; dragging black pilot to death, 250; economic boom, roots of later, 100; escapes from, 259, 261; going native in, 87; goods taken by Japan, 280; government, Chinese in, 100, 142; Hong Kong defense corps, 63, 69–70, 74, 75–76; Indians during, 144–46, 212; Japanese hatred of English, 264–65; Japanese in, 104; lack of resistance, 104, 297; liquor destroyed, 285; looting, 80, 285, 294; monitoring of German nationals, 273; physical destruction, 279; police, 88; prohibition on whites living on The Peak, 83–84,

(China), 134; Osaka (China), 135; postwar-
Hong Kong capitalism's roots, 100–101,
153–54; punishment of women, 155; racial
reversal in, 81–89, 96–97, 99, 147; Santo
Tomas (Philippines), 157–58; segregation of
women and children from men, 156;
Shamshuipo (Hong Kong), 86, 148, 153–54,
287; slave mentality in, 97–98; in Sumatra,
156; on Taiwan, 135; U.S. sailors in, 91;
Warm Road Goal (Shanghai), 212; women,
emotionally expressive, 155; women frater-
nizing with captors, 152; Yokohama
(Japan), 97. *See also* Stanley internment
camp
Ireland, Kevin: on threat of invasion of New
Zealand, 171–72
Irian Jaya: black soldiers in, 183
Irish: collaboration by, 309–10; in prewar
Hong Kong, 24
Isamu Ishara: collaboration with Japan, 307
Isherwood, Christopher: bathhouse beauties,
335n77
Ishihara ("The Beast of the East"): Japanese
American in Japanese occupation forces,
134, 136
Ishii Kikujiro, Viscount: on rectifying racial
discrimination, 164–65
Ismail Zain: on fall of Singapore, 194–95; on
postwar Britons, 198
Isogai: collaborator friends, 292
Isoroku Yamamoto: on defeating U.S., 129
Issei: alien land law and, 54; contributions to
Japanese war effort, 13; harassment of, 39;
outflow of, 131. *See also* Japanese Ameri-
cans; Nisei
Italians: in Australia, 174
Italy: invasion of Ethiopia, 155, 231–32; Tri-
partite Pact and, 274
Iwao Oyama: in Russo-Japanese War (1904-
1905), 45
Izumiya Tatsuro: on British armed forces in
Burma, 203

Jamaica: anti-British talk in, 106; black nationalists from, 48; emigrants to Britain, 314–15;
whites in, 234
Jansen, Marius B.: on Sun Yat-Sen, 251
Japan: advantage among African Americans,
59; African American press in, 59; African
American travelers, 54; African Americans,
appeal to, vii–viii, xiii, 57–58, 324; African
Americans' admiration for, 43–48; Africans
in defeating, 3; alliance with African Americans, 15, 43, 48–49, 53–54, 55–56; alliance
with China, 12; alliance with Nazi Germany, Fascist Italy (Tripartite Pact), 108,

165, 268–75; alliance with Soviet Union, 12,
365n8; alliance with/trust in Britain, 62, 95,
160, 188, 200–201, 255, 266–67, 295; anti-
Chinese policies in Southeast Asia, 6; anti-
Semitism lacking in, 271–72; anti-white behavior in, 37; anticommunism in, xiv; appeal to African Americans, vii–viii, xiii,
57–58, 324; appeal to Asians, viii; its appeal
to Asians, 11; armed forces (*see* Japanese
armed forces); "Asia for Asiatics" ("Aji,
Ajino, Ajia!"), 26–27, 209, 284, 313; Asians'
hatred for Euro-Americans, 4; Asians in defeating, 3; banditry by, 130–31; bigotry in, x;
black market, 271; in British Empire's undoing, 280; British racism's effect on, viii; brutality in China, viii; its challenge to Western
domination, x, xiii–xiv; as "champion of
colored races," ix, 114; China, trade with,
258; China compared to, to African Americans, 110–13; Chinese in, 271; Chinese students in, 252–53; classes of nations created
by, 273; collaboration with (*see* Collaboration with Japan); colonizing neighbors, policy of, 32; competition with British in
Africa, 229–31; cultural influence, postwar,
322–23; defeat, acceptance of, 279, 280; defeat questioned, 291; detestation for, xiv;
driving wedge between Britain and U.S.,
265–66; Du Bois's attitude toward, 110;
early successes, viii; effect of U.S.'s Negrophobia, 329n2; effect on British Empire in
Asia, xv; Ethiopia and, 155, 231–32; Europeans in, 282; failure to declare war on the
Soviet Union, 274–75; fears of it allying
with Russia and China, 12; global domination, poised for, 147; Hong Kong's role in its
war effort, 101; immigration exclusion laws,
view of U.S.'s, 38; "imperial preferences"
to, 218; International Military Tribunal for
the Far East's accusations, 3; Jews in, 271;
Jews in Manchuria, assistance to, 271; Jews
in occupied territories, 272; Korean intervention (1910), 32, 35; League of Nations
and, 165; Liberia and, 45; lynching Negroes,
sales of novel about, 51; Manchurian conquest (1931), 74, 112; Meiji Restoration (*see*
Meiji Restoration); Mexico and, 53, 275–78;
mobilization against white supremacy, 160;
multiculturalism of, 142, 172; national independence for others, 14–15, 326; nationalism, 272, 323; Nazi Germany compared to,
x, xiv; Nazi Germany's ability to deflect hatred toward it, 270; Nisei with Canadian or
American citizenship, 302; pacifism in,
329n2; Pan-Asianism, 3, 5, 251; popularity
of acting against racial discrimination, 35;

cies in, 6; Japanese interregnum, importance of, 189–90; Kesatuan Melaya Muda (Malay Youth Movement), 195; pro-Japan sentiments, 189, 195–98, 207; racial discrimination on trains, 207

Malays: in Singapore, 197

Malliet, A. M. Wendell: on African Americans' pro-Japan sentiments, 115–16; on attention to racial consequences of the war, 121; on racial reversal, 107

Maltby, C. M.: on Japanese agents in Hong Kong, 64; Scots to, 71

Maltese: concerns about their identity, 41

Manansala, Policarpio: Black Dragon Society link, 119; pro-Japan sentiments, 119

Manchuria: Japanese armed forces in postwar, 290; Japan's assistance to Jews in, 271; Japan's conquest (1931), 74, 112; rape in, 152; white supremacy slain in, 112

March, Leo: volunteering for service in British armed forces, 235–36

Marijuana: effect on sexual desire, 239–40; effect on women's sexual desires, 239–40

Marriage: Chinese wives of army personnel in Australia, 170; to Chinese women, 28, 282; Eurasians' prospects for, 31, 282; of Filipinos and those of European descent, 124; in internment camps, 150; internment's effects, 157–58; interracial marriage in China, 20; Japanese husbands of African Americans, 57; mixed marriage, reaction to, 28–30, 317; spotting children of mixed marriages, 29

Marshall, David: on Singapore Volunteers Corps, 191

Marsman, Jan Henrik: on German-Japanese relations in Hong Kong, 274; on Japanese hatred for English, 265–66

Martel, Charles, 45

Martin, Mary Erwin: on kindness by Japanese American in Japanese occupation forces, 136

Masanobu Tsuji: on British armed forces, 190

Masao Dodo: on Japan's treatment of blacks, 58

Massaquoi, Hans J.: on Japans' independence of Nazi Germany, 275

Matsuda ("Cardiff Joe"): in Japanese occupation forces, 136

Matsutaro Shoiki: murdered, 38–39

Matthews, Clifford: on end of white supremacy, 78–79; humiliation of Eurasians in postwar Hong Kong, 317; on Japanese captors, 325

Maugham, W. Somerset: attitudes toward Chinese, xii–xiii

Maxwell, George: on color bar in Malaya's civil service, 188

McCarthy, Joseph: Schuyler and, 112

McCoin, Theodore Roosevelt: on racism in U.S., 123–24

McKinney, T. Nimrod: alien land law and, 54; Japanese ties, 53–54

Meiji Restoration: Japanese racial ideology's roots, 273; motivation for, 32; Perry's landing and, 8; white supremacy, refutation of, 8–9

Mein Kampf: on Japan, 271; Japanese translation, 270

Melanesia: Australians in prewar, 19

Melbourne, Duke of: on subversives among black troops in Britain, 240

Men: gender reversal in Japanese internment camps, 147–49, 155–56

Merigo, Juan: on Mexico's role in U.S.-Japan war, 278

Merrett, Victor: on British defeat at Hong Kong, 67

Mexico: Japan and, 53, 275–78

Meyer, Father (priest interned at Stanley internment camp): opposition to abortion, 151

Michitsura Nodzu: in Russo-Japanese War (1904-1905), 45

Middle East: use of Basuto troops in British armed forces in, 241

Milholland, John: on Russo-Japanese War's impact, 44

Minear, Richard: on Tokyo War Crimes Trials, 375*n*161

Miroir de la Guadeloupe: justification for anti-Jewish decrees, 127

Mishima, B.: on Chinese in Stanley internment camp, 141–42; on Indians prison guards in Hong Kong, 145

Miya Sannomiya Kikuchi: in Alabama, 137

Moko, Peter: handling insults to Maoris, 162

"Monkey": European and Euro-American usage, 10

Moore, Mrs. A.: arrested, 346*n*73

Morris, John: on Japanese dislike of Germans, 273; on war betweeen Japan and Nazi Germany, 268–69; writing anti-Nazi articles in Japan, 272–73

Morrison, Ian: on white supremacy in the Far East, 2

Motosada Zumoto: on possibility of race war, 109

Moy, Hubert: collaboration with Japan, 142

Muhammad, Elijah: arrested, 116, 346*n*73; on brotherhood among blacks and Japanese, 48

About the Author

GERALD HORNE teaches at the University of North Carolina, Chapel Hill. He is the author, most recently, of *Race Woman: The Lives of Shirley Graham Du Bois.*